W9-AIQ-127

MONTANA, WYOMING & IDAHO CAMPING

BECKY LOMAX

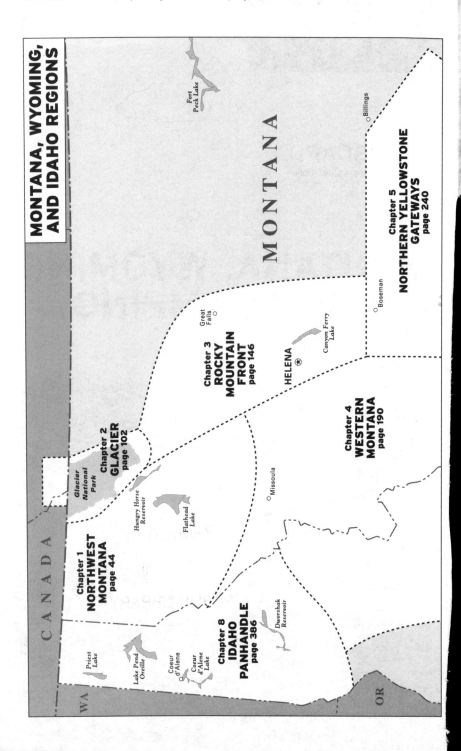

MONTANA, WYOMING, AND IDAHO REGIONS

CANADA

WA

Priest Lake

Lake Pend Oreille

Coeur d'Alene

Coeur d'Alene Lake

Chapter 8 IDAHO PANHANDLE page 386

Dworshak Reservoir

OR

Chapter 1 NORTHWEST MONTANA page 44

Glacier National Park

Chapter 2 GLACIER page 102

Hungry Horse Reservoir

Flathead Lake

Missoula

Chapter 4 WESTERN MONTANA page 190

HELENA

Canyon Ferry Lake

Great Falls

Chapter 3 ROCKY MOUNTAIN FRONT page 146

Fort Peck Lake

MONTANA

Boseman

Billings

Chapter 5 NORTHERN YELLOWSTONE GATEWAYS page 240

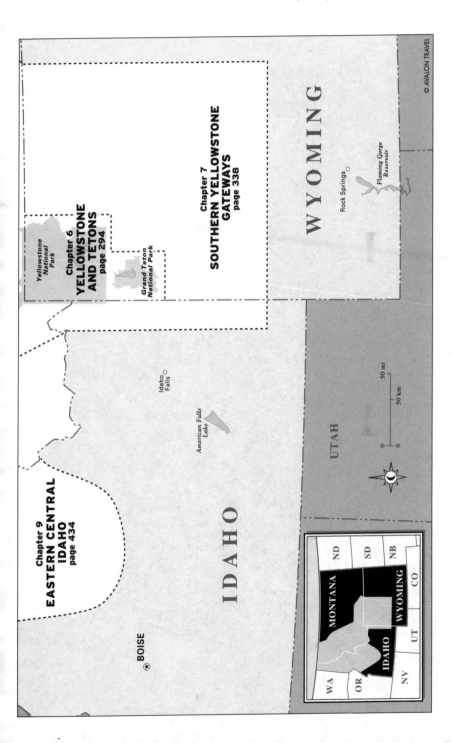

Contents

How to Use This Book

ABOUT THE CAMPGROUND PROFILES

The campgrounds are listed in a consistent, easy-to-read format to help you choose the ideal camping spot. If you already know the name of the specific campground you want to visit, or the name of the surrounding geological area or nearby feature (town, national or state park, forest, mountain, lake, river, etc.), look it up in the index and turn to the corresponding page. Here is a sample profile:

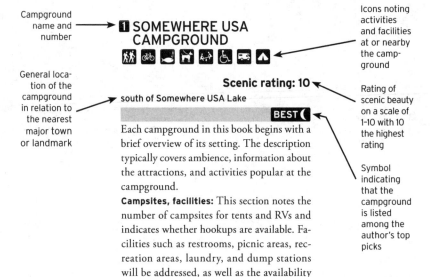

Campground name and number

General location of the campground in relation to the nearest major town or landmark

Icons noting activities and facilities at or nearby the campground

Rating of scenic beauty on a scale of 1-10 with 10 the highest rating

Symbol indicating that the campground is listed among the author's top picks

1 SOMEWHERE USA CAMPGROUND

Scenic rating: 10

south of Somewhere USA Lake

BEST (

Each campground in this book begins with a brief overview of its setting. The description typically covers ambience, information about the attractions, and activities popular at the campground.

Campsites, facilities: This section notes the number of campsites for tents and RVs and indicates whether hookups are available. Facilities such as restrooms, picnic areas, recreation areas, laundry, and dump stations will be addressed, as well as the availability of piped water, showers, playgrounds, stores, and other amenities. The campground's pet policy and wheelchair accessibility is also mentioned here.

Reservations, fees: This section notes whether reservations are accepted, and provides rates for tent sites and RV sites. If there are additional fees for parking or pets, or discounted weekly or seasonal rates, they will also be noted here.

Directions: This section provides mile-by-mile driving directions to the campground from the nearest major town or highway.

Contact: This section provides an address, phone number, and website, if available, for the campground.

ABOUT THE ICONS

The icons in this book are designed to provide at-a-glance information on activities, facilities, and services available on-site or within walking distance of each campground.

- Hiking trails
- Biking trails
- Swimming
- Fishing
- Boating
- Canoeing and/or kayaking
- Hunting

- Winter sports
- Hot springs
- Pets permitted
- Playground
- Wheelchair accessible
- RV sites
- Tent sites

ABOUT THE SCENIC RATING

Each campground profile employs a scenic rating on a scale of 1 to 10, with 1 being the least scenic and 10 being the most scenic. A scenic rating measures only the overall beauty of the campground and environs; it does not take into account noise level, facilities, maintenance, recreation options, or campground management. The setting of a campground with a lower scenic rating may simply not be as picturesque that of as a higher rated campground, however other factors that can influence a trip, such as noise or recreation access, can still affect or enhance your camping trip. Consider both the scenic rating and the profile description before deciding which campground is perfect for you.

MAP SYMBOLS

Expressway	(80)	Interstate Freeway	✗	Airfield
Primary Road	(101)	U.S. Highway	✗	Airport
Secondary Road	(21)	State Highway	O	City/Town
Unpaved Road	66	County Highway	▲	Mountain
Ferry		Lake	▲	Park
National Border		Dry Lake	⁄⟋	Pass
State Border		Seasonal Lake	◉	State Capital

Best Campgrounds

INTRODUCTION

© BECKY LOMAX

Author's Note

Fire and ice dominate the Montana, Wyoming, and Idaho mountain corridor of the Northern Rockies. The earth fumes into boiling geysers from one of the biggest supervolcanoes in the world while craggy peaks cradle centuries-old ice. Yellowstone, the nation's first national park, resounds with the roar of vents spewing steam, and Glacier, the nation's tenth national park, retains fast-melting vestiges of ice snuggled in a scoured, jagged landscape that exposes some of the oldest sedimentary rocks in North America.

Wrapped in winter cloaks of snow for half the year, the parks draw campers in summer because of their wildlife-watching, beauty, and singularity. Along with Yellowstone and Glacier, Grand Teton National Park contributes a toothy landscape, with much younger mountains. For campers, the region also harbors 14 national forests, 9 national wildlife refuges, 38 state parks, and countless fishing accesses to explore. It also contains national historic sites, multi-state historic trails following the routes of Lewis and Clark and the Nez Perce, and the new Ice Age Floods National Geologic Trail.

The corridor of the Northern Rockies also forms a citadel for nature at its wildest. The region includes not only 16 wilderness areas, but also the largest roadless wilderness in the Lower 48. You can camp so far off the grid here that your cell phone won't pick up calls from the office.

The Northern Rockies harbor the nation's largest carnivores, as well as wild native trout, and one of the country's biggest migration flyways cruises overhead. Grizzly bears and gray wolves top the food chain, just as they did in Lewis and Clark's day. Moose, elk, and antelope browse the lowlands while bighorn sheep and mountain goats stand as icons of the alpine. Blue-ribbon streams abound where anglers can catch native westslope cutthroat trout. In the air, the Rocky Mountain flyway draws avian traffic twice a year with golden eagles, raptors, and songbirds.

With less than 1 percent of the nation's population dotted across the three states in cow towns and blink-and-you'll-miss-it rural villages, the region offers big expanses of public land where you won't see a house for miles. Contrary to other states where private homes rim every inch of rivers and lakes, in this area waterways abound with easy access for the public. Montana houses Flathead Lake, the largest freshwater lake in the West, and some of the West's largest rivers—the Yellowstone, Missouri, Snake, and Salmon—find their headwaters in the mountains of Montana, Wyoming, and Idaho. Fed by chilly waters from snowmelt and glaciers, lakes provide campers with scenic places to boat, fish, paddle, water-ski, and swim, while rivers bring on small riffles for fishing and floating as well as some of the country's biggest white water.

In researching campgrounds for this book, I drove the equivalent of coast to coast—several times. Montana, Wyoming, and Idaho are big places. Many first-time visitors assume they can pop between Glacier and Yellowstone National Parks in a couple of hours, but the distance requires a full day's drive, minimum. For an enjoyable visit, plan camping trips that cover reasonable distances and include plenty of days; you want to avoid marathon drives that preclude time to sit around the campfire. Also, many campground gems hide on remote gravel roads. I logged so many potholed dirt roads with one friend that she nicknamed them in my notes as AFBRs (Another Flipping Bumpy Road).

The corridor between the two national parks and their surrounding mountains is bear country. Both black and grizzly bears live in the Northern Rockies. But while black bears thrive across the United States, grizzly bears have been squeezed into 1 percent of their traditional range in the Lower 48—the Glacier–Yellowstone corridor. Camping in bear country demands conscientious habits for storing food and garbage. Although some campgrounds, like those in Glacier, staple reminders to picnic tables and levy substantial fines for failure to keep a bear-proof camp, others do not. While a few campgrounds listed in this book haven't seen a bear in decades, others do frequently. To keep both you and the bears safe, assume you are in bear country at all campgrounds in the Northern Rockies.

While I've made every endeavor to provide accurate information in this guide, the status of campgrounds changes fast. Storms, snows, floods, and fires destroy campgrounds. Even as current stimulus money is funding construction of new campgrounds in the Northern Rockies, depleted Forest Service maintenance budgets are forcing shorter seasons and closures of some lesser-used campgrounds.

One small creature, however, is changing the face of campgrounds faster than anything else. Pine bark beetles are rampantly killing trees across western mountains—up to 40 percent in some national forests. Their presence can be recognized by rust-colored pines. Many national forests have been forced into spraying programs to protect campground trees. When an infestation causes dead trees to pose a danger to the public, campgrounds close to logging companies can thin out the dead timber. The logging converts campgrounds once in deep shade into sunny open sites.

While private RV campgrounds spread across Montana, Idaho, and Wyoming, only select ones were included in this book: those nearest the national parks, those that offer access to recreation, and those on travel corridors. Public campgrounds in national parks and national forests make up the bulk of the book's selections. Primitive campsites—a personal favorite—are also included for those who prefer the quiet, solitude, and seclusion they provide.

Ultimate memories from camping are forged not just from stunning views and roasting marshmallows around the campfire. They come from rare experiences—listening to raucous tent-shaking thunderclaps in Montana's Swan Valley, gagging on the stench from Yellowstone's mudpots, standing in utter blackness in the Lewis and Clark Caverns, and spying a pair of wolverines romping in Glacier. The best camping memories are also created from those with whom we share the experience. Among the indelible camping images etched in my memory, I have visions of paddling the sluggish Marge the Barge with my youngest sister up the Priest River Thoroughfare, mountain biking the Hiawatha rail trail with my intrepid 10-year-old niece, gazing with my college roommate at a sky blazing with stars on the remote North Fork of the Clearwater River, and hiking with friends through a wealth of yellow, purple, and red wildflower blooms in the Beartooth Mountains.

Camping disasters yield fodder for humor. While pulling over with my 17-year-old niece to let a vehicle pass on Montana's narrow gravel Rock Creek Road, I caught my camper's back jack on a rock, ripping it off. When punchy from driving to camp in Idaho's Island Park, I mistakenly called a tow truck to fix the truck, when I just needed to switch gas tanks.

Regardless of the adventure, all camping trips have one thing in common—they simply increase the desire to camp again. The Northern Rockies are a place to smell rich pine, taste the dry air, and cool hot hiking feet in ice-cold streams. Bring the toys—hiking boots, boats, rafts, kayaks, canoes, and mountain bikes—to enjoy all it has to off

Mammoth, Yellowstone and Tetons, page 298.
Granite Creek, Southern Yellowstone Gateways, page 372.
Jerry Johnson, Eastern Central Idaho, page 436.
Easley, Eastern Central Idaho, page 473.

◖ Best of Idaho
Indian Creek, Yellowstone and Tetons, page 299.
Big Springs, Southern Yellowstone Gateways, page 341.
Grandview, Southern Yellowstone Gateways, page 347.
Priest River Recreation Area (Mudhole), Idaho Panhandle, page 404.
North Fork of the Clearwater River Primitive, Idaho Panhandle, page 424.
Wilderness Gateway, Eastern Central Idaho, page 435.
Stanley Lake, Eastern Central Idaho, page 461.
Sockeye, Eastern Central Idaho, page 469.

◖ Best Lake Camping
Big Arm State Park, Northwest Montana, page 79.
Kintla Lake, Glacier, page 104.
Sprague Creek, Glacier, page 125.
Cliff Point, Northern Yellowstone Gateways, page 254.
Grant, Yellowstone and Tetons, page 317.
Beaver Creek, Idaho Panhandle, page 391.
Sam Owen Recreation Area, Idaho Panhandle, page 406.
Hawley's Landing, Idaho Panhandle, page 416.
Dent Acres, Idaho Panhandle, page 427.
Outlet, Eastern Central Idaho, page 467.

◖ Best of Montana
Big Therriault Lake, Northwest Montana, page 55.
Spotted Bear, Northwest Montana, page 86.
Bowman Lake, Glacier, page 106.
Rising Sun, Glacier, page 127.
Cave Mountain, Rocky Mountain Front, page 150.
Devil's Elbow, Rocky Mountain Front, page 171.
Missouri Headwaters State Park, Northern Yellowstone Gateways, page 241.
Lewis and Clark Caverns State Park, Northern Yellowstone Gateways, page 242.
Red Mountain, Northern Yellowstone Gateways, page 243.
Beaver Creek, Northern Yellowstone Gateways, page 251.

◖ Best River Camping
Bull River, Northwest Montana, page 63.
Big Creek, Glacier, page 115.
Dalles, Western Montana, page 215.
Warm River, Southern Yellowstone Gateways, page 348.
Aquarius Creek, Idaho Panhandle, page 423.
Washington Creek, Idaho Panhandle, page 424.
Wild Goose, Eastern Central Idaho, page 441.

O'Hara Bar, Eastern Central Idaho, page 443.
Upper and Lower O'Brien, Eastern Central Idaho, page 458.
Mormon Bend, Eastern Central Idaho, page 459.

◖ Best Wildlife-Watching
Swan Lake, Northwest Montana, page 85.
Freezeout Lake, Rocky Mountain Front, page 158.
Departure Point, Rocky Mountain Front, page 167.
Brown's Lake, Western Montana, page 196.
Upper Red Rock Lake, Northern Yellowstone Gateways, page 255.
Indian Creek, Yellowstone and Tetons, page 299.
Slough Creek, Yellowstone and Tetons, page 300.
Pebble Creek, Yellowstone and Tetons, page 301.
Canyon, Yellowstone and Tetons, page 313.
Albeni Cove Recreation Area, Idaho Panhandle, page 403.

◖ Best of Wyoming
Beartooth Lake, Northern Yellowstone Gateways, page 287.
Madison, Yellowstone and Tetons, page 311.
Cave Falls, Yellowstone and Tetons, page 320.
Grassy Lake Primitive, Yellowstone and Tetons, page 321.
Signal Mountain, Yellowstone and Tetons, page 326.
Clearwater, Southern Yellowstone Gateways, page 354.
Brooks Lake, Southern Yellowstone Gateways, page 360.
Pinnacles, Southern Yellowstone Gateways, page 361.

Camping Tips

TRAVELING THE NORTHERN ROCKIES
Roads and Routes

Traveling the Northern Rockies of Montana, Wyoming, and Idaho requires an understanding of roads. Interstates are few and far between. Rough, narrow, paved two-laners are common, and dirt roads are as ubiquitous as pavement.

HIGHWAYS AND INTERSTATES

Only two interstates bisect the region. I-15 runs through Montana and Idaho, connecting Calgary with Salt Lake City, and I-90 crosses Montana en route from Seattle to Chicago and Boston. State highways crisscross the region, providing the main thoroughfares. These can be two or four lanes, or they may be dirt roads. To navigate the area, use a current detailed map that shows pavement and gravel roads.

CROSSING THE CONTINENTAL DIVIDE AND HIGH PASSES

The Continental Divide skitters along the highest summits of the Rocky Mountains, making the division between water flowing to the Atlantic and water flowing to the Pacific. For campers, driving over the Continental Divide provides a challenge. In winter, some high passes are closed for several months, while others struggle with intermittent closures due to avalanches. Glacier's Going-to-the-Sun Road, the Beartooth Highway northeast of Yellowstone, and much of Yellowstone National Park closes for winter, and remote Forest Service roads convert to snowmobile routes.

But even in summer, you can encounter snow on the higher passes through the mountains from Glacier to the Tetons. Wyoming's Beartooth Pass tops out at 10,947 feet, and Togwotee Pass is 9,658 feet. Both have amassed snow in August. But perhaps the most notorious is Teton Pass on the south end of Grand Teton National Park. While it only touches 8,431 feet high, its 10 percent grade proves a grunt for RVs and those hauling camping trailers. Make a practice of downshifting into second gear for descents rather than burning your brakes.

Current pass conditions are available on each state's Department of Transportation website. Some even have webcams on the summits so you can see the weather.

DIRT ROADS

Many of the prized campgrounds in the Northern Rocky Mountains are accessed via dirt or gravel roads. The best roads—wide, graveled double-laners that may be graded regularly—hold the washboards to a minimum. Others bounce along with large washboards, rocks, eroded stream beds, and small potholes. The worst contain monstrous chuckholes that can nearly swallow small cars and grab trailer hitches. Do not bring prized paint jobs on dirt roads! Take a hint from locals, who all drive rigs with dings and window chips. Rigs with four-wheel drive are helpful to get out of rough spots, but they are not required to reach any of the campgrounds in this book. If you are concerned about your vehicle's ability to navigate a certain dirt road, call the appropriate national forest for a road update.

DISTANCES

Many campers visiting the Northern Rockies for the first time expect to whiz between Glacier and Yellowstone National Parks in a few hours. The distance between the two is the same as driving from San Francisco to Los Angeles or from Boston to Baltimore, only without an interstate most of the way. To drive between the two parks, most campers take a full day without stopping or sightseeing.

GAS

Don't wait until you're empty to look for gas. Always plan ahead for filling up, as gas stations sometimes can be 60 miles or

ENTRY FEES

While many national forests and public lands require no entry fee, national parks, national historic sites, and some special Forest Service and Bureau of Land Management sites require entry fees. Rates vary by site.

NATIONAL PARK FEES

Entry for one private vehicle to Glacier, Grand Teton, or Yellowstone National Park costs $25 for a seven-day pass. No single-day passes are sold. Those entering one of the parks on foot or by bicycle pay $12. Motorcycle entry fee to Glacier costs $12, but it's $20 for Yellowstone and Grand Teton National Parks. Passes for Yellowstone or Grand Teton National Park are good for both parks.

Yellowstone has the same fees year-round, but Glacier reduces the entry fee in winter to $15, and Grand Teton reduces it to $5. Glacier also offers free entry June 20-21, July 18-19, and August 15-16. All three parks waive entry fees on National Public Lands Day on September 26 and Veterans Day on November 11.

For those camping longer than seven days, annual passes are available, too, for each of the parks. A combined annual Yellowstone-Teton pass costs $50, and the Glacier annual pass costs $35.

INTERAGENCY PASSES

Since 2007, the America the Beautiful Interagency Pass has been available. The $80 nontransferable annual pass grants entrance to federal sites run by the National Park Service, Fish and Wildlife Service, Bureau of Land Management, Bureau of Reclamation, and the U.S. Forest Service. The pass covers all occupants in a single, noncommercial vehicle. At walk-up sites, the pass is good for the pass-holder plus three adults. Children under 16 camp for free. Passes are available at entrance stations or online (store.usgs.gov/pass).

Seniors can purchase lifetime nontransferable interagency passes for $10. The pass is available to U.S. citizens or permanent residents age 62 or over. The pass admits the pass-holder and passengers in a noncommercial vehicle at per-vehicle fee areas and the pass-holder plus three adults at per-person fee areas. Lifetime passes can only be obtained in person at park entrances. Bring proof of age (state driver's license, birth certificate, passport). The pass provides a 50 percent discount on many campgrounds in the Northern Rockies.

Access passes are available free to U.S. citizens or permanent residents with permanent disabilities. The nontransferable lifetime pass admits the pass-holder and passengers in a noncommercial vehicle at per-vehicle fee areas and pass-holder plus three adults at per-person fee areas. Passes may only be purchased in person at entrance stations with proof of medical disability or eligibility for receiving federal benefits. The Access Pass provides a 50 percent discount on many campgrounds in the Northern Rockies.

more away. Gas prices tend to be cheaper in Wyoming than in Montana or Idaho; they are also cheaper in cities compared to small rural stations.

REPAIRS

Repairs to vehicles and RVs are available. Even in the national parks or on remote national forest roads, mechanics can come take a look at your vehicle and tow it back to the shop, if necessary. In some places, mobile repair services are available. Most repair services coming to your campsite will charge by the hour for their services rather than by the mile, to account for the extra time spent traveling slow dirt roads and scenic byways.

RVs

Most RVers are well aware that different campgrounds have size restrictions based on the size of parking pads and configuration of the campground road. However, RVers will want to consider the road status in their choices of campgrounds, too. Dirt national forest roads do not usually post warnings on status. Call the local ranger station to check on road status before driving. Most paved roads, except for the Logan Pass stretch of Glacier's Going-to-the-Sun Road, are suitable for any size RV. The Logan Pass stretch is closed to vehicles over 21 feet in length, taller than 10 feet, and wider than 8 feet.

MOTORCYCLES

Montana, Wyoming, and Idaho are popular for motorcycle touring. Many bikers haul their tents and mini-trailers to camp in the national parks and ride the high scenic passes. None of the three states require helmets—except for those 17 years old and younger. Motorcyclists riding the high passes should be prepared for

inclement weather and cold temperatures even in August.

Navigational Tools

MAPS

The dirt roads into many campgrounds in the Northern Rockies do not even appear on the state road maps. More detailed maps will provide you with a better view of where you are driving. Overall, U.S.G.S. seven-minute maps yield the most detail for driving forest roads, hiking, and camping; however, the dollars can rack up fast on a big trip requiring a load of maps. *National Geographic Trails Illustrated* maps (800/962-1643, www.natgeomaps. com) are available for Glacier, Grand Teton, and Yellowstone National Parks. Each national forest also sells huge maps with one-mile grids; find these at ranger stations or purchase online (www.nationalforeststore.com). Beartooth Publishing (406/585-7205 or 800/838-1058, www.beartoothpublishing.com) produces regional recreation maps for southern Montana,

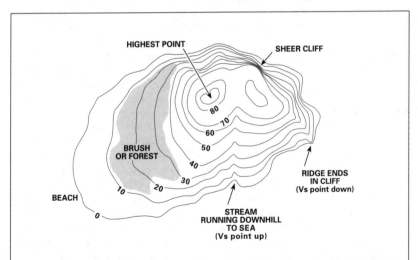

The **topographical map** is easier to read than many believe. Lines close together mean steep gradients; lines farther apart mean gentle gradients; V-shaped sets of lines pointing to higher elevations mean gulleys or stream-beds; V-shaped sets of lines pointing to lower elevations mean ridges.

northwestern Wyoming, and eastern Idaho; maps include latitude and longitude grids, trail mileages, and campgrounds.

GPS, COMPASSES, AND PERSONAL LOCATING DEVICES

GPS units and compasses are useful for navigation but require knowledge on how to use them. Learn to use them before you depart on a trip where your safety may rely on them. Large vehicle GPS units work well on most areas accessed by paved roads, but head off on remote Forest Service roads and they become useless without the detailed maps to make them functional. Both vehicle and hand-held GPS units rely on access to satellites; in many deep canyons in the Northern Rockies, you may not be able to pick up enough satellites for them to work. A compass, which always works, can provide a good backup.

While personal locating devices will transmit everywhere a GPS works, they require conscientious use. Across the West, rescue organizations are being called out for frivolous reasons or accidentally sent signals—risking the lives of the rescuers. Signals should only be transmitted in life-threatening situations. Personal locating devices should not be used as tickets to hike, climb, bike, or boat beyond one's abilities; go only those places you would visit without one and preplan self-rescue options.

Cell Phones

Visitors to the Northern Rockies expect cell phones to work everywhere as they do in virtually all populated areas. The dead zones here are vast. Even though a cell tower sits near Old Faithful in Yellowstone National Park, much of the mountainous terrain plummets into narrow canyons where signals do not reach. Don't expect to find reception deep in the forests, in canyons, or in the mountains.

One of the best inventions for emergencies, cell phones allow immediate access to help. But do not rely on a cell phone as your sole means of rescue in case of an emergency. Whether you are backpacking in a wilderness or driving 20 miles on a gravel road into a national forest, be prepared to self-rescue.

When cell phones do work in campgrounds, use of them requires etiquette. Turn off ringers because phone noise catapults hikers and campers from a natural experience back into the hubbub of modern life. If you must make a call, move away from campsites and other hikers to avoid disrupting their experience. On trails, refrain from using phones in the presence of other hikers. Be considerate of other campers and their desire to get away from it all.

CLIMATE

The Northern Rockies from Glacier to Yellowstone sit on a collision course between Arctic Continental and Pacific Maritime weather. Storms race inland from the Pacific, with accompanying moderate temperatures and precipitation. They crash into weather systems from the north that bring cold temperatures, resulting in snow in the high mountains—even in August. Yet when maritime jet streams chug north into Canada, southern heat waves creep into Montana, Idaho, and Wyoming, shooting the summer thermometer into the 90s or above.

The Northern Rockies region is a land of weather extremes. North of Helena, Montana, Rogers Pass ranks in the top 10 coldest places in the world, alongside Antarctica and Siberia. From Glacier National Park to Helena, the Rocky Mountain Front frequently makes the record books for extreme winds, cold, and heat. Loma recorded the most extreme temperature change in a 24-hour period in the United States when the January thermometer yo-yoed over 100 degrees from -54 °F to 49 °F. Lander, Wyoming, ranks in the top 10 snowiest cities in the country. Of all 50 states, Montana holds the record for the most variation in extremes—a 187-degree difference between its record high and low, and Great Falls holds the record for the most rapid temperature change recorded in the United States—47 degrees in seven minutes.

Although precipitation drops equally on both sides of the Continental Divide, wind produces more weather extremes on its east side. While winter winds often blow snow from slopes, providing forage for ungulates, they also have pushed trains off their tracks in East Glacier, Montana. Chinook winds—high warm winds with speeds reaching over 90 miles per hour—blow any time of the year, but they are most obvious in winter. Native Americans called them "snow eaters" for rapidly melting snow. In summer, high passes can rage with unpredictable winds, causing hikers to crawl on all fours across them.

Seasons

The mountains of Montana, Idaho, and Wyoming enjoy four distinct seasons, each with its own quirks. With the appropriate equipment and preparation, you can enjoy camping year-round, even in snow.

SPRING

Spring first enters the lower elevations beginning in late March and April. Winter snow melts, turning miles of dirt roads into muddy tracks. While March, April, and May are appealing off-months to travel, in the Northern Rockies they are wet and cold, still clinging to winter. Weather bounces between soggy rains one day and 70-degree blue skies the next. Snow buries the high country, including scenic routes such as Going-to-the-Sun Road in Glacier National Park and the Beartooth Highway access to Yellowstone National Park, often preventing opening until after Memorial Day. May still brings tempestuous storms to the mountains, with rains and snows increasing the potential for avalanches and mudslides, but stretches of sunny days hint at summer. Spring temperatures range from the mid-50s to the mid-70s with nighttime lows from 20 to 40 degrees F.

SUMMER

Summer brings the most campers to the national parks and forests, but the mountainous terrain of the Northern Rockies often reels with its own weather agenda. While cool breezes are welcome on baking summer days, they can also bring snows to the mountains in August. During summer months, June habitually monsoons, but July and August usher in warmer, drier skies. Temperatures run at a pleasant 70–80 degrees with very little humidity. Most areas will see several days each summer in the 90s (locals consider anything over 90 to be sweltering), but rarely does the thermometer stretch up to triple digits. Nighttime lows dip into the 40s and 50s.

FALL

The first frosts usually descend in September. Autumn's cool nights usher in warm, bug-free days. While golds paint aspen and larch trees, temperatures bounce through extremes—from warm shorts-wearing weather during the day to below freezing at night. Plenty of 70-degree days keep summer outdoor recreation alive as schizophrenic weather jerks between rain with snow at higher elevations for a few days followed by clear, warming trends. Daytime highs vacillate between the 40s and 60s, while nighttime lows can reach the 20s.

WINTER

While winter temperatures vary in elevation, most of the Northern Rockies hang in the 10–25 degree range, producing voluminous snows. While Yellowstone National Park sees about 150 inches of snowfall, Logan Pass in Glacier National Park buries under 350–650 inches of snow per year. Temperatures can spike above freezing, with its companion rain, or plummet below zero for several days with an arctic front.

DAYLIGHT AND TIME

Given the northern latitude and placement of Montana and Wyoming on the Mountain Time Zone's west edge, hours of daylight fluctuate wildly during the year. In June, over 16 hours of daylight floods the mountains. First light fades in around 5 A.M., and dark doesn't descend until almost 11 P.M. By late August, however, dark descends by 9 P.M. with daylight cruising on a shorter ride until December's slim 8.5 hours of daylight. Around the winter solstice, the sun rises around 8 A.M. and sets at 4:30 P.M. The Idaho Panhandle, which operates on Pacific time, sees both daylight and darkness an hour earlier.

ELEVATION

Due to the mountainous terrain, temperatures vary by elevations. Mountaintops are cooler than valley floors—up to 15 degrees cooler. Boaters may enjoy 82-degree weather camping on Montana's Flathead Lake in August, while hikers less than 60 air miles away in Glacier National Park hit trails with temperatures in the high 60s. Yellowstone National Park sits on a high-elevation plateau with most of the park above 7,500 feet, and the highest campgrounds on the Beartooth Plateau in Wyoming top out at 9,600 feet. Campgrounds in these locations are substantially cooler than those at lower elevations, such as Montana's Missouri Headwaters State Park at 4,045 feet.

Weather

Locals have a saying about the weather in the Northern Rockies: "Wait five minutes, and the weather will change." The mountain terrain lends itself to wild swings in weather. You can begin hiking in shorts but by afternoon be pulling on gloves and fleece hats as gray clouds lob sheets of sleet on slopes. Calm, glassy lakes can give way to four-foot high whitecaps as storms blow in.

LIGHTNING AND THUNDERSTORMS

Afternoon thundershowers and lightning storms are common across much of the Northern Rocky Mountains. In some locations—particularly around Yellowstone National Park and Wyoming's Beartooth Plateau—they roll in daily, almost on schedule in the late afternoon. During lightning storms, boaters should get off the water, and those enjoying beaches should move to a sheltered location. Hikers should descend from summits, ridges, and exposed slopes, and stay away from isolated trees. Some thunderstorms bring hail; other dump pelting rains.

WINDS

The Continental Divide causes high winds. With eastern air masses trying to equalize with western jet streams, the result is strong winds optimal for migrating golden eagles and wind farms. But the open, eastern slopes of the Continental Divide can pose tricky driving for large RVs, with wind gusts threatening to push them off the road. Likewise, treeless campgrounds on the prairie often bluster with winds. Montana's Rocky Mountain Front and the Absaroka Front receive the most notorious winds, on an average day blowing 7–20 mph with gusts up to 50 mph.

PRECIPITATION

While Montana, Wyoming, and Idaho are drier than the Pacific Northwest, their mountain areas receive substantial precipitation. The amount depends largely upon topography. Across the area, most snow falls November–March, but heavy snowstorms can occur as early as mid-September or as late as May—especially in the high mountains. Annual snowfall averages 300 inches in many of the mountain ranges—hence the region's numerous ski resorts. Valley floors receive about 50 inches of snowfall. Nearly half of the region's annual average precipitation falls from May through July in the form of valley rain, sleet, or snow. Heavy rains falling during the spring thaw contribute to late season avalanches and flooding.

FOREST FIRES

Like snow, wind, or rain, lightning-caused fire is a natural process. It is healthy for the ecosystem, for it removes bug infestations, reduces deadfall and nonnative plants, releases nutrients into the soil like a good fertilizer, and maintains a natural mix of vegetation. Following decades of heavy fire suppression policy, forest fuels have built up across the Northern Rocky Mountain forests to high levels, with some forests suffering under severe attack from pine beetles and blister rust—conditions that kill trees and make them ripe for fire. You can check on current forest fire locations and their status at www.inciweb.org/.

CAMPING CONCERNS

Camping Regulations and Red Tape

NATIONAL PARKS
National parks are set aside for their historical, geological, cultural, or biological significance, and geared toward public recreation. Hunting is not permitted, nor is picking wildflowers or berries for commercial use. Dogs are not allowed on trails; neither are mountain bikes. Camping is limited to designated campgrounds and generally limited to 14 days in one campsite, unless otherwise posted. Permits are needed for backcountry camping. National parks require entrance fees, and each campground requires fees.

Waterton Lakes National Park in Canada borders Glacier National Park and is used to access parts of Glacier. U.S. national park passes are not valid in Waterton. Passports are required to drive to Waterton; only U.S. and Canadian citizens with passports are permitted to travel into Glacier past Goat Haunt.

NATIONAL FORESTS
National forests are used for their resources, with timber harvesting, commercial berry picking, mushroom harvesting, mining, and recreation permitted. Hunting is permitted with licenses administered by the state. Trails permit dogs and mountain bikes as long as no special designation says otherwise. Designated campgrounds usually allow stays up to 14–16 days in the same campsite; a few high-use areas employ shorter limits. Unless otherwise designated, primitive camping is usually permitted anywhere outside of developed campgrounds. Permits are not needed for backcountry camping. National forests usually do not charge entrance fees, but some specific visitor sites do. Some developed campgrounds require fees; others are free, as is primitive camping.

Wilderness areas are administered usually by the national forest that contains the wilderness boundaries. They permit no mechanical transports, including mountain bikes. Hunting is permitted. Fido can go along on the trail, and permits are not needed for backcountry camping, which is free.

OTHER GOVERNMENT LANDS
Bureau of Land Management and Bureau of Reclamation terrain operates much like national forest land, with most developed campgrounds charging fees. Entrance fees are usually not charged; however, some sites charge day-use fees. Stays are limited to 14 days in the same spot, unless posted otherwise. Free primitive camping is permitted outside of developed campgrounds.

Montana, Wyoming, and Idaho **state parks** vary in campgrounds and amenities under the auspices of each state. State parks charge fees for day use and camping. Most campground fees include day use, too. Montana residents have free day use of Montana state parks. Wyoming residents receive discounts on day use and camping fees in Wyoming state parks. Camping is permitted in a Montana or Wyoming state park for 14 days out of a 30-day period; in Idaho, the limit is 15 days.

Camping with Children
Children learn to enjoy camping when they can participate in the activities. Have them help with camp chores—building fires, collecting garbage, and bear-proofing the camp.

Kids can earn **Junior Ranger Badges** by completing self-guided activities in Glacier, Yellowstone, and Teton National Parks. Activities, which target ages 5–12, vary by park but are an excellent way to help children learn about the park and wildlife. Junior Ranger activity books or newspapers are available at all visitors centers in the parks (free in Glacier, $3 in Yellowstone, $1 in Teton). When kids return the completed newspaper to any visitors center, they are sworn in as Junior Rangers and receive park-specific badges.

Plan ahead with kids by taking along extra clothing and shoes. If kids can get wet, they will. Replacing wet soggy clothing with warm dry gear improves their attitude and their enjoyment of camping. When hiking, even for short walks, take along water and snacks to maintain the energy level for children.

Camping with Pets

NATIONAL PARKS
Pets are allowed in national parks, but only in limited areas. Campgrounds, roadsides, and parking lots are all okay for pets. When outside a vehicle, pets must be on a six-foot or shorter leash or be caged. Pets are not permitted on national park trails, with the exception of Waterton Lakes National Park north of Glacier. Two main reasons are to protect fragile vegetation and thermal areas and to prevent conflicts with wildlife. Bears are a major argument for leaving the pooch home. Pets are also not permitted in visitors centers or at beaches. If necessary, pets can stay in your vehicle while you are viewing roadside attractions, but provide ventilation for the animal's survival.

NATIONAL FORESTS
Contrary to national parks, national forests permit pets on most trails. (Read trailhead signs carefully because some trails do not permit pets.) Keep in mind that many hikers in the Northern Rockies have heightened sensitivity to movement, due to being on alert for

In setting up camp, always be mindful of potential ecological disturbances. Pitch tents and dispose of human waste at least 200 feet from the water's edge. In grizzly bear territory, increase the distance between your tent and your cooking area, food-hang, and the water's edge threefold. In other words, if you're in grizzly country, do all your cooking 100 yards (not feet) downwind of your sleeping area. If you can establish an escape tree nearby, all the better.

bears. To prevent bear conflicts and to avoid scaring other hikers with a dog charging down the trail, keep Fido on a leash. Pets are also allowed in campgrounds, but they must be leashed, rather than running free.

In bear country, store pet food, bowls, and toys in a hard-sided vehicle or bear box when not in use. Like humans, pets should leave no traces other than footprints. Clean up and dispose of all pet feces in the garbage.

Camping Ethics

Protection of public lands and campgrounds is up to those of us who use them. Be respectful of nature and campground facilities, taking care of them as if they were your own. Follow Leave No Trace ethics when camping in developed campgrounds or the backcountry.

LEAVE NO TRACE

Visitors to the Northern Rockies need to take an active role in maintaining the environment.

Plan ahead and prepare. Plan ahead for camping with fluctuating weather in mind, and choose appropriate hiking routes for mileage and elevation gain. Carry hiking essentials.

Travel and camp on durable surfaces. In both developed and backcountry campgrounds, camp in designated sites only. Protect fragile trailside plants by staying on the trail, refusing to cut switchbacks, and walking single file on trails even in the mud. If you must walk off-trail, step on rocks, snow, or dry grasses rather than on wet soils and fragile plants.

Leave what you find. Flowers, rocks, and goat fur tufts on shrubs are protected resources in national parks. Even on other public lands, they should be left for others to enjoy. For lunch stops and camping, sit on rocks or logs where you find them rather than moving them to accommodate your camp.

Properly dispose of waste. Whatever you bring in, you must pack out or deposit in garbage receptacles. Do not burn garbage in fire pits. If toilets are not available, urinate on rocks, logs, gravel, or snow to protect fragile soils and plants from salt-starved wildlife. Bury feces 6–8 inches deep at least 200 feet from water. Pack out used toilet paper in your trash.

Minimize campfire impacts. Make fires in designated fire pits only. Use small, wrist-size dead and down wood, not live branches. Be aware that fires or firewood collecting is not permitted in many places in national parks.

Respect wildlife. Bring along binoculars, spotting scopes, and telephoto lenses to aid in watching wildlife. Keep your distance. Do not feed any wildlife, even ground squirrels. Once fed, they become more aggressive. Maintain a distance of a football-field length from bears and wolves and 25 yards from all other wildlife.

Be considerate of other visitors. Minimize use of electronics, generators, and other noise-makers in campgrounds, and keep dogs from barking. Follow posted quiet hours, departing and arriving as silently as possible before or after hours.

RECREATION

Hiking

The Northern Rockies are crisscrossed with hiking trails—some short day-hike destinations and others stringing long miles back into remote roadless wilderness areas. While links still remain to be built, the Continental Divide Trail forms the longest trail system, running through the Wind River Range in Wyoming, Yellowstone National Park, the Bitterroot Mountains along the border of Montana and Idaho, several national forests and wilderness area, and finishing in Glacier National Park. Also, Montana's Bob Marshall Wilderness and Yellowstone National Park each contain over 1,000 miles of trails, while Glacier National Park contains over 700 miles of trails. Outfitters are available for guided hiking and backpacking in Glacier, Grand Teton, and Yellowstone National Parks.

HIKING ESSENTIALS

Hiking in the Northern Rockies of Montana, Wyoming, and Idaho demands preparedness. High elevations, unpredictable winds, fast-changing weather, and summer snowstorms can catapult a lazy day walk into a nightmare if one is not prepared. Take the following:

Extra clothing: Rain pants and jackets can double as wind protection, while gloves and a lightweight warm hat will save fingers and ears. Carry at least one extra water-wicking layer for warmth. Avoid cotton fabrics that stay soggy and fail to retain body heat.

Extra food and water: Take lunch and snacks, like compact high-energy food bars. Low-odor foods will not attract animals. Heat, wind, and elevation dehydrate hikers quickly; always carry extra water. Don't drink directly from streams or lakes due to bacteria; always filter (with a one-micron filter) or treat water sources before drinking.

Navigation: Although national park trails are well-signed, national forest and wilderness trails are not. Take a detailed topographical map of the area to best ascertain the distance traveled and location. A compass or GPS will also help, but only if you know how to use them.

Flashlight: Carry a small flashlight or headlamp with extra batteries. In an after-dark emergency, the light becomes invaluable.

First-aid kit: Two Band-Aids are not enough! Carry a fully equipped standard first-aid kit with blister remedies. Don't forget personal requirements such as bee-sting kits and allergy medications.

Sun protection: Altitude, snow, ice, and lakes all increase ultraviolet radiation. Protect yourself with 30 SPF sunscreen, sunglasses, and a sunhat or baseball cap.

Emergency bathroom supplies: To accommodate alfresco bathrooms, carry a small trowel, plastic bags, and toilet paper. Move at least 200 feet away from water sources. For urinating, aim for a durable surface, such as rocks, logs, gravel, or snow, rather than fragile plants, campsites, or trails. Bury feces 6–8 inches deep in soil. Pack the toilet paper out in a Ziploc bag.

Feminine hygiene: Carry heavy-duty Ziploc bags for packing tampons and pads out rather than burying them.

Insect repellent: Insect repellents containing 50 percent DEET work best with the mosquitoes and black flies. Purchase applications that rub or spray in a close range rather than aerosols that become airborne onto other people, plants, and animals.

Pepper spray: Use an eight-ounce can of pepper spray for charging bears, but do not bother unless you know how to use it and what influences its effectiveness. It is not to be used like bug repellent.

Cell phones: Take the cell phone along for emergencies, but don't rely on it for rescue. In much of the Northern Rockies, cell phones do not work. Plan to self-rescue. If you do carry a cell phone, turn it off to save the batteries for an emergency and to avoid offending fellow hikers who seek solitude, quiet, and the sounds of nature.

Miscellaneous: Pack along a knife, a few feet of nylon cord, and duct tape wrapped around a flashlight handle. Many hikers have repaired boots and packs with duct tape and a little ingenuity.

TRAILS AND SIGNS

Conditions on trails vary depending on the season, elevation, recent severe weather, and wildlife. In places where swinging or plank bridges are removed annually across rivers and creeks, crews re-install them in late May or early June. Steep snowfields inhibit early hiking at higher elevations until July. Avalanches and severe storms—wind microbursts, heavy snows, and torrential rains—can cause miles of downed trees across trails. Depending on the location, crews may or may not be available for immediate clearing. Some trails in Glacier, Grand Teton, and Yellowstone National Parks are closed temporarily due to increased bear activity. Yellowstone also has annual closures in feeding areas. To find out about trail conditions before hiking, stop at ranger stations and visitors centers for updates. In general, trails in the national parks are maintained in better condition than in national forests, due to funding of bigger trail crews.

National park trails tend to be well-signed with direction and mileage. Some signs, however, may be in kilometers, rather than miles. (To convert kilometers to miles, multiply the kilometers listed by 0.6.) National forests and wilderness areas tend to have both less specific signage and fewer signs. Carry a good map and a compass or GPS to navigate the maze of trails. In the Northern Rockies, some trails have names while some use numbers with names or without names. The numbers, which are assigned by the U.S. Forest Service, identify the trails on U.S.F.S. maps and many topographical maps of the region.

In the national parks, where the concentration of bears is high, you may also see **bear warning signage.** Use extreme caution and all your bear country savvy when bears frequent a trail. Obey closures: They usually mean that a bear has been aggressive or is feeding on a carcass, which it will forcefully defend.

BACKCOUNTRY CAMPING

Backcountry camping is by permit only in Glacier, Grand Teton, and Yellowstone National Parks. Backcountry campgrounds vary in size, but most separate sleeping sites from communal cooking areas. No food, garbage, toiletries, or cookware should ever be kept in the tent sites. Near the cook sites, a bear pole, bar, or box allows for safe food storage. Take along a 30-foot rope and stuff bags to hang your food in Glacier and Yellowstone; backpackers in Grand Teton are required to carry bear-resistant food containers, available for free. Many backcountry campsites do not allow fires. Carry a lightweight stove for cooking.

To plan backcountry camping trips by foot, horseback, or boat in Glacier, Grand Teton, or Yellowstone National Park, follow the directions in each park's Backcountry Trip Planner, available online (www.nps.gov/glac, www.nps.gov/grte, www.nps.gov/yell). Permits may be reserved by mail for $20–25 (a limited number of sites are assigned this way, and you still have to pay your per person fee when you pick up the actual permit), or you can pick up permits in person, no more than 24 hours in advance. Permits are not issued over the phone. Permits are free except in Glacier ($4 per person per night). Permits are not needed for backpacking in national forests or wilderness areas.

Backcountry campers in the Northern Rockies need to take a 30-foot rope for hanging food, a small screen or strainer for sifting food particles out of gray water, a water purifier, and a small trowel for human waste when a pit toilet is unavailable.

Mountaineering and Climbing

The peaks of Montana, Idaho, and Wyoming draw mountaineers for their rugged, challenging routes to the summits. The quality of the rock varies between the crumbling sedimentary shales in the north and the harder granitic rocks in the south, making the type of climbing different. Ice routes, too, are shrinking due to the rapid melting of the region's glaciers. Mountaineers shimmy routes up through most of the region's mountain ranges, but a few specific locales gain above-average reputations.

While technical rock-climbing routes are available in Glacier National Park, the bulk of the summits are reached via Class 3 or 4 scrambles. Long, loose scree fields lead to tight goat walks along cliffs. Use Gordon Edwards's *A Climber's Guide to Glacier National Park* for route descriptions. Even though more technical routes exist, all six summits over 10,000 feet can be reached via scrambles. You're on your own, though, as the park has no permitted guides for off-trail scrambles.

Teton National Park harbors the region's best rock-climbing opportunities. With over 50 major routes to the summit, the Grand Teton tops the Northern Rockies' highest elevation at 13,770 feet. For those with the expertise to climb self-guided, check out Aaron Gams's *Teton Rock Climbs* for route descriptions. Two companies in Jackson offer instruction and guided trips to Teton summits—including the Grand. Other popular rock-climbing routes string down the Wind River Mountains, particularly Cirque of the Towers in the Popo Agie Wilderness.

With the glaciers across the Northern Rockies fast melting into extinction, the routes that utilize ice are changing. However, winter ascents on skis and ice climbing are available.

Bicycling

ROAD BIKING

Road bicyclists relish the Northern Rockies for the long dramatic climbs over the Continental Divide and the miles of pedal-free descents. The **TransAmerica Trail** cuts through the region, too, as does the **Lewis & Clark Trail,** among other long-distance rides. Route descriptions and maps are available from Missoula's Adventure Cycling Association (800/721-8719, www.adventurecycling.org).

Narrow, curvy roads with no shoulders and drivers gawking at scenery instead of the road all shove the biker into a precarious position.

Wear a helmet and bright colors to ensure your safety.

Two scenic byways rank with bicyclists for both their challenge and their scenery. In Glacier National Park, the 52-mile **Going-to-the-Sun Road** requires planning. Early-season up-and-back riding is available in spring and fall while road construction has the route closed to vehicles. But due to snow at Logan Pass, riders usually cannot bike across the summit. Once the road is open (mid-June–mid-Sept.), bicycling restrictions close two narrow sections of the road on the west side 11 A.M.–4 P.M. until Labor Day. Eastbound riders must be at Logan Pass by 11 A.M. or dismount and wait.

Starting from Red Lodge, Montana, the 68-mile **Beartooth Highway** climbs a lung-busting route up to 10,947 feet to cross Beartooth Pass on a high tundra plateau. Riding westbound towards Yellowstone National Park lets you get the full wow of the snowcapped peaks of the Absaroka Range. The route, which bounces from Montana into Wyoming and back into Montana, passes scads of lakes, which produce mosquito swarms into August that plague bicyclists. Snow buries the highway much of the year, but it usually is open mid-May to mid-October.

For riders looking for flat spins instead, Idaho's 72-mile paved **Trail of the Coeur d'Alenes** runs from Mullan to Plummer, following rivers, passing wetlands brimming with wildlife, and crossing the Chacolet Bridge. Interpretive signs, picnic areas, and rest stations dot the route, which changes so little in elevation that you're never sure if you're riding uphill or down. The trail is usually snow-free April–November.

Glacier and Yellowstone National Parks maintain a handful of campsites at most of their developed campgrounds for bicyclists. The shared campsites ($5 per person) have bear boxes for storing food and room for several small tents, and the campsites are first come, first served.

MOUNTAIN BIKING

While single-track mountain bike trails are

sprouting up around the region faster than weeds, rail trail projects are converting defunct tracks into wide bike paths. Idaho's 15-mile **Route of the Hiawatha** (208/744-1301, www.ridethehiawatha.com), the region's most popular mountain bike trail, crosses seven trestles and rides through nine dark tunnels, with the longest (1.7 miles) running under the Idaho-Montana state line. The Route of the Hiawatha (open late May–early October, $9 adults, $5 kids) also offers a shuttle ($9 adults, $6 kids) for those who only want to ride downhill. Eastern Idaho's 42-mile **Railroad Right of Way Trail** also runs from Warm River to West Yellowstone.

Many national forest trails permit bicycles, except in wildernesses or areas with special designations. Mountain bikes also are not permitted on national park trails, except for special routes designated in each national park.

Fishing

The movie *A River Runs Through It* catapulted Montana's rivers into the national consciousness with dreams of clear waters and wild trout. But that's the true nature of fly-fishing in the Northern Rockies, which harbor 18 blue-ribbon trout streams populated with rainbow, brown, brook, Yellowstone cutthroat, westslope cutthroat, and bull trout—many wild-bred. Lowland lakes also fill with lake trout (mackinaw), kokanee salmon, northern pike, and bass.

NATIONAL PARK FISHING

Each of the national parks has different licensing regulations for fishing. Glacier requires no license. Yellowstone National Park requires a fishing permit for anglers 16 years and older ($15 for three days, $20 for seven days, or $35 for a season); anglers 15 and younger may fish without a permit if they are fishing under the direct supervision of an adult who has a valid park fishing permit, or they can obtain a free permit (signed by a responsible adult) to fish without direct adult supervision. Grand Teton requires a Wyoming fishing license. Waterton

Native cutthroat trout are one of the prized fish in Northern Rockies streams.

© BECKY LOMAX

Lakes National Park requires a national park fishing license (one day CDN$10 or annual CDN$35). Purchase national park fishing licenses at ranger stations and visitors centers.

Each park has slightly different fishing regulations with seasons, catch-and-release laws, closure locations, and creel limits designed to protect the resources in the area. You'll need to be able to identify species that are catch-and-release only—especially the endangered bull trout. Fishing regulations are available online and at ranger stations and visitors centers.

STATE FISHING LICENSES

Outside the national parks, state fishing licenses are required. Some states offer discounts for those who are disabled. Licenses are available online and at sporting goods stores. The one exception is on Indian reservations; each has its own tribal fishing permits and rates.

Montana fishing licenses (http://fwp. mt.gov/fishing/license/default.html) cost $13

for two days or $26 for the season for resident adults. Conservation licenses for resident seniors age 62 and older and kids ages 12–14 cost $8. Resident teens ages 15–17 pay $16 for the season. Kids 11 and under fish free. Nonresident licenses for ages 15 and older cost $25 for two days, $53.50 for 10 days, or $60 for the season. Additional permits are required for warm-water game fish, paddlefish, and bull trout.

Idaho fishing licenses (http://fishandgame. idaho.gov/fish/) for residents cost $11.50 for a single day and $5 for each consecutive day; for the season, they cost $13.75 for ages 14–17 and $25.75 for adults. Nonresident licenses cost $12.75 for one day and $6 for each consecutive day, or season licenses cost $21.75 for kids up to 17 and $98.25 for adults. Nonresidents can also purchase a three-day salmon/ steelhead license for $37.50.

Wyoming fishing licenses (http://gf.state. wy.us/fish/fishing/index.asp) for residents cost $6 per day; for the season, they cost $3 for youths and $24 for adults. Nonresidents pay a daily license fee of $14 or $92 for an annual license. Nonresident youths pay $15 for an annual fee.

Boating

Small reservoirs dot the Northern Rockies, but big lakes command most of the boating interest from visitors. Montana's Flathead Lake is the largest freshwater lake west of the Mississippi. Montana, Wyoming, and Idaho each require boats to be registered. Rates vary depending on the state and the size of boat.

In **Montana,** all sailboats 12 feet long and longer and all motorized boats and personal watercraft must be registered. Nonmotorized sailboats less than 12 feet long and manually propelled boats, regardless of length, are exempt. Boats from out of state or country may be used in Montana for up to 90 consecutive days without registering with the state.

Wyoming requires all motorized boats to be registered. Motorboats that are properly registered in another state may be used on Wyoming's waters for up to 90 consecutive days without registration.

Idaho requires all boats with mechanical propulsion to be registered. Boats currently registered in another state may be used on Idaho's waterways for 60 consecutive days or less without registering with the state.

WATERSKIING

Water-skiers from warm-water areas often are shocked by their first contact with water in the Northern Rockies. It's cold. Frigid in places. The ice-fed deep lakes maintain a chill even in summer. Surface water may only heat up in August into the low 60s. Bring a wetsuit for more enjoyable waterskiing.

Rafting

The Northern Rockies spill with Class III–V white water—frothy waves with big holes. Other Class I–II rivers make for more leisurely float trips. Thirteen major rivers contain Class III and above white-water sections that you can run on your own if you have the expertise or go with local guides. In Montana, head for the Clark Fork, Middle Fork of the Flathead, Yellowstone, Gallatin, Madison, or Stillwater River for white-water thrills. Where Wyoming's Shoshone, Green, and Snake Rivers squeeze through canyons, you can bounce through rapids. In Idaho, the Lochsa, Selway, and Main Salmon provide single-day options for white water, but the Middle Fork of the Salmon requires a multi-day trip through the River of No Return Wilderness. Most of these rivers have nearby drive-to campgrounds available, and some are lined with primitive campgrounds for overnight float trips. Check on current water levels through state hydrology departments or American Whitewater (www. americanwhitewater.org).

Floating most of these rivers on an overnight trip does not require a permit. However, Idaho's Selway, Middle Fork of the Salmon, and Main Salmon Rivers do. These are acquired via an annual computerized lottery drawing. Between December 1 and January 31, you can

Whitewater rafting and kayaking is available on the Middle Fork of the Flathead as well as on other rivers in the Northern Rockies.

apply for all three rivers with one application (www.fs.fed.us/r4/sc/recreation/4rivers/index. shtml); launch winners are notified in mid-February. Permits are not available by phone, except for acquiring permits from cancelled launches after the February drawing.

Outfitters guide trips on most of the Northern Rockies' major rivers and some of their tributaries. Trips include half-day, full-day, and multi-day excursions. Locate outfitters in the towns nearest the rivers. Check with state agencies to be sure they are licensed.

Canoeing and Kayaking

The Northern Rockies also harbor lakes and slow-moving rivers—gems for multi-day paddling trips. In Montana, the Missouri River through Gates of the Mountains offers paddling along the route of Lewis and Clark, plus hiking and camping. Connected lakes, such as Idaho's Priest Lake and Upper Priest Lake, include camping on islands as well as paddling the two-mile Thoroughfare to the roadless upper lake, where the Forest Service maintains four campgrounds. A paddle route

around Montana's Flathead Lake makes use of six state parks.

Canoes and kayaks are available to rent in select places, but to guarantee you have a boat, bring your own or call ahead to reserve the rental. Rentals and guided paddle trips are available in Yellowstone and Grand Teton National Parks, plus Flathead Lake.

GEAR SELECTION AND MAINTENANCE

Camping in the Northern Rocky Mountains requires planning for all types of weather and conditions. The proper equipment can make the difference between enjoying a trip when the temperatures plummet or the air drips soggy and hating the experience.

Tents

Tents come in a variety of shapes, sizes, weights, and prices—tailored to different types of camping. Any reputable outdoor store will provide comparative ratings for their tents. Due to elevation, erratic weather, and

© BECKY LOMAX

Rain flies should cover tents completely for the best protection.

the potential for snow even in August, tents for the Northern Rockies should be double walled—with a tent wall and a rain fly that covers the complete tent to the ground. Purchase a tent with sealed seams to prevent water seeping into the tent. Bug netting is also essential for the voracious mosquitoes and black flies that proliferate during June and July. While many campers go without footprints or tarps below their tents, in wet, muddy conditions or snow, ground cloths can keep the tent floor dry. They also will prolong the life of a tent. Three-season tents work the best in the Northern Rockies for camping in summer, spring, or fall—even with erratic summer snowstorms. But for winter camping, invest in a four-season tent.

After use, dry tents completely before storing to prevent mildew. They also should be stored in a dry location rather than a damp garage, attic, or crawl space. If possible, store them loose rather than folded or rolled up

tight to prevent breakdown of the fabric on the folds.

Sleeping Bags and Pads

Sleeping bags are available with synthetic or goose down insulation. Either works well in the Northern Rockies, although those with goose down need to take extra precaution to keep their bags dry because down loses its insulation value if it gets wet. Invest in a waterproof stuff sack to keep sleeping bags dry. Bags for summer camping should be rated to 20 degrees; however, if you plan on camping in spring or fall in the Northern Rockies, you'll be more prepared for the weather mood swings with a bag rated to zero. The cut of mummy bags as opposed to rectangular bags will allow your body to heat up the space faster.

A sleeping bag alone will not keep you warm without an insulating layer between the ground and your body. Sleeping pads range from a thin 0.5-inch layer of foam to large thick air mattresses that require a compressor to inflate. Assess your needs before purchasing. If backpacking, go for the lightest weight in foam or inflatable. If car camping, you can afford to pack along more weight. Self-inflating and blow-up air mattresses allow you to camp more quietly than if you must turn on an air compressor.

Both sleeping bags and pads should be stored loose to extend their life as long as possible. A tall closet works well for hanging both. Launder sleeping bags according to the manufacturer's instruction.

Day Packs

If you plan on hiking on your camping trip, bring along a day pack. While you can get away with carrying just a water bottle for a one-hour hike, you should be prepared for the weather to change abruptly on longer day hikes. Mountain weather can mutate from blue skies to rain squalls, raging winds, hail, and even snow during summer. Bring a day pack that can fit extra clothing—rain jacket and pants, warm hat, gloves, and a light

CAMPING EQUIPMENT CHECKLIST

Group Gear
- 30-foot bear pole rope
- Aluminum foil
- Camp chairs
- Camp table
- Can opener
- Coffee cone and filters
- Cooking utensils
- Cooler
- Corkscrew
- Dishwashing tubs
- Duct tape
- Eating utensils
- Firewood
- Food
- Footprint or ground tarp
- Fuel
- Garbage bags
- Hatchet
- Kindling and newspaper
- Lanterns
- Lighter and matches
- Maps, GPS, and compass
- Mugs, plates, bowls
- Parachute cord for tarps
- Pot-holder
- Pots and pans with lids
- Rain tarps
- Salt, pepper, and spices
- Soap and sponge
- Stove
- Tent with rain-fly
- Toilet paper and trowel
- Utility knife
- Water filter
- Water jugs
- Ziploc bags

Safety
- First-aid kit
- Insect repellent
- Pepper spray
- Sunscreen

Personal Gear
- Bandana
- Batteries
- Flashlight or headlamp
- Fleece top and pants
- Gloves
- Hiking boots
- Rain jacket and pants
- Sleeping bag and pad
- Sunglasses
- Sun hat or ball cap
- Swimsuit
- Toiletries
- Warm hat
- Water bottle
- Water sandals

Recreational Gear
- Binoculars and spotting scopes
- Camera
- Cribbage board
- Day pack
- Fishing rod and tackle
- Kayak, raft, or canoe
- Mountain bike and helmet
- Paddles and personal flotation devices
- Playing cards
- Trekking poles

fleece layer. Your pack should also be able to fit lunch, snacks, first-aid kit, sunscreen, bug juice, headlamp, and water. Consider the size of optional items you may enjoy, such as a camera and binoculars.

Good day packs will include small padded hip belts to keep the weight from pulling on your neck. The hip belts also work for attaching pepper spray holders for bears. Try day packs on for size in the store, as different brands work better for different body types. Air out packs after use and store them in a dry location.

Food and Cooking Gear

Cooking while camping can be as simple as

Stoves are available in many styles and burn a variety of fuels. These are three typical examples. Top left: **White gas stoves** are the most popular because they are inexpensive and easy to find; they do require priming and can be explosive. Top right: **Gas canister stoves** burn propane, butane, isobutane, and mixtures of the three. These are the easiest to use but have two disadvantages: 1) Because the fuel is bottled, determining how much fuel is left can be difficult. 2) The fuel is limited to above-freezing conditions. Bottom: **Liquid fuel stoves** burn Coleman fuel, denatured alcohol, kerosene, and even gasoline; these fuels are economical and have a high heat output, but most must be primed.

boiling water for quick instant freeze-dried meals or as involved as slow roasting on the fire. Your mode of travel will most likely dictate the type of cooking you choose to do. If backpacking, bicycling, kayaking, or canoeing, quick-cooking meals require less gas, they weigh less, and they need fewer pots. Slow roasting on the fire requires aluminum foil, aluminum pots, or Dutch ovens. Traveling by RV, car, or boat allows for more room to pack along meals that are entertaining to cook. Virtually any recipe can be adapted to cooking outdoors with a little ingenuity.

Stoves and cooking pots also come in a variety of sizes to suit different uses. Smaller versions are available for backpacking, kayaking, and canoeing, while larger, heavier options are only suitable for vehicle-assisted camping. Most stoves are heated with white gas and propane, both available across the Northern Rockies. Butane canisters are convenient, but replacement canisters may not be as easy to find, and they add to landfills. Most outdoor lightweight cooking pots are now available with nonstick surfaces.

In bear country, low-odor foods mean less scent to attract wildlife. Store all food, cooking gear, utensils, coolers, pet food, and garbage inside hard-sided vehicles when not in use or at night. For those traveling by foot, bicycle, or motorcycle, bear boxes are available at some campgrounds. Carry 30 feet of rope for hanging food and cooking gear in case bear boxes are not available. Hang food 20 feet from the ground and 10 feet from the trunk of a tree.

Water Treatment

While the water in developed campgrounds is usually safe to drink, most streams and lakes in the West run the risk of carrying giardia and cryptosporidium, the two most common cysts in the Northern Rockies. At campgrounds where potable water is not available, plan to purify or boil water to kill potential trouble causers.

Boiling water requires no extra equipment—just a stove and extra fuel. The Wilderness Medical Society recommends heating the water to a rapid boil for one minute to kill microorganisms.

Water filters and purifiers pump water by hand through filters that are rated to strain out certain sizes of critters. A 1.0-micron filter will remove giardia and cryptosporidium, but a 0.2-micron filter will also remove bacteria while a 0.0004-micron purifier will remove viruses, too.

Chemical treatments include the use of chlorine or iodine tablets, crystals, or liquid. Follow the manufacturer's instructions for their use, most of which require waiting 30 minutes before drinking. While many campers dislike the taste left from iodine, it can work as a backup in an emergency.

UV light is now available in a compact instrument about the size of an electric toothbrush for killing microorganisms. Immerse the light tube into the water for 60 seconds. Batteries are required.

What to Wear

LAYERS

Dress in layers to adapt to the quick-changing mountain conditions and weather. Mornings can start with blue skies and temperatures for T-shirts and shorts, but by afternoon, winds

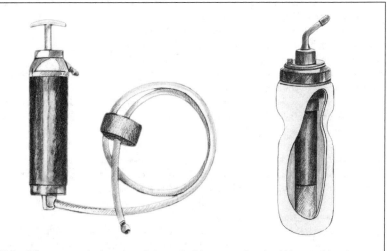

Water filters are a wise investment since all wilderness water should be considered contaminated. Make sure the filter can be easily cleaned or has a replaceable cartridge. The filter pores must be 0.4 micron or less to remove bacteria.

can usher in storm fronts delivering hail and even snow. The opposite can happen, too, with frosty mornings warming by afternoon. Layers allow adapting to the changing conditions by putting on additional clothing for protection from the elements or taking a layer off to cool down. Prepare for mountain extremes by packing a fleece or wool hat and gloves.

Sun Protection

The sun's intensity increases at high elevations. With much of the Northern Rocky Mountains stretching above 6,000 feet in elevation, protection from the glaring sun is important for preventing blistering sunburns. Add white snowfields and glaciers to the elevation, and the sun's rays wax more intense. Ball caps or sun hats protect the face from the sun's scorching rays, and sunglasses will protect the eyes from burns and snowblindness.

Rain Gear

Breathable rain gear is essential camp clothing for the Northern Rockies. Breathable rain fabrics let you recreate outdoors without getting equally as wet beneath your jacket as outside. Both rain shells and pants are useful, especially when hiking in brushy meadows laden with moisture. Arm pit zippers let you adjust the ventilation of shells. Hoods allow for closing off the neck area to chilling, wet winds, and ankle zippers on pants allow for putting them on and taking them off without removing your hiking boots.

Shoes, Socks, and Foot Care

Footwear needs to adapt to the recreation you plan to do while camping. Hikers need boots with a sturdy tread, which are available in lightweight, waterproof, and leather options. Ill-fitting shoes and incorrect socks cause blisters—preventable by shoe choice and fit. Squished toes and loose heels are the biggest culprits for blisters. To prevent toes from blistering by rubbing on each other, a shoe with a larger toe box is essential. If heels fit too loosely, two remedies can prevent blisters: Wearing one liner sock inside a heavier sock allows socks to rub against each other rather than against the heels, and footbeds, either custom or market-ready, will absorb excess space and provide more support for the foot.

Appropriate socks can also prevent blisters. Although cotton socks feel good, they aren't the best choice for hiking. Cotton absorbs water from the feet and holds it, providing a surface for friction. Synthetic, silk, or wool blend socks wick water away from the skin. Socks should fit smoothly over the feet with no added bunching. A comfortable fit, but not loose, is paramount for preventing blisters.

Those including water sports in their itineraries should also bring sturdy water sandals or shoes that will protect the feet on rough algae-slick rocks. Flip-flops do not protect the feet; use sandals or water shoes with a thick, solid tread. During spring and fall, booties will keep the feet warm in chilly waters.

SAFETY AND FIRST AID

Plants

Poison Ivy

Montana, Wyoming, and Idaho have pockets of poison ivy. Recognize the below-knee-height plant by its three leaves, often tinged with red and clustering in river corridors. If your skin comes into contact with poison ivy, wash immediately with soap and water. Do not scratch infected areas as it can spread. Avoid contact with eyes, mouth, and open sores. If you have a reaction, an antihistamine can relieve symptoms. Seek medical help.

Nettles and Cow Parsnip

Lush, forested slopes of the Northern Rockies sprout with two irritating plants. Stinging nettles vary in height 2–4 feet. Recognize them by the serrated-edged leaves and minuscule flowers hanging on a drooping stem. If skin comes into contact with nettles, you can use sting-relief products such as those for mosquito bites. Calydene also provides relief.

Some people react to cow parsnip. Recognize the plants by their 10-inch-diameter heads of white flowers and gigantic leaves shaped like maple leaves. Reactions can vary from redness to blistering. For the latter, seek medical help.

Mosquitoes and Ticks

Bugs are irritants, but more importantly, they can carry diseases such as West Nile virus and Rocky Mountain spotted fever. Protect yourself by wearing long sleeves and pants as well as using bug repellents in spring and summer when mosquitoes and ticks are common. Also, avoid areas heavily trafficked by ungulates (deer, sheep, elk), which transport ticks. If a tick bites you, remove it and disinfect the bite; keep your eye on it for lesions or a rash, consulting a doctor if either appears.

Wildlife

BEARS

Safety in bear country starts from knowledge and behaving appropriately. With the exception of Alaska and Canada, the Northern Rockies harbor the highest density of grizzly bears, and black bears find likable habitat here, too. For safety while watching bears, maintain the distance of a football field between you.

Hike safely by making noise on the trails with your voice. Do not rely on the bells sold in gift shops to alert bears to your presence. (Guides jokingly call them "dinner bells.") Bells are ineffective and may incur wrathful glares from fellow hikers who loathe them. To check the bells' effectiveness out hiking, see how close you are to oncoming hikers before you hear their ringing. Sometimes, it's too close! Bear bells are best as a souvenir, not as a substitution for human noise on the trail. Talk, sing, hoot, and holler. You'll

feel silly at first, but after a while, you'll realize it's something everyone does.

Many hikers carry **pepper spray** to deter aggressive, attacking bears; however, they are not repellents like bug sprays to be sprayed on the human body, tents, or gear. Instead, spray the capsicum derivative directly into a bear's face, aiming for the eyes and nose. While pepper sprays have repelled some attacking bears, wind and rain may reduce effectiveness, as will the product's age. Small, purse-sized pepper sprays are not adequate for bears; carry an eight-ounce can, which can be purchased in most outdoor stores in the Northern Rockies, and practice how to use it. Pepper spray is not protection: Carrying it does not lessen the need for making noise in bear country. Pepper sprays are not allowed by airlines unless checked in luggage, and only brands with USEPA labels may cross through Canadian customs.

Bears are dangerous around food—be it a carcass a bruin may be guarding in the woods or a cooler left unwittingly in a campsite. Protecting bears and protecting yourself starts with being conscious of food—including wrappers and crumbs. Gorp tidbits dropped along the trail attract wildlife, as do "biodegradable" apple cores chucked into the forest. Pick up what you drop and pack out all garbage so you will not be leaving a Hansel and Gretel trail for bears.

MOUNTAIN LIONS

Mostly unseen because of their nocturnal wanderings, these large cats are a sight to behold in daylight. They rarely prey on humans, but they can—especially small kids. While hiking, make noise to avoid surprising a lion. Hike with others, and keep kids close. If you do stumble upon a lion, do not run. Be calm. Group together and look big, waving arms overhead. Look at the cat from peripheral vision rather than staring straight on as you back slowly away. If the lion attacks, fight back with everything: rocks, sticks, or kicking.

CAMPING IN BEAR COUNTRY

Most of the Northern Rocky Mountains of Montana, Wyoming, and Idaho comprise both prime grizzly bear habitat and black bear territory. Where bears are plentiful, campgrounds require strict food and garbage management practices. Even in areas with less frequent bear visitation, properly storing food and garbage prevents problems with other wildlife – deer, squirrels, jays, and rodents.

When not in immediate use, all food, meat, cooking appliances, utensils, pots, pans, canned foods, toiletries, and empty or full food storage containers should be kept in a closed, hard-sided vehicle during the day and at night. Coolers and beverage containers should also be stored inside vehicles, as should garbage.

For campers traveling on bicycles, motorcycles, or open vehicles, many campgrounds provide food lockers or bear boxes for storing food. Use these to store food, cooking gear, toiletries, and garbage, but do not leave the garbage in the bear box. Dispose of it properly in a bear-resistant trash container.

Store all pet items that may attract or provide a reward to wildlife inside vehicles. This includes pet food, empty food dishes, and toys. Stock feed should also be stowed in hard-sided vehicles.

When hiking or walking in the woods, make noise. To avoid surprising a bear, use your voice – sing loudly, hoot, holler, or clap your hands. Bears tend to recognize human sounds as ones to avoid and usually wander off if they hear people approaching. Consciously make loud noise in thick brushy areas, around blind corners, near babbling streams, and against the wind.

Hike with other people in broad daylight, avoiding early mornings, late evenings, and night. Avoid hiking alone. Keep children near.

BISON, MOOSE, AND OTHER WILDLIFE

Bison can be as dangerous as bears. Gorings all too frequently occur despite the docile appearance of the animals. Moose also can be lethal with both antlers and hooves. For safety, maintain a distance of 25 yards from most wildlife and 100 yards from bears and wolves.

First Aid

DEHYDRATION

Many first-time visitors find the Northern Rockies to be surprisingly arid, despite the green appearance. Fight fluid loss by drinking plenty of water—especially when hiking. Altitude, sun overexposure, wind, and exercise can all lead to dehydration, which manifests in yellow urine (rather than clear), lightheadedness, headaches, dizziness, rapid breathing and heart rate, and fatigue. If you feel a headache coming on, try drinking water. If you hike with children, monitor their fluid intake. For mild dehydration, sports drinks on the market today can restore the balance of body fluids, electrolytes, and salt. Severe cases of dehydration may need intravenous fluids; treat these as a medical emergency and get to a hospital.

GIARDIA

Lakes and streams can carry parasites such as *Giardia lamblia*, which if ingested causes cramping, nausea, and severe diarrhea for an exceptionally long period of time. Tap water in the park campgrounds and picnic areas has been treated (you'll definitely taste the strong chlorine in some systems), but if you drink

Avoid bear-feeding areas. Since bears must gain weight before winter, feeding is their prime motive. Often, bears will pack in 20,000 calories in a day. In the early season, glacier lily bulbs attract grizzlies for their high nutritional value. By midseason, cow parsnip patches provide sustenance, in between high protein carrion. If you stumble across an animal carcass, leave the area immediately and notify a ranger. In August, huckleberry patches provide high amounts of sugar. Detour widely around feeding bears.

Never approach a bear. Watch the body language. A bear that stands on hind legs may just be trying to get a good smell or better viewpoint. On the other hand, head swaying, teeth clacking, laid-back ears, a lowered head, and huffing or woofing are signs of agitation: Clear out!

If you do surprise a bear, take care of yourself. Contrary to all inclinations, do not run! Instead, back away slowly, talking quietly and turning sideways or bending your knees to appear smaller and nonthreatening. Avoid direct eye contact, as the animal kingdom interprets eye contact as a challenge; instead, avert your eyes. Leave your pack on; it can protect you if the bear attacks.

In case of an attack by a bear you surprised, use pepper spray if you have it. Protect yourself and your vulnerable parts by assuming a fetal position on the ground with your hands around the back of your neck. Play dead. Only move again when you are sure the bear has vacated the area.

If a bear stalks you as food, which is rare, or attacks at night, fight back, using any means at hand – pepper spray, shouting, sticks, or rocks – to tell the bear you are not an easy food source. Try to escape up something, like a building or tree.

untreated water from streams and lakes, you run the risk of ingesting the cysts. Seek medical attention if you suspect a case of giardia.

WATER HAZARDS

Contrary to popular opinion, grizzly bears are not the number one cause of death and accidents in the Northern Rockies; drowning is. Be extremely cautious around lakes, streams, and especially waterfalls. Waters here are swift, frigid, plumb-full of submerged obstacles, and unforgiving. Be especially careful on rocks and logs around fast-moving streams; these often have moss and clear algae that makes the rocks slippery.

Yellowstone's gorgeous hydrothermic features can be deadly, too. In many, water bubbles above boiling, and what looks like solid ground may only be a thin crust that can give way with the weight of a human. Stay on designated boardwalks and trails. Toxic gases spew in some of the geyser basins. If you feel sick, leave the area immediately.

ALTITUDE

The Northern Rockies climb in elevation. Some visitors from coastal regions may feel the effects of altitude—a lightheadedness, headache, or shortness of breath—in high zones like Logan Pass in Glacier, the Yellowstone plateau, and the Beartooth Highway. In most cases, slowing down a hiking pace helps, along with drinking lots of fluids and giving the body time to acclimatize. If symptoms are more dramatic, descend in elevation as soon as possible.

Altitude also increases the effects of UV radiation. Above the tree line, you can actually feel cool but still redden with sunburn. Use a strong sunscreen to prevent burning. Sunglasses and a hat will also help protect you.

CREVASSES AND SNOWBRIDGES

While ice often looks solid to step on, it harbors unseen caverns beneath. Crevasses (large vertical cracks) are difficult to see, and snowbridges can collapse easily as a person crosses. Unless you have training in glacier travel, you're safer staying off the ice. Even Glacier's tiny icefields have caused fatalities. Snowfields also demand respect. Steep slopes can run out into rocks, trees, or over cliffs. If sliding for fun, choose a location with a safe runout. Do not travel across steep snowfields unless appropriately equipped with an ice axe and the knowledge to use it.

HYPOTHERMIA AND FROSTBITE

Because mountain weather can disintegrate rapidly from a summer balm to a winter snowstorm, hypothermia is a very real threat. At onset, the body's inner core loses heat, thus reducing mental and physical functions. It's insidious and progressively subtle: Watch for uncontrolled shivering, incoherence, poor judgment, fumbling, mumbling, and slurred speech. Exhausted, physically unprepared, and ill-clad hikers are most at risk. You can avoid becoming hypothermic by donning rain gear and warm layers. Don't let yourself get wet. Also, leave the cotton clothing back in the car; instead wear moisture-wicking layers that you can adjust to stay dry.

If someone in your party is hypothermic, get him or her sheltered and into dry clothing immediately. Warm liquid can help heat the body, but be sure it's nonalcoholic and noncaffeinated. Build a fire for warmth. If the victim cannot regain body warmth, get into a sleeping bag with the victim, with you and the victim stripped for skin-to-skin contact, and seek medical help.

Frostbite, which usually affects extremities when exposed to very cold temperatures, causes the tissues to freeze, resulting in hard, pale, and cold skin. As the area thaws, the flesh becomes red and painful. Prevent frostbite by watching the hands, feet, nose, and ears for discoloration and wearing appropriate clothing. Warm the hands in armpits, and cover the nose and ears with dry, gloved hands. If frostbitten, do not rub the affected skin, let thawed areas refreeze, or thaw frozen areas if a chance of refreezing exists. Seek medical help immediately.

BLISTERS

Blister prevention starts with recognition of "hot spots" or rubs. Before any blister forms, apply Moleskin or New Skin to the sensitive area. Both act as another layer of skin. Moleskin adheres to the skin, like a thick Band-Aid, with its fuzzy covering absorbing friction. New Skin, looking and smelling like fingernail polish, rubs off gradually, absorbing friction instead of the skin. Be aware that New Skin must be reapplied frequently and should not be used on open sores. In a pinch, duct tape can be slapped on potential trouble spots.

Once a blister occurs, apply Second Skin, a product developed for burns that cools the blister off and cushions it. Cover Second Skin with Moleskin, which absorbs future rubbing and holds the Second Skin in place. Also, marketed under several brand names, specialty blister bandages promote healing. Apply the adhesive bandage carefully with hand heat to mold it to the foot surface. Leave it in place until the blister begins to callus. Check placement often, as these bandages and moleskin tend to migrate away from the blister.

HANTAVIRUS

The hantavirus infection is contracted by inhaling the dust from deer mice urine and droppings. Once infected, you'll feel flu-like symptoms set in; seek medical attention immediately if you suspect contact with the virus. To protect yourself, avoid areas thick with rodents, their burrows, and woodpiles. Store all food in rodent-proof containers. If you find rodent dust in your gear or tent, spray with a mix of water and bleach (1.5 cups bleach to one gallon water).

NORTHWEST MONTANA

© BECKY LOMAX

BEST CAMPGROUNDS

(Boat-in Camping
Elk Island, page 76.

(Hiking
Little Therriault Lake, page 54.
Holland Lake, page 90.

(Hot Springs
Cascade, page 89.

(Lake Camping
Big Arm State Park, page 79.

(Montana
Big Therriault Lake, page 55.
Spotted Bear, page 86.

(River Camping
Bull River, page 63.

(Wildlife-Watching
Swan Lake, page 85.

Ice carved out the jagged, snowcapped north-
west Montana mountains, leaving wet thumbprints of ponds, lakes, and
alpine tarns. As the ice receded, water etched valleys, frothing white in
rocky drops and smoothing placidly into clear, blue-green glass through
the flats. Campgrounds line the rivers and lakes, from high alpine passes
to the lowest elevation in Montana.

In contrast with other states where luxury homes and posh resorts
take up every inch of shore along rivers and lakes, in Montana the public
maintains access to miles of water. Plus, the region teems with wildlife:
grizzly bears, wolves, mountain lions, elk, moose, mountain goats, and
bighorn sheep. Accessibility and wildlife lure campers, but the area has
even more attributes.

More than five million acres of public, accessible forests envelop northwest Montana. That's comparable to the size of New Jersey. The region
also holds more state parks than any other area of Montana. Seven mountain ranges, five wilderness areas, four national forests, and two special
hiking areas gain the region a reputation as a camping mecca. Add more
than 500 lakes, three major rivers, three huge reservoirs, and 3,000
miles of streams, and the options for camping multiply far beyond what
you can visit in months of travel.

But, while many campgrounds are accessible by paved two-lane
roads, a substantial number are accessed only by dirt roads that crawl
deep into the forest. To camp at Spotted Bear – the springboard into
the Bob Marshall Wilderness – you must drive almost 60 dusty miles
of washboards.

The most popular camping areas cluster around lakes, where waters
buzz with water-skiers, anglers, sailors, sea kayakers, and canoeists. Flathead Lake, the largest freshwater lake west of the Mississippi River, attracts the most boaters; its five state parks have campgrounds rimming
its shoreline. The sheer size of the lake – almost 30 miles long – makes
it seem more on par with an inland sea, and its whitecaps attest to winds
that can whip up several-foot-high waves. The lake's 50-pound mackinaw
trout attract sport anglers, and its Wild Horse Island – a day-use park –

lures hikers for its wild horses, bighorn sheep, wildflowers, and views of the peak-rimmed lake from its summit.

Two other large reservoirs also attract boaters, but in far fewer numbers than at Flathead Lake. East of Flathead Lake, Hungry Horse Reservoir squeezes between two mountain ranges with 14 campgrounds. Anglers especially relish its fishery, which harbors westslope cutthroat trout. Several islands dot the 35-mile-long reservoir – two contain campgrounds. Northwest of Flathead Lake, Lake Koocanusa sprawls 90 miles, crossing the border into Canada. Its name combines the Kootenai River plus the names of its two countries. Campgrounds rim the lake, which offers boating and fishing for kamloops trout.

Those who enjoy camping at smaller lakes head to Tally Lake, Montana's deepest lake, which plummets to nearly 500 feet. Other lake getaways include two valleys lining lakes up in strings. Southeast of Flathead Lake, the narrow Highway 83 corridor cradles seven large lakes between the Mission and Swan Mountains. You can watch bald eagles fishing and wake up to the call of loons. These lakes attract not only boaters and anglers, but hikers as well, as trails lead both east and west into wilderness areas. West of Flathead Lake, the Thompson Chain of Lakes along Highway 2 links up another seven large lakes with a handful of smaller ponds – all loaded with state-run and national forest campgrounds.

Campers looking for special places to hike will find campgrounds at the base of mountains that climb from cedar canopies to wildflower meadows. Ten Lakes Scenic Area, with its two campgrounds, weaves hiking trails along ridges right on the border with Canada; views encompass tiny subalpine lakes, the northern Whitefish Range, and Glacier Park in the distance. The Cabinet Mountain Wilderness – topped by glaciers on Snowshoe Peak – offers lakes, huckleberry picking, and high passes as destinations for hikers. Jewel Basin, with its 27 alpine lakes, has trails with views of Flathead Lake and the wild interior of the Great Bear Wilderness.

For campers, northwest Montana is one vast playground. Rarely do campgrounds swell to over 50 campsites, and many are small free sites with room for only a few tents.

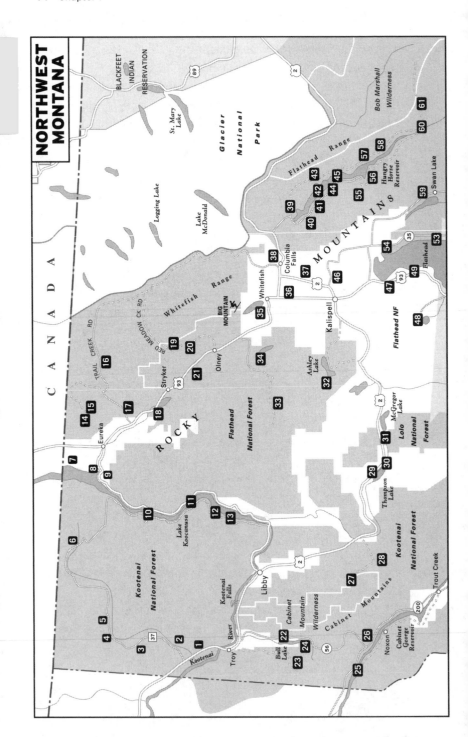

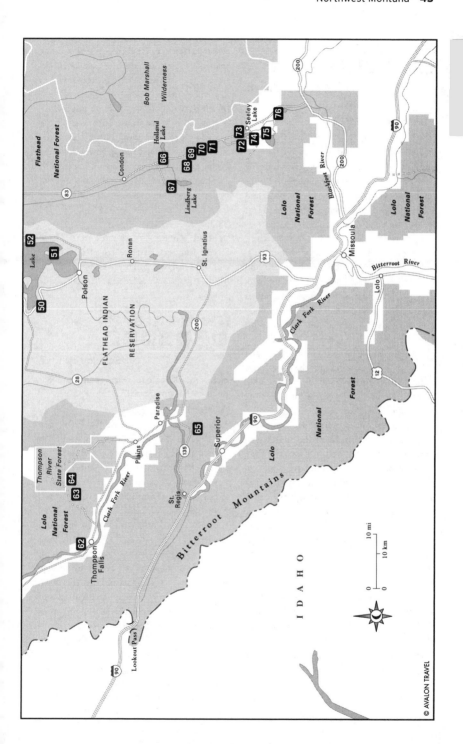

© AVALON TRAVEL

◼ YAAK RIVER

Scenic rating: 8

on the Yaak River in the Purcell Mountains in Kootenai National Forest

At 1,900 feet at the confluence of the Kootenai and Yaak Rivers, the campground is the only developed Forest Service campground right on the highway between the Idaho border and Libby. It also has the fame of being the lowest in Montana and frequently fills up, particularly on weekends. The 53-mile Yaak River, which drains the remote Purcell Mountains, holds rainbow trout, mountain whitefish, and brook trout. The fishing is best from the bank or by wading. The color of the river changes from crystal clear most of the year to cloudy gray during the May and June runoff. With only a few riffles, the lower Kootenai River is also a favorite with locals for floating rafts and fishing in drift boats. Put in at the Troy Bridge to float about nine miles to the campground. A primitive boat ramp works for launching canoes and small boats.

The campground, which has two paved loops, sits on both sides of the Yaak River, with turnoffs north and south of the Yaak River Bridge. Shaded by tall larches and cedars, both loops have access to both the Yaak and Kootenai Rivers, although the north loop has a larger sandy beach. Campsites are spaced out for privacy, with tall brush between sites. You'll hear some trucks at night on the highway above. Eight sites offer pull-through paved parking pads, and several parking pads are double-wide.

Campsites, facilities: The campground has 44 RV or tent campsites. RVs are limited to 32 feet. Facilities include picnic tables, fire rings with grills, vault toilets, garbage service, campground hosts, and drinking water. You can collect downed limbs for firewood from the surrounding national forest. Leashed pets are permitted. A wheelchair-accessible toilet is available.

Reservations, fees: Reservations are not available. Campsites cost $10. Cash or check. Open year-round, with limited services September–May.

Directions: From Troy, drive on Highway 2 northwest for seven miles. Turn west off the highway into the campground. Entrances flank the Yaak River Bridge; however, the fee station and campground hosts are on the south side before crossing the river. From the Idaho border, drive about seven miles southeast. GPS Coordinates: N 48° 33.662' W 115° 58.335'

Contact: Kootenai National Forest, Three Rivers Ranger District, Troy Ranger Station, 12858 Hwy. 2, Troy, MT 59935-8750, 406/295-4693, www.fs.fed.us/r1/kootenai/.

◼ YAAK FALLS

Scenic rating: 7

on the Yaak River in the Purcell Mountains in Kootenai National Forest

Sitting at 2,400 feet on the Yaak River in the Purcell Mountains, the campground is named for the nearby falls 0.3 mile to the north. The falls, named after the Yaak Indians who once populated the area, cascade through some of the oldest rock in the world. Due to the eastward shift of the Pacific plate, rocks 800 million to 1.5 billion years old shoved up to the surface. The 53-mile Yaak River cuts through these slabs, which you can sit on to view the two falls. During high water in late May and early June, they roar. The river harbors westslope cutthroat and rainbow trout. Above the falls, pools work for fly-fishing and the access is easy due to the road's proximity. Larger rainbows hang out below the falls. White-water rafters and kayakers also float the Yaak. Below the falls, the canyon holds expert Class IV–V drops. Above the falls in the four-mile stretch from Seventeen Mile Bridge, the rapids rank more around Class II–III; experience in navigating boulders is a must.

The campground receives filtered sunlight through larch and cedar trees. Underbrush alternates with open rocky areas, granting some sites privacy. You can hear the roar of the river in the campground.

Campsites, facilities: The campground has seven RV or tent campsites. RVs are limited to 32 feet. Facilities include picnic tables, fire rings, and a vault toilet, but no drinking water. Bring water with you, or haul it from the fishing access. If you plan to use the river water, purify or boil it before drinking. Sometimes firewood is available, but you can also collect downed limbs for firewood from the surrounding national forest. Pack out your trash. Leashed pets are permitted.

Reservations, fees: Reservations are not available. Campsites are free. Open year-round, but services are limited September–May.

Directions: On Highway 2, drive 10 miles west from Troy or four miles east from the Idaho-Montana border. Turn north onto Highway 508, a paved road, and drive for seven miles. Turn right into the campground.

GPS Coordinates: N 48° 38.656' W 115° 53.229'

Contact: Kootenai National Forest, Three Rivers Ranger District, Troy Ranger Station, 12858 Hwy. 2, Troy, MT 59935-8750, 406/295-4693, www.fs.fed.us/r1/kootenai/.

3 RED TOP

Scenic rating: 6

in the Purcell Mountains in Kootenai National Forest

Sitting at 2,920 feet in the Purcell Mountains, Red Top Campground is used mostly by those touring the Yaak River drainage. However, the campground does not sit on the river, but rather across the road on Red Top Creek. Fishing is available in Red Top Creek, but most of the Yaak River adjacent to the campground is flanked by private land, although fishing accesses are available both north and south on the river. The campground is named for the 6,226-foot summit of Red Top Mountain to the west.

Dense conifers shade the tiny campground, which is bordered on the north side by the creek. Its location on the road to Yaak allows for road noise to enter the campground, but at night, traffic quiets so you can hear the creek. The dirt campground road is narrow, affording limited maneuvering space for trailers.

Campsites, facilities: The campground has five RV or tent campsites. RVs are limited to 32 feet. Facilities include picnic tables, fire rings with grills, and a vault toilet, but no drinking water. Bring water with you, or haul it from Red Top Creek. If you plan to use the creek water, purify or boil it before drinking. Pack out your trash. You can collect downed limbs for firewood from the surrounding national forest. Leashed pets are permitted.

Reservations, fees: Reservations are not available. Campsites are free. Open year-round, but services are limited September–May.

Directions: On Highway 2, drive 10 miles west from Troy or five miles east from the Idaho-Montana border to Highway 508. Turn north onto the paved road and drive for 16 miles. Turn west into the campground.

GPS Coordinates: N 48° 45.660' W 115° 55.070'

Contact: Kootenai National Forest, Three Rivers Ranger District, Troy Ranger Station, 12858 Hwy. 2, Troy, MT 59935-8750, 406/295-4693, www.fs.fed.us/r1/kootenai/.

4 WHITETAIL

Scenic rating: 7

on the Yaak River in the Purcell Mountains in Kootenai National Forest

Sitting at 3,080 feet in the heavily forested Purcell Mountains, Whitetail is one of four campgrounds accessed by pavement along the lower Yaak River. The river, which is slow-flowing in this area, is good for floating from the Yaak Bridge in the town of Yaak to the campground. The distance is about six miles, and the river stretches wide enough for canoes, inflatable kayaks, small rafts, and drift boats. Larger rafts are better only in the last half from Pete Creek to the campground. The river has occasional logjams, so keep alert. A primitive boat ramp in the campground allows for launching or loading canoes and small boats. The river also harbors rainbow and brook trout. Forest Road 4354 leads to a trailhead into the Northwest Peak Scenic Area, and mountain bikers can ride to Mount Baldy Lookout.

A loose coniferous forest lends partial shade to the campground, which tucks between the road and the river. Thick, lush brush and grass envelops the shoreline, but trails weave through it to reach the water. Sites are spread out for privacy, and a few of them overlook the river. Some also back into the hillside against the road. At night, the road noise dwindles, and the sound of the river is pervasive, especially in early summer. A paved road loops through the campground, which is a good place for sighting moose.

Campsites, facilities: The campground has 12 RV or tent campsites. RVs are limited to 32 feet. Facilities include picnic tables, fire rings with grills, a vault toilet, drinking water, campground hosts, a boat ramp, and limited firewood for sale. Leashed pets are permitted. A wheelchair-accessible toilet is available.

Reservations, fees: Reservations are not available. Campsites cost $7. Cash or check. Open year-round, with limited services September–May.

Directions: On Highway 2, drive 10 miles west from Troy or four miles east from the Idaho-Montana border. Turn north onto the paved Highway 508 and drive for 24 miles to the campground, located on the south side of the road. From Yaak, the campground is 5.5 miles to the west.

GPS Coordinates: N 48° 49.667' W 115° 49.035'

Contact: Kootenai National Forest, Three Rivers Ranger District, Troy Ranger Station, 12858 Hwy. 2, Troy, MT 59935-8750, 406/295-4693, www.fs.fed.us/r1/kootenai/.

5 PETE CREEK

Scenic rating: 8

on the Yaak River in the Purcell Mountains in Kootenai National Forest

Pete Creek sits at 3,120 feet along the Yaak River in the Purcell Mountains. A primitive boat launch in the campground works for rafts, kayaks, and canoes. You can float from the Yaak Bridge 2.6 miles east or three miles from the campground to Whitetail Campground, but larger rafts should stick to the section below Pete Creek. Floaters must be on the lookout for logjams. The Yaak River also harbors rainbow and brook trout. To explore the 19,100-acre Northwest Peak Scenic Area, drive 19 miles north on Forest Road 338. From the trailhead, a 2.3-mile path leads to the top of 7,705-foot-high Northwest Peak for views in Canada and glimpses of the Cabinet Mountains toward the southwest. Plenty of Forest Service roads are also available for mountain biking, hunting, and winter snowmobiling. The campground is also the closest to Yaak, a tiny, remote year-round community.

Dense, tall conifers and lush undergrowth lend both shade and privacy to this intimate campground tucked between the road, Pete Creek, and Yaak River. With both the creek and the river, the sound of flowing water is heard at most of the campsites. Rock walls provide bouldering right in the campground. Three sites overlook Pete Creek, and two small, private walk-in campsites are best for tenters.

Campsites, facilities: The campground has 11 RV or tent campsites, plus two walk-in campsites for tents. RVs are limited to 32 feet. Facilities include picnic tables, fire rings, a vault toilet, drinking water, campground hosts, firewood for sale, and a boat ramp. Leashed pets are permitted. A wheelchair-accessible toilet is available.

Reservations, fees: Reservations are not available. Campsites cost $7. Cash or check. Open year-round, with limited services September–May.

Directions: On Highway 2, drive 10 miles west from Troy or four miles east from the Idaho-Montana border. Turn north onto the paved Highway 508 and drive for 27 miles to the campground, which is on the south side of the road. From Yaak, the campground is 2.5 miles to the west.

GPS Coordinates: N 48° 49.867' W 115° 45.960'

Contact: Kootenai National Forest, Three Rivers Ranger District, Troy Ranger Station, 12858 Hwy. 2, Troy, MT 59935-8750, 406/295-4693, www.fs.fed.us/r1/kootenai/.

6 CARIBOU

Scenic rating: 8

in the Purcell Mountains in Kootenai National Forest

At an elevation of 3,700 feet in the Purcell Mountains, Caribou Campground requires a long drive from everywhere. Caribou Creek runs adjacent to Caribou Campground, which sits only 3.5 miles from the Canadian border. Fishing is available in the creek. The campground works as a base camp for exploring the remote northern Yaak. Upper Yaak Falls is about 10 miles west of the campground, and much of the area along the road provides good wildlife-watching. The Caribou Trail (#56), which begins about 0.5 mile northwest of the campground, traverses Caribou Mountain and peters out near the border. The Vinal–Mount Henry–Boulder National Recreation Trail sits in the mountains south of the campground. Trails 7 and 17 lead to Mount Henry Lakes and the summit of Mount Henry, while connecting with the trail.

The tiny secluded campground is the epitome of quiet. Located miles from pavement in both directions, the forest road passing the campground produces minimal traffic and none at night. The creek, which flows on the west side of the campground, is the only sound you'll hear beside wildlife: owls, coyotes, and ravens. The campsites rim a meadow surrounded by a loose forest of conifers.

Campsites, facilities: The campground has three RV or tent campsites. RVs are limited to 32 feet. Facilities include picnic tables, fire rings, and a vault toilet. No drinking water is available. Bring your own, or if you plan to use creek water, then filter or boil it before drinking. Leashed pets are permitted.

Reservations, fees: Reservations are not available. Campsites are free. Open mid-April–mid-November, but services are limited until May and after early September.

Directions: On Highway 2, drive 10 miles west from Troy or four miles east from the Idaho-Montana border. Turn north onto the Highway 508 and drive for 30 miles to Yaak, where the road becomes dirt and changes to Forest Road 92. Drive 19 more miles and turn north into the campground. From the Eureka area, cross the Lake Koocanusa Bridge and drive six miles north on Forest Road 92 and turn left after crossing Sullivan Creek, driving about 19 miles west on Forest Road 92.

GPS Coordinates: N 48° 56.900' W 115° 30.226'

Contact: Kootenai National Forest, Three Rivers Ranger District, Troy Ranger Station, 12858 Hwy. 2, Troy, MT 59935-8750, 406/295-4693, www.fs.fed.us/r1/kootenai/.

7 SWISHER LAKE

Scenic rating: 8

northwest of Eureka in Kootenai National Forest

Located at 2,480 feet, Swisher Lake is one of several small ponds sitting northwest of Eureka. The tiny grassland- and forest-surrounded nine-acre lake is also within two miles of Lake Koocanusa and two miles from the Canadian border. A 0.3-mile foot and horse trail leads to the campsites on the northwest shore of the lake. The trailhead for horses sits 0.2 mile past the campground gate, but no equine loading ramp is available. The campground includes a primitive boat ramp with a dock, and the lake harbors brook and westslope cutthroat trout, but also is stocked regularly with rainbow trout. The campground sits about one mile from the Murray Spring Fish Hatchery, where you can take tours. The lake works for hand-carried watercraft, such as small rafts and canoes.

Swisher Lake is a walk-in campground for tents only. Parking is available for only four vehicles at the trailhead. The quiet campground sits on the grassy shore of the lake in a mixed open forest—a good location to spot wildlife.

Campsites, facilities: The tent-only campground has only four campsites. Facilities include picnic tables, fire rings, a vault toilet, and boat ramp. You can collect downed limbs for firewood from the surrounding national forest. No drinking water is available. Bring your own, or if you plan to use lake water, then filter or boil it before drinking. Pack out your trash. Leashed pets are permitted.

Reservations, fees: Reservations are not available. Campsites are free. Open year-round.

Directions: From just north of Eureka, turn west on Highway 37 and drive 2.5 miles to the junction with the Sophie Lake and Tetrault Lake Road. Turn north and drive five miles to the gate at the Swisher Lake entrance and the tiny parking lot. (The pavement ends about 0.5 mile before the gate.)

GPS Coordinates: N 48° 58.128' W 115° 8.020'

Contact: Kootenai National Forest, Rexford Ranger District, Eureka Ranger Station, 949 Hwy. 93 N., Eureka, MT 59917-9550, 406/296-2536, www.fs.fed.us/r1/kootenai/.

8 REXFORD BENCH COMPLEX

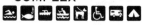

Scenic rating: 8

on Lake Koocanusa in Kootenai National Forest

Contrary to many of Kootenai National Forest's quiet remote campgrounds, the Rexford Bench Complex is not wilderness. The campground sits at 2,470 feet on Lake Koocanusa, a 90-mile-long reservoir spanning the international boundary. (Hence, the invented name that combines KOOtenai, CANada, and USA.) The Libby Dam formed the lake when it was completed in 1974. The huge lake garners plenty of recreational boaters around bays, but the main lake always seems empty. During droughts, late summer draw-downs drop the lake very low, sometimes prohibiting launching boats. The complex includes a boat launch with low- and high-water concrete ramps, docks, fish-cleaning stations, trailer parking, and a buoyed swimming beach. The campground sits on a narrow, sheltered side bay that is popular for waterskiing, canoeing, and fishing for kokanee salmon.

A paved road loops through the campground, which is shaded by firs. The campsites have no views of the lake, and the open understory permits visibility of neighboring campers. Vehicle noise from the highway floats through the campground. Six campsites have pull-through parking pads.

Campsites, facilities: The campground has 34 RV or tent campsites and 20 campsites for tents only. RVs are limited to 32 feet. Facilities include picnic tables, fire rings with grills, flush toilets, drinking water, garbage service, campground hosts, a disposal station ($2), a boat ramp, a swimming beach, and overflow overnight parking for RVs, but no hookups. Without designated parking spaces, the Kamloops Terrace overflow area fits about 25 RVs and has flush toilets, drinking water, tables, and fire rings. Leashed pets are permitted. A wheelchair-accessible toilet is available.

Reservations, fees: Reservations are available (877/444-6777, www.recreation.gov). Campsites cost $12. Cash or check. Open mid-May–early September, but the swimming beach doesn't open until June and the boat launch is available whenever reservoir water levels allow launching. Kamloops Terrace overflow camping costs $9 and has services only mid-June–mid-September.

Directions: From Highway 93 north of Eureka, drive five miles west on Highway 37 to reach Rexford. Turn north off the highway into the campground. From the Lake Koocanusa Bridge, drive eight miles northeast.

GPS Coordinates: N 48° 53.908' W 115° 9.480'

Contact: Kootenai National Forest, Rexford Ranger District, Eureka Ranger Station, 949 Hwy. 93 N., Eureka, MT 59917-9550, 406/296-2536, www.fs.fed.us/r1/kootenai/.

9 CAMP 32

Scenic rating: 5

east of Lake Koocanusa in Kootenai National Forest

The turnoff to Camp 32 sits 1.5 miles northwest of the Lake Koocanusa Bridge, the longest and tallest bridge in Montana. The bridge, built in 1970, is 2,437 feet long. You can park in the lot just south of the bridge and walk across the half-mile span. To get to the campground, the road follows Pinkham Creek, which draws anglers going after rainbow trout. Few people come here because of the narrow, rough access road, which also offers a few large secluded dispersed camping sites along the creek.

Since the campground is off the main Lake Koocanusa highway, the campground is ultra quiet. The campground circles around one loop under Douglas firs, with small vine

maples and wild rosebushes forming privacy barriers between campsites. All of the sites are pull-ins, and some of the tables are in disrepair. The campsites are also fairly small. A large field parallels the entrance to the campground. Two campsites with less privacy back up to the dirt entrance road rather than the creek.

Campsites, facilities: The campground has eight RV or tent campsites. The sites can accommodate a maximum RV size of 20 feet, and trailers are not recommended. Facilities include picnic tables, rough rock fire rings, vault toilets, drinking water from a hand pump, and limited firewood. Leashed pets are permitted. A wheelchair-accessible toilet is available.

Reservations, fees: Reservations are not accepted. Campsites are free. Open year-round, but serviced only mid-May–early September.

Directions: From Highway 93 north of Eureka, drive 12 miles southwest on Highway 37. Turn east onto the dirt Rondo Road (Forest Road 7182). Drive 2.5 miles on the single-lane, narrow, potholed road to the campground. From the Lake Koocanusa Bridge, the signed turnoff sits 1.5 miles northeast.

GPS Coordinates: N 48° 50.238' W 115° 11.458'

Contact: Kootenai National Forest, Rexford Ranger District, Eureka Ranger Station, 949 Hwy. 93 N., Eureka, MT 59917-9550, 406/296-2536, www.fs.fed.us/r1/kootenai/.

10 PECK GULCH

Scenic rating: 9

on Lake Koocanusa in Kootenai National Forest

Peck Gulch is a unique campground. People either love it or hate it, depending on tastes. At 2,470 feet, the campground sits on a flat, wide, treeless sandbar jutting several hundred feet out into Lake Koocanusa's east shore. The rocky cliffs, broken with open grassy areas between Peck Gulch and the Lake Koocanusa Bridge, provide excellent habitat for bighorn sheep, and the cliffs also attract rock climbers. From the campground, a steep 0.5-mile trail climbs to Peck Gulch. Two boat ramps—one for high water and one for low water—allow for launching when the reservoir water reaches different levels during the season. An adjacent paved parking lot provides a place to drop the trailer before claiming a campsite.

Raised grassy areas circle the campground around four large, round gravel parking lots with no designated parking strips or campsite boundaries. No vegetation—no trees, no bushes—grows on the sandbar, so campsites have no privacy and no wind blocks. Sidle up to a place that looks good and claim it. Many of the campsites sit right on the edge of the bar, with unobstructed views of the reservoir and the Purcell Mountains rising from the opposite shore. More-protected sites tuck up against the firs and ponderosas along the hillsides.

Campsites, facilities: The campground has undesignated campsites on a flat, open, dirt, table-like sandbar with room for 22 RV or tent camping units. Vehicles over 32 feet are not permitted. Facilities include picnic tables, rock fire rings with grills, vault toilets, drinking water, and a campground host. Firewood is available. Leashed pets are permitted. A wheelchair-accessible toilet is available.

Reservations, fees: Reservations are not accepted. Campsites cost $9. Cash or check. Open mid-April–September but serviced only mid-May–early September.

Directions: From Highway 93 north of Eureka, drive 21 miles southwest on Highway 37, or from Libby, drive 48 miles northeast on Highway 37. Turn west off the highway at the sign, which leads to a narrow, steep, paved single-lane road that drops to the campground.

GPS Coordinates: N 48° 43.456' W 115° 18.459'

Contact: Kootenai National Forest, Rexford Ranger District, Eureka Ranger Station, 949 Hwy. 93 N., Eureka, MT 59917-9550, 406/296-2536, www.fs.fed.us/r1/kootenai/.

11 ROCKY GORGE

Scenic rating: 8

on Lake Koocanusa in Kootenai National Forest

Located at 2,470 feet on the east shore of 90-mile-long Lake Koocanusa, Rocky Gorge Campground sits at one of the narrowest stretches of the reservoir. A cement boat launch allows for getting out on the reservoir. At low pool (when water level is at its lowest seasonal levels), plenty of beach opens up with its combination of clay sand and rocks. Watch for bald eagle nests and ospreys fishing along this side of the reservoir.

Islands of bushes and trees divide up the campground, but the rough-paved, parking lot effect is evident. No designated parking spaces denote campsites. Just roll in and claim a spot that looks good. The campground sits under ponderosa pines, but with the open parking, little privacy is available. Sites along the west perimeter have peek-a-boo views of the reservoir and work better for those with tents. Two walk-in tent sites sit right on the bluff with broad views of the reservoir. Recent thinning added more views, too. Spring brings on blooms of yellow arrowleaf balsamroot in the campground.

Campsites, facilities: The campground has undesignated campsites with room for 60 RV or tent camping units. The maximum vehicle length is 32 feet. Facilities include picnic tables, rock fire rings with grills, vault toilets, drinking water, and a campground host. While you can collect firewood in the surrounding forest, the downed limbs have mostly been plucked up. Pack out your trash. Leashed pets are permitted. A wheelchair-accessible toilet is available.

Reservations, fees: Reservations are not accepted. Campsites cost $9. Cash or check. Open year-round, but serviced only mid-May–early September.

Directions: From Highway 93 north of Eureka, drive 31 miles southwest on Highway 37, or from Libby, drive 40 miles northeast on Highway 37. Turn west off the highway into the campground entrance at milepost 41.4.

GPS Coordinates: N 48° 39.132' W 115° 18.683'

Contact: Kootenai National Forest, Rexford Ranger District, Eureka Ranger Station, 949 Hwy. 93 N., Eureka, MT 59917-9550, 406/296-2536, www.fs.fed.us/r1/kootenai/.

12 BARRON FLATS

Scenic rating: 7

on Lake Koocanusa in Kootenai National Forest

On Lake Koocanusa, known for its kokanee salmon fishery, Barron Flats sits at 2,500 feet on the reservoir's west side. A snowmobile destination in winter and a quiet getaway in summer, the campground serves as a west-side stop on the Koocanusa Scenic Byway, which loops 67 miles around the reservoir via the Lake Koocanusa Bridge on the north and Libby Dam on the south. The west-side road, which is closed in winter, usually melts out by April and receives snow again in November. Take binoculars, for the region provides habitat for bighorn sheep, black bears, and bald eagles. A concrete boat launch allows launching of powerboats, kayaks, and canoes.

The quiet campground sits above the reservoir in a large, grassy field with two loops through the west side of the meadow. The sites are undesignated; just pull over next to a patch of grass. Camping on the open west sides of the loops grants views of the surrounding terrain, but no privacy; for tidbits of shade and a semblance of privacy, camp along the

south and east perimeters adjacent to the forest. Three rock fire rings are tucked along the southwest perimeter in the trees.

Campsites, facilities: The campground has dispersed RV or tent camping with no designated campsites or picnic tables, but space to accommodate 15 rigs. The maximum vehicle length is 32 feet. Facilities include a few rock fire rings and vault toilets. No drinking water is provided. Plan on bringing your own; lake water must be filtered or boiled before drinking. Pack out your trash. Leashed pets are permitted. A wheelchair-accessible toilet is available.

Reservations, fees: Reservations are not accepted. Campsites are free. Open year-round, but serviced only mid-May–early September.

Directions: Approach the campground from the north via the Koocanusa Bridge, about an hour's drive on the curvy but paved Forest Road 228. At milepost 12.5, turn east onto the paved road to the boat launch and turn right onto a dirt road dropping into the campground's huge meadow. From the south, turn off Highway 37 one mile northeast of the Canoe Gulch Ranger Station and drive 13 miles north.

GPS Coordinates: N 48° 30.960' W 115° 17.638'

Contact: Kootenai National Forest, Libby Ranger District, Canoe Gulch Ranger Station, 12557 Hwy. 37, Libby, MT 59923-8212, 406/293-7773, www.fs.fed.us/r1/kootenai/.

13 MCGILLIVRAY

Scenic rating: 7

on Lake Koocanusa in Kootenai National Forest

On Lake Koocanusa, McGillivray is the closest designated Forest Service campground to Libby Dam. It sits on the reservoir's west side and is a snowmobile destination in winter on the snow-covered west-side road. The Libby Dam Visitor Center is located on the same side of the dam as the campground. Between Memorial Day and Labor Day, four dam tours depart daily for 90-minute guided walks through the dam and powerhouse. The 422-foot-tall dam retains 90 miles of water in Lake Koocanusa, with 48 of the lake's miles in the United States and the other miles over the international border in Canada. Near the dam, the Souse Gulch picnic area is home to nesting bald eagles. The two boat ramps accommodate both high and low reservoir levels, plus a dock and boat trailer parking. Set back in the firs above the reservoir—a kokanee salmon fishery—the campground connects to the swimming and boating beaches via either roads or trails. Trails also loop around the bluffs for views of the reservoir and Salish Mountains. The swimming beach is formed by a narrow inlet at high pool (when water level is at its highest seasonal levels).

The two campground loops sit under thick ponderosas and firs with no views. Recent thinning has opened up some of the campground to filtered sunlight, but most of the campsites are shaded. Campsites are spread apart for privacy, and the campground is ultra-quiet.

Campsites, facilities: The campground has 22 RV or tent campsites. The maximum vehicle length is 32 feet. Facilities include picnic tables, fire rings with grills, vault and flush toilets, drinking water, campground hosts, a boat ramp, a covered picnic shelter, and a swimming beach. Limited firewood is available. Leashed pets are permitted. A wheelchair-accessible toilet is available.

Reservations, fees: Reservations are not accepted. Campsites cost $10. Cash or check. Open year-round, but serviced only mid-May–early September.

Directions: From north side of the Lake Koocanusa Bridge, drive south on the curvy, paved Forest Road 228 for about an hour to milepost 10.1. Turn east into the campground. From the south, turn north onto Forest Road 228

one mile northeast of Canoe Gulch Ranger Station and drive 10 miles north.

GPS Coordinates: N 48° 29.174' W 115° 18.277'

Contact: Kootenai National Forest, Libby Ranger District, Canoe Gulch Ranger Station, 12557 Hwy. 37, Libby, MT 59923-8212, 406/293-7773, www.fs.fed.us/r1/kootenai/.

14 LITTLE THERRIAULT LAKE

Scenic rating: 9

in Ten Lakes Scenic Area in Kootenai National Forest

BEST (

Tucked under Ten Lakes Scenic Area at 5,650 feet, idyllic Little Therriault Lake provides a convenient base camp for exploring proposed alpine wilderness area in the north end of the Whitefish Range. Less than 0.5 mile from the campground, the nearest trailhead (#83) leads 1.5 miles up to a pair of subalpine lakes. Surrounded by wildflower meadows, Paradise and Bluebird Lakes make the best kid-friendly destinations, but the trail also connects with the longer Galton Range Trail (#88), which runs along the crest of Ten Lakes toward Poorman Peak, the site of an old lookout at 7,832 feet. Starting from the horse camp above the campground, an 11-mile loop trail with both lakes and ridge walking links the Wolverine Lakes with the Bluebird Basin on trails #82, 84, 88, and 83. Plan for a long, dusty, dirt-road drive to get here. A rough ramp provides for launching boats for fishing or canoeing; powerboats are not permitted, and the trout-filled lake is best for smaller boats and canoes. Snowmobilers ride here in winter.

The small, secluded one-acre campground sits right on the lake. Bring the bug spray, for the area sometimes breeds voracious mosquitoes. Campsites are spread out for privacy and shaded. Due to the proximity of the campsites on the lakeshore, they often fill first before those just around the corner at Big Therriault Lake.

Campsites, facilities: The campground has six RV or tent campsites. RVs are limited to 32 feet in length. Facilities include picnic tables, fire rings, a vault toilet, and drinking water (July–early September). Leashed pets are permitted. A wheelchair-accessible toilet is available.

Reservations, fees: No reservations are accepted. A campsite costs $5. Cash or check. Open year-round, but snowbound November–mid-June.

Directions: From Eureka, drive eight miles south on Highway 93 to Graves Creek Road and turn east. Follow the road, which turns from pavement into the dirt Forest Road 114, for 12 miles as it heads east and circles north. Where Trail Creek Road (Forest Road 114) veers east, drive north for 16 miles on Forest Road 319. Turn right at the sign for the campground.

GPS Coordinates: N 48° 56.633' W 144° 53.3660'

Contact: Kootenai National Forest, Fortine Ranger District, Murphy Lake Ranger Station, P.O. Box 116, 12797 Hwy. 93 S., Fortine, MT 59918-0116, 406/882-4451, www.fs.fed.us/r1/kootenai/.

15 BIG THERRIAULT LAKE

Scenic rating: 9

in Ten Lakes Scenic Area in Kootenai National Forest

BEST (

On the edge of Ten Lakes Scenic Area at 5,650 feet in elevation, Big Therriault Lake provides a convenient base camp for exploring proposed alpine wilderness area in the north end of the Whitefish Range. Departing from the lake, a trail climbs 1.5 miles up to Therriault Pass, which in itself isn't much of a destination in the trees, but it links to several other trails. The Galton Range Trail (#88)

walks north across the entire Ten Lakes Scenic Area just under the ridge toward Poorman Peak, the highest mountain in the area. From the pass, a trail also leads 1.75 miles farther to Stahl Lookout at 7,392 feet. The lookout provides views of the northern Whitefish Range, plus Glacier Park's peaks in the distance. A one-mile, often muddy trail also loops around the lakeshore, climbing through boulders and meandering near shoreline so you can stare into the clear water at the multicolored sedimentary rocks. A rough ramp provides for launching boats for fishing or canoeing; no power boating is permitted on the lake. The campground is a snowmobile destination in winter.

The dusty dirt-and-gravel drive to get to the campground goes on forever. The campground sprawls its few campsites into private locations tucked into five acres of thick Douglas and subalpine firs, with heavy vegetation between most of the sites.

Campsites, facilities: This campground has 10 RV or tent campsites. RVs are limited to 32 feet in length. Facilities include picnic tables, fire rings, a vault toilet, and drinking water (July–early September). Leashed pets are permitted. A wheelchair-accessible toilet is available.

Reservations, fees: No reservations are accepted. A campsite costs $5. Cash or check. Open year-round, but snowbound November–June.

Directions: From Eureka, drive eight miles south on Highway 93 to Grave Creek Road and turn east. Follow the road, which turns from pavement into the dirt Forest Road 114, for 12 miles as it heads east and circles north. Where Trail Creek Road (Forest Road 114) veers east, drive north for 16 miles on Forest Road 319. Turn right at the sign for the campground. The lake sits at the end of the road.

GPS Coordinates: N 48° 56.200' W 114.G> 52.650'

Contact: Kootenai National Forest, Fortine Ranger District, Murphy Lake Ranger Station, P.O. Box 116, 12797 Hwy. 93 S., Fortine, MT

59918-0116, 406/882-4451, www.fs.fed.us/
r1/kootenai/.

16 TUCHUCK

Scenic rating: 6

east of Eureka in the Whitefish Range in
Flathead National Forest

A night or two at Tuchuck lets you explore
some of the remote trails at the north end
of Flathead National Forest. Thoma Lookout, in particular, is worth the grunt up its
1,900 vertical feet in three miles because of its
panoramic view of Glacier's Kintla-Kinnerly
peaks. Miles below, on the Flathead Valley
floor, the international boundary swath cuts
through the forest, and north of it sit the peaks
of Canada's Akamina-Kishenena Provincial
Park. Locate the trailhead about 6.6 miles east
of the campground and up Forest Road 114a,
where the road dead-ends. A faint trail also
connects to Mount Hefty from the Thoma
trail. The forested campground is near the
confluence of the Yakinikak and Tuchuck
Creeks at 4,500 feet in elevation at the confluence of Trail Creek. Fishing is available in
the creeks.

Regardless of the approach road, accessing
this two-acre campground requires driving
long, bumpy, dusty gravel and dirt roads. Its
quiet location miles from highways gives it
appeal. Sites are spread out for privacy in a
forested loop.

Campsites, facilities: The small, two-acre
campground has seven RV or tent campsites.
RVs are limited to 22 feet. Facilities include
picnic tables, fire rings, and a vault toilet.
Drinking water is not available; filter or boil
any water dipped from the creeks. Pack out
your trash. Collecting firewood from the surrounding forest is permitted. Leashed pets
are permitted. A wheelchair-accessible toilet
is available.

Reservations, fees: Reservations are not

accepted. Campsites are free. Open mid-
May–September.

Directions: From Polebridge, drive 15 miles
north on the North Fork Road to Trail Creek
Road (Forest Road 114) and turn west for nine
miles. Turn south into the campground. From
Eureka, drive eight miles south on Highway
93 to Graves Creek Road and drive east, north,
and then east for 20 miles to the campground.
Note: Graves Creek Road turns from pavement into the dirt Forest Road #114, which
becomes Trail Creek Road.
GPS Coordinates: N 48° 55.406' W 114°
36.034'

Contact: Flathead National Forest, Glacier
View District, 10 Hungry Horse Dr., Hungry
Horse, MT 59919, 406/387-3800, www.fs.fed.
us/r1/flathead/.

17 GRAVE CREEK

Scenic rating: 6

south of Eureka in Kootenai National Forest

At 3,000 feet on the east edge of the Tobacco Valley in the north end of the Whitefish
Range, Grave Creek Campground provides
a base camp for exploring trails in Ten Lakes
Scenic Area. A 12-mile drive ends at the south
trailhead to Stahl Peak Lookout. A four-mile
climb on trail #81 leads to the lookout, which
sits at 7,435 feet in elevation with views of
Therriault Pass, Gibralter Ridge, and tidbits
of Glacier Park in the distance. The nearest
trailhead, however, departs from two miles
away to climb Gibralter Ridge (#335) for
views down into the Tobacco Valley. While
the trail continues farther, it tops out at
7,131 feet on Mount Gibralter after a five-
mile ascent. With the campground set on
Grave Creek at the site of a historical dam,
anglers who prefer stream fishing should drop
in a line.

An open mixed forest of birches, cottonwoods, and firs dominates the narrow canyon

that houses the campground. The first camp-site, which looks like a huge parking area, sits across from the dam. The first two campsites view less of the road across the creek than the last two. The campsites, which line up along the creek, are run-down. The third site is missing a picnic table.

Campsites, facilities: The campground has four RV or tent campsites. The maximum vehicle length is 20 feet, and trailers must be 12 feet or less. Facilities include picnic tables, fire rings, and a vault toilet. The campground has no water, so plan on purifying creek water or boiling it. Pack out your trash. Leashed pets are permitted. A wheelchair-accessible toilet is available.

Reservations, fees: No reservations are accepted, and the campsites are free. Open year-round, but serviced only mid-May–early September and snow-covered in winter.

Directions: From Eureka, drive Highway 93 eight miles south to Grave Creek Road 114. Turn east and drive three miles before turning right onto dirt Stoken Road 7019. Cross the bridge, continue for 0.5 mile, and make a left turn, dropping down the steep, narrow gravel road into the campground.

GPS Coordinates: N 48° 47.885' W 114° 57.102'

Contact: Kootenai National Forest, Fortine Ranger District, Murphy Lake Ranger Station, P.O. Box 116, 12797 Hwy. 93 S., Fortine, MT 59918-0116, 406/882-4451, www.fs.fed.us/r1/kootenai/.

18 NORTH DICKEY LAKE
🚶 🚴 ⛵ 🛶 🎣 ⛴ ❄ 🐕 ♿ 🍴 ⛺

Scenic rating: 8

south of Eureka on the west flank of the Whitefish Range in Kootenai National Forest

Located adjacent to Highway 93 at 3,200 feet, North Dickey Lake Campground is a cinch to reach compared to many of the other Kootenai National Forest campgrounds. Its day-use area includes a boat ramp, dock, roped-off swimming area, and grassy beach. The 800-acre lake lures anglers looking to hook kokanee salmon and rainbow trout. It is also a popular for waterskiing, with room in the day-use parking lot for boat trailers. The Mount Marston Trailhead sits on the east side of Highway 93 just opposite the entrance road. The nine-mile climb slogs up to the lookout, sitting at 7,343 feet, for views of the Whitefish Range. Paddlers find both raptors and songbirds at the lake as well as waterfowl. In the spring and early summer, listen for the sound of the loon as a morning wake-up call. From the campground, a short wheelchair-accessible trail leads to a platform for viewing the lake, and a descent down the hill on a footpath is required to reach the lake. Cyclists can tour the bucolic paved roads to Trego.

The shady hillside campground is tucked back from the shoreline in the lodgepole pine and larch forest, with low brush as ground cover, allowing visibility of other campsites. With a paved loop through the trees, the campground has a secluded feel, but you can still hear commercial trucks on the two-lane highway and see the highway from the beach.

Campsites, facilities: The campground has 25 RV or tent campsites. RVs are limited to 32 feet. Facilities include picnic tables, fire rings with grills, vault toilets, tent pads, garbage service, drinking water, and a disposal station. Leashed pets are permitted. A wheelchair-accessible toilet is available.

Reservations, fees: Reservations are accepted (877/444-6777, www.recreation.gov). Campsites cost $10. Cash or check. Open mid-April–November, but serviced only mid-May–early September.

Directions: On Highway 93, drive 14.8 miles south from Eureka or 35.3 miles north from Whitefish to the signed Trego turnoff. Turn west and drive 0.2 mile to a left turn into the campground.

GPS Coordinates: N 48° 43.128' W 114° 49.908'

North Dickey Lake swimming beach and dock in Kootenai National Forest

Contact: Kootenai National Forest, Fortine Ranger District, Murphy Lake Ranger Station, P.O. Box 116, 12797 Hwy. 93 S., Fortine, MT 59918-0116, 406/882-4451, www.fs.fed.us/r1/kootenai/.

19 RED MEADOW LAKE

Scenic rating: 10

in the Whitefish Range of Flathead National Forest

Red Meadow Lake perches like a jewel at 5,500 feet atop the Whitefish Divide on the midway crossover from the Flathead Valley to the North Fork Valley. Mountain bikers ride the route, but many drivers are deterred by the miles of bumpy, dusty, jarring road. About 0.5 mile south of the lake, the Ralph Thayer Memorial Trail ascends to the Whitefish Divide crest and traverses 17 miles south to Werner Peak Lookout, with big views of the Whitefish Range and Glacier Park; turn around at Diamond Peak for a 10-mile day.

Other trails within a 10-minute drive from the lake climb to Chain Lakes (a very steep 2 miles), Link Lake (1.5 miles), or Nasukoin Mountain (5.8 miles), the highest peak in the Whitefish Range. Small hand-carried boats, canoes, and kayaks can be launched from the shoreline for paddling or fishing.

The small campground is quite open with exceptional views, but at the cost of privacy. Winter avalanches keep much of the mature timber pruned out around the lake. A couple of the campsites sit right on the lakeshore only inches off the road; others are across the road from the lake. Despite the road slicing right through the campground, this is a quiet location, with the rough dirt miles deterring lots of traffic.

Campsites, facilities: The campground has six RV or tent campsites. RVs are limited to 32 feet. Facilities include picnic tables, fire rings, and a vault toilet. Drinking water is not available; bring water, or plan on purifying or boiling lake water. Pack out your trash. Leashed pets are permitted. A wheelchair-accessible toilet is available.

Reservations, fees: No reservations are

accepted. Camping is free. Open mid-May–September.

Directions: From the North Fork Road five miles north of the Polebridge junction, drive 11 miles west on Red Meadows Road (#115). From Highway 93 north of Whitefish, turn east onto the Olney Crossover Road across the highway from Olney and drive 8.5 miles to a signed three-way junction. Turn left and continue another 11 miles, staying on the main road and climbing steeply in the last two miles.

GPS Coordinates: N 48° 45.234' W 114° 33.787'

Contact: Flathead National Forest, Glacier View District, 10 Hungry Horse Dr., Hungry Horse, MT 59919, 406/387-3800, www.fs.fed.us/r1/flathead/.

20 UPPER WHITEFISH LAKE

Scenic rating: 9

north of Whitefish in Stillwater State Forest in the Whitefish Range

A favorite with anglers in summer and hunters in fall, the 80-acre Upper Whitefish Lake sits at 4,549 feet in elevation at the base of the Whitefish Divide. While fly-fishing and spin-casting can work from shore, a boat helps to catch the bigger native westslope cutthroat. (A dirt launch is available.) Canoeists enjoy paddling the placid lake in the morning and evening calm because the waterfowl, songbirds, and raptors make for good bird-watching. Most of the hiking trails in the area depart from trailheads in the vicinity of Red Meadows Lake, about six miles up the road. The trail to three destinations—Link Lake (1.5 miles), Lake Mountain (3.5 miles), and Nasukoin Mountain (5.8 miles)—departs off a spur road, Road 589. Look for the Link Lake sign and drive 1.3 miles to the trailhead. The forest road is a favorite for mountain bikers.

Sitting on the southeastern corner of the lake, the six-acre quiet campground clusters around both sides of the road north of the bridge that crosses the outlet stream. A few sites are accessed via a spur road to the left just before the lake comes into view. Foliage and mature trees maintain privacy between the sites. Most of the campsites rest in the trees along the lake, with short trails running down to the shore, but a couple are on the opposite side of the road with more open views of the surrounding mountains.

Campsites, facilities: The campground has 13 RV or tent campsites. RVs are limited to 32 feet. Facilities include picnic tables, fire rings with grills, vault toilets, and a boat launch. No drinking water is available; bring your own, or purify or boil the lake water. Pack out your trash. Leashed pets are permitted. A wheelchair-accessible toilet is available.

Reservations, fees: No reservations are accepted, and campsites are free. The campground is open June–October.

Directions: From Highway 93 north of Whitefish, turn east onto the Olney Crossover Road across the highway from Olney and drive 8.5 miles to a signed three-way junction. Turn left and continue another five miles to the campground, which sits on both sides of the creek and road.

GPS Coordinates: N 48° 41.068' W 114° 34.441'

Contact: Stillwater State Forest, P.O. Box 164, Olney, MT 59919, 406/881-2371, http://dnrc.mt.gov.

21 STILLWATER LAKE

Scenic rating: 7

north of Whitefish on Upper Stillwater Lake in Flathead National Forest

Located at 3,250 feet on Upper Stillwater Lake, this tiny campground is favored by anglers year-round; there's ice fishing in winter, and stream fishing in the slow-moving Stillwater River nearby can land a 20- to 30-pound pike. Canoeists enjoy the lake but should be wary of logjams when floating the river. A boat ramp works for launching small watercraft. Mountain bikers hit the forest roads around the lake. For hikers, a nearby 1.5-mile trail tours the LeBeau Natural Area through old-growth larches and ancient Belt Sea formation rocks to large bluffs above Finger Lake. A spur trail cuts off to Hole-in-the-Wall Lake. Hunters also use the campground in fall.

Sitting right on the Stillwater lakeshore in sparse tall trees, the campsites may have you waking up to the slap of beavertails on the water. The small campground with four sites received an overhaul in 2008 with new picnic tables, fire rings, leveled gravel parking pads, and a bench for viewing the lake and the beaver lodge just offshore. Watch here for moose, otter, and songbirds. Campsites 1, 2, and 4 overlook the lake.

Campsites, facilities: The campground has four RV or tent campsites. Trailers are limited to 12 feet. Facilities include picnic tables, fire rings with grills, and a vault toilet. Drinking water is not available; bring water, or plan on purifying or boiling lake water. Pack out your own garbage. A bear pole is available for hanging food. Leashed pets are permitted. A wheelchair-accessible toilet is available.

Reservations, fees: Reservations are not accepted, and camping is free. Open late April–November.

Directions: From Whitefish, drive 21 miles north on Highway 93 and turn west at the Stillwater Lake Campground sign at milepost 151.5. Follow the signs two miles to the campground. The dirt road snakes left, then right, before crossing the railroad tracks and turning left to climb over a hill.

GPS Coordinates: N 48° 36.224' W 114° 39.370'

Contact: Flathead National Forest, Talley Lake Ranger District, 650 Wolfpack Way, Kalispell, MT 59901, 406/758-5204, www.fs.fed.us/r1/flathead/.

22 DORR SKEELS

Scenic rating: 9

on Bull Lake in Kootenai National Forest

Bull Lake, which sits at 2,350 feet in elevation, tucked between the Cabinet Mountains and Scotchman Peaks, runs 4.5 miles in length—the largest lake on Bull River—and harbors rainbow trout, kokanee salmon, and largemouth bass. While the lake borders public land on its west shore, the east shore contains private land and homes. The campground sits on the north end of the lake, with a warm, sunny, south-facing swimming beach. The day-use area sees heavy weekend visitation from locals. At the campground, a concrete ramp and dock aid those launching boats, kayaks, and canoes, and several boat tie-up anchors are available near the campsites. A buoyed sand-and-pebble swimming beach separates swimmers from boaters. The Ross Creek Scenic Area, with its giant cedars, requires a seven-mile drive from Dorr Skeels Campground. If you're pulling a trailer and planning to visit Ross Creek Cedars, leave the trailer in the designated parking area because the curvy road and parking area at the trailhead do not accommodate larger RVs.

Sitting on a forested bluff under cedars and firs, the shaded tent campsites have peek-a-boo views of the lake. Sites 6 and 7 offer the most privacy. Some of the flat sleeping spaces will accommodate only two-person tents. The self-contained RV campsites consist of a parking lot with no privacy.

Campsites, facilities: The campground has seven walk-in tent campsites and two RV campsites that can fit trailer combinations up to 32 feet. Facilities include picnic tables and fire rings with grills at tent sites only, vault toilets, campground hosts, drinking water, garbage service, a boat launch, and swimming beach. Leashed pets are permitted. A wheelchair-accessible toilet is available.

Reservations, fees: Reservations are not

China Rapids on the Kootenai River between Libby and Troy, Montana

accepted. Campsites are free. Open year-round, but serviced mid-May–early September.

Directions: On Highway 2, from Libby drive 15.2 miles west, or from Troy drive three miles east. Turn south onto Highway 56 and drive 13 miles. Turn west onto the 0.5-mile road that leads to the campground. From Highway 200, drive 21.6 miles north on Highway 53 to the campground turnoff on the left. GPS Coordinates: N 48° 16.024' W 115° 51.209'

Contact: Kootenai National Forest, Three Rivers Ranger District, Troy Ranger Station, 12858 Hwy. 2, Troy, MT 59935-8750, 406/295-4693, www.fs.fed.us/r1/kootenai/.

23 SPAR LAKE

Scenic rating: 7

in Scotchman Peaks in Kootenai National Forest

At 3,300 feet in the Scotchman Peaks, the 383-acre Spar Lake is so popular with locals that the Forest Service expanded the campground in 2009. The small lake with a dirt boat ramp is good for small motorboats, canoes, and kayaks. Fish species include kokanee salmon, brook trout, and lake trout. Two hiking trails in the Scotchman Peaks—a proposed wilderness area—sit about three miles south of the campground, starting from the same trailhead. Gaining 2,300 feet in elevation over three miles, the Little Spar Lake Trail (#143) ascends along Spar Creek through lush forest to the small lake, which harbors native westslope cutthroat trout. With 3,000 feet of elevation gain, the Spar Peak Trail (#324) climbs a steep 3.2-mile path along Cub Creek through bear grass meadows to the summit. At 6,585 feet in elevation and waltzing above tree line, the peak grants a 360-degree view of both the Scotchman Peaks and Cabinet Mountains.

The ultra-quiet campground is tucked in tall firs above the lake at the head of a west side bay. The expansion added a new toilet and four more campsites, but the campground is so far removed from roads and towns that it guarantees solitude. Campsites are spread out for privacy.

Campsites, facilities: The campground has 12 RV or tent campsites. Sites can fit RVs and trailer combinations up to 32 feet long. Facilities include picnic tables, fire rings with grills, vault toilets, and drinking water. You can collect downed limbs for firewood from the surrounding national forest. Pack out your trash. Leashed pets are permitted.

Reservations, fees: Reservations are not accepted. Campsites are free. Open May–November, but serviced late May–early September.

Directions: From two miles east of Troy on Highway 2, drive 19 miles south on Lake Creek Road (Forest Road 384). The paved road passes by small ranches for 10 miles before turning to dirt. It crosses Lake Creek, enters the national forest, and climbs to the lake.

GPS Coordinates: N 48° 16.268' W 115° 57.382'

Contact: Kootenai National Forest, Three Rivers Ranger District, Troy Ranger Station, 12858 Hwy. 2, Troy, MT 59935-8750, 406/295-4693, www.fs.fed.us/r1/kootenai/.

24 BAD MEDICINE

Scenic rating: 8

on Bull Lake in Kootenai National Forest

At an elevation of 2,350 feet on the southwest corner of 4.5-mile-long Bull Lake, below Scotchman Peaks and the Cabinet Mountains, Bad Medicine is the closest campground for those hiking the one-mile Ross Creek Cedars interpretive trail. Located four miles from the campground, the 100-acre ancient grove of western red cedar trees—some that were saplings when Columbus landed in the New World—survived the ravages of floods, fires, and insects. Great-grandfather trees span eight feet in diameter and stand over 175 feet tall. The campground also has a boat ramp, dock, and small swimming beach. Paddling the lake early or late in the day yields calmer waters with big views of the surrounding mountains.

A paved road loops through the campground, parts of which are reminiscent of dark, coastal cedar rain forests dripping with moss. Dense vegetation and thick trees close off the views from the campsites but also provide seclusion and cool shade for hot days. Sites 3, 4, and 9–12 are especially private. Sites 1 and 2 sit closest to the lake. For views, head to the beach for beautiful reflections of the Cabinet Mountains on calm days. Prepare for mosquitoes.

Campsites, facilities: The campground has 17 RV or tent campsites. RVs are limited to 32 feet. Facilities include picnic tables, fire rings or grates, vault toilets, campground hosts, drinking water, garbage service, a boat launch, and swimming beach. You can collect downed limbs for firewood from the surrounding national forest. Leashed pets are permitted. A wheelchair-accessible toilet is available.

Reservations, fees: Reservations are not accepted. Campsites cost $10. Cash or check. Open April–November, but managed mid-May–early September.

Directions: From Libby drive 15 miles west, or from Troy drive three miles east to Highway 56. Turn south and drive 21 miles to Ross Creek Cedars Road (Forest Road 398), between mileposts 16 and 17. From Highway 200, drive 13.5 miles north on Highway 53 to the Ross Creek Cedars turnoff on the left. On Forest Road 398, drive two paved miles to the campground, passing the turnoff to Ross Creek Cedars about halfway.

GPS Coordinates: N 48° 13.236' W 115° 51.425'

Contact: Kootenai National Forest, Three Rivers Ranger District, Troy Ranger Station, 12858 Hwy. 2, Troy, MT 59935-8750, 406/295-4693, www.fs.fed.us/r1/kootenai/.

25 BIG EDDY

Scenic rating: 7

on Cabinet Gorge Reservoir in Kootenai National Forest

At an elevation of 2,200 feet, eight miles east of the Montana-Idaho border, Big Eddy Campground sits on the north shore of Cabinet Gorge Reservoir, closest to the dam. The dam's viewing platform (open spring–fall) affords a bird's-eye view of the spillway and is an interpretive site for the new Ice Age Floods National Geologic Trail, created by Congress in 2009. The site marks the location of an ice dam that formed Glacial Lake Missoula 14,000 years ago and repeatedly failed, flooding Idaho, Washington, and Oregon. One of the best hikes is to the west in the proposed Scotchman Peak Wilderness Area, on a beargrass-flanked trail to Scotchman Peak. The trail requires only a 3.5-mile climb up switchbacks, but with 3,700 feet of elevation gain, it's a grunt to get to the views of the Clark Fork River and Lake Pend Oreille. The boat ramp at the campground accesses the Cabinet Gorge Reservoir for fishing, waterskiing, paddling, and bird-watching.

The tiny campground has small campsites and short parking pads. A narrow dirt road loops through the old-growth forest of hemlock and cedar, which admits filtered sunlight. An overnight parking area with undesignated campsites provides overflow camping. Noise from trucks and trains seeps into the campground.

Campsites, facilities: The campground has three RV or tent campsites. RVs are limited to 20 feet. Facilities include picnic tables, fire grates, a vault toilet, and a boat ramp, but no drinking water. Bring water with you, or if you plan to use the reservoir water, filter or boil it before drinking. Leashed pets are permitted. A wheelchair-accessible toilet is available.

Reservations, fees: Reservations are not accepted. Campsites are free. Open year-round, but serviced only mid-May–early September.

Directions: From Noxon, drive eight miles west on Highway 200. From Libby, drive 55 miles, heading west on Highway 2 and then south on Highway 56. Turn west on Highway 200 for three miles. From Sandpoint, Idaho, drive 41 miles east on Highway 200. The campground sits on the south side of the highway at milepost 7.

GPS Coordinates: N 48° 4.016' W 115° 55.144'

Contact: Kootenai National Forest, Cabinet Ranger District, Trout Creek Ranger Station, 2693 Hwy. 200, Trout Creek, MT 59874-9503, 406/827-3533, www.fs.fed.us/r1/kootenai/.

26 BULL RIVER

Scenic rating: 8

on Bull River in Kootenai National Forest

BEST (

Located in the Bull River Recreation Area at 2,200 feet on the south flank of the Cabinet Mountains, the campground sits at the confluence of the Bull River and the eight-mile-long Cabinet Gorge Reservoir. On the east shore of a narrow, sheltered north bay, the campground is one of the most popular in the area due to its diverse activities. The boat ramp sits right at the entrance to the campground, allowing boaters, water-skiers, anglers, and paddlers to launch on the bay. Paddlers can tour the bay to look for wildlife, while anglers head out on the reservoir to fish for bass, trout, and large northern pike. The campground also makes a good base camp for exploring trails on the west side of the Cabinet Mountain Wilderness, and mountain bikers ride the Old Bull River Road.

Set in thick, green conifers, the campground loops with paved roads linking to paved parking pads. Sites 12, 13, and 15–18 overlook the water, but the upper loop campsites have more privacy—especially site 6. From the campsite loops, two sets of stairs drop down the bank to the water. Campsites are spread out for privacy, but you will see neighbors. You can also hear a few commercial trucks on the highway and trains across the water at night. Only two of the campsites are pull-throughs. Claim a site early in high season.

Campsites, facilities: The campground has 26 RV or tent campsites. RVs are limited to 32 feet. Facilities include picnic tables, fire grates, vault and flush toilets, drinking water, campground hosts, and a boat ramp. Firewood is available during the serviced season. Leashed pets are permitted. A wheelchair-accessible toilet is available.

Reservations, fees: Reservations are not accepted. Campsites cost $10. Cash or check. Open mid-April–November, but serviced only mid-May–early September.

Directions: From Noxon drive four miles west on Highway 200, or from Libby drive 55 miles, heading west on Highway 2, south on Highway 56, and then east on Highway 200 for 0.5 mile. Turn north into the campground. GPS Coordinates: N 48° 1.806' W 115° 50.597'

Contact: Kootenai National Forest, Cabinet Ranger District, Trout Creek Ranger Station, 2693 Hwy. 200, Trout Creek, MT 59874-9503, 406/827-3533, www.fs.fed.us/r1/kootenai/.

27 HOWARD LAKE

Scenic rating: 8

in the Cabinet Mountains in Kootenai National Forest

Tiny Howard Lake, which is popular with Libby locals for fishing, sits serene in a deep pocket amid a thick, mature forest. At 4,100 feet in elevation, the lake is only 33 acres in size, making it best for canoeing and fishing from small boats. It is stocked with rainbow trout. The Gold Panning Recreation Area is one mile from the lake, and nearby hiking trails climb up creek drainages into the Cabinet Mountain Wilderness. Unfortunately, the most popular hiking trail requires a long drive back out to the highway and a nine-mile drive up Bear Creek Road to the Leigh Lake Trailhead. The 1.5-mile trail climbs a steep ascent, gaining 1,000 feet past Leigh Falls and following rock cairns to find the easiest route into the alpine bowl where Leigh Lake clings.

The ultra-quiet campground sits half under big shade-producing conifers and half on the open edge of the forest adjacent to the lake. The campground's one road loops between the campsites and the lake, with a boat ramp that doubles as a swimming beach. Because it has little underbrush and several open sites, you will see neighbors.

Campsites, facilities: The campground has nine RV or tent campsites. Three of them accommodate small RVs up to 20 feet in pull-through sites; five are tent sites that will not fit RVs. Facilities include picnic tables, fire grates, a vault toilet, garbage service, and drinking water. Leashed pets are permitted. A wheelchair-accessible toilet is available.

Reservations, fees: Reservations are not accepted. Campsites cost $8. Cash or check. Open late May–September.

Directions: On Highway 2, drive 13 miles east from Libby or 75 miles west from Kalispell to the junction of Libby Creek Road (Forest Road 231). Turn south onto this road, which turns into dirt, and drive 14 miles to the campground sign. As you drive, stay on the well-traveled route, veering left at all junctions. At the junction with the campground sign, go right, climbing up the hill and driving about one mile. The campground entrance sits on the left. GPS Coordinates: N 48° 6.001' W 115° 31.838'

Contact: Kootenai National Forest, Libby Ranger District, Canoe Gulch Ranger Station, 12557 Hwy. 37, Libby, MT 59923-8212, 406/293-7773, www.fs.fed.us/r1/kootenai/.

Leigh Lake, a steep 1.5-mile hike, in the Cabinet Mountains of Kootenai National Forest

© BECKY LOMAX

28 LAKE CREEK

Scenic rating: 8

in the Cabinet Mountains in Kootenai National Forest

At 3,360 feet on the east flank of the Cabinet Mountains, Lake Creek Campground sits at the confluence of Lake and Bramlet Creeks. For stream anglers going after mountain whitefish and rainbow trout, nearby rivers also include Fourth of July and West Fisher. Each can be reached via narrow forest roads or trails. The best hike in the area goes to Geiger Lakes, a pair of subalpine pools sitting near the crest in the Cabinet Mountains Wilderness. The trailhead sits about two miles from the campground up Forest Road 6748, and a steady grade climbs through lodgepole pines to the first lake, which has large boulders on a peninsula that makes a good destination. To reach the second lake in a scenic alpine meadow below Lost Buck Pass, grunt up 600 feet in elevation. Another trailhead requiring a longer drive on the Silver Butte

Road leads to Baree Lake, a six-mile round-trip climb to one of the Cabinet's most southern lakes, known for its wealth of huckleberries in July and August.

The tiny campground tucks into a conifer forest, offering seclusion and utter quiet with only the sound of the creek filtering through the trees. The campground's one small loop spreads out the campsites for privacy.

Campsites, facilities: The campground has four RV and tent campsites. RVs are limited to 32 feet. Facilities include picnic tables, fire grates, and a vault toilet, but no drinking water. Bring your own water, or if you plan to use the creek water, purify or boil it first. Pack out your trash. Leashed pets are permitted.

Reservations, fees: Reservations are not accepted. Campsites are free. Open year-round, but serviced only late May–early September.

Directions: On Highway 2, drive 22 miles southeast from Libby or 66 miles west from Kalispell to the junction with W. Fisher Road (Forest Road 231). Turn onto this dirt road and drive approximately 4.5 miles, swinging left onto Forest Road 2332 at the fork. Drive 0.5 mile to the turnoff to the campground on the left.

GPS Coordinates: N 48° 2.331' W 115° 29.371'

Contact: Kootenai National Forest, Libby Ranger District, Canoe Gulch Ranger Station, 12557 Hwy. 37, Libby, MT 59923-8212, 406/293-7773, www.fs.fed.us/r1/kootenai/.

29 THOMPSON CHAIN OF LAKES PRIMITIVE

Scenic rating: 7

on several lakes in Thompson Chain of Lakes

The Thompson Chain of Lakes consists of 4,655 acres of land containing 18 lakes running in a 20-mile string along Highway 2 between Libby and Kalispell. Some of the lakes are small four-acre ponds; the largest lake tops 1,500 acres. Receding glaciers formed the lakes in a trail of water pockets separated by moraines. Crystal, Horseshoe, and Loon comprise the smaller lakes at the west end. The three Thompson Lakes (Upper, Middle, and Lower) cover the most miles, while McGregor Lake is the largest. The lakes are popular for trout and bass fishing as well as magnets for wildlife. Wake up to the call of loons and watch ospreys dive for fish. Concrete boat ramps for motorboats, canoes, and kayaks are located at Little McGregor, McGregor, Lower Thompson, Upper Thompson, Horseshoe, and Loon Lakes. Some of the lakes have no-wake speed limits.

The campsites are sprinkled along the shorelines singly or in pairs or groups on both sides of the lakes. To locate the Thompson Chain of Lakes primitive campsites, pick up a map at one of the eight pay stations on the road entrances to the lakes. Those campsites adjacent to the highway are the most popular. Most of the campsites are accessed via narrow potholed dirt roads unsuitable for anything larger than a truck camper; however, some of those adjacent to the highway can fit larger rigs.

Campsites, facilities: Thompson Chain of Lakes has 83 primitive campsites and eight group campsites. Sites can have a maximum of two tents, trailers, or RVs, but many can only fit one. Where campsites are concentrated together, a vault toilet is available, but not at the single sites. Facilities include fire rings and some picnic tables. No drinking water is available. Bring your own, or plan to filter or boil the lake water. Leashed pets are permitted.

Reservations, fees: Reservations are not accepted. Campsites cost $7 for those who already have Montana fishing licenses. Otherwise, camping costs $12. Cash or check. Open year-round unless snowbound.

Directions: From Kalispell, drive between 35 and 55 miles westward on Highway 2 to reach Thompson Chain of Lakes.

GPS Coordinates: N 48° 1.451' W 115° 2.446'

Contact: Montana Fish, Wildlife, and Parks, Region 1, 490 N. Meridian Rd., Kalispell, MT 59901, 406/752-5501, http://fwp.mt.gov.

30 LOGAN STATE PARK

Scenic rating: 8

on Middle Thompson Lake in Thompson Chain of Lakes

Sitting midway between Libby and Kalispell on the Highway 2 corridor at 3,300 feet, the Thompson Chain of Lakes strings the Upper, Middle, and Lower Thompson Lakes together with sloughs to make up about 3,000 acres for water recreation. The lakes garner their share of locals, especially on weekends and holidays, and are popular for waterskiing, paddling, and largemouth bass fishing. The bass can range 1–3 pounds in size. Logan Campground sits on the north shore of the middle lake, with a cement boat ramp, dock, trailer parking, and a swimming beach. A half-mile hiking trail leads along the lakeshore to good birdwatching spots. Watch for herons, ospreys, and waterfowl. Loons nest on the lakes, too.

The 17-acre grassy campground circles its two loops under a canopy of western larch, ponderosa pine, and Douglas fir. Without underbrush, the campsites do not have much privacy from each other. Loop B sits closers to the swimming beach and boat launch. Loop A, which leads to the hiking trail, has the playground and showers, and sites 13, 14, 15, and 17 are close to the beach. Squeezed between the lake and the highway, the campground picks up noise from passing vehicles on the highway.

Campsites, facilities: The campground has 37 RV or tent campsites. RVs are limited to 30 feet. Facilities include picnic tables, fire rings with grills, flush toilets, showers, drinking water, a playground, a boat launch, a swimming beach, campground hosts, garbage service, a disposal station, and a horseshoe pit. Firewood is for sale. Leashed pets are permitted. A wheelchair-accessible toilet is available and there's an ADA campsite with an electrical hookup.

Reservations, fees: Reservations are not accepted. For day use, Montana residents have free admission, but all others pay $5 per vehicle. Bikers or hikers cost $3. Campsites cost $15 May–September and $13 October–April. Cash or check. Open year-round.

Directions: From Kalispell drive 45 miles westward on Highway 2, or from Libby drive 40 miles southeast on Highway 2. Turn south at the signed entrance to the campground. GPS Coordinates: N 48° 2.635' W 115° 5.811'

Contact: Montana Fish, Wildlife, and Parks, Region 1, 490 N. Meridian Rd., Kalispell, MT 59901, 406/752-5501, http://fwp.mt.gov.

31 MCGREGOR LAKE

Scenic rating: 8

on McGregor Lake in Kootenai National Forest

At an elevation of 3,998 feet on the easternmost lake in a long chain along Highway 2, McGregor Lake Campground sits on the west end of the long, narrow McGregor Lake. With its short 35-minute drive from Flathead Valley, the 1,522-acre lake is surrounded by summer homes and a small resort. On weekends, the lake packs with water-skiers, boaters, paddlers, and anglers trolling for lake trout or the frequently stocked rainbow trout. The campground allows access to the lake via its boat ramp and a beach for swimming. The lake sits surrounded by a patchwork of Kootenai National Forest and state lands, which offer mountain biking and hiking, but not to exceptionally scenic destinations.

Tucked under large conifers, the campground has two loops with a few of the campsites sitting along the lakeshore. Those rimming the shore are more open and less private than those shaded under trees away from the shore, but they offer views and immediate access to the beach. Truck noise from the highway seeps into the campground.

Campsites, facilities: The campground has 22 RV or tent campsites. RVs are limited to 32 feet. Facilities include picnic tables, fire rings, vault toilets, drinking water, a boat ramp, a campground host, and garbage service, and some firewood is available. Leashed pets are permitted. A wheelchair-accessible toilet is available.

Reservations, fees: Reservations are not accepted. Campsites cost $12. Cash or check. Open mid-May–fall, but serviced only late May–early September.

Directions: From Kalispell, drive 32 miles westward on Highway 2, or from Libby, drive 53 miles southeast on Highway 2. Turn south off the highway at the west end of the lake onto the dirt road leading into the campground. GPS Coordinates: N 48° 1.925' W 114° 54.189'

Contact: Kootenai National Forest, Libby Ranger District, Canoe Gulch Ranger Station, 12557 Hwy. 37, Libby, MT 59923-8212, 406/293-7773, www.fs.fed.us/r1/kootenai/.

32 ASHLEY LAKE NORTH

Scenic rating: 7

west of Kalispell in Flathead National Forest

West of Kalispell in Flathead National Forest, Ashley Lake sits at 3,500 feet. Campers head to Ashley Lake for swimming, canoeing, fishing, and waterskiing, but due to the many homes around the lake—some of them multimillion-dollar summer homes—the area doesn't feel much like wilderness. The lake, which is about five miles long and one mile wide, gets substantial day use from locals. Anglers go after kokanee salmon, westslope cutthroat trout, yellow perch, and large rainbow trout. Some of the rainbow-cutthroat hybrids can get up to five pounds. The boat ramp sits about 0.5 mile west of the campground. Mountain bikers tour the scads of forest roads that crisscross the area, and bird-watchers catch sight of loons and other waterfowl.

The campground is tucked into the north shore of the lake under conifers for shade. The location away from the highway provides quiet once the personal watercraft leave the lake at night. Sites are spread out for privacy, but neighboring campers are visible.

Campsites, facilities: The campground has five RV or tent campsites. RVs are limited to 12 feet. Facilities include picnic tables, fire rings, a vault toilet, swimming area, and boat ramp. Drinking water is not available, so bring your own or plan to purify or boil the lake water. Pack out all garbage. Leashed pets are permitted. A wheelchair-accessible toilet is available.

Reservations, fees: Reservations are not accepted, and camping is free. Open late May–mid-September.

Directions: From Highway 93 in Kalispell, drive west on Highway 2 for 16 miles. Turn north onto the gravel Ashley Lake Road and drive 13 miles following the signs to the campground. (Stay left at the big junction about seven miles up.)

GPS Coordinates: N 48° 12.176' W 114° 37.996'

Contact: Flathead National Forest, Talley Lake Ranger District, 650 Wolfpack Way, Kalispell, MT 59901, 406/758-5204, www. fs.fed.us/r1/flathead/.

33 SYLVIA LAKE

Scenic rating: 7

west of Whitefish in the Salish Mountains in Flathead National Forest

Anglers head to Sylvia Lake for its arctic grayling and westslope cutthroat trout. The 23-acre lake, which sits at 5,189 feet in elevation, is stocked on a frequent cycle by the state. The lake is also popular with canoeists and bird watchers. A trail (#171) across the road climbs 3.5 miles to the summit of Ingalls Mountain, with some views of the Salish Mountains. The area also attracts mountain bikers for its single-track riding on trails and double-track riding on old forest roads. Hunters also use the camp as a base area for hunting in fall. A rough boat ramp aids in launching smaller watercraft onto the lake.

Surrounded by conifers, the campground sits on the lake where you might hear the haunting call of loons in the morning. Due to its distance from pavement, the ultra-quiet campground is usually a place to garner solitude.

Campsites, facilities: The campground has three RV or tent campsites. The maximum length for a trailer is 12 feet. Facilities include picnic tables, rock-ring fire pits, and a pit toilet. Drinking water is not available, so bring your own or plan to purify or boil the lake water. Pack out your trash. Leashed pets are permitted.

Reservations, fees: Reservations are not accepted, and camping is free. Open Memorial Day–Labor Day.

Directions: From Whitefish, drive Highway

93 northwest to Farm to Market Road. Drive 1.8 miles and turn right onto Star Meadows Road (Forest Road 539), which becomes Forest Road 113 when the pavement changes to dirt about 15 miles up. Stay to the left at the next two junctions, following the signs about six miles to Sylvia Lake.

GPS Coordinates: N 48° 20.562' W 114° 49.194'

Contact: Flathead National Forest, Talley Lake Ranger District, 650 Wolfpack Way, Kalispell, MT 59901, 406/758-5204, www.fs.fed.us/r1/flathead/.

34 TALLY LAKE

Scenic rating: 9

west of Whitefish in the Salish Mountains in Flathead National Forest

At 492 feet deep, Tally Lake claims the record as Montana's deepest lake. Located in the heavily forested Salish Mountains at 3,500 feet, the lake attracts weekend campers as well as those out for a day of fishing, waterskiing, paddling, or swimming on the sandy beach. A cement boat ramp, dock, and trailer parking are available. An interpretive site has a spotting scope for watching bald eagles fishing or migratory waterfowl. Several hiking and mountain-biking trails explore the surrounding forest. The 1.25-mile Tally Lake Overlook trail departs from the campground to climb through mature timber. While the walk through the trees provides a close-up view of old-growth forest, the overlook is fast losing its view to crowding trees. Also departing near the campground, a nine-mile loop trail through old-growth forest and in spring fairy slipper orchids also climbs 1,955 vertical feet up Tally Mountain, where it connects with the Boney Gulch Trail to drop back to the road two miles south of the trailhead.

The 23-acre, quiet campground sits on the lake's north shore. The campground loops through mature timber that provides filtered

paddling below the cliffs at Tally Lake, the deepest lake in Montana, in Flathead National Forest

shade. Most of the sites are set back from the lakeshore and spread out for privacy, but several on the northwest loop have not only lake frontage, but views of the lake and surrounding mountainside.

Campsites, facilities: The campground has 40 RV or tent campsites. Maximum trailer length for the campground is 40 feet. Facilities include picnic tables, fire rings with grills, vault toilets, drinking water, a disposal station, garbage service, a boat launch, a swimming beach, volleyball, horseshoe pits, and firewood. Leashed pets are permitted. A wheelchair-accessible toilet is available.

Reservations, fees: Reservations are accepted (877/444-6777, www.recreation.gov). Campsites cost $15. Cash or check. Open mid-May–September.

Directions: From Whitefish, drive Highway 93 west 2.5 miles and turn south on Twin Bridges Road for two miles until it reaches Farm to Market Road. Turn left for two more miles and then turn west onto Forest Road

913. Drive nine miles on the dusty dirt road to the campground.

GPS Coordinates: N 48° 24.888' W 114° 35.190'

Contact: Flathead National Forest, Talley Lake Ranger District, 650 Wolfpack Way, Kalispell, MT 59901, 406/758-5204, www.fs.fed.us/r1/flathead/.

35 WHITEFISH LAKE STATE PARK

Scenic rating: 9

in Whitefish on Whitefish Lake

The state park, which sits at 3,000 feet on the south side of Whitefish Lake, with a view of Big Mountain from the beach, is a place to camp more for convenience than quiet. Around 40 trains per day rumble on the tracks adjacent to the campground, which kids and train fanatics love but light sleepers abhor. Local anglers, water-skiers, paddlers, and lake sightseers use the boat launch for the day, and the cordoned-off swimming area attracts families from town to cool off in the summer heat. Downtown Whitefish, with shops, restaurants, groceries, gas, and nightlife, is only two miles away. Whitefish Golf Course with 36 holes is only one mile away. Whitefish Mountain Resort above the lake runs its chairlift in the summer for sightseeing and mountain biking, and the four-mile Danny On Trail connects the summit of Big Mountain with the resort.

With a paved campground road and parking pads, the campsites tuck under a mature forest with substantial undergrowth foliage. None of the campsites sit right on the shoreline, but sites 7, 8, 26, and 25 are closest. Sites 2–13 cluster around a loop separated from the road that day users drive to reach the boat ramp, beach, and parking lot. Sites 14, 15, 22, and 23–25 sit just beneath the slope leading up to the railroad tracks; sites 2–9 are the farthest away from the tracks.

Campsites, facilities: The campground has 25 RV or tent campsites. RVs or trailer combinations are limited to 35 feet. One site is reserved for hikers or bicyclists. Facilities include picnic tables, fire rings with grills, flush toilets, showers, drinking water, a boat ramp with a dock, and a swimming area. Firewood is for sale. Leashed pets are permitted. A wheelchair-accessible toilet is available.

Reservations, fees: No reservations are accepted. Montana residents have free day use, but nonresidents must pay $5 per vehicle. Campsites cost $15. Cash or check. Open May–September.

Directions: From downtown Whitefish, drive Highway 93 west for 1.3 miles. Veer right at the state park sign around the golf course. Take the next right onto State Park Road and follow it about one mile until it crosses the railroad tracks. The entrance sits just past the tracks on the left.

GPS Coordinates: N 48° 25.500' W 114° 22.247'

Contact: Montana Fish, Wildlife, and Parks, Region 1, 490 N. Meridian Rd., Kalispell, MT 59901, 406/752-5501, http://fwp.mt.gov.

36 WHITEFISH KOA

Scenic rating: 7

south of Whitefish

At 3,100 feet, the campground is conveniently near Whitefish as well as only a 35-minute drive from the west entrance to Glacier National Park. Downtown Whitefish, four miles north of the campground, clusters shopping, restaurants, and nightlife within a few blocks. Grocery stores, gas, and other shops line the two miles leading into town. Recreation abounds around town: boating on Whitefish Lake, canoeing the Whitefish River, hiking on Big Mountain, and bicycling the Fish Trails.

A thick forest hides the campground from the highway. Campsites sprinkle across 33 acres of mature forest connected by a gravel road. Open pull-through sites for large RVs allow for satellite reception. Deluxe RV sites include wooden decks. Tent sites sit closer to the bathhouse in grassy or forested locations with options including electricity and water.

Campsites, facilities: There are 25 sites for tents or RVs with a maximum length of 40 feet. RV hookups include sewer, water, and electricity up to 50 amps. Facilities include picnic tables, fire rings, flush toilets, showers, a camp store, a seasonal restaurant, a games center, a playground, and indoor/outdoor pool (mid-April–September only), an adults-only hot tub, wireless Internet, free mini-golf, a disposal station, and firewood. Leashed pets are permitted. A wheelchair-accessible toilet is available.

Reservations, fees: Reservations are accepted. RV hookups run $30–60; tent sites cost $20–36. Cash, check, or credit card. Add on a 7 percent Montana bed tax. Open mid-April–mid-October.

Directions: From Whitefish at the junction of Highways 93 and 40, drive two miles south on Highway 93, or from the junction of Highways 2 and 93 in Kalispell, drive nine miles north on Highway 93. At mile marker 123, turn east into the campground.

GPS Coordinates: N 48° 20.823' W 114° 19.799'

Contact: Whitefish KOA, 5121 Hwy. 93 S., Whitefish, MT 59937, 406/862-4242 or 800/562-8734, www.glacierparkkoa.com.

37 ROCKY MOUNTAIN HI

🚲 🏊 ⛵ 🚣 🏕 ♿ 🚐 ⛺

Scenic rating: 7

in Kalispell

At 2,950 feet on the east side of Kalispell, Rocky Mountain Hi sits on Spring Creek, almost equidistant from Whitefish, Columbia Falls, and Bigfork. Three golf courses—Northern Pines, Village Greens, and Buffalo Hills—are within six miles. Within five miles of the campground are two fishing access sites on the Flathead River and shopping, box stores, and restaurants in Kalispell. A 25-minute drive connects with the west entrance to Glacier National Park, and 20 minutes on the road leads to Flathead Lake. For kids, the campground has a large playground with a miniature western town and swimming in the creek. A grassy beach lines the creek, and the slow-moving stream works for fishing and canoeing.

The quiet, forested campground sits on the east side of Spring Creek away from the highway noise. Sites 90–98 sit closest to the creek, along with the tent campsites. Many of the pull-through sites sit in a large open area good for clear satellite reception, but with little privacy between sites. Tent sites are separated by wooden privacy fences. The campground has some long-term RVers.

Campsites, facilities: The campground has 98 RV campsites and 10 tent campsites. Pull-through sites can fit the largest RVs. Hookups include sewer, water, electricity up to 50 amps, and cable TV. Facilities include picnic tables, flush toilets, showers, a launderette, swimming area with dock, canoe landing, and camp store. Leashed pets are permitted.

Reservations, fees: Reservations are accepted and recommended for July and August. Hookups run $25–28 for one or two people. Extra people over 12 years old cost $4. Tent sites cost $19. Add on 7 percent Montana bed tax. Cash, check, or credit card. Open year-round.

Directions: From Kalispell, drive Highway 2 north toward Columbia Falls. Turn right on East Reserve Drive and go one mile before turning left onto Helena Flats Road. About 0.8 mile up the road, turn right into the campground.

GPS Coordinates: N 48° 14.969' W 114° 15.279'

Contact: Rocky Mountain Hi RV Park and

Campground, 825 Helena Flats Rd, Kalispell, MT 59901, 406/755-9573 or 800/968-5637, www.glaciercamping.com.

38 COLUMBIA FALLS RV PARK

Scenic rating: 7

in Columbia Falls

Tucked under Columbia Mountain at 3,100 feet, this RV park works for those who want the convenience of driving 20 minutes to the west entrance of Glacier National Park and the quick access to Flathead Valley shopping, restaurants, and recreation. The Columbia Falls post office, outdoor community pool, coffee shop, and restaurants sit within a six-block walk. Big Sky Waterslides, one mile east, opens June–Labor Day. A mountain-biking and hiking trail runs six miles up to the summit of Columbia Mountain for broad views of the valley. At a fishing access and boat launch 0.5 mile to the east, you can float the Flathead River with drift boats, kayaks, rafts, and canoes, and anglers drop lines off the bridge.

Nothing blocks the campground from the highway, so light sleepers should bring ear plugs. Not much privacy exists between sites either; however, the open sites appeal to those requiring satellite reception. Most of the sites are gravel pull-throughs with some extra-large spaces accommodating RVs with double slide-outs. Some seasonal RV residents are here. Most sites garner views of Columbia Mountain or the Whitefish Range. Tent sites sit in a separate large, grassy lawn area. The campground has plans to add 20 new RV super sites for 2010.

Campsites, facilities: The campground has 42 RV campsites and 10 tent campsites. Hookups include sewer, water, electricity up to 50 amps, and cable TV, and some of the sites have phone lines. Facilities include picnic tables, flush toilets, showers, a launderette, wireless Internet, and camp store. Leashed pets are permitted. A wheelchair-accessible toilet is available.

Reservations, fees: Reservations are accepted and highly recommended for July and August. Hookups cost $34; tent sites cost $24–28. Rates cover two people per site; each extra person costs $5. Cash, check, or credit card. Add on 7 percent Montana bed tax. Open mid-April–mid-October.

Directions: From the intersection of Highway 2 and Nucleus Avenue in Columbia Falls, drive 0.25 mile east. The campground sits on the north side of the highway. For those coming from the east, the campground is 0.5 mile west of the bridge over the Flathead River.

GPS Coordinates: N 48° 22.185' W 114° 10.623'

Contact: Columbia Falls RV Park, 103 Hwy. 2 E., Columbia Falls, MT 59912, 406/892-1122 or 888/401-7268, www.columbiafallsrvpark.com.

39 EMERY BAY

Scenic rating: 9

on the east side of Hungry Horse Reservoir in Flathead National Forest

At 3,600 feet on the east side of Hungry Horse Reservoir, Emery Bay Campground is the closest east-side campground to the highway. A cement boat ramp helps launch watercraft for boating, fishing, waterskiing, and paddling. Canoes and kayaks can explore the more sheltered inlets rather than venture out onto the open reservoir where winds can crop up. Mountain-biking and hiking trails are available four miles north in the Coram Experimental Forest. Five miles northeast of the campground, trail #331 also leads to the crest of the Flathead Mountains for stunning views into the Great Bear Wilderness and Glacier National Park.

The quiet campground huddles under a conifer forest that provides partly sunny or shaded sites; however, peek-a-boo views of the reservoir do exist from the bluff that overlooks the main reservoir, Emery Bay, and the Flathead and Swan Mountains. The spacious campsites are spread out, with young trees and tall grass lending privacy between sites. Wildflowers bloom in early summer, too. The parking pads are gravel-and-grass back ins, except for two pull-throughs.

Campsites, facilities: Emery Bay has 26 RV or tent campsites. Trailers are limited to 32 feet. Facilities include picnic tables, fire rings with grills, vault toilets, drinking water, bear boxes, a boat ramp, and campground hosts. Pack out your trash. Leashed pets are permitted. A wheelchair-accessible toilet is available.

Reservations, fees: No reservations are accepted. Campsites cost $13. Cash or check. Open mid-May–September.

Directions: From the town of Hungry Horse, drive 0.6 mile to Martin City and turn east, following signs to the Hungry Horse Reservoir East Road for six miles and veering right at the Y, where the road turns to dusty rough dirt and gravel. Veer right at the campground sign and drop 0.4 mile to the campground.

GPS Coordinates: N 48° 20.062' W 113° 56.957'

Contact: Flathead National Forest, Hungry Horse Ranger District, 10 Hungry Horse Dr., Hungry Horse, MT 59919, 406/387-3800, www.fs.fed.us/r1/flathead/.

40 LOST JOHNNY AND LOST JOHNNY POINT

Scenic rating: 9

on the west side of Hungry Horse Reservoir in Flathead National Forest

At an elevation of 3,600 feet on the west side of Hungry Horse reservoir, Lost Johnny and Lost Johnny Point Campgrounds sit less than 0.2 mile apart on Doris Creek inlet's south side. Lost Johnny Point has a cement boat ramp to launch boats for sightseeing, waterskiing, fishing, and paddling, but you can launch hand-carried watercraft from Lost Johnny Campground. North of the inlet, mountain bikers can climb the eight-mile Beta Road, while from its terminus, hikers can ascend three miles to Doris Lake or five miles to Doris Peak for dramatic views of Flathead Valley, the reservoir, and Glacier National Park.

Deep, thick conifers cover both of these quiet campgrounds, providing shade, and underbrush works well as a privacy fence. Lost Johnny Creek runs adjacent to the smaller campground, while Lost Johnny Point Campground, with its paved road and parking pads, tops a bluff on a steep hill with a more open forest and some sites overlooking the reservoir. Due to the paved road access and the proximity to Hungry Horse, the pair fill up faster than other campgrounds on the reservoir. The Forest Service also plans to build a third campground with a three-lane boat ramp and 10 campsites on the inlet's north side at Doris Point.

Campsites, facilities: Lost Johnny Camp has five private RV or tent campsites that can accommodate trailers up to 50 feet, and Lost Johnny Point has 21 RV or tent campsites that can fit trailers up to 40 feet. Facilities include picnic tables, fire rings with grills, drinking water, vault toilets, a boat ramp, and a campground host. Pack out your trash. Leashed pets are permitted. A wheelchair-accessible toilet is available at Lost Johnny Point.

Reservations, fees: No reservations are accepted. The campsites cost $13. Cash or check. Open mid-May–September.

Directions: From the town of Hungry Horse, drive south on the paved West Reservoir Road for nine miles, crossing the dam. Turn left into both campgrounds, located 0.2 mile apart. Lost Johnny GPS Coordinates: N 48° 18.323' W 113° 58.085'

Lost Johnny Point GPS Coordinates: N 48° 18.601' W 113° 57.813'

Contact: Flathead National Forest, Hungry Horse Ranger District, 10 Hungry Horse Dr., Hungry Horse, MT 59919, 406/387-3800, www.fs.fed.us/r1/flathead/.

41 LID CREEK

Scenic rating: 9

on the west side of Hungry Horse Reservoir in Flathead National Forest

At 3,600 feet on the west side of Hungry Horse Reservoir, Lid Creek sits just at the end of the paved road. A fishing access is at the bottom of the campground, where you can carry small boats, rafts, kayaks, and canoes to the water. A motor or paddle about one mile across the reservoir reaches Fire Island. The nearest large boat launch is at Lost Johnny Point, five miles to the north. The nearest hiking and mountain-biking trail is at the end of Forest Road 895C, about two miles from the campground entrance and 3.5 miles up the Wounded Buck drainage. A three-mile trail climbs to the top of the Swan Crest, meeting up with the Alpine 7 trail, where you can head south to the summit of Strawberry Mountain or Strawberry Lake. The area is favored by huckleberry pickers. Due to the longer drive to reach the campground, it sees fewer people than Lost Johnny.

Known for its quiet and seclusion, the campground sits in thick mixed conifer forest on a large loop on the slope above the reservoir. Tent spaces are tight, small, or lacking in some campsites; you may need to pitch the tent on the parking pad. The campsites are spaced out for privacy. An upper spur offers more primitive campsites. Views from the beach include the rugged Flathead Range across the reservoir.

Campsites, facilities: The campground has 23 RV or tent campsites. Trailers longer than 32 feet are not recommended in the campground. Facilities include picnic tables, fire rings with grills, vault toilets, and campground hosts. No drinking water is available; if you use reservoir water, boil or filter it. Pack out your garbage. Leashed pets are permitted.

Reservations, fees: No reservations are accepted. Campsites cost $11. Cash or check. Open mid-May–September.

Directions: From the town of Hungry Horse, take the Hungry Horse Reservoir's West Reservoir Road south for 15 miles. The paved road crosses the reservoir on the dam and traverses south along the shore. Turn left at the signed entrance onto a gravel road for one mile (go straight through the intersection) into the campground.

GPS Coordinates: N 48° 17.185' W 113° 54.616'

Contact: Flathead National Forest, Hungry Horse Ranger District, 10 Hungry Horse Dr., Hungry Horse, MT 59919, 406/387-3800, www.fs.fed.us/r1/flathead/.

42 FIRE ISLAND

Scenic rating: 8

on Hungry Horse Reservoir in Flathead National Forest

Fire Island is a boat-in campground. While Hungry Horse Reservoir has several islands (all of which permit dispersed camping), only two have established designated campgrounds on them—Elk and Fire. At 3,600 feet, Fire Island sits farther north than Elk and requires no dirt road driving to get to its closest launch ramp at Lid Creek Campground. However, the island's location in the reservoir requires paddling or motoring across open water. The reservoir offers fishing for westslope cutthroat trout. Beach boats completely at night in case winds crop up.

Located on the southwest side of the island, the campsites are primitive, with small spaces for tents tucked into an open forest. The campsites are spread out for privacy in the tall brush and white bear grass blooming in early summer. Unlike Elk Island's gentle beach, Fire Island requires a steep climb up the bank to the campsites. Nonetheless, it still offers quiet and solitude.

Campsites, facilities: The island has four designated tent campsites. Facilities include picnic tables, fire rings with grills, and a pit toilet. Drinking water is not available; bring your own or filter or boil any water dipped from the reservoir. Pack out your trash. Collecting firewood from the beach and downed limbs in the forest is permitted. Leashed pets are permitted.

Reservations, fees: Reservations are not accepted. Campsites are free. Open mid-May–September.

Directions: From the town of Hungry Horse, take the Hungry Horse Reservoir's West Reservoir Road south for 15 miles to Lid Creek Campground. The paved but curvy road crosses the reservoir on the dam and traverses the west shoreline. Turn left at the signed entrance onto a gravel road for one mile to reach the boat launch.

GPS Coordinates: N 48° 17.675' W 113° 53.773'

Contact: Flathead National Forest, Hungry Horse Ranger District, 10 Hungry Horse Dr., Hungry Horse, MT 59919, 406/387-3800, www.fs.fed.us/r1/flathead/.

43 MURRAY BAY

Scenic rating: 9

on the east side of Hungry Horse Reservoir in Flathead National Forest

At 3,600 feet on the east side of Hungry Horse Reservoir, Murray Bay is one of the more coveted campgrounds on the reservoir. The campground's boat ramp aids boaters going for fishing, waterskiing, and sightseeing. Murray Bay is one of the reservoir's better places for paddling, due to the inlets, islands, and more protected water. On Forest Road 1048, the trail to Great Northern Mountain shoots up 4,300 feet in 4.5 miles to the summit for spectacular views of Grant Glacier and Glacier National Park. If snow clings to the upper mountain, the climb can be treacherous and should not be attempted without an ice axe. Mountain bikers ride up to Firefighter Mountain Lookout for panoramic views of the reservoir and knife-like Great Northern Mountain.

The 19-acre ultra-quiet campground sits on a loosely forested, partly sunny larch- and fir-covered square peninsula that sticks out toward Kelly Island. When the reservoir water drops low enough, you can swim or wade across the narrow channel to explore the island. Most of the secluded, roomy campsites have views of the reservoir and the Swan Mountains; however, low underbrush that blooms in July with tall white bear grass permits visibility of other campers. The gravel campground road is narrow and so are the sites; some large RVs may have trouble maneuvering. If the campground is full, more campsites are available at Riverside boat launch one mile north.

Campsites, facilities: The campground has 18 RV or tent campsites. Trailers are limited to 32 feet. Facilities include picnic tables, fire rings with grills, vault toilets, and campground hosts. Pack out your garbage. No drinking water is available; bring your own or filter or boil the lake water. Leashed pets are permitted.

Reservations, fees: No reservations are accepted. Campsites cost $11. Cash or check. Open mid-May–September.

Directions: From the town of Hungry Horse, go east on Highway 2 for 0.6 mile to Martin City and turn eastward, following the signs leading toward the east side of Hungry Horse Reservoir and veering right at the Y, where the road becomes a battle with dust and washboards. Drive 22 miles south on Forest Road 38. Turn right into the campground.

GPS Coordinates: N 48° 15.980' W 113° 48.670'

Contact: Flathead National Forest, Hungry Horse Ranger District, 10 Hungry Horse Dr., Hungry Horse, MT 59919, 406/387-3800, www.fs.fed.us/r1/flathead/.

44 LAKEVIEW

Scenic rating: 8

on the west side of Hungry Horse Reservoir in Flathead National Forest

Lakeview Campground, with an elevation of 3,600 feet, is one of the less crowded destinations on the west side of Hungry Horse Reservoir. Boating and fishing on the reservoir is only available via hand-carried watercraft carried down the bank to the beach. To the west on Forest Road 1633, the 2.5-mile trail #420 climbs to Clayton Lake in Jewel Basin Hiking Area. Locate the road about 3.5 miles north of Lakeview and drive 2.5 miles to the trailhead. The lake is known for its native westslope cutthroat fishery. Due to the campground's late closing in the fall, it is popular with hunters.

The campground sits on a forested slope between the road and the reservoir. The quiet campsites, sitting in a mix of firs and spruce, spread out for privacy and are partly shaded with peek-a-boo views of the lake. Spectacular views greet you at the beach; the knife-like Great Northern and Grant Peak across the lake are snow-covered still in June.

Campsites, facilities: The campground has five RV or tent campsites. Trailers longer than 22 feet are not recommended in the campground. Facilities include picnic tables, fire rings with grills, and a vault toilet. No drinking water is available. Bring your own, or plan to filter or boil water from the creek. Pack out your garbage. Leashed pets are permitted.

Reservations, fees: Reservations are not accepted. Camping is free. Open June–November.

Directions: From the town of Hungry Horse, drive the Hungry Horse Reservoir's West Reservoir Road south for 24 miles. The road crosses the reservoir on the dam and is paved as far as Lid Creek before turning to dirt for about nine miles. Turn left into the campground.

GPS Coordinates: N 48° 13.109' W 113° 48.301'

Contact: Flathead National Forest, Hungry Horse Ranger District, 10 Hungry Horse Dr., Hungry Horse, MT 59919, 406/387-3800, www.fs.fed.us/r1/flathead/.

45 ELK ISLAND

Scenic rating: 10

in Hungry Horse Reservoir in Flathead National Forest

BEST (

Located on the east side of Hungry Horse Reservoir, Elk Island is a boat-in campground at 3,600 feet. Paddling to Elk Island in a sea kayak or canoe yields gorgeous views of Great Northern and Grant Peak, along with the northern Swan Range. (You can also motorboat to the island, launching from any one of the four boat ramps at the north end of the reservoir.) Put in at the Riverside boat launch, which has a cement ramp. Paddle or motor between the Murray Bay Campground and Kelly Island south to Elk Island, beaching on the north side of the island to reach the campsites. If winds come up, stay near the shoreline. If the waters are calm, add tours around Kelly and Elk Islands. On Elk, a 90-minute walk will tour you around the shoreline. Beach boats completely at night in case winds crop up.

The campsites are primitive with small spaces for tents. With lower water levels, some flat sites appear on the beaches. In June, the island blooms with both bear grass and a good crop of mosquitoes. Pull out the camera for the sunset over the Swan Range and the sunrise from the Great Bear Wilderness. The songs of birds, water lapping the shore, and wind are the only sounds on the island.

Campsites, facilities: The island has seven designated tent campsites, plus several more primitive sites. Facilities include picnic tables, fire rings with grills, and pit toilets. Pack out your trash. Drinking water is not available; bring your own or filter or boil any water dipped from the reservoir. Collecting firewood from the beach and downed limbs in the forest is permitted. Leashed pets are permitted.

Reservations, fees: Reservations are not accepted. The campsites are free. Open mid-May–September.

Directions: From the town of Hungry Horse, go east on Highway 2 for 0.6 mile to Martin City and turn eastward, following the signs leading toward the east side of Hungry Horse Reservoir and veering right at the Y onto the gravel road. Drive 21 miles south on the dusty washboard of Forest Road 38. Turn right into Riverside boat launch.

GPS Coordinates: N 48° 14.452' W 113° 47.932'

Contact: Flathead National Forest, Hungry Horse Ranger District, 10 Hungry Horse Dr., Hungry Horse, MT 59919, 406/387-3800, www.fs.fed.us/r1/flathead/.

46 SPRUCE PARK ON THE RIVER

Scenic rating: 8

in Kalispell on the Flathead River

At an elevation of 2,900 feet, Spruce Park mixes the convenience of being a few minutes from downtown Kalispell with the ambiance of a riverfront setting backdropped by mountain views. Sitting right on the Flathead River, the campground lures anglers who

want to try to hook rainbows or westslope cutthroat trout from the campground's dock. Three golf courses are within seven miles, and the renowned Eagle Bend Golf Club requires only a 20-minute drive. Glacier Park is 30 miles to the northeast. Several fishing accesses on the Flathead River allow for launching boats, rafts, kayaks, and canoes for floating the river.

Most of Spruce Park's campsites sit under large mature firs and cottonwoods with some sites bordering the Flathead River. A paved road loops through the mowed lawn campground, with some large pull-through spaces for big rigs towing boats or cars; sites along the river have views of the northern Swan Mountains. Sites are set close together with little privacy, and highway noise enters the campground.

Campsites, facilities: The campground has 70 RV campsites and 17 tent campsites. Pull-through sites can fit the largest RVs. Hookups include cable TV, sewer, water, and electricity up to 50 amps. Facilities include picnic tables, fire rings, flush toilets, showers, a launderette, wireless Internet, a disposal station, a pet-walking area, a playground, a dock, horseshoes, a game room, a volleyball court, and a camp store. Leashed pets are permitted.

Reservations, fees: Reservations are accepted. Hookups cost $25–28. Tent sites cost $19. Rates are based on one family with their minor children per site or four adults. Add on 7 percent Montana bed tax. Cash, credit card, check, or Canadian currency. Open year-round.

Directions: From Kalispell, drive east on Highway 35 toward Creston. Turn left into the campground about 1.5 miles past the LaSalle/Highway 2 junction.

GPS Coordinates: N 48° 13.440' W 114° 14.825'

Contact: Spruce Park on the River RV Park and Campground, 1985 Hwy. 35, Kalispell, MT 59901, 406/752-6321, www.spruceparkrv.com.

47 EDGEWATER RV RESORT

Scenic rating: 6

on the west side of Flathead Lake

Located on the west side of Flathead Lake in Lakeside, the Edgewater RV Resort sits on one side of the two-lane highway while a marina covers the shoreline. The marina rents power boats, personal watercraft, and paddleboats. Charter fishing and lake cruises are also available. Downtown Lakeside spans only five blocks, so you can walk to the grocery store or restaurants. The town is also home to Tamarack Brewing Company Alehouse and Grill, which serves its microbrews, such as Bear Bottom Blonde and Old 'Stache Whiskey Barrel Porter, along with lunch and dinner.

The campground loops on a paved road through the resort with mowed lawn flanking each paved parking apron. The campground is wide open with no trees for shade, but grabs a clear shot of the sky for satellite reception. Three sites (44–46) sit across the highway closer to the lakeshore. The RV park is adjacent to the resort's motel, and those camping have access to the resort's private swimming beach and dock.

Campsites, facilities: The campground has 38 RV sites. Hookups include water, sewer, and electricity up to 50 amps, and 20 of the sites are pull-throughs at 27 feet wide by 70 feet long—wide enough to accommodate slide-outs. Facilities include picnic tables, pedestal barbecues, flush toilets, showers, a disposal station, modem hookups, a launderette, and access across the highway to the lake, a dock, and swimming. Leashed pets are permitted. A wheelchair-accessible toilet is available.

Reservations, fees: Reservations are accepted. Hookups cost $34. Cash, check, or credit card. Open May–September.

Directions: On Highway 93, find Lakeside 13 miles south of Kalispell and 38 miles north of Polson. The resort sits on the opposite side of the highway from the lake at the north end of town.

GPS Coordinates: N 48° 1.349' W 114° 13.547'

Contact: Edgewater RV Resort, 7140 Hwy. 93 S., Lakeside, MT 59922, 406/844-3644 or 800/424-3798, www.edgewaterrv.com.

48 LAKE MARY RONAN

Scenic rating: 6

on Lake Mary Ronan in the Salish Mountains

Lake Mary Ronan, which sits seven miles west of Flathead Lake at 3,800 feet in the Salish Mountains, doesn't get nearly the traffic that the Flathead Lake parks see, but the lake draws its share of people. At 1,513 acres, the lake is considerably smaller than Flathead Lake, but it still attracts bird-watchers, swimmers, kayakers, canoeists, water-skiers, and mushroom and huckleberry pickers. Anglers go after kokanee, largemouth bass, pumpkinseed, rainbow trout, yellow perch, and westslope cutthroat trout. Trails lead to the beach, which has a concrete boat ramp with an adjacent dock, a small swimming beach, and paved parking for boat trailers.

The quiet, 120-acre park shaded by Douglas firs and western larches tucks its campground back in the shady woods on one gravel loop. The sites around the outside rim of the loop are more private than those inside the circle.

Campsites, facilities: The campground has 31 RV or tent campsites. RVs are limited to 35 feet. Facilities include picnic tables, fire rings with grills, vault toilets, drinking water, a boat launch, and garbage service. Firewood is for sale. Leashed pets are permitted. A wheelchair-accessible toilet is available.

Reservations, fees: No reservations are accepted. Montana residents may use the park free during the day; nonresidents must pay $5 per vehicle or $3 per bike. Camping costs $15, cash or check. The park is open all year but only has services May–September.

Directions: From Kalispell, drive 20 miles south on Highway 93. From Polson, drive 32 miles north on Highway 93. Look for the sign on the west side of the road.

GPS Coordinates: N 47° 55.615' W 114° 22.917'

Contact: Montana Fish, Wildlife, and Parks, Region 1, 490 N. Meridian Rd., Kalispell, MT 59901, 406/752-5501, http://fwp.mt.gov.

49 WEST SHORE STATE PARK

Scenic rating: 9

on the west side of Flathead Lake

Located at 2,900 feet, Flathead Lake has 128 miles of shoreline with waters like clear glass. The glacially fed lake, which draws its waters from Glacier Park, Canada, and the Bob Marshall Wilderness area, grew from ice age glaciers melting 10,000 years ago. Located on the west shore with sunrise views over the Mission and Swan Mountains, the West Shore State Park has the reputation of being the most private state park on the lake. The campground sits on a bluff on Goose Bay with tiny Goose Island about 0.3 mile out in the lake. A concrete boat ramp facilitates launching watercraft for fishing, waterskiing, sailing, kayaking, canoeing, and sightseeing.

The quiet 129-acre park spans a forested hillside with a rocky beach. Filtered sunlight hits the campsites through tall larches and pines. Some of the campsites have peek-a-boo views across the lake to the mountains rising above the opposite shore about eight miles away. The campground road is paved, but parking pads are gravel.

Campsites, facilities: The campground has 31 RV or tent campsites. RVs are limited to 30 feet. Facilities include picnic tables, fire rings with grills, vault toilets, drinking water, garbage service, a playground, and a boat launch. For bicyclists, a bear-resistant food storage locker is available. Firewood is for sale. Leashed pets are permitted. A wheelchair-accessible toilet is available, and an ADA campsite has electrical and water hookups.

Reservations, fees: No reservations are accepted. Montana residents may use the park free during the day; nonresidents must pay $5 per vehicle or $3 per bike. Camping costs $15. Cash or check. Open all year, but serviced only May–September.

Directions: From Kalispell drive 20 miles south on Highway 93, or from Polson drive 32 miles north on Highway 93. Turn east at the signed entrance to drop into the campground.

GPS Coordinates: N 47° 56.958' W 114° 11.027'

Contact: Montana Fish, Wildlife, and Parks, Region 1, 490 N. Meridian Rd., Kalispell, MT 59901, 406/752-5501, http://fwp.mt.gov.

50 BIG ARM STATE PARK

Scenic rating: 10

on the west side of Flathead Lake

BEST (

Flathead Lake covers 188 square miles, but from the vantage of Big Arm State Park, islands cut off some of the wide open water and shrink the size of the lake in appearance. Located on the lake's west side on Big Arm Bay at 2,900 feet, the park faces the morning sunrise coming over the Mission Mountains. Wild Horse Island—a day use state park renowned for its wild horses, bighorn sheep, birds, and wildflowers—sits 5.5 miles across the lake; boat to the island to hike around it. Kayakers and canoeists should watch the weather carefully, as winds can whip the lake into a white-capped frenzy in minutes. The park also sits on Confederated Salish Kootenai land of the Flathead Reservation; tribal fishing permits are required to fish the lake. The campground includes a cement boat ramp, dock, and trailer parking. With a 2.5-mile nature trail through its prairie grasslands and forest, the park is also good for bird-watching—especially with bald eagles and ospreys fishing in the lake.

Large ponderosa pines and junipers bring filtered shade to the campground. A long swimming beach runs from the boat ramp and dock north to the end of B loop. Campsites are tucked around two narrow, long, paved loops with gravel aprons. Both loops have half of the sites overlooking the lake.

Campsites, facilities: The campground has 40 RV or tent campsites. RVs are limited to 30 feet. Facilities include picnic tables, fire rings with grills, vault toilets, flush toilets, showers, drinking water, garbage service, and a boat launch. The campground also includes a bear-resistant food storage locker for those traveling by bicycle. Firewood is for sale. The campground also rents a yurt. Leashed pets are permitted. A wheelchair-accessible toilet is available.

Reservations, fees: No reservations are accepted. While Montana residents may use the park free during the day, nonresidents must pay $5 per vehicle or $3 per bike. Camping costs $15. Cash or check. Open May–September.

Directions: From Polson, drive 14 miles north on Highway 93, or from Kalispell, drive about 38 miles south on Highway 35. Turn right at the signed entrance.

GPS Coordinates: N 47° 48.770' W 114° 18.612'

Contact: Montana Fish, Wildlife, and Parks, Region 1, 490 N. Meridian Rd., Kalispell, MT 59901, 406/752-5501, http://fwp.mt.gov.

51 FINLEY POINT STATE PARK

Scenic rating: 9

on the east side of Flathead Lake

Flathead Lake is the largest natural freshwater lake west of the Mississippi. Finley Point State Park sits at 2,900 feet on the lake's south end on the Flathead Reservation below the Mission Mountains. The point is actually a half-mile-wide spit that sticks out into the lake, forming Skidoo Bay to the northeast and Polson Bay to the southeast—both littered with summer homes along the shores. The proximity to Polson 15 minutes away brings heavy day use to the park. Anglers come here to fish for whitefish, rainbow and bull trout, northern pike, and lake trout that grow up to 20 pounds. A tribal fishing license is required. A boat ramp, marina, boat pump-out, and trailer parking are available. The National Bison Range and Ninepipes National Wildlife Refuge are about 40 minutes south.

The 28-acre campground sits on the shore of Flathead Lake with all of its cramped campsites lined up along the lake facing the sunset. The grassy campground, shaded by mature firs and birches, lacks privacy. From the beach, you'll see summer homes and Polson across the bay. However, the campground's popularity comes from its prime waterfront campsites. Sites 1–4 with tent pads are designated for tents only. Tents are not permitted in the RV sites, which line up in parking-lot fashion in front of their tables and fire rings.

Campsites, facilities: The campground has 12 RV campsites, four tent campsites, and 16 boat campsites. RV hookups include electricity with 30 amps, and the maximum RV length is 40 feet. Facilities include picnic tables, fire rings with grills, flush toilets, drinking water, boat facilities, and a swimming area. Firewood is for sale. Four of the 16 boat slips also have electrical and water hookups. Boats are limited to 25 feet. Leashed pets are permitted. A wheelchair-accessible toilet is available.

Reservations, fees: No reservations are accepted. While Montana residents may use the park for free during the day, nonresidents must pay $5 per vehicle. Campsites and boat camping slips cost $15. Hookups cost $5 additional. Cash or check. Open May–September.

Directions: From Polson, drive seven miles north on Highway 35. Turn left and follow the signs four miles northwest on narrow Finley Point Road. Turn left into the campground. GPS Coordinates: N 47° 45.249' W 114° 5.165'

Contact: Montana Fish, Wildlife, and Parks, Region 1, 490 N. Meridian Rd., Kalispell, MT 59901, 406/752-5501, http://fwp.mt.gov.

52 BLUE BAY

Scenic rating: 10

on the east side of Flathead Lake

Blue Bay commands a spectacular location on Flathead Lake's east side, with views of Wild Horse Island. The campground, which faces southeast down the lake, sets up the majority of its campsites with prime real estate on the waterfront. Owned and operated by the Confederated Salish and Kootenai Tribes, Blue Bay has three parts: a lodge area reserved for groups, the day-use beach and marina, and the campground. The marina includes 32 boat slips, a concrete ramp and boat docks, a fishing pier, boat trailer parking, and a fish-cleaning station. The day-use swim beach has picnic tables, a dock, and a buoyed off area to protect swimmers. Personal watercraft are not permitted.

The campground, on the opposite side of the marina from the day-use area, has another buoyed swim area with a dock at the group shelter and another swim dock with no buoy line located between sites 18 and 19. Large ponderosa pines shade some of the grassy area. Sites 1–6, 41, and 51 are farther apart from their neighbors, while the remainder of the sites line up close to each other. Sites 7–33 line the waterfront. In a row on a bluff behind the waterfront campsites are the sites with hookups. No alcohol is permitted in the campground. Most of the campsites are buffered from the highway by the bluff with the lodges.

Campsites, facilities: The campground has 55 campsites. RV hookups are available at 17 sites with hookups for sewer and water, and some have electricity. Facilities include picnic tables, fire rings, drinking water, garbage service, and flush toilets.

Reservations, fees: Reservations are not accepted. Day use for the area costs $5 per vehicle. Camping costs $15 per vehicle. Hookups cost $30. Cash or check. Open May–September.

Directions: From Polson, drive 13.5 miles north on Highway 35. From Bigfork, drive 14.5 miles south on Highway 35. Turn west at the signed entrance.

GPS Coordinates: N 47° 49.650' W 114° 1.689'

Contact: Confederated Salish and Kootenai Tribes, 51383 Hwy. 93 N., Pablo, MT 59855, 406/675-2700 or 406/253-3813 (campground), www.cskt.org.

53 YELLOW BAY STATE PARK

Scenic rating: 8

on the east side of Flathead Lake

For those looking for a little less hectic experience on Flathead Lake, Yellow Bay may be the answer. It's on the flanks of the Mission Mountains in cherry orchard country. In July, look for stands selling freshly picked cherries along Highway 35; on hot days, you can smell the fruit in the air. Located on the lake's east side, the park sits across from Wild Horse Island—a day use state park with bighorn sheep, eagles, and wild horses. With 10 miles of water in between, power boaters go from this eastern side, but kayakers and canoeists tend to stick to the east shoreline, visiting the island only from the west side of the lake. The park also sits on the Flathead Reservation; tribal fishing permits are required to fish the lake. Located in sheltered Yellow Bay, the 15-acre park sidles up to the Flathead Lake shoreline with a wide, sandy southeast-facing beach for swimming and Yellow Bay Creek running through the park. A concrete ramp with a dock aids boat launchers for fishing, waterskiing, and sightseeing.

Although the access off the highway is paved, the road is steep and narrow. Picking up traffic noise, the tent sites sit back from the beach, tucked under a thick canopy of trees between the campground and the highway.

Campsites, facilities: The campground has only four walk-in tenting sites. Facilities include picnic tables, pedestal grills, flush toilets, drinking water, and garbage service. Wood fires are not permitted; bring your own charcoal. Bear-resistant food storage lockers are also available, a boon for bicyclists. Leashed pets are permitted.

Reservations, fees: No reservations are accepted. While Montana residents may use the park free during the day, nonresidents must pay $5 per vehicle or $3 per bike. Camping costs $15. Cash or check. Open May–September.

Directions: From Polson, drive 15 miles north on Highway 35, or from Bigfork, drive 13 miles south on Highway 35. Turn west at the signed entrance to the park.

GPS Coordinates: N 47° 52.532' W 114° 1.728'

Contact: Montana Fish, Wildlife, and Parks, Region 1, 490 N. Meridian Rd., Kalispell, MT 59901, 406/752-5501, http://fwp.mt.gov.

54 WAYFARERS STATE PARK

Scenic rating: 9

on the east side of Flathead Lake

Sitting at 2,900 feet on the largest natural freshwater lake in the West, Wayfarers State Park hops in high season with fishing, sailing, waterskiing, paddling, and sightseeing. For boaters, a concrete launch ramp, boat trailer parking, dock, and pump-out service are available. A 1.5-mile hiking trail climbs through the 67-acre forested park with scenic overlooks of the lake. The park is also adjacent to Bigfork, with its summer theater, restaurants, and shopping. Wayfarers is the closest designated campground to Jewel Basin, a 15,349-acre hiking area in mountain goat terrain with 50 miles of trails that loop between 27 alpine lakes. The Wild Mile of the Swan River yields advanced white-water kayaking right outside Bigfork.

The paved entrance road passes an osprey nest as it drops to the lake, where the boat launch and picnic area sit on the beach, with the campground a five-minute walk away. Most of the campground loops through a shady canopy of mature firs and ponderosa pines. Sites 10–15 have more privacy than sites 19–25, which sit on a big meadow. Sites 1–4 also sit on the meadow, right at the campground entrance with more traffic. A couple of tight sites are pull-throughs reserved for RVs only; maximum trailer combination is 50 feet. A few sites are for tents only.

Campsites, facilities: The campground has 26 RV or tent campsites. RVs are limited to 50 feet. Facilities include picnic tables, fire rings with grills, vault and flush toilets, showers, drinking water, garbage service, a disposal station, a playground, and a bear-resistant food storage locker for bikers. Firewood is for sale. Leashed pets are permitted. A wheelchair-accessible toilet is available, and there's a 30-amp electrical hookup at site 24, an ADA site.

Reservations, fees: No reservations are accepted. Montana residents may use the park free during the day; nonresidents must pay $5 per vehicle or $3 per bike. Camping costs $15. Cash or check. Open all year, but serviced only May–September.

Directions: From Bigfork, drive 0.5 mile south on Highway 35. Turn west at the signed entrance into the park.

GPS Coordinates: N 48° 4.120' W 114° 4.849'

Contact: Montana Fish, Wildlife, and Parks, Region 1, 490 N. Meridian Rd., Kalispell, MT 59901, 406/752-5501, http://fwp.mt.gov.

55 HANDKERCHIEF LAKE

Scenic rating: 7

west of Hungry Horse Reservoir in Flathead National Forest

At 3,850 feet on the west side of Hungry Horse Reservoir above Graves Bay, the 30-acre Handkerchief Lake sits only two miles from Graves Bay. The lake makes for nice canoeing; no boat launch is available, but trails lead to the shore. Fishing is available for native trout, too. Continue up the road another two miles to reach the Graves Creek Trailhead. The trail climbs in five miles to Black Lake—a native westslope cutthroat fishery—in Jewel Basin Hiking Area, with views of Mount Aeneas and the Great Bear Wilderness across the reservoir. The campground is used by hunters in the fall.

The campground has a unique layout. You park on a pull-off on the road, but sites are spread out all along the shore below the road. The campsites sit in a deep forest of thick spruce and firs with privacy between campsites created from abundant underbrush. Only natural sounds fill the campground, making it prized for its quiet.

Campsites, facilities: The campground has nine RV or tent campsites. Trailers are limited to 22 feet. Facilities include picnic tables, fire rings with grills, and vault toilets. No drinking water is available; bring your own, or plan to filter or boil water from the creek. Pack out your trash. Leashed pets are permitted.

Reservations, fees: Reservations are not accepted. Camping is free. Open June–November.

Directions: From the town of Hungry Horse, take the Hungry Horse Reservoir West Road south for 35 miles. The road crosses the reservoir on the dam and is paved as far as Lid Creek (halfway) before turning to dusty washboards and potholes. At 35 miles, turn right onto Forest Road 897 and drive two miles to the campground.

GPS Coordinates: N 48° 8.631' W 113° 49.574'

Contact: Flathead National Forest, Hungry Horse Ranger District, 10 Hungry Horse Dr., Hungry Horse, MT 59919, 406/387-3800, www.fs.fed.us/r1/flathead/.

56 GRAVES BAY

Scenic rating: 8

on the west side of Hungry Horse Reservoir in Flathead National Forest

On the west side of the reservoir, Graves Bay Campground (sometimes called Graves Creek) sits on the largest bay—stretching almost three miles long. The elevation is 3,600 feet. A primitive boat launch is available—best for hand-carried small boats, canoes, and kayaks. The narrow bay's water offers a protected place to paddle. Waters tumble from Jewel Basin down to the bay, which increases beach size as the reservoir drops during the summer. The Graves Creek Trail, which departs from above Handkerchief Lake, climbs to Black Lake into Jewel Basin Hiking Area for views of Mount Aeneas and the Great Bear Wilderness across the reservoir.

The quiet, forested campground sits at the head of Graves Bay. The campsites sit along the creek on a spur road opposite the bay. The Forest Service has plans to remove the campsites on the reservoir side of the road and develop the sites on the west side of the road with a vault toilet and an ADA camping site. If this campground is full, try Handkerchief Lake three miles away.

Campsites, facilities: The campground has 10 RV or tent campsites. Trailers longer than 22 feet are not recommended in the campground. Facilities include picnic tables, fire rings with grills, and vault toilets. No drinking water is available. Bring your own, or plan to filter or boil water from the creek. Pack out your garbage. Leashed pets are permitted.

Reservations, fees: Reservations are not accepted. Camping is free. Open June–September.

Directions: From the town of Hungry Horse, take the Hungry Horse Reservoir West Road south for 35 miles. The road crosses the reservoir on the dam and is paved as far as Lid Creek, about halfway. After that, the curvy dirt road becomes interminable dust and washboards. Turn west into the campground. GPS Coordinates: N 48° 7.625' W 113° 48.643'

Contact: Flathead National Forest, Hungry Horse Ranger District, 10 Hungry Horse Dr., Hungry Horse, MT 59919, 406/387-3800, www.fs.fed.us/r1/flathead/.

57 DEVIL'S CORKSCREW

Scenic rating: 7

on the east side of Hungry Horse Reservoir in Flathead National Forest

The long dirt road on the east side of the reservoir into Devil's Corkscrew deters many people. Before departing from the town of Hungry Horse, gas up and check the spare tire in preparation for the dust, washboards, and lack of services. Located at 3,600 feet, the campground has a primitive boat launch for small boats, kayaks, and canoes. Larger boats must launch from ramps located 10 miles in either direction. The 35-mile-long Hungry Horse Reservoir is known for its native fishery. Within short drives north and east on the forest road, you can find trailheads. The six-mile Logan Creek Trail (#62) climbs into the Great Bear Wilderness, and a four-mile rougher trail leads to the site of Baptiste Lookout for views of the reservoir.

The Forest Service thinned the campground area several years ago, opening up the thick forest for partial sun. The quiet small campground sits back in the trees from the shore with campsites spread out for privacy. This is one prized for its quiet and solitude.

Campsites, facilities: The campground has four RV or tent campsites. Trailers are limited to 32 feet. Facilities include picnic tables, fire rings with grills, and a vault toilet. Drinking water is not available; bring your own. Pack out your trash. Leashed pets are permitted.

Reservations, fees: Reservations are not accepted. The campsites are free. Open mid-May–September.

Directions: From the town of Hungry Horse, go east on Highway 2 for 0.6 mile to Martin City and turn eastward, following the signs leading toward the east side of Hungry Horse Reservoir and veering right at the Y onto the gravel road. Drive 32 miles south on Forest Road 38. Turn right into the campground. GPS Coordinates: N 48° 6.610' W 113° 41.801'

Contact: Flathead National Forest, Spotted Bear Ranger District, 10 Hungry Horse Dr., Hungry Horse, MT 59919, 406/387-3800, www.fs.fed.us/r1/flathead/.

58 PETER'S CREEK

Scenic rating: 8

on the east side of Hungry Horse Reservoir in Flathead National Forest

The long, dusty road on the east side of the reservoir into Peter's Creek deters many people. Gas up, and check the spare tire before you depart. At an elevation of 3,600 feet on the east shore of the 35-mile-long reservoir, the campground is prized for its sheer remoteness. You can launch hand-carried watercraft from the campground, but larger boats need to launch from the Crossover boat launch about 4.5 miles farther south of Peter's Creek. It offers a cement low-water boat ramp for water-skiers, sightseers, and anglers going for the native species in the reservoir. Mountain biking is available on a tangle of forest roads on the flanks of the Flathead Mountains.

A thick forest of larch and Douglas fir covers the small two-acre campground, but with enough openings through the trees for views of the Swan Range across the reservoir. The quiet, secluded campsites are spaced out along the reservoir, with loads of undergrowth for privacy, but they are small and cramped, with very small tent spaces. Short trails lead down to the reservoir, where the beach grows larger throughout the summer as the dam draws the water down.

Campsites, facilities: The campground has seven RV or tent campsites. Trailers are limited to 22 feet. Facilities include picnic tables, fire rings with grills, and a vault toilet. Drinking water is not available; filter or boil any water dipped from the creeks. Pack out your trash. Leashed pets are permitted. A wheelchair-accessible toilet is available.

Reservations, fees: Reservations are not accepted. Camping is free. Open mid-May–September.

Directions: From the town of Hungry Horse, go east on Highway 2 for 0.6 mile to Martin City. Turn eastward, following the signs leading toward the east side of Hungry Horse Reservoir and veering right at the Y onto the gravel road. Drive 37 miles south on Forest Road 38. Turn right to drop into the campground.

GPS Coordinates: N 48° 3.408' W 113° 38.678'

Contact: Flathead National Forest, Spotted Bear Ranger District, 10 Hungry Horse Dr., Hungry Horse, MT 59919, 406/387-3800, www.fs.fed.us/r1/flathead/.

59 SWAN LAKE

Scenic rating: 9

in Swan Valley in Flathead National Forest

BEST (

At 3,100 feet, Swan Lake—a long, skinny cold-water lake located just southeast of Bigfork in the Swan Valley—gets packed with recreational boaters and water-skiers. The lake, with a swimming beach, dock, and boat ramp, is surrounded by the high Swan Mountains. The south end of the lake attracts paddlers for bird-watching along the Swan River National Wildlife Refuge, and anglers go for the rainbow and westslope cutthroat trout. Local hikes lead to lookouts and lakes. A four-mile climb tops Sixmile Mountain, the site of an old lookout at the north end of the southern Swan Crest Trail (Alpine 7), and a seven-mile trail ascends to Bond and Trinkus Lakes, which cuddle in basins just below the crest.

Shaded by big cedars, the picnic area sits right on the beach of Swan Lake, while the campground tucks its two loops back into trees on the opposite side of the highway. Underbrush lends a sense of privacy between many of the campsites; those on the outsides of the loops have more privacy than those on the inside. The Forest Service holds campfire programs in the evenings. Catering to cyclists, the campground has bike lanes and one bicycle-only campsite.

Campsites, facilities: The campground has 36 RV or tent campsites. The campground can accommodate trailers up to 50 feet. Facilities include picnic tables, fire rings with grills, vault toilets, drinking water, campground hosts, and garbage service. Leashed pets are permitted. A wheelchair-accessible toilet is available.

Reservations, fees: Reservations are accepted (877/444-6777, www.recreation.gov). Campsites cost $15. Cash or check. Open mid-May–September.

Directions: From two miles north of Bigfork, drive east on Highway 83 and 19.7 miles south to Swan Lake. From Seeley Lake, drive 56.5 miles north on Highway 83. Turn east into the campground.

GPS Coordinates: N 47° 56.187' W 113° 51.033'

Contact: Flathead National Forest, Swan Lake Ranger District, 200 Ranger Station Rd.,

Bigfork, MT 59911, 406/837-7500, www. fs.fed.us/r1/flathead/.

60 SPOTTED BEAR

Scenic rating: 9

south of Hungry Horse Reservoir in Flathead National Forest

BEST (

Gas up the vehicle to drive to Spotted Bear, and take along emergency tire repair equipment, for no services exist on the long dusty access road, and cell phones won't work. Located at 3,700 feet at the confluence of the Spotted Bear River and South Fork of the Flathead River, the campground features fishing in both rivers. A Wild and Scenic River, the South Fork also provides Class II rafting, canoeing, or kayaking. Nearby trails for hiking, mountain biking, and horseback riding depart to Spotted Bear Lake (2 miles), Spotted Bear Lookout (a long 7-mile climb), and Meadow Creek Gorge (10 miles). The Spotted Bear Ranger Station, which is staffed seven days per week, sits across Spotted Bear River, and the Diamond R Guest Ranch is across the road. Find the footbridge across the South Fork River behind ranger station to reach the river for fishing and swimming holes.

Located on a bench above the confluence of the rivers, the campground sits partly shaded under a loose forest of Douglas firs and western larch, with underbrush adding to privacy. Due to its distance from pavement, the campground offers the rare commodities of silence and solitude. The campsites, with gravel parking pads, are spread out on both sides of the campground loop, with half of the sites high above Spotted Bear River.

Campsites, facilities: The campground has 13 campsites for RVs or tents. Trailers are limited to 32 feet. Facilities include picnic tables, fire rings with grills, a vault toilet, drinking water, garbage service, bear boxes, and campground hosts. Leashed pets are permitted. A wheelchair-accessible toilet is available.

Reservations, fees: No reservations are accepted. Campsites cost $10. Cash or check. Open mid-May–September.

Directions: From the town of Hungry Horse, go east on Highway 2 for 0.6 mile to Martin City and turn eastward, following the signs leading toward the east side of Hungry Horse Reservoir and veering right at the Y just outside Martin City, where the road becomes an interminable battle with dust and washboards. Drive 54 miles south on Forest Road 38. Turn right into the campground.

GPS Coordinates: N 47° 55.531' W 113° 31.700'

Contact: Flathead National Forest, Spotted Bear Ranger District, 10 Hungry Horse Dr., Hungry Horse, MT 59919, 406/387-3800, www.fs.fed.us/r1/flathead/.

61 BEAVER CREEK

Scenic rating: 8

south of Hungry Horse Reservoir in Flathead National Forest

At 4,150 feet on Spotted Bear River over 60 miles from pavement, Beaver Creek is the last campground before jumping off into the Bob Marshall Wilderness. Don't go here on a whim: The distance will take you several hours, and no services are available en route. Be sure your spare tire is pumped up and ready for use. Within five miles of the campground are five trailheads—Silvertip, Upper Big Bill, Lower Big Bill, South Creek, and Meadow Creek—with trails winding up long drainages into the heart of the wilderness. The 34-mile-long Spotted Bear River south of the campground supports mountain whitefish, native westslope cutthroat, and the threatened bull trout for fly-fishing. Due to flooding, the riverbed is broad, with braided streams weaving through rocks and sand in late summer. Hunters use the campground in fall.

Due to its remote location, the tiny campground offers utter quiet, except for the sound of the river. The secluded forested campground spreads out its sites for privacy, and undergrowth adds to it. Should the campground be full, the Forest Service permits dispersed camping in this area. Choose a site that shows previous use rather than starting a new site, and follow Leave No Trace principles.

Campsites, facilities: The campground has four RV or tent campsites. Trailers are limited to 32 feet. Facilities include picnic tables, fire rings with grills, and a vault toilet. Drinking water is not available; filter or boil any water dipped from the river. Pack out your trash. Leashed pets are permitted.

Reservations, fees: Reservations are not accepted. The campsites are free. Open June–November.

Directions: From the town of Hungry Horse, go east on Highway 2 for 0.6 mile to the Martin City turnoff and head eastward, veering right at the Y onto the dusty gravel road that traverses the east side of Hungry Horse Reservoir. Drive 54 miles south on Forest Road 38 and then 8.5 miles east on Forest Road 568. Turn right into the campground.
GPS Coordinates: N 47° 55.458' W 113° 22.442'

Contact: Flathead National Forest, Spotted Bear Ranger District, 10 Hungry Horse Dr., Hungry Horse, MT 59919, 406/387-3800, www.fs.fed.us/r1/flathead/.

62 THOMPSON FALLS STATE PARK

Scenic rating: 8

west of Thompson Falls on the Clark Fork River

Located less than five minutes from downtown Thompson Falls or Rivers Bend Golf Course,

the 36-acre state park sits under firs and tall ponderosa pines right on the Clark Fork River. The campground overlooks the river, flowing with a few riffles to slow downriver in Noxon Reservoir. The campground's boat ramp, located between the B and C loops, is suitable for small boats. For a full-sized boat launch, head 0.5 mile north on Blue Slide Road across the bridge. The river is popular for boating, waterskiing, paddling, and fishing. Seven miles east of the campground, you can see bighorn sheep at the KooKooSint viewing area November–mid-April. In the campground, a trail tours the riverbank and loops around a small pond that houses turtles, frogs, and fish. The park also provides good bird-watching: ospreys, hawks, Canadian geese, and songbirds.

Recent thinning at the campground increased the filtered sunlight reaching the grassy campsites, which sit in two loops. C loop's sites 16 and 17 are the most private and closest to the river. Bring earplugs for sleeping, as the trains pass on the railroad tracks across the river all night long.

Campsites, facilities: The campground has 17 RV or tent campsites. Fourteen sites can accommodate RVs up to 30 feet. Facilities include picnic tables, fire rings with grills, vault toilets, drinking water, a boat launch, nature trail, campground hosts, and a group site with covered tables. Firewood is available for purchase. Leashed pets are permitted. A wheelchair-accessible toilet is available.

Reservations, fees: Reservations are not accepted. Camping costs $15. For day use, state parks charge $5 per vehicle for nonresidents; Montana residents have free day use. Cyclists only need to pay $3 for day use. Cash or check only. Open May–September.

Directions: From Thompson Falls, drive Highway 200 one mile northwest. At milepost 49.5, turn right onto Blue Slide Road. Drive 1.5 miles to the entrance on the west side of the road. Coming from the west on Highway 200, turn left onto Birdland Bay Road at mile marker 47.5 and drive 0.5 mile to the entrance on the right.

GPS Coordinates: N 47° 35.564' W 115° 20.256'

Contact: Montana Fish, Wildlife, and Parks, Region 1, 490 N. Meridian Rd., Kalispell, MT 59901, 406/752-5501, http://fwp.mt.gov.

63 COPPER KING

Scenic rating: 7

on the Thompson River in Lolo National Forest

Drive up the Thompson River Road, and you'll find your neck craning upward. Huge rock outcroppings and cliffs frame the steep-walled valley. Sitting at 2,700 feet, Copper King is the only campground accessible via pavement. Anglers visit Copper King to fish the river for brook, brown, or rainbow trout. Floaters also paddle the river. During high water, some Class II and Class III rapids add froth to the river just below the campground.

Tucked under large cedar trees, the tiny campground encompasses two acres. The campground's tight corners and short parking pads relegate this campground to truck campers, mini-bus campers, and tents. The first campsite is the only one set back in the trees away from the river; the others all border the river. Sites 2 and 5 are more private, but sites 3 and 4 have mountain views. Site 5 is the largest, with a double-sized table. (If this campground is full, you can drive one more mile to the Clark Memorial Campground.) Only one thing encroaches on the singing robins and sound of the river—the rumble from logging trucks hidden in the woods across the river. However, they do not drive at night.

Campsites, facilities: The campground has five RV or tent campsites. RVs are limited to small vehicles. Trailers are not recommended on the Thompson River Road. Facilities include picnic tables, fire rings with grills, and a vault toilet, but no drinking water. Bring your own water, or if you plan to use the river water, boil or purify it before drinking. Pack out your trash. Leashed pets are permitted. A wheelchair-accessible toilet is available.

Reservations, fees: Reservations are not accepted. Campsites cost $5. Cash or check. Open late May–late September.

Directions: From Thompson Falls, drive five miles northeast on Highway 200. On the west side of the Thompson River, turn north onto the paved Thompson River Road and drive four miles. Turn right into the campground. (Stay off the east side road. It sees logging trucks kicking up dust and turns into a private road.)

GPS Coordinates: N 47° 37.165' W 115° 11.344'

Contact: Lolo National Forest, Plains/Thompson Falls Ranger District, P.O. Box 429, Plains, MT 598859, 406/826-3821, www.fs.fed.us/r1/lolo/.

64 CLARK MEMORIAL

Scenic rating: 7

on the Thompson River in Lolo National Forest

Located at 2,400 feet in elevation one mile north of Copper King, Clark Memorial Campground sits on the Thompson River near a memorial grove of huge western red cedars, which grow only in areas that receive abundant moisture. The Thompson River cuts through the steep-walled canyon, home to bighorn sheep. You can launch rafts and kayaks from the campground to paddle Class II–III rapids down to Copper King or all the way to the Clark Fork River. The river, which usually runs clear even during high water, produces only small 8- to 12-inch trout.

Contrary to the heavily forested Copper King, this campground sits more in the open, with views of the rugged mountains that pinch the river. Unfortunately, the open area also allows for watching loud logging trucks on the road across the river. Luckily, they don't drive at night. The grassy campground lines the river, with the site at the south end claiming the most privacy.

Campsites, facilities: The campground has five RV or tent campsites. Trailers are not recommended on the Thompson River Road due to its skinny width and sharp corners, and the campground is suitable only for small RVs. Facilities include picnic tables, fire rings with grills, a vault toilet, but no drinking water. Bring your own water, or if you plan to use the river water, boil or purify it before drinking. Leashed pets are permitted. A wheelchair-accessible toilet is available.

Reservations, fees: Reservations are not accepted. Campsites cost $5. Cash or check only. Open late May–late September.

Directions: From Thompson Falls, drive six miles northeast on Highway 200. On the west side of the Thompson River, turn north onto the paved Thompson River Road and drive five miles. The road turns to dirt and narrows just past Copper King. A few pullouts sit along the road to deal with oncoming vehicles. (Stay off the east side road. It sees logging trucks kicking up dust and turns into a private road.)

GPS Coordinates: N 47° 37.937' W 115° 10.417'

Contact: Lolo National Forest, Plains/Thompson Falls Ranger District, P.O. Box 429, Plains, MT 598859, 406/826-3821, www.fs.fed.us/r1/lolo/.

65 CASCADE

Scenic rating: 7

on the Clark Fork River in Lolo National Forest
BEST (

Across the road from the Clark Fork River, sitting at 2,900 feet, Cascade is the only designated campground on Highway 135, so it frequently fills up—especially with its close proximity to a hot spring resort. Four miles east of the campground, Quinn's Hot Springs welcomes drop-ins for about $9 per person. Sink into the two hot tubs and four soaking pools before hopping in the 65-degree cold pool. The resort, which is open daily and refills the pools nightly rather than using chemicals, also has a swimming pool, a restaurant, and tavern. Five miles west of the campground, a fishing access allows for launching drift boats, rafts, canoes, and kayaks onto the Clark Fork River. The Cascade National Recreation Trail begins at the campground, and a one-mile nature walk leads to Cascade Falls overlook and views of the Clark Fork River.

Adjacent to the paved highway, the four-acre campground is tucked under a shady canopy of ponderosa pines and larch. The narrow canyon walls shade the campground until filtered sun arrives late in the morning. Both truck and train noise enters the campground. Low brush lends some privacy, but you'll see a few neighboring campers. If the campground fills up, locate free dispersed, primitive campsites between the campground and the fishing access. As long as no sign is posted banning camping, it is legal to camp at large in the national forest.

Campsites, facilities: The campground has nine RV or tent campsites. Facilities include picnic tables, fire grates, vault toilets, and drinking water. Pack out your trash. Leashed pets are permitted. A wheelchair-accessible toilet is available.

Reservations, fees: Reservations are not accepted. Campsites cost $10. Cash or check. Open late May–late September.

Directions: From St. Regis drive 17 miles northeast on Highway 135, or from Paradise drive south on Highway 200 across the Clark Fork River and turn west onto Highway 135 for 6.2 miles. Turn south into the campground.

GPS Coordinates: N 47° 18.385' W 114° 49.504'

Contact: Lolo National Forest, Plains/Thompson Falls Ranger District, P.O. Box 429, Plains, MT 598859, 406/826-3821, www.fs.fed.us/r1/lolo/.

66 HOLLAND LAKE

Scenic rating: 10

in Swan Valley in Flathead National Forest

BEST (

At an elevation of 4,150 feet near the southern end of the Swan Valley, Holland Lake provides a leap-off point into the Bob Marshall Wilderness. Both backpackers and horse-packing trips depart from here. Surrounded by the rugged Swan Mountains, the lake itself is very popular for boating, waterskiing, fishing, and paddling, but weekdays and off-season offer quieter exploration. Hiking trails depart right from the campground. A 1.5-mile easy hike hugs the lake to Holland Falls, roaring and spewing mist. A steep 3.5-mile trail climbs to Holland Lookout for dramatic views into the wilderness area, and a 12-mile loop ties together Upper Holland Lake and the smaller Sapphire Lake in an alpine bowl of wildflowers and huckleberry bushes. The historic lodge—which has a restaurant and bar—also rents canoes and kayaks and leads horseback trail rides. Owl Creek Packer Camp, with two stock ramps, vault toilets, and drinking water, sits 0.5 mile away.

The quiet campground snuggles under a fir forest canopy on the lake and adjacent to the rustic Holland Lake Lodge, with trails that run between the campsites and the lake. Lakefront sites include 1, 2, 3, 5, 6, 18, 20, 21, 23, 30, 32, 34, and 36. Some of the sites are very private due to thick foliage; others are more open with minimal understory.

Campsites, facilities: The campground has 40 RV or tent campsites. RVs are limited to 50 feet. Facilities include picnic tables, fire rings with grills, flush and vault toilets, drinking water, campground hosts, a boat ramp, a disposal station, and garbage service. Leashed pets are permitted. A wheelchair-accessible toilet is available.

Reservations, fees: Reservations are accepted (877/444-6777, www.recreation.gov). Campsites cost $15. Cash or check. Open mid-May–September.

Directions: From the start of Highway 83 two miles north of Bigfork, drive 35.2 miles south past Condon to Holland Lake Road. From Seeley Lake, drive 19.3 miles north on Highway 83 to Holland Lake Road. Turn east and drive 2.5 miles to the Y, and turn left. Follow the signs to the campground.
GPS Coordinates: N 47° 27.099' W 113° 36.526'
Contact: Flathead National Forest, Swan Lake Ranger District, 200 Ranger Station Rd., Bigfork, MT 59911, 406/837-7500, www.fs.fed.us/r1/flathead/.

67 LINDBERGH LAKE

Scenic rating: 7

in Swan Valley in Flathead National Forest

Southwest of Holland Lake, at an elevation of 4,400 feet, Lindbergh Lake draws fewer campers. It still sees its share of water-skiers, anglers, and paddlers, but the four-mile-long lake is nearly twice as big as Holland Lake, allowing more room to spread out. A boat ramp allows launching onto the lake. Streams from the Mission Mountain Wilderness feed the 815-acre lake, which sits at 4,494 feet in elevation and fosters several trout species plus mountain whitefish, kokanee salmon, northern pike minnow, longnose suckers, and yellow perch. Recent years have seen stocking of kokanee and westslope cutthroat trout. The campground lends itself well for mountain biking with a maze of old logging roads in the area. Most of the hiking trails require dirt road drives to get to the trailheads, but they lead to high clear lakes in the Mission Mountain Wilderness.

The campground tucks under a thick forest of spindly conifers, with plenty of shrubs and small trees lending privacy to most of the campsites. The sites are small but spread out. Due to the distance from the highway, the campground is quiet.

Campsites, facilities: The campground has 22 RV or tent campsites. The maximum length for RVs is 20 feet. Facilities include picnic tables, fire rings with grills, and vault toilets. No drinking water is available. Bring your own, or haul it from the lake. Be sure to purify or boil the lake water before use. Pack out your trash. Leashed pets are permitted. A wheelchair-accessible toilet is available.

Reservations, fees: Reservations not accepted. The campground has been free, but the Forest Service plans to start charging a fee for camping. Open May–September.

Directions: From the start of Highway 83 two miles north of Bigfork, drive 36.5 miles south past Condon to Forest Road 79. From Seeley Lake, drive 18 miles north on Highway 83 to Forest Road 79. Turn west and drive four miles to the campground road (79C).

GPS Coordinates: N 47° 24.241' W 113° 43.588'

Contact: Flathead National Forest, Swan Lake Ranger District, 200 Ranger Station Rd., Bigfork, MT 59911, 406/837-7500, www.fs.fed.us/r1/flathead/.

68 RAINY LAKE

Scenic rating: 8

north of Seeley Lake in Lolo National Forest

Accessed via a short, dirt forest road, Rainy Lake is a favorite of those who like small, primitive off-beat campgrounds. The campground sits at 4,100 feet on the divide at the southern end of the Swan Valley. Although the campground itself holds debris from recent thinning in the form of stumps and small slash piles, and some of the campsites show excessive wear, the small lake attracts float tube anglers and visitors who want to lounge on the grassy shore with the snow-covered Swan Range reflecting in the water. The lake is also close enough to the parking lot to carry lightweight canoes and kayaks down to the shore.

Three of the walk-in sites sit back in the mixed forest, two with peek-a-boo views of the lake. But the one walk-in site on the peninsula commands a view not only of most of the lake, but also the Swan Mountains. The one small, open drive-up site has no views. Except for the drive-up site, the campsites are spread out, but all are within sight of each other, which makes for little privacy but a very quiet location.

Campsites, facilities: The campground has one RV or tent campsite suitable only for a small RV and four walk-in tent campsites. Facilities include picnic tables, fire rings with grills, a vault toilet, and bear pole. The walk-in sites provide large flat areas for tents. No drinking water is available; if you plan to use lake water, boil or purify it before drinking. Leashed pets are permitted. Pack out your trash.

Reservations, fees: Reservations are not accepted. Camping is free. Open May–November.

Directions: Turn west off Highway 83 at milepost 27 onto Forest Road 4357. Drive 0.5 mile on the dirt road to where the road loops in a dead end.

GPS Coordinates: N 47° 20.205' W 113° 35.603'

Contact: Lolo National Forest, Seeley Lake Ranger District, HC-31, Box 3200, Seeley Lake, MT 59868, 406/677-2233, www.fs.fed.us/r1/lolo/.

69 LAKE ALVA

Scenic rating: 7

north of Seeley Lake in Lolo National Forest

Located north of Seeley Lake, Alva is one of the string of lakes tied along the upper Clearwater River. Sitting at 4,198 feet in elevation, the 298-acre lake is fed by cold water from the Mission Mountains and the Swan Mountains. With a small grassy swimming beach, a boat launch, and boat trailer parking, the lake yields four species of trout plus an array of lake fish—redside shiners, suckers, and yellow perch—and has been stocked with westslope cutthroat trout and kokanee. The lake also harbors nesting loons—both at the head and on the tiny island. To see the knife-like Swan Range, paddle or boat to the opposite shore of the lake. (Wish the campground had those views!) For hiking, drive five miles up the Clearwater Loop Road 4370, following the signs, to hike the Clearwater Lake Loop trail. The loop road also works for mountain biking.

Sitting between the highway and the lake, Alva picks up road noise through the trees. Large spruces, larches, and subalpine firs tower over the campground, which sprinkles its campsites around three paved loops with paved parking pads set above the lake. The loop nearest the lake holds two group campsites. Due to the thick foliage, none of the campsites has a view of the lake, but the sites are private and loaded with clumps of bear grass. The campground offers interpretive programs; check the bulletin board for the schedule.

Campsites, facilities: The campground has 41 RV or tent campsites. RVs are limited to 22 feet long. Facilities include picnic tables, fire rings with grills, vault toilets, drinking water, garbage service, and campground hosts. Leashed pets are permitted. A wheelchair-accessible toilet is available.

Reservations, fees: Reservations are not accepted, except for the two group campsites (877/444-6777, www.recreation.gov). Campsites cost $10. Each extra vehicle costs $5. Cash or check. Open Memorial Day weekend–September.

Directions: At milepost 26.1 on Highway 83 north of Seeley Lake, turn west on Forest Road 1098 for 0.4 mile to enter the campground. GPS Coordinates: N 47° 19.470' W 113° 35.078'

Contact: Lolo National Forest, Seeley Lake Ranger District, HC-31, Box 3200, Seeley Lake, MT 59868, 406/677-2233, www.fs.fed.us/r1/lolo/.

70 LAKESIDE

Scenic rating: 7

north of Seeley Lake in Lolo National Forest

As the name implies, the Lakeside campground sits at 4,100 feet right on the side of a lake—Lake Alva. The campground may be listed on older maps as Old Alva Campground. Lakeside also squeezes in the Clearwater River Valley between the Alva and Inez campgrounds. With shoreline campsites, launching hand-carried watercraft is easy. Those who want to launch larger boats must do so at Alva Campground. Fishing is available. The lake also harbors nesting loons—both at the head and on the tiny island. To see the knife-like Swan Range, paddle or boat to the opposite shore of the lake. For hiking, drive five miles up Clearwater Loop Road 4370, following the signs, to hike the Clearwater Lake Loop trail. The loop road also works for mountain biking.

While you can camp overlooking the lake, only a short steep slope separates the sites from the highway, which is within earshot and sight. The long, skinny campground is in two parts, connected by a 0.3-mile single-lane, narrow, curvy dirt road with a few pullouts in case vehicles meet. Trailers will have trouble backing up on this stretch. The campground road dead-ends in a small loop. Each section has three campsites and a vault toilet. The large sites are separated from each other under fir trees. Site 2 is a walk-in site on a shaded bluff overlooking the lake. Handicapped-accessible site 3 is very large, with extra tables and parking spots. Sites 4, 5, and 6 require driving the narrow road to the end of the campground.

Campsites, facilities: The campground has five RV or tent campsites and one walk-in tent campsite. Only small RVs are suitable; trailers are not recommended. Facilities include picnic tables, fire rings with grills, vault toilets, and garbage service. Bring your own water; or if you use lake water, boil or purify it first.

Leashed pets are permitted. A wheelchair-accessible toilet is available.

Reservations, fees: Reservations are not accepted. Campsites cost $10. Each extra vehicle costs $5. Cash or check. Open Memorial Day weekend–September.

Directions: From Highway 83 north of Seeley Lake, turn west into the entrance of the campground at milepost 25.6.

GPS Coordinates: N 47° 18.903' W 113° 34.705'

Contact: Lolo National Forest, Seeley Lake Ranger District, HC-31, Box 3200, Seeley Lake, MT 59868, 406/677-2233, www.fs.fed.us/r1/lolo/.

71 LAKE INEZ

Scenic rating: 7

north of Seeley Lake in Lolo National Forest

Tucked between the Swan and Mission Mountains two miles south of Lake Alva sits another one of the Clearwater River's chain of lakes. At 4,100 feet, the 288-acre Lake Inez is popular for swimming, fishing, boating, and waterskiing. Get out on the lake for the views of the southern Swan Mountains. Due to its location, it has the same fishing, mountain-biking, and hiking options as Lake Alva. For those with canoes to paddle its willow-laden north shore, bird-watching is prime. Look for red-necked grebes, bald eagles, rufous hummingbirds, American redstarts, flycatchers, and sparrows. The lakes along this chain make good habitat for loons, too, with suitable nesting areas protected from human disturbance and a substantial supply of fish. Listen in the morning or evening for the haunting call of the loon. About 60 pairs of loons nest in this chain of lakes, but only about 30 offspring survive.

The campground sits at the north end of Lake Inez on a dirt road. Find the primitive boat ramp with small grassy parking for boat trailers at the campground's north end as well as the three main campsites with the vault toilet. Undeveloped sites 4 and 5 sit farther south on the road, with lake views. Site 5 only has parking for a small vehicle.

Campsites, facilities: The campground has three RV or tent campsites, plus two primitive campsites. Facilities include fire rings with grills at all campsites, but picnic tables and a vault toilet for the first three campsites. Drinking water is not available. Bring your own, or if you plan to use lake water, purify it by filtering or boiling. Pack out your trash. Leashed pets are permitted.

Reservations, fees: Reservations are not accepted. Camping is free. Open May–November.

Directions: From Highway 83 north of Seeley Lake, the campground has two entrances, neither marked by obvious signs on the road. Turn west into the north entrance at milepost 24.1 or into the south entrance at milepost 22.9.

GPS Coordinates: N 47° 17.701' W 113° 34.111'

Contact: Lolo National Forest, Seeley Lake Ranger District, HC-31, Box 3200, Seeley Lake, MT 59868, 406/677-2233, www.fs.fed.us/r1/lolo/.

72 SEELEY LAKE

Scenic rating: 9

on Seeley Lake in Lolo National Forest

At 4,000 feet between the Swan and Mission Mountains, Seeley Lake is the largest of the upper Clearwater River's lakes. The 1,031-acre lake cranks with the noise of water-skiers, Jet Skiers, and power boaters. The big picnic area spans a long grassy beach that includes a cordoned-off swimming area, cement boat launch, and boat trailer parking. The campground also attracts quiet paddlers because of the Clearwater Canoe Trail, which feeds into the lake from the Clearwater River. The

© BECKY LOMAX

paddling the Clearwater Canoe Trail to Seeley Lake in Lolo National Forest

Campsites, facilities: The campground has 29 RV or tent campsites. The maximum recommended trailer length is 32 feet. Facilities include picnic tables, fire rings, flush toilets, drinking water, garbage service, a swimming beach, and a boat launch. Leashed pets are permitted. A wheelchair-accessible toilet is available.

Reservations, fees: Reservations are not accepted. Campsites cost $10. Each extra vehicle costs $5. Cash or check. Open Memorial Day weekend–Labor Day.

Directions: From milepost 14 on Highway 83 in the town of Seeley Lake, turn west onto Boy Scout Road and drive 3.2 miles. Turn right into the campground.

GPS Coordinates: N 47° 11.560' W 113° 31.214'

Contact: Lolo National Forest, Seeley Lake Ranger District, HC-31, Box 3200, Seeley Lake, MT 59868, 406/677-2233, www.fs.fed.us/r1/lolo/.

73 BIG LARCH

Scenic rating: 8

on Seeley Lake in Lolo National Forest

3.5-mile trail paddles through a dense willow marsh full of the music of songbirds such as ruby crowned kinglets. Located on the west side of the lake just opposite the River Point campground, Seeley Lake campground grabs a bigger view of the south Swan Mountains from the beach than other campgrounds in the area. The popular campground fills up on weekends and holidays.

A paved road leads up the west side of the lake to the 11-acre campground. The campground's road is narrow and curvy; large trees pinch the corners as it winds through the two loops. While the road is paved, the parking aprons are mostly dirt. Large spruces, monster larches, and subalpine firs shade most of the campground. The sites have little privacy, but they are very roomy. None of the campsites sit right on the lake, but sites 28 and 29 are right across from the beach. Sites 5, 7, and 8 are more private because they're on a side inlet from the lake.

Big Larch is a busy campground, thanks to its location one mile from the town of Seeley Lake and right on the east side adjacent to the highway. At 4,000 feet, it sits on the largest of the upper Clearwater River's lakes and offers fishing, boating, waterskiing, paddling, and swimming. Two sandy swimming beaches sprawl along the shoreline. The campground also has a 0.5-mile nature trail. Loaded with bird-watching, the Clearwater Canoe Trail is easy to access from this side of the lake as the put-in and take-out sit 5–10 minutes up the highway. The campground also sits closest to the most popular trail in the area—the Morrell Falls National Recreation Trail. Located seven miles up Morrell Creek Drive, the easy-walking 2.5-mile trail (open to mountain bikers and hikers) wanders past a series of small lakes and ponds before finishing at the 90-foot-tall falls. The trail sees a steady stream of hikers on weekends. Forest roads attract mountain bikers.

A paved road wanders through the campground with a mix of dirt, gravel, and paved parking aprons in the three overlapping loops. As the name suggests, huge larch trees along with some equally large Ponderosa pines shade much of the campground. In this type of forest, however, little underbrush survives, so most of the campsites are open beneath the trees, affording very little privacy. Sites 1–30 in the first two loops have shorter but wider campsites. Sites 34–49 are longer but narrower. Check the bulletin board at the check-in station for evening interpretive programs.

Campsites, facilities: The campground has 50 RV or tent campsites. Trailers are limited to 32 feet. Facilities include picnic tables, fire rings with grills, vault toilets, drinking water, garbage service, a large swimming beach, and a concrete boat launch. Leashed pets are permitted. A wheelchair-accessible toilet is available.

Reservations, fees: Reservations are not accepted. Campsites cost $10. Each extra vehicle costs $5. Cash or check. Open Memorial Day weekend–September.

Directions: From Seeley Lake, drive one mile north on Highway 83. Turn west at the signed entrance into the campground.

GPS Coordinates: N 47° 11.533' W 113° 29.638'

Contact: Lolo National Forest, Seeley Lake Ranger District, HC-31, Box 3200, Seeley Lake, MT 59868, 406/677-2233, www.fs.fed.us/r1/lolo/.

74 RIVER POINT

Scenic rating: 9

on Seeley Lake in Lolo National Forest

Of the three campgrounds on Seeley Lake in between the Mission and Swan Mountains,

the eight-acre River Point is the smallest. It sits at 4,000 feet at the foot of the lake where the broad, slow-moving Clearwater River exits the lake. With the proximity to the town of Seeley Lake, the campground is convenient for running to town for groceries, gas, gift shops, and restaurants. This campground is also the closest to Seeley Lake's golf course south of town. The Morrell Falls National Recreation Trail is within an 11-mile drive. The day-use area of the campground sits on both Seeley Lake and the Clearwater River. Views from the beach include the south Swan Peaks. The campground, however, only borders the river. Despite the lake frontage, no boat launch ramp is available. Use the one at Seeley Lake Campground 1.2 miles north. However, you can launch rafts, canoes, and kayaks from the river campsites, plus the beach in the day-use area.

A paved road leads to and through the one-loop campground, which has paved parking aprons. Large spruces, larches, and subalpine firs shade most of the roomy campsites, but with little understory and only short brush, the campsites have little privacy. Sites 11, 12, 14, 17, 19, and 20 sit on the river.

Campsites, facilities: The campground has 26 RV or tent campsites. Trailers are limited to 22 feet. Facilities include picnic tables, fire rings with grills, vault toilets, drinking water, garbage service, and a swimming beach. Leashed pets are permitted. A wheelchair-accessible toilet is available.

Reservations, fees: Reservations are not accepted. Campsites cost $10. Each extra vehicle costs $5. Cash or check. Open Memorial Day weekend–Labor Day.

Directions: In the town of Seeley Lake at milepost 14 on Highway 83, turn west onto Boys Scout Road on the north side of Pyramid Lumber Company. Drive two miles to the campground, which sits on the north side of the road.

GPS Coordinates: N 47° 11.252' W 113° 30.889'

Contact: Lolo National Forest, Seeley Lake

Ranger District, HC-31, Box 3200, Seeley Lake, MT 59868, 406/677-2233, www.fs.fed.us/r1/lolo/.

75 PLACID LAKE STATE PARK

🏃 🏊 🚤 🚣 🐕 ♿ 🚐 ⛺

Scenic rating: 8

south of Seeley Lake in Lolo National Forest

At 4,100 feet, Placid Lake State Park sits on one of the smaller pools in the upper Clearwater River's chain of lakes. The 31-acre lake is tiny in comparison to its northern sisters, but still attracts boaters for waterskiing, fishing, sightseeing, paddling, and wildlife-watching. Look for ospreys fishing, but keep your distance from nesting loons. Because private homes surround much of the shoreline, the water hops with Jet Skiers and boat noise (not exactly placid!) on weekends and hot August days. A short foot trail departs from site 18 to tour the shoreline. The boat docks include slips for 13 boats.

The 32-acre campground sits on the shore of Placid Lake, with the campsites tucked on three loops in the trees. A wide, potholed dirt road leads to the campground, but the campground road and parking pads are paved. Sites 1, 2, 3, 5, 6, 7, 12, 16, and 17 sit adjacent to the beach. Large ponderosas and firs partly shade campsites, but the lack of undergrowth yields little privacy.

Campsites, facilities: The campground has 40 RV or tent campsites. RVs are limited to 25 feet. Up to eight people and two camping units (vehicles or tents) are allowed per site. Facilities include picnic tables, fire grates, flush toilets, pay showers, drinking water, a disposal station, a swimming beach, boat docks, boat trailer parking, and a concrete boat ramp. Firewood is for sale. Leashed pets are permitted. A wheelchair-accessible toilet is available, and sites 16 and 17 are reserved for disabled campers.

Reservations, fees: No reservations are accepted. Day use costs $5 per vehicle for nonresidents while Montana residents get in for free. Campsites cost $15. Seniors and campers with disabilities pay $7.50. Hookups cost an addition $5. Cash or check. Open May–November.

Directions: From the Clearwater Junction (look for the big cow at the junction of Highways 83 and 200), drive 10 miles north on Highway 83. From Seeley Lake, drive Highway 83 south for three miles. Turn west onto the Placid Lake Road at milepost 10.2, and drive 2.7 miles. At the campground sign, turn left, then make an immediate right to reach the entrance in 0.3 mile.

GPS Coordinates: N 47° 7.102' W 113° 30.147'

Contact: Montana Fish, Wildlife, and Parks, Region 1, 490 N. Meridian Rd., Kalispell, MT 59901, 406/752-5501, http://fwp.mt.gov.

76 SALMON LAKE STATE PARK

🏃 🏊 🚤 🚣 🐕 ♿ 🚐 ⛺

Scenic rating: 8

south of Seeley Lake in Lolo National Forest

At 3,900 feet, the 631-acre Salmon Lake is the last lake in the chain of the Clearwater lakes. Small steep-walled mountains constrict the valley into a narrow channel that holds the lake, forming a natural impoundment for the Clearwater River. A few islands—some with private homes—also sit in the lake, which is popular for fishing, boating, paddling, and waterskiing. The 42-acre long, narrow park has separate entrances for the campground and day use area, which holds the cement boat ramp, boat trailer parking, 60-foot boat dock, and cordoned-off swimming beach. A foot trail with lupines, arrowleaf balsamroot, and shooting stars in spring connects the campground loop with the day-use area.

North of the day-use area, the campground

squeezes between the lake and highway, with most of the campsites in one loop under firs and larch. Sites 1, 2, and 21 sit closest to the lake. Sites 22 and 23 sit in the old boat ramp area on the beach. Sites 1, 2, 4, 5, and 7 have lake views. Sites 10–15 sit adjacent to the highway, but given how narrow the campground is, no one is far from the lake nor the highway noise. The amphitheater hosts evening interpretive programs.

Campsites, facilities: The campground has 20 RV or tent campsites. RVs are limited to 25 feet. Facilities include picnic tables, fire rings with grills, flush toilets, pay showers, drinking water, a disposal station, campground hosts, a swimming beach, and a boat launch. Firewood is for sale. Leashed pets are permitted. A wheelchair-accessible toilet is available, and the ADA site has electrical hookups.

Reservations, fees: No reservations are accepted. Day use costs $5 per vehicle for nonresidents but is free for Montana residents. Campsites cost $15. Seniors and campers with disabilities are charged $7.50. Hookups cost $5 more. Cash or check. Open May–November.

Directions: From the Clearwater Junction (look for the big cow at the junction of Highways 83 and 200), drive seven miles north on Highway 83. From Seeley Lake, drive Highway 83 south for six miles. At milepost 7, turn west into the campground. The day-use entrance is at milepost 6.5.

GPS Coordinates: N 47° 5.542' W 113° 23.831'

Contact: Montana Fish, Wildlife, and Parks, Region 1, 490 N. Meridian Rd., Kalispell, MT 59901, 406/752-5501, http://fwp.mt.gov.

GLACIER

© BECKY LOMAX

BEST CAMPGROUNDS

Looking like teeth gnawing at the heavens, Glacier National Park's chiseled ramparts – some of the most ancient rocks in North America – scratch the sky. Ice-filled cirques glimmer above blooming blue, magenta, and neon-yellow wildflower meadows before plummeting into deep verdant green valleys speckled with turquoise lakes. Grizzly bears, mountain goats, bighorn sheep, and moose dine on the landscape, while wolves hunt down the weaker ungulates.

For visitors to Glacier, the best way to experience these Crown of the Continent's wonders is camping. You can wake to songbirds in early summer and see deer wander through campgrounds. The park, which is a National Heritage Site and UNESCO Biosphere Reserve, harbors 13 drive-to park service campgrounds within its boundaries – many of which fill by noon in midsummer and on holiday weekends. You can also boat to an additional handful of backcountry campgrounds. The surrounding national forests provide less-crowded campgrounds and primitive places to camp with access to trailheads. Three small towns dotting the park's perimeter offer RVers places to hook up to services.

Located a full day's drive north of Yellowstone, Glacier Park's one million acres split along a north-south line – the Continental Divide – that runs from the Canadian border to Marias Pass. Clad in thick evergreens, the western mountains tuck campgrounds into thick forests or at the toe of long lakes that feed into the Flathead River's Middle Fork and North Fork, which form the park's western and southwestern boundaries. On the eastern flanks, campgrounds cluster in a mix of grasslands and aspen groves, as the mountains tumble onto the Blackfeet Reservation's prairie. The border with Canada divides Glacier from its northern sister, Waterton Lakes National Park; together they formed the world's first international peace park, adding international camping to the mix.

Only one road bisects the core of Glacier Park. In a feat of ingenious 1920s engineering, Going-to-the-Sun Road slices through cliffs as it crawls on a narrow, precipitous path to Logan Pass. Tunnels, arches, and retaining walls give the road its unique character while leading cars into an alpine wonderland where marmot whistles ride air currents through top-of-the-world scenery. Five campgrounds flank its natural wonders, such as a pocket of rain forest harboring huge western red cedars up to 500 years old.

On the west side of the Continental Divide, several long, forested valleys spill from Glacier's peaks. The most popular houses the park's largest body of water – Lake McDonald – and three campgrounds, including two of the park's biggest. Forming the park's southern boundary, the Middle Fork of the Flathead River, which parallels Highway 2, runs from a canyon into West Glacier, the local capital for white-water rafting, fishing, float trips, and a string of private RV parks and campgrounds. To the north, long dirt roads cut through the bucolic backwoods of the North Fork of the Flathead River Valley to primitive river campsites or remote lake campgrounds that provide solitude.

On the east side of the Continental Divide, private campgrounds on the Blackfeet Reservation offer hookup services unavailable at the park's five campgrounds. St. Mary's private campgrounds garner views of Red Eagle Mountain's maroon slopes, with peaks rising straight up from the prairie. Of the east-side park service campgrounds, two are the most popular: Two Medicine on the southeast corner ranks as highest drive-to lake in the park, and Many Glacier in the Swiftcurrent Valley is a hub for well-traveled trails that lead to lakes floating with icebergs even in August.

Over 700 miles of trails crisscross Glacier, making it a hiker's playground. Paths climb to glaciers, duck under cascading waterfalls, tunnel through a mountain, lead to lookout perches with panoramic views, and reach lakes teeming with native westslope cutthroat trout. Two of the park's campgrounds sit at trailheads where you can stay for multiple days, hiking to a different place each day without traveling in your car.

For over a century, campers have come to Glacier to explore its rare country. With plenty of places to pitch a tent, plan to linger here for several days to a week.

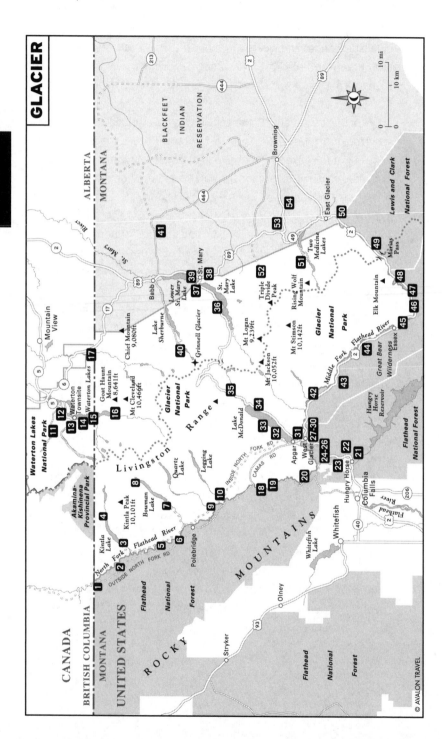

1 NORTH FORK BORDER PRIMITIVE

Scenic rating: 7

on the North Fork of the Flathead River in Flathead National Forest

The North Fork of the Flathead River enters the United States at the northwest corner of Glacier National Park. At the Border River Access for floating the river, a few dispersed tent-only campsites line the river near the parking lot. The campsites make a good base for rafting, canoeing, or fishing the river. The camp is also a 10-minute drive from the trailhead to climb 2,917 feet in five miles to Thoma Lookout for views that stretch across Glacier's entire northern panorama of peaks as well as down to the camp, across the border swath, and into Canada. While the border patrol still uses the station near the river, the crossing into Canada has been closed for over a decade after a flood washed out the Canadian road.

The primitive, partially shaded tent campsites with views of the river sit south of the parking lot. Since the bumpy, potholed drive to the border takes so long, the campsites are the most remote in the North Fork of the Flathead River Valley, guaranteeing privacy with only the sound of the river and the crackling campfire. Tucked under cottonwoods and firs, the campsites sit in their own cubbyholes, but within earshot of each other. During a midsummer day, the river access sees traffic, but at night there are only wolf howls.

Campsites, facilities: The river access has three primitive tent campsites. Facilities include rock fire rings and a vault toilet in the parking lot. (No fires are permitted in the parking lot.) Boil or purify river water before drinking. Pack out your trash. Camping is limited to three days. This is bear country: practice safe food storage. Leashed pets are permitted.

Reservations, fees: No reservations are accepted. Camping is free. Open year-round, although the last 0.1 mile is not plowed to the parking lot.

Directions: From Polebridge, drive north on the North Fork Road (Forest Road 486) for 22 miles to the U.S. border station. Turn right for 0.1 mile to the river access parking lot.

GPS Coordinates: N 49° 0.019' W 114° 28.538'

Contact: Flathead National Forest, Glacier View District, 10 Hungry Horse Dr., Hungry Horse, MT 59919, 406/387-3800, www.fs.fed.us/r1/flathead/.

2 NORTH FORK OF THE FLATHEAD RIVER PRIMITIVE

Scenic rating: 9

flanking Glacier National Park's west boundary in Flathead National Forest

With its headwaters in Canada, the North Fork of the Flathead River flows 59 miles from the border along the western boundary of Glacier National Park. Its route through the North Fork Valley flows through one of the most ecologically diverse areas of Montana, home to rare plants, woodpeckers and birds, and wildlife from the pygmy shrew to the wolf. The river, designated as Wild and Scenic, runs with Class II–III rapids, and the flow peaks in early June. Life jackets are required. Eight river accesses accommodate those rafting, kayaking, and canoeing: the border, Ford, Polebridge, Coal Creek, Big Creek, Great Northern Flats, Glacier Rim, and Blankenship. The river is best for rafting mid-May–early September.

Accessed only via rafts, canoes, or kayaks, primitive campsites flank the river's west bank. Camping on the east bank in Glacier is not permitted, except for Round Prairie (permit required). Most campsites tuck under cottonwoods and firs within view of the river, and most are not in sight of each other, which guarantees solitude. At night, you'll hear the sound of the river and moose walking through the water.

Campsites, facilities: About 15 primitive tent campsites that can accommodate 4–6 people line the river. Campers are required to take a groover for human waste and a fire pan to minimize burn scars. Purchase the *Three Forks of the Flathead River Floating Guide* from the Hungry Horse Ranger Station to aid in finding sites and avoiding private land. A permit is not required to camp overnight in the river corridor. Vault toilets are available at the eight river access sites. Pack out your trash. Pets are permitted. Practice safe food storage to deter bears.

Reservations, fees: No reservations are accepted. Camping is free. Open April–November.

Directions: From Columbia Falls, drive the potholed washboard North Fork Road (Forest Road 486) to the river access site of your choice. The border put-in is the farthest away at 53 miles. The other river access sites require turning east off the North Fork Road and driving less than 0.5 mile to reach launch sites. Each river access site is signed.

Contact: Flathead National Forest, Glacier View District, 10 Hungry Horse Dr., Hungry Horse, MT 59919, 406/387-3800, www.fs.fed.us/r1/flathead/.

3 KINTLA LAKE

Scenic rating: 8

on Kintla Lake in Glacier National Park

BEST (

Located at 4,015 feet in elevation between Starvation and Parke Ridges, Kintla Lake defines remote. Not only do you have to drive the bumpy, dusty miles of dirt road to reach the Polebridge entrance station to Glacier, but then you need to drive another hour of dirt road to reach the lake. Due to the cantankerous road, which is not recommended for large RVs and trailer combinations, and distance from pavement, the lake attracts few people; campers who come here find the rewards of solitude. No motorboats or personal watercraft are permitted on the lake, leaving paddlers to ply its waters in quiet. Anglers—especially those who can get away from shore in a boat—can pull in native westslope cutthroat trout and bull trout. One trail departs the campground along the north shore and reaches the head of the lake in 6.2 miles. Backpackers continue on to Upper Kintla and over Boulder Pass to end at Goat Haunt at Waterton Lake (32 miles total) or Bowman Lake (37 miles total).

The tiny, quiet campground cuddles under big trees in one loop. Several of the campsites near Kintla Creek have their parking spot on the loop but their tent sites, tables, and campfires down an embankment below the road. Sites 10 and 12 sit closest to the lake; sites 1–3 sit the farthest away. Sites 4–10 border Kintla Creek. Little privacy remains due to stripped underbrush.

Campsites, facilities: The 13 RV and tent campsites can accommodate only small RVs, although the park service discourages RVs or trailer combinations. Facilities include picnic tables, fire rings with grills, hand pumps for potable water, vault toilets, garbage service, and a boat ramp. During primitive camping, when the water is turned off, boil or purify lake water. Strict food storage regulations are in effect for bears. Bring firewood; collecting is illegal. Leashed pets are permitted.

Reservations, fees: No reservations are accepted. Campsites cost $15 late May–mid-September. Cash, check, or credit card. Depending on snow, primitive camping ($10) is available mid-September–November and earlier in May.

Directions: From the Polebridge entrance station to Glacier National Park, drive 14.3 miles north on the Inside Road. The road terminates in the campground.

GPS Coordinates: N 48° 56.144' W 114° 20.743'

Contact: Glacier National Park, P.O. Box 128, West Glacier, MT 59936, 406/888-7800, www.nps.gov/glac.

④ HEAD OF KINTLA LAKE

Scenic rating: 8

on Kintla Lake in Glacier National Park

BEST (

Huddling between Starvation and Parke Ridges in Glacier's remote northwest corner, the six-mile-long Kintla Lake sees very few people at its upper end. Those who visit its campground at 4,100 feet in elevation enjoy solitude and watching bald eagles and bears. A 2.7-mile trail from the campground continues on to Upper Kintla Lake, where scenery unfolds with glaciers hanging off Kintla Peak and Kinnerly Peak rising straight from the lake. Take a brisk swim in the glacial waters before hiking back to the campground.

Reach the campground at the head of the lake by hiking 6.2 miles or paddling up the lake from Kintla Campground at the foot of the lake. At the head of the lake, the remote, quiet campground is built on a hillside with two communal cooking sites in the cedars near the shore and tent sites scattered on shaded terraces in the forest above. There are bears, so bring a rope for hanging food and cooking gear. In spring, high water floods some of the beach, but in summer as the water level drops, the smooth-stoned beach provides an easier place to pull boats out of the water. Tie up all boats at night in case winds arise!

Campsites, facilities: The campground has six designated tent campsites, and each holds up to four people each. Facilities include rock-rimmed fire pits, log benches, a food hanging cable, and a pit toilet. Boil or purify lake water for drinking. Pack out your trash. Pets are not permitted.

Reservations, fees: Backcountry permits are required. Advance reservations ($20) for three of the campsites are available starting April 15. Get permits for remaining sites in person 24 hours in advance at the Apgar Backcountry Office in Apgar. Permits cost $5 per adult per night and $2.50 for children 8–15. They are free for children 7 and under. Cash, check, or credit card. Open June–November. With early snowmelt, the campground may be available by late May.

Directions: From the Polebridge entrance station to Glacier National Park, drive 14.3 miles north on the Inside Road to the Kintla Campground.

GPS Coordinates: N 48° 58.538' W 114° 15.186'

Contact: Glacier National Park, P.O. Box 128, West Glacier, MT 59936, 406/888-7800, www.nps.gov/glac.

⑤ ROUND PRAIRIE

Scenic rating: 7

on the North Fork of the Flathead River in Glacier National Park

At 3,850 feet in elevation, Round Prairie is the only campground on the North Fork of the Flathead River's east bank in Glacier National Park. It is one of four Palouse prairies in the North Fork Valley, blooming with wheatgrass, fescues, oatgrass, sagebrush, and rare plants. Due to Whitefish Mountain's rain shadow, Round Prairie sees only 20 inches of annual precipitation. Access the campground by floating the river or driving the bumpy, dirt Inside Road to walk through 0.5 mile of Round Prairie.

A mixed forest of firs and cottonwoods lines the river around the quiet, remote campground, which sits on the edge of Round Prairie. Bring a rope for hanging food and cooking gear. A large gravel bar allows boats to be beached. In the campground, a communal cooking site is available, and three tent sites are separated for privacy in the trees. The campground faces the sunset over the Whitefish Mountains.

Campsites, facilities: The walk-in or boat-in campground has three tent campsites, each holding up to four people. Facilities include a rock fire ring, log benches, a pit toilet, and food-hanging cable. Boil or purify river water for drinking. Pack out your trash. Permits for two of the three sites are reserved until 3 P.M. each day for river floaters. No pets are permitted.

Reservations, fees: Backcountry permits are required. Advance reservations ($20) for two of the campsites are available starting April 15. Get permits for other sites in person 24 hours in advance at the Apgar Backcountry Office in Apgar. Permits cost $5 per adult per night and $2.50 for children 8–15. They are free for children 7 and under. Cash, check, or credit card. Opens June–November. With early snowmelt, the campground may be available in late May.

Directions: For walking in, drive from the Polebridge park entrance station 7.6 miles north on the Inside Road to the trailhead on the left. For boating, drive north from the town of Polebridge on the dirt North Fork Road for 21 miles to the border or 10 miles to Ford to launch onto the river.

GPS Coordinates: N 48° 51.463' W 114° 21.985'

Contact: Glacier National Park, P.O. Box 128, West Glacier, MT 59936, 406/888-7800, www.nps.gov/glac.

6 SONDERSON MEADOW

Scenic rating: 9

on the North Fork of the Flathead River in Flathead National Forest

North of the town of Polebridge in the North Fork Valley, Sonderson Meadow sprawls into large open fields surrounded by fir forests and beaver ponds. The North Fork of the Flathead River runs around the perimeter of the meadow, making it popular for camping with those floating the river, but you can also drive to it. A skinny dirt road accesses the meadow, which used to harbor an old airstrip. Unmarked game trails good for morning and evening wildlife-watching hikes wander around the meadow. Call the Forest Service first to be sure the gate on the access road is open.

From campsites along the meadow and river, you get shots of the rugged, remote Livingston Range of Glacier National Park with the sunrise coming over the park. The primitive, quiet campsites sit along the river's bank with wide-open views of the night sky and the music of the river. The campsites are very spread out for privacy at the north and south ends of the meadows, accessed by two rough jeep trails.

Campsites, facilities: Sonderson Meadow has three RV or tent campsites, but the road is only suitable for small RVs—not trailers. Facilities include only rock fire rings, and fire pans are recommended instead. To use river water, boil or filter it first. Campers are required to use a self-contained system for solid waste and carry it out to an RV dump station. This is bear country, so practice safe food storage. Pack out your trash. Follow Leave No Trace principles in camping, using previous fire rings rather than making new ones and placing your tent on ground or rocks rather than sensitive vegetation. Leashed pets are permitted.

Reservations, fees: Reservations are not accepted. Camping is free. Open April–November.

Directions: Drive seven miles north from the town of Polebridge on the North Fork Road. Turn right at the sign for Schnauss Cabin onto Forest Road 10372 and follow the narrow road as it drops one mile down the steep hill to the river.

GPS Coordinates: N 48° 50.052' W 114° 20.407'

Contact: Flathead National Forest, Glacier View District, 10 Hungry Horse Dr., Hungry Horse, MT 59919, 406/387-3800, www.fs.fed.us/r1/flathead/.

7 BOWMAN LAKE

Scenic rating: 10

on Bowman Lake in Glacier National Park

BEST (

Sitting at 4,030 feet in elevation, Bowman Lake is one of two remote drive-to lakes in

© BECKY LOMAX

bear pole for hanging food at Head of Bowman Lake campground in Glacier

Glacier's northwest corner. Even though access to the campground requires miles of potholed dirt road driving—on either the Outside North Fork Road or the Inside North Fork Road, both equally nasty in dust—it is the most popular campground in the North Fork Valley. Trailheads lead to Numa Lookout (5.6 miles) for stunning views across to the Rainbow-Carter massif, Quartz Lake Loop (12.4 miles) for fishing, and the Bowman Lake Trail (7.1 miles) along the north shore. Motorboats of 10 horsepower or less are permitted, but not Jet Skiing and waterskiing. Canoeists and kayakers tour the shoreline to watch for bald eagles. The best fishing is from a boat; anglers go after westslope cutthroat and bull trout.

Sitting at the foot of Bowman Lake, the quiet campground winds one large loop through the brushy mixed forest. Filtered sunlight warms most of the campsites. A short road and trails connect to the beach and boat launch. Campsites are spread out for privacy,

but you will see a few other campsites through the trees. Sites on the east side of the loop sit closer to the beach, but none border the shoreline. Walk to the lakeshore after dark for a stunning look at the stars.

Campsites, facilities: The campground has 48 RV or tent campsites, which can fit small RVs. The park service does not recommend large RVs or trailer combinations on the rough, narrow access road. Facilities include picnic tables, fire rings with grills, pit toilets, drinking water, and garbage service. During primitive camping, the water is turned off, but you can boil or purify water from the lake. Leashed pets are permitted. Strict food storage regulations are in effect for bears. Bring firewood; collecting is illegal.

Reservations, fees: No reservations are accepted. Campsites cost $15. Cash, check, or credit card. Open late May–mid-September; however, primitive camping ($10) is possible mid-September–November and sometimes in early May depending on snow.

Directions: From the Polebridge entrance station to Glacier, drive 0.3 mile north to the Bowman Lake Road. Turn right and drive six miles to the campground on the left.

GPS Coordinates: N 48° 49.709' W 114° 12.087'

Contact: Glacier National Park, P.O. Box 128, West Glacier, MT 59936, 406/888-7800, www.nps.gov/glac.

⑧ HEAD OF BOWMAN LAKE
🏃 🏊 🚣 🛶 🎣 ⛺

Scenic rating: 10

on Bowman Lake in Glacier National Park

BEST (

In Glacier Park's remote northwest corner, six-mile-long Bowman Lake cuts through a steep-walled valley between the hulks of Rainbow and Numa Peaks. Craggy Thunderbird Peak rises out of the lake's head. At an elevation of 4,100 feet at the lake's head, the backcountry campground is favored by canoeists, kayakers, boaters, and hikers for its rugged remote setting and very few people. Paddling to the campground takes about two hours; hiking the 7.1 miles along the northwest shore takes about 3 hours. A boat ramp at the foot of the lake assists launching, and a parking lot is available for overnight parking. Watch for winds; the half-mile-wide lake kicks up big whitecaps fast.

The quiet campground sprawls on both sides of a creek, with tent sites scattered in the trees for privacy and two communal cooking sites. Bring a rope for hanging food and cooking gear. In spring, high water floods some of the beach, but in summer as the water level drops, the smooth-stoned beach provides an easier place to pull boats out of the water. Beach all boats at night in case winds arise!

Campsites, facilities: The campground has six tent campsites, each holding up to four people. Facilities include rock fire pits, food hanging cables, and a pit toilet. Boil or purify lake water for drinking, and pack out your trash. Pets are not permitted.

Reservations, fees: Backcountry permits are required. Advance reservations ($20) for three of the campsites are available starting April 15. Get permits for remaining sites in person 24 hours in advance at the Apgar Backcountry Office in Apgar. Plan to be in the office as soon as it opens as the popular campground fills its sites fast. Permits cost $5 per adult per night and $2.50 for children 8–15. They are free for children 7 and under. Cash, check, or credit card. Opens mid-June–November. With early snowmelt, the campground may be available in late May and early June, too.

Directions: From the Polebridge entrance station to Glacier, drive 0.3 mile north on the Inside Road to the Bowman Lake Road. Turn right and drive six miles to the foot of Bowman Lake.

GPS Coordinates: N 48° 54.219' W 114° 7.264'

Contact: Glacier National Park, P.O. Box 128, West Glacier, MT 59936, 406/888-7800, www.nps.gov/glac.

9 QUARTZ CREEK

Scenic rating: 6

on the Inside North Fork Road in Glacier National Park

Located on the Inside North Fork Road through Glacier's western forests, tiny Quartz Creek Campground is used by campers looking for quiet and solitude. Its access requires driving miles of dirt road that is as notorious for its jarring potholes and bumpy washboards as it is for its clouds of dust. Adjacent to the campground, an infrequently maintained trail follows Quartz Creek for 6.8 miles to Lower Quartz Lake. Mountain bikers use this camp on North Fork tours, and anglers fish the creek and Quartz Lakes for native westslope cutthroat trout. Some camping supplies are available at the Polebridge Mercantile, 1.5 miles from the Polebridge entrance station; cookies and cinnamon rolls are freshly baked there daily.

The campground, which is tucked under a mix of large shade-producing firs and sunny brush, rarely fills up due to its remoteness. Sites 4, 5, and 6 border the creek. Bring bug juice as the riparian area tends to breed mosquitoes in droves. The small sites also have small dirt parking pads.

Campsites, facilities: The campground has seven RV and tent campsites that can accommodate small RVs. Large RVs and trailer combinations are not recommended on the Inside Road. Facilities include picnic tables, fire rings with grills, and a pit toilet. Water is available from the creek, but be sure to boil or purify it before use. Pack out your trash. Collecting of downed firewood is permitted on the Inside North Fork Road, but not in the campground. Leashed pets are permitted. Strict food storage regulations are in effect for bears.

Reservations, fees: No reservations are accepted. Campsites cost $10. Cash, check, or credit card. Open July–early November.

Directions: From the Polebridge entrance

station to Glacier National Park, drive 5.7 miles south on the Inside North Fork Road (Glacier Route 7). From Fish Creek Campground, drive 21.3 miles north on the Inside Road. The campground sits on the east side of the road.

GPS Coordinates: N 48° 43.297' W 114° 13.456'

Contact: Glacier National Park, P.O. Box 128, West Glacier, MT 59936, 406/888-7800, www.nps.gov/glac.

10 LOGGING CREEK

Scenic rating: 8

on the Inside North Fork Road in Glacier National Park

Located on Glacier's western forest slopes, Logging Creek sits on the Inside North Fork Road a long distance from pavement. Top speeds for driving the potholed, washboarded, curvy road reach about 20 mph. Sullivan Meadows, a few miles south of the campground, was home to the first pack of wolves that migrated from Canada in the 1980s. A nearby trail departs for Logging Lake, a 4.4-mile forested hike. The lake harbors westslope cutthroat trout, but fly-fishing requires wading away from the brushy shore. Many campers—including mountain bikers—use this remote campground for looping on a scenic tour through the North Fork Valley. Pack a birding field guide, for the area around the Logging Ranger Station and Logging Creek provides good bird-watching. Over 196 species of birds have been documented in the North Fork, including at least 112 that nest in the valley.

Logging Creek burbles adjacent to the campground, and across the road the idyllic Logging Ranger Station is staffed intermittently in summer. The quiet campground's one loop swings through large cedars and firs that admit filtered sunlight to the small campsites. Due to its remoteness, the campground rarely fills up. The damp vicinity also is a breeding ground for mosquitoes, so come prepared with repellent. Listen at night for wolf howls.

Campsites, facilities: The campground has seven RV and tent campsites that can accommodate small RVs. Large RVs and trailer combinations are not recommended on the Inside Road. Facilities include picnic tables, fire rings with grills, and a pit toilet. Water is available only from the creek, but be sure to boil or purify it before use. Pack out your trash. Collecting of downed firewood is permitted on the Inside North Fork Road, but not in the campground. Leashed pets are permitted. Strict food storage regulations are in effect for bears.

Reservations, fees: No reservations are accepted. Campsites cost $10. Cash, check, or credit card. Open July–early November.

Directions: From the Polebridge entrance station to Glacier Park, drive 8.3 miles south on the Inside North Fork Road, also called Glacier Route 7 on some maps. Or from the Fish Creek Campground, drive 18 miles north on the Inside Road. The campground sits on the east side of the road.

GPS Coordinates: N 48° 41.897' W 114° 11.535'

Contact: Glacier National Park, P.O. Box 128, West Glacier, MT 59936, 406/888-7800, www.nps.gov/glac.

11 CRANDELL MOUNTAIN

Scenic rating: 9

on Blakiston Creek in Waterton Lakes National Park, Canada

On the opposite side of Crandell Mountain from the Waterton Townsite, this campground tucks into a red-rock valley with outstanding wildlife-watching opportunities. Wildlife frequents its narrow paved access road—the Red Rocks Parkway. The campground nestles in the woods along Blakiston Creek, where you can see bears and moose. Bighorn sheep also graze on the slopes across the creek. An easy 3.1-mile round-trip walk to Crandell Lake departs from the campground, and a 10-minute drive leads to the end of Red Rocks Parkway, where trailheads depart to Blakiston Falls (0.6 mile), Goat Lake (3.9 miles), and Avion Ridge (14 miles). You can also mountain bike five miles to Snowshoe Cabin or around Crandell Mountain. Fishing is available in Blakiston Creek; Waterton Park and Alberta fishing licenses are both required.

With many campsites tucked deep in mixed forest, the campground's eight loops have a remote feel, with trees and brush providing some privacy between sites. A, B, C, and D loops sit in thicker trees; E, F, G, and H loops are more open with views of surrounding peaks. Tight loops and back-ins can cramp some RVs. Plan on arriving at the campsite office by noon in July and August to get a campsite.

Campsites, facilities: Crandell has 129 RV or tent campsites; some can accommodate mid-sized RVs. Facilities include picnic tables, fire rings, flush toilets, drinking water, kitchen shelters, firewood, a disposal station, interpretive programs, and bear-resistant food storage lockers. Strict food storage regulations are in effect. Leashed pets are permitted. A wheelchair-accessible toilet is available.

Reservations, fees: Reservations are not accepted. Campsites cost CDN$22. Add on CDN$8 for a burning permit for fires. Cash, check, or credit card. Open mid-May–early September.

Directions: Drive the 30-mile Chief Mountain International Highway across the border (open mid-May–September), turn west for 0.7 mile to the park entrance, then go 2.8 miles south on the park entrance road and turn west onto Red Rocks Parkway. Find the campground entrance on the left 3.8 miles up the parkway.

GPS Coordinates: N 49° 5.947' W 113° 56.758'

Contact: Waterton Lakes National Park, Box 200, 215 Mount View Rd., Waterton Park, AB T0K 2M0, Canada, 403/859-2224, www. pc.gc.ca/pn-np/ab/waterton.

12 PASS CREEK

Scenic rating: 9

on Blakiston Creek in Waterton Lakes National Park, Canada

Located 3.1 miles north of the Waterton Townsite, the Pass Creek Campground is a picnic area that converts to a campground in winter, when the town dwindles to a few hundred residents and offers only a few services. All of the park's campgrounds close by mid-October, except for Pass Creek. The campground is convenient for ducking in to town for a dinner out at Kilmorey Lodge—especially if the weather turns brutal. Heated washrooms and running water are available at the fire hall. The campground also provides excellent wildlife-watching in the shoulder seasons as animals, such as elk, move to lower ground. In spring, nearby Lower Waterton Lake and Maskinonge Lake attract scads of migrating birds. In winter, the cross-country skiers hit the two designated trails on the upper Akamina Parkway. Bertha Falls also provides a popular four-mile round-trip snowshoe destination. For those with avalanche gear, the park also has ski touring routes and ice climbing.

Located just south of Red Rocks Parkway and right on the Blakiston River, where you can fish, the campground has big views of the Waterton Valley. Be prepared, however, for winds, for the campground also hovers on the edge of the open prairie. A few cottonwood trees provide windbreaks, but the area is open, and the campsites are visible from the entrance road to the park.

Campsites, facilities: The campground has eight RV or tent campsites that can accommodate midsized RVs. Facilities include picnic tables, a kitchen shelter with a wood stove, and a pit toilet. Bring your own water, or if you plan on using creek water, purify or boil it first.

Leashed pets are permitted. Because of bears, strict food storage regulations are in effect.

Reservations, fees: No reservations are accepted. Camping is free. Open mid-October–mid-April.

Directions: From Highway 3 at Pincher Creek, drive 30 miles south on Highway 6 to the entrance to Waterton Lakes National Park. Turn south and drive 2.8 miles to the campground on the right. (Chief Mountain Highway is closed October–May.)

GPS Coordinates: N 49° 4.584' W 113° 52.901'

Contact: Waterton Lakes National Park, Box 200, 215 Mount View Rd., Waterton Park, AB T0K 2M0, Canada, 403/859-2224, www.pc.gc.ca/pn-np/ab/waterton.

13 WATERTON TOWNSITE

Scenic rating: 10

on Waterton Lake in Waterton National Park, Canada

Located in Waterton Townsite, the campground garners spectacular views and wildlife. It borders Waterton Lake, with large peaks rising to the north and east of town. Paved walking paths circle the campground, linking to restaurants in town, Cameron Falls, the beach, and the boat tours on the lake. Do not bicycle on the walking paths, only on the town roads or the several mountain-bike trails in the area. From the campground, the Waterton Lake hiking trail departs to roaring Bertha Falls (2 miles), Bertha Lake (3.5 miles), or Goat Haunt, U.S.A. (8.7 miles).

A paved road with paved parking pads circles through the mowed lawn campground, which is divided by Cameron Creek. The RV hookup sites line up in the open. A few trees shade some sites but offer no privacy. For lake views, go for unserviced spots in the G loop (sites 26–46), but be prepared for strong winds off the lake. For more sheltered scenery, go for the Cameron

Creek E loop sites (even numbers 2–16). In July and August, arrive by noon to claim a site, or make reservations. In shoulder seasons without reservations, you'll have your pick of sites.

Campsites, facilities: The campground has 95 hookup campsites that can accommodate large RVs and 143 unserviced RV or tent campsites. Hookups include sewer, water, and electricity. Facilities include flush toilets, showers, a disposal station, drinking water, kitchen shelters, bear-resistant food storage lockers, and firewood. Fires are permitted only in kitchen shelters. Because of bears, strict food storage regulations are in effect. Leashed pets are permitted. A wheelchair-accessible toilet is available.

Reservations, fees: Reservations are available (877/737-3783, www.pccamping.ca). Hookups cost CDN$39. Unserviced sites cost CDN$23–28. A burning permit for fires costs $9. Cash, check, or credit card. Opens April–mid-October.

Directions: Drive the 30-mile Chief Mountain International Highway across the border (open mid-May–September), go west for 0.7 mile to the Waterton entrance, and then go five miles south to the Waterton Townsite. At the townsite, turn left on Mount View Drive for two blocks and right on Windflower Avenue for three blocks to the campground entrance.

GPS Coordinates: N 49° 2.917' W 113° 54.560'

Contact: Waterton Lakes National Park, Box 200, 215 Mount View Rd., Waterton Park, AB T0K 2M0, Canada, 403/859-2224, www.pc.gc.ca/pn-np/ab/waterton.

14 BERTHA BAY

Scenic rating: 9

on Waterton Lake in Waterton National Park, Canada

On the western shore of Upper Waterton Lake, Bertha Bay is accessible only by a 1.5-

mile hike or by boat. Boaters must scope the weather out carefully before launching trips because winds kick up fast on the lake, churning up monstrous whitecaps. The backcountry campsite does not have a boat ramp or dock; boats should be completely beached overnight. From the campground, a trail ascends 1.3 miles to Bertha Falls and then switchbacks up another 1.7 miles to Bertha Lake.

For protection from the wind, the campsites are set in the woods back from the rock and pebble shore. A designated cooking site separates food handling, storing, and eating from the tent platforms for sleeping. Keep all food in the cooking area to avoid attracting wildlife into the sleeping zone. Bring a gas stove for cooking and 30 feet of rope for hanging food at night.

Campsites, facilities: Bertha Bay has four tent platforms, which each can hold one tent. The campground can accommodate a total of 12 people, but only six are allowed per party. Facilities include a bear pole for hanging food and garbage, a pit toilet, and a fire pit. Bring your own drinking water, or purify or boil lake or stream water. Pack out your trash. Pets are not permitted.

Reservations, fees: Reservations for required wilderness passes are available by phone 90 days in advance beginning April 1 of each year. The park charges a nonrefundable CDN$12 reservation fee, plus a modification fee for any additional changes. April–mid-May, call the warden's office (403/859-5140); after then, call the visitors center (403/859-5133). Wilderness passes can also be picked up in person no sooner than 24 hours in advance of the starting date. Backcountry camping costs CDN$10 per person per night. Children 16 years old and under camp for free. Open May–November.

Directions: Hikers can locate the trailhead at the end of Evergreen Avenue on the west end of the Waterton Townsite. Kayakers and canoeists should launch from the Cameron Bay picnic area. Boat ramps for larger boats are available at Linnet Lake picnic area and the marina in the Townsite.

GPS Coordinates: N 49° 1.736' W 113° 54.530'

Contact: Waterton Lakes National Park, Box 200, 215 Mount View Rd., Waterton Park, AB T0K 2M0, Canada, 403/859-2224, www.pc.gc.ca/pn-np/ab/waterton.

15 BOUNDARY BAY

Scenic rating: 10

on Waterton Lake in Waterton National Park, Canada

BEST (

Boundary Bay sits near the international border between Canada and the United States on the western shore of Upper Waterton Lake. Reach the campground by hiking a 3.7-mile rolling trail or by boating. Boaters should check the weather forecast before departing because winds kick up fast into whitecaps. Since the campground does not have a boat ramp or dock, beach boats completely for overnighting. From the campground, the trail continues another 4.3 miles on to Goat Haunt. Bring your passport to go through customs at Goat Haunt.

Boundary Bay campground is set in a mixed forest of firs and cottonwoods back from the shore for protection from winds. A designated communal cooking site is separated from the tent platforms for sleeping. Keep all food in the cooking area to avoid attracting wildlife into the sleeping zone. Bring a gas stove for cooking and 30 feet of rope for hanging food.

Campsites, facilities: The campground has three tent sites, which allow one tent each. While the campground can accommodate nine campers total, only six are allowed per group. Facilities include a bear pole for hanging food and garbage, a pit toilet, and a fire pit. Bring your own drinking water, or if you plan to use lake or stream water, purify or boil it before drinking. Pack out your trash. Pets are not permitted.

Reservations, fees: Reservations for required wilderness passes are available by phone 90 days in advance beginning April 1 for a nonrefundable CDN$12 reservation fee, plus a modification fee for any additional changes. April–mid-May, call the warden's office (403/859-5140); after then, call the visitors center (403/859-5133). Wilderness passes can also be picked up in person no sooner than 24 hours in advance of the starting date. Backcountry camping costs CDN$10 per person per night. Kids 16 years old and under camp for free. Open May–November.

Directions: Hikers can locate the trailhead at the end of Evergreen Avenue on the west end of Waterton Townsite. Kayakers and canoeists should launch from the Cameron Bay picnic area. Boat ramps for larger boats are available at Linnet Lake picnic area and the marina in the Townsite.

GPS Coordinates: N 49° 0.002' W 113° 54.320'

Contact: Waterton Lakes National Park, Box 200, 215 Mount View Rd., Waterton Park, AB T0K 2M0, Canada, 403/859-2224, www.pc.gc.ca/pn-np/ab/waterton.

16 GOAT HAUNT

Scenic rating: 10

on Waterton Lake in Glacier National Park, U.S.A.

No roads reach Goat Haunt, which sits at the south end of Waterton Lake. Visitors must hike or boat. Backpackers hike to Goat Haunt in three- to five-day trips that start at six trailheads in Glacier. All others must travel through Canada and take either the tour cruise or a private boat from Waterton Townsite to reach Goat Haunt. Bring a passport. An 8.7-mile trail also leads from the townsite to Goat Haunt. When hiking or boating south on Waterton Lake, you cross the international boundary again back into Montana. Only those with U.S. or Canadian

© BECKY LOMAX

The Goat Haunt shelters sit behind the boat dock area and visitor center.

passports are allowed to stay overnight in Goat Haunt or hike past the International Peace Park Pavilion.

Sitting above the boat dock and the open-air visitors center, the campground comprises smaller shelters with cement floors bordered with two walls for privacy from other campers. (Bring a good pad for your back.) During the day, the area bursts with mayhem when the tour boat disgorges tourists, but nighttime brings quiet on your own private beach. Day hikes lead from Goat Haunt to Rainbow Falls (0.7 mile), an overlook (1 steep mile), and Kootenai Lakes (2.8 miles) to spot moose.

Campsites, facilities: The campground has seven designated campsites; each holds up to four people. A community cooking site sits behind the shelters with a bear pole for hanging food. Facilities include flush toilets and drinking water from the sinks. Campfires are permitted in the cooking site, but you'll need to gather your own wood. Pets are not permitted.

Reservations, fees: Backcountry permits are required. Advance reservations ($20) for four of the campsites are available starting April 15. Get permits for other sites in person 24 hours in advance at the Apgar Backcountry Office or St. Mary Visitor Center. Permits cost $5 per adult per night and $2.50 for children 8–15. They are free for children 7 and under. Cash, check, or credit card. Open mid-June–November, although the tour boat runs only through mid-September.

Directions: From Waterton, Alberta, take a private boat or the tour cruise boat across the lake to reach Goat Haunt, Montana. Contact Waterton Shoreline Cruises (403/859-2362, www.watertoncruise.com) for tour boat prices and departure times.

GPS Coordinates: N 48° 57.574' W 113° 53.277'

Contact: Glacier National Park, P.O. Box 128, West Glacier, MT 59936, 406/888-7800, www.nps.gov/glac.

17 BELLY RIVER

Scenic rating: 6

on Chief Mountain International Highway in Waterton Lakes National Park, Canada

For those who want to shoot back across the border from Canada first thing in the morning, the Belly River Campground sits five minutes north of Chief Mountain Customs. Trout anglers looking to fish here will need a Waterton Lakes National Park fishing license as well as an Alberta fishing license; you can get both at the visitors center in Waterton. A short trail, mostly used by anglers, leads up the Belly River but fizzles before the international boundary or any real destination. Some floaters also launch at the Belly River Campground to paddle the Class II river.

A mixed forest surrounds the campground, but the quaking aspen groves give it character. When breezes blow, the leaves chatter. That and the burbling of the Belly River are about the only noises you'll hear. The campsites are located in a mix of shady sites and open sites. Those that are open have forest views. The campground is also a good site for wildlife-watching and birding, particularly along the river. Look for moose, bears, and foxes.

Campsites, facilities: The campground has 24 RV or tent campsites that can accommodate midsized RVs. Facilities include picnic tables, fire rings, pit and flush toilets, kitchen shelters, group camping sites, firewood, a campground host, and bear-resistant food storage lockers. Bring your own drinking water, or boil or purify river water. Because of bears, strict food storage regulations are in effect. Leashed pets are permitted.

Reservations, fees: Reservations are not accepted. Campsites cost CDN$16. Burning permits for fires cost CDN$8. Group campsites are available by reservation only, with a minimum of 25 people; call the park for reservations. Cash or check. Open mid-May–early September.

Directions: Drive 19 miles up Chief Mountain International Highway, crossing the border (open mid-May–September). The campground is on the left about five minutes north of the border before you cross the Belly River. Coming from the north, look for the signed turnoff on the right as soon as you cross the Belly River Bridge.

GPS Coordinates: N 49° 2.840' W 113° 41.368'

Contact: Waterton Lakes National Park, Box 200, 215 Mount View Rd., Waterton Park, AB T0K 2M0, Canada, 403/859-2224, www.pc.gc.ca/pn-np/ab/waterton.

18 BIG CREEK

Scenic rating: 9

on the North Fork of the Flathead River in Flathead National Forest

BEST (

Located on the North Fork of the Flathead River's west bank across from Glacier National Park, Big Creek nestles below Huckleberry Mountain, which blocks direct sun until late morning. Evidence of the 2001 Moose Fire still surrounds the campground, but the forest is regenerating with lodgepole pines and pink fireweed. The fire bypassed the campground, leaving its trees green. At 2.5 miles north of the campground, the Glacier View Trail climbs the steep 2.3 miles up to a ridgetop meadow that yields panoramic views of Glacier Park. Anglers fish both Big Creek and the North Fork of the Flathead River for westslope cutthroat and rainbow trout. The campground sits adjacent to a boat launch for rafting and kayaking.

Tall lodgepoles and firs shade most of the campsites, with a few cottonwoods sprinkled along the river. More than half of the campsites overlook the river or sit adjacent to it. Backing in to alcoves of trees on a gravel loop and spur road, the spacious campsites spread out for privacy, but you'll see neighboring tents through the trunks with no underbrush. Some

of the river campsites capture more sun along the meadows, and you'll only hear the sound of the river.

Campsites, facilities: The campground has 22 RV and tent campsites that can accommodate RVs up to 40 feet. The huge group campsite fits up to 200 people. Facilities include picnic tables, fire rings with grills, drinking water, vault toilets, a boat ramp, firewood for sale, and a campground host. Pack out your trash. Leashed pets are permitted. A wheelchair-accessible toilet is available.

Reservations, fees: Reservations are not accepted, except for the large group campsite ($25, 977/444-6777, www.recreation.gov). Campsites cost $13. Cash or check. Open mid-May–mid-October.

Directions: From Apgar, drive 11.5 miles north on the Camas Road. Turn left on the North Fork Road and drive 2.5 miles south to the campground entrance. From Columbia Falls, drive 20 miles north on the North Fork Road. Find the signed entrance road on the road's east side. When you drive in, bypass the road to the river launch site and the group campsite loop to reach the individual campsites.

GPS Coordinates: N 48° 36.126' W 114° 9.862'

Contact: Flathead National Forest, Glacier View District, 10 Hungry Horse Dr., Hungry Horse, MT 59919, 406/387-3800, www.fs.fed.us/r1/flathead/.

19 GREAT NORTHERN FLATS PRIMITIVE

Scenic rating: 7

on the North Fork of the Flathead River in Flathead National Forest

Along the North Fork of the Flathead River, Great Northern Flats has been revamped from a park-and-camp-anywhere place to designated campsites. The flats, a large river bar on the west bank opposite Glacier National Park, are also a river access for rafters, kayakers, and anglers to float the river. From the flats to Glacier Rim includes the Class II–III Fools Hen Rapids. Only hand-carried watercraft can be launched. From here downriver, motorboats with a 10-horsepower limit are also permitted. The flats huddle under the Apgar Mountains, which rise in steep semi-arid faces across the river. In 2001, the Moose Fire swept through here, part of a 73,000-acre fire that raged for two months. Despite the fire, Great Northern Flats is now fast regenerating with lodgepole pines and wildflowers.

Growing with grass, wildflowers, and tiny new lodgepoles, the arid, dusty, sunny flats are wide open with no shade and no privacy. The primitive back-in campsites tuck close together around a small gravel loop near the river. At night, after the daytime river traffic disappears, the campground goes quiet, with only the sound of the wind and the river. Tents are usually set up on the gravel parking pads, as no additional tent space is available.

Campsites, facilities: The campground has three RV or tent campsites that can accommodate only small RVs. Facilities include fire rings with grills and a vault toilet. Bring your own water, or boil or filter the water taken from the river. Camping is limited to three days. Leashed pets are permitted. A wheelchair-accessible toilet is available.

Reservations, fees: No reservations are accepted. Camping is free. Open late April–November.

Directions: From Apgar, drive 11.5 miles north on Camas Road. Turn left on North Fork Road and drive 5.8 miles to the campground. From Columbia Falls, drive 16 miles north on North Fork Road to the campground. Turn east into the river access site, marked only with a small sign saying "1070."

GPS Coordinates: N 48° 34.119' W 114° 7.861'

Contact: Flathead National Forest, Glacier View District, 10 Hungry Horse Dr., Hungry Horse, MT 59919, 406/387-3800, www.fs.fed.us/r1/flathead/.

20 GLACIER RIM PRIMITIVE

Scenic rating: 7

on the North Fork of the Flathead River in Flathead National Forest

Located on the North Fork of the Flathead River at 3,179 feet in elevation, the Glacier Rim River Access sits on the west bank opposite Glacier National Park. It's close to Columbia Falls (about 15 minutes south), so this is a popular place to camp, due to its access via pavement instead of dirt road. The area is also popular for local anglers, rafters, kayakers, and canoeists buzzing out for the evening after work to float to Blankenship Bridge. Motorboats with a 10-horsepower limit are also permitted on the river.

The two campsites are strikingly different. The RV site sits on a sloped gravel spur north of the parking lot. The site is sunny, visible from the cars driving in, and requires a five-minute walk to see the river. The idyllic tent site sits on the river adjacent to the boat ramp under heavy shade and filled with the sound of the river. Vehicles for the tent site must park up the hill 50 feet or in the parking lot. Plan to arrive early to claim a spot.

Campsites, facilities: Glacier Rim has two campsites. Facilities include rock fire rings, a boat launch, boat trailer parking, and a vault toilet. Bring your own water; if you plan to drink river water, purify or boil it first. A three-day maximum for camping is enforced. Leashed pets are permitted. A wheelchair-accessible toilet is available.

Reservations, fees: Reservations are not accepted. Camping is free. Open late April–November.

Directions: From Apgar, drive 11.5 miles north on Camas Road. Turn left on North Fork Road and drive 11.8 miles to Glacier Rim. From Columbia Falls, drive 10 miles north on North Fork Road to reach Glacier Rim. Look for the river access sign and turn off toward the east.

GPS Coordinates: N 48° 29.573' W 114° 7.588'

Contact: Flathead National Forest, Glacier View District, 10 Hungry Horse Dr., Hungry Horse, MT 59919, 406/387-3800, www.fs.fed.us/r1/flathead/.

21 TIMBER WOLF RESORT

Scenic rating: 7

on Highway 2 west of West Glacier

Timber Wolf Resort is the farthest west in the string of private RV campgrounds that line Highway 2 west of West Glacier. It sits about 10 minutes from Glacier National Park's west entrance station. The tiny town of Hungry Horse is 0.5 mile west. Less than two miles away, a frontage road parallels the dam-controlled section of the South Fork of the Flathead River, making for easy shoreline access to cast flies for rainbows and cutthroat. The resort's large group campfire serves as a place to meet other campers. A hiking trail loops around part of the campground, and a bike trail parallels the highway.

The campground, in 20 wooded acres on a terraced hillside, offers peek-a-boo views of Glacier's Apgar Range. Most of the narrow pull-through RV campsites have a tree for partial shade but garner plenty of sunshine views of the traffic. Tucked at the back of the campground, the tent sites have more shade and privacy from the road. You'll hear highway noise at this campground.

Campsites, facilities: The campground has 24 RV campsites that can accommodate RVs up to 40 feet, as well as five tent campsites. Hookups include sewer, water, and electricity up to 50 amps. Facilities include picnic tables, fire rings, pedestal charcoal grills (bring your own charcoal), flush toilets, showers, high-speed modem hookups, wireless Internet, a camp store, a playground, and firewood for sale. Leashed pets are permitted.

Reservations, fees: Reservations are accepted. Hookups cost $27–36. Tent sites cost $21 for one tent; each additional tent costs $5. Spring and fall rates run $5 less. Check the resort's website for specials. Rates cover two people, and up to six are permitted per campsite. Kids under age six camp for free, but additional adults are charged $3 per night. Pets are also charged $3 per day. The 7 percent Montana bed tax will be added on. Cash, check, or credit card. Open May–September.

Directions: From Hungry Horse, on Highway 2 drive eastward 0.25 mile past Hungry Horse Dam Road. From West Glacier, drive west on Highway 2 for 9 miles. Find the resort entrance on the south side of the highway. GPS Coordinates: N 48° 23.217' W 114° 2.874'

Contact: Timber Wolf Resort, P.O. Box 190800, 9105 Hwy. 2 E., Hungry Horse, MT 59919, 406/387-9653, www.timberwolfresort.com.

22 MOUNTAIN MEADOWS

Scenic rating: 8

on Highway 2 west of West Glacier

Located nine miles west of Glacier National Park's west entrance, Mountain Meadows is one of the many private campgrounds lining the highway between West Glacier and Hungry Horse. Forty private acres behind the campground contain trails for walking in the forest. A paved walking-bicycle path leads 0.6 mile to the tiny town of Hungry Horse for browsing funky antique shops and huckleberry stores. About two miles east, the Coram Experimental Forest, which houses several 500-year-old larch trees, loops with trails through an area used by the Forest Service for research. You can also fish their private catch-and-release stocked rainbow trout pond. (No license needed.)

The campground sits on 77 natural forested

acres with views of Glacier's Apgar Range from its pond. Benches are available to watch the sun set over the peaks. Less railroad and highway noise filters into the campground than in others in the area. The back-in campsites gain partial shade and privacy from the tall forest of mixed trees. Big-rig sites are more open and sunny.

Campsites, facilities: The campground has 52 RV sites that can accommodate RVs up to 45 feet long with slide-outs and awnings. Hookups are available for water, sewer, and electricity up to 30 amps. Facilities include picnic tables, fire rings with grills, flush toilets, showers, a coin-operated launderette, a disposal station, a camp store, firewood for sale, and wireless Internet. Leashed pets are permitted.

Reservations, fees: Make midsummer reservations in winter to guarantee a spot. Hookups run $35–38. Check for Internet specials. Rates are based on two-person occupancy per site. Additional adults cost $4 and children $2. A 7 percent Montana bed tax will be added on. Cash, check, or credit card. Open May–September.

Directions: From Hungry Horse, drive east on Highway 2 up the hill 0.6 mile. From West Glacier, drive west on Highway 2 for nine miles. Find the park entrance on the highway's east side.

GPS Coordinates: N 48° 23.259' W 114° 2.749'

Contact: Mountain Meadows RV Park, P.O. Box 190442, 9125 Hwy. 2 E., Hungry Horse, MT 59919, 406/387-9125, www.mmrvpark. com.

23 CANYON RV AND CAMPGROUND

Scenic rating: 7

on Highway 2 west of West Glacier

Located between the tiny blips on Highway 2 of Coram and Martin City, Canyon RV and Campground is the only campground with river access. An eight-mile drive leads to the west entrance to Glacier National Park and West Glacier, with its rafting, golf, shopping, and restaurants. The campground neighbors Montana Fur Traders and sits across the highway from a paved walking-bicycling path that parallels the road. The campground sits on a treed plateau above the Flathead River, but its property runs right down to the river's bank. You can cast a line from the shore for rainbow or cutthroat trout, or just sit to watch rafts float by. A trail through the woods connects to the river.

A few sparse mature trees offer a wee bit of shade in the sunny campground. A narrow dusty gravel road loops through the grassy narrow pull-through and back-in campsites, which are lined up in RV parking lot fashion— close to the neighbors. Due to the proximity of the railroad tracks across the river and the highway, noise seeps into the campground.

Campsites, facilities: The campground has 50 RV and tent campsites that can accommodate RVs up to 45 feet. Hookups include water, sewer, and electricity up to 50 amps. Facilities include picnic tables, flush toilets, showers, a launderette available only by appointment, a disposal station, a camp store, a playground, and wireless Internet. Leashed pets are permitted. A wheelchair-accessible toilet and campsites are available.

Reservations, fees: Reservations are accepted. Hookups cost $33–36, but only $30 in May and September. Tent sites and RVs without hookups cost $24. Rates are based on two people; each extra person costs $3. Sometimes the park offers the seventh night free. A 7 percent Montana bed tax will be added to the bill. Cash, check, or credit card. Open May–September.

Directions: On Highway 2, from Hungry Horse, drive one mile east, or from West Glacier, drive eight miles west. Turn west into the campground entrance.

GPS Coordinates: N 48° 23.834' W 114° 2.500'

Contact: Glacier National Park, P.O. Box 7,

9540 Hwy. 2 E., Hungry Horse, MT 59919, 406/387-9393, www.montanacampground.com.

24 SUNDANCE CAMPGROUND AND RV PARK

🏠 🚶 ♿ 🚐 ⛺

Scenic rating: 5

on Highway 2 west of West Glacier

Sundance sits in the middle of the line of private RV parks and campgrounds strung along Highway 2 to the west of West Glacier. The entrance to Glacier National Park is 6.5 miles to the east. For those with pets, Sundance offers one amenity that other campgrounds do not: While you tour Glacier for the day, you can kennel Fido at the campground. For hikers, kenneling the dog allows you to explore the national park trails on which pets are not permitted. The neighboring Great Bear Adventure Park—a drive-through habitat with captive black bears—sits over the fence on the campground's east side.

A natural forest surrounds the campground, with little in the way of understory between the tall trees. Most campsites are grassy, and a dirt road loops through the campground for access to sites with gravel parking. The north-end sites are farthest from the highway but are closest to the railroad tracks. The east-side sites border the bear park. The campground also welcomes walk-ins after the office closes at 9 P.M.

Campsites, facilities: The campground has 22 RV sites that are pull-throughs with hookups for water and electricity up to 50 amps. Nine tent sites include water and fire rings. Facilities includes flush toilets, hot showers, a disposal station, truck pump service, a camp store, wireless Internet, a launderette, a day kennel, a playground, and a dishwashing station for tenters. Leashed pets are permitted. A wheelchair-accessible toilet is available.

Reservations, fees: Reservations are accepted.

Hookups cost $26; tent sites cost $18. Rates cover two people; additional campers over 10 years old cost $2 each. Inquire about pet kenneling costs. Add on 7 percent Montana bed tax. Cash, check, or credit card. Open May–October.

Directions: From West Glacier, drive six miles west on Highway 2. The campground is on the north side of the road between mileposts 147 and 148. Look for a red sign.

GPS Coordinates: N 48° 26.031' W 114° 2.589'

Contact: Sundance Campground and RV Park, P.O. Box 130037, 10545 Hwy. 2 E., Coram, MT 59913, 406/387-5016 or 866/782-2677.

25 NORTH AMERICAN RV PARK

🏠 🚶 🚐 ⛺

Scenic rating: 5

on Highway 2 west of West Glacier

North American RV Park sits six miles west of West Glacier and its rafting, fishing, and horseback riding companies, plus the West Glacier Golf Course. It is also 6.5 miles west from the entrance to Glacier National Park. The gravel roads through the campground use names of famous places in Glacier Park.

Recent growth in the past decade put a fir tree barrier between the highway and the campground. Cabins and yurts also added to the wall. Growing trees are breaking up the parking lot feel and lending a bit of shade to some back-in sites. Most of the campsites, however, are sunny, open, and surrounded by mowed lawn. Big-rig drivers prefer this park because its fewer trees and pull-through sites allow for easier maneuvering, and satellites can often gain a clear shot at the sky. Campfires are not permitted in midsummer. Highway noise creeps into the campground, and trains run all night on the tracks on the opposite side of the highway. Sites 7–9 sit the farthest from the highway with the most privacy. Sites

43, 45, 47, 49, 51, 53, 54, and 55 also back up towards woods rather than other campers.

Campsites, facilities: The campground has 55 RV sites, which can fit RVs up to 45 feet, and 10 tent campsites. Hookups are available for sewer, water, and electricity up to 50 amps. Facilities include picnic tables, campfire rings, flush toilets, showers, a launderette, wireless Internet, a playground, and camp store. Leashed pets are permitted.

Reservations, fees: Reservations are highly recommended in midsummer. The office opens to begin taking reservations around mid-April. Hookups cost $33–38. Off-season (until mid-June, after September 1) rates are discounted by $5. Rates are for two people. Each additional person costs $5, but kids 12 years old and under camp for free. Add on 7 percent Montana bed tax. Cash, check, or credit card. Open mid-April–October.

Directions: From West Glacier, drive 5.5 miles west on Highway 2 to milepost 147.5. Turn south into the campground.

GPS Coordinates: N 48° 26.260' W 114° 2.495'

Contact: North American RV Park, P.O. Box 130449, 10784 Hwy. 2 E., Coram, MT 59913, 800/704-4266, www.northamericanrvpark.com.

26 DANCING BEAR CAMPGROUND

Scenic rating: 7

on Highway 2 west of West Glacier

Located four miles from the west entrance to Glacier National Park, Dancing Bear Campground provides something different in the string of private campgrounds between West Glacier and Hungry Horse. West Glacier's newest campground opened in 2008 for a test drive but is planning its big opening for 2010. The owners plan to develop the campground in an eco-friendly way with an emphasis on innovative green power and recycling. It is also aiming for the budget-conscious traveler, offering primitive camping in a natural setting. The owners, however, who have worked in Glacier Park for nearly two decades, are loaded with knowledge about where to hike, fish, raft, and see scenery.

A thick natural forest surrounds the campground; a few campsites have views of the mountains forming Bad Rock Canyon. A gravel road loops through the campground for access to sites. The large sites give a sense of privacy, as campers are not stacked right next to each other. The campsites—none of which have hookups—are suitable for tents, small RVs, truck campers, and small pop-up tent trailers, but not big RVs. Call to check on the current status of the campground.

Campsites, facilities: The campground has 20 RV or tent sites. Facilities include picnic tables, fire rings with grills, vault toilets, garbage service, drinking water, and a solar shower.

Reservations, fees: Reservations are accepted. Campsites cost $5 per person. Cash or check. Open mid-April–October.

Directions: From West Glacier, drive four miles west on Highway 2. Look for a sign tucked in the trees on the south side of the highway at about milepost 147.8. (The sign is easier seen coming from the west. From the east, by the time you see the sign, you've gone too far.) Turn south into the campground.

GPS Coordinates: N 48° 26.561' W 114° 2.297'

Contact: Dancing Bear Campground, 10780 Hwy. 2 E., Coram, MT 59913, 406/471-0640, www.dancingbearcampground.com.

27 LAKE FIVE RESORT

Scenic rating: 7

on Lake Five west of West Glacier

Lake Five Resort sets its cabins and campground on a 235-acre lake west of West Glacier. Due to the shallow lake depth, its waters are warmer than the chilly glacier-fed Lake McDonald five miles away in Glacier National Park—hence the tiny lake's attraction for waterskiing, canoeing, and swimming. Waterskiing lessons are available, and canoes can be rented. The lake buzzes with motorboats on hot summer days. Bicyclists can ride the local paved and dirt back roads to circle the lake or ride to the confluence of the Middle Fork and the North Fork of the Flathead River.

Unfortunately, most of the cabins claim the front spots on the lake, with the campground lining up most of it its tiny, cramped back-in sites close together behind them in a grassy, wooded setting that offers partial shade. Six campsites have beachfront, and the resort also has two tipis right on the shoreline for those who want the experience of camping in a Native American tradition. Set off Highway 2 on a side road, Lake Five Resort is quieter than some of the other area campgrounds, but like all in the area, it still picks up noise from the trains.

Campsites, facilities: The resort has 45 RV campsites that can fit RVs up to 40 feet. Hookups include sewer, water, and electricity up to 50 amps, but only 14 sites include sewer hookups. Facilities include fire rings, flush toilets, showers, a disposal station, a boat launch, a boat dock, a playground, and horseshoes. Tipis sleep up to six people. Leashed pets are permitted.

Reservations, fees: Reservations are highly recommended during midsummer. Campsites cost $40–45. The rate covers two people. Extra campers are charged $5 per night. Tipis rent for $50–60 per night. Dogs cost $5 per day. Add on 7 percent Montana bed tax. Cash, check, or credit card. Open May–October.

Directions: Drive 2.7 miles westward from West Glacier on Highway 2 and turn right onto the Lake Five Road. After driving 0.4 mile to Belton Stage Road, turn right and go 0.5 mile. Turn right into the campground.
GPS Coordinates: N 48° 27.726' W 114° 1.104'

Contact: Lake Five Resort, P.O. Box 338, 540 Belton Stage Rd., West Glacier, MT 59936, 406/387-5601, www.lakefiveresort.com.

28 SAN-SUZ-ED RV PARK

Scenic rating: 4

on Highway 2 west of West Glacier

Located on Highway 2, this RV park is one of the closer private campgrounds to Glacier National Park's west entrance three miles to the east. It is also 2.5 miles from West Glacier activities: trail rides, white-water rafting, float trips, fishing, golf, and shopping. Instead of individual campfire rings at each site, the campground has one large community campfire every night. Bring your own marshmallows or hot dogs for roasting and glean news from fellow campers: where the fish are biting, where the bears are feeding, and where the huckleberries are ripe. The owners also bake homemade pies and, during the summer, serve a breakfast of Belgian waffles and sourdough hotcakes with homemade syrup.

Set in a mix of forest—with some sites shaded and others sunny—the campground sits between Highway 2 and the railroad tracks, which allows some noise to percolate through the trees. Light sleepers should bring earplugs. Part of the campground is paved, with paved pull-through and back-in parking pads, which eliminates dust. Wide sites allow for RV slide-outs and awnings. Each campsite has a different colored picnic table.

Campsites, facilities: The park contains 21 tent sites and 38 RV sites that can accommodate RVs up to 45 feet. Hookups include sewer, water, and electricity up to 50 amps. Facilities include picnic tables, flush toilets, showers, wireless Internet, a launderette, a convenience store, and three enclosed shelters without utilities. Leashed pets are permitted. A wheelchair-accessible toilet is available.

Reservations, fees: Reservations are

appreciated. Hookups cost $31–34. Tent campsites cost $27. Rates are for two people. Extra campers cost $5 per person, but kids under 10 years old stay free. The enclosed shelters cost $35 for up to four people. Add on the 7 percent Montana bed tax. Cash, check, or credit card. Open May–October.

Directions: On Highway 2, from West Glacier drive west for 2.5 miles, or from Hungry Horse drive east for 6.5 miles. The campground sits on the north side of the highway between mileposts 150 and 151.

GPS Coordinates: N 48° 27.753' W 114° 0.124'

Contact: San-Suz-Ed RV, P.O. Box 387, 11505 Hwy. 2 W., West Glacier, MT 59936, 406/387-5280 or 800/630-2623, www.san-suzedrvpark.com.

29 WEST GLACIER KOA

Scenic rating: 7

south of Highway 2 west of West Glacier

Located one mile south of the busy Highway 2 to the west of West Glacier, the KOA is 2.5 miles from Glacier National Park's west entrance. It is also two miles from West Glacier's rafting companies, horseback rides, golf, restaurants, and gift shops. The campground boasts the only swimming pool on the park's west side. While the heated outdoor pool is open June–mid-September, the two hot tubs steam all season long. The campground serves breakfast, ice cream, and an evening barbecue during summer months, and rotates a Tom Ulrich wildlife slide show with a Forest Service program and Glacier videos for evening entertainment.

Set in lodgepole pines, the campsites are separated from the pool area by a large grassy lawn, good for a game of Frisbee. Sites 121–152, which are grassy and more open, do not permit tents or campfires; the other sites have fire rings. Sites 113–125 sit at the back, away from the main camp hubbub but close to one restroom; tent sites 100–112 also gain privacy with larger spaces and picnic tables.

Campsites, facilities: The KOA has 139 RV sites that can accommodate 45-foot RVs. Fifty of the campsites are pull-throughs. Hookups include sewer, water, and electricity up to 50 amps. Facilities include picnic tables, fire rings, flush toilets, showers, a coin-operated launderette, a swimming pool, hot tubs, a playground, a game room, wireless Internet, a disposal station, and a dog-walk area. Leashed pets are permitted. Wheelchair-accessible facilities are available.

Reservations, fees: Reservations are accepted. Hookups run $46–49; no hookups and tent sites cost $29. Rates are based on two people. Extra adults cost $4.50 each, but kids 17 years old and under stay free. In shoulder seasons (May–early June, mid-September–October 1) campsite rates are discounted by $1–2. Add on 7 percent Montana bed tax. Cash, traveler's check, or credit card. Open May–September.

Directions: From West Glacier, drive west on Highway 2 for 2.5 miles. Turn south onto paved Half Moon Flats Road and drive one mile.

GPS Coordinates: N 48° 27.881' W 113° 58.874'

Contact: West Glacier KOA, 355 Half Moon Flats Rd., West Glacier, MT 59936, 406/387-5341 or 800/562-3313, www.westglacierkoa.com.

30 GLACIER CAMPGROUND

Scenic rating: 6

on Highway 2 west of West Glacier

Located one mile from the west entrance to the Glacier National Park, Glacier Campground is the closest private campground to the park in the long string of RV park campgrounds between West Glacier and Hungry Horse. Golf, restaurants, gift shops, an espresso stand, a post office, and the train depot sit 0.5 mile to the east. Four rafting companies that run white-water and float trips on the Middle Fork of the Flathead also have their offices within a five-minute drive. The park's historic red bus tours also will stop by the campground to pick up riders. For evening entertainment, the campground sponsors Forest Service presentations.

The family-owned campground is on 40 timbered acres set back a bit from the highway. The trees not only reduce the highway and railroad noise (you'll still hear it) but grant shade for hot days. Firs, birches, and copious underbrush verging on jungle help to maintain privacy for the campsites. Big rigs can get a few pull-through sites, but otherwise, parking requires a tight squeeze to back into the forest slot. Not all of the campsites have picnic tables and fire rings; ask specifically for these when you arrive or reserve a spot. The campground also has grassy sites for bicyclists and backpackers.

Campsites, facilities: The campground has 80 RV sites, with some pull-through sites that can accommodate RVs up to 40 feet, and 80 tent campsites. Hookups include water and electricity up to 30 amps. Facilities include flush toilets, showers, a pumper truck for sewer service ($10), a camp store, coin-operated launderette, wood-heated recreation room, a playground, and wireless Internet. Leashed pets are permitted.

Reservations, fees: Reservations are accepted. Hookups cost $24–29; no hookup and tent sites cost $19–20. For bikers and hikers, the campground charges $7 per person. Add on 7 percent Montana bed tax. Cash, check, or credit card. Open May–September.

Directions: On Highway 2, from West Glacier drive 0.5 mile west, or from Hungry Horse drive 8.5 miles east. Turn south off the highway at the signed entrance.

GPS Coordinates: N 48° 28.977' W 113° 59.806'

Contact: Glacier Campground, P.O. Box 447,

12070 Hwy. 2 W., West Glacier, MT 59936, 406/387-5689 or 888/387-5689, www.glaciercampground.com.

31 APGAR

Scenic rating: 9

on Lake McDonald on Going-to-the-Sun Road in Glacier National Park

At the foot of Lake McDonald on Glacier's west side, Apgar campground bustles with campers walking to Lake McDonald for a swim, bicycling to the Middle Fork of the Flathead River, or hopping shuttles up Going-to-the-Sun Road to Logan Pass. Adjacent to Apgar Village, the campground connects via paved trails to the Apgar Visitor Center, Eddy's Restaurant, a camp store, ice cream stand, and gift shops. Lake McDonald's only boat ramp

Boats are available for rent on Lake McDonald in Apgar.

© BECKY LOMAX

sits between the picnic area and the village. You can rent canoes, kayaks, or boats with small horsepower engines. Lower McDonald Creek sees heavy fishing and is a warm-day favorite for floating on kayaks, rafts, or tubes to Quarter Circle Bridge. Hikers drive 10 minutes to the trailhead to climb 2.8 miles to Apgar Lookout, which overlooks McDonald Valley and Glacier's jagged peaks.

None of the campsites sit right on Lake McDonald; however, the amphitheater where the park service holds evening programs does. Surrounded by birch and hemlocks, the campground is Glacier's largest, with open campsites beneath the trees and some road noise from Going-to-the-Sun Road. Vehicles over 21 feet must access this campground from West Glacier.

Campsites, facilities: The campground has 194 RV or tent campsites, including 25 that can accommodate RVs up to 40 feet and group sites for 9–24 people. Facilities include picnic tables, fire rings with grills, flush toilets, drinking water, raised gravel tent platforms, shared sites for hikers and bikers, garbage service, interpretive programs, and a disposal station. Bring firewood; collecting it is illegal. During the primitive camping season (April, mid-October–Nov) the campground has only pit toilets and no running water. In winter, camp at the picnic area—a plowed parking lot with a pit toilet. Leashed pets are permitted. A wheelchair-accessible toilet is available.

Reservations, fees: Reservations are not accepted. Sites cost $20 per night May–mid-October. Biker and hiker sites cost $5 per person. Primitive camping costs $10; winter camping is free. Cash, check, or credit card. Open year-round.

Directions: From the west entrance of Glacier National Park, drive northeast on Going-to-the-Sun Road one mile to the Apgar Junction. Turn right, driving for one mile, then turn left at the sign to Apgar Village and drive 0.3 mile to the campground entrance on the left.

GPS Coordinates: N 48° 31.592' W 113° 59.069'

Contact: Glacier National Park, P.O. Box 128, West Glacier, MT 59936, 406/888-7800, www.nps.gov/glac.

32 FISH CREEK

Scenic rating: 8

on Lake McDonald in Glacier National Park

Fish Creek Campground is located on Lake McDonald's north shore three miles from Apgar on Glacier's west side. While Fish Creek flows through the campground, the stream is closed to fishing. Anglers still fish nearby in Lake McDonald, especially where the creek runs into the lake. Built on a hillside in deep cedars, lodgepoles, and larches, the campground and picnic area border the shoreline with its multicolored perfect rock-skipping stones. As the water level drops throughout the summer, the beaches become larger and more appealing for sunbathing, swimming, and sunset-watching. The Lake McDonald Trail departs from loop C for a one-mile jaunt to Rocky Point—a rock bluff with views of Mount Edwards and Mount Brown. Hike farther up the lake to remote beaches, or loop back through the 2003 fire zone, which has interpretive signs. You can launch hand-carried watercraft from the picnic area, but no boat launch is available.

Loops C and D have the best sites for the quickest access to the lake. Some of their southern campsites have peek-a-boo water views, too. If privacy is valued, ask for one of the smaller campsites on the outer, uphill side of loop B. The shaded campground sits far enough away from the Apgar hubbub to be a peaceful, quiet place. Be prepared for mosquitoes.

Campsites, facilities: Fish Creek has 178 RV or tent campsites, including 18 campsites accommodating RVs up to 35 feet long and 62 sites fitting RVs up to 27 feet. Facilities include picnic tables, fire rings with grills, flush toilets, drinking water, shared hiker and biker campsites, garbage service, and a disposal station. Bring firewood; collecting it is illegal. Strict food storage regulations are in effect due to bears. Leashed pets are permitted. A wheelchair-accessible toilet is available.

Reservations, fees: Reservations are available (877/444-6777, www.reservations.gov). Campsites cost $23 per night; shared hiker or biker sites cost $5 per person. Cash, check, or credit card. Open June–early September.

Directions: From Glacier's west entrance, drive one mile northeast to the Apgar Junction. Turn left and drive 1.25 miles north on Camas Road and turn right at the campground sign, dropping one mile down past the picnic area to the staffed campground entrance station.

GPS Coordinates: N 48° 32.873' W 113° 59.139'

Contact: Glacier National Park, P.O. Box 128, West Glacier, MT 59936, 406/888-7800, www.nps.gov/glac.

33 LAKE MCDONALD

Scenic rating: 9

on Lake McDonald's north shore in Glacier National Park

At 10 miles long and 1.5 miles wide, Lake McDonald is the largest lake in Glacier National Park. Its southern flank is bordered by Going-to-the-Sun Road, but its north side—where the Lake McDonald backcountry campground sits—is accessed only by hiking the Lake McDonald Trail from Fish Creek Campground or by boating the lake. The Robert Fire in 2003 closed the campground, but the National Park Service opened it up again in 2009. From the shore near the camp, you get views of Mount Brown, Edwards, and Jackson Peak—mountains not visible from the Sun Road. The lake harbors kokanee salmon and lake trout. Paddling to the campground takes about 90 minutes from Apgar; traveling with a motorboat takes about

30 minutes. No dock is available; completely beach all boats at night in case winds arise.

The campground sits about halfway up the north side of the lake, with the communal cooking site and sleeping campsites set back in the trees from the lakeshore. In June, the rocky beach is minimal, but by August, it increases to a quiet spacious place to relax on the shore in the sun. The campground is prized for its quiet and solitude. Take 30 feet of rope for hanging food and cooking gear.

Campsites, facilities: The campground has two tent campsites; each holds up to four people. Facilities include a rock fire pit, food-hanging cables, communal cooking site with log benches, and a pit toilet. Boil or purify lake water for drinking. Pack out your trash. Pets are not permitted.

Reservations, fees: Backcountry permits are required. Advance reservations ($20) for one of the campsites is available starting April 15. Get permits for remaining sites in person 24 hours in advance at the Apgar Backcountry Office in Apgar. Permits cost $5 per adult per night and $2.50 for children 8–15. They are free for children 7 and under. Opens mid-May–November.

Directions: For boating, launch from the Apgar boat ramp. Parking for trailers is available across the street. For hiking, park at the Fish Creek picnic area.

GPS Coordinates: N 48° 35.610' W 113° 55.816'

Contact: Glacier National Park, P.O. Box 128, West Glacier, MT 59936, 406/888-7800, www.nps.gov/glac.

34 SPRAGUE CREEK

Scenic rating: 10

on Lake McDonald on Going-to-the-Sun Road in Glacier National Park

BEST (

Sitting at 3,200 feet on Lake McDonald's southeast shore, Sprague Creek is one of five campgrounds lining Going-to-the-Sun Road. It is the smallest drive-to campground on Lake McDonald and the first to fill up. Paths access the lake for launching canoes or kayaks, but large boats must go to Apgar for the boat ramp. Anglers fish the lake for lake trout and kokanee salmon. Squeezed in between Going-to-the-Sun Road and the lake, the campground sits one mile from historic Lake McDonald Lodge, restaurants, boat tours, red bus tours, a camp store, horseback riding, and the Sperry Trailhead. The trail ascends to Snyder Lake (4.4 miles), historic Sperry Chalet (6.4 miles), Sperry Glacier (10.4 miles), and Mount Brown Lookout (5.8 steep miles), with its dizzying view down to Lake McDonald. A shuttle stop at the campground connects with 17 places on Going-to-the-Sun Road, including Logan Pass.

Shaded by large cedars, the campsites cluster tight in the forest with little to no underbrush between them to add privacy. Strung around a narrow, curvy, paved road, sites 1, 2, 5, 7, 8, 10, 12, 13, 15, and 16 overlook the lake. The backs of sites 17, 20, 21, 22, and 24 flank the busy Going-to-the-Sun Road, but traffic quiets after dark. Due to the campground's popularity, plan on arriving around 11 A.M. in midsummer.

Campsites, facilities: The campground has 25 RV or tent campsites that can accommodate RVs up to 21 feet. No towed units are allowed. Facilities include picnic tables, fire rings with grills, raised gravel tent platforms, drinking water, and garbage service. Bring firewood; collecting is illegal. Strict food storage regulations—stapled to the picnic tables—are in effect for bears. Leashed pets are permitted. A wheelchair-accessible toilet is available.

Reservations, fees: No reservations are accepted. Campsites cost $20. Shared sites for hikers and bikers cost $5 per person. Cash, check, or credit card. Open mid-May–mid-September.

Directions: From the west entrance to Glacier National Park, drive 9.5 miles east on Going-to-the-Sun Road. From the St. Mary entrance, drive 40.5 miles west over Logan Pass. Find the campground entrance on the lake side of the road.

GPS Coordinates: N 48° 36.371' W 113° 53.082'

Contact: Glacier National Park, P.O. Box 128, West Glacier, MT 59936, 406/888-7800, www.nps.gov/glac.

35 AVALANCHE

Scenic rating: 9

in McDonald Valley on Going-to-the-Sun Road in Glacier National Park

Tucked into a narrow canyon between massive peaks, Avalanche Campground sits at 3,550 feet on Going-to-the-Sun Road in Glacier National Park. This is the closest west-side campground to Logan Pass, 16 miles east. Named for the nearby avalanches that rip down Mount Cannon's slopes, the campground sits in a pocket of rain forest preserved from fire. The 0.7-mile, wheelchair-accessible, paved and boardwalk Trail of the Cedars loops from the campground through ancient cedars and past red-rocked Avalanche Gorge. A spur trail climbs two miles up to Avalanche Lake, where giant waterfalls plummet from a hanging valley. In midsummer, the trail sees a constant stream foot traffic heading to the lake for swimming, fishing, or gazing at mountain goats on the cliffs. The free Going-to-the-Sun Road shuttles stop at the campground. Vehicles over 21 feet are not permitted farther east on Going-to-the-Sun Road past this campground.

Driving into the shady campground is akin to driving into a jungle. Grandfather cedar trees and thick underbrush crowd into campsites, and boggy places can produce prodigious numbers of mosquitoes. Avalanche Creek runs adjacent to the campground. You'll be able to see a couple other campsites, but the campground goes silent after dark. Due to the campground's popularity, plan on arriving before 3 P.M. during midsummer and before noon on Saturday. Vehicles over 21 feet must access this campground from West Glacier, not St. Mary.

Campsites, facilities: The campground has 87 RV or tent campsites that can accommodate RVs up to 26 feet. Facilities include picnic tables, fire rings with a grills, drinking water, flush toilets, garbage service, shared hiker and biker campsites, and an amphitheater for evening interpretive programs. Strict food storage regulations are in effect because of bears. Bring firewood; collecting is illegal. Leashed pets are permitted. A wheelchair-accessible toilet is available.

Reservations, fees: No reservations are accepted. Campsites cost $20. Shared sites for hikers and bikers cost $5 per person. Cash, check, or credit card. Open early June–early September.

Directions: From the west entrance to Glacier National Park, drive 15.7 miles up Going-to-the-Sun Road. From the St. Mary entrance, drive 34 miles west over Logan Pass. The entrance is on the south side of the road.

GPS Coordinates: N 48° 40.791' W 113° 49.152'

Contact: Glacier National Park, P.O. Box 128, West Glacier, MT 59936, 406/888-7800, www.nps.gov/glac.

36 RISING SUN

🚶 🚴 ⛱ 🎣 🚌 ⛴ 🐕 ♿ 🚐 ⛺

Scenic rating: 10

in St. Mary Valley on Going-to-the-Sun Road in Glacier National Park

BEST (

Below Otokomi and Goat Mountains north of St. Mary Lake, Rising Sun is one of two eastside campgrounds on Going-to-the-Sun Road. As daylight shifts, streaks of red argillite douse peaks, offset by the lake's turquoise water. The Rising Sun complex includes cabins, a restaurant, a camp store, a boat ramp, boat tours, a picnic area, shuttle stop, and trailhead. Walk across the road to swim in the lake, or hop a boat tour around Wild Goose Island. If boating or fishing, watch the winds; in minutes, fierce winds can kick up huge whitecaps on St. Mary Lake. On Going-to-the-Sun Road a five-minute drive west, photographers will want to shoot Wild Goose Island in early morning light. From the campground, hike five miles up to Otokomi Lake to watch mountain goats climb on the cliffs, or hop a free shuttle up to other popular trailheads around Logan Pass. Vehicles over 21 feet must access the campground from St. Mary, not West Glacier.

The campground's two loops feature different types of sites. Many are set under firs and cottonwoods for shade, but some are grassy, with wide-open views of peaks and the night sky—particularly those on the west loop's southwest side. Rising Sun bustles during the day but quiets after dark when traffic diminishes on Going-to-the-Sun Road.

Campsites, facilities: The campground has 83 RV or tent campsites. Only 10 campsites can accommodate RVs or trailer combinations up to 25 feet long. Facilities include picnic tables, fire rings with grills, drinking water, flush toilets, a disposal station, shared hiker and biker campsites, and an amphitheater for interpretive programs. Purchase tokens from the camp store for showers at the adjacent motel. Leashed pets are permitted. A wheelchair-accessible toilet is available.

Reservations, fees: No reservations are accepted. Campsites cost $20. Shared sites for hikers and bikers cost $5 per person. Cash, check, or credit card. Open late May–mid-September.

Directions: From the St. Mary entrance to Glacier, drive six miles west up Going-to-the-Sun Road. From the west entrance to Glacier National Park, drive 43.5 miles over Logan Pass. The campground entrance is on the north side of the road.

GPS Coordinates: N 48° 41.638' W 113° 31.278'

Contact: Glacier National Park, P.O. Box 128,

West Glacier, MT 59936, 406/888-7800, www.nps.gov/glac.

37 ST. MARY

Scenic rating: 9

in St. Mary Valley on Going-to-the-Sun Road in Glacier National Park

St. Mary marks the east entrance to Glacier National Park, in a place where the mountains sweep up right out of the lakes. The campground, which sits just inside the park entrance, requires a half-mile walk to reach the visitors center, where interpretive programs are held and free shuttles depart up Going-to-the-Sun Road for trailheads and Logan Pass. A 2.5-mile drive toward the 1913 ranger station ends at a trailhead that departs for Red Eagle Lake, where a state record 16-pound native westslope cutthroat was caught. The 7.5-mile trail to the lake passes through broad, colorful wildflower meadows blooming with lupines and crosses the outlet river twice on Indiana Jones–type suspension bridges. A one-mile walk or drive from the campground takes you outside the park to the town of St. Mary, with its restaurants, gift shops, launderette, and gas station. Vehicles over 21 feet must access this campground from Highway 89, not Going-to-the-Sun Road from West Glacier.

The campground circles around a wide-open prairie comprising grasses, currant bushes, and ground squirrel holes, but with views of Divide and Red Eagle Mountains, particularly in the C loop. Some of the small campsites are tucked into aspen groves that afford some shade, but most are hot, windy, or within sight of each other. From the campground, a rough game trail with downed trees climbs four miles along the park boundary to the top of Napi Point, named for the creator of Blackfeet legends. Traffic on Going-to-the-Sun Road quiets after dark.

Campsites, facilities: The campground has 148 RV or tent campsites. Only 25 of the sites can accommodate RVs or trailer combinations up to 35 feet long. Facilities include picnic tables, fire rings with grills, flush toilets, drinking water, a disposal station, large group sites, and shared hiker and biker campsites. During winter and primitive camping (April–mid-May, late September–November) periods, there are only pit toilets, and no potable water is available. Leashed pets are permitted.

Reservations, fees: Reservations are accepted (877/444-6777, www.recreation.gov). Campsites cost $23 late May–mid-September. Shared sites for hikers and bikers cost $5 per person. Primitive camping (April–mid-May and late September–November) costs $10. Winter camping is free. Cash, check, or credit card.

Directions: From the St. Mary entrance station to Glacier, drive 0.5 mile on Going-to-the-Sun Road. Turn right into the campground.
GPS Coordinates: N 48° 45.053' W 113° 26.811'

Contact: Glacier National Park, P.O. Box 128, West Glacier, MT 59936, 406/888-7800, www.nps.gov/glac.

38 JOHNSON'S OF ST. MARY

Scenic rating: 9

in St. Mary on the Blackfeet Reservation

Johnson's of St. Mary is located on a knoll above the tiny seasonal town of St. Mary at the east entrance station to Going-to-the-Sun Road in Glacier National Park. The town—with its restaurants, gift shops, lodges, cabins, and grocery store—packs out with visitors in summer. Since vehicles over 21 feet are not permitted past Sun Point on Going-to-the-Sun Road, those with big RVs can catch park tours from the campground on the historic red jammer buses or Native American Sun Tours. Cyclists on Highway

89 use the campground for its convenience, and a five-minute drive leads to trailheads for a 0.1-mile stroll to the historic ranger station or a 7.5-mile hike to Red Eagle Lake. Fishing is also available at St. Mary Lake and on the St. Mary River.

For many of the RV sites, the knoll affords spectacular views of the St. Mary Valley and sunsets over Glacier's peaks. From the campground, views include Napi Point to the north. The rocky outcrop was named for the creator in Blackfeet legends. A dirt road, which can be dusty in late summer, winds through the campground to get to the tent sites—all in grassy open meadows for sun or aspen groves for shade. The RV sites here are notoriously narrow, cramping the use of awnings and slide-outs. The grassy tenting area has an old cinder-block restroom and shower house, but campers can hike down the hill to the newer RV restroom and showers.

Campsites, facilities: Johnson's has 82 RV sites with pull-throughs that can fit large RVs, plus over 50 tent sites. Hookups include water, sewer, and electricity up to 30 amps. Facilities include picnic tables, fire rings, flush toilets, showers, coin-operated launderette, wireless Internet, a disposal station, propane, restaurant, and small camp store. Johnson's also has overnight facilities for horses. Leashed pets are permitted.

Reservations, fees: Reservations are accepted. Hookups run $33–40. RVs using no hookups cost $26; tents cost $23. Fees include two adults, two kids, and two vehicles per site. Extra people and vehicles cost $5 each. Add on 7 percent Montana bed tax. Cash, check, or credit card. Open late April–late September.

Directions: In St. Mary, drive 0.5 mile north of the Going-to-the-Sun and Highway 89 intersection. Turn right up the hill at the sign for the campground.

GPS Coordinates: N 48° 45.005' W 113° 25.569'

Contact: Johnson's of St. Mary, HC 72-10, Star Route, St. Mary, MT 59417-9701, 406/732-4207, www.johnsonsofstmary.com.

39 ST. MARY KOA

Scenic rating: 9

in St. Mary on the Blackfeet Reservation

Located east of the town of St. Mary, the KOA sits on the west end of St. Mary Lake bordering the St. Mary River. The east entrance to Glacier Park and Going-to-the-Sun Road sits less than two miles away, with restaurants, groceries, and gas in the town one mile west. At the KOA, you can rent a kayak or canoe to paddle the lake, hone golf skills on the campground's putting green, and tour back roads on a mountain bike. With a Blackfeet fishing license available on site, anglers can fish the lake or river. Elk frequent the campground, and the riparian habitat along the water attracts scads of birds, including eagles. Since vehicles over 21 feet are not permitted past Sun Point on Going-to-the-Sun Road, you can catch the Blackfeet-led Sun Tours from here.

Pull-through RV sites line up parking-lot style on gravel, with dramatic views of Singleshot Mountain. Tent sites are scattered in grassy sunny meadows or among the aspens and firs for partial shade. The complex centers around an outdoor pool and a 22-person hot tub, both with views of Glacier's peaks and stars at night. Campground views include, to the north, Napi Point, named for the creator in Blackfeet legends. Several tent sites in the L and K loops border the river.

Campsites, facilities: The campground has 100 RV sites (65 full hookups and 35 partial hookups) and 59 tent campsites. Hookups include water, sewer, and electricity up to 50 amps. Facilities include picnic tables, fire rings with grills, flush toilets, showers, wireless Internet, a pool, a hot tub, a disposal station, a playground, a camp store, and a café that serves breakfast and dinner in the summer. Leashed pets are permitted. A wheelchair-accessible toilet is available.

Reservations, fees: Reservations are accepted.

Hookups cost $25–50. Tents cost $25–31. Rates cover two people. Additional adults cost $7. Kids 17 and under camp free. Add on 7 percent Montana bed tax. Cash, check, or credit card. Open May–September.

Directions: From Babb, drive 8.7 miles south on Highway 89 and turn right heading north on W. Shore Road. From St. Mary Resort gas station, drive 0.4 mile north on Highway 89 and turn left on W. Shore Road. The campground is 0.9 mile north from the turnoff. GPS Coordinates: N 48° 45.487' W 113° 26.156'

Contact: St. Mary KOA, 106 W. Shore, St. Mary, MT 59417, 406/732-4122 or 800/562-1504, www.goglacier.com.

40 MANY GLACIER

Scenic rating: 10

in Swiftcurrent Valley in Glacier National Park

BEST (

Park the car for days at this most coveted campground on the Continental Divide's east side in Glacier National Park! Located below Grinnell Point, the campground sits at a hub of trails. Hike 4.5 miles to Iceberg Lake to swim with icebergs in August. Ascend the 5.5 miles to see Grinnell Glacier melting fast into a turquoise pool. Grunt up the 5.2 miles to the Ptarmigan Tunnel for views of the Belly River drainage. Slog 8 miles of switchbacks to the top of the Continental Divide at Swiftcurrent Lookout. Shorter walks lead to waterfalls, wildflowers meadows, and blue lakes with moose feeding. Launch canoes, kayaks, and small motorboats onto Swiftcurrent Lake for paddling or fishing. Boats are also available for rent.

Set in firs and aspens, the small, shaded campsites pack in tight next to the busy Swiftcurrent parking lot and the ranger station. Across the Swiftcurrent parking lot you'll find a restaurant, a camp store, and showers (buy tokens in the store), and often the park service erects telescopes for viewing bighorn sheep and grizzly bears on the surrounding slopes. A few campsites get peek-a-boo views of Grinnell Point, especially those on the south side of the southern loop and

© BECKY LOMAX

A 5.5-mile hike leads to Grinnell Glacier, perched below the Continental Divide.

the northwest corner of the northwest loop. Due to the campground's extreme popularity, claim a site before 11 A.M. during July and August.

Campsites, facilities: The campground has 110 RV or tent campsites. Only 13 sites can accommodate RVs up to 35 feet long. Facilities include picnic tables, fire rings with grills, flush toilets, drinking water, a disposal station, large group sites, bear boxes, shared hiker and biker campsites, garbage service, and campground hosts. Primitive camping (late September–October) offers only pit toilets and no potable water. Due to bears, strict food storage regulations are in effect. Leashed pets are permitted. A wheelchair-accessible toilet is available.

Reservations, fees: No reservations are accepted. Campsites cost $20 late May–mid-September. Primitive camping costs $10. Shared sites for hikers and bikers cost $5 per person. Cash, check, or credit card. Open late May–October.

Directions: From Babb, drive 12 miles on Many Glacier Road (Glacier Route 3). Turn left at the ranger station sign and veer right into the campground.

GPS Coordinates: N 48° 47.831' W 113° 40.452'

Contact: Glacier National Park, P.O. Box 128, West Glacier, MT 59936, 406/888-7800, www.nps.gov/glac.

41 DUCK LAKE LODGE

Scenic rating: 7

west of Duck Lake on the Blackfeet Reservation

At 5,015 feet in elevation, Duck Lake on the Blackfeet Reservation is renowned for its fishing, including ice fishing in winter. From Duck Lake, Glacier's peaks spread across the horizon, with Chief Mountain taking prominence to the northwest, and the

east entrance to Glacier's Going-to-the-Sun Road is 10 minutes to the west. The lake harbors rainbow and brown trout averaging 8 pounds, but a few lucky anglers pluck out 15-pounders. Float tubes or boats work best in the lake for fishing, rather than casting from shoreline, and motorized boats are restricted to a 10 mph speed limit. Anglers are required to purchase a tribal fishing license and recreation tags for boats. The lodge sells both.

Duck Lake Lodge with its small campground sits two miles west of Duck Lake. Ponds border the gravel access road leading to Duck Lake Lodge, and aspens surround the campground. Tents fit on an open grassy field with no privacy, catching the full sun and wind, and the RV campsites stack very close together along the edge of the aspens. The campground mostly attracts anglers and hunters coming to experience the reservation. The lodge draws on a collection of reliable Blackfeet outfitters for guided fishing or hunting trips on the reservation. The small lodge also has a restaurant and bar.

Campsites, facilities: The campground has five RV sites that can fit midsized RVs, plus room for five tents in a grassy meadow. Hookups include electricity, water, and sewer. Facilities include flush toilets, showers, a launderette, and wireless Internet in the lodge. Leashed pets are permitted.

Reservations, fees: Reservations are recommended. Hookups cost $40. Tent camping costs $10. Cash, check, or credit card. The lodge is open year-round, but camping runs May–October.

Directions: From St. Mary, drive eight miles south on Highway 89 and turn right onto Highway 464. Drive 1.3 miles to milepost 29. At the lodge sign, turn right onto the gravel entrance road.

GPS Coordinates: N 48° 50.314' W 113° 23.562'

Contact: Duck Lake Lodge, P.O. Box 210, 3215 Hwy. 464, Babb, MT 59411, 406/338-5770, www.montanaducklakelodge.com.

42 MIDDLE FORK OF THE FLATHEAD

Scenic rating: 9

on the Middle Fork of the Flathead River in Flathead National Forest

The Middle Fork of the Flathead River churns with white water for some of its 87 miles. The Wild and Scenic River, which springs from headwaters deep within the Bob Marshall Wilderness Complex, races through John F. Stevens Canyon en route to its confluence with the North Fork of the Flathead River near Coram. From Bear Creek, the river flows along the southeast boundary of Glacier National Park, where scenic float sections alternate with Class II–IV white water. Rapids such as Jaws, Bonecrusher, and Screaming Right Hand Turn require technical finesse to navigate. Seven river accesses (Bear Creek, Essex, Paola, Cascadilla, Moccasin Creek, West Glacier, and Blankenship) allow boaters to vary the length of the trips. Most overnight trips take 2–3 days and can add on hiking adventures in the park or the national forest. Most of the white water packs into the section between Moccasin Creek and West Glacier, and notorious logjams litter the Cascadilla to Moccasin Creek float. During high water in late May, some rapids can reach Class IV. Life jackets are required.

The campsites all sit on the south shore of the river on rocky river bars, on willow and grass flats, or in cottonwood, cedar, and fir forests. You can hear the highway at some, but views at all of them look across the river to Glacier.

Campsites, facilities: No camping is permitted between Bear Creek and Essex, but below Essex, you'll find at least 10 tent campsites. Campers are required to take a groover for human waste and a fire pan to minimize burn scars. Camping is only permitted on the south shore in Flathead National Forest; no camping is permitted on the Glacier Park side to the north. Get a copy of *Three Forks of the Flathead Floating Guide* from the Forest Service to help with campsite selection; the national forest side also has private property to avoid. The river accesses all have vault toilets. Pets are permitted.

Reservations, fees: Reservations are not available. No permit is needed; camping is free. The rafting and kayaking season runs mid-May–early September.

Directions: From West Glacier, drive east on Highway 2 to reach the various signed river accesses.

GPS Coordinates: N 48° 14.035' W 113° 33.929'

Contact: Flathead National Forest, Hungry Horse District, 10 Hungry Horse Dr., Hungry Horse, MT 59919, 406/387-3800, www.fs.fed. us/r1/flathead/.

43 STANTON CREEK LODGE

Scenic rating: 4

on Highway 2 in Flathead National Forest

At 3,550 feet in Flathead National Forest across from the southwestern boundary to Glacier National Park, Stanton Creek Lodge is one of the old fixtures on the Highway 2 corridor. The lodge, campsites, and cabins sit right next to the highway, with the railroad tracks across the street. (Bring earplugs for a good night's sleep here.) A one-mile trail climbs to Stanton Lake in the Great Bear Wilderness. Anglers drop lines into the lake for native westslope cutthroat trout. Those looking for bigger views of glaciers and ridgetop walking continue climbing the Grant Ridge Loop, which returns to the lodge in 10.2 miles. A half mile west of the lodge at Coal Creek, a 10-minute trail cuts down to the Middle Fork of the Flathead River, also for fishing.

Hailing from 1932, the lodge itself was one of a string of wild bars dotting the Marias Pass route within a day's horse ride of each other.

Drunken visitors rode horses through the bar, and bullets flew at passing trains. You can still see bullet holes in the original floor inside the bar. Because of the adjacent highway and railroad tracks, the camping experience here is not quiet wilderness. The tight, small RV campsites sit in the sun between the cabins; tent campsites are shaded under firs. Views are of the forest, highway, and a snippet of Glacier's southern peaks.

Campsites, facilities: The campground has four tent campsites and eight RV campsites that can accommodate midsized RVs. Hookups are available for sewer, water, and electricity up to 30 amps. Facilities include picnic tables, a community fire pit, flush toilets, showers, a restaurant, and bar.

Reservations, fees: Reservations are accepted. RV hookups cost $25; tent sites cost $15. Prices are for two people. Extra campers pay $5 each. Children camp for free. Cash, check, Canadian currency, or credit card. Open late May–mid-September.

Directions: From West Glacier, drive 16 miles east on Highway 2. From East Glacier, drive 44 miles west on Highway 2. The lodge and campground are at milepost 170 on the south side of the highway.

GPS Coordinates: N 48° 24.139' W 113° 42.971'

Contact: Stanton Creek Lodge, HC 36 Box 2C, Essex, MT 59916, 406/888-5040 or 866/883-5040, www.stantoncreeklodge.com.

44 GLACIER HAVEN RV

Scenic rating: 7

on Highway 2 west of Essex surrounded by Flathead National Forest

Located west of Essex on Highway 2, the Glacier Haven RV and Campground opened in summer 2009. It sits in the Middle Fork of the Flathead River corridor across from Glacier National Park. For RVs over 21 feet long that are not permitted to drive over Going-to-the-Sun Road, the campground added one more RV campground on Highway 2. A five-minute drive east to Essex or west to Paola leads to fishing accesses, also places to launch rafts and kayaks to float the Middle Fork of the Flathead River. Also within a five-minute drive, Dickey Lake Road turns south to reach trailheads into Great Bear Wilderness. Marion Lake requires an elevation change of 1,810 feet over 1.7 miles, and 2.4-mile Dickey Lake trail climbs up a steep, brushy headwall to reach into a hanging valley. The campground is five minutes from the historical Izaak Walton Inn, with bike trails in summer.

Glacier Haven added the new campground adjacent to its hotel and a small restaurant, which serves home-style meals. The campground does not permit smoking, even outdoors. The forested campground with one gravel loop squeezes in between the highway and the railroad tracks; bring earplugs to help with sleeping as trains rumble by at night. Most of the RV spots are gravel back-ins. One open area is available for tents with undesignated sites. Views include the forest, highway, and railroad tracks.

Campsites, facilities: The campground has 19 RV campsites, including three that can accommodate large RVs on pull-through gravel parking pads, and room for five tents in a large camping zone. Hookups include water, sewer, and electricity. Facilities include flush toilets, showers, a launderette, and restaurant. Leashed pets are permitted.

Reservations, fees: Reservations are accepted. RV sites cost $35. Tent sites cost $25. Rates are for two people; additional people are charged $5 each. Children ages nine and under camp for free. The pet fee is $2.

Directions: On Highway 2 west of Essex, look for milepost markers 173 and 174. Turn south into the campground on the gravel road west of the Glacier Haven Inn.

GPS Coordinates: N 48° 21.830' W 113° 39.752'

Contact: Glacier Haven, 14297 Hwy. 2 E., Essex, MT 59916, 406/888-9987 or 406/888-5720, www.glacierhavenrv-campground.com.

45 ESSEX PRIMITIVE

🚶🚲🛶⛴🎣🦌🚙🏕

Scenic rating: 6

on the Middle Fork of the Flathead River in Flathead National Forest

Walton picnic area marks the southernmost tip of Glacier National Park, and across the Middle Fork of the Flathead River sits the tiny community of Essex. The Essex river access site provides a place to launch onto the river for floating or fishing; it is also a location along the river where you can camp right on the bank. Essex also houses the historical Izaak Walton Inn, which offers summer mountain biking, and the Half-Way House convenience store and restaurant. From Walton picnic area, a trail climbs 4.7 miles to Scalplock Lookout for a dramatic view of Mount St. Nicholas. From the Dickey Lake Road (Highway 2, milepost 178.7), you can access two trailheads in Flathead National Forest. A popular, steep trail climbs 1.7 miles to Marion Lake, and a 2.4-mile trail leads up to Dickey Lake in a hanging valley.

The Essex river access site sits on a sandy bar, which increases in size as the river level drops during the season. Primitive camping is permitted on the bar, but it is without privacy. A few cottonwoods provide some shade for the campsites. A bridge above the site crosses the river, blocking the view of Scalplock Mountain. Traffic dwindles at night, but between the road, the river, and the railroad track above, this is not a place for quiet.

Campsites, facilities: The campground has three primitive RV or tent campsites, which can fit midsized RVs. Facilities include rock fire rings and a portable toilet June–August. Boil or filter water taken from the river. Pack out your trash. This is bear country, so practice safe food storage. Camping is limited to three days. Leashed pets are permitted.

Reservations, fees: No reservations are accepted. Camping is free. It's open May–November, but during late May and early June high water can flood the sandbar.

Directions: On Highway 2 between Essex and Walton, turn north at milepost 180. The unsigned exit sits on the west side of the bridge over the river and swings under the bridge to reach the sandbar.

GPS Coordinates: N 48° 16.492' W 113° 36.301'

Contact: Flathead National Forest, Hungry Horse District, 10 Hungry Horse Dr., Hungry Horse, MT 59919, 406/387-3800, www.fs.fed.us/r1/flathead/.

46 BEAR CREEK PRIMITIVE

🚶🛶⛴🎣🦌🚙🏕

Scenic rating: 7

on the Middle Fork of the Flathead River in Flathead National Forest

At the confluence of Bear Creek and the Middle Fork of the Flathead River, Bear Creek river access site sits where the Middle Fork of the Flathead River plunges from the Bob Marshall Wilderness Area to then form Glacier National Park's southern boundary. It is a large site used for launching onto the river to float for day-long or overnight float trips and for hikers and horse-packers heading into the Bob Marshall Wilderness. Day hikers also use the trail heading up the Middle Fork, which spurs off up Edna Creek for a 3.5-mile steep grunt up to scenic Tranquil Basin Overlook, and a 0.5-mile climb farther to summit 7,394-foot Mount Furlong yields views of Glacier's peaks.

The area roars equally with churning rapids and noise from the highway and railroad. Those camping here may want to bring earplugs. The wide-open, giant dusty parking lot yields big views of the surrounding mountains—the Great Bear Wilderness and Glacier—but at a cost to privacy. The area is not designed with designated campsites, but the big parking lot permits plenty of room for primitive camping for those needing campsites while traveling over Marias Pass.

Campsites, facilities: The area has room for three RVs or tent campsites. Facilities include a wheelchair-accessible vault toilet. Boil or filter water taken from the river. Pack out your trash. Camping is limited to three days. Because of bears, practice safe food storage. Leashed pets are permitted.

Reservations, fees: No reservations are accepted. Camping is free. Open May–November.

Directions: On Highway 2, between Essex and Marias Pass, find Bear Creek River Access at milepost 185 on the south side of the highway.

GPS Coordinates: N 48° 14.032' W 113° 33.942'

Contact: Flathead National Forest, Hungry Horse District, 10 Hungry Horse Dr., Hungry Horse, MT 59919, 406/387-3800, www.fs.fed.us/r1/flathead/.

47 DEVIL CREEK

Scenic rating: 6

on Highway 2 in Flathead National Forest

At 4,450 feet in elevation along Highway 2, Devil Creek is close to both river recreation and hiking trails in the Great Bear Wilderness, which surrounds it, and trails across the narrow valley in Glacier National Park. Across the highway from the campground, Bear Creek harbors brook trout and westslope cutthroat trout. Five miles to the west, the creek collides with the Middle Fork of the Flathead River as it roars out of the Bob Marshall Wilderness Area, and a 3.5-mile trail climbs to Tranquil Basin. At the Bear Creek river access site, rafters and anglers launch to float a portion or all of the 44 miles to the North Fork of the Flathead River. Hikers drive two miles east to catch the trail up Elk Mountain in Glacier National Park. The 3.5-mile trail slogs up 3,355 feet for top-of-the-world views. From the campground, a trail also leads to Elk Lake (5.9 miles) and Moose Lake (8.2 miles).

© BECKY LOMAX

hiking down from Elk Mountain on Glacier's southern end

The small campground tucks into the forest adjacent to Devil Creek. One loop holds all the campsites, with those at the top of the loop being farthest from the highway. All of the sites are shaded under firs and lodgepole pines. The small sites are spread out, but you can still see neighboring campers. You'll hear both highway and railroad noise in the campground. Due to the limited campgrounds along Highway 2, plan on arriving before 3 P.M. during midsummer to claim a campsite.

Campsites, facilities: The campground has 14 RV or tent campsites that can fit RVs up to 40 feet. Facilities include picnic tables, fire rings with grills, drinking water, vault toilets, and campground hosts. Pack out your trash. Firewood is not provided, but you're free to scour the surrounding forest for downed limbs. Leashed pets are permitted. A wheelchair-accessible toilet is available.

Reservations, fees: No reservations are accepted. Campsites cost $10. Cash or check. Open late May–mid-September.

Directions: On Highway 2 between Essex and Marias Pass, turn south at milepost 190 into the campground.

GPS Coordinates: N 48° 15.103' W 113° 27.919'

Contact: Flathead National Forest, Hungry Horse District, 10 Hungry Horse Dr., Hungry Horse, MT 59919, 406/387-3800, www.fs.fed.us/r1/flathead/.

48 GLACIER MEADOW RV PARK

Scenic rating: 7

on Highway 2 in Flathead National Forest

Located at 4,450 feet in elevation on Highway 2, Glacier Meadow RV Park has Flathead National Forest on its south boundary and Glacier National Park a mile to the north. From the campground, river rafters and anglers head seven miles to the west to the Middle Fork of the Flathead River. Hikers drive less than 0.5 mile to reach the Elk Mountain Trailhead and its strenuous 3,355-foot, 3.5-mile climb to an old lookout site with views into Glacier National Park. For those traveling with RVs over 21 feet long that are not permitted over Going-to-the-Sun Road, the red buses stop at Glacier Meadow to pick up riders for the 8.5-hour tour that loops over Logan Pass. Nearby Skyland Road is also available for ATV riding.

The campground, which sits on 58 acres, adjoins a large meadow that attracts elk in May and June. A gravel road connects the campsites, and for large RVs, the campground's wide-open large grassy field makes for easy parking. Sites in the open have full views of the surrounding peaks. Some sites along the campground's east side receive morning shade from a mixed forest of firs and lodgepoles. The 25 pull-through sites have electric and water hookups; 16 sites along the woods have electricity only. Only some of the sites have picnic tables.

Campsites, facilities: The campground has 41 RV campsites, which can fit RVs up to 40 feet, and 16 tent campsites. Facilities include picnic tables, drinking water, flush toilets, showers, a launderette, a shuffleboard floor, horseshoe pits, wireless Internet, a playground, and a disposal station. The management can also provide horse boarding. Leashed pets are permitted. A wheelchair-accessible toilet is available.

Reservations, fees: Reservations are accepted. Hookups cost $30–32. Tent sites cost $20. Rates include two people; each additional person is charged $5. Kids 10 years old and under camp for free. The Montana bed tax of 7 percent will be added to the bill. Cash or credit card. Open mid-May–mid-September.

Directions: From East Glacier, drive 16 miles west on Highway 2. From West Glacier, drive 44 miles east on Highway 2. Turn south between mileposts 191 and 192.

GPS Coordinates: N 48° 15.981' W 113° 26.605'

Contact: Glacier Meadow RV Park, P.O. Box 124, East Glacier, MT 59936, 406/226-4479, www.glaciermeadowrvpark.com.

49 SUMMIT

Scenic rating: 7

at Marias Pass in Lewis and Clark National Forest

Of all the passes crossing the Rocky Mountains, Marias Pass is the lowest at 5,220 feet. It sits in Lewis and Clark National Forest across from Glacier National Park. Ironically, the pass eluded Lewis and Clark. John F. Stevens discovered it in 1889 while looking for a route for the Great Northern Railway to cut through the mountains. The pass also marks the Continental Divide, the split where waters flow to the Atlantic and Pacific, and the place where geologists first discovered the Lewis Overthrust Fault, where 1.6 billion-year-old rocks buried younger layers from the dinosaur age. Departing across the highway, the Continental Divide Trail enters Glacier Park and passes Three Bears Lake in 0.6 mile—a good place to fish, spot moose, and go bird-watching. At 1.1 miles, the trail intersects with Autumn Creek Trail, which parallels the front range of peaks.

The small forested campground tucks into the lodgepole pines for partial shade on the east side of the Marias Pass rest area. Both the highway and the railroad tracks pass in front of the campground, admitting noise all night long, especially from the railway. Bring earplugs for a good night's sleep. A few sites on the north side of the loop have peek-a-boo views of Glacier's peaks. Because campgrounds are limited along Highway 2, plan on arriving before 3 P.M. during midsummer to claim a campsite.

Campsites, facilities: The campground has 17 RV or tent campsites that can fit midsized RVs. Facilities include picnic tables, fire rings with grills, vault toilets, and potable water. Pack out your trash. Firewood is not provided, but you're free to scour the surrounding national forest for downed limbs. Leashed pets are permitted. A wheelchair-accessible toilet is available.

Reservations, fees: No reservations are accepted. Camping costs $10. Cash or check. Open early June–mid-September.

Directions: From East Glacier, drive Highway 2 west for 11.3 miles to Marias Pass at milepost 198. From West Glacier, drive 48.9 miles east. On the east side of the Marias Pass rest area, locate the campground entrance.

GPS Coordinates: N 48° 19.121' W 113° 21.109'

Contact: Lewis and Clark National Forest, Rocky Mountain Ranger District, 1102 N. Main Ave., P.O. Box 340, Choteau, MT 59422, 406/466-5341, fax 406/466-2237, www.fs.fed.us/r1/lewisclark.

50 Y LAZY R RV PARK

Scenic rating: 7

in East Glacier on the Blackfeet Reservation

South of the main road through East Glacier, this campground appears at first to be little more than a large grassy field, but the views of Glacier's peaks, from the Calf Robe to Dancing Lady—especially at sunset—make up for the setting. From the campground, a quick two-block walk puts you in tiny East Glacier, where you'll find groceries, a few gift shops, three restaurants, and a post office. Walk under the railroad overpass to see the historic East Glacier Park Hotel, with its monstrous Douglas firs in the lobby. The lodge's golf course (its nine holes are named for former Blackfeet chiefs) has the oldest grass greens in Montana. Drive 12 miles north to Two Medicine Lake for picnicking, hiking, fishing, boating, and sightseeing. Two hiking trails depart from the north side of town; pick up Blackfeet Tribal recreation licenses before hiking these.

The campground covers three acres, most of which is mowed grass with only a couple of trees for shade. The campsites with the trees tend to get snagged early. Sites on the south end at the edge of the bluff overlook Midvale Creek and grab views of the mountains, too. A gravel road accesses the tight sites, and while the overall campground is level, the individual sites can present a challenge for leveling an RV. You can hear both the highway and the railroad tracks from the campground. Be aware that East Glacier's water supply often requires boiling for purification. Ask when you check in about the current water quality and any "boil orders."

Campsites, facilities: The campground has 30 RV campsites that can fit large RVs, plus 10 tent sites. Hookups are available for sewer, water, and electricity. Facilities include picnic tables, flush toilets, coin-operated showers, a playground, a disposal station, and a huge coin-operated launderette with 17 commercial washers.

Reservations, fees: Reservations are accepted. Hookups cost $20–23. Tent sites cost $18. The Montana bed tax is included in the price. Cash or check. Open June–mid-September.

Directions: In East Glacier, coming from the east on Highway 2, turn left at the fourth street. From the west on Highway 2, take the first right in town. Then, drive two blocks south to Washington Street and turn right to reach Lindhe Avenue. Turn left for 1.5 blocks.

The campground sits west of the junction of Lindhe Avenue and Meade Street.
GPS Coordinates: N 48° 26.405' W 113° 12.958'
Contact: Lazy R RV Park, P.O. Box 146, East Glacier, MT 59936, 406/226-5505.

51 TWO MEDICINE

Scenic rating: 10

on Pray Lake in the southeast corner of Glacier National Park

BEST (

Huddling below the massive hulk of Rising Wolf Mountain, Two Medicine Campground sits on Pray Lake, a small outlet pond for the much larger Two Medicine Lake. Sitting a mile high, the campground offers hikers, sightseers, boaters, and anglers a taste of Glacier's less-crowded realm. From the campground, the 18.8-mile Dawson-Pitamakin Trail loops around Rising Wolf, along the Continental Divide. A mile up the road, the Scenic Point Trail climbs 3.1 miles to a bluff overlooking

© BECKY LOMAX

Two Medicine Campground surrounds Pray Lake in Glacier.

the lakes and staring out onto the plains. The *Sinopah* tours the lake several times daily for sightseers, and rental canoes, kayaks, and motorboats are available near the boat dock. The historical dining hall from the park's early days now houses a camp store, and the staffed ranger station keeps track of bear sightings on a large map.

Set in stunted subalpine firs, the quiet campground curls around Pray Lake, a good fishing and swimming outlet pool from Two Medicine Lake. At least half of the campsites at Two Medicine have stunning views—most of Rising Wolf. You can sit in your campsite with a pair of binoculars and watch mountain goats or grizzly bears crawl around the slopes. Find these sites in loops A and C. Sites 92–100 yield closer views of the slopes. Due to the campground's popularity, plan on arriving before noon during July and August.

Campsites, facilities: The campground has 99 RV or tent campsites. Only 13 sites can accommodate RVs or trailer combinations up to 35 feet. Facilities include picnic tables, fire rings with grills, flush toilets, drinking water, a disposal station, large group campsites, interpretive programs, shared hiker and biker campsites, and campground hosts. Primitive camping (late September–October) offers only pit toilets, and there's no potable water. Leashed pets are permitted. A wheelchair-accessible toilet is available.

Reservations, fees: No reservations are accepted. Campsites cost $20 late May–mid-September. Primitive camping costs $10. Hikers and bikers pay $5 per person. Cash, check, or credit card.

Directions: From East Glacier, drive four miles north on Highway 49 and then swing left onto Two Medicine Road for 7.5 miles. Turn right at the ranger station to enter the campground.

GPS Coordinates: N 48° 29.301' W 113° 22.045'

Contact: Glacier National Park, P.O. Box 128, West Glacier, MT 59936, 406/888-7800, www.nps.gov/glac.

52 CUT BANK

Scenic rating: 7

in Cut Bank Valley on the east side of Glacier National Park

At 5,200 feet in a rugged, remote valley on Glacier's east side, Cut Bank sits between East Glacier and St. Mary. Two barriers deter RVs from going to Cut Bank—the narrow curvy Highway 89 and the five miles of potholed dirt road leading to the campground. The campground is a favorite for tenters, who relish the quiet and the campground's real rusticity. A 7.2-mile trail departs up-valley from here towards Triple Divide Pass, so named for the peak above that feeds water to the Atlantic, Pacific, and Hudson Bay drainages. A less strenuous hike ends in six miles at Medicine Grizzly Lake, a lure for anglers and bears alike because of its 12-inch rainbow trout. Frequently, the lake closes because of bear sightings. Another spur leads to Atlantic Creek Falls at 4.1 miles; add on another 2.5 miles to reach Morning Star Lake, in a small cirque below cliffs that hold a golden eagle nest and mountain goat paths.

Tucked under a deep shaded forest, the ultra-quiet campground stays cool even on hot August days. Atlantic Creek burbles adjacent to the campground. Unfortunately, most of the undergrowth beneath the canopy is gone, leaving little privacy between sites. The sites are small but do have room for tents. Those with small RVs may find it a challenge to level them.

Campsites, facilities: The campground has 14 RV and tent campsites that can fit only small RVs. The park service discourages RVs and trailers from using this campground. Facilities include picnic tables, fire rings with grills, and pit toilets. Bring your own water, or boil or filter water taken from the creek for drinking. Bring firewood, as gathering even downed limbs is prohibited in the park. Pack out your trash. Leashed pets are permitted.

Reservations, fees: No reservations are accepted. The fee is $10 per night. Cash, check, or credit card. Open late May–mid-September.

Directions: From St. Mary, drive 14.5 miles south on Highway 89. From East Glacier, drive 13.5 miles north on Highway 49 and 5.5 miles north on Highway 89. At the campground sign on Highway 89, turn west onto the dirt road for five miles.

GPS Coordinates: N 48° 36.116' W 113° 23.020'

Contact: Glacier National Park, P.O. Box 128, West Glacier, MT 59936, 406/888-7800, www.nps.gov/glac.

53 ASPENWOOD RESORT

Scenic rating: 8

west of Browning on the Blackfeet Reservation

Located west of Browning below Glacier's eastern front range, the campground and resort sit on the Blackfeet Reservation, where just about the only sound is the incessant wind. On the prairie to the east, Browning has a little over 1,000 residents. The small Museum of the Plains Indians provides the best look at the tribe's history, with dioramas and clothing made with phenomenal beadwork. The Blackfeet Heritage Center and Gallery also provides a venue for locals to market their art. Recently, the tribe built the Glacier Peaks Casino, a 33,000-square-foot gaming facility with more than 300 slot machines. For four days each year, the annual North American Indian Days festival brings out dancing, singing, storytelling, and a rodeo during the second weekend in July, at the powwow grounds behind the museum. Two beaver ponds offer fishing, paddleboating, wildlife-watching, and hiking. The resort also arranges for Native American guided fishing trips, tours, and horseback riding.

The resort includes a small lodge with rooms, a restaurant, and a campground. The resort's restaurant—the Outlaw Grill—serves breakfast, lunch, and dinner, and does takeout orders if you prefer to eat at your campsite. The RV sites are gravel pull-throughs surrounded by grass with no trees; however, the open venue allows for views of Glacier's peaks. Tent sites are tucked in between the aspen groves for shade and wind protection.

Campsites, facilities: The campground has 10 RV campsites and eight tent campsites. The pull-through RV sites can fit large rigs; eight of the RV spaces have hookups, with two for dry camping. Hookups are available for electricity and water only. Facilities include picnic tables, fire pits, flush toilets, showers, a disposal station, firewood, a game and exercise room, and paddleboats. Leashed pets are permitted. Horse boarding is also available.

Reservations, fees: Reservations are accepted and are highly recommended for powwow weekends—the second weekends of July and August. Hookups cost $30–35. Tent sites cost $18. Cash, check, or credit card. Open mid-May–mid-October.

Directions: From the junction of Highway 2 and Highway 89 in Browning, drive west on Highway 89 for 9.5 miles. From Kiowa Junction, drive 2.3 miles east on Highway 89. The resort sits on the north side of the road.

GPS Coordinates: N 48° 32.467' W 113° 13.514'

Contact: Aspenwood Resort, HC-72, Box 5150, Hwy. 89, Browning, MT 59417, 406/338-3009, www.aspenwoodresort.com.

54 LODGEPOLE TIPI VILLAGE

Scenic rating: 9

west of Browning on the Blackfeet Reservation

Located on the Blackfeet Reservation below Glacier's eastern front range, the Lodgepole

Tipi Village offers a different type of camping—camping in a tipi with cultural insight into the traditional life of the Blackfeet. The tipi village sprawls across 200 acres of wildflower prairie with a spring-fed lake and unobstructed views of Glacier's southern ramparts. A small herd of Spanish mustangs runs wild on the property. The village also contracts with Blackfeet guides to offer horseback riding trips on the rolling foothills below Glacier's peaks and fly fishing for rainbow trout on the reservation's renowned lakes. The owner also leads cultural history tours to historical buffalo jumps, tipi rings, and medicine lodges.

Camping in the tipi village is expensive, but you're paying for the cultural experience provided by its Blackfeet owner, Darrell Norman. Tour his small gallery, or add on an art workshop to make a drum or parfleche. Breakfast and a Blackfeet wild game dinner are also available by reservation. With a campfire in the tipi, it glows under the night sky. The sun brightens the inside early when the sunrise hits the prairie. Wind and the hooves of the Spanish mustangs are the only sounds you'll hear.

Campsites, facilities: Camping is permitted only in tipis here—not RVs nor tents. The seven double-walled lodgepole tipis remain cool in the summer heat but retain warmth in cooler months. Each tipi centers around a rock-ringed fire pit (firewood provided). Facilities include picnic tables, flush toilets, and showers. A large communal campfire is sheltered from wind by a wooden arbor built to resemble a traditional Blackfeet ceremonial lodge. Bring your own sleeping bag and pad as well as a flashlight. Tipis have no floors, so your sleeping pad will go on the ground.

Reservations, fees: Reservations are wise—especially for Browning powwow weekends during the second weekends of July and August. The first person in the tipi is charged $50 per night, and for each additional person its $15. Children under 12 years old are charged $8. Check or credit card. Open May–September.

Directions: From Browning, drive 2.5 miles west on Highway 89. Locate the entrance on the south side of the road.

GPS Coordinates: N 48° 33.261' W 113° 4.492'

Contact: Lodgepole Tipi Village, P.O. Box 1832, Browning, MT 59417, 406/338-2787, www.blackfeetculturecamp.com.

ROCKY MOUNTAIN FRONT

© BECKY LOMAX

BEST CAMPGROUNDS

In eastern Montana, the sage-scented prairie

churns forever. With very few trees, it rolls westward, broken only by a pot-hole pond here or a river there. But in one abrupt sweep, the Rocky Mountain Front pops up like a wall, looming as monstrous snow-clad purple peaks. For campers, the Front yields a wondrous combination of campgrounds where the flat prairie collides with the rugged peaks of the Continental Divide.

The open prairie dotted with cow towns offers wind-blown places to camp along reservoirs, while long river valleys snake into the mountains with shaded, more-protected campgrounds. The Front attracts campers for fishing, boating, hiking, horseback riding, hunting, and mountain biking. It also acts as a gateway into the Bob Marshall Wilderness Area, where 9,000-foot-high summits flank a towering 22-mile-long, 1,000-foot-high limestone escarpment called the Chinese Wall.

Prepare for weather extremes while camping and recreating on the Front. High winds contort ridgeline trees into avant garde sculptures, blow trains off their tracks in winter, and cause white-knuckled driving in RVs. The Front also fluctuates wildly in temperatures, having set records for swinging up to 100 degrees in 24 hours, and Rogers Pass claims fame as one of the top 10 coldest spots in the world.

How ironic that such a harsh environment produces quirks that sustain abundant wildlife. The Front's winds turn it into one of the largest golden eagle migratory flyways in North America. The national forests, game preserves, and wildlife refuges burgeon with elk, bighorn sheep, deer, grizzly bears, mountain lions, coyotes, pronghorn antelope, and birds.

From the Blackfeet Reservation in the north to the Canyon Ferry Reservoir in the south, large tracts of unpopulated public land with campgrounds flank towns. Helena, Montana's capital, houses only 28,000 people — a population comparable to 3 percent of the downtown San Francisco population. Great Falls, which holds double the population of Helena, is the largest city in the area, but most of the Front's population is centered in tiny towns like Choteau (pronounced "SHOW-toe"), which has a mere 1,800 residents.

Campers exploring the Rocky Mountain Front find themselves confined to minimal roads. Only one freeway (I-15) runs north to south through the prairie, linking up Great Falls with Helena. A narrow, more-scenic two-lane highway (Highway 89) that requires several hours to drive parallels the freeway farther west, connecting the tiny towns closer to the Front mountain ranges. Routes over the Continental Divide dwindle to two: Highway 200 squeezes over Rogers Pass north of Helena, and Highway 12 scoots even higher over MacDonald Pass west of Helena. Beyond that, the more-common paved, skinny two-laners and the more-pervasive washboard gravel or potholed dirt routes comprise the web of the Front's roadways to reach campgrounds.

On the Front, waterways draw the most campers. Upper Missouri River dams create reams of reservoirs, each holding shoreline campgrounds that fill on hot summer days with water-skiers, sailors, canoeists, Jet Skiers, and swimmers. Holter Lake butts up against the Beartooth Wildlife Management Area, providing opportunities for watching elk and raptors. Hauser Lake forms the entrance to Gates of the Mountains Wilderness, the route of Lewis and Clark. Canyon Ferry Lake, the largest, sees the most use of any lake in the state. Anglers go after its rainbow trout, walleye, perch, and ling, as do the bald eagles that nest here.

Those looking for more remote places to camp wrestle the bumpy dirt roads that creep into the Lewis and Clark or Helena National Forest. The forests form several doorways to the immense Bob Marshall Wilderness Complex — a roadless area the size of Rhode Island. The wilderness is crisscrossed with hiking and horse-packing trails that snake past bighorn sheep herds and climb through wildflower fields to precipice-clinging lookouts. Streams teem with native trout, and big game attracts hunters. Front country campers find Forest Service campgrounds the norm, rather than manicured RV parks.

The Rocky Mountain Front is unique. From its glimmering peaks to its golden prairie echoing with the lone cry of red-tailed hawk, it yields a rare beauty that hasn't been marred by the creep of million-dollar homes.

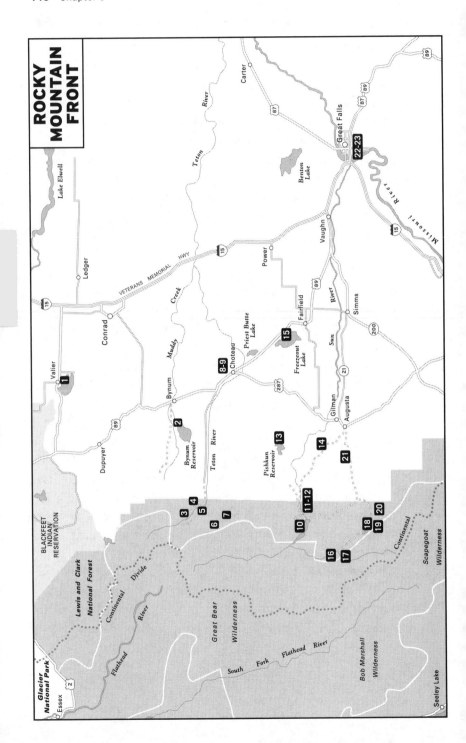

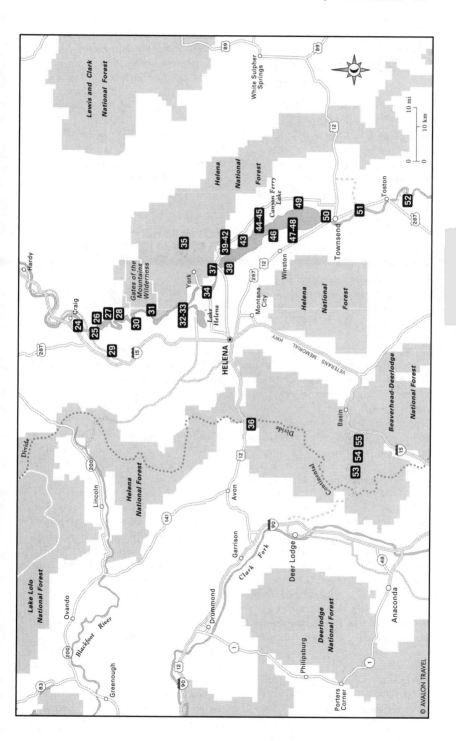

1 LAKE FRANCES

Scenic rating: 7

in Valier on the Blackfeet Indian Reservation

At an elevation of 3,800 feet on the prairie on the Blackfeet Indian Reservation, Lake Frances attracts campers for water recreation. In summer, swimming, fishing, boating, waterskiing, sailing, windsurfing, and Jet Skiing are favored. In winter, ice fishing and snowmobiling are popular. The lake has three boat ramps and docks—on the east end, in Valier, and on the west end—but as water levels drop in late summer, sometimes launching can be difficult. Anglers go after walleye, northern pike, and yellow perch. From the hiking and biking trail along the lakeshore, you get a view of the Rocky Mountains in the distance.

The campground is composed of three interconnected loops, all with back-in parking pads. Eleven sites sit right on the shoreline, but several others also have lake views. Perimeter trees provide spots of shade in the sunny campground. Sites are close together, offering little privacy, but with its location across the little-used air strip from town and away from the highway, the campground is quiet. An additional overflow primitive campground with only a pit toilet is at the southeast end of the lake.

Campsites, facilities: The campground has 50 RV campsites that can accommodate large RVs and 10 primitive tent campsites. Facilities include picnic tables, fire rings with grills, flush toilets, a disposal station, garbage service, a boat ramp, a fish-cleaning station, and a playground. Leashed pets are permitted.

Reservations, fees: Reservations are not accepted. Campsites cost $15 for electrical hookups; tent sites cost $7. Cash or check. Open year-round.

Directions: From Highway 44 on the west end of Valier, turn south onto Teton Avenue, which becomes Lake Frances Road. Drive 0.9 mile to the campground entrance on the right. To find the primitive overflow campground on the lake's southeast end, drive 2.2 miles east of Valier on Highway 44 and turn south onto Division Street for 2.1 miles. The campground is on the right just before the dam.

GPS Coordinates: N 48° 18.046' W 112° 15.591'

Contact: Valier Area Development Corporation, P.O. Box 568, Valier, MT 59486, 406/279-3600.

2 BYNUM RESERVOIR

Scenic rating: 7

west of Bynum northwest of Choteau

The 3,205-acre Bynum Reservoir is one of the myriad of small lakes dotting the prairie of the Rocky Mountain Front. Sitting at 4,198 feet in elevation west of the small village of Bynum, the lake draws anglers for its rainbow trout and yellow perch. It also contains walleye, but a fish consumption advisory is in effect for that species here due to mercury buildup. A concrete boat ramp is available, but it is unusable during drought conditions. Contact the Region 4 office for the reservoir's current water levels. Find a small general store, post office, and the Two Medicine Dinosaur Center in Bynum. The center displays bones from the world's longest dinosaur, a model skeleton of a seismosaurus, and the first baby dinosaur remains found in North America. The Blackleaf Wildlife Management Area—home to mountain goats, elk, and golden eagles—is about 25 minutes to the west.

The campground is primitive and part of the fishing access site run by the state. The sites line up along the shore of the reservoir in a hot, sunny, treeless, grassy area along the dirt campground road. The campground and lake yield expansive views of the Front range peaks in the distance, but when winds crop up, no trees are available as windbreaks. The campground is far enough away from the highway that the only sounds you'll hear are the wind, the waterfowl, and sometimes the western chorus frog. When water levels drop low in August, the rim becomes dusty.

Campsites, facilities: The campground has four RV and tent campsites that can accommodate only smaller RVs. Facilities include picnic tables, fire rings with grills, vault toilets, and boat ramp. Pack out your trash. Leashed pets are permitted. A wheelchair-accessible toilet is available.

Reservations, fees: Reservations are not accepted. Campsites cost $7 with a Montana fishing license and $12 without a Montana fishing license. Cash or check. Open year-round.

Directions: From Bynum at the signed turnoff, drive west on the dirt county road for 4.2 miles. Veer left at the signed fork for 0.6 mile, and turn left for 1.2 miles to reach the reservoir. Follow the road 0.6 mile eastward to reach the fishing access site and campground.

GPS Coordinates: N 47° 57.593' W 112° 24.382'

Contact: Montana Fish, Wildlife, and Parks, Region 4, 4600 Giant Springs Rd., Great Falls, MT 59405, 406/454-5840, http://fwp.mt.gov.

3 WEST FORK

Scenic rating: 7

on the West Fork of the Teton River in Lewis and Clark National Forest

At 5,700 feet in elevation, the West Fork campground sits at the confluence of the West Fork with the Teton River in a narrow, forested valley dwarfed by high peaks. Hiking trails with trailheads located within 0.25 mile depart to several destinations. Mount Wright requires a steep four-mile climb to reach the summit and its panoramic wilderness views, bighorn sheep, and mountain goats. Three other trails depart for drainages in the Bob Marshall Wilderness Area—the shortest is the West Fork Trail (#114), which climbs over Teton Pass at the Continental Divide in about seven miles. The wilderness boundary is only one mile from the campground. Brown and rainbow trout as well as mountain whitefish inhabit both the West Fork and the Teton River. The campground is a favorite for hunters in the fall.

The access to reach the forested campground requires long miles of dirt road driving, but the reward is solitude, along with the sound of the West Fork of the Teton River. The Forest Service discourages RVs and trailers from the campground; however, smaller RVs and truck campers will fit on the dirt parking pads and narrow road. Campsites are a mix of shade and partial sun.

Campsites, facilities: The campground has six tent sites that also work for small RVs. Facilities include picnic tables, fire rings with grills, pit toilets, and a hand pump for drinking water. Pack out your trash. Leashed pets are permitted.

Reservations, fees: No reservations are accepted. Camping is free. Open late May–November.

Directions: From four miles north of Choteau, turn off Highway 89 at milepost 46.5, heading west on Teton River Road (also Forest Road 144) toward Teton Pass Ski Area. Drive 33 miles to the campground, climbing up to the ski area and dropping again to the river. (The pavement turns to gravel and dirt, loaded with washboards and potholes, around milepost 18.)

GPS Coordinates: N 47° 57.741' W 112° 48.474'

Contact: Lewis and Clark National Forest, Rocky Mountain Ranger District, 1102 N. Main Ave., P.O. Box 340, Choteau, MT 59422, 406/466-5341, fax 406/466-2237, www.fs.fed.us/r1/lewisclark.

4 ELKO

Scenic rating: 7

on the West Fork of the Teton River in Lewis and Clark National Forest

At 5,300 feet in elevation, Elko Campground sits in the Lewis and Clark National Forest about five air miles east of the boundary of the Bob Marshall Wilderness. The campground isn't necessarily a destination in itself, but works as a good overflow site should Cave Mountain fill up. Across the road from the campground, the exceptionally clear waters of the West Fork of the Teton River contain rainbow, brown, and brook trout. The North Fork Teton River Trail (#107) departs nearby and heads four miles through Box Canyon. It's a cool trail for hot days since it requires fording the river several times. The campground is popular with hunters in fall.

The campground sits very close to the dusty road, although road traffic abates into silence after dark. Two of the sites are well-used, with broad spaces for tents. The third, less-used site is overgrown with thimbleberry and thistle. Tall firs partially shade the campsites, which sit very close together. The site on the right as you drive in sits near a seasonal stream.

Campsites, facilities: The campground has three RV or tent campsites. Due to the uneven, rocky, short parking pads and little turnaround room, only small RVs can squeeze in here. Facilities include picnic tables, fire rings with grills, and a pit toilet. No water is available; bring your own, or if you use river water, boil or purify it first. Pack out your trash. Leashed pets are permitted.

Reservations, fees: No reservations are accepted. Camping is free. Open late May–November.

Directions: From Choteau, drive about four miles north on Highway 89 to milepost 46.5. Turn west onto Teton River Road (Forest Road 144) and drive 27 miles. The pavement will turn to gravel and dirt with copious washboards around milepost 18. The campground is unsigned on the east side of the road.

GPS Coordinates: N 47° 55.476' W 112° 45.792'

Contact: Lewis and Clark National Forest, Rocky Mountain Ranger District, 1102 N. Main Ave., P.O. Box 340, Choteau, MT 59422, 406/466-5341, fax 406/466-2237, www.fs.fed.us/r1/lewisclark.

5 CAVE MOUNTAIN

Scenic rating: 8

on the West Fork of the Teton River in Lewis and Clark National Forest

BEST (

At 5,200 feet in elevation, Cave Mountain Campground sits in the Lewis and Clark National Forest at the confluence of the Middle Fork with the West Fork of Teton River—both trout fisheries in exceptionally clear waters after spring runoff. The Bob Marshall Wilderness is accessed via the Route Creek Trail (#108) over a high pass six miles up the Middle Fork. The trailhead, which is equipped for stock (hitch rails, feeding trough, loading ramp) is a five-minute drive up the road. The same trail also connects with the Lonesome Ridge Trail (#154), which crosses into the South Fork of the Teton River drainage. The campground is popular with hunters in fall.

The quiet campground is surrounded by a rail fence to keep out cattle grazing under permit in the area. Aspens, pines, and firs shade many of the campsites, with low vegetation between them. However, sites are spread out to offer privacy, especially site 14 at the end of the loop. Seven sites overlook the river; the others back up to the hillside. Sites 8, 10, and 12 offer views of the area's dramatic cliffs and better river views. Sites 3 and 4 have spaces for large or multiple tents.

Campsites, facilities: The campground has 14 RV or tent campsites. The gravel back-in

© BECKY LOMAX

The Teton River flows from the Bob Marshall Wilderness past Cave Mountain Campground on the Rocky Mountain Front.

parking pads can fit RVs up to 50 feet. Facilities include picnic tables, fire rings with grills, vault toilets, and drinking water. Pack out your trash. Leashed pets are permitted. One vault toilet is wheelchair accessible.

Reservations, fees: No reservations are accepted. Campsites cost $6. Cash or check. Open late May–November.

Directions: From Choteau, drive four miles north on Highway 89 to milepost 46.5. Turn west onto Teton River Road (Forest Road 144) and drive 22.6 miles. The pavement will turn to gravel and dirt with copious washboards around milepost 18. At the sign for the campground, turn left and drive for 0.4 mile. The entrance road crosses a one-lane bridge, swings right, crosses a second short bridge, and continues straight past the next junction to the campground entrance on the right.

GPS Coordinates: N 47° 53.399' W 112° 43.595'

Contact: Lewis and Clark National Forest, Rocky Mountain Ranger District, 1102 N. Main Ave., P.O. Box 340, Choteau, MT 59422, 406/466-5341, fax 406/466-2237, www.fs.fed.us/r1/lewisclark.

6 MILL FALLS

Scenic rating: 8

on the South Fork of the Teton River in Lewis and Clark National Forest

BEST (

Mill Falls Campground sits in the Lewis and Clark National Forest near the South Fork of the Teton River, a trout fishery. From the campground, you can hike 0.1 mile to its namesake waterfall. A popular trailhead departs 1.5 miles farther up the road for the small scenic alpine Our Lake (2.5 miles) and Headquarters Pass (3 miles), which marks the entrance to the Bob Marshall Wilderness. The Headquarters Pass Trail is also used to scramble up the Class 4 slopes to the summit of Rocky Mountain, one of the highest peaks in the region. The area also is popular for fall hunting.

The tiny, shaded, quiet campground is tucked back off the road. Its entrance looks like a jeep trail, and its narrow, rocky, potholed, rutted road with overhanging branches can only accommodate smaller RVs. Trailers will not have room to turn around. Sites 3 and

4 pair up close together on the right as you drive in. Also close together, sites 1 and 2 sit at the back of the campground, with large tent spaces adjacent to a small creek.

Campsites, facilities: The campground has four RV or tent campsites. The small uneven, rocky parking pads, however, can only fit smaller camper-truck RVs. Facilities include picnic tables, fire rings with grills, and a pit toilet. No drinking water is provided; bring your own. Pack out your trash. Leashed pets are permitted.

Reservations, fees: No reservations are accepted. Camping is free. Open late May–November.

Directions: From Choteau, drive four miles north on Highway 89 to milepost 46.5. Turn west onto Teton River Road (Forest Road 144) and drive 16.9 miles to the Ear Mountain Outstanding Area sign. Turn left onto the gravel road and cross the single-lane bridge. Immediately after the bridge, turn right onto South Fork Road. Drive 3.1 miles, veering right at the Nature Conservancy Pine Butte Guest Ranch sign. Follow the bumpy, washboard Forest Road 109 for 5.4 miles to the signed campground entrance on the right.

GPS Coordinates: N 47° 51.519' W 112° 46.389'

Contact: Lewis and Clark National Forest, Rocky Mountain Ranger District, 1102 N. Main Ave., P.O. Box 340, Choteau, MT 59422, 406/466-5341, fax 406/466-2237, www.fs.fed.us/r1/lewisclark.

7 GREEN GULCH

Scenic rating: 7

on the South Fork of the Teton River in Lewis and Clark National Forest

Tiny Green Gulch primitive campground sits at 5,560 feet in elevation in the Lewis and Clark National Forest near the South Fork of the Teton River. The river is a trout fishery with rainbows, brook, and brown trout. The 12-mile-long Green Gulch Trail (#127) tours a deeply wooded valley after fording the river and reaches a pass at 7,232 feet, where it drops into Sheep Gulch. The area is popular for fall hunting. It also has quick access within a 10-minute drive to the trailhead for Our Lake (2.5 miles) and Headquarters Pass (3 miles)—both much more scenic trails than the Green Gulch trail.

The shaded, quiet, primitive campground is tucked on the Green Gulch side road closer to the South Fork of the Teton River than Mill Falls. Both sites offer ample room for tents, and with only two sites, you get privacy.

Campsites, facilities: The campground has two RV or tent campsites. The small parking pads, however, can only fit smaller RVs and trailers. Facilities include picnic tables, fire rings with grills, and a pit toilet. No drinking water is provided; bring your own. Pack out your trash. Leashed pets are permitted.

Reservations, fees: No reservations are accepted. Camping is free. Open late May–November.

Directions: From Choteau, drive four miles north on Highway 89 to milepost 46.5. Turn west onto Teton River Road (Forest Road 144) and drive 16.9 miles to the Ear Mountain Outstanding Area sign. Turn left onto the gravel road and cross the single-lane bridge. Immediately after the bridge, turn right onto South Fork Road. Drive 3.1 miles, veering right at the Nature Conservancy Pine Butte Guest Ranch sign. Follow the bumpy, washboard Forest Road 109 for 4.4 miles to Green Gulch Road and veer left onto it for 0.2 mile to the campground.

GPS Coordinates: N 47° 51.839' W 112° 45.466'

Contact: Lewis and Clark National Forest, Rocky Mountain Ranger District, 1102 N. Main Ave., P.O. Box 340, Choteau, MT 59422, 406/466-5341, fax 406/466-2237, www.fs.fed.us/r1/lewisclark.

8 CHOTEAU

Scenic rating: 4

in Choteau west of Great Falls

Located in Choteau, the campground is convenient for exploring the town. The community swimming pool is within one mile, and the nine-hole golf course is less than 0.5 mile away, north of the campground across a field. Open daily in summer, the Old Trail Museum on the north end of town includes fossils, Native American artifacts, pioneer history, and wildlife exhibits. Choteau's Rodeo Grounds host rodeo events and music concerts. Eureka Reservoir, eight miles northwest on Teton Canyon Road, provides fishing and boating. Four miles south of town, Freezeout Lake annually draws bird-watchers in March, when the lake crowds with 300,000 snow geese and 10,000 tundra swans on their migration north, but birding is also good in the fall.

The campground sits on the outskirts of town, but right on the highway. However, the route isn't a major trucking thoroughfare, so road noise dwindles at night. A handful of small trees dot the campground, but most of the grassy campsites are open, sunny, and close to each other. Because it lacks trees for windbreaks, the campground can see hefty winds. From the campground, views span pastures and neighboring houses.

Campsites, facilities: The campground has 55 RV and 20 tent campsites. Facilities include picnic tables, fire rings, drinking water, flush toilets, showers, a launderette, a store, a disposal station, a playground, a game room, horseshoe pits, and hookups for sewer, water, and electricity. Leashed pets are permitted.

Reservations, fees: Reservations are accepted. Hookups cost $28–32. Tent sites cost $18. Montana bed tax will be added. Cash, check, or credit card. Open mid-April–mid-November.

Directions: From Choteau at the junction of Highways 89 and 221, drive 0.75 mile east on Highway 221 to the campground. The campground sits on the north side of the road. GPS Coordinates: N 47° 48.956' W 112° 9.985'

Contact: Choteau Campground, 85 Hwy. 221, Choteau, MT 59422, 406/466-2615 or 800/562-4156.

9 CHOTEAU CITY PARK

Scenic rating: 4

in Choteau west of Great Falls

The city park campground is one block off the downtown main strip in Choteau, an easy option for those bicycling the Rocky Mountain Front. A two-block walk leads to restaurants downtown and the community swimming pool. The nine-hole golf course is less than one mile away. Open daily in summer, the Old Trail Museum on the north end of town includes fossils, Native American artifacts, pioneer history, and wildlife exhibits. Choteau's Rodeo Grounds host rodeo events and music concerts. Eureka Reservoir, eight miles northwest on Teton Canyon Road, provides fishing and boating. Four miles south of town, Freezeout Lake draws bird-watchers in March, when the lake crowds with 300,000 snow geese and 10,000 tundra swans on their migration north, but also offers birding in the fall.

The campground is part of Choteau's city park. Nine of the campsites sit on the hot west side, with views of a warehouse and grain silos and only a few perimeter willow and cottonwood trees for shade. The other five campsites are more secluded, tucked on the east side under bigger, thicker trees next to a tiny creek. Due to the shade, these sites usually have green grass while the others are brown dry grass. A gravel walking path runs through the park. You may want to bring earplugs—the park is only a half block away from the railroad tracks. The campground road is a combination of gravel and pavement, with level sites for tents or RVs.

Campsites, facilities: There are 14 RV and tent campsites. The west-side campsites can accommodate any length of RV. Facilities include picnic tables, a few fire pits or rock fire rings at some of the sites, drinking water, flush toilets, a dump station, and garbage service. Leashed pets are permitted.

Reservations, fees: No reservations are accepted. Campsites cost $8 per night. Open May–September.

Directions: In downtown Choteau, turn east off Highway 89 at the campground sign onto 1st Street NE and drive one block. Turn right at the park sign, drive 0.1 mile, and turn left into the campground. You can also get to the campground entrance via 1st Street SE.

GPS Coordinates: N 47° 48.695' W 112° 10.719'

Contact: Choteau Park and Campground, City of Choteau, P.O. Box 619, Choteau, MT 59422, 406/466-2510.

Trail (#201), which heads along the reservoir's shore. You can mountain bike the trail up to the wilderness boundary (7 miles) and continue on to climb Sun Butte (9.5 miles) for a panoramic view of the area. The Mortimer Gulch National Recreation Trail (7 miles) offers views of Sawtooth Ridge and the reservoir.

The quiet campground's two loops feature partially shaded, partially private campsites. Some are tucked under aspens, others under large Douglas firs. Those in the upper loop tend to have more shade than those in the lower loop. One of the campsites has a pull-through parking pad, but the remainder are paved back-ins.

Campsites, facilities: The campground has 28 RV or tent campsites that can accommodate vehicles up to 48 feet. Facilities include picnic tables, fire rings with grills, vault toilets, and drinking water. Pack out your trash. Leashed

🔟 MORTIMER GULCH

🚶🚴🛶🎿🛻🚣🎣🐕🏕️♿🚐⛰️

Scenic rating: 9

on Gibson Reservoir in Lewis and Clark National Forest

Located near 5,000 feet in the Lewis and Clark National Forest, Mortimer Gulch is the only designated campground on the 1,289-acre Gibson Reservoir. The reservoir is surrounded by dramatically steep upthrust ridges that mark the edge of the Front. A steep cement ramp, a dock, and trailer parking aid in launching boats for fishing, sightseeing, and waterskiing. The reservoir also houses rainbow, brook, and westslope cutthroat trout, and arctic grayling. The campground is popular in early summer when the reservoir's water levels are higher; in fall, hunters flock to the campground because it's a seven-mile hike away from the Sun River Game Preserve. A hiking trail drops from the campground to the boat launch area and connects with the North Fork of the Sun River

© BECKY LOMAX

Bighorn sheep are just one of the game species on the Sun River Game Preserve, near Gibson Reservoir.

pets are permitted. A wheelchair-accessible toilet is available.

Reservations, fees: No reservations are accepted. Campsites cost $8. Cash or check. Open late May–November; however, water is turned off after Labor Day.

Directions: Drive out of town on Manix Street in Augusta, which becomes the Sun River Road (Forest Road 108). Drive 3.7 miles to a signed intersection. Turn right and drive 15 miles on dirt, where the road turns to pavement again. Continue driving 6.8 miles on the pavement, which climbs up above the dam. Turn left into the campground at the sign.

GPS Coordinates: N 47° 36.748' W 112° 46.133'

Contact: Lewis and Clark National Forest, Rocky Mountain Ranger District, 1102 N. Main Ave., P.O. Box 340, Choteau, MT 59422, 406/466-5341, fax 406/466-2237, www.fs.fed.us/r1/lewisclark.

11 SUN CANYON LODGE

Scenic rating: 7

east of Gibson Reservoir in Lewis and Clark National Forest

At 4,600 feet in Lewis and Clark Forest, the rustic Sun Canyon Lodge is a bucolic Montana outfitter with trophy antlers on the wall of the octagon 1920s log lodge. The lodge nestles below the towering cliffs one mile south of the North Fork of the Sun River below the Gibson Reservoir dam. The river contains rainbow, brook, and cutthroat trout that can be caught by wade fishing. Within a 10-minute drive to the west, Gibson Reservoir offers lake fishing, hiking and mountain-biking trails, boating, and swimming. Departing from Sun Canyon Lodge, the Home Gulch–Lime Trail (#267, 15 miles) offers spring wildlife-watching opportunities, but more scenic trails depart from the reservoir area.

The campground is part of the Sun Canyon

Lodge complex of restaurant, cabins, and corrals, with campsites lined up along the perimeter of a grassy meadow against aspen trees. Its location off the Sun Canyon Road yields quiet, but the campsites are visible from the restaurant and the parking area.

Campsites, facilities: The campground has 10 RV or tent campsites that can accommodate large RVs. Facilities include picnic tables, drinking water, flush toilets, showers, a disposal station, garbage service, a coin-operated launderette, a restaurant, a bar, trail rides, a playground, boat tours, horse corrals, and outfitting services for fishing and hunting. Leashed pets are permitted. A wheelchair-accessible toilet is available.

Reservations, fees: Reservations are accepted. RV camping costs $10 without electrical hookups and $15 with electrical hookups. Tent camping costs $5. Using the disposal station costs $10, and showers cost $3 per person. Cash, check, or credit card. Open May–November.

Directions: From Augusta, follow the signs to Gibson Reservoir. Drive out of town on Manix Street, which becomes Sun River Road (Forest Road 108). Drive 3.7 miles to a signed intersection. Turn right and drive 15 miles on dirt to where the road turns to pavement again. Continue three more miles to the Sun Canyon Lodge sign and turn left, traveling for one more mile.

GPS Coordinates: N 47° 36.303' W 112° 43.296'

Contact: Sun Canyon Lodge, P.O. Box 327, Sun River Rd., Augusta, MT 59410, 406/562-3654 or 888/749-3654, www.suncanyonlodge.com.

12 HOME GULCH

Scenic rating: 7

on Sun River east of Gibson Reservoir in Lewis and Clark National Forest

Located at 4,580 feet in Lewis and Clark National Forest, Home Gulch nestles below the towering cliffs along the North Fork of the Sun River below the Gibson Reservoir dam. Within a five-minute drive, funky Sun Canyon Lodge offers a coin-operated launderette, showers, trail rides, a disposal station, and a cafe displaying the stuffed trophies from local hunts. The campground is popular with hunters in the fall, and the North Fork of the Sun River contains rainbow, brook, and cutthroat trout that can be caught by wade fishing. Gibson Reservoir, with fishing, hiking and mountain-biking trails, boating, and swimming is a 10-minute drive to the west. Departing from Sun Canyon Lodge, the Home Gulch–Lime Trail (#267, 15 miles) offers spring wildlife-watching opportunities, but more scenic trails depart from the reservoir area.

The campground squeezes between the Sun Canyon Road and the North Fork of the Sun River. Aspen and alder trees lend partial shade to the campsites. The campground is quiet but does get a fair amount of weekend traffic during the day on the adjacent road, but not at night when the sound of the river is pervasive. A narrow dirt road winds through the campground, which has gravel parking pads; one is a pull-through and the rest are back-ins. Most of the campsites overlook the river.

Campsites, facilities: The campground has 15 RV or tent campsites that can accommodate vehicles up to 45 feet long. Facilities include picnic tables, fire rings with grills, vault toilets, and hand pumps for drinking water. Pack out your trash. Leashed pets are permitted. A wheelchair-accessible toilet is available.

Reservations, fees: No reservations are accepted. Campsites cost $6. Cash or check. Open late May–November, but the water is shut off after Labor Day.

Directions: From Augusta, follow the signs to Gibson Reservoir. Drive out of town on Manix Street, which becomes Sun River Road (Forest Road 108). Drive 3.7 miles to a signed intersection. Turn right and drive 15 miles on dirt to where the road turns to pavement again. Continue 1.8 miles farther on the pavement and turn right at the sign into the campground.

GPS Coordinates: N 47° 36.981' W 112° 43.698'

Contact: Lewis and Clark National Forest, Rocky Mountain Ranger District, 1102 N. Main Ave., P.O. Box 340, Choteau, MT 59422, 406/466-5341, fax 406/466-2237, www.fs.fed.us/r1/lewisclark.

13 PISHKUN RESERVOIR

Scenic rating: 8

north of Augusta and southwest of Choteau

The 1,518-acre Pishkun Reservoir is a prairie lake below the Rocky Mountain Front. Long, rough, gravel and dirt access roads lead to it from Choteau or Augusta. Sitting at 4,370 feet in elevation, the lake draws anglers for its northern pike, rainbow trout, and yellow perch. Used also in winter for ice fishing, it is stocked regularly with rainbow trout and sometimes kokanee. The concrete boat ramp is unusable during drought conditions. Contact the Region 4 office for current water levels. Also a wildlife management area, the reservoir is a good place for watching waterfowl, loons, and peregrine falcons.

The primitive campground is part of the fishing access site run by the state. Its campsites line up along the shore in a hot, sunny, windy, treeless, grassy area along the dirt campground road facing the dramatic, expansive views of the Front range peaks. The campground is so distant from any highway that wind is the only sound. The state discourages trailers and RVs from using the campground due to the rough condition of the access road, but smaller RVs and truck-campers often visit the campground anyway. Despite how spread out the campsites are, you'll still see your neighboring campers.

Campsites, facilities: The campground has five RV and tent campsites that can accommodate only smaller RVs. Facilities include picnic tables with shelters, fire rings with grills, vault toilets, and a boat ramp. Pack out your trash. Leashed pets are permitted.

Reservations, fees: Reservations are not accepted. Campsites cost $7 with a Montana fishing license and $12 without a Montana fishing license. Cash or check. Open year-round.

Directions: From Choteau, drive 0.5 mile south on Highway 287 and turn southwest for 19 miles on the Pishkun Road. Turn left at the signed entrance to the fishing access site to reach the campground. From Augusta, drive 11.3 miles north on Highway 287 and turn left onto West Spring Valley Road for 7.3 miles as it jogs north and west again. Turn right onto the Pishkun Access Road for 4.8 miles and then turn left onto Pishkun Road for 0.8 mile to the campground entrance on the left.

GPS Coordinates: N 47° 41.666' W 112° 28.650'

Contact: Montana Fish, Wildlife, and Parks, Region 4, 4600 Giant Springs Rd., Great Falls, MT 59405, 406/454-5840, http://fwp.mt.gov.

14 WILLOW CREEK RESERVOIR

Scenic rating: 8

north of Augusta

The 1,314-acre Willow Creek Reservoir is a prairie lake below the Rocky Mountain Front accessible via a rough gravel road. At 4,150 feet in elevation, the lake draws anglers for its rainbow and brook trout. Used also in winter for ice fishing, it is stocked regularly with rainbow trout. The concrete boat ramp is unusable during drought conditions and late in the summer; contact the Region 4 office for current water levels. Also a wildlife management area, the reservoir is a good place for watching waterfowl and loons, and it attracts hunters in fall.

The primitive campground is part of the fishing access site run by the state. Its spread-out campsites line up along the shore in a hot, sunny, windy, treeless, grassy area along the dirt campground road. Some of the campsites face east toward the lake's island, but the Front peaks are also in view to the west. Other campsites can nab reflections of the Front peaks in the water on calm days. The campground is so distant from any highway that wind is the only sound. The state discourages trailers and RVs from using the campground because of the rough condition of the access road, but smaller RVs and truck-campers often visit the campground anyway.

Campsites, facilities: The campground has six RV and tent campsites that can accommodate only smaller RVs. Facilities include picnic tables, fire rings with grills, vault toilets, and a boat ramp. Pack out your trash. Leashed pets are permitted.

Reservations, fees: Reservations are not accepted. Campsites cost $7 with a Montana fishing license and $12 without a Montana fishing license. Cash or check. Open year-round.

Directions: From Augusta, drive out of town on Manix Street, which becomes the Sun River Road (Forest Road 108). Drive 3.7 miles to a signed intersection. Turn right for 1.6 miles and turn right again at the fishing access site sign onto Willow Creek Road for 1.2 miles. Turn left for 0.1 mile to reach the campground.

GPS Coordinates: N 47° 32.842' W 112° 26.358'

Contact: Montana Fish, Wildlife, and Parks, Region 4, 4600 Giant Springs Rd., Great Falls, MT 59405, 406/454-5840, http://fwp.mt.gov.

15 FREEZEOUT LAKE

🏃 🚤 🛶 🎣 🏠 ♿ 🚐 ⛺

Scenic rating: 8

south of Choteau

BEST (

Freezeout Lake sits on a 11,466-acre wildlife state management area at 3,770 feet in elevation south of Choteau. The lake—actually one lake and six ponds—provides outstanding wildlife-watching. In late March and early April, as many as 300,000 snow geese and 10,000 tundra swans congregate on the lake amid a cacophony of squawks on their migration northward. For the best experience, watch in early morning as thousands of birds lift off the lake to go feed in nearby grain fields to prepare for their flight to Saskatchewan and then the arctic. Over 200 species of birds use the Freezeout area—either for migration or nesting. Winter brings upland game birds and raptors, spring and fall have waterfowl migrations, and summer includes ducks, herons, shorebirds, sandhill cranes, swans, and raptors. You can call 406/467-2646 for an automated waterfowl update. Perimeter roads are open year-round. Interior roads are closed during hunting season (October–mid-January) for upland game birds and waterfowl. Dike roads are closed to motorized vehicles but open for hiking. A paved walking path leads to a waterfowl blind. Only nonmotorized boats are permitted on the lake.

The primitive campground squeezes between the highway and Pond 5 in an open field divided by hedgerows of brush into back-in grassy campsites. The campground is sunny and windy, and receives noise from a handful of trucks at night. But that doesn't compare with the deafening noise of thousands of snow geese at once.

Campsites, facilities: The campground has 12 RV and tent campsites that can accommodate small RVs. Facilities include picnic tables, vault toilets, and primitive boat ramps. Pack out your trash. Leashed pets are permitted. A wheelchair-accessible toilet and campsite are available, along with a paved trail to a viewing blind.

Reservations, fees: Reservations are not accepted. Camping is free. Open year-round; however, motorized vehicles are restricted

© BECKY LOMAX

Freezeout Lake, a popular birding campground, sees thousands of snow geese in March.

October–mid-January when internal roads are closed.

Directions: From Choteau, drive Highway 89 southeast for 12.3 miles. Turn west at the headquarters office. Drive 0.3 mile to a four-way junction. Turn right, continuing for 0.3 mile. Turn right and go 0.1 mile to the campground entrance.

GPS Coordinates: N 47° 40.180' W 112° 0.947'

Contact: Montana Fish, Wildlife, and Parks, Region 4, 4600 Giant Springs Rd., Great Falls, MT 59405, 406/454-5840, http://fwp.mt.gov.

16 SOUTH FORK SUN RIVER
🚶 🛶 🎣 🐕 ♿ 🚐 ⛺

Scenic rating: 7

on the South Fork of the Sun River in Lewis and Clark National Forest

At 5,300 feet, the South Fork of the Sun River Campground is in Lewis and Clark National Forest at one of the most popular trailheads to access the wilderness for backpacking, horse packing, fishing, hunting, and mountain climbing. The 22-mile-long Chinese Wall can be reached via trail in about 18 miles. The Sun River attracts anglers for brown trout, mountain whitefish, and rainbow trout. The South Fork of the Sun Trail (#202), which is part of the Continental Divide Trail, parallels the South Fork of the Sun River to access the Scapegoat Wilderness to the south and the Bob Marshall Wilderness to the north.

This campground is busy and dusty, due to the trailhead. The campground loop is adjacent to parking for hikers and for stock trailers, which can be packed with up to 20 trucks and trailers that are visible from every campsite. Even though the campground sits on the river, none of the campsites have private river frontage, although you can walk the 100 feet to it. Lodgepole pines lend partial shade to the campground, with campsites surrounded by tall grass. While Benchmark offers much more privacy and camping ambiance, some hikers prefer camping here for the convenience to the trailhead.

Campsites, facilities: The campground has seven RV or tent campsites that can accommodate smaller RVs. Facilities include picnic tables, fire rings, hand pumps for drinking water, and vault toilets. Pack out your trash. Leashed pets are permitted. A wheelchair-accessible toilet and campsite are available, although the campsite has become overgrown.

Reservations, fees: No reservations are accepted. Camping costs $8. Cash or check. Open late May–November.

Directions: From Augusta, follow County Road 435 for 0.3 mile to the Nilan Reservoir sign. Turn right onto Eberl Street. Follow the road as it swings south and then west again, where the road turns to gravel, becoming Forest Road 235. Drive 14.2 miles to an intersection and continue straight for 16.2 miles until the road dead-ends in the campground.

GPS Coordinates: N 47° 30.108' W112°53.283'

Contact: Lewis and Clark National Forest, Rocky Mountain Ranger District, 1102 N. Main Ave., P.O. Box 340, Choteau, MT 59422, 406/466-5341, fax 406/466-2237, www.fs.fed.us/r1/lewisclark.

17 BENCHMARK
🚶 🛶 🎣 🐕 ♿ 🚐 ⛺

Scenic rating: 7

on Straight Creek in Lewis and Clark National Forest

Located at 5,300 feet in the Lewis and Clark National Forest, Benchmark is a remote Forest Service station with an airstrip and a popular access for those entering the wilderness for hiking, backpacking, horse packing, fishing, and hunting. The 22-mile-long Chinese Wall can be reached via trail in about

18 miles. The campground sits between Straight and Wood Creeks, both tributaries to the South Fork of the Sun River that harbor mottled sculpin and rainbow trout. The 15.2-mile Straight Creek Trail (#212) departs 0.2 mile from the campground, and one mile north the South Fork of the Sun Trail (#202), which is part of the Continental Divide Trail, parallels the river to access the Scapegoat Wilderness to the south and the Bob Marshall Wilderness to the north.

A mixed aspen and conifer forest shades the campground, which is suited for those with stock. The two loops on the right have feeding troughs for horses, plus hitching rails and loading ramps are available. To accommodate stock trailers, the parking pads are large, triple-wide back-ins. The loop to the left is not set up for horses. Low grass covers the forest floor, while lodgepole pines lend partial shade. The spaced out sites are private due to shorter pine trees growing between sites. Sites 18, 19, 20, 24, and 25 have views but also look across the airstrip. Site 16 has a bear pole for hanging food. Most of the campsites have large, flat tent spaces.

Campsites, facilities: The campground has 25 RV or tent campsites that can accommodate RVs up to 30 feet. Facilities include picnic tables, fire rings, hand pumps for drinking water, stock equipment, and pit and vault toilets. Pack out your trash. Leashed pets are permitted. A wheelchair-accessible toilet is available.

Reservations, fees: No reservations are accepted. Campsites cost $6. Cash or check. Open late May–November.

Directions: From Augusta, follow County Road 435 for 0.3 mile to the Nilan Reservoir sign. Turn right onto Eberl Street. Follow the road as it swings south and then west again, where the road turns to gravel, becoming Forest Road 235. Drive 14.2 miles to an intersection and turn left for another 15.2 miles on the Benchmark Road. At the campground sign, turn left, driving across the single-lane bridge, and swing left for another 0.2 mile.

GPS Coordinates: N 47° 29.207' W 112° 52.942'

Contact: Lewis and Clark National Forest, Rocky Mountain Ranger District, 1102 N. Main Ave., P.O. Box 340, Choteau, MT 59422, 406/466-5341, fax 406/466-2237, www.fs.fed.us/r1/lewisclark.

18 WOOD LAKE

Scenic rating: 9

at Wood Lake in Lewis and Clark National Forest

At 5,799 feet in elevation, Wood Lake is a small, shallow lake on Benchmark Road in the Lewis and Clark National Forest just east of the Scapegoat Wilderness Area. The lake is popular with anglers for its westslope cutthroat trout; you can often see six or more people fly-fishing along its shore. A primitive boat ramp is available, but motors are not permitted.

Sitting across the road from the lake, the aspen, lodgepole, and fir campground is enclosed with a rail fence to keep cattle grazing under permit in the area from entering. It sits very close to Benchmark Road, where every vehicle kicks up dust, which filters into the campsites adjacent to the road. Sites 2, 3, and 5 are more open, with views of the forested slopes. In July, cow parsnips, black-eyed susans, and cinquefoil bloom around the campsites, which are close together and lacking foliage. Site 7 is a small, private site with a view of a small rocky gorge; a rough trail cuts through the fence and tours it. Sites 11 and 12 sit in a second area to the left when you drive in. These sites are open, with views of Wood Lake across the road, and with extra parking pads for trailers or additional vehicles.

Campsites, facilities: The campground has 12 RV or tent campsites that can accommodate a maximum RV length of 22 feet. Facilities include picnic tables, fire rings with grills, vault toilets, and hand pumps for drinking water. Leashed pets are permitted. A wheelchair-accessible toilet is available.

Reservations, fees: No reservations are accepted. Camping costs $6. Cash or check. Open late May–November.

Directions: From Augusta, follow County Road 435 for 0.3 mile to the Nilan Reservoir sign. Turn right onto Eberl Street. Follow the road as it swings south and then west again, where the road turns to gravel, becoming Forest Road 235. Drive 14.2 miles to an intersection and turn left onto Benchmark Road. Drive nine miles to Wood Lake. The campground entrance is on the right just before the lake.

GPS Coordinates: N 47° 25.706' W 112° 47.697'

Contact: Augusta Information Station, 405 Manix St., P.O. Box 365, Augusta, MT 59410, 406/562-3247.

19 FORD AND WOOD CREEKS PRIMITIVE

Scenic rating: 7

on the Benchmark Road in Lewis and Clark National Forest

At an elevation of 5,600 feet in Lewis and Clark National Forest, the Benchmark Road parallels Ford and Wood Creeks, two Rocky Mountain Front trout streams. Dispersed primitive campsites flank both sides of the road, some on the creeks and others in pine forest settings on the opposite side of the road. A few are open and visible from the road. Locate the campsites on dirt spur roads. Some are marked with numbered tent icon signs; others are unmarked. Scout the roads first before driving in blind—especially if you are pulling a small trailer or driving an RV. Not all of the sites have turnaround room.

The primitive campsites along the road are attractive for their solitude and privacy broken only by the sounds of nature. Some are forested while others sit in partly sunny aspen groves. Follow Leave No Trace principles when camping at these dispersed sites, using only pre-existing fire rings and driving only on jeep trails.

Campsites, facilities: The Benchmark Road has 13 dispersed campsites for small RVs or tents. Facilities include rock fire rings. No drinking water is available. If you choose to use the creek water, boil or purify it first. Pack out your trash. Leashed pets are permitted.

Reservations, fees: No reservations are accepted. Camping is free. Open May–November.

Directions: From Augusta, follow County Road 435 for 0.3 mile to the Nilan Reservoir sign. Turn right onto Eberl Street. Follow the road as it swings south and then west again, where the road turns to gravel becoming Forest Road 235. Drive 14.2 miles to an intersection and turn left onto the Benchmark Road. Find dispersed campsites on both sides of the road between MP 4.5 and the Benchmark airstrip.

Contact: Lewis and Clark National Forest, Augusta Ranger Station, 1102 N. Main Ave., P.O. Box 340, Choteau, MT 59422, 406/466-5341, fax 406/466-2237, www.fs.fed.us/r1/lewisclark.

20 DOUBLE FALLS

Scenic rating: 7

on Wood Creek in Lewis and Clark National Forest

At 5,500 feet on Ford Creek in Lewis and Clark National Forest, Double Falls sits on the road to Benchmark, one of the most popular entrances to the Scapegoat and Bob Marshall Wildernesses. It is named for the falls just east of the campground. A 0.1-mile trail follows the north side of the creek to the falls. The campground is also the trailhead for Petty Ford Creek Trail (#244). With views of Crown and Steamboat Mountains, the 3.5-mile trail climbs out of Ford Creek and drops to Petty Creek. Ford Creek harbors brook trout.

This small, primitive campground is reached via a steep, narrow, rocky dirt road. The road can be muddy in wet weather. While high clearance vehicles are not mandatory, they will manage the rocks better. Both campsites sit right on the river, hence the campground's appeal despite its primitive status. One campsite is open with a views across the meadow (full of pink sticky geraniums in July) and of the mountainsides. The other campsite on the east end of the campground is tucked behind tall firs for more privacy. Both have large, flat spaces for tents and rough dirt parking pads.

Campsites, facilities: The campground has two RV or tent campsites that can accommodate only smaller RVs and trailers. Facilities include picnic tables, fire rings with grills, and a vault toilet. No drinking water is available. Pack out your trash. If you choose to use the creek water, boil or purify it first. Leashed pets are permitted.

Reservations, fees: No reservations are accepted. Camping is free. Open May–November.

Directions: From Augusta, follow County Road 435 for 0.3 mile to the Fishing Access for Nilan Reservoir sign. Turn right onto Eberl Street. Follow the road as it swings south and then west again, where the road turns to gravel, becoming Forest Road 235. Drive 14.2 miles to an intersection and turn left onto the Benchmark Road. Continue on 4.5 miles to the campground entrance, which sits on the left.
GPS Coordinates: N 47° 24.443' W 112° 43.329'

Contact: Augusta Information Station, 405 Manix St., P.O. Box 365, Augusta, MT 59410, 406/562-3247.

21 NILAN RESERVOIR

Scenic rating: 9

west of Augusta

At an elevation of 4,440 feet, west of Augusta on the road to Benchmark, Nilan Reservoir is one of the most scenic of the Rocky Mountain Front reservoirs due to its surrounding prairie and the looming peaks. The 520-acre reservoir offers boating for motorized craft as well as canoes and kayaks. For anglers, the reservoir houses rainbow and brown trout. It is also a popular ice-fishing location in winter. Bird-watchers can see a variety of birds, from raptors to American pelicans.

The campground sprawls along the south shore of Nilan Reservoir, with open gravel, rock, and dry grass campsites in pairs. The lack of trees makes them sunny and affords outstanding views of the front range, but winds whip right through them. Mornings tend to be calm, with the water often reflecting the peaks, but breezes pick up in the afternoon. Sites 1–6, which are large gravel pull-throughs, have the best views but, due to the road, get dusted by passing vehicles; sites 7 and 8 sit adjacent to the dusty road away from the water on the boat ramp spur. Sites 3 and 4 each have their own small jetty; site 2 has a small windbreak from cottonwood trees. Due to the rough road access, the state does not recommend the campground for trailers or RVs, but plenty of people drive in with both.

Campsites, facilities: The campground has eight RV or tent campsites that can accommodate midsized RVs. Facilities include picnic tables, fire rings with grills, vault toilets, and a boat ramp. No drinking water is available. If you choose to use the reservoir water, boil or purify it first. Pack out your trash. Leashed pets are permitted.

Reservations, fees: No reservations are accepted. Camping costs $7 if you have a Montana fishing license or $12 without. Cash or check. Open year-round.

Directions: From Augusta, follow County Road 435 for 0.3 mile to Fishing Access for Nilan Reservoir sign. Turn right onto Eberl Street. Follow the road as it swings south and then west again, where the road turns to gravel, becoming Forest Road 235. Drive seven miles to the campground. Sites will be on the right side of the road over the next 0.3 mile.

GPS Coordinates: N 47° 28.387' W 112° 31.074'

Contact: Montana Fish, Wildlife, and Parks, Region 4 Office, 4600 Giant Springs Rd., Great Falls, MT 59405, 406/454-5840, http://fwp.mt.gov.

22 DICK'S RV PARK

🚶 🚴 🛶 ⛴ 🚐 🎣 🐕 ⛺ ♿ 🚙 ⛰

Scenic rating: 5

in Great Falls

At an elevation of 3,505 feet, Dick's RV Park is convenient for exploring the C.M. Russell Museum, which celebrates the work of the famous western artist, and the Lewis and Clark Interpretive Center, with displays about the Corps of Discovery, as well as hiking trails and bicycling paths. Although the campground sits along the Sun River, the confluence of the Sun River with the Missouri River is less than a five-minute drive away. The campground is also a five-minute drive from two golf courses and fishing, boating, and floating on the Missouri River, along with hiking and biking trails at Giant Springs Heritage State Park.

The older campground squeezes between the Sun River and a four-lane freeway with trucking traffic, and it picks up noise from the nearby railroad. Both pull-through and back-in sites are available, with small plots of grass between sites. The cramped sites are very close together with no privacy. The sunny campground has only a few trees. Some long-term residents live here.

Campsites, facilities: The campground has 141 RV sites that can fit large RVs, 20 tent campsites, and 30 unserviced overflow sites. Hookups include water, sewer, electricity, and cable TV. Facilities include picnic tables, flush toilets, showers, a coin-operated launderette, coin-operated car wash, drinking water, store with movie rentals, wireless Internet, cable TV, a dog walk, propane for sale, and a recreation hall. Leashed pets are permitted.

Reservations, fees: Reservations are accepted. Hookups cost $26–36. Tent sites cost $19. Cash, check, or credit card. Open year-round.

Directions: From I-15 at Great Falls, take Exit 278 (10th Avenue S.) onto Highway 87/89/200 heading east. Take Exit 0, turning north onto 14th Street. Turn right at 13th Avenue SW and drive two blocks, going under the railroad bridge. The campground entrance is on the right.

GPS Coordinates: N 47° 29.456' W 111° 19.998'

Contact: Dick's RV Park, 1403 11th St. SW, Great Falls, MT 59404, 406/452-0333, www.dicksrvpark.com.

23 GREAT FALLS KOA

🚶 🚴 🛶 ⛴ 🚐 🎣 🐕 ⛺ ♿ 🚙 ⛰

Scenic rating: 5

in Great Falls

At an elevation of 3,505 feet, the Great Falls KOA is convenient for exploring three of the town's main attractions: the C.M. Russell Museum Complex, Giant Springs Heritage State Park, and the Lewis and Clark Interpretive Center. Great Falls also has three golf courses and fishing, boating, and floating on the Missouri River, along with hiking and biking trails.

This manicured grassy campground provides partial shade from the cottonwood trees, and some of the sites have privacy from bushes. Sites include full hookups, partial hookups, dry camping, and tent villages with partial shade and fenced grass. The quiet location on the edge of town still picks up a little noise from large trucks on the highway. Shower facilities include family rooms, and a covered outdoor kitchen is available. Mornings start with an all-you-can-eat pancake breakfast with chokecherry syrup. On summer evenings, entertainment includes bluegrass music and cowpoke poetry performed by the River Town Rounders.

Campsites, facilities: The campground has 120 RV and tent campsites that can accommodate rigs of any length. Hookups include water, sewer, and electricity (50 amps available), and the tent village area includes hookups for water and electricity. Facilities include picnic tables, pedestal grills, flush toilets, showers, a coin-operated launderette, drinking water, a playground, a swimming pool, water slides and park, a hot tub, a game room, movie nights, fresh veggies in the garden, basketball and volleyball courts, a dog walk, wireless Internet, modem dataports, cable TV, café, a camp store, firewood for free, propane for sale, and a dump station. Leashed pets are permitted.

Reservations, fees: Reservations are accepted. Hookups cost $49–56. Tent sites cost $38–45. Rates cover two people. For over two people, add on $10 per adult and $8 per child. Children five years old and under stay free. Six people maximum are permitted per campsite. Kamping cabins cost $65–87. Cash, check, or credit card. Open year-round.

Directions: From I-15 in Great Falls, take Exit 278 and drive five miles east on Highways 87/89/200 (also called 10th Avenue S.) to the east edge of the city. Turn south onto 51st Street S. and drive 0.3 mile to the campground entrance on the corner where the road turns west.

GPS Coordinates: N 47° 29.269' W 111° 13.304'

Contact: Great Falls KOA, 1500 51st St. S, Great Falls, MT 59405, 406/727-3191 or 800/562-6584, www.greatfallskoa.com.

24 WOLF BRIDGE

Scenic rating: 4

on the Missouri River north of Helena

On the Missouri River north of Holter Dam, Wolf Bridge, at 3,500 feet, is a popular fishing

and boating access, but not a prime camping location. You can launch upriver at Holter Dam Campground and float two miles back to the camp, or you can float from Wolf Bridge eight miles north to Craig. Anglers go after a variety of game fish, which include black crappie, brown trout, burbot, channel catfish, mountain whitefish, northern pike, paddlefish, rainbow trout, sauger, shovelnose sturgeon, smallmouth bass, walleye, and yellow perch.

Squeezed up against the road and bridge, the campground is really a strip of dry grass along the edge of a large gravel parking lot and boat launch—a fishing access site run by the state. It's a place to camp for convenience rather than ambiance. Two of the sites have flat spaces for tents. The campground has no trees for shade or to block wind. The area does have a bench along the river for watching the passing boats. Campsite 1 is the closest to the river. Individual parking pads do not exist; just pull up next to a picnic table.

Campsites, facilities: The campground has five RV or tent campsites that can accommodate larger RVs. Facilities include picnic tables, fire rings with grills, vault toilets, and a boat ramp. No drinking water is available. If you choose to use the river water, boil or purify it first. Pack out your trash. Leashed pets are permitted. A wheelchair-accessible toilet is available.

Reservations, fees: No reservations are accepted. Camping costs $7 if you have a Montana fishing license or $12 without. Cash or check. Open year-round.

Directions: From I-15 north of Helena, take Exit 226 at Wolf Creek. From Wolf Creek on the south side of the freeway, drive Recreation Road for 3.3 miles and turn left after crossing the bridge over the Missouri River.

GPS Coordinates: N 47° 1.198' W 112° 0.612'

Contact: Montana Fish, Wildlife, and Parks, Region 4 Office, 4600 Giant Springs Rd., Great Falls, MT 59405, 406/454-5840, http://fwp.mt.gov.

25 HOLTER DAM

Scenic rating: 6

on Holter Lake north of Helena

Below Holter Dam on the west bank of the Missouri River, at 3,550 feet, Holter Dam Campground drones with the constant noise of the dam, and views are of the dam as well as the surrounding arid mountain slopes. Yet it attracts many anglers, who fish from shore or hop on rafts or drift boats to float the Missouri River for its game fish. During high water, the dam may need to release water; a siren and lights alert those in the river channel to move up into the campground.

The campground is in two parts, adjacent to the boat launch area. The first part (sites 1–11) centers around a large gravel parking lot with picnic tables with shade covers. Sites 1 and 11 sit on the water, but the remainder line up on the grass on the opposite side of the parking lot from the river. Only a couple of large willow trees provide shade. Sites 13–17 line up with double-wide back-in gravel parking pads and no covers on the tables. Neither of the sections affords privacy due to the lack of trees and close quarters.

Campsites, facilities: There are 33 RV or tent campsites that can accommodate midsized RVs. Facilities include picnic tables, fire rings with grills, vault toilets, drinking water, a gravel boat launch, boat trailer parking, dock, garbage service, firewood for sale, and a campground manager on site. Leashed pets are permitted. Site 7 and toilets are wheelchair-accessible.

Reservations, fees: No reservations are accepted. Campsites cost $10. Day use of the park costs $2. Cash or check. Open early May–October.

Directions: From I-15 north of Helena, take Exit 226 at Wolf Creek. From Wolf Creek on the south side of the freeway, drive Recreation Road for 3.3 miles and turn right just before the bridge over the Missouri River. Drive two miles. The road has large washboards and potholes that make driving the two miles a challenge.

GPS Coordinates: N 46° 59.705' W 112° 00.682'

Contact: Bureau of Land Management, 106 N. Parkmont, P.O. Box 3388, Butte, MT 59702, 406/533-7600, www.blm.gov/mt/st/en.html.

26 HOLTER LAKE

Scenic rating: 8

on the Missouri River north of Helena

Located at 3,600 feet on the east shore of Holter Lake north of Helena, this campground sits on the Missouri River in a lake created by Holter Dam. From the campground, you can boat south into Gates of the Mountains Wilderness for sightseeing along the route that Lewis and Clark traveled. The lake is popular for waterskiing and fishing for black crappie, brown trout, burbot, channel catfish, mountain whitefish, northern pike, paddlefish, rainbow trout, sauger, shovelnose sturgeon, smallmouth bass, walleye, and yellow perch. A marina with boat rentals and gas sits 0.5 mile south on Beartooth Road.

Sitting on a bluff above the lake, the campground appears as a green, mowed-lawn oasis amid the surrounding dry grassland and pine hills. Two interconnected paved loops waltz through the cramped, crowded open campground, which has no privacy between sites. Only a few short cottonwoods offer shade for hot days, causing most campers to cower in the cool shadow of their trailer or RV. Paved walkways connect the campground to the beach, boat launch, and fishing jetty. Sites 3, 5, 6, 7, 8, 10, 12, 13, 15, and 18 overlook the lake. A separate walk-in tent area is available.

Campsites, facilities: There are 33 RV or tent campsites, plus an additional open walk-in tenting area without assigned sites. The gravel parking pads can accommodate midsized RVs.

© BECKY LOMAX

Holter Lake, home to several campgrounds, is formed on the Missouri River by a downstream dam.

Facilities include picnic tables, fire rings with grills, vault toilets, drinking water, a paved multi-lane boat launch, boat trailer parking, docks, boat slips, a fish-cleaning station, garbage service, swimming area, and campground manager on-site. Leashed pets are permitted. Toilets are wheelchair-accessible. Camping is limited to seven days.

Reservations, fees: No reservations are accepted. Campsites cost $10. Day use of the park costs $2. Cash or check. Open early May–October.

Directions: From I-15 north of Helena, take Exit 226 at Wolf Creek. From Wolf Creek on the south side of the freeway, drive Recreation Road for 3.3 miles until you cross the Missouri River on a bridge; turn right onto paved Beartooth Road for 2.3 miles. The campground is on the right.

GPS Coordinates: N 46° 59.640' W 111° 59.436'

Contact: Bureau of Land Management, 106 N. Parkmont, P.O. Box 3388, Butte, MT 59702, 406/533-7600, www.blm.gov/mt/st/en.html.

27 LOG GULCH

Scenic rating: 9

on the Missouri River north of Helena

Log Gulch, at 3,600 feet on the east shore of Holter Lake, a reservoir on the Missouri River, provides access for fishing and a sandy swimming beach. It is the closest launch for boating up the Oxbow to Gates of the Mountains Wilderness. Once at the Gates, you can hike one hour into Mann Gulch, a National Historic Landmark that marks the site of a tragic wildfire in 1949 that killed 13 firefighters. Crosses up the steep hillside mark where each firefighter died.

The campground flanks a hillside with three different options for camping—none with privacy. The main campground circles in several paved loops upslope in the gulch. A few of these lawn campsites have pull-through gravel parking pads, a cottonwood or pine tree for partial shade, and views of the lake (from the sites at the top of the loop). A second area—Little Log—climbs a steep hill with staggered terraced campsites, some with peek-a-boo views of the lake. A third area—a large, flat, treeless, gravel parking lot for RVs to back into—offers prime views of spiny Sleeping Giant Mountain and the lake. Watch for rattlesnakes around the campground.

Campsites, facilities: There are 70 RV or tent campsites; some can accommodate the largest RVs. Facilities include picnic tables, fire rings with grills, vault toilets, drinking water, a paved multi-lane boat launch, boat trailer parking, docks, boat slips, a fish-cleaning station, garbage service, swimming area, and campground manager on-site. Leashed pets are permitted. Toilets are wheelchair-accessible.

Reservations, fees: No reservations are accepted. Campsites cost $10. Day use of the park costs $2. Cash or check. Open early May–October.

Directions: From I-15 north of Helena, take Exit 226 at Wolf Creek. From Wolf Creek on the south side of the freeway, drive Recreation Road for 3.3 miles until you cross the bridge over the Missouri River; turn right onto Beartooth Road for 6.5 miles. After passing Holter Lake campground, the paved road turns to bumpy oiled dirt and narrows with sharp, blind corners, but pavement resumes just before the campground.

GPS Coordinates: N 46° 57.683' W 111° 56.601'

Contact: Bureau of Land Management, 106 N. Parkmont, P.O. Box 3388, Butte, MT 59702, 406/533-7600, www.blm.gov/mt/st/en.html.

28 DEPARTURE POINT

Scenic rating: 8

on the Missouri River north of Helena

BEST (

At 3,600 feet on Holter Lake's east shore, Departure Point is a tiny campground one bay south of Log Gulch. A narrow paved road connects it with the larger campground, but be prepared for its sharp, blind corners. The campground is as far as you can drive along the shoreline of Holter Lake's east side, and it sits at the northern entrance to the Beartooth Wildlife Management Area, where you can see elk, deer, bighorn sheep, and a variety of raptors and birds. Go for wildlife drives either in early morning or evening when sightings are usually best.

The tiny campground has only four sites on a paved parking lot set above the day use area and beach. The double-wide parking strips cram together, but the sunset views across the lake are stunning. A paved trail connects the parking lot with the day-use area and swimming beach. The distance is short enough that you can launch canoes and sea kayaks from here to tour the Oxbow. Larger boats can be launched at Log Gulch and beached here. Rattlesnakes are in the area; caution is advised.

Campsites, facilities: Four RV campsites can accommodate midsized RVs. Facilities include picnic tables, fire rings with grills, vault toilets, drinking water, garbage service, and a buoyed swimming area. Leashed pets are permitted. Toilets are wheelchair-accessible.

Reservations, fees: No reservations are accepted. Campsites cost $10. Day use of the park costs $2. Cash or check. Open early May–October.

Directions: From I-15 north of Helena, take Exit 226 at Wolf Creek. From Wolf Creek on the south side of the freeway, drive Recreation Road for 3.3 miles until you cross the bridge over the Missouri River; turn right onto paved Beartooth Road for seven miles. The paved surface will change to a rough, oiled dirt road about a lane and a half wide for a couple of miles. Drive slowly—it is narrow with blind corners.

GPS Coordinates: N 46°57.391' W 111° 56.418'

Contact: Bureau of Land Management, 106 N. Parkmont, P.O. Box 3388, Butte, MT 59702, 406/533-7600, www.blm.gov/mt/st/en.html.

29 PRICKLY PEAR RIVER

Scenic rating: 6

on the Prickly Pear River north of Helena

On the Prickly Pear River, a tributary of the Missouri River, three state-run fishing access campsites dot this stream, which attracts anglers with its brown and rainbow trout. At 3,760 feet in elevation, the camps snuggle into Prickly Pear Canyon—a dramatic geological slice through layered pink rock. The campsites are divided into two locations—the Lichen Cliff on the north and Prickly Pear to the south.

Despite the side road locations, both campgrounds fill with noise from the paralleling I-15 and railroad tracks. The Prickly Pear campsite sits 20 feet from the tracks. The two Lichen Cliff campsites are pull-overs off the road, better suited to midsized RVs, even though the state does not recommend trailers or RVs. The Prickly Pear campsite, tucked down a short spur road, offers a better tent area secluded from the road. Lichen Cliff campsites sit right on the stream, but at Prickly Pear, you must walk across the railroad tracks to several two-minute trails to reach the creek.

Campsites, facilities: The campgrounds have three RV or tent campsites. Lichen Cliff can accommodate larger RVs, but the Prickly Pear spot is suitable only for smaller RVs. Small trailers can fit, but the campsite has minimal turnaround space. Facilities include picnic tables, fire rings with grills, and vault toilets. No drinking water is available. If you choose to use the stream water, boil or purify it first. Pack out your trash. Leashed pets are permitted.

Reservations, fees: No reservations are accepted. Camping costs $7 if you have a Montana fishing license or $12 without. Cash or check. Open year-round.

Directions: From I-15 north of Helena, take Exit 226 at Wolf Creek and drive south on Recreation Road, or take Exit 219 and drive north on Spring Creek Road. The milepost numbering starts at the south and begins re-numbering again at Lyons Creek Road around milepost 3. Find Prickly Pear at milepost 0.8 between Exit 219 and Lyons Creek Road. Find Lichen Cliff at milepost 1.6 between Lyons Creek Road and Wolf Creek.

GPS coordinates for Lichen Cliff: N 46° 56.316' W 112° 7.300'

GPS coordinates for Prickly Pear: N 46° 55.004' W 112° 7.371'

Contact: Montana Fish, Wildlife, and Parks, Region 4 Office, 4600 Giant Springs Rd., Great Falls, MT 59405, 406/454-5840, http://fwp.mt.gov.

30 BEARTOOTH LANDING

Scenic rating: 8

on the Missouri River north of Helena

On west shore of the Missouri River on Holter Lake, at 3,600 feet, Beartooth Landing is a small boat-in only campground below the Sleeping Giant. It sits just downstream from the 2,225-mile mark on the Missouri, across from Ming Bar, which has shallow water over a sandy swimming basin. Boating from the north requires navigating 10.2 river miles through the convoluted Oxbow from Log Gulch, roughly double the air miles. You can also boat in 6.8 miles from the south through the steep-walled canyon of Gate of the Mountains. The campground sits 1.8 miles upstream from Mann Gulch National Historic Site and the north entrance to Gates of the Mountains and across the river from the Beartooth Wildlife Management Area, with pronghorns, deer, elk, bighorn sheep, raptors, and songbirds.

The tiny, north-facing, partially shaded campsites sit along the shore, with views of Beartooth Mountain. No dock is available, so boats must be beached. During the day, the area bustles with motorboats—water-skiers, sightseers, and anglers—but in the evening, quiet pervades the river. Rattlesnakes are in the area; caution is advised.

Campsites, facilities: The campground has four tent sites. Facilities include picnic tables, fire rings with grills, and a vault toilet. No drinking water is available. Pack out your trash. Leashed pets are permitted.

Reservations, fees: No reservations are accepted. Camping is free. Open early May–October.

Directions: To launch from the north on Holter Lake, drive I-15 north of Helena to Exit 226 at Wolf Creek. From Wolf Creek on the south side of the freeway, drive Recreation Road for 3.3 miles until you cross the bridge over the Missouri River; turn right onto Beartooth Road for 6.5 miles. The paved road turns to bumpy oiled dirt and narrows with sharp, blind corners, but pavement resumes just before the Log Gulch Campground, where you can launch a boat. Kayaks and canoes can also launch 0.6 mile farther south at Departure Point Recreation Area. To launch from the south, drive 20 miles north of Helena on I-15 to Exit 209 and then east on Gates of the Mountains Road for 2.7 miles to Gates of the Mountains Marina.

GPS Coordinates: N 46° 53.131' W 111° 56.458'

Contact: Bureau of Land Management, 106 N. Parkmont, P.O. Box 3388, Butte, MT 59702, 406/533-7600, www.blm.gov/mt/st/en.html.

31 COULTER

Scenic rating: 10

in Gates of the Mountains in Helena National Forest

BEST (

Located on the Missouri River at 3,610 feet in elevation, Coulter is a boat-in only campground in the Gates of the Mountains, a steep-walled narrow gorge named by Lewis

and Clark. The campground sits about midway through the canyon on the east shore. You can launch from Gates of the Mountains Marina ($5 for boats from trailers and $3 for kayaks and canoes) and travel 3.3 miles downstream, or launch from the north at Log Gulch or Departure Point to travel 11.7 miles upstream. Both routes can be windy. The campground sits about 1.5 miles south of the entrance to Mann Gulch, a National Historic Landmark honoring 13 firefighters who lost their lives in 1949 (their crosses still stand on the hillside), and 0.8 mile south of the Meriwether picnic area, which has trails, interpretive displays, and a boat dock. A fire burned some of the surrounding wilderness in 2007. Trails also go upstream from the campground to several overlooks. Watch for ospreys and bald eagles fishing.

The campground sits on a grassy hillside with campsites in the open sun or tucked back in more secluded pines and junipers that offer

© BECKY LOMAX

Coulter campground is located on the Missouri River in the Gates of the Mountains canyon.

partial shade. After the day boaters and the tour boat disappear, a quiet descends on the canyon.

Campsites, facilities: The campground has seven tent sites. Facilities include picnic tables, fire rings, a vault toilet, and boat docks. Pack out your trash. Leashed pets are permitted.

Reservations, fees: No reservations are accepted. Camping is free. Open late May–September.

Directions: To launch boats from the south, drive 20 miles north of Helena on I-15 to Exit 209 and then east on Gates of the Mountains Road for 2.7 miles to Gates of the Mountains Marina. To launch boats from the north, drive I-15 north of Helena to Exit 226 at Wolf Creek. From Wolf Creek on the south side of the freeway, drive Recreation Road for 3.3 miles and turn right onto the half paved/half bumpy oiled dirt Beartooth Road for 6.5 miles to Log Gulch Campground, where you can launch a boat. Kayaks and canoes can also launch 0.6 mile farther south at Departure Point Recreation Area.

GPS Coordinates: N 46° 51.570' W 111° 54.439'

Contact: Helena National Forest, Helena Ranger District, 2001 Poplar, Helena, MT 59601, 406/449-5490, www.fs.fed.usfr1/helena.

32 BLACK SANDY

Scenic rating: 8

on Hauser Lake north of Helena

On the west side of Hauser Lake, south of Hauser Dam at 3,835 feet in elevation, the 43-acre campground, which sits just north of White Sandy Campground, has the benefit of both a lake and canyon scenery as the walls rise straight from the water. The lake is a reservoir on the Missouri River, and the campground sits on the Lewis and Clark Trail; interpretive information is available. A hiking trail leads one mile along the lake. Hauser Lake is popular for waterskiing, swimming, boating, and fishing for kokanee salmon, trout, and other game fish.

Most of the campsites cram along the river frontage with no privacy and nearly on top of each other. Grass surrounds cement pads under the picnic tables. The campground bakes on hot days; only one-third of the sites have willows to offer some shade. The sun drops behind the canyon walls early to begin cooling off the campground for evening. Level, back-in gravel parking pads access most campsites. Two of the walk-in tent sites have river frontage; the other two sit up on a flat bench with views. The tent sites are dry, dusty, and lack trees.

Campsites, facilities: The campground has 29 RV or tent campsites, plus four walk-in tent sites. Parking pads can accommodate trailers up to 35 feet. Facilities include picnic tables, fire rings with grills, vault and flush toilets, a boat ramp, dock, boat slips, drinking water, garbage service, a dump station, campfire programs, and a campground host. Leashed pets are permitted. Toilets are wheelchair-accessible.

Reservations, fees: No reservations are accepted. Camping costs $15. For day use, Montana residents get in free; nonresidents pay $5 per vehicle. Cash or check. Open year-round.

Directions: From I-15 north of Helena, take Exit 200 and drive west on Lincoln Road for 5.1 miles. Turn left at the signed junction onto Hauser Dam Road for three miles, which turns to a wide gravel boulevard in 0.2 mile. At the fork where the pavement resumes, swing left, following the sign to Black Sandy State Park. The campground entrance will be on the right after the dump station and sign.

GPS Coordinates: N 46° 44.848' W 111° 53.185'

Contact: Montana Fish, Wildlife, and Parks, Region 4 Office, 4600 Giant Springs Rd., Great Falls, MT 59405, 406/454-5840, http://fwp.mt.gov.

33 WHITE SANDY

Scenic rating: 8

on Hauser Lake north of Helena

Located on the west side of Hauser Lake south of Hauser Dam, the campground sits at 3,835 feet in elevation just south of Black Sandy Campground. The lake is on the Missouri River where it begins to narrow into a canyon with steep cliff walls. The campground sits on the Lewis and Clark Trail. Hauser Lake is popular for fishing, swimming, boating, and waterskiing. The lake houses kokanee salmon, walleye, yellow perch, mountain whitefish, and several species of trout.

White Sandy is a new campground. As such, its trees are very small, affording no shade or windbreaks yet. The sites, however, are bigger and more spacious than in the adjacent state park, so they gain more privacy by distance, even though you can see the neighbors. The grassy campground has two separate areas for campsites. The upper spur has five sites that back in against a hill with a turnaround loop at the end; these have views of the lower bluff and lake. The lower bluff area is more popular for its 14 lakefront sites. Most of the gravel back-in parking pads are double-wide.

Campsites, facilities: The campground has 34 RV or tent campsites that can accommodate larger RVs. Facilities include picnic tables, fire rings with grills, vault toilets, a boat ramp, a dock, a fish-cleaning station, drinking water, garbage service, firewood for sale, and a campground host. Leashed pets are permitted. Site 14 and toilets are wheelchair-accessible.

Reservations, fees: No reservations are accepted. Camping costs $10. Cash or check. Open May–October.

Directions: From I-15 north of Helena, take Exit 200 and drive west on Lincoln Road for 5.1 miles. Turn left at the signed junction onto Hauser Dam Road for three miles, which turns to a wide gravel boulevard in 0.2 mile. At the fork where the pavement resumes, swing right, following the sign to Black Sandy State Park. The road climbs over a bluff and drops into the campground in 0.2 mile.

GPS Coordinates: N 46° 44.503' W 111° 53.251'

Contact: Bureau of Land Management, 106 N. Parkmont, P.O. Box 3388, Butte, MT 59702, 406/533-7600, www.blm.gov/mt/st/en.html.

34 DEVIL'S ELBOW

Scenic rating: 9

on the Missouri River north of Helena

BEST (

At an elevation of 3,700 feet on the west side of Hauser Lake on the Missouri River, the Devil's Elbow campground sits where the river makes a sharp oxbow around a peninsula before entering a steep-walled slot canyon. The campground sits on that peninsula about one mile north of the York Bridge, the access to the Gates of the Mountains Wilderness and Helena National Forest. The scenic drive through the narrow rocky canyon across the bridge is worth the time. The campground sits below the Two Camps Vista, which affords a dramatic view of the area as well as interpretive information on the Lewis and Clark expedition. Hiking trails connect to Clark's Bay picnic area and the vista. Hauser Lake is popular for swimming, boating, waterskiing, and fishing for kokanee salmon, trout, and other game fish.

The spacious, sunny campground has three grassy loops on a sagebrush bluff above the lake. Young trees scatter throughout the open camp's double-wide gravel parking pads. Some areas are fenced above steep cliffs. Sites are spread out to feel private, but you can see the neighbors. In loop A, sites 1, 3, 5, 6, and 7 overlook the water. In loop B, sites 18, 20,

21, 22, and 24 have water views. Loop C sits farther back from the edge of the bluffs, but with expansive views across the water to distant mountains.

Campsites, facilities: The campground has 41 RV or tent campsites that can accommodate larger RVs on their double-wide parking pads. Facilities include picnic tables, fire rings with grills, vault toilets, a boat ramp, docks, boat slips, boat trailer parking, a fish-cleaning station, drinking water, garbage service, firewood for sale, and a campground host. Leashed pets are permitted. Toilets are wheelchair-accessible.

Reservations, fees: No reservations are accepted. Camping costs $10. Day-use only costs $2. Cash or check. Open May–October.

Directions: From I-15 in Helena, take Exit 193 to the east side of the freeway and go north on Washington Street for 0.8 mile. Turn east onto Canyon Ferry Road for 0.7 mile. Turn north onto York Road and drive 11.6 miles to the signed campground entrance on the right. Drop 0.5 mile down into the campground. GPS Coordinates: N 46° 42.021' W 111° 48.272'

Contact: Bureau of Land Management, 106 N. Parkmont, P.O. Box 3388, Butte, MT 59702, 406/533-7600, www.blm.gov/mt/st/en.html.

35 VIGILANTE

Scenic rating: 8

in the Big Belt Mountains of Helena National Forest

Tucked at an elevation of 4,400 feet at the west end of the deep Trout Creek Canyon in the Big Belt Mountains, Vigilante Campground is the only designated campground for exploring this area of Helena National Forest. The Vigilante Trail (#247)—a National Recreation Trail—begins at the campground and climbs six miles into a hanging valley with an overlook into Trout Creek Canyon. The last 300-foot section requires climbing through steep crevasses in the rocks. The Trout Creek Canyon Trail (#270), which begins with a one-mile wheelchair-accessible paved section, traverses up the canyon for three miles, with clear views of its limestone walls. Shaded areas of the canyon stay cool in the heat of summer, and an interpretive brochure identifies features along the trail, including the original road, which was washed out in a 1981 flood. The canyon is also good for bird- and wildlife-watching.

The quiet, secluded campground snuggles at the bottom of a canyon, where you have a choice of shady or sunny campsites. Some campsites have a forest duff floor; others are grassy. The campground is small, so you will see the neighbors, but enough undergrowth is present in places to make you feel private. Prepare for an onslaught of mosquitoes in early summer.

Campsites, facilities: The campground has 18 RV or tent campsites that can accommodate only smaller RVs. Facilities include picnic tables, fire rings, drinking water, and vault toilets. Pack out your trash. Leashed pets are permitted. A wheelchair-accessible toilet is available.

Reservations, fees: No reservations are accepted. Campsites cost $5. Cash or check. Open late May–September.

Directions: From I-15 in Helena, take Exit 193 to the east side of the freeway and go north on Washington Street for 0.8 mile. Turn east onto Canyon Ferry Road for 0.7 mile. Turn north onto York Road and drive 12.6 miles to the York Bridge. After crossing the bridge, drive 10 miles on the York-Trout Creek Road to the campground. The entrance is on the right. GPS Coordinates: N 46° 46.020' W 111° 39.024'

Contact: Helena National Forest, Helena Ranger District, 2001 Poplar, Helena, MT 59601, 406/449-5490, www.fs.fed.usfr1/helena.

36 CROMWELL DIXON

Scenic rating: 6

on MacDonald Pass in Helena National Forest

At 6,260 feet in elevation at the top of Mac-Donald Pass west of Helena, Cromwell Dixon Campground sits on the Continental Divide. Bicyclists use the campground while doing long-distance rides. The campground is more one for convenience when traveling west from Helena rather than a destination in itself.

With the campground's proximity to Highway 12—a trucking route—noise pervades the area even at night. The paved campground road loops around a hillside of mature Douglas fir and lodgepole pines. A few of the pines are turning rust-colored due to attacking beetles. Fireweed and cow parsnip meadows also flank the campground, offering a mix of choices for campsites. Open to the wind, grassy sites 6 and 8 have sunny expansive views across meadows; other sites tuck protected and shaded under big trees with a forest duff floor. Some sites include large, shapely granitic boulders that kids find fun for climbing. Most of the gravel parking pads are back-ins. Because of the hillside, only some of the sites have level tent spaces. The sites at the end of the loop are closer together than those that are further spaced out at the beginning of the loop.

Campsites, facilities: The campground has 15 RV or tent campsites. Some of the sites can fit midsized RVs, and site 9 offers a big pull-through. Facilities include picnic tables, fire rings, vault toilets, and drinking water. Pack out your trash. Leashed pets are permitted. A wheelchair-accessible toilet is available.

Reservations, fees: No reservations are accepted. Campsites cost $8. Cash or check. Open late May–September.

Directions: From Helena, go 15 miles west on Highway 12. At milepost 27.8, turn south off the highway at the campground sign and immediately turn right over the cattle grate for 0.2 mile to the campground entrance.

GPS Coordinates: N 46° 33.427' W 112° 18.892'

Contact: Helena National Forest, Helena Ranger District, 2100 Poplar, Helena, MT 59601, 406/449-5490, www.fs.fed.us/r1/helena.

37 RIVERSIDE

Scenic rating: 7

on the Missouri River north of Canyon Ferry Dam

Most people who visit Riverside Campground, which sits at 3,700 feet, head onto the Missouri River. You can launch from here to float, motor, or paddle downstream as far as Hauser Dam, which is 15 river miles north. Campers stay here rather than up on Canyon Ferry Reservoir because they prefer the feel of the slow-moving river to the lake. A primitive, dirt boat ramp and dock aid in launching small motorboats, rafts, drift boats, kayaks, and canoes. Boat trailer parking is available. One wheelchair-accessible fishing platform is also available.

Surrounded by dry sagebrush and juniper hillsides, the wide-open, breezy, and sunny campground sits just below the Canyon Ferry Dam, which is visible and emits a constant audible drone. Four interconnected loops make up most of the campground, and the bulk of the campsites circle two of them. Sites 1–4, 6–9, and 20 have river frontage, with their picnic tables a few feet from the shoreline. The lack of trees equals no privacy, shade, or windbreaks, but the flat grassy sites afford plenty of room for setting up large tents. Site 21 sits off by itself overlooking the boat launch.

Campsites, facilities: The campground has 38 RV or tent campsites. Facilities include picnic tables (three are covered), fire rings with grills, vault toilets, garbage service, drinking water, a boat ramp, horseshoe pits, and campground hosts. Leashed pets are permitted. A wheelchair-accessible toilet and campsite (site 1) on the river are available.

Reservations, fees: No reservations are accepted. Campsites cost $8. Cash or check. Open May–September.

Directions: From I-15 in Helena, take Exit 193 to the east side of the freeway and go north on Washington Street for 0.8 mile. Turn east onto Canyon Ferry Road for 14.3 miles to the Canyon Ferry Dam. Cross the dam, driving 1.2 miles. Turn north onto Jimtown Road for one mile, veering left at both junctions, until you reach the campground entrance on the right.

GPS Coordinates: N 46° 39.376' W 111° 44.194'

Contact: Bureau of Reclamation, Montana Area Office, Canyon Ferry Field Office, 7661 Canyon Ferry Rd., Helena, MT 59602, 406/475-3921, www.usbr.gov/gp/mtao/canyonferry/.

38 FISHHAWK

Scenic rating: 8

on the northwest shore of Canyon Ferry Reservoir

On bluffs at 3,850 feet above Canyon Ferry Reservoir, Fishhawk Campground is a treat for tent campers. While it does not have lake access for boating, it does provide views of the intricate web of islands, peninsulas, and coves at the north end of the lake, and you can climb down to the rocky lakeshore. The campsites face the sunrise, with views of the Big Belt Mountains flanking the lake's east side.

The unnumbered walk-in campsites are divided by rocky outcrops and tall ponderosa pines that offer a bit of shade and privacy, but most of the campsites are quite sunny—especially the one adjacent to the toilet. Many campers bring tarps for shade as well as rain protection. Sagebrush and junipers also grow on the hillside, casting a scent into the air after rains. Each of the sites has flat spaces for tents, and some can fit more than one tent. Even from the vantage point of the bluffs, you can hear motorboats on the lake during the day, but the noise disappears at night. Bring binoculars for watching bald eagles and ospreys fishing. The gravel entry road is narrow and curves sharply around the loop that contains the parking areas. Bear in mind that you must hike uphill to the toilet here from most of the campsites.

Campsites, facilities: The campground has five walk-in tent campsites. Facilities include picnic tables and fire rings with grills at some of the campsites and a vault toilet. Bring your own water. Pack out your trash. Leashed pets are permitted. A wheelchair-accessible toilet and one site are available.

Reservations, fees: No reservations are accepted. Campsites cost $8. Cash or check. Open year-round; however, services are available only May–September.

Directions: From I-15 in Helena, take Exit 193 to the east side of the freeway and go north on Washington Street for 0.8 mile. Turn east onto Canyon Ferry Road for 13.4 miles to West Shore Drive. Turn south and drive 0.5 mile on the narrow, paved, hilly single-lane road. The campground entrance is on the left.

GPS Coordinates: N 46° 37.935' W 111° 43.063'

Contact: Bureau of Reclamation, Montana Area Office, Canyon Ferry Field Office, 7661 Canyon Ferry Rd., Helena, MT 59602, 406/475-3921, www.usbr.gov/gp/mtao/canyonferry/.

39 COURT SHERIFF

Scenic rating: 7

on the northeast shore of Canyon Ferry Reservoir

On the rugged north end of Canyon Ferry Reservoir at 3,800 feet, Court Sheriff is the closest campground to the Canyon Ferry Visitor Center, 0.7 mile to the west. While it doesn't have a boat ramp, it has plenty of easy-access shoreline for launching hand-carried watercraft. (You can launch larger boats at Chinamen's Gulch, 0.3 mile south, or at Kim's Marina about 0.5 mile south.) A few islands sit offshore, and lagoons divide parts of the campground, giving the landscape a playful look. The islands also grant destinations for exploration. Much of the shoreline is muddy and willowy, but open areas are available for beaching boats. Anglers go after walleye, rainbow trout, brown trout, ling, and perch in the lake and ice fish in winter.

Almost half of the campsites have waterfront—on either the lake or one of the lagoons. The grassy, open, sunny campground affords little privacy or shade, but a few sites have large pines for partial shade. Large flat tent spaces are available, and several campsites have paved, double-wide, back-in parking to accommodate trailers. A few pull-through sites are also available. This is a busy end of the lake, humming with the noise of personal watercraft and motorboats until the sun goes down. The campground faces the sunset.

Campsites, facilities: The campground has 49 RV or tent campsites that can accommodate midsized RVs. Facilities include picnic tables, fire rings with grills, vault toilets, drinking water, garbage service, boat trailer parking, and campground hosts. Leashed pets are permitted. Wheelchair-accessible toilets are available.

Reservations, fees: No reservations are accepted. Campsites cost $10. Cash or check. Open year-round; however, services are available only May–September.

Directions: From I-15 in Helena, take Exit 193 to the east side of the freeway and go north on Washington Street for 0.8 mile. Turn east onto Canyon Ferry Road for 14.3 miles to the Canyon Ferry Dam. Continue 1.7 miles past the dam to milepost 10.8 and turn right. GPS Coordinates: N 46° 39.488' W 111° 42.608'

Contact: Bureau of Reclamation, Montana Area Office, Canyon Ferry Field Office, 7661 Canyon Ferry Rd., Helena, MT 59602, 406/475-3921, www.usbr.gov/gp/mtao/canyonferry/.

40 CHINAMEN'S GULCH

Scenic rating: 7

on the east shore of Canyon Ferry Reservoir

Located on the west shore of the north end of Canyon Ferry Reservoir at 3,800 feet, Chinamen's Gulch sits in a small, narrow canyon that descends to the lakeshore. Contrary to other campgrounds that spread out along the shore, this campground has a tiny beach area. But it includes a shallow area for swimming, a primitive gravel boat launch, and a small dock. The beach flanks a small bay off the main lake, which offers game fishing in summer and ice fishing in winter.

Chinamen's Gulch Campground is a slice of a hot, dry, dusty narrow canyon that faces the sunset. Large ponderosa pines cover some of the upper sites, offering shade, but some of these are dying due to attacking pine beetles. The lower 12 campsites are small and terraced with views of the water and each other. Most sit west-facing in full sun. The upper campsites are more spread out, with large boulders and big trees dividing some of the sites for a little privacy. You'll still be able to see a few neighbors, though. Most of the sites have dirt floors with little surrounding ground cover. Even though the campground is on the busy north end of the lake, it quiets at night.

Campsites, facilities: The campground has 45 RV or tent campsites that can accommodate smaller RVs and trailers. Facilities include picnic tables, fire rings with grills, vault toilets, drinking water, garbage service, a boat ramp, dock, and campground hosts. Leashed pets are permitted. Wheelchair-accessible toilets are available.

Reservations, fees: No reservations are accepted. Campsites cost $8. Cash or check. Open year-round; however, services are available only May–September.

Directions: From I-15 in Helena, take Exit 193 to the east side of the freeway and go north on Washington Street for 0.8 mile. Turn east onto Canyon Ferry Road for 14.3 miles to the Canyon Ferry Dam. Continue two miles past the dam to milepost 11.1 and turn right, descending on a dirt washboard road down into the campground.

GPS Coordinates: N 46° 39.046' W 111° 42.540'

Contact: Bureau of Reclamation, Montana Area Office, Canyon Ferry Field Office, 7661 Canyon Ferry Rd., Helena, MT 59602, 406/475-3921, www.usbr.gov/gp/mtao/canyonferry/.

41 KIM'S MARINA AND RV RESORT

Scenic rating: 6

on the east shore of Canyon Ferry Lake

Kim's Marina is one of three marinas on the 33,500-acre Canyon Ferry Lake. Located at 3,800 feet in elevation, the marina and RV resort sit on the northeast corner of the lake in a sheltered bay. The resort services boaters, water-skiers, and anglers going after the walleye, rainbow trout, brown trout, ling, and perch that inhabit the reservoir.

The campground is cramped wall-to-wall with RVs. Premium sites on the water for dry camping and electrical-only hookups cost more than those off the waterfront. Full hookup sites are set back in the campground, some on a large, dry, gravel hillside. A paved road loops through the grassy campground, but the parking pads—all back-ins—are gravel. A few big willows dot the shoreline along the waterfront sites for partial shade, but most of the sites are sunny. The campground has several

permanent trailer homes, plus rents long-term RV sites, and the bay is busy with motorboats during the day as the marina houses around 165 boats.

Campsites, facilities: The campground maintains 105 RV sites. Facilities include picnic tables, pedestal grills, flush toilets, showers, drinking water, a token-operated launderette, a store with fishing tackle, a disposal station, horseshoe pits, tennis courts, boat rentals, docks, boat trailer parking, boat slips, buoyed swimming beach, and hookups for sewer, water, and electricity. Leashed pets are permitted.

Reservations, fees: Reservations are accepted. Hookups cost $24–27. Dry camping costs $15–16. Fees are based on four people per site; each additional person costs $3. A 7 percent Montana bed tax will be added to camping fees. Showers cost $2. Use of the RV and boat disposal station costs $5. Launching a boat costs $10. Open year-round; however, services are available only May–September.

Directions: From I-15 in Helena, take Exit 193 to the east side of the freeway and go north on Washington Street for 0.8 mile. Turn east onto Canyon Ferry Road for 14.3 miles to the Canyon Ferry Dam. Cross the dam, driving another 2.5 miles around the head of the lake. The marina is on the right at milepost 11.5.

GPS Coordinates: N 46° 39.144' W 111° 42.070'

Contact: Kim's Marina and RV Resort, 8015 Canyon Ferry Rd., Helena, MT 59602, 406/475-3723, www.kimsmarina.com.

42 JO BONNER

Scenic rating: 6

on the east shore of Canyon Ferry Reservoir

Located on the east shore of Canyon Ferry Reservoir at 3,800 feet, Jo Bonner Campground sits at the head of a long bay that is flanked with summer homes. It is the farthest south of the busy north-end campgrounds, which attract water-skiers, sailors, Jet Skiers, windsurfers, and anglers. Game fish opportunities include brook trout, brown trout, burbot, rainbow trout, walleye, and yellow perch. In winter, the lake is popular for ice fishing. Opposite the campground turnoff, the Magpie Creek Road leads to a back route (trail #248) that connects with the Hanging Valley National Recreation Trail, which climbs and then drops through a narrow rocky chasm to an overlook above Trout Creek Canyon.

The campground sits on an open grassy slope speckled with a few cottonwoods and junipers and flanked with large trees and willows along the lakeshore. The gravel campground loop connects the grassy, sloped, uneven parking pads. Most of the campsites are sunny and open with no privacy; the four campsites on the shore gain partial afternoon shade from the trees. The shoreline camps are muddy and overused; one even floods in high water. The remainder of the campground doesn't see much use, so you can feel like you have the place to yourself. At nighttime, the campground and bay quiet.

Campsites, facilities: The campground has 28 RV or tent campsites that can accommodate smaller RVs. Facilities include picnic tables, fire rings with grills, vault toilets, drinking water, garbage service, a boat ramp, boat dock, and campground hosts. Leashed pets are permitted. A wheelchair-accessible toilet is available.

Reservations, fees: No reservations are accepted. Campsites cost $8. Cash or check. Open year-round; however, services are available only May–September.

Directions: From I-15 in Helena, take Exit 193 to the east side of the freeway and go north on Washington Street for 0.8 mile. Turn east onto Canyon Ferry Road for 14.3 miles to the Canyon Ferry Dam. Cross the dam, driving another 3.7 miles around the head of the lake. At milepost 12.7, where you'll see the campground sign, turn right for 0.1 mile. The campground entrance sits at the junction between East Shore Drive and East Shore Drive N.

GPS Coordinates: N 46° 39.074' W 111° 42.484'

Contact: Bureau of Reclamation, Montana Area Office, Canyon Ferry Field Office, 7661 Canyon Ferry Rd., Helena, MT 59602, 406/475-3921, www.usbr.gov/gp/mtao/canyonferry/.

43 HELLGATE

Scenic rating: 6

on the east shore of Canyon Ferry Reservoir

Hellgate sits on along the south shore of a long, narrow bay at 3,800 feet on the east side of Canyon Ferry Reservoir, known for its fishing. While the bay is somewhat protected, this section of the lake is known for wind, and the nearly treeless peninsula housing the campground offers little protection from breezes. The bay lacks summers homes, making it a much more wild location than some of the campgrounds farther north.

The 1.2-mile-long campground offers a variety of terrain for camping. The first section flanks a creek with large cottonwoods and lush grass. Even though the sites here are south-facing, they are separated from each other by lush undergrowth (you can still see the campground road, though). On the bay, three loops with back-in gravel parking pads have waterfront sites. These vary between partial shade with willows and cottonwoods along the shore where you can beach a boat to full sun with overlooks of the water. Some have a little privacy, but you can see your neighboring campers from most of them. A last loop curves around the barren bluff at the end of the peninsula. The sites here garner grand views of the lake but are very windy and have zero privacy.

Campsites, facilities: The campground has 96 RV or tent campsites that can accommodate large RVs. Facilities include picnic

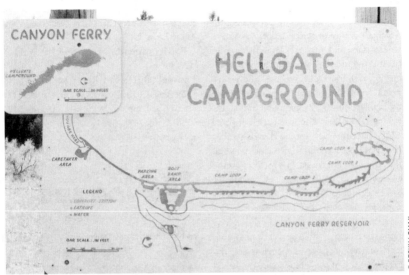

Hellgate is one of the largest campgrounds on Canyon Ferry Reservoir.

© BECKY LOMAX

tables, fire rings with grills, vault toilets, one flush toilet, drinking water, garbage service, boat ramps, boat docks, a life jacket loan station, and campground hosts. Leashed pets are permitted. Wheelchair-accessible toilets are available.

Reservations, fees: No reservations are accepted. Campsites cost $8. Cash or check. Open year-round; however, services are available only May–September.

Directions: From I-15 in Helena, take Exit 193 to the east side of the freeway and go north on Washington Street for 0.8 mile. Turn east onto Canyon Ferry Road for 14.3 miles to the Canyon Ferry Dam. Continue driving for eight miles. At the campground sign at milepost 17.1, turn west onto the gravel road for 0.7 mile. The gravel soon gives way to rutted dirt with potholes and bumpy washboards as it descends to the campground.

GPS Coordinates: N 46° 39.079' W 111° 42.476'

Contact: Bureau of Reclamation, Montana Area Office, Canyon Ferry Field Office, 7661 Canyon Ferry Rd., Helena, MT 59602, 406/475-3921, www.usbr.gov/gp/mtao/canyonferry/.

44 GOOSE BAY MARINA

Scenic rating: 6

on the east shore of Canyon Ferry Reservoir

At 3,800 feet in elevation on the east shore of Canyon Ferry Reservoir, Goose Bay sits midway downlake in a remote area without crowds on the water for fishing, waterskiing, or boating. Contrary to the lake's rugged and semiforested north end, this section of the reservoir is surrounded by low, arid sagebrush, sparse grassland, and ranches. Trees are a rarity. The marina sits in a finger inlet protected from lake winds. The concessionaire's contract for this marina and RV campground runs out in 2010; call first to inquire on the campground's status and possible changes to its services.

The RV campground sits behind the store and adjacent to the marina; sites are stacked side by side in parking lot fashion with no privacy and no lake views. With no trees for shade, the campground is hot, but it's marginally protected by trailer homes, a few cottonwood trees, and the store if winds come from the west. The marina area also has 31 year-round trailer homes.

Campsites, facilities: The marina campground has 68 RV sites that can accommodate large RVs and 20 tent sites. Facilities include flush toilets, showers, hookups for water and electricity up to 50 amps, drinking water, garbage service, a disposal station, a boat ramp, a gas station, a convenience store, propane for sale, and a coin-operated launderette. The marina has 88 boat slips. Leashed pets are permitted.

Reservations, fees: Reservations are accepted. Campsites with hookups cost $17.50–19.50. Tent sites cost $12. Montana bed tax of 7 percent is added on. Cash, check, or credit card. Open April–early November.

Directions: From I-15 in Helena, take Exit 193 to the east side of the freeway and go north on Washington Street for 0.8 mile. Turn east onto Canyon Ferry Road for 26.5 miles, circling around the north end of the lake and down the east side to the Goose Bay sign. Turn right onto the rough gravel road and drive 2.8 miles. The road tours around one bay before reaching Goose Bay Marina. From Townsend at the lake's south end, drive east on Highway 12 for 3.3 miles and then north on Highway 284 for 20.3 miles to the Goose Bay turnoff.

GPS Coordinates: N 46° 32.513' W 111° 34.269'

Contact: Goose Bay Marina, 300 Goose Bay Ln., Townsend, MT 59644, 406/266-3645.

45 GOOSE BAY PRIMITIVE

Scenic rating: 6

on the east shore of Canyon Ferry Reservoir

At 3,800 feet on Canyon Ferry Reservoir's east shore, Goose Bay sits midway in a

remote area less crowded than the north end. Goose Bay houses a marina, RV campground, a coin-operated launderette, and a store with gas, fishing tackle, propane, and minor groceries. Primitive undesignated campsites are scattered from the dirt-ramp boat launch west of the marina around the two peninsulas and two small bays to the north. The lake attracts anglers for its game fish and winter ice fishing. Five undesignated beaches surround the peninsulas, offering places to swim, water-ski, and beach boats overnight.

Primitive campsites flank the lake, offering solitude, privacy, quiet, and views. However, the undesignated area around the boat launch gets crowded with RVs. Away from the boat launch, sites tuck into the rare cottonwoods for wind and shade protection; others sit open on the barren bluffs above the lake, catching the brunt of winds and heat. Follow Leave No Trace principles in choosing an undesignated campsite, using only pre-existing fire rings. Scout the rough roads first for possible mudholes and large ruts as well as turnaround spots before driving in blind. Dirt roads circle both peninsulas, with campsites along the perimeters and plenty of flat space for tents.

Campsites, facilities: Goose Bay has 43 RV and tent campsites that can accommodate large RVs. Facilities include the occasional rock fire ring and two wheelchair-accessible vault toilets—one on each peninsula. Nine sites have picnic tables. Leashed pets are permitted.

Reservations, fees: No reservations are accepted. Camping is free. Open year-round.

Directions: From I-15 in Helena, take Exit 193 to the east side of the freeway and go north on Washington Street for 0.8 mile. Turn east onto Canyon Ferry Road for 26.5 miles, circling the lake's north end and dropping down the east side to the Goose Bay sign. Turn right onto the gravel road and drive 2.8 miles. The road tours around one bay before reaching Goose Bay. From

Townsend at the lake's south end, drive east on Highway 12 for 3.3 miles and then north on Highway 284 for 20.3 miles to the Goose Bay turnoff.

GPS Coordinates: N 46° 32.420' W 111° 33.663'

Contact: Bureau of Reclamation, Montana Area Office, Canyon Ferry Field Office, 7661 Canyon Ferry Rd., Helena, MT 59602, 406/475-3921, www.usbr.gov/gp/mtao/canyonferry/.

46 WHITE EARTH

Scenic rating: 6

on the west shore of Canyon Ferry Reservoir

At an elevation of 3,800 feet on the west shore of Canyon Ferry Reservoir, White Earth is named for its white sand and pebble beaches, although the sand is more like silty clay. As the reservoir level drops during the summer, the beaches get bigger. Call the Canyon Ferry Field Office for current water levels. The cement boat ramp, dock, and trailer parking aid those launching boats onto the lake for waterskiing, sightseeing, and fishing. In winter, anglers turn to ice fishing. The 29-mile-long lake is a trout fishery and also has ling, walleye, and perch.

The campground is open, treeless, windy, hot, and sunny. Many of the campsites line up along the north shore of a bay while others flank the main lakeshore. A few also rim a small lagoon. With no shrubs and trees, the grassy campground offers no privacy, protection from the afternoon winds, or shade. The campground does, however, gain good views of the sunrise over the Big Belt Mountains on the east side of the lake.

Campsites, facilities: The campground has 38 RV or tent campsites that can accommodate larger RVs. Facilities include picnic tables, fire rings with grills, vault toilets, drinking water, garbage service, a boat ramp, boat dock, and campground hosts. Leashed pets are permitted. Wheelchair-accessible toilets are available.

Reservations, fees: No reservations are accepted. Campsites cost $8. Cash or check. Open year-round; however, services are available only May–September.

Directions: From Winston on Highway 12/287 between Townsend and Helena, drive 5.3 miles northeast on dirt Beaver Creek Road, turning right at 2.3 miles to reach the campground.

GPS Coordinates: N 46° 31.292' W 111° 35.253'

Contact: Bureau of Reclamation, Montana Area Office, Canyon Ferry Field Office, 7661 Canyon Ferry Rd., Helena, MT 59602, 406/475-3921, www.usbr.gov/gp/mtao/canyonferry/.

47 CANYON FERRY LAKE KOA

Scenic rating: 6

on the west shore of Canyon Ferry Reservoir

At 3,850 feet on the west slopes of Canyon Ferry Reservoir, the KOA provides access to the lake even though it doesn't have waterfront. A Bureau of Reclamation boat ramp sits 0.2 mile to the east, and slip rental is available at The Silos Marina on Broadwater Bay. Designated swimming areas are also available near the marina. The campground is about five miles north of the 5,000-acre Canyon Ferry Wildlife Management Area, where birders and wildlife watchers can access trails to wildlife-viewing spots.

The KOA sits on an arid hillside above Canyon Ferry Lake, with views across to the Big Belt Mountains. Small pines and firs lend partial shade and windbreaks, but overall the site is very sunny and hot in midsummer. The campground road is gravel, along with the parking pads, which are stacked close together with no privacy in KOA fashion. The upper part of the campground is more open, drier, and dustier than the lower portion, which is built around patches of lawn. The KOA also runs the on-site Flamingo Grill, which is open for breakfast, lunch, and dinner.

Campsites, facilities: The campground has 47 RV campsites with a maximum pull-through length of 75 feet and 12 tent campsites. Facilities include picnic tables, fire rings, flush toilets, showers, drinking water, garbage service, a disposal station, coin-operated launderette, wireless Internet, a convenience store, a café, a playground, a dog walk, propane, a recreation room with TV, and horseshoe pits. Hookups include sewer, water, and electricity for up to 50 amps. Leashed pets are permitted. Wheelchair-accessible toilets are available.

Reservations, fees: Reservations are accepted. Hookups cost $25–43. Tent campsites cost $15–20 for one tent and $10 for a second tent. Tipis cost $45. Kamper Kabins cost $55–60. Rates are for two adults and two children under 16 years old. A 7 percent Montana bed tax will be added on. Use of the disposal station costs $4. Cash, check, or credit card. Open year-round.

Directions: From Townsend, drive Highway 12/287 north for 7.5 miles to milepost 70. Turn east onto Silos Road. (You'll see the two big, red brick silos.) Drive 0.8 mile east to the campground entrance on the left.

GPS Coordinates: N 46° 24.852' W 111° 34.839'

Contact: Townsend-Canyon Ferry Lake KOA, 81 Silos Rd., Townsend, MT 59644, 406/266-3100, www.canyonferrylakekoa.com.

48 SILOS

Scenic rating: 6

on the west shore of Canyon Ferry Reservoir

At 3,800 feet on the west shore of Canyon Ferry Reservoir, Silos is popular for its ease of access off the highway. You only have to drive one mile of the dusty washboard, gravel road. Despite its popularity, this end of the lake is less congested than the more popular north end. The lake attracts boaters, water-skiers, windsurfers, anglers, Jet Skiers, and, in winter, ice anglers. The campground inlets contain beaches that grow larger throughout the summer as the reservoir levels drop. These work for swimming and beaching boats for the night. The boat launch includes cement ramps and docks. In the evening, the post-boating crowd heads to the Silos Bar and Restaurant, located at the highway turnoff to the campground. The campground is about five miles north of the Canyon Ferry Wildlife Management Area, which has trails for accessing wildlife-viewing spots to see waterfowl, songbirds, raptors, moose, and deer.

Located on large, flat, treeless, grassy plateaus, the campground comprises four main loops, each divided by a small, narrow inlet. Two additional small loops on the southern peninsulas contain undesignated campsites. The dirt loops kick up dust. The campsites offer a semblance of privacy because they are spread out, but since there is no vegetation taller than grass, you will still see neighboring campers. Some small willows flank a few of the more popular campsites along the inlets. Even from a mile away, you can hear some of the faint trucking noise at night along the highway.

Campsites, facilities: The campground has 63 RV or tent campsites that can fit larger RVs. Facilities include picnic tables, fire rings with grills, vault toilets, drinking water, garbage service, a boat ramp, and campground hosts. Leashed pets are permitted. Wheelchair-accessible toilets are available.

Reservations, fees: No reservations are accepted. Campsites cost $10. Cash or check. Open year-round.

Directions: From Townsend, drive Highway 12/287 north for 7.5 miles to milepost 70. Turn east onto Silos Road. (You'll see the two big, red brick silos.) Drive one mile east to the boat launch area. Turn right to access the campground loops.

GPS Coordinates: N 46° 24.687' W 111° 34.574'

Contact: Bureau of Reclamation, Montana Area Office, Canyon Ferry Field Office, 7661 Canyon Ferry Rd., Helena, MT 59602, 406/475-3921, www.usbr.gov/gp/mtao/canyonferry/.

49 CONFEDERATE

Scenic rating: 6

on the east shore of Canyon Ferry Reservoir

Located at 3,800 feet on the east shore of Canyon Ferry Reservoir, the campground flanks the north and south sand and pebble beaches of Confederate Bay. This remote area draws only a few people due to the rough condition of the access road, which waffles between ruts, washboards, jarring cattle grates, large potholes, and rocky sections. The road narrows to one lane and can be a mudhole when wet. Even though the campground doesn't have a boat ramp, you can launch from your campsite any hand-carried watercraft for fishing, sightseeing, or wind-surfing. In winter, the bay draws ice anglers. The beaches grow larger as the lake level drops throughout the summer.

The primitive campsites string along two sandy beaches. The south beach offers more trees and willows for a bit of shade and wind protection, but the north beach has only one cottonwood tree. While you won't have privacy from neighboring campers, the campground as a whole offers solitude, quiet, and privacy from the hubbub at the north end of the lake. Both beaches are sunny, hot in midsummer, and windy, but you can have your tent door a few feet from the water.

Campsites, facilities: The campground has 16 undesignated RV or tent campsites that can accommodate midsized RVs. Facilities include rock fire rings at some sites and two wheelchair-accessible vault toilets, one at each beach. Leashed pets are permitted.

Reservations, fees: No reservations are accepted. Camping is free. Open year-round.

Directions: From Townsend on Highway 12/287, drive east on Highway 12 for 3.3 miles and then north on Highway 284 for 16.8 miles to the Confederate turnoff. At milepost 25, turn west onto the gravel Lower Confederate Lane and drive 4.2 miles. Turn right to reach the north beach or continue 0.5 mile around the bay to reach the south beach. From I-15 in Helena, take Exit 193 to the east side of the freeway and go north on Washington Street for 0.8 mile. Turn east onto Canyon Ferry Road for 30 miles, circling around the lake's north end and down the east side to the Confederate sign.

GPS Coordinates: N 46° 29.324' W 111° 31.516'

Contact: Bureau of Reclamation, Montana Area Office, Canyon Ferry Field Office, 7661 Canyon Ferry Rd., Helena, MT 59602, 406/475-3921, www.usbr.gov/gp/mtao/canyonferry/.

50 INDIAN ROAD

Scenic rating: 6

on the Missouri River south of Canyon Ferry Reservoir

At 3,850 feet, Indian Road Campground, as its name implies, sits on an ancient Native American route that the Lewis and Clark expedition also followed. The campground, with its interpretive displays, is on the Missouri River just before it enters Canyon Ferry Reservoir. A lush oasis amid the arid surrounding hills, the park includes a children's fishing pond, which is ringed by a gravel walking trail and crossed by a bridge. Swimming is not permitted in the pond. Several breaks through the willows afford access to the Missouri River for fishing and wading. A paved bicycling and walking path parallels the highway into Townsend. North of the Missouri River, the

Canyon Ferry Wildlife Management Area also offers short trails to wildlife-viewing spots. It's an excellent place for bird-watching and good moose habitat.

A gravel campground road circles the park, with a few pull-through gravel parking pads. The remainder of the parking pads are short back-ins. A few cottonwood trees and shorter willows provide some shade, but the mowed-lawn campground affords no privacy between the close sites. You can, however, have views of the surrounding mountains. At night, the trucks on the highway are loud.

Campsites, facilities: The campground has 32 RV or tent campsites that can accommodate midsized RVs. Facilities include picnic tables, fire rings with grills, pedestal grills, vault toilets, drinking water, and garbage service. Leashed pets are permitted. A wheelchair-accessible toilet, paved walkway, and fishing platform are available.

Reservations, fees: No reservations are accepted. Camping is free. Open year-round.

Directions: From the north end of Townsend, drive Highway 12/287 north for 0.5 mile. (Turn off before the bridge over the Missouri River.) Turn east onto Centerville Road and drive 0.1 mile. Turn north into the campground.

GPS Coordinates: N 46° 20.065' W 111° 31.763'

Contact: Bureau of Reclamation, Montana Area Office, Canyon Ferry Field Office, 7661 Canyon Ferry Rd., Helena, MT 59602, 406/475-3921, www.usbr.gov/gp/mtao/canyonferry/.

51 YORK'S ISLANDS

Scenic rating: 6

south of Townsend on the Missouri River

Compared to the surrounding arid countryside, York's Islands is a lush oasis along the Missouri River, at 3,838 feet in elevation.

The area is named for York, Captain William Clark's servant, who accompanied him on the Corps of Discovery expedition, and is a place where the Missouri River fragments into different channels around eight islands due to beaver dams shifting the water flows. The campground is primitive, part of the fishing access site run by the state. Rafters, kayakers, anglers, and river floaters can launch eight river miles upstream at Tosten and float back to camp. A downstream float leads to Townsend and farther into the Canyon Ferry Wildlife Management Area, but no watercraft are permitted March–August to protect nesting waterfowl.

The grassy sites, which are crammed together and small, are partially shaded under tall cottonwoods. Junipers, willows, and lots of brush provide some privacy between sites, especially those ringing the outside of the loop. You can hear the railroad and the highway at night as the river here is slow-moving and quiet. You can find flat spaces on the grass for pitching tents.

Campsites, facilities: The campground has 10 RV or tent campsites that can accommodate trailers up to 30 feet. Facilities include picnic tables, fire rings with grills, vault toilets, and a concrete boat ramp. Pack out your trash. Leashed pets are permitted. A wheelchair-accessible toilet is available.

Reservations, fees: Reservations are not accepted. Campsites cost $7 with a Montana fishing license and $12 without a Montana fishing license. Cash or check. Open year-round.

Directions: From Townsend, drive south on Highway 287 for four miles to milepost 81.5. Turn west and cross the railroad tracks, driving one mile on the potholed gravel road. (Watch for cows on the road.) The road dead-ends at the campground.

GPS Coordinates: N 46° 15.995' W 111° 29.529'

Contact: Montana Fish, Wildlife, and Parks, Region 3, 1400 S. 19th Ave., Bozeman, MT 59718, 406/994-4042, http://fwp.mt.gov.

52 LOWER TOSTEN DAM RECREATION AREA

Scenic rating: 6

south of Townsend on the Missouri River

Lower Tosten Dam Recreation Area sits at 4,000 feet in a small canyon cut through dramatic sedimentary layers of orange and white stone amid surrounding sagebrush and juniper hillsides. Below the dam, the Missouri River rolls at a slow pace. Rafters, kayakers, and anglers launch boats from here to float down to Tosten fishing access site or farther to York's Islands. Above the dam, a small reservoir affords fishing, swimming, and boating. You can motor around a broad oxbow and islands in the river. Both sides of the dam are good for watching American pelicans.

The recreation area is divided into two campgrounds—one below the dam and one above. The lower area has two grassy, unshaded campsites adjacent to the cement boat ramp and squeezed between the road and the river. Large willow brush blocks the view of the river. The upper area has three grassy campsites on the shore of the lake formed by the dam. The picnic tables are covered, and small trees lend minimal shade. A cement boat ramp and dock are available. All five campsites are small, close together, and open, and you can hear humming from the dam in both areas. The road to access the dam is rough dirt with potholes, but the campground roads are gravel.

Campsites, facilities: The campground has five RV or tent campsites that can accommodate midsized RVs. Facilities include picnic tables, fire rings with grills, vault toilets, a boat dock, and boat ramps. Leashed pets are permitted. A wheelchair-accessible toilet is available.

Reservations, fees: No reservations are accepted. Camping is free. Open May–October.

Directions: From Townsend, drive Highway 287 south for 12.6 miles, passing Tosten and crossing the Missouri River. Turn east at the BLM sign onto Tosten Dam Road and drive 4.3 miles to the lower campground or 5.2 miles to the upper campground. The rough dirt road has a one-lane bridge. Watch for cattle on the road.

GPS Coordinates: N 46° 20.065' W 111° 31.763'

Contact: Bureau of Land Management, 106 N. Parkmont, P.O. Box 3388, Butte, MT 59702, 406/533-7600, www.blm.gov/mt/st/en.html.

53 WHITEHOUSE

Scenic rating: 7

in the Boulder Mountains in Beaverhead-Deerlodge National Forest

At 6,000 feet, Whitehouse sits along the Boulder River in the Boulder Mountains, a mecca for ATV riders. The river houses mountain whitefish along with brook, brown, and rainbow trout, although the stream shores are quite willowy. The 2.5-mile Cottonwood Lake Trailhead (#65) sits about three miles from the campground. From the lake, trails also climb farther to Thunderbolt Mountain and Electric Peak. Call the Forest Service on the status of this campground, as it may close temporarily for diseased tree removal. Be prepared for a rough, potholed, rutted road into the campground.

Of the three campgrounds on the Boulder River, Whitehouse is the most popular. The campground, which sits on the Boulder River, surrounds large meadows with a perimeter of aspens and a few lodgepole pines that are dying due to beetle attacks. The sites are spread out for privacy, but with the open, sunny meadow, you'll have views of neighboring campers. Some sites also command views of forested slopes as well as views of a few power lines. The meadows bloom in midsummer with harebells, yarrow, and purple asters. You'll find plenty of large, flat tent spaces here. Should the campground be full, you can find an additional five dispersed primitive campsites, also on the Boulder River, 0.5 mile east just opposite the junction the Red Rock Road. Other than the ATV noise, the campground is quiet.

Campsites, facilities: The campground has 10 RV or tent campsites. The Forest Service recommends a maximum trailer length of 22 feet. Facilities include picnic tables, rock fire rings or fire rings with grills, drinking water, and a vault toilet. Pack out your trash. Leashed pets are permitted. A wheelchair-accessible toilet is available.

Reservations, fees: No reservations are accepted. Camping is free. Open late June–November.

Directions: From I-15 between Helena and Butte, take Exit 151 (4.6 miles south of Basin). Cross to the west side onto Boulder River Road (Forest Road 82). Drive 3.25 miles, turning right at the fork and crossing the Boulder River. Continue for 3.9 miles. Turn left at the signed entrance to the campground.

GPS Coordinates: N 46° 15.480' W 112° 28.755'

Contact: Beaverhead-Deerlodge National Forest, Jefferson Ranger District, 3 Whitetail Rd., Whitehall, MT 59759 406/287-3223, http://fs.usda.gov.

54 LADYSMITH

Scenic rating: 4

in the Boulder Mountains in Beaverhead-Deerlodge National Forest

Ladysmith, at 5,800 feet, is a small, little-used forest campground. The Boulder River near the campground is on private land, so you must drive three or so miles to public land, where you can fish for trout. As in much of the national forest here, the lodgepole pines are dying due to attacking beetles. Entire slopes of rust-colored trees in the area attest to the pervasiveness of the attack. This campground is scheduled for logging to remove the diseased

trees; call the ranger station to check on its status before visiting.

A rough-paved, potholed narrow road loops through the campground, which sits on a meadow and open forest slope. Buffalo berries, sticky pink geraniums, and yellow cinquefoil dot the slope. The dirt back-in parking pads are small, bumpy, and sloped. Much of the lodgepole forest is dead and marked for removal, which will convert the currently partial-shade campground to a sunny site. The upper campsites have views of meadows. While the access road has some noise during the day from forest travelers and ATVs, the night brings quiet.

Campsites, facilities: The campground has six RV or tent campsites that can accommodate only small RVs. Facilities include picnic tables, fire rings with grills, a large group fire ring with three benches, and pit toilets. Pack out your trash. Leashed pets are permitted.

Reservations, fees: No reservations are accepted. Camping is free. Open late June–September.

Directions: From I-15 between Helena and Butte, take Exit 151 (4.6 miles south of Basin). Cross to the west side onto the Boulder River Road (Forest Road 82). Drive 3.2 miles, turning left at the signed entrance to the campground. Drive over the cattle grate.

GPS Coordinates: N 46° 15.127' W 112° 24.261'

Contact: Beaverhead-Deerlodge National Forest, Jefferson Ranger District, 3 Whitetail Rd., Whitehall, MT 59759 406/287-3223, http://fs.usda.gov.

55 MORMON CREEK

Scenic rating: 4

in the Boulder Mountains in Beaverhead-Deerlodge National Forest

Mormon Creek—also called Mormon Gulch—is a small, little-used forest campground at an elevation of 5,800 feet with a tiny creek trickling through the campground. The Boulder River near the campground is on private land, so you must drive four or so miles to public land, where you can fish for trout. As in much of the national forest here, the lodgepole pines are dying due to attacking beetles. Entire slopes of rust-colored trees in the area attest to the pervasiveness of the attack. This campground is scheduled for logging to remove the diseased trees; call the ranger station to check on its status before visiting.

Campsites are set close together in a grassy area blooming with wild roses, penstemon, cow parsnip, and bedstraw. The tree canopy, which provides filtered shade, is dead. Once this is removed, the campground will turn into an open meadow with a young crop of aspens growing into the shade trees. Some of the sites are overgrown and show little use. The flat spaces available in some sites will fit only smaller tents. The two sites at the top of the loop see the most use because of the partial privacy they afford.

Campsites, facilities: The campground has nine RV or tent campsites that can hold trailers up to 16 feet. Facilities include picnic tables, fire rings with grills, and pit toilets. Pack out your trash. Leashed pets are permitted.

Reservations, fees: No reservations are accepted. Camping is free. Open late June–September.

Directions: From I-15 between Helena and Butte, take Exit 151 (4.6 miles south of Basin). Cross to the west side onto Boulder River Road (Forest Road 82). Drive one mile and turn left at the campground sign. Climb on the single-lane, rough pavement over the cattle grate and dodge chuckholes 0.1 mile to the campground.

GPS Coordinates: N 46° 15.440' W 112° 21.735'

Contact: Beaverhead-Deerlodge National Forest, Jefferson Ranger District, 3 Whitetail Rd., Whitehall, MT 59759 406/287-3223, http:// fs.usda.gov.

WESTERN MONTANA

© BECKY LOMAX

BEST CAMPGROUNDS

The Continental Divide weaves through western

Montana, leaping between high rugged mountain ranges that stretch far above the green forest. Large rivers carve through valleys that swing between broad, fertile ranching plains and narrow canyons pinching waters into white, roaring froth. Tall mountain ranges lend the landscape craggy, snow-covered peaks that turn in August to dark blocks of seemingly inhospitable rock.

For campers, the extremes that baffled Lewis and Clark on their travels yield a variety of camping opportunities along blue-ribbon trout streams and mountain lakes. The region, known for its rich history, also sports rivers with rapids for white-water rafting, wilderness areas where hiking trails abound, and terrain fostering a wealth of wildlife.

With campgrounds speckling historic paths, campers can trace the 1805 footsteps of Lewis and Clark down the Bitterroot River. In the Bitterroot Mountains, the expedition suffered the worst fatigue of their journey, compounded by cold and hunger. Following much of the same route in 1877, Chief Joseph and the Nez Perce ran from the U.S. Army trying to force them onto a reservation. Their route down the Lolo River to Fort Fizzle culminated in the Battle of the Big Hole; the site, west of Wisdom, is now a national battlefield with a visitors center, interpretive displays, and encampments. Montana's Wild West mining heritage also left a swath of ghost towns – vacated as inhabitants disappeared to another gold-frenzied town. Bannack State Park, west of Dillon, offers both camping and a look at life in the 1860s through the 60 buildings left standing.

Those looking for trout streams will find them in western Montana. A third of the state's 12 renowned blue-ribbon trout streams flow through the region. The Big Hole, which runs 155 miles from the Beaverhead Mountains to the prairies, winds through the idyllic Big Hole River Valley, with its postcard Montana views and prime trout fishery. Hopping with brown and rainbow trout, the Beaverhead River runs 69 miles from Clark Canyon Reservoir to meet up with the Big Hole. The 127-mile Blackfoot River is seeing a restoration of native trout species – especially westslope cutthroat – as its waters plummet from the Continental Divide westward.

Rock Creek, another westslope cutthroat trout fishery, flows 52 miles through a canyon dotted with campgrounds. Other top fisheries include the Clark Fork and Bitterroot Rivers. All six of these rivers offer a combination of Forest Service, Bureau of Land Management, and state-run river access campgrounds.

Campers seeking serene pools and frothing white water for rafting, canoeing, and kayaking will find floating stretches on these rivers. Most of western Montana's rivers run with Class II water, broken by boulder-strewn patches of Class III rapids. The one exception is the Clark Fork River, which adds the ferocity of challenging Class III-IV white water through Alberton Gorge. Camping options include Forest Service, BLM, state, and private campgrounds.

Lake camping, with boating opportunities such as waterskiing, is best at three large dammed reservoirs in western Montana. Georgetown Lake, Lake Como, and Clark Canyon Reservoir offer the best options, with multiple campgrounds rimming the shorelines of each.

Hikers will find plenty of places to camp that offer trails to stunning vistas. The Pioneer Mountains, sliced by the campground-loaded Pioneer Scenic Byway, top out at 11,000 feet, with trails wrapping around several of its peaks. Destinations include summits as well as small alpine lakes. The Bitterroot Mountains, which flank the Selway-Bitterroot Wilderness Area and the Montana-Idaho border, yield deep-gouged glacier-carved high valleys full of well-traveled trails. Stunning vertical walls line trails such as Blodgett Canyon, and campgrounds are available at many trailheads.

Western Montana also offers prime wildlife-watching. Mountain goats and bighorn sheep populate the alpine terrain, while pronghorn antelope graze in fields adjacent to cattle. Moose browse through willows along streams. South of Missoula, the Bitterroot Valley Birding Trail links up hot spots for bird-watching in the Lee Metcalf Wildlife Refuge. State and federal campgrounds accommodate those toting binoculars, and many campgrounds include interpretive information about local species.

Along with peaks, rivers, and wildlife, western Montana bubbles with hot springs. What better way to top off camping!

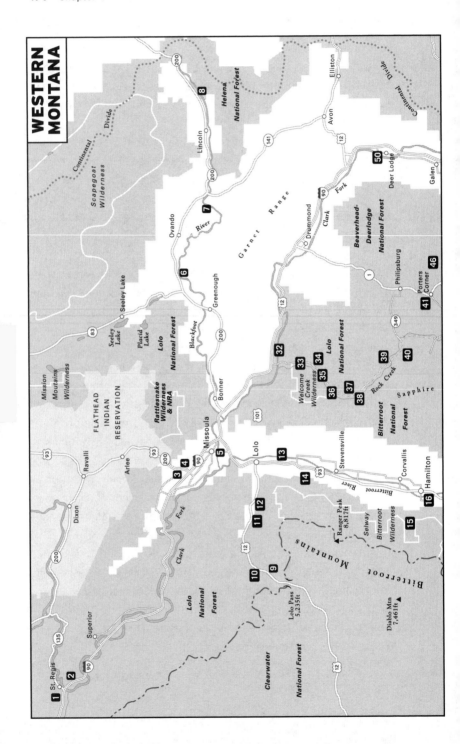

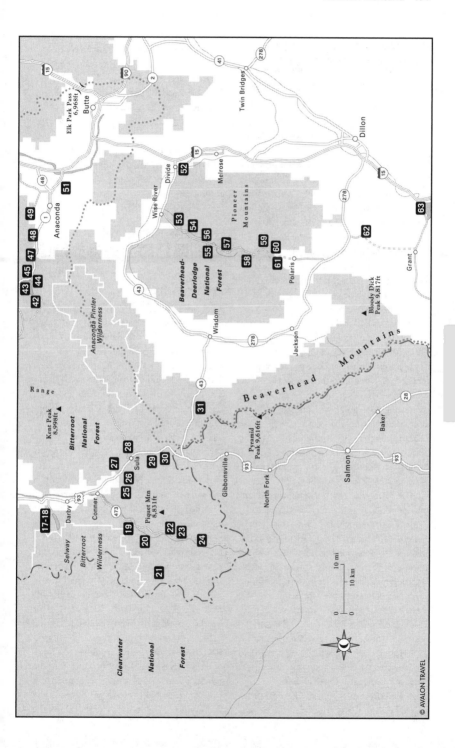

■ CAMPGROUND ST. REGIS

Scenic rating: 6

on I-90 in St. Regis

At 2,800 feet, Campground St. Regis sits about two miles west of the tiny two-block town of St. Regis and the Clark Fork River. Local outfitters guide fishing and floating trips on the river. On the west side of town, a conservation trail weaves through the St. Regis Community Park. The campground also sits about 30 minutes from the west entrance of the Route of the Hiawatha bike trail, a 15-mile rail trail with 10 tunnels and seven trestles. (Bring a headlamp for the tunnels!) Class II rafting, canoeing, and kayaking is available on the Clark Fork River from St. Regis downstream.

Paved roads lead to the campground, but past the entrance the road becomes gravel. Open sites with little privacy compose most of the campground, with a few large ponderosa pines for shade on the loop to the right of the office. Most of its largest loop circles a playground, tiny swimming pool, and lawn. The campground also has a separate broad grassy site for tents. Due to the proximity to the freeway, traffic noise permeates the campground.

Campsites, facilities: The campground has 47 RV sites and 28 tent sites. Some sites accommodate 75-foot-long pull-throughs. Hookups include water, sewer, and electricity up to 50 amps. Facilities include picnic tables (albeit rickety), fire rings, flush toilets, drinking water, a tiny pool, wireless Internet, a disposal station, propane, a camp store, a dog walk, firewood for sale, a playground, and a coin-op launderette. Leashed pets are permitted.

Reservations, fees: Reservations are accepted. Hookup campsites with water and electricity cost $23–26. Add on a sewer connection for $2 and additional people for $3 each. Also add the 7 percent Montana bed tax. Cash, check, Visa, or Mastercard. Open all year.

Directions: From I-90, take Exit 33 at St. Regis. Head to the north side of the freeway to the four-way stoplight. Turn left onto Old Highway 10 for 0.7 mile. Turn left onto Little Joe Road and drive 0.5 mile. Turn right onto Frontage Road W. and drive 0.6 mile. Then, turn right into the campground.

GPS Coordinates: N 47° 18.072' W 115° 8.027'

Contact: Campground St. Regis, Drawer A, 44 Frontage Rd. W., St. Regis, MT 59866, 406/247-8734 or 888/247-8734, www.campgroundstregis.com.

■ NUGGET RV PARK

Scenic rating: 7

on I-90 in St. Regis

At an elevation of 2,800 feet, east of St. Regis above the Clark Fork River, this RV park is convenient for golfing, fishing, rafting, hiking, or mountain biking. The nine-hole Trestle Creek Golf Course sits across the road. The Clark Fork River offers fishing and floating with guides in St. Regis. Class II rafting, canoeing, and kayaking is available on the Clark Fork River from St. Regis downstream. On the west side of town, a conservation trail weaves through the St. Regis Community Park. Less than a 30-minute drive leads to the west entrance of the Hiawatha trail—a 15-mile rail mountain bike path with trestles and long tunnels.

A miniature mining camp—log cabin, blacksmith shop, and hotel—sits at the paved campground entrance, and the historical theme continues with a small fort in the playground. Interior gravel roads connect gravel parking pads. RV sites 1–4 sit up on a bluff with views overlooking the valley and forested mountains. The big-rig RV sites—mostly pull-throughs—sit in an open terraced area. Tent campsites ring the border of the campground, separated from the RV areas. No fires are permitted in the campground. Up on its high knoll above the river valley, the campground is removed from freeway noise.

Campsites, facilities: The campground has 66 RV campsites and 21 tent sites. All sites, including tent sites, have hookups for water and electricity up to 50 amps. RV sites add sewer hookups, too. Facilities include picnic tables, flush toilets, showers, drinking water, wireless Internet, a swimming pool, a basketball court, a launderette, propane, and a disposal station. Leashed pets are permitted. A wheelchair-accessible toilet is available.

Reservations, fees: Reservations are accepted. Full hookups cost $30. Tent sites and truck-camper sites cost $24. Rates include two people; any additional people over five years old cost $3 each. Montana also adds on a 7 percent bed tax. Cash, check, or credit card. Open April–October.

Directions: From I-90, take Exit 33 at St. Regis. Go to the north side of the freeway and turn east at the four-way stop onto Old Highway 10. Drive one mile, crossing the Clark Fork River and climbing a hill. Look for the entrance on the left.

GPS Coordinates: N 47° 17.369' W 115° 4.958'

Contact: Nugget RV Park, 105 Old Hwy. 10 E., St. Regis, MT 59866, 406/649-2122 or 888/800-0125, www.nuggetrvpark.com.

3 JELLYSTONE PARK

Scenic rating: 6

at the junction of I-90 and Highway 93 on the west side of Missoula

With an elevation of 3,300 feet at the intersection of I-90 and Highway 93, Jellystone Park is convenient for those traveling to the National Bison Range, Ninepipes National Wildlife Refuge, and Glacier National Park. The Rocky Mountain Elk Museum and Smoke Jumper Center are within a five-minute drive. A 15-minute drive leads to downtown Missoula and the University of Montana to hike the 1.75 miles passing the "M" to Mount Sentinel's summit. A trail used by runners, walkers, and bicyclers, the two-mile Clark Fork Riverfront Trail runs through town from the Van Buren Street Footbridge to Caras Park, where a hand-carved carousel spins year-round. The Clark Fork River provides kayaking, canoeing, and rafting. Of Missoula's four golf courses, the Ranch Club is a 10-minute drive away.

Sitting in the open for easy satellite reception, the sunny campsites with small trees are close together, with some views of sagebrush hills. Paved roads loop through the campground, but the parking pads are gravel surrounded by mowed lawns. Yogi Bear shows up every night in summer, starting about July 4. Kids can take wagon rides with Yogi, plus dig into huckleberry ice cream at the nightly social. A nightly campfire is also available. Freeway noise is audible.

Campsites, facilities: The campground has 110 RV campsites and seven tent campsites. For big RVs, 81 pull-through sites fit combinations up to 70 feet. Hookups include water, sewer, and electricity up to 50 amps. Facilities include picnic tables, flush toilets, showers, drinking water, wireless Internet, an outdoor heated swimming pool, mini-golf, a basketball court, horseshoes, a TV and game room, a launderette, a camp store, propane, a disposal station, and a pet walk. Leashed pets are permitted. A wheelchair-accessible toilet is available.

Reservations, fees: Reservations are highly recommended for July and August. Hookups cost $36–38. Tent sites cost $29. All rates are for two people; additional people over six years old are charged $3–4 per person. Add on a 7 percent bed tax. Cash, check, or credit card. Open May–September.

Directions: From I-90, take Exit 96 on the west side of Missoula. Go north on Highway 93 to milepost 1. Turn left onto Jellystone Avenue to enter the park.

GPS Coordinates: N 46° 57.645' W 114° 8.106'

Contact: Yogi Bear's Jellystone Park, 900 Jellystone Ave., Missoula, MT 59808, 406/543-9400 or 800/318-9644, www.campjellystoneMT.com.

4 JIM AND MARY'S RV PARK

Scenic rating: 6

at the junction of I-90 and Highway 93 on the west side of Missoula

Just north of the I-90 and Highway 93 junction at 3,300 feet, this RV park works for those heading north to the National Bison Range, Ninepipes National Wildlife Refuge, Flathead Valley, and Glacier National Park. A 10-minute drive leads to downtown Missoula, which offers art galleries, shopping, restaurants, farmers markets, breweries, theaters, museums, the University of Montana, and city parks. The campground is also convenient for touring the Smoke Jumper Center or the Rocky Mountain Elk Foundation, both within a five-minute drive. Outdoor activities—hiking, mountain biking, cycling, golf, kayaking, and river rafting—are all in the area, too.

Drive into Jim and Mary's in summer, and you'll be greeted by colorful flowers grown in their own greenhouse. Surrounded partially by shade-producing fir trees, but not smothered in darkness under them, the lawn campground has a park feel. A paved road loops through the campground with gravel parking pads. About 75 percent of the campsites are pull-throughs. A few sites on the southern end are very open for those who prefer heavy sunshine. The A row sites are a little more spacious than those in rows B–F. Several sites are filled by permanent residents. Freeway noise is audible.

Campsites, facilities: The campground has 68 RV sites that can fit large RVs. Hookups include sewer, water, and electricity up to 50 amps. Facilities include picnic tables, flush toilets, showers, drinking water, free wireless Internet, and a coin-op launderette. Leashed pets are permitted. A wheelchair-accessible toilet is available.

Reservations, fees: Reservations are highly recommended. Campsites cost $34. The 7 percent state bed tax is included. Cash, check, or credit card. Open year-round.

Directions: From I-90, take Exit 96 on the west side of Missoula. Go north on Highway 93 to milepost 1.2. Turn right onto Lady Slipper Lane and right again to enter the RV park.

GPS Coordinates: N 46° 57.875' W 114° 7.834'

Contact: Jim and Mary's RV Park, 9800 Hwy. 93 N., Missoula, MT 59808, 406/549-4416, www.jimandmarys.com.

5 MISSOULA KOA

Scenic rating: 4

in downtown Missoula

At an elevation of 3,500 feet in Missoula, surrounded by residential and commercial property, the KOA is Missoula's largest campground. It's a five-minute drive from Missoula's hand-built carousel—Dragon Hollow—a monster-sized playground shaped like a three-headed dragon, and Caras Park, which holds a kayak play wave (an artificial wave for river kayakers to practice skills) on the Clark Fork. Caras also hosts weekly summer music festivals and farmers markets. Boating, floating, fishing, walking, and biking are available on the Clark Fork River, which runs through town.

All of the campsites in the KOA are pull-throughs, and the campground's premium sites include a patio, log swing, fire pit, and two sewer hookups. Tent sites—some with electricity and water—sit in a separate grassy area from the RV campsites. Campsites are packed in close together with little privacy, and traffic noise from the busy four-lane Reserve Street is audible. The campground has a café that serves breakfast daily, rental bikes for the paved trail looping the campground, and nightly community bonfires and ice cream socials.

Campsites, facilities: The campground has 146 RV campsites and 31 tent sites. RV combinations are limited to 70 feet. Hookups include sewer, water, and electricity up to 50 amps. Facilities include picnic tables, flush toilets, showers, a launderette, a disposal station, cable TV, free modem dataport hookups in the café, a heated outdoor swimming pool, two outdoor hot tubs, firewood for sale, a game center, mini-golf, a camp store, a café, and three fenced dog walks. Tent sites have fire pits, but RV sites do not. Leashed pets are permitted. A wheelchair-accessible toilet is available.

Reservations, fees: Reservations are accepted by phone or online. RV sites cost $32–63. Tent sites cost $27–31. Rates are for two people; the cost for additional campers is $3. Kids nine years old and under stay free. Add on 7 percent tax. Cash, check, or credit card. Open year-round.

Directions: From I-90, take Exit 101 and drive south for 1.5 miles on Reserve Street. Turn right at the light onto England Boulevard. Turn right onto Tina Avenue. Coming from south of Missoula, go to the junction of Highway 93 and Highway 12. Turn north onto Reserve Street and drive four miles. Turn left at the light onto England Boulevard and right onto Tina Avenue. GPS Coordinates: N 46° 53.731' W 114° 2.612'

Contact: Missoula KOA, 3450 Tina Ave., Missoula, MT 59808, 406/549-0881 or 800/562-5366, www.missoulakoa.com.

⑥ RUSSELL GATES MEMORIAL

🚶 🚵 🛶 🚣 🛟 🐕 ♿ 🚐 ⛺

Scenic rating: 7

between Lincoln and Clearwater Junction on the Blackfoot River

BEST (

Located at 3,865 feet in elevation on the Blackfoot River, Russell Gates Memorial Campground is tucked into a narrow river canyon in the Blackfoot-Clearwater Wildlife Management Area. The river—one of Montana's blue-ribbon trout streams—harbors brown, rainbow, and westslope cutthroat trout. Anglers wade-fish, shore-fish, or float the river to fish. A primitive boat launch allows for launching rafts, kayaks, and canoes. Put in at Harry Morgan to float the Class II section to the campground, or launch at the campground to float to Clearwater Junction. Boulder-crammed rapids clog the river below Clearwater Junction. Hiking trails and mountain biking roads loop through the wildlife management area across the highway.

The south-facing campground swelters in midsummer in the narrow canyon, but the water cools off the campers. Partly shaded by large ponderosas, the grassy campsites sit in the open with views of neighboring campers, the river, and the canyon. Seven of the campsites overlook the river, with sites 10 and 11 the most private at the end but also the closest to the highway. While the sound of rushing water fills the campground, so does noise from the two-lane highway—especially when large commercial hauling trucks pass.

Campsites, facilities: The campground has 11 campsites. Trailer length is limited to 25 feet. Facilities include picnic tables, fire rings with grills, vault toilets, drinking water, and garbage service. Leashed pets are permitted. A wheelchair-accessible toilet is available.

Reservations, fees: Reservations are not accepted. Campsites cost $12 for those without Montana fishing licenses and $7 for those who have licenses. Open year-round.

Directions: On Highway 200, drive 3.7 miles east of Clearwater Junction or 20 miles west of the Highway 141 junction to the signed turnoff at milepost 35.5. Turn south into the campground. GPS Coordinates: N 47° 1.379' W 113° 18.418'

Contact: Montana Fish, Wildlife, and Parks, Region 2 Headquarters, 3201 Spurgin Rd.,

Missoula, MT 59804, 406/542-5500, http:// fwp.mt.gov.

7 BROWN'S LAKE

Scenic rating: 7

between Lincoln and Clearwater Junction in the Blackfoot River Valley

BEST (

At 4,308 feet in elevation in the Blackfoot River Valley, Brown's Lake is a large, 516-acre lake that sits between Ovando and Lincoln. Because of the marshy wetlands, Brown's Lake is a favorite spot for bird-watchers in spring, with nesting areas adjacent to the Blackfoot Waterfowl Production Area— open only to foot traffic. Watch for bald eagles, ospreys, great blue herons, American white pelicans, American avocets, and sandhill cranes. A concrete boat ramp and boat trailer parking area aids those launching onto the lake for fishing. A portion of the lake, marked by barrel booms, is closed to all boats April–mid-July. Anglers fish for annually stocked rainbow trout that can get up to 20 inches. Windsurfers also cruise the lake in summer afternoons, and ice fishing is popular in winter.

The quiet campground sits on an almost treeless spit of land protruding out into the lake's south end. Most of the shadeless campsites are out in the open, so expect winds in the afternoon. While views from the campsites include other campers, they also swing to panoramic swaths of the peaks of the Scapegoat Wilderness Area. Outside of the developed campground, plenty of primitive campsites surround the lake. Use previous fire rings and follow Leave No Trace practices if you use these.

Campsites, facilities: The campground has 10 RV or tent campsites that can fit large RVs. Facilities include picnic tables, fire rings with grills, and vault toilets, but no drinking water. Bring your own water, or if you plan on using lake water, boil or purify it first. Pack out your trash. Leashed pets are permitted. A wheelchair-accessible toilet is available.

Reservations, fees: Reservations are not accepted. Campsites cost $12 for those without Montana fishing licenses and $7 for those who have licenses. Open year-round.

Directions: From Highway 200, locate the Brown's Lake turnoff seven miles east of Ovando or 2.7 miles west of the Highway 141 junction. Turn south onto County Road 112. Follow it around the east side of the lake for 3.5 miles and then north onto the spit into the campground.

GPS Coordinates: N 46° 57.062' W 113° 0.657'

Contact: Montana Fish, Wildlife, and Parks, Region 2 Headquarters, 3201 Spurgin Rd., Missoula, MT 59804, 406/542-5500, http:// fwp.mt.gov.

8 ASPEN GROVE

Scenic rating: 7

east of Lincoln on the Blackfoot River in Helena National Forest

On the west side of the Continental Divide, Aspen Grove, elevation 4,800 feet, is the only Forest Service campground between Missoula and Great Falls along Highway 200. It sits about 11.5 miles from the Rogers Pass on the Continental Divide, where you can climb up 1.5 miles on the Continental Divide Trail for expansive views of the mountains and the prairie. The campground attracts anglers for the famed Blackfoot River, which harbors several species of trout: brown, westslope cutthroat, brook, and rainbow.

Aspen Grove includes both an overnight camping area and a day-use area. Contrary to the name, the quiet eight-acre campground sits in a large grove of shady cottonwood trees. There are some aspens, but they're not the dominant trees. Some of the sites sit in more open grassy areas with a mix of sagebrush. Two gravel loops with gravel parking aprons have sites that border the Blackfoot River, which fills the campground with the sound of flowing water.

Campsites, facilities: The campground has 20 RV or tent campsites. Most of the parking pads are 20 feet long, but a couple can handle RVs up to 45 feet long. Facilities include picnic tables, fire rings with grills, drinking water, vault toilets, garbage service, and campground hosts. Leashed pets are permitted. A wheelchair-accessible toilet is available.

Reservations, fees: Reservations are not accepted. Campsites cost $8. Open late May–early September.

Directions: From Lincoln east of Missoula, drive 6.5 miles east on Highway 200. Turn south at the Aspen Grove Campground sign. Drive 0.5 mile on the gravel road to the campground.

GPS Coordinates: N 46° 58.665' W 112° 31.864'

Contact: Helena National Forest, Lincoln Ranger District, 1569 Hwy. 200, Lincoln, MT 59639, 406/362-4265, www.fs.fed.us/r1/helena/.

⑨ LEE CREEK

🥾 🚴 🛶 🛟 ♨ 🏕 ♿ 🚐 ⛺

Scenic rating: 7

between Lolo and Lolo Pass in Lolo National Forest

BEST (

Of the Highway 12 campgrounds between Lolo and Lolo Pass in the Bitterroot Mountains, Lee Creek sits the closest to the pass at 4,200 feet in elevation. A portion of the historic Lolo Trail, once used by the Nez Perce, Salish, and Kootenai tribes and explored by Lewis and Clark, parallels the opposite side of the highway, accessed 0.5 mile away at Fish Creek Road, which is a mountain-biking

road. Lolo Hot Springs Resort, with its outdoor hot pool, sits one mile to the east, and the Lolo Pass Visitor Center is six miles to the west. You can hike to the hot springs or the visitors center via the Lolo Trail. For anglers, Lolo Creek contains brook, brown, westslope cutthroat, and rainbow trout as well as mountain whitefish. A one-mile trail also leads up Lee Ridge.

The campground comprises two loops, serviced by paved roads and connected to paved parking pads. Six of the campsites have pull-through parking. Sites 1–5 in the lower right-hand loop are spread out between the lodgepoles and wild roses for more privacy. In a loop up the hill on the left, the remaining sites cram together on a hillside of scrawny lodgepole pines with little undergrowth to lend privacy from the neighbors. A stairway connects the upper loop to the lower loop.

Campsites, facilities: The campground has 22 RV or tent campsites. RVs are limited to 30 feet. Facilities include picnic tables, fire rings with grills, vault toilets, drinking water, campground hosts, and garbage service. During September, the drinking water may be turned off and garbage service ended. If so, pack out your trash. Site 22 has a bear box for bicyclists. Leashed pets are permitted. A wheelchair-accessible toilet is available.

Reservations, fees: Reservations are not accepted. Campsites cost $10. Additional vehicles cost $4. Cash or check only. Open late May–September.

Directions: From Lolo, drive 26 miles west on Highway 12. From Lolo Pass, drive six miles east. Locate the campground road on the south side of the highway past a small bridge over Lolo Creek.

GPS Coordinates: N 46° 42.357' W 114° 32.210'

Contact: Lolo National Forest, Missoula Ranger District, Bldg. 24A, Fort Missoula, Missoula, MT 59804, 406/329-3814, www.fs.fed.us/r1/lolo.

10 LOLO HOT SPRINGS RESORT

Scenic rating: 7

between Lolo and Lolo Pass in Lolo National Forest

Sitting at 4,000 feet, Lolo Hot Springs Resort has two natural year-round pools—one hot pool indoors and another cooler outdoor pool, both open daily (10 A.M.–10 P.M. summers; pools close at 8 P.M. winters, $7 for adults, $5 for kids 12 and under). The 32-mile Lewis and Clark National Historic Trail, also called the Lolo Trail, parallels the north side of the highway. Hike either direction to follow in the 1805 footsteps of the Corps of Discovery and later the Nez Perce in their flight from the U.S. Army. The trail is for hikers only, but Fish Creek Road to the north works for mountain biking. For anglers, Lolo Creek contains brook, brown, westslope cutthroat, and rainbow trout. In winter, the resort is a base for snowmobiling in the national forest and cross-country skiing at Lee Creek and Lolo Pass.

Located in an open grassy sunny area, the campground sits across the highway and Lolo Creek from the hot pools, restaurant, bar, and casino. The sites cram close together, and some of the tent sites snuggle up against the forest. Privacy is minimal, and highway noise from commercial hauling trucks is audible.

Campsites, facilities: The campground has 70 RV campsites with hookups for water, sewer, and electricity; 60 tent and RV dry campsites are also available. Parking pads can accommodate large RVs. Facilities include picnic tables, fire rings, flush toilets, showers, horseshoe pits, volleyball nets, tipis for rent, and a disposal station. Wireless Internet is available in the bar and restaurant across the street. Leashed pets are permitted. A wheelchair-accessible toilet is available.

Reservations, fees: Reservations are accepted. Full hookups cost $25.00. Seniors camp at a discounted rate of $21.25. Dry camping or tent sites cost $16. Tipi camping costs $25. Pets cost $2–5. Add on 7 percent tax. Cash, check, or credit card. Open year-round.

Directions: From Lolo, drive 25 miles west on Highway 12, or from Lolo Pass, drive seven miles east. Locate the resort on both sides of the road at milepost 7. The campground sits south of the highway and the pools are on the north side.

GPS Coordinates: N 46° 43.496' W 114° 31.864'

Contact: Lolo Hot Springs Resort, 38500 Hwy. 12, Lolo, MT 59847, 406/273-2294 or 877/541-5117, www.lolohotsprings.com.

11 EARL TENANT

Scenic rating: 6

between Lolo and Lolo Pass in Lolo National Forest

In the Bitterroot Mountains between Missoula and Lolo Pass, Earl Tenant Campground sits on Lolo Creek at 3,900 feet in elevation. Across the highway, the historic Lolo Trail—also called the Lewis and Clark National Historic Trail—parallels the highway for over 32 miles. Hop onto the hiking-only trail at the Howard Creek Trailhead and walk where the Nez Perce, Salish, and Kootenai tribes once traveled. The Corps of Discovery passed through here in fall of 1805. For anglers, Lolo Creek houses brook, brown, westslope cutthroat, and rainbow trout as well as mountain whitefish. The campground is named in honor of the first ranger at Lolo Ranger Station. Lolo Hot Springs sits seven miles to the west. The campground is on the TransAmerica Trail bicycle route.

Surrounded by wild grasses, the campground, looping on a gravel road, waxes dry and dusty in late August. The graveled, wide parking pads have been leveled, and all of the sites are visible from each other and receive sunlight with a little shade from a few tall ponderosa pines. The highway is also visible through the willows on the creek. Sites 1, 2, 3, and 7 tuck up against the forest on the outside of the loop.

Campsites, facilities: The campground has seven RV or tent campsites. RVs are limited to 30 feet. Facilities include picnic tables, fire rings with grills, vault toilets, and garbage service, but no drinking water. You can get drinking water two miles west at Lolo Creek Campground. Leashed pets are permitted. A wheelchair-accessible toilet is available.

Reservations, fees: Reservations are not accepted. Campsites cost $8. A second vehicle costs $4. Cash or check. Open late May–September.

Directions: From Lolo, drive 16 miles west on Highway 12, or from Lolo Pass, drive 14 miles east. Locate the campground at milepost 14.3. The campground sits south of the highway across a small bridge over Lolo Creek.

GPS Coordinates: N 46° 45.092' W 114° 30.377'

Contact: Lolo National Forest, Missoula Ranger District, Bldg. 24A, Fort Missoula, Missoula, MT 59804, 406/329-3814, www.fs.fed.us/r1/lolo.

12 LOLO CREEK

Scenic rating: 7

between Lolo and Lolo Pass in Lolo National Forest

Midway between Lolo and Lolo Pass in the Bitterroot Mountains, this campground sits on Lolo Creek at 3,800 feet in elevation. It is still called Lewis and Clark Campground on some maps, but the name has changed to Lolo Creek. For hikers, the 32-mile Lewis and Clark National Historic Trail parallels the highway. The campground is about 11 miles west from the Fort Fizzle Historic Site,

where the U.S. Army erected a wooden barricade to stop the advance of Chief Joseph during the Nez Perce war. The Nez Perce, however, dodged the barricade and climbed a ravine with their horses and possessions to evade the soldiers. For anglers, Lolo Creek houses brook, brown, westslope cutthroat, and rainbow trout. Highway 12 is part of the TransAmerica Trail bicycle route; cyclists use this campground for its ease of access before crossing Lolo Pass. Of the Forest Service campgrounds on Highway 12, this one is the closest to services—gas, groceries, shopping, and restaurants—in Lolo.

A paved road loops through the campground with paved parking pads. Several campsites have tiny pull-through parking. The campground sits on a hillside of mixed open forest. Although the several of the campsites are small, tenters can find some with large flat spaces. Sites 1 and 2, on a spur road nearest the creek, do not have turnaround room for trailers. The campground is quiet, but it does pick up noise from trucks on the highway.

Campsites, facilities: The campground has 17 RV or tent campsites. RVs are limited to 30 feet. Facilities include picnic tables, fire rings with grills, vault toilets, garbage service, and drinking water. Leashed pets are permitted. A wheelchair-accessible toilet is available.

Reservations, fees: Reservations are not accepted. Campsites cost $10. A second vehicle costs $4. Cash or check. Open mid-May–September.

Directions: From Lolo, drive 15 miles west on Highway 12. From Lolo Pass, drive 17 miles east. Locate the campground at milepost 17. Turn south off the highway and immediately right again to cross the bridge over Lolo Creek into the campground.

GPS Coordinates: N 46° 46.535' W 114° 23.082'

Contact: Lolo National Forest, Missoula Ranger District, Bldg. 24A, Fort Missoula, Missoula, MT 59804, 406/329-3814, www.fs.fed.us/r1/lolo.

13 CHIEF LOOKING GLASS FISHING ACCESS

Scenic rating: 6

on the Bitterroot River south of Lolo

Located 21 miles upstream from the mouth of the Bitterroot River and just south of the town of Lolo and the junction with Highway 12, Chief Looking Glass is a 13-acre fishing access site sitting at an elevation of 3,182 feet. Here the Bitterroot River divides into several channels with broad sand and rock beaches that open up as water levels drop during summer. Chief Looking Glass is one of a dozen fishing access sites on the Bitterroot River, but one of the few with a campground. The river, which runs deep, quiet, and slow-moving without rapids in this stretch, harbors brown trout, rainbow trout, mountain whitefish, and swimming holes. The area is also rich with nesting birds in June. The campground has several sites where you can launch a boat by hand, perfect for rafts and canoes (only nonmotorized craft are allowed here). You can also launch at the Florence Bridge, about five miles upstream, and float back to camp.

While pavement reaches the entrance, the campground road and parking aprons are gravel. The quiet, sunlit campground has a mix of tall ponderosas, short aspens, and open meadows. Sites 1, 2, 4, 5, 6, and 7 border the river. Site 4 is very private, with brush blocking off other campsites. The others are open with little privacy. Sites 8–10 have a little more privacy at the north end of the campground. The sounds of nature—birds and water—fill the campground.

Campsites, facilities: The campground has 19 RV or tent campsites. RVs are limited to 28 feet. Facilities include picnic tables, fire rings, drinking water, vault toilets, campground hosts, and garbage service. Leashed pets are permitted. A wheelchair-accessible toilet is available.

Reservations, fees: Reservations are not accepted. Campsites cost $12 for those without Montana fishing licenses and $7 for those with licenses. Cash or check. Open May–November.

Directions: From Lolo, go six miles south on Highway 93 to milepost 77. Turn east onto Chief Looking Glass Road and drive one mile to the campground entrance on the left. GPS Coordinates: N 46° 39.668' W 114° 3.247'

Contact: Montana Fish, Wildlife, and Parks, 3201 Spurgin Rd., Missoula, MT 59804, 406/542-5500, http://fwp.mt.gov.

14 CHARLES WATERS

Scenic rating: 7

in the eastern Bitterroot Mountains south of Florence in Bitterroot National Forest

Charles Waters Campground tucks under the east flank of the Bitterroot Mountains. A paved bike trail parallels the highway, and the campground reserves one campsite for bicyclists. Sitting at 3,520 feet in elevation, the campground is near the Bass Creek Trailhead and Bass Creek Overlook. From the campground, a half-mile nature trail tours a dry ponderosa pine forest and a moist old-growth forest adjacent to Bass Creek. Trail #4 also follows Bass Creek for 9.1 miles to Bass Lake. To reach the overlook at 6,100 feet, with its views of the Bitterroot Valley, turn left when leaving the campground and take the dirt, single-lane Forest Road 1136 for about seven miles, swinging left at the T intersection. Fives miles east is the Lee Metcalf National Wildlife Refuge, with nature trails (including a 0.5-mile wheelchair-accessible path), bird-watching, hunting, and fishing.

The road is paved all the way to the ultra-quiet campground, plus the two campground loops are newly paved, along with a few of the parking pads that are pull-throughs or large enough for two vehicles. The remaining parking pads are gravel. Most of the campsites sit under large ponderosas, except for sites 9–11, which border a large meadow with views of the base of the mountains. Campsites on the south side of the loop—13, 15, 16, 17, 18, 20, 22, and 25—have privacy in the woods adjacent to Bass Creek.

Campsites, facilities: The campground has 26 RV or tent campsites. The maximum length for RVs and trailer combinations is 70 feet. Facilities include picnic tables, fire rings with grills, drinking water, vault toilets, garbage service, and a camp host. Leashed pets are permitted. A wheelchair-accessible toilet is available.

Reservations, fees: Reservations are not accepted. Campsites cost $10. An extra vehicle costs $5. Cash or check. Open May–October.

Directions: From Florence, drive Highway 93 south for 3.1 miles to milepost 71.5. Watch for the Bass Creek Recreation Site sign and turn west onto Bass Creek Road just after crossing North Bass Creek. Drive two miles to the entrance. (You'll see the campground sign about 0.3 mile before you actually reach the entrance.)

GPS Coordinates: N 46° 34.462' W 114° 8.063'

Contact: Bitterroot National Forest, Stevensville Ranger District, 88 Main St., Stevensville, MT 59870, 406/777-5431, www.fs.fed.us/r1/bitterroot/.

15 BLODGETT CANYON

Scenic rating: 9

in the eastern Bitterroot Mountains west of Hamilton in Bitterroot National Forest

At 4,300 feet, Blodgett Canyon is one of the Bitterroot Mountain's hidden treats, offering dramatic spires and cliff faces. Surrounded by the Selway-Bitterroot Wilderness, the canyon houses huge 500-foot walls that attract rock climbers. Departing from the campground, the Blodgett Canyon Trail looks up to the rugged canyon walls above Blodgett Creek. Destinations include a 20-foot waterfall (3.6 miles), High Lake (8 miles), and Blodgett Lake (12.5 miles). A second interpretive trail—departing 4.5 miles from the campground—climbs a fire-ravaged slope to overlook the canyon.

The small campground nestles at the base of the canyon next to roaring Blodgett Creek. Even though a potholed dirt road leads up to the campground, the campground loop is paved and so are the parking pads. Mature trees shade the campsites, and thick underbrush lends privacy. Large boulders litter some of the campground—fun bouldering for those with a hankering for rock climbing.

Campsites, facilities: The campground has five RV or tent campsites, plus one walk-in tent campsite. RVs are limited to 45 feet.

A hiker at Blodgett Canyon overlook stares down several thousand feet to the canyon floor.

© BECKY LOMAX

Facilities include picnic tables, fire rings with grills, vault toilets, campground hosts, and drinking water. Pack out your trash. Due to its popularity, the campground has a five-day stay limit; arrive early to claim a campsite. Leashed pets are permitted. A wheelchair-accessible toilet is available.

Reservations, fees: Reservations are not accepted. Camping is free. Open year-round, but snowbound usually December–April.

Directions: Just north of Hamilton on Highway 93 at milepost 50.2 on the north side of the bridge over the Bitterroot River, turn west onto Bowman Road. Follow the signs on this route for Blodgett Canyon Trailhead. Drive 0.7 mile and then swing left onto Ricketts Road for two miles to a stop sign. (At 1.7 miles, it will turn 90 degrees to head straight for the Bitterroot Mountains and reach the stop sign 0.3 mile later.) Go straight through the stop sign onto Blodgett Camp Road. Follow it 1.9 miles until the pavement ends. In 0.6 mile farther, the road to Blodgett Canyon Overlook Trailhead turns west, but continue straight for 1.4 miles to the road's terminus at the campground.

GPS Coordinates: N 46° 16.155' W 114° 14.624'

Contact: Bitterroot National Forest, Stevensville Ranger District, 88 Main St., Stevensville, MT 59870, 406/777-5431, www.fs.fed.us/r1/bitterroot/.

16 ANGLER'S ROOST

Scenic rating: 5

on the Bitterroot River south of Hamilton

At an elevation of 3,750 feet about four miles south of Hamilton, Angler's Roost is a combination state-run fishing access site and private campground. The cement boat ramp accommodates launching onto the river for floating and fishing. You can also launch at Wally Crawford fishing access site about

10 miles upstream to float back to Angler's Roost, or launch at the campground to float half that distance to Demmons in Hamilton. The river is known for its long fishing season and multiple species of trout: brown, rainbow, brook, bull, westslope cutthroat. It also contains largemouth bass, northern pike, and redside shiners. Only nonmotorized boats are allowed on the river throughout most of the year, but October–January, you can use motorized craft of 15 horsepower or less. Fishing equipment (boats, waders, and rods) is for rent. A bicycle/walking path connects with downtown Hamilton.

The campground squeezes in between the highway and the river, with most of the sites lined up in a large grassy open meadow. Those sites along the river have cottonwood trees for shade. The RV area lines up rigs in parking-lot fashion within sight and sound of the highway. Sites 6–23 are closest to the river—some have river frontage. The treed tenting area sits on the river on the north end of the campground.

Campsites, facilities: The campground has nine tent campsites and 59 RV campsites, 14 that can fit RVs up to 65 feet. Hookups include sewer, water, and electricity up to 50 amps. Facilities include picnic tables, fire rings with grills, flush and vault toilets, showers, a launderette, a store, firewood for sale, a dog exercise area, gas, propane, and a disposal station. Leashed pets are permitted. A wheelchair-accessible toilet is available.

Reservations, fees: Reservations are accepted, especially for the busy May–September season. Hookups cost $23–30. Tent campsites cost $19. Cash or check. Open year-round.

Directions: From Hamilton on Highway 93, drive four miles south to the campground. The entrance is on the right just before the bridge crosses the Bitterroot River.

GPS Coordinates: N 46° 11.981' W 114° 10.011'

Contact: Angler's Roost, 815 Hwy. 93 S., Hamilton, MT 59840, 406/363-1268, www.anglersroost-montana.com.

17 LOWER LAKE COMO
🏃 🚲 🏊 ⛵ 🚣 🛶 🏕 ♿ 🚐 ⛺

Scenic rating: 9

on Lake Como northwest of Darby in
Bitterroot National Forest

Tucked at 4,250 feet on the west side of the
Bitterroot Valley, Lake Como sits right at the
base of the Selway-Bitterroot Wilderness in
the Bitterroot Mountains. The Rock Creek
Trail and the Lake Como National Recreation
Trail form mountain-biking and hiking routes
on the south and north shores of the lake,
meeting a half mile before the wilderness
boundary. Popular for boating and fishing,
the lake, which was formed by a dam built
in 1905, stays at full pool through mid-July.
Boating usually goes until mid-August, before
water levels drop too low, shrinking the head
of the lake to mud and a small stream. The
boat launch includes a concrete ramp, dock,
and trailer parking 1.5 miles from the campground. The recreation area also contains a
horse camp, and between the lower and upper

campgrounds a day-use area has a buoyed
swimming beach, changing shelters, vault
toilets, and picnic tables. Overflow camping
is available east of the boat launch.

Located below the dam along the creek, the
shaded quiet campground, which is designed
for RVs minus hookups, has a paved road
and paved parking pads, most of them pull-
throughs. The campsites are spread out beneath ponderosa pines and Douglas firs; even
though you can see other campers through
the woods, the roominess affords privacy for
most of the sites. Sites 5A and 5B overlook
the creek.

Campsites, facilities: The campground has 11
RV or tent campsites. The campsite parking
pads can fit trailer combinations up to 125
feet. Facilities include picnic tables, fire rings
with grills, a few pedestal grills, vault toilets,
drinking water, garbage service, boat trailer
parking, and campground hosts. Leashed pets
are permitted. A wheelchair-accessible toilet
is available.

Reservations, fees: Reservations are not accepted. Campsites cost $14. Day use costs

Lake Como in the Bitterroot Mountains offers swimming, paddling, boating, and fishing with
views into the Selway-Bitterroot Wilderness.

$5. Cash or check. Open late May–early September.

Directions: About four miles north of Darby, look for milepost 35.1 on Highway 93. Turn west onto Lake Como Road and drive for three miles. Turn right at the signed junction for the campgrounds and go 0.8 mile. Turn left and immediately left again to reach the campground entrance.

GPS Coordinates: N 46° 4.099' W 114° 14.150'

Contact: Bitterroot National Forest, Stevensville Ranger District, 88 Main St., Stevensville, MT 59870, 406/777-5431, www.fs.fed.us/r1/bitterroot/.

18 UPPER LAKE COMO
🏃 🚴 🏊 ⛵ 🎣 🚤 🐕 ♿ 🚐 ⛺

Scenic rating: 9

on Lake Como northwest of Darby in Bitterroot National Forest

Lake Como sits at 4,300 feet on the west side of the Bitterroot Valley, tucked adjacent to the Selway-Bitterroot Wilderness. The lake, formed by a dam built in 1905, retains water at nearly full pool from spring through mid-July but can be boated through mid-August. The large, popular recreation area includes a boat launch, which is about two miles away on the other side of the lake. The launch—with a cement ramp and dock—can handle up to 40 boats. The day-use area that sits between the lower and upper campgrounds has a sandy beach with a buoyed area for swimming, dressing shelters, vault toilets, and picnic tables. For hikers, mountain bikers, and equestrians, the Rock Creek Trail tours the south end of the lake and the Lake Como National Recreation Trail travels the north side. Adjacent to the recreation area, the Lick Creek Auto Tour—a one-hour interpretive drive through a research forest—departs for seven miles to Lost Horse Creek Road. Overflow camping is available east of the boat launch.

The ultra-quiet campground loops around Kramis Pond, with spacious shaded sites set far apart for privacy on a mixed forest hillside. Sites 2 and 3 overlook the lake. A narrow gravel road loops through the campground, which has gravel parking pads.

Campsites, facilities: The campground has 11 RV or tent campsites. The parking pads can handle a maximum RV length of 30 feet. Facilities include picnic tables, fire rings with grills, drinking water, campground hosts, and garbage service. Leashed pets are permitted. A wheelchair-accessible toilet is available.

Reservations, fees: Reservations are not accepted. Campsites cost $8 in summer. Day-use fees are $5 per vehicle. Cash or check. Open year-round, but usually snowbound December–April.

Directions: About four miles north of Darby, look for milepost 35.1 on Highway 93. Turn west onto Lake Como Road and drive for three miles. Turn right at the signed junction for the campgrounds and go 0.8 mile. Turn left and immediately right. Drive 0.5 mile. (Pavement ends at 0.2 mile.) The campground is a half mile west of Lower Como Campground with the swimming beach and picnic area in between.

GPS Coordinates: N 46° 3.982' W 114° 14.829'

Contact: Bitterroot National Forest, Stevensville Ranger District, 88 Main St., Stevensville, MT 59870, 406/777-5431, www.fs.fed.us/r1/bitterroot/.

19 SAM BILLINGS MEMORIAL
🏃 ⛵ 🎣 🚤 🐕 ♿ 🚐 ⛺

Scenic rating: 6

on the West Fork of the Bitterroot River in the Bitterroot National Forest

Located at 4,500 feet in the southern Bitterroot Mountains, Sam Billings Campground is the first developed campground you reach while driving south on the long West Fork of the Bitterroot River. A launch site for canoes, kayaks, and rafts for floating or fishing the West Fork is 0.2 mile farther south on the highway. One mile of potholed dirt road leads off the highway to the campground, which sits on Boulder Creek, a tributary of the West Fork. The trailhead for the Boulder Creek trail is 0.5 mile farther up the road. The route leads in 4.5 miles to Boulder Creek Falls in the Selway-Bitterroot Wilderness and farther into the Boulder Lakes Basin.

Sprawled out under ponderosa pines, the large campsites hug the gravel campground loop, but far enough away from each other to gain a sense of privacy. Several of the campsites have new gravel parking pads, and recent thinning cleaned up scraggly small-growth trees, making more room for tents. A trail cuts down to the creek between sites 7 and 8. The campground is very quiet with the only noise coming from the tumbling of Boulder Creek.

Campsites, facilities: The campground has 12 RV or tent campsites. The maximum length for RVs is 30 feet. Facilities include picnic tables, fire rings with grills, a few pedestal grills, and vault toilets. No drinking water is available. Bring your own, or if you plan on using creek water, boil or purify it first. Pack out your trash. Leashed pets are permitted. A wheelchair-accessible toilet and several campsites are available.

Reservations, fees: Reservations are not accepted. Camping is free. Open year-round, but usually closed by snow December–April.

Directions: From Highway 93 four miles south of Darby, drive south on the West Fork Road for 13.1 miles. Turn right onto Forest Road 5631 and drive 0.9 mile. After you cross a single-lane bridge, the campground entrance will be on the left.

GPS Coordinates: N 45° 49.493' W 114° 14.891'

Contact: Bitterroot National Forest, West Fork Ranger District, 6735 West Fork Rd., Darby, MT 59829, 406/821-3269, www.fs.fed.us/r1/bitterroot/.

20 ROMBO

Scenic rating: 5

on the West Fork of the Bitterroot River in the Bitterroot National Forest

On the riverside at 4,500 feet, on the West Fork of the Bitterroot River in the southern Bitterroot Mountains, Rombo is a campground for those who want to fish or float the river. The campground, however, does not permit launching boats, so you must launch just upstream 0.2 mile across the bridge on the opposite side of the river. It does, however, have plenty of fishing access along the river. The 42-mile river is a favorite of fly-casters going after brown, rainbow, bull, brook, and westslope cutthroat trout. Sites to launch rafts for fishing or floating are primitive on the West Fork.

Shaded by mature ponderosa pines, the gravel road loops through the quiet campground, which has gravel back-in parking pads. Some of the campsites (13 and 14, in particular) have views of the surrounding forested hills. Sites 1, 2, 5, 6, 8, and 13 also border the river, but mostly without views of the river. Short trails through the brush connect to it. Site 14 on the north end is more secluded. Sites are spread out for privacy, but neighboring camps are visible.

Campsites, facilities: The campground has 15 RV or tent campsites. With the short parking pads, the maximum RV length is 30 feet. Facilities include picnic tables, fire rings with grills, a few pedestal grills, vault toilets, drinking water, garbage service, and campground hosts. Leashed pets are permitted. A wheelchair-accessible toilet is available.

Reservations, fees: Reservations are accepted (www.recreation.gov, 877/444-6777). Campsites cost $8 per night. Cash or check. Open late May–mid-October.

Directions: From Darby, go four miles south on Highway 93 to the West Fork Road. Drive south past milepost 17 for 0.9 mile and take a sharp right-hand turn to enter the campground.

GPS Coordinates: N 45° 45.825' W 114° 16.923'

Contact: Bitterroot National Forest, West Fork Ranger District, 6735 West Fork Rd., Darby, MT 59829, 406/821-3269, www.fs.fed.us/r1/bitterroot/.

21 FALES FLAT

Scenic rating: 7

on Magruder Road Corridor east of Nez Perce Pass in Bitterroot National Forest

At 5,125 feet in the southern Bitterroot Mountains, Fales Flat is the only designated Montana campground on the 101-mile primitive Magruder Road Corridor over the 6,598-foot high Nez Perce Pass into Idaho. The pass, which is also a good mountain-biking destination, affords views into the Selway-Bitterroot and Frank Church River of No Return Wildernesses. Fourteen miles of pavement—the remnant of thwarted timber sales—starts one mile before the campground and continues the seven miles to the pass. Watch for falling rocks, downed trees, and large sinkholes on the unmaintained and unplowed road. At 1.5 miles south of the campground, the Watchtower Creek Trailhead (#669) departs.

The ultra-quiet campground sprawls across a large, open, grassy meadow bordered by mixed forest. If the group campsite is not reserved, you may use it. Most of the campsites tuck into the edge of the trees for shade and weather protection, with the exception of the primitive sites in the meadow.

Campsites, facilities: The campground has seven RV or tent campsites. The campsites can fit midsized RVs, but the condition of the road may dissuade interest. Facilities include picnic tables, fire rings with grills or rock fire rings, vault toilets, and a fenced stock area, but no drinking water. If you use the creek water, boil or purify it. Pack out your trash. Leashed pets are permitted. A wheelchair-accessible toilet is available.

Reservations, fees: Reservations are not accepted except for the group site (www.recreation.gov, 877/444-6777, $15). Camping is free. Open year-round, but usually buried under snow December–April.

Directions: From Highway 93 four miles south of Darby, drive south on the West Fork Road. At 0.3 mile past milepost 14, turn right onto the Nez Perce Road, which is also known as the Magruder Road Corridor and Forest Road 468. At 3.7 miles up the road at Little West Fork Creek, the pavement ends, and large potholes and bumpy washboards litter the dirt road for the next six miles before rough pavement resumes. Reach the campground on the left at 10.6 miles. Enter the campground at the group sign.

GPS Coordinates: N 45° 44.770' W 114° 26.612'

Contact: Bitterroot National Forest, West Fork Ranger District, 6735 West Fork Rd., Darby, MT 59829, 406/821-3269, www.fs.fed.us/r1/bitterroot/.

22 SLATE CREEK

Scenic rating: 7

east of Painted Rocks Lake in the West Fork of the Bitterroot River Drainage in the Bitterroot National Forest

At 4,875 feet, Slate Creek Campground sits east of Painted Rocks Lake. Unfortunately, from its position tucked in a narrow side gorge, the campground has no views of the stunning orange-lichen-covered rocks or the lake. From its location, you can drive or mountain bike across the dam on a narrow, single-lane dirt road to reach remote trailheads such as Castle Rock and the natural undeveloped hot springs on Forest Road 362. The 143-foot-high and 800-foot-long dam was built in 1939 for irrigating Bitterroot Valley. Boating on the lake is best before August, when irrigation demand reduces the lake level significantly. The lake harbors mountain whitefish and five species of trout—westslope cutthroat, rainbow, brown, brook, and bull. The campground sits on the west side of the paved lake road opposite a primitive boat launch, beach, and fishing access. Locate the lake's developed boat launch, which has paved trailer parking and a concrete ramp, near the dam.

Along a narrow, gravel road loop, the tiny quiet, shaded campground lines up along Slate Creek, which flows into the lake. The campground's sites each have access to the creek and only room for small tents. The entrance road looks down on the campground, affording little privacy from passing motorists.

Campsites, facilities: The campground has four RV or tent campsites. The parking pads can fit RVs up to 25 feet in length. Facilities include picnic tables, fire rings with grills, and a vault toilet, but no drinking water. Bring your own, or if you choose to use the creek water, boil or purify it first. Pack out your trash. Leashed pets are permitted. A wheelchair-accessible toilet is available.

Reservations, fees: Reservations are not accepted. Camping is free. The campground is open year-round but usually snowbound December–April.

Directions: From Darby, go four miles south on Highway 93 to the West Fork Road. Drive south to milepost 23 and continue another 0.5 mile up the east side of Painted Rocks Lake. Turn left onto a narrow gravel road and drive 0.1 mile to the entrance on the right. GPS Coordinates: N 45° 41.894' W 114° 17.128'

Contact: Bitterroot National Forest, West Fork Ranger District, 6735 West Fork Rd., Darby, MT 59829, 406/821-3269, www.fs.fed.us/r1/bitterroot/.

23 PAINTED ROCK STATE PARK

Scenic rating: 8

on Painted Rocks Lake in the West Fork of the Bitterroot River Drainage in the Bitterroot National Forest

On the south end of Painted Rocks Lake in the southern Bitterroot Mountains, the 23-acre state park, elevation 4,750 feet, is the only

The Painted Rocks, colored with lichen, tower above Painted Rocks Lake.

© BECKY LOMAX

campground that sits right on the lake. It is named for the dramatic orange, black, and tan colors that smear the rocky outcrops at the north end of the lake. From the boat launch, you can glimpse them, but you'll get the best views from the water or pullouts along the road. The colors are a result of lichens growing on the 70–90 million-year-old granitic and rhyolite cliffs. The campground's boat launch includes a cement ramp, dock, and trailer parking. The lake is a trout fishery.

The quiet campground squeezes together campsites under lodgepoles and firs with little privacy. If you're going for views, a few line the lake frontage. One in the north sits in the open next to the boat launch; if you don't mind the commotion, you'll get prime lakeside views. While the road is paved to the entrance, the campground loop is a dirt road with mostly back-in parking pads—muddy when wet and dusty when dry. Most sites have big flat spaces for tents. The six lakefront sites in the south loop are more spread out, offering a little privacy.

Campsites, facilities: The campground is a primitive state park with 21 RV or tent campsites. Facilities include picnic tables, fire rings with grills, and vault toilets, but no drinking water. Bring your own, or if you use lake water, boil or purify it first. You can also get water four miles up the road at Alta Campground. Pack out your trash. Leashed pets are permitted. A wheelchair-accessible toilet is available.

Reservations, fees: Reservations are not accepted. Camping is free, but donations are accepted. Open year-round, but snow-covered in winter.

Directions: From Darby, go four miles south on Highway 93 to the West Fork Road. Drive south to milepost 25 on the east side of Painted Rocks Lake and continue another 0.2 mile. Turn right into the campground.

GPS Coordinates: N 45° 40.879' W 114° 18.069'

Contact: Montana Fish, Wildlife, and Parks, 3201 Spurgin Rd., Missoula, MT 59804, 406/542-5500, http://fwp.mt.gov.

24 ALTA

Scenic rating: 6

south of Painted Rocks Lake in the West Fork of the Bitterroot River Drainage in Bitterroot National Forest

Located the farthest south of the developed campgrounds in the West Fork of the Bitterroot River, Alta Campground gives access to the river for fishing, but at this end of the river at 5,000 feet, only small, hand-carried rafts, canoes, and kayaks work. Painted Rocks Reservoir sits less than five miles to the north—another option for fishing and boating. The surrounding Bitterroot Mountains zigzag with myriad forest roads that are popular with ATV riders and mountain bikers.

Large ponderosa pines shade the campground, which is set in a small community of cabins and homes. The tiny day-use area includes a long bench for sitting by the river, bird-watching, or soaking up the sounds of the forest. The quiet campsites are a mix of sizes, with varying degrees of privacy. Some have room for large tents (sites 12 and 13); others only fit small, two-person tents. Sites 6, 7, and 12 border the river. The campground loop road is gravel, and the sites have gravel parking pads.

Campsites, facilities: The campground has 15 RV or tent campsites. The parking pads can accommodate RVs up to 30 feet in length. Facilities include picnic tables, fire rings with grills, a few pedestal grills, vault toilets, drinking water, overflow parking, campground hosts, and garbage service. Leashed pets are permitted. A wheelchair-accessible toilet is available.

Reservations, fees: Reservations are accepted (www.recreation.gov, 877/444-6777). Campsites cost $8. Cash or check. Open year-round, but the campground is usually buried by snow December–April.

Directions: From Darby, go four miles south

on Highway 93 to the West Fork Road. Drive south to milepost 29, passing Painted Rocks Lake. Continue another 0.4 mile up the road and turn right into the campground.

GPS Coordinates: N 45° 37.430' W 114° 18.089'

Contact: Bitterroot National Forest, West Fork Ranger District, 6735 West Fork Rd., Darby, MT 59829, 406/821-3269, www.fs.fed. us/r1/bitterroot/.

25 CRAZY CREEK

Scenic rating: 8

west of the East Fork of the Bitterroot River in Bitterroot National Forest

At the confluence of Warm Spring Creek and Crazy Creek at 4,800 feet, the campground is actually a pair of adjacent campgrounds squeezed into a narrow canyon. The upper campground services tent and RV campers with sites along the river or with views up the valley. The lower campground is equipped with a watering trough, hitch rails, and stock ramps for horse-packers. Trails for hikers, equestrians, and mountain bikers depart from here both up-valley and down—to Warm Springs (#103), Porcupine Creek (#205), and Shields Creek (#673)—via a footbridge that crosses Warm Springs in the upper campground. Crazy Creek contains several species of trout, but most prominently rainbow trout.

Both of the ultra-quiet campgrounds sit along Warm Springs Creek in a mixed forest with shaded sites, but Crazy Creek tumbles through the upper campground. Sites 1 and 2 have views of the rocky cliffs of the canyon. Sites 3, 6, and 7 look up-valley with mountain views. Due to the hillside placement of the campsites, many can only accommodate small tents.

Campsites, facilities: The upper campground has seven RV or tent campsites, and

the horse camp has five sites. Both have a maximum RV length of 26 feet. Facilities include picnic tables, fire rings with grills, and vault toilets. Drinking water is available in the upper campground but not the lower. Pack out your trash. Leashed pets are permitted. A wheelchair-accessible toilet is available.

Reservations, fees: Reservations are not accepted. Campsites cost $8 per night during summer. Cash or check. The campgrounds are open year-round but usually snowbound December–April.

Directions: From Highway 93 between Darby and Sula, turn west at milepost 15.7 opposite Spring Gulch Campground onto the rough pavement of Medicine Springs Road. Drive 0.8 mile to the campground sign for Warm Springs, where the pavement ends, and continue driving for three more miles to reach both campground entrances—the horse camp downhill to the left and the individual campsites up and straight ahead.

GPS Coordinates: N 45° 48.729' W 114° 4.130'

Contact: Bitterroot National Forest, Sula Ranger District, 7338 Hwy. 93 S., Sula, MT 59871, 406/821-3201, www.fs.fed.us/r1/bitterroot/.

26 WARM SPRINGS

Scenic rating: 6

west of the East Fork of the Bitterroot River in Bitterroot National Forest

Located at 4,500 feet on Warm Springs Creek, a tributary of the East Fork of the Bitterroot River in the southern Bitterroot Mountains, the campground is an alternative if Crazy Creek and Spring Gulch are full. It doesn't have the things to commend it that the other two campgrounds do and is in need of some TLC, but it works if you need a campground in this general location and want the quiet of being away from the long-haul truck noise on the highway. It sits one mile off the highway from Spring Gulch Campground and three miles below Crazy Creek Campground. On the way to the campground, you'll pass the Warm Springs Trailhead (#166) for hikers, equestrians, and mountain bikers that follows the drainage upstream. The stream contains rainbow trout for fishing.

Tall grass and out-of-control brush are taking over the campground, which makes claiming tent space difficult. The campground has a mix of open meadow sites and shaded tree sites. Although the narrow campground road is paved, the pavement is old with cracks and bumps. Surrounding the meadow, sites 1, 2, 3, and 14 sit in the open with views of the rocky hillsides. Sites 4–13 are in the trees. Site 8 is more private than the others.

Campsites, facilities: The campground has 14 RV or tent campsites. No RVs larger than 26 feet should try to camp here. Facilities include picnic tables, fire rings with grills, vault toilets, drinking water, and garbage service. Leashed pets are permitted. A wheelchair-accessible toilet is available.

Reservations, fees: Reservations are accepted for seven of the sites (www.recreation.gov, 877/444-6777). Campsites cost $8. Cash or check. Open late May–September.

Directions: From Highway 93 between Darby and Sula, turn west at milepost 15.7 opposite Spring Gulch Campground onto the rough pavement of Medicine Springs Road. Drive 1.2 miles to the campground sign and turn left, going up the hill past a few cabins to the campground entrance. (The pavement ends just past the sign.)
GPS Coordinates: N 45° 50.583' W 114° 2.339'

Contact: Bitterroot National Forest, Sula Ranger District, 7338 Hwy. 93 S., Sula, MT 59871, 406/821-3201, www.fs.fed.us/r1/bitterroot/.

27 SPRING GULCH

Scenic rating: 7

on the East Fork of the Bitterroot River in the Bitterroot National Forest

One of the last few campgrounds in Montana before you pop over Lost Trail Pass into Idaho, Spring Gulch is conveniently right on the highway just north of Sula at 4,500 feet. Of course, the trade-off for convenience is road noise. Since it sits right on the East Fork of the Bitterroot River, you can launch rafts, kayaks, and canoes from the campground—but nothing larger. A small parking area can accommodate boat trailers. The view across the river holds some striking rock outcroppings. A very short paved trail connects with the river, where a large fishing deck allows you to soak up the views and the sounds of the water. Hiking and mountain biking are available on Medicine Springs Road across the highway.

Tucked under large ponderosa pines, the campground picks up some shade where it squeezes in between the river and the highway. It is also grassy and brushy, which yields some privacy to a couple of the campsites. Campsites 2, 4, 5, and 8 sit close to the river. Site 8 is wide open in a meadow and offers views, as does site 6, which is closer to the highway. Sites 2, 6, 11, and 12 have room for tents. The campground loop and parking aprons—all of which are back-ins—are both paved. Rattlesnakes sometimes frequent this campground.

Campsites, facilities: The campground has 11 RV or tent campsites. Only a couple of parking pads can handle RVs and trailer combinations up to 50 feet. Facilities include picnic tables, fire rings with grills, vault toilets, drinking water, a campground host, and garbage service. Leashed pets are permitted. A wheelchair-accessible toilet is available.

Reservations, fees: Reservations are accepted (www.recreation.gov, 877/444-6777). Campsites cost $12. Cash or check. Open late May–September.

Directions: From Highway 93 between Darby and Sula, turn east at milepost 15.7 opposite Medicine Creek Road into the campground. GPS Coordinates: N 45° 51.510' W 114° 1.415'

Contact: Bitterroot National Forest, Sula Ranger District, 7338 Hwy. 93 S., Sula, MT 59871, 406/821-3201, www.fs.fed.us/r1/bitterroot/.

28 SULA COUNTRY STORE AND RESORT

Scenic rating: 6

in Sula in the Bitterroot Mountains

Squeezed in between the southern ranges of the Bitterroot and Sapphire Mountains at 4,450 feet, the Sula Country Store is an icon of Montana for those driving the remote roads here that cross into Idaho or Montana's Big Hole. The roadside store and restaurant that serves home-style meals (the breakfast specialty is homemade country sausage gravy with biscuits) are favorite stops in winter for locals heading to Lost Trail for downhill skiing, Chief Joseph Pass for cross-country skiing, or the myriad national forest snowmobile trails in the mountains. In summer, the resort serves as a base for fishing the Bitterroot forks, hiking, rafting, and cycling. In fall, the area attracts hunters. The resort sits adjacent to a path leading 0.1 mile to the Lewis and Clark Discovery Trail interpretive site. The East Fork of the Bitterroot River flows behind the campground. Lost Trail Hot Springs is seven miles to the south.

The 16-acre campground is right on Highway 93, behind the Sula Country Store, surrounded by cabins, large ponderosas, and mowed lawns. The gravel road and parking pads weave around the kids' fishing pond. Most of the sites are back-ins, but at least seven are pull-throughs. Expect highway noise and little privacy with tight campsites.

Campsites, facilities: The campground has 19 RV sites and 10 tent campsites. Hookups are available for sewer, water, and electricity up to 50 amps. Five RV pull-through sites can fit combinations up to 68 feet. Facilities include picnic tables, fire rings or pedestal grills, flush toilets, showers, a coin-op launderette, gas, diesel, propane, a store, a disposal station, cabins, mini-golf, kids' fishing pond, and hot tub. Leashed pets are permitted. A wheelchair-accessible toilet is available.

Reservations, fees: Reservations are accepted. Hookups cost $18–20. Tent sites cost $13. Rates are for one or two people. It's $4 for each additional person. Cash, check, or credit card. Open year-round.

Directions: Locate the resort on the north side of Highway 93. It sits 13 miles north from the Idaho-Montana border at Lost Trail Pass. GPS Coordinates: N 45° 50.184' W 113° 58.935'

Contact: Sula Country Store, Campground, and RV Park, 7060 Hwy. 93 S., Sula, MT 59871, 406/821-3364, http://bitterroot-montana.com.

29 INDIAN TREES

Scenic rating: 7

between Sula and Lost Trail Pass in Bitterroot National Forest

BEST (

In the southern Bitterroot Mountains at 5,200 feet, Indian Trees Campground is named for the scarring left on its huge ponderosa pines when the Salish people in the 1800s fed on the cambium layers. Located 0.3 mile south of the campground exit off the highway, the Nee-Me-Poo Trail—the four-state Nez Perce National Historic Trail—traces the flight of the Nez Perce from the U.S. Army over Gibbons Pass to Trail Creek. The gravel auto and mountain-biking route connects to Highway 43 and Big Hole National Battlefield. The Porcupine Saddle Trailhead is within a

10-minute drive. Lost Trail Hot Springs is a five-minute drive.

Large ponderosas provide a semi-open forest, where some brush between campsites helps create privacy. Most of the sites are grassy. One large loop swings through the campground, which has a paved road and paved parking pads. Campsite 2 is reserved for bicyclists. Even though the campground sits back from the highway, you'll still hear long-haul trucks gearing up and down. This campground has better tent places than the hot springs.

Campsites, facilities: The campground has 16 RV or tent campsites. RVs are limited to 50 feet. Facilities include picnic tables, fire rings with grills, vault toilets, drinking water, garbage service, and campground hosts. Leashed pets are permitted. A wheelchair-accessible toilet is available.

Reservations, fees: Reservations are accepted (www.recreation.gov, 877/444-6777). Campsites cost $10 per night. Cash or check. Open late May–September.

Directions: From Sula, go six miles south on Highway 93. Turn west on Forest Road 729 for 0.5 mile past a right turn. Follow the dirt road for 0.2 mile over a cattle guard, veering right to where the road turns back to pavement. Turn left at the entrance sign.
GPS Coordinates: N 45° 45.387' W 113° 57.208'

Contact: Bitterroot National Forest, Sula Ranger District, 7338 Hwy. 93 S., Sula, MT 59871, 406-821-3201, www.fs.fed.us/r1/bitterroot/.

30 LOST TRAIL HOT SPRINGS RESORT

Scenic rating: 7

between Sula and Lost Trail Pass in Bitterroot National Forest

In the southern Bitterroot Mountains just north of Lost Trail Pass and the Idaho-Montana border at 5,200 feet, Lost Trail Hot Springs Resort features a natural hot springs pool with water temperatures that hang around 93 degrees year-round and no chemicals added. One end of the pool plunges deep; the other end is 10 inches deep for wading. In winter, the pool is covered by a dome. The resort provides a base for those downhill skiing at Lost Trail, cross-country skiing at Chief Joseph Pass, and snowmobiling in the surrounding national forest. In the summer, the resort attracts hikers, mountain bikers, sightseers, and anglers. In fall, it's a hunting destination. The resort, which also includes cabins and a restaurant, can help arrange white-water rafting and connect you with fishing or hunting outfitters. Five minutes north on the highway, the Nee-Me-Poo Trail—the four-state Nez Perce National Historic Trail—traces the flight of the Nez Perce from the U.S. Army over Gibbons Pass to Trail Creek. The gravel auto and mountain-biking route connects to Highway 43 and Big Hole National Battlefield.

The resort is surrounded by Bitterroot National Forest and sits down in treed ravine within earshot of commercial trucks on the highway. A gravel road loops through the resort. Campsites have gravel parking pads and are tucked close together with minimal privacy.

Campsites, facilities: The resort has 18 RV and four tent campsites. Eight have full hookups with sewer, water, and electricity. Facilities include flush toilets, showers, a restaurant, casino, lounge, and lodge. Leashed pets are permitted. A wheelchair-accessible toilet is available.

Reservations, fees: Reservations are accepted. Hookups cost $25. Dry camping sites (RV or tent) cost $10 per night. Fees cover six people. Admission to the hot pool is extra: children 2–12 $5, adults $7, and seniors over 60 years old $6. Cash, check, or credit card. Open year-round.

Directions: From Highway 93 between Sula and Lost Trail Pass, turn west off the highway six miles north of the Idaho-Montana border at the signed entrance. Drive 0.25 mile.

GPS Coordinates: N 45° 45.081' W 113° 56.640'

Contact: Lost Trail Hot Springs Resort, 8321 Hwy. 93 S., Sula, MT 59871, 406/821-3574 or 800/825-3574, www.losttrailhotsprings.com.

31 MAY CREEK

Scenic rating: 7

between Chief Joseph Pass and Wisdom in Beaverhead-Deerlodge National Forest

At 6,300 feet in elevation in the Beaverhead Mountains, May Creek is the only designated campground on the highway between Chief Joseph Pass and Wisdom. Miles of willow bogs line the streams—good habitat for moose. The Nee-Me-Poo Trail, a gravel driving or mountain-biking route from Highway 93 over Gibbons Pass to 1.6 miles west of the campground, follows the path of the Nez Perce fleeing after the seizure of their lands. The route is part of the four-state Nez Perce National Historic Trail. East of the campground after you descend into the Big Hole Valley, the Big Hole National Battlefield lies north of the road. Adjacent to May Creek, the campground attracts anglers and those looking to hike May Creek Trail (#103), which follows the creek up two miles to a cabin. The campground's west side has a horse corral with a stock ramp and pasture. The trail departs from across the creek on the other side of the pasture.

The quiet campground is surrounded by log fences to keep grazing cattle out. Campsites 4, 6, 7, 9, and 10 border the meadow and willows along the perimeter of the campground, which is mostly shaded by lodgepoles. While the sites are spread out for privacy, you'll still see neighboring campers from each site.

Campsites, facilities: The campground has 21 RV or tent campsites. The parking pads can fit a maximum trailer length of 30 feet. Facilities include picnic tables, fire rings with grills, pedestal grills at some campsites, vault toilets, and drinking water. Pack out your trash. Leashed pets are permitted. A wheelchair-accessible toilet is available.

Reservations, fees: Reservations are not accepted. Campsites cost $7. An extra vehicle costs $3. Cash or check. Open mid-June–early September.

Directions: From Wisdom, go 17 miles west on Highway 43 to the campground. From Highway 93, drive 9.7 miles west on Highway 43. The campground sits on the south side of the highway and is entered via a rough, potholed dirt road that crosses a cattle guard.

GPS Coordinates: N 45° 39.239' W 113° 46.810'

Contact: Beaverhead-Deerlodge National Forest, Wisdom Ranger District, P.O. Box 238, Wisdom, MT 59761, 406/689-3243, www.fs.fed.us/r1/b-d.

32 BEAVERTAIL HILL STATE PARK

Scenic rating: 6

east of Missoula on the Clark Fork River

At an elevation of 3,615 feet, east of Missoula on the north bank of the Clark Fork River, Beavertail Hill State Park is named for a large hill to the west that resembles a beavertail. Unfortunately, I-90 sliced the beavertail in half. The 65-acre park has a half mile of river frontage: Gates from the campground access the shoreline for fishing and launching hand-carried boats. The next take-out downstream is Schwartz Creek about seven miles to the west. The campground is the closest to Garnet Ghost Town—home in 1898 to 1,000 people digging for gold. Locate the road to Garnet eight miles east on I-90. Hiking and mountain-biking trails are also available around Garnet.

The campground tucks its campsites on a gravel loop and spur under large cottonwoods and pines. The grassy sites are very close together, but sites 7, 9, 11, 12, 19, 20, 21, and 22 have river frontage. A fence divides the river and the campground to protect children from running into the river, but several gates allow access. Those campsites on the end of the spur are closest to the freeway, with campsite 22 even having views of it. Be prepared for freeway noise to seep in at night, especially from trucks. A one-mile interpretive trail circles the campground—a good place to watch for nighthawks and great horned owls at dusk.

Campsites, facilities: The campground has 28 RV or tent campsites. Most of the gravel parking pads can fit trailers up to 28 feet in length. Facilities include picnic tables, fire rings with grills, flush and vault toilets, drinking water, campground hosts, garbage service, interpretive amphitheater programs, firewood for sale, two tipis for rent, two horseshoe pits, a nature trail, and river access. Leashed pets are permitted. A wheelchair-accessible toilet is available.

Reservations, fees: Reservations are not accepted. Campsites cost $15. Seniors and disabled campers pay half price. Nonresident day use costs $5; it's free for Montana residents. Tipi rental is $25 per night. Cash or check. Open May–September.

Directions: From I-90 between Missoula and Drummond, take Exit 130. Head south following the signs for 0.3 mile and turn left into the campground.

GPS Coordinates: N 46° 43.200' W 113° 34.515'

Contact: Montana Fish, Wildlife, and Parks, 3201 Spurgin Rd., Missoula, MT 59804, 406/542-5500, http://fwp.mt.gov.

33 NORTON

Scenic rating: 9

on Rock Creek in Lolo National Forest

West of Missoula beneath the Sapphire Mountains, Rock Creek spills into the Clark Fork River in the I-90 corridor. Of the campgrounds lining Rock Creek's 41-mile road, Norton Campground sits the farthest north—the only one accessible by pavement and the lowest in elevation at 3,900 feet. A 10-minute drive north, the Valley of the Moon 0.5-mile boardwalk trail tours the riparian corridor with interpretive signs on the natural history, native fishery, small mammals, and vegetation. The river is popular for rafting, kayaking, and fishing, while Rock Creek Road works for mountain biking.

South of a string of cabins, the quiet campground has a unique layout. The campsites sit jumbled willy-nilly on the inside of a dirt loop under firs and lodgepoles. You park around the ring in pull-over spaces and walk in to the picnic tables, which are quite close together and have zero privacy from each other. Flat spaces for tents are small. A trail leads from the campground to the river.

Campsites, facilities: The campground has 12 RV or tent campsites. RVs are limited to small rigs. Facilities include picnic tables, fire rings with grills, pit toilets, and campground hosts. From mid-May–September, drinking water and garbage service are available. When the water is turned off, you can boil or purify creek water. Pack out your trash when the garbage service closes down. Leashed pets are permitted. A wheelchair-accessible toilet is available.

Reservations, fees: Reservations are not accepted. Campsites cost $6 mid-May–September but are otherwise free. Cash or check. Open year-round, but snow-covered in winter.

Directions: From I-90, locate Rock Creek at Exit 126 halfway between Missoula and Drummond. From the freeway, drive south on the paved part of Rock Creek Road (Forest Road 102) to milepost 10.6. The campground sits between the road and the river. Coming from Philipsburg, drive 14 miles on Highway 348 to reach Forest Road 102. Turn right at the bridge over Rock Creek and drive 30.4 miles north on the bumpy dirt road. Between mileposts 30 and 25, the skinny road shrinks to one lane with turnouts and steep cliff sections—unsuitable for large RVs and trailers. GPS Coordinates: N 46° 35.420' W 113° 40.179'

Contact: Lolo National Forest, Missoula Ranger District, Bldg. 24A, Fort Missoula, Missoula, MT 59804, 406/329-3814, www. fs.fed.us/r1/lolo.

34 GRIZZLY

Scenic rating: 7

east of Rock Creek in Lolo National Forest

Located east of the Rock Creek drainage on a tributary, Grizzly Campground sits at 4,200 feet in elevation. The Grizzly Trailhead, on Rock Creek Road 0.25 mile north of the campground turnoff, is used by mountain bikers and hikers heading up the creek to Grizzly Point. Fishing the Ranch Creek that flows past the campground provides its challenges due to the brushy banks.

With well-spread-out sites under a mix of ponderosa and fir, the ultra-quiet campground tucks in between a large black talus slope and brushy Ranch Creek. The dirt road makes two loops through the campground. The loop to the right houses only two sites—both very private. The loop to the left contains sites 3–9, which have some peek-a-boo views of surrounding slopes. Sites 2–5 back up to the talus slope, and sites 7–9 border the creek.

Campsites, facilities: The campground has nine RV or tent campsites. RVs are limited to small rigs, and trailers are discouraged because of the road. Facilities include picnic tables, fire rings with grills, pit toilets, horseshoe pits, and a volleyball court (bring your own net). From mid-May–September, drinking water and garbage service are available. When the water is turned off, you can boil or purify creek water. Pack out your trash when the garbage service closes down. Leashed pets are permitted. A wheelchair-accessible toilet is available.

Reservations, fees: Reservations are not accepted. Campsites cost $6 May–September but are otherwise free. Cash or check. Open year-round, but covered by snow in winter.

Directions: From I-90, take the Rock Creek Exit 126 halfway between Missoula and Drummond. From the freeway, drive south on the paved part of Rock Creek Road (Forest Road 102) to milepost 11.2. Turn east onto the dirt Forest Road 4296 for 0.7 mile and then turn right, driving over Ranch Creek to enter the campground. Coming from Philipsburg, drive 14 miles on Highway 348 to reach Forest Road 102. Turn right at the bridge over Rock Creek and drive 29.8 miles north on the bumpy dirt road. Between mileposts 30 and 25, the skinny road shrinks to one lane with turnouts and steep cliff sections—unsuitable for large RVs and trailers.

GPS Coordinates: N 46° 34.357' W 113° 39.625'

Contact: Lolo National Forest, Missoula Ranger District, Bldg. 24A, Fort Missoula, Missoula, MT 59804, 406/329-3814, www. fs.fed.us/r1/lolo.

35 DALLES

Scenic rating: 7

on Rock Creek in Lolo National Forest

BEST (

Rock Creek borders tiny Welcome Creek Wilderness, a pocket nine miles long and seven miles wide in the Sapphire Mountains west of Missoula. At 4,200 feet, Dalles Campground provides a major entrance to the wilderness with the Welcome Creek Trailhead located 0.4 mile north of the campground. A swinging bridge crosses Rock Creek into the wilderness, where the trail climbs 7.5 miles to the steep, rocky Sapphire Range divide. Mountain bikers are not allowed in the wilderness but can bike the road. From the campground, paths lead down to the riverbank for fishing on the blue-ribbon trout stream that is also popular for rafting, kayaking, and canoeing. Only small RVs should attempt to come from the south.

Sitting on a bluff overlooking the river, Dalles Campground provides large, spread-out campsites good for tenting. Sites 4, 6, and 8 overlook the river. A mature forest lends partial shade to the campsites, which are spread out for privacy and quiet enough to hear the river.

Campsites, facilities: The campground has 10 RV or tent campsites. Some parking pads can accommodate midsized RVs. Facilities include picnic tables, fire rings with grills, and pit toilets. From mid-May–September, drinking water and garbage service are available. When the water is turned off, you can boil or purify river water. Pack out your trash when the garbage service closes down. Leashed pets are permitted. A wheelchair-accessible toilet is available.

Reservations, fees: Reservations are not accepted. Campsites cost $6 May–September; otherwise they're free. Cash or check. Open year-round, but snow-covered in winter.

Directions: From I-90, take Rock Creek Exit 126 halfway between Missoula and Drummond. Drive south on Rock Creek Road (Forest Road 102) to milepost 14.1. (The pavement ends after 11.5 miles.) The campground is between the road and the river. Coming from Philipsburg, drive 14 miles on Highway 348 to reach Forest Road 102. Turn right at the bridge over Rock Creek and drive 26.9 miles north on the bumpy dirt road. Between mileposts 30 and 25, the skinny road shrinks to one lane with turnouts and steep cliff sections—unsuitable for large RVs and trailers.

GPS Coordinates: N 46° 33.444' W 113° 42.672'

Contact: Lolo National Forest, Missoula Ranger District, Bldg. 24A, Fort Missoula, Missoula, MT 59804, 406/329-3814, www.fs.fed.us/r1/lolo.

36 HARRY'S FLAT

Scenic rating: 5

on Rock Creek in Lolo National Forest

Rock Creek, which flows through a canyon hanging east of the Sapphire Mountains, is home to bighorn sheep and mountain goats. Harry's Flat Campground, at 4,200 feet, perches in the narrow canyon's lower end, where steep talus slopes tumble into the river. Across the river is the Welcome Creek Wilderness. The blue-ribbon trout stream attracts rafters, kayakers, and anglers. Mountain bikers ride the road, and hikers can find trailheads south of the campground.

The quiet campground spreads out around two loops under large ponderosa pines. The loop housing sites 10–19 has a pit toilet; the loop with sites 1–9 has a vault toilet, plus more private sites, especially site 8. Most of the campsites have large flat spaces for tents. Sites 1, 2, 3, and 5 claim riverfront.

Campsites, facilities: The campground has 19 RV or tent campsites. The configuration of the dirt loops and the size of the parking pads can accommodate larger RVs. However, be aware that the drive requires more than five miles on a rough narrow dirt road from the north; only small RVs should attempt access from the south. Facilities include picnic tables, fire rings with grills, and vault toilets. From mid-May–September, drinking water and garbage service are available. When the water is turned off, you can boil or purify river water. Pack out your trash when the garbage service closes down. Leashed pets are permitted. A wheelchair-accessible toilet is available.

Reservations, fees: Reservations are not accepted. Campsites cost $6 May–September. Cash or check. Open year-round, but snow-covered in winter.

Directions: From I-90, take Rock Creek Exit 126 halfway between Missoula and Drummond and drive south on Rock Creek Road (Forest Road 102) to milepost 16.5. (The pavement ends after 11.5 miles.) The campground is between the road and the river. Coming from Philipsburg, drive 14 miles on Highway 348 to reach Forest Road 102. Turn right at the bridge over Rock Creek and drive 24.5 miles north on the bumpy dirt road. Between mileposts 30 and 25, the skinny road shrinks to one lane with turnouts and steep cliff sections—unsuitable for large RVs and trailers.

GPS Coordinates: N 46° 32.850' W 113° 44.367'

Contact: Lolo National Forest, Missoula Ranger District, Bldg. 24A, Fort Missoula, Missoula, MT 59804, 406/329-3814, www.fs.fed.us/r1/lolo.

37 ROCK CREEK PRIMITIVE

Scenic rating: 7

on Rock Creek in Lolo National Forest

Rock Creek—a 52-mile blue-ribbon trout river draining the Sapphire Mountains southwest of Missoula—flows north into the Clark Fork River with Rock Creek Road paralleling most of its distance. Camping in dispersed sites is not permitted in this area of Lolo National Forest except for 15 designated primitive sites between mileposts 12 and 33. Most may be accessed from the river for those who want to overnight while rafting or kayaking; all may be accessed via the rugged 41-mile dirt Forest Road 102, which parallels the river.

Each signed primitive campsite is different and identified by number. These forested locations are attractive for the quiet and solitude they provide. Two sit in the woods on the east side of the road, but the others command river frontage. Primitive sites 4, 7, 8, and 11 are walk-in sites for tenting.

Campsites, facilities: Fifteen primitive camps line the Rock Creek Road. Most have one campsite; camp 14 has three sites. Eleven camps accommodate small RVs or tents; four camps are tents only. Facilities include pit toilets at two camps and metal or rock fire rings. Those with no toilets require campers to follow Leave No Trace ethics for human waste. No drinking water is available; boil or purify river water. (You can get water at Norton, Dalles, Harry's Flat, and Bitterroot Flat campgrounds, also on Rock Creek Road.) Pack out your trash. Leashed pets are permitted.

Reservations, fees: Reservations are not accepted. Camping is free. Open year-round, but snow covers sites in winter.

Directions: From I-90, take Rock Creek Exit 126 halfway between Missoula and Drummond and drive south on Rock Creek Road (Forest Road 102) about 12 miles to where the pavement ends to reach the first primitive campsite. Those coming from Philipsburg direction need to access Forest Road 102 via 14 miles of pavement on Highway 348. Primitive campsite 15 sits at milepost 33, eight miles north of the bridge crossing Rock Creek. The remaining primitive campsites sprinkle along Rock Creek Road every one to three miles. Five of the single-lane, steep miles from milepost 25 to 30 have very few turnouts and are only suitable for small RVs. Trailers are not recommended.

GPS Coordinates: N 46° 34.411' W 113° 41.091' (Milepost 12); N 46° 22.591' W 113° 38.866' (Milepost 33)

Contact: Lolo National Forest, Missoula Ranger District, Bldg. 24A, Fort Missoula, Missoula, MT 59804, 406/329-3814, www.fs.fed.us/r1/lolo.

38 BITTERROOT FLAT

Scenic rating: 6

on Rock Creek in Lolo National Forest

Popular for rafting and kayaking, Rock Creek—a blue-ribbon trout-fishing tributary of the Clark Fork River—squeezes in between the Sapphire and Long John Mountains east of Missoula. At 4,450 feet, Bitterroot Flat is almost equidistant from either end of the rugged forest road along the creek, but coming from the north gains the advantage of 11.5 miles of pavement. Heading into the Sapphires, the Wahlquist Trailhead is three miles to the north.

The grassy campground with low brush sits under a canopy of firs. A group fire pit with benches is available. Sites 1, 2, 3, 5, 8, 10, 11, 13, and 14 have river frontage—some right on the bank staring across the river at the huge talus slope. Since most campers head for these, the sites on the inside of the loop are more overgrown from less use. Site 14 is large enough for two big tents, and several sites have double-wide parking. Site 2 also has a bear box for mountain bikers or those floating the river.

Campsites, facilities: The campground has 15 RV or tent campsites that can fit midsized RVs. Facilities include picnic tables, fire rings with grills, and three vault toilets. From mid-May–September, drinking water and garbage service are available. When the water is turned off, you can boil or purify river water. Pack out your trash when the garbage service closes down. Leashed pets are permitted. A wheelchair-accessible toilet is available.

Reservations, fees: Reservations are not accepted. Campsites cost $6 May–September. Cash or check. Open year-round, although the campground and road may be snowbound in winter.

Directions: From I-90, take Rock Creek Exit 126 halfway between Missoula and Drummond and drive south on Rock Creek Road (Forest Road 102) to milepost 22.5. (The pavement ends after 11.5 miles.) The campground sits between the road and the river. Coming from Philipsburg, drive 14 miles on Highway 348 to reach Forest Road 102. Turn right at the bridge over Rock Creek and drive 18.5 miles north on the bumpy dirt road. Between mileposts 30 and 25, the skinny road shrinks to one lane with turnouts and steep cliff sections—unsuitable for large RVs and trailers.

GPS Coordinates: N 46° 28.153' W 113° 46.635'
Contact: Lolo National Forest, Missoula Ranger District, Bldg. 24A, Fort Missoula, Missoula, MT 59804, 406/329-3814, www.fs.fed.us/r1/lolo.

39 SIRIA

Scenic rating: 5

on Rock Creek in Lolo National Forest

Only those with a hankering for driving the long, slow miles of bumpy, potholed dirt road of Rock Creek should head to Siria Campground, located at 4,600 feet. The campground grants utter solitude, quiet, and remoteness, but it is a chore to reach. The last few miles on either side of the campground squeeze down to one lane, with a few turnouts, plus steep cliff sections. Two fishing accesses and places to launch rafts and kayaks are within 0.6 mile north of the campground. Trailheads also are within two miles of both sides of the campground. At milepost 25.1, an interpretive site explains the impressive display across the river of destruction from a microburst. Mountain bikers also ride the road. The river is known for its blue-ribbon trout fishery.

The campground sits opposite the historical ranger station. Large, tall ponderosa pines shade the ultra-quiet campground. Grass and brush are overgrowing the campsites. Paths lead to the river.

Campsites, facilities: The campground has three RV or tent campsites. The campground and the road are only suitable for small RVs; trailers are not recommended. Facilities include picnic tables, fire rings with grills, and a pit toilet, but no drinking water. Bring your own, or if you plan to use river water, boil or purify it first. Pack out your trash. Leashed pets are permitted.

Reservations, fees: Reservations are not accepted. Camping is free. Open year-round, although the campground and road may be snowbound in winter.

Directions: From I-90, take Rock Creek Exit 126 halfway between Missoula and Drummond and drive south on Rock Creek Road (Forest Road 102) to milepost 27.9. The pavement ends after 11.5 miles. Starting at milepost 25, the already narrow road shrinks to one lane with turnouts and a steep cliff section. North of the ranger station, turn west into Siria Campground. Coming from Philipsburg, drive 14 miles on Highway 348 to reach Forest Road 102. Turn right at the bridge over Rock Creek and drive 13.1 miles north on the bumpy dirt road. At milepost 30, the skinny road narrows to a single-lane to traverse around a steep bluff. GPS Coordinates: N 46° 25.359' W 113° 43.066'

Contact: Lolo National Forest, Missoula Ranger District, Bldg. 24A, Fort Missoula, Missoula, MT 59804, 406/329-3814, www.fs.fed.us/r1/lolo.

40 STONY

Scenic rating: 9

west of Rock Creek in Beaverhead-Deerlodge National Forest

At an elevation of 4,800 feet, northwest of Philipsburg, Stony Campground is the most southern of the campgrounds lining Rock Creek. The river maintains a high reputation among anglers for fly-fishing after rainbow, cutthroat, brown, and bull trout. Hatches of mayflies and caddis flies last season long. Boat accesses for the river are on both sides of the campground at the bridges at mileposts 41 and 35.5. The campground is in the upper end of the canyon across from huge orange and rust cliffs that light up with the setting sun. At the end of Forest Road 241, trail #2 follows Stony Creek up to Stony Lake in the Sapphire Mountains, a destination for hikers and mountain bikers.

The long, narrow campground sits adjacent to Stony Creek. Most of the sites tuck under firs, but three sites (8, 9, and 10) command

prime views of the cliffs from an open meadow. (Too bad houses and phone lines are in the view, too.) The gravel parking pads for these sites are overgrown with weeds. Sites 3 and 6 have creek frontage.

Campsites, facilities: The campground has 10 RV or tent campsites. Parking pads can fit trailers up to 32 feet in length. Facilities include picnic tables, fire rings with grills, vault toilets, and drinking water. Pack out your trash. Leashed pets are permitted. A wheelchair-accessible toilet is available.

Reservations, fees: Reservations are not accepted. Camping is free. Open mid-May–late September.

Directions: From I-90, take Rock Creek Exit 126 halfway between Missoula and Drummond and drive south on Rock Creek Road (Forest Road 102) to milepost 36.6. Those coming from the north will encounter five miles (mileposts 25–30) of steep, skinny road suitable only for small RVs (trailers not recommended). The easier drive enters from Philipsburg: Go west about 14 miles on paved Highway 348 to the bridge crossing Rock Creek and turn right onto the dirt Forest Road 102 for 4.4 miles. At the campground sign, turn west onto Forest Road 241 and drive 0.1 mile to turn left into the campground over the cattle guard. GPS Coordinates: N 46° 20.936' W 113° 36.545'

Contact: Beaverhead-Deerlodge National Forest, Pintler Ranger District, 88 Business Loop, Philipsburg, MT 59858, 406/859-3211, www.fs.fed.us/r1/b-d.

41 FLINT CREEK

Scenic rating: 5

north of Georgetown Lake in Beaverhead-Deerlodge National Forest

Located on the Pintler Scenic Byway, Flint Creek Campground suffers repeated flooding during high water releases from the dam at Georgetown Lake. Flint Creek flows north from the lake, cuts through the bedrock, and then tumbles through a chiseled steep gorge to the valley floor, where the campground sits at 5,650 feet. The scenic byway in this section is equally dramatic, as it climbs the steep grade to reach Georgetown Lake's elevation. Due to the flooding, much of the area is sandy. In June, it can also be muddy and wet, with some of the upper campsites nearly containing small lakes. Those camping here during high-water season (May–June) must be ready to evacuate if an alarm sounds, indicating a release from the dam. Flint Creek and the small pond that forms in early summer in the campground provide fishing.

A potholed dirt road leads into the campground, where all of the campsites line up along the creek. Near the upper end of the campground, the road crosses a small dam to reach campsites 10 and 11, which sit above the pond. The campsites are spread out, affording privacy, but the road overhead adds noise from trucks.

Campsites, facilities: The campground has 12 RV or tent campsites. Trailers are limited to 16 feet. Facilities include picnic tables, fire rings with grills, and vault toilets. Leashed pets are permitted. A wheelchair-accessible toilet is available.

Reservations, fees: Reservations are not accepted. Camping is free. Open early May–late September.

Directions: From Philipsburg, drive eight miles south on the Pintler Scenic Byway (Highway 1) to reach the campground at milepost 30.3. Turn south to enter the campground. From Georgetown Lake, drive north on the highway, descending through the gorge.

GPS Coordinates: N 46° 14.093' W 113° 18.103'

Contact: Beaverhead-Deerlodge National Forest, Pintler Ranger District, 88 Business Loop, Philipsburg, MT 59858, 406/859-3211, www.fs.fed.us/r1/b-d.

42 PINEY

Scenic rating: 8

on Georgetown Lake in Beaverhead-Deerlodge National Forest

Located on Georgetown Lake, which sits between Philipsburg and Anaconda on the Pintler Scenic Byway, Piney Campground is one of two popular Forest Service lakeside campgrounds at 6,400 feet. Both Piney and Philipsburg Bay grace the lake's western shores, with entrances less than a mile apart. Trails run through Piney's campground to the beach, where the lake splays out at the base of the Pintler Mountains—a gorgeous view in June with snow on the peaks. The campground's concrete boat ramp, dock, and trailer parking aid launching for fishing, waterskiing, kayaking, and canoeing. Bicyclists can tour the lake loop, but use caution—the road is narrow.

Located on a bay off the main lake, the campground—shaded by lots of tall lodgepole pines—has two paved loops with paved parking aprons. A handful of sites have prime lake frontage: 7, 9, 37, 44, and 46. Others sit across the loop from the lake with peek-a-boo views of the water: 8, 11, 38, 39, 40–43, and 45. The remaining campsites stack up the hillside. Short whortleberry provides groundcover (taste the red berries), but at only a few inches tall, it does not add privacy to the branchless lodgepoles between the sites. The sites are roomy, and most have spaces for large tents. The campground is locked nightly between 10 P.M. and 6 A.M. for security.

Campsites, facilities: The campground has 48 RV or tent campsites. The large parking pads can handle trailers up to 32 feet long. Facilities include picnic tables, fire rings with grills, vault toilets, drinking water, and garbage service. Leashed pets are permitted. A wheelchair-accessible toilet is available.

Reservations, fees: Reservations are not accepted. Campsites cost $12. Extra camping units (tent, RV, trailer) cost an additional $12. Cash or check. Open mid-May–late September.

Directions: From the Pintler Scenic Byway (Highway 1), take the northern Georgetown Lake Road west along the lakeshore for 2.4 miles. Turn left into the campground. (Note: Georgetown Lake Road loops completely around the lake. For the shortest route, take the north end of the loop at the dam rather than the one at the southeast corner of the lake.)

GPS Coordinates: N 46° 11.837' W 113° 18.243'

Contact: Beaverhead-Deerlodge National Forest, Pintler Ranger District, 88 Business Loop, Philipsburg, MT 59858, 406/859-3211, www. fs.fed.us/r1/b-d.

43 PHILIPSBURG BAY

Scenic rating: 8

on Georgetown Lake in Beaverhead-Deerlodge National Forest

On Georgetown Lake, which sits between Philipsburg and Anaconda on the Pintler Scenic Byway, Philipsburg Bay Campground is one of two popular Forest Service lakeside campgrounds less than one mile apart at 6,400 feet. Trails run through the Philipsburg Bay Campground to the beach, which is on a small, sheltered bay ringed with summer homes rather than on the main lake. At the top of the entrance road just off Georgetown Lake Road, a grassy trail traverses the ridge from the overlook, granting big views of the lake and the Anaconda Range. At the campground, a cement boat ramp, dock, and trailer parking aid launching onto the lake for fishing, waterskiing, kayaking, and canoeing.

Contrary to Piney, where a few campsites sit on the shoreline or have views of the lake, the quiet Philipsburg Bay campsites all sit on three paved loops with paved parking pads, up the hillside from the beach with no views of the lake. Trails through the campground access the beach area, which contains the boat launch and an area for swimming. Many of the roomy campsites have ample tent spaces, but thanks to the whortleberry groundcover and lodgepole tree trunks, you can see the neighboring campers. The campground is locked nightly between 10 P.M. and 6 A.M. for security.

Campsites, facilities: The campground has 69 RV or tent campsites. RVs are limited to 32 feet. Facilities include picnic tables, fire rings with grills, vault toilets, drinking water, garbage service, and a campground host. Leashed pets are permitted. A wheelchair-accessible toilet is available.

Reservations, fees: Reservations are not accepted. Campsites cost $12. Extra camping units (tent, RV, trailer) cost an additional $12 each. Cash or check. Open mid-May–late September.

Directions: From the Pintler Scenic Byway (Highway 1), take the northern Georgetown Lake Road west along the lakeshore for 1.5 miles. Turn left and descend 0.5 mile downhill into the campground. (Note: Georgetown Lake Road loops completely around the lake. For the shortest route in, take the north end of the loop at the dam rather than at the southeast corner of the lake.)

GPS Coordinates: N 46° 12.368' W 113° 17.184'

Contact: Beaverhead-Deerlodge National Forest, Pintler Ranger District, 88 Business Loop, Philipsburg, MT 59858, 406/859-3211, www. fs.fed.us/r1/b-d.

44 STUART MILL BAY

Scenic rating: 9

on Georgetown Lake west of Anaconda

Off the Pintler Scenic Byway on Georgetown Lake's south side, Stuart Mill Bay is a 363-acre state fishing access park that contains wetlands, grasslands, and forest. The area houses moose, deer, ospreys, bald eagles, coots, red-necked grebes, and great blue herons. Georgetown Lake harbors brook trout, rainbow trout, and kokanee salmon. The park, at 6,400 feet, has two boat launches—a primitive ramp to accommodate smaller hand-carried crafts such as canoes, kayaks, and rafts and a concrete ramp with a dock to launch power boats. Trailer parking is also available. Both launches are in the campground.

Nearly every campsite in the park has waterfront or water views of the Anaconda Mountains dominated by Mount Haggin. Large gravel parking pads are surrounded by grass, and some willows break up the shoreline. Only a few trees shade a couple of the sites; most are wide open, allowing winds to whip through them. Sites 1–11 sit in pods of three or four campsites; the remaining campsites (12–16) line up along the water. Some of the campsites have double-wide parking pads; a few are pull-throughs.

Campsites, facilities: The campground has 15 RV or tent campsites. Trailers are limited to 30 feet. Facilities include picnic tables, fire rings with grills, a few pedestal grills, and vault toilets. No drinking water is available. Bring your own, or if you plan to use lake water, boil or purify it first. Pack out your trash. Leashed pets are permitted. A wheelchair-accessible toilet is available.

Reservations, fees: Reservations are not accepted. Campsites cost $12 for those without Montana fishing licenses and $7 for those with licenses. Cash or check. Open year-round.

Directions: From the Pintler Scenic Byway (Highway 1), take the southern Georgetown Lake Road west along the lakeshore for 1.4 miles. Turn right into the park. You'll come to the primitive launch first, then a sign for the large boat launch and two campground loops. (Note: Georgetown Lake Road loops completely around the lake. For the shortest route in, do not take the north end of the loop at the dam but the one at the southeast corner of the lake.)

GPS Coordinates: N 46° 10.435' W 113° 16.456'

Contact: Montana Fish, Wildlife, and Parks, 3201 Spurgin Rd., Missoula, MT 59804, 406/542-5500, http://fwp.mt.gov.

45 LODGEPOLE

Scenic rating: 7

east of Georgetown Lake in Beaverhead-Deerlodge National Forest

At 6,400 feet, Lodgepole Campground is the easiest campground to reach on Georgetown Lake, as it is located right on the Pintler Scenic Byway between Anaconda and Philipsburg. However, it is not as popular as the Piney and Philipsburg Bay Campgrounds because it is older, sits on the two-lane highway, and requires crossing the highway to reach the Red Bridge boat launch. Open early May until late September, the boat launch includes a cement boat ramp, dock, and large parking lot for boat trailers. At the back of the campground unmarked trails depart into the forest for hiking and walking dogs.

The two loops of the shady hillside campground have old, rough pavement that connects to dirt parking pads, some of which are very narrow. While the campsites are spaced out, you can still see other campers through the lodgepole forest. Some of the sites accommodate tents; others do not. Those on the upper sides of the loops tend to be built into steep hills and very sloped. Sites 15, 16, 17, and 22 are more private.

Campsites, facilities: The campground has 31 RV or tent campsites. RVs are limited to 32 feet. Facilities include picnic tables, fire rings with grills, drinking water, pit toilets, garbage service, and a campground host. Leashed pets are permitted. A wheelchair-accessible toilet is available.

Reservations, fees: Reservations are not accepted. Campsites cost $12 for one camping unit (RV, tent, or trailer). Each additional camping unit costs $12, too. Cash or check. Open late May–late September.

Directions: On the Pintler Scenic Byway (Highway 1) at Georgetown Lake halfway between Anaconda and Philipsburg, turn east at milepost 26.9 opposite the Red Bridge boat launch.

GPS Coordinates: N 46° 12.652' W 113° 16.421'

Contact: Beaverhead-Deerlodge National Forest, Pintler Ranger District, 88 Business Loop, Philipsburg, MT 59858, 406/859-3211, www.fs.fed.us/r1/b-d.

46 CABLE MOUNTAIN

Scenic rating: 5

east of Georgetown Lake in Beaverhead-Deerlodge National Forest

East of Georgetown Lake halfway between Anaconda and Philipsburg, Cable Mountain Campground, elevation 6,700 feet, sits east of the Pintler Scenic Byway south of Discovery Basin Ski Area. In winter, the area provides parking for snowmobiles taking off to explore the Flint Creek Range. In summer, the campground is popular with anglers and ATV enthusiasts. Echo Lake boat launch and fishing access, which is open mid-May to late September, is 2.4 miles away on a rugged, bumpy dirt road unsuitable for trailers. The North Fork of Flint Creek runs adjacent to several campsites. It is closed to fishing until July 1 every year to protect spawning rainbow trout.

Just before you cross North Flint Creek into the campground, you'll hit the first campsite. It sits right on the creek and right on the entrance road with no privacy. The other campsites line up along the opposite creek bank and sprawl into the woods. Sitting close together, sites 5, 6, and 7 border the creek. The other campsites, with roomy flat areas for tents, are more spread out under the lodgepole pines. The campground road

is dirt, as are the parking pads. The campground is quiet unless ATVs are driving around the area.

Campsites, facilities: The campground has 11 RV or tent campsites. RVs are limited to 22 feet. Facilities include picnic tables, fire rings with grills, pit and vault toilets, and drinking water. Pack out your trash. Leashed pets are permitted. A wheelchair-accessible toilet is available.

Reservations, fees: Reservations are not accepted. Campsites cost $10 for the first camping unit (tent, RV, trailer) and $10 for each additional unit. Cash or check. Open late June–mid-September.

Directions: From the Pintler Scenic Byway (Highway 1) at Georgetown Lake, halfway between Philipsburg and Anaconda, turn east onto the road with the ski area sign at milepost 25.2. At the three-way split, continue left and follow the route to the ski area. At 2.8 miles from the highway, turn right onto the dirt Forest Road 242 and drive 0.2 mile. Turn right to reach the first campsite and the narrow bridge into the campground.

GPS Coordinates: N 46° 13.284' W 113° 14.798'

Contact: Beaverhead-Deerlodge National Forest, Pintler Ranger District, 88 Business Loop, Philipsburg, MT 59858, 406/859-3211, www.fs.fed.us/r1/b-d.

47 SPRING HILL

Scenic rating: 5

in the Flint Creek Mountains of Beaverhead-Deerlodge National Forest

Located on the Pintler Scenic Byway on the south slopes of the Flint Creek Mountains, Spring Hill may be a better choice than Warm Springs just for sheer convenience to the highway without a bumpy dirt road. Spring Hill, however, doesn't have a river for fishing, but it does spread out its campsites out more than Warm Springs and provides larger parking spaces. Its entrance is only 0.2 mile farther west from the access road to Warm Springs. Within four miles west of the campground, Silver Lake is a favorite haunt for bird-watchers, but due to the lake's clarity, coldness, and changing water depth, it lacks fish. (If you're itching to fish a lake, drive two miles farther to Georgetown Lake.)

One gravel loop circles the shady campground, with roomy campsites under thick lodgepole pines. Two sites—7 and 9—have raised, gravel tent pads, but most of the other campsites can accommodate large tents, too. Site 10 has more privacy than the others as it sits off by itself. Site 5 is a walk-in campsite. You'll hear truck noise from the highway in the campground.

Campsites, facilities: The campground has 15 RV or tent campsites. Trailers are limited to 22 feet. Facilities include picnic tables, fire rings with grills, a few pedestal grills, vault toilets, garbage service, and drinking water. Pack out your trash. Leashed pets are permitted.

Reservations, fees: Reservations are not accepted. Campsites cost $8. An extra camping unit (trailer, tent, or RV) costs $8. Cash or check. Open late June–mid-September.

Directions: At milepost 19.4 on the Pintler Scenic Byway (Highway 1), turn north into the campground.

GPS Coordinates: N 46° 10.235' W 113° 9.902'

Contact: Pintler Ranger District, Philipsburg Office, 88 Business Loop, Philipsburg, MT 59858, 406/859-3211.

48 WARM SPRINGS

Scenic rating: 4

in the Flint Creek Mountains of Beaverhead-Deerlodge National Forest

Just north of the Pintler Scenic Byway, Warm Springs is an older campground that attracts ATVers and anglers. It's one of the closest designated Forest Service campgrounds to Anaconda, the turnoff being about 10 miles west of town. It is one of two campgrounds that access the south Flint Creek Range, a lower elevation set of peaks in Montana's western mountains. The jarring Forest Service road passing bucolic farms packs in the potholes, and you'll notice the number of beetle-killed lodgepole pines compared to the healthy aspens. Warm Springs Creek harbors trout (brook, bull, brown, rainbow, westslope cutthroat, and hybrids) plus longnose suckers, mountain whitefish, and sculpin. Mountain bikers can explore the forest roads north of the campground.

After crossing a cattle guard and Warm Springs Creek on a skimpy bridge, the narrow campground road weaves between lodgepoles with barely enough room to breathe. The small shaded campsites are packed in close together, making you immediate buddies with the neighbors. The parking pads are quite small. Campsites on the north end of the loop have good views up the Warm Springs Creek drainage. Due to its location back from the highway, the campground is quieter than Spring Hill.

Campsites, facilities: The campground has six RV or tent campsites. The maximum length for trailers is 16 feet. Facilities include picnic tables, fire rings with grills, pit toilets, and drinking water. Pack out your trash. Leashed pets are permitted.

Reservations, fees: Reservations are not accepted. Camping is free. Open late June–mid-September.

Directions: At milepost 19.2 on the Pintler Scenic Byway (Highway 1), turn north onto Forest Road 170. Dodge the copious potholes on the dirt road for 2.4 miles and turn left into the campground.

GPS Coordinates: N 46° 11.423' W 113° 11.911'

Contact: Pintler Ranger District, Philipsburg Office, 88 Business Loop, Philipsburg, MT 59858, 406/859-3211.

49 LOST CREEK STATE PARK

Scenic rating: 8

north of Anaconda in the Flint Creek Mountains

North of Anaconda, 502-acre Lost Creek State Park hides in a narrow canyon at 6,250 feet on the southeast corner of the Flint Creek Mountains. The 1,200-foot-tall granite and limestone cliffs dance with an array of colors: gray, pink, beige, orange, and rust. Large granite dikes cut stripes into the rock where igneous intrusions surfaced. Rock climbers navigate various routes on cliff faces and spires, as do the mountain goats and bighorn sheep that sometimes frequent the area. A 100-foot paved trail leads to Lost Creek Falls, which tumbles 50 vertical feet in its descent through the canyon. The interpretive site in the upper campground includes benches for watching the falls or wildlife on the cliffs. A Forest Service trail follows Lost Creek west into the canyon in Beaverhead-Deerlodge National Forest for several miles.

The quiet campground has lower and upper sections, both serviced by gravel roads and small gravel parking pads. While both have views of the cliffs and sit along Lost Creek, the upper is by far the more scenic campground. One campsite with its own toilet also sits alone halfway between the two campgrounds. The lower campground straddles the road in a rough, clearcut area. The upper campground loops through lodgepole pines with sites close together. The trees in both areas suffer from bark beetle attacks, resulting in their rust color.

Campsites, facilities: The campground has 25 RV or tent campsites. RVs are limited to 23 feet. Facilities include picnic tables, fire rings with grills, and vault toilets, but drinking water is only available in the upper campground. The host usually camps in the lower campground. Pack out your trash. Leashed pets are permitted. A wheelchair-accessible toilet is available.

Reservations, fees: Reservations are not accepted. Camping is free, but donations are accepted. Open May–November.

Directions: From east of Anaconda, head northwest on road 273. After 1.8 miles, turn left. Follow the road for 5.8 miles to the state park entrance. Continue on the paved road, which turns to dirt in 0.4 mile. You'll reach the lower campground first and the upper campground one mile later.

GPS Coordinates: N 46° 12.536' W 113° 0.154'

Contact: Montana Fish, Wildlife, and Parks, 3201 Spurgin Rd., Missoula, MT 59804, 406/542-5500, http://fwp.mt.gov.

50 DEER LODGE KOA

Scenic rating: 7

on the Clark Fork River in Deer Lodge

In Deer Lodge, the KOA sits on the Clark Fork River within walking distance of restaurants in town. From the campground, you can fish for rainbow trout in the river. But the main reason to stay here is to visit the Grant-Kohrs Ranch National Historic Site about 1.5 miles from the campground. The 1,600-acre ranch, which preserves 80 historic buildings, is a working cattle ranch that preserves the cowboy life of the American West. The ranch (open daily 9 A.M.–5:30 P.M. Memorial Day–Labor Day, until 4:30 P.M. September–May; free admission) offers guided tours, children's activities, walking trails, and special events. Wagon tours ($5 per person, $15 per family) run hourly throughout the summer.

The campground sits between the railroad tracks and the river, so be prepared for some noise. Tent sites sit in a big grassy area shaded by mature trees, and some sites are available with water and electrical hookups. The RV sites have gravel parking pads, half of which are pull-throughs with room for slide-outs. In RV park fashion, the sites are close together, but several line up along the riverfront. Views of the Flint Creek Mountains are available from some locations.

Campsites, facilities: The campground has 40 RV campsites and 25 tent campsites. RVs are limited to 75 feet, and hookups are available for water, sewer, and electricity up to 50 amps. Facilities include picnic tables, fire rings with grills, flush toilets, showers, drinking water, garbage service, wireless Internet, a Kamping Kitchen, a playground, firewood for sale, and a camp store. Leashed pets are permitted.

Reservations, fees: Reservations are accepted (800/562-1629). Hookups cost $32–35; tent sites cost $23–27. Rates include two people. Cost is $5 per additional adult, $3 per additional child ages 13–17, free for children under 13 years old. Add on 7 percent Montana bed tax. Open April–October.

Directions: From I-90 at Deer Lodge, take Exit 184 or 187 onto Main Street. Drive north or south to the stoplight at Milwaukee Avenue and turn west. Drive three blocks and turn right at the sign.

GPS Coordinates: N 46° 23.932' W 112° 44.454'

Contact: Deer Lodge KOA, 330 Park St., Deer Lodge, MT 59722, 406/846-1629, www.koa.com.

51 FAIRMONT RV PARK

Scenic rating: 6

east of Anaconda

BEST (

Fairmont RV Park neighbors Fairmont Hot Springs Resort (406/797-3337 or 800/332-3272, www.fairmontmontana.com), with two Olympic-sized swimming pools, two mineral soaking pools, a 350-foot enclosed five-story-tall water slide, and an 18-hole golf course. The pools are open to the public, usually 8 A.M. to 10 P.M., with lifeguards on duty. Admission to the pools costs $5 for kids 10

and under, $4.50 for seniors 65 and above, and $8.25 for all others. For the pools and the water slide, kids pay $11.25 and all others pay $15.25. The par-72 golf course is known for its mile-high, mile-long fifth hole and five ponds adding to the difficulty. The last hole finishes with a fountain pond.

The mowed-lawn campground has very few shade trees. Most of the sites are wide open and close together. RV camping choices consist of 36 pull-through sites, 49 back-in sites, 52 partial hookups, and 11 dry sites. The campground is quiet, but you can hear trucks on the freeway in the distance unless the wind drowns them out.

Campsites, facilities: The campground has 147 RV campsites and 13 tent sites. Hookups are available for sewer, water, and electricity up to 50 amps; the park accommodates large RVs. Facilities include picnic tables, a fire stand, flush toilets, showers, a launderette, free wireless Internet, three rental tipis that sleep four people each, a camp store, gas, diesel, movie rentals, horseshoe pits, a disposal station, a dog walk, and a recreation center. Leashed pets are permitted. A wheelchair-accessible toilet is available.

Reservations, fees: Reservations are accepted. Hookups cost $30–35. Dry camping and tent sites cost $20. Tipi rentals cost $25. A 7 percent Montana bed tax will be added on. Rates are for two people. Extra people cost more: children $2.50 and adults $5. Cash, check, or credit card. While the hot springs are open all year long, the campground is only open mid-April–mid-October.

Directions: On I-90, drive west for 15 miles from Butte or east for 108 miles from Missoula to Exit 211. Follow the signs southwest for four miles to Fairmont RV Park on the left. Fairmont Hot Springs Resort is next door to the southwest.

GPS Coordinates: N 45° 2.545' W 112° 48.308'

Contact: Fairmont RV Park, 700 Fairmont Rd., Fairmont, MT 59711, 866/797-3505 or 406/797-3505, www.fairmontrvresort.com.

52 DIVIDE BRIDGE

Scenic rating: 7

on the Big Hole River northwest of Dillon

BEST (

Near I-15 northwest of Dillon, the Divide Bridge Campground, at 5,500 feet, is one of the river access points for the famous Big Hole River. The 153-mile-long free-flowing river gathers its headwaters in southwest Montana's Beaverhead Mountains and joins the Beaverhead River at Twin Bridges northeast of Dillon. Its fishery—arctic grayling, mountain whitefish, and trout—is considered blue ribbon. A large boat ramp between the bridge and the campground allows those with trailers to launch rafts or drift boats. The fishing access also has a large parking area for trailers. Those with small hand-carried rafts, canoes, or kayaks can launch from the primitive ramp in the campground. The Big Hole is closed to all motorboats but is good for rafting mid-May–mid-July. From the campground, a three-mile destination-less trail departs for Sawmill Gulch, good for exploring the arid high desert environment and sometimes wildlife-watching.

Accessed via a 0.4-mile potholed dirt road, the campground divides into two sections, both with back-in sites. One section has mowed lawns in between the gravel parking pads on a loop (sites 1–13); the other is a spur surrounded by rugged sagebrush and high desert grasses (sites 14–22). All the gravel parking pads on the spur are wide enough to accommodate two vehicles. Both areas are wide open with no shade—except for the few sites along the river (sites 10–13) tucked into the cottonwoods and aspens. Views include the hillsides forming the entrance for Sawmill Gulch.

Campsites, facilities: The campground has 24 RV or tent campsites. Facilities include picnic tables, fire rings with grills, vault toilets, and a campground host. Drinking water is not available. Bring your own, or if you plan to use river water, boil or purify it first. Pack out your trash. Leashed pets are permitted. A wheelchair-accessible toilet is available.

Reservations, fees: Reservations are not accepted. Campsites cost $12. Cash or check. Open year-round.

Directions: From I-15 north of Dillon, take Highway 43 west toward Divide. After crossing the Big Hole River, turn left at milepost 75 and drive 0.4 mile to the campground. Coming from the west on Highway 43, drive 2.5 miles past the town of Divide.

GPS Coordinates: N 45° 45.215' W 112° 46.472'

Contact: Bureau of Land Management, 106 N. Parkmont, Butte, MT 59701, 406/533-7600.

53 PETTINGILL

Scenic rating: 7

in the Pioneer Mountains in Beaverhead-Deerlodge National Forest

At 6,200 feet on the 44-mile Pioneer Mountains Scenic Byway, Pettingill Campground is the first campground you'll reach coming from the north. It is the tiniest of the campgrounds along the byway and often fills up because of its location and size. The campground is less than a mile from Pattengail Road, which heads into the western Pioneer Mountains. The road accesses the trailhead for Grouse Lakes (4 miles), stock camp areas, and the Pattengail Jeep Trail, which is open to ATVs, mountain bikes, and motorcycles.

Squeezed between the Wise River and the byway, the tiny campground with nighttime quiet spreads its three sites on a hillside just south of a large day-use parking lot, where you can grab views up to surrounding hillsides. Lodgepole pines shade the campsites, and all three sites border the river. A paved road services the campground, and each campsite has a paved parking pad.

Campsites, facilities: The campground has three RV or tent campsites. The parking pads can fit trailers up to 24 feet in length. Facilities include picnic tables, fire rings with grills, vault toilets, and garbage service. The campground has no drinking water. Bring your own, or if you choose to use the river water, boil or purify it first. You can also get drinking water 1.2 miles south at Fourth of July Campground. Leashed pets are permitted. A wheelchair-accessible toilet is available.

Reservations, fees: Reservations are not accepted. Campsites cost $8. An extra vehicle costs $3. Cash or check. Open mid-June–September.

Directions: From the junction of Highway 43 and the Pioneer Mountains Scenic Byway, drive 10 miles south. Turn east off the byway into the campground. From the junction of Highway 278 and the scenic byway, drive 35.1 miles north.

GPS Coordinates: N 45° 40.863' W 113° 3.650'

Contact: Beaverhead-Deerlodge National Forest, Wise River Ranger District, P.O. Box 100, Wise River, MT 59762, 406/832-3178, www.fs.fed.us/r1/b-d.

54 FOURTH OF JULY

🚶 🚴 🏊 🐎 ♿ 🚐 ⛺

Scenic rating: 7

in the Pioneer Mountains in Beaverhead-Deerlodge National Forest

At an elevation of 6,400 feet on the 44-mile Pioneer Scenic Byway, Fourth of July Campground offers a paved wheelchair-accessible trail that loops around the entire campground—including along the Wise River. Access for fishing the Wise River is easy from the trail, too. The 26-mile river harbors several species of trout, including brook, brown, rainbow, Yellowstone cutthroat, and westslope cutthroat. Pattengail Road, departing west from the byway two miles north of the campground, leads to the Grouse Lakes Trailhead (#219). The steep trail climbs four miles to Grouse Lakes, which sit in granite basins, and the Pattengail Jeep Trail is open to mountain bikes, motorcycles, and ATVs.

The narrow campground, which is quiet at night, squeezes between the byway and the river, but contrary to other forested campsites along the byway, this one is an open lodgepole forest broken up by large sagebrush and wildflower meadows that offer views of the timbered hillsides surrounding the campground. In June, the meadows bloom with purple larkspur. The campsites have varying degrees of privacy depending on whether they are in the meadows or under the lodgepole forest. Sites 1, 2, and 5 sit in the wide-open meadows. The remainder have a few trees for shade and privacy. The campground loop is paved, and each campsite has a paved parking pad.

Campsites, facilities: The campground has five RV or tent campsites. Parking pads can accommodate trailers up to 30 feet. Facilities include picnic tables, fire rings with grills, vault toilets, drinking water, and garbage service. Leashed pets are permitted. A wheelchair-accessible toilet is available.

Reservations, fees: Reservations are not accepted. Campsites cost $8. An extra vehicle costs $3. Cash or check. Open mid-June–September.

Directions: From the junction of Highway 43 and the Pioneer Mountains Scenic Byway, drive 11.2 miles south. Turn east into the campground. From the junction of Highway 278 and the scenic byway, drive 33.9 miles north.

GPS Coordinates: N 45° 39.818' W 113° 3.872'

Contact: Beaverhead-Deerlodge National Forest, Wise River Ranger District, P.O. Box 100, Wise River, MT 59762, 406/832-3178, www.fs.fed.us/r1/b-d.

55 LODGEPOLE

Scenic rating: 7

in the Pioneer Mountains in Beaverhead-Deerlodge National Forest

At 6,550 feet on the 44-mile Pioneer Mountains Scenic Byway, Lodgepole Campground sits right across the highway from Boulder Campground. Some of Boulder's campsites overlook the Wise River from a high bench, while some of Lodgepole's sit right on it. The river crosses the highway just north of both campgrounds. The canyon narrows up here, forcing the Wise River to pick up speed compared to the meandering slower segments near the summit of the byway, and the canyon prevents seeing the 10,000-foot-high peaks of the Pioneer Mountains. The campground is convenient for hiking the Boulder Trail; the trailhead is 0.25 mile up the byway on the east side. The trail links in with the Sheep Creek and Gold Creek drainage trails, used mostly by anglers and horse-packers, but is also open to mountain bikers.

The two-acre campground lines up all of its campsites along the river. The paved campground road connects with paved parking aprons; sites 1, 2, 7, 8, and 9 all have double-wide parking pads. As the name indicates, the campground is shaded by lodgepole pines, and its location fills the campground with the sound of rushing water.

Campsites, facilities: The campground has 10 RV or tent campsites. The parking pads can handle trailers up to 30 feet. Facilities include picnic tables, fire rings with grills, a few pedestal grills, vault toilets, drinking water, and garbage service. Leashed pets are permitted. A wheelchair-accessible toilet is available.

Reservations, fees: Reservations are not accepted. Campsites cost $8. Extra vehicles cost $3. Cash or check. Open mid-June–September.

Directions: From the junction of Highway 43 and the Pioneer Mountains Scenic Byway, drive 12.2 miles south. Turn west into the campground. From the junction of Highway 278 and the scenic byway, drive 32.9 miles north.

GPS Coordinates: N 45° 38.913' W 113° 4.247'

Contact: Beaverhead-Deerlodge National Forest, Wise River Ranger District, P.O. Box 100, Wise River, MT 59762, 406/832-3178, www.fs.fed.us/r1/b-d.

56 BOULDER CREEK

Scenic rating: 7

in the Pioneer Mountains in Beaverhead-Deerlodge National Forest

Located at 6,550 feet on the 44-mile Pioneer Mountains Scenic Byway, Boulder Creek Campground sits right across the highway from Lodgepole Campground. Some of Boulder's campsites overlook the Wise River from a high bench, while some of Lodgepole's sit right on it. Boulder Creek runs right behind the campground. Both campgrounds are convenient for hiking the Boulder Trail, a one-mile secondary trail following Boulder Creek. It links to a trail running between Sheep Creek and Gold Creek, used mostly by anglers and horse-packers, but is also open to mountain bikers. The trailhead is 0.25 mile from the byway on the east side. Fishing is available in the Wise River, although reaching the river is easier from Lodgepole Campground across the byway.

With a paved campground road and parking aprons, the campground lines up several campsites along the top of a bench overlooking the Wise River—sites 1–7 and 9—but those sites not overlooking the river tend to be roomier and more private. Most of the campsites have large tent spaces. At the end of the campground, a single-lane dirt road continues on to a couple of primitive dispersed sites. The campground is shaded by large firs and fills with the sound of the river.

Campsites, facilities: The campground has 13 RV or tent campsites. Several of the sites have long pull-throughs to accommodate trailers up to 30 feet. Facilities include picnic tables, fire rings with grills, vault toilets, drinking water, garbage service, and a campground host. Leashed pets are permitted. A wheelchair-accessible toilet is available.

Reservations, fees: Reservations are not accepted. Campsites cost $8. Extra vehicles cost $3. Cash or check. Open mid-June–September.

Directions: From the junction of Highway 278 and the Pioneer Mountains Scenic Byway, drive 32.9 miles north. Turn east off the byway into the campground. From the junction of Highway 43 and the scenic byway, drive 12.2 miles south.

GPS Coordinates: N 45° 38.909' W 113° 4.099'

Contact: Beaverhead-Deerlodge National Forest, Wise River Ranger District, P.O. Box 100, Wise River, MT 59762, 406/832-3178, www.fs.fed.us/r1/b-d.

57 WILLOW

Scenic rating: 7

in the Pioneer Mountains in Beaverhead-Deerlodge National Forest

On the 44-mile Pioneer Mountains Scenic Byway, Willow Campground sits right on the 26-mile Wise River, where it begins to drop in elevation as the canyon narrows. The river tumbles and froths white here in June's high water in contrast to the slow-moving willow bottoms upstream. Anglers here go after multiple species of trout: brook, brown, rainbow, westslope cutthroat, and Yellowstone cutthroat. Even though the campground sits 1,200 feet below the summit of the byway, it still has an elevation of 6,600 feet. Locate the road to the popular nearby Lacy Creek Trail (#259) on the west side of the byway four miles south of the campground. The trailhead, which sits up Lacy Creek Road, and leads in 5.5 miles to Lake of the Woods and Odell Lake, part of the Pioneer Loop National Scenic Recreation Trail, currently open to hikers and mountain bikers. Watch for moose along this trail. From Lacy Creek Road, you can also reach the Bobcat Trail (#50) for an eight-mile hike to Bobcat Lakes, located in glacial cirques.

One small loop forms the tiny campground, with campsite 5 sitting right in the middle of the loop. Sites 1, 2, and 3 have river frontage, with site 3's picnic table just a few feet from the water. The large campsites can accommodate tents, and sites 4 and 5 have raised, gravel tent pads. Site 4 has the most privacy off by itself. The campground loop and parking aprons are paved. The sound of the river fills the campground.

Campsites, facilities: The campground has five RV or tent campsites. The parking aprons can accommodate trailers up to 26 feet. Facilities include picnic tables, fire rings with grills, a vault toilet, drinking water, and garbage service. Leashed pets are permitted. A wheelchair-accessible toilet is available.

Reservations, fees: Reservations are not accepted. Campsites cost $8. Extra vehicles cost $3. Cash or check. Open mid-June–September.

Directions: From the junction of Highway 43 and the Pioneer Mountains Scenic Byway, drive 13.1 miles south. Turn east into the campground. From the junction of Highway 278 and the scenic byway, drive 32 miles north.

GPS Coordinates: N 45° 38.460' W 113° 4.234'

Contact: Beaverhead-Deerlodge National Forest, Wise River Ranger District, P.O. Box 100, Wise River, MT 59762, 406/832-3178, www.fs.fed.us/r1/b-d.

58 LITTLE JOE

Scenic rating: 7

in the Pioneer Mountains in Beaverhead Deerlodge-National Forest

On the 44-mile Pioneer Mountains Scenic Byway, Little Joe Campground offers a quiet place to camp along the Wise River at 6,800 feet in elevation. The river meanders through large willow meadows here, and this is a good place for spotting moose. Anglers go after brook, brown, and rainbow trout along with mountain whitefish, but often must battle brushy willow along the riverbanks. Just 0.7 mile north of the campground, the Grand Vista Viewpoint is worth visiting for its views up the Wise River toward the 10,000-foot summits of the Pioneer Mountains. A paved wheelchair-accessible interpretive nature trail drops to the river willow bottom. Hiking and mountain biking are also available out of the Mono Creek area, 0.5 mile south.

Although the tiny campground crams its sites close together on a very small loop (sites 3 and 4 almost sit on top of each other), the few sites give the campground an intimate feel, and it quiets at night. Sites 2 and 5 have large spaces for tents, and site 2 includes peek-a-boo views of the river. The campground loop is paved, as are the parking pads.

Campsites, facilities: The campground has five RV or tent campsites. Trailers are limited to 28 feet. Facilities include picnic tables, fire rings with grills, vault toilets, drinking water, and garbage service. Leashed pets are permitted. A wheelchair-accessible toilet is available.

Reservations, fees: Reservations are not accepted. Campsites cost $8. Extra vehicles cost $3. Cash or check. Open mid-June–September.

Directions: From the junction of Highway 43 and the Pioneer Mountains Scenic Byway, drive 20.5 miles south. Turn west into the campground. From the junction of Highway 278 and the scenic byway, drive 25 miles north.

GPS Coordinates: N 45° 33.400' W 113° 5.454'

Contact: Beaverhead-Deerlodge National Forest, Wise River Ranger District, P.O. Box 100, Wise River, MT 59762, 406/832-3178, www.fs.fed.us/r1/b-d.

59 MONO CREEK

Scenic rating: 7

in the Pioneer Mountains in Beaverhead-Deerlodge National Forest

At an elevation of 7,000 feet, about halfway on the 44-mile Pioneer Mountains Scenic Byway in the Pioneer Mountains, Mono Creek is convenient for those intending to explore Coolidge Ghost Town. The relic from mining days is reached by driving four miles past the campground on a single-lane dirt road with pullouts. After a Montana politician bought up mining claims, the town sprang up in 1919 to support the tunnel silver mine, but within 20 years most residents left. Mono Creek is also in the summit area of the byway, where miles of high meadows attract wildlife in the evening for feeding. Look especially for elk, deer, and moose. Fishing is available in the Wise River, and tiny Mono Creek runs through the campground. A backpacking and stock trailhead departs adjacent to the campground. The trail for hikers, mountain bikers, and motorcycles climbs through Jacobson Meadows to the David Creek Trail (#56, 8 miles) and Brownes Lake Trail (#2, 6 miles)—both with multiple lake destinations.

Tucked under lodgepoles, the tiny, quiet Mono Creek Campground sits back off the byway. The grassy campsites are roomy and spaced out enough to afford some privacy among the thinned trees. Two sites with tent pads are reserved for those with tents, as the other sites accommodate small RVs.

Campsites, facilities: The campground has three RV or tent campsites plus two sites reserved for tents only. RVs are limited to 18 feet. Facilities include picnic tables, fire rings with grills, a few pedestal grills, vault toilets, drinking water, and garbage service. Leashed pets are permitted. A wheelchair-accessible toilet is available.

Reservations, fees: Reservations are not accepted. Campsites cost $8. Extra vehicles cost $3. Cash or check. Open mid-June–September.

Directions: From the junction of Highway 43 and the Pioneer Mountains Scenic Byway, drive 21 miles south. Turn east off the byway onto Forest Road 484 and drive 0.8 mile to the campground. From the junction of Highway 278 and the scenic byway, drive 24.1 miles north. GPS Coordinates: N 45° 32.514' W 113° 4.803'

Contact: Beaverhead-Deerlodge National Forest, Wise River Ranger District, P.O. Box 100, Wise River, MT 59762, 406/832-3178, www.fs.fed.us/r1/b-d.

60 PRICE CREEK

Scenic rating: 8

in the Pioneer Mountains in Beaverhead-Deerlodge National Forest

On the 44-mile Pioneer Mountains Scenic Byway, Price Creek sits at 7,600 feet near the summit of the byway, where miles of high meadows allow wildlife-watching for elk, moose, and bears. The 10,212-foot Saddleback Mountain looms to the east, but you only get snippets of views through the trees. One mile north of the campground, Crystal Park attracts rock hounds, who dig for amethyst, smoky quartz, and clear quartz crystals. The day-use area charges $5 for parking, but digging for crystals is free. Multi-use trails open to hikers, mountain bikers, equestrians, and motorcycles lead into the highest peaks of the Pioneer Mountains—attractions for mountain climbers—and connect with the trails from Mono Creek.

The largest of the byway campgrounds, Price Creek has several paved loops that wander through firs and lodgepoles. Most of the large campsites have back-in paved parking aprons, but sites 2, 4, 6, 8, and 11 accommodate larger RVs with pull-throughs. Lining the edge of one loop, sites 14, 15, and 16 are more private. For views and possible evening wildlife-watching, walk to the large meadow adjacent to the campground along the fence. Set back from the byway, the campground is quiet. In fall, listen for elk bugling in the night.

Campsites, facilities: The campground has 28 RV or tent campsites. The maximum trailer length is 30 feet. Facilities include picnic tables, fire rings with grills, log benches, vault toilets, drinking water, garbage service, and campground hosts. Leashed pets are permitted. A wheelchair-accessible toilet is available.

Reservations, fees: Reservations are not accepted, except for the group campsite (call the ranger station). Campsites cost $8. Extra vehicles cost $3. Cash or check. Open June–September.

Directions: From the junction of Highway 43 and the Pioneer Mountains Scenic Byway, drive 28.3 miles south. Turn east off the byway and drive 0.5 mile to the campground entrance. From the junction of Highway 278 and the scenic byway, drive 16.8 miles north. GPS Coordinates: N 45° 28.788' W 113° 5.002'

Contact: Beaverhead-Deerlodge National Forest, Dillon Ranger District, 420 Barrett St., Dillon, MT 59725, 406/683-3900, www.fs.fed.us/r1/b-d.

61 GRASSHOPPER

Scenic rating: 7

in the Pioneer Mountains in Beaverhead-Deerlodge National Forest

BEST (

Located at 7,000 feet on the southern end of the 44-mile Pioneer Mountains Scenic Byway,

Grasshopper attracts campers for its many campsites along the creek, plus Elkhorn Hot Springs 0.3 mile up the road. The hot springs—open year-round—have two outdoor pools, showers, flush toilets, and an indoor sauna. The pool water is high in mineral content but without sulfur. The large pool's temperature ranges 95–100 degrees F and the smaller pool ranges 102–106 degrees F. Admission to the pools costs $6 for adults and $4 for kids. While the hot springs are open year-round, unfortunately the campground is not. Hikers, equestrians, and mountain bikers can tour the Blue Creek Trail for fishing and wildlife-watching, with the trailhead located 0.3 mile south of the campground.

The grassy campground spreads out in an aspen and lodgepole forest on the hillside along Grasshopper Creek. Eleven of the campsites have creek frontage, with sites 9–12 and 14–17 being the farthest from the campground entrance. The campground has a large group campsite, too, which can be used by drop-ins

© BECKY LOMAX

Elkhorn Hot Springs in the Pioneer Mountains are open year-round.

if it is not reserved. Trails climb the hillside behind the campground to go above the rocky outcrop. At night, you'll fall sleep to the sound of aspen leaves clicking in the breeze.

Campsites, facilities: The campground has 24 RV or tent campsites. Trailers are limited to 25 feet. Facilities include picnic tables, fire rings with grills, a few pedestal grills, vault toilets, drinking water, garbage service, and campground hosts. Leashed pets are permitted. A wheelchair-accessible toilet is available.

Reservations, fees: Reservations are not accepted except for the group campsite. (Call the ranger station.) Campsites cost $8. An extra vehicle costs $3. Cash or check. Open mid-June–mid-September.

Directions: From the junction of Highway 43 and the Pioneer Mountains Scenic Byway, drive 32.5 miles south. Turn northwest off the byway at the well-signed campground entrance. From the junction of Highway 278 and the scenic byway, drive 12.6 miles north. GPS Coordinates: N 45° 27.054' W 113° 7.123'

Contact: Beaverhead-Deerlodge National Forest, Dillon Ranger District, 420 Barrett St., Dillon, MT 59725, 406/683-3900, www.fs.fed.us/r1/b-d.

62 BANNACK STATE PARK

Scenic rating: 6

southwest of Dillon and south of the Pioneer Mountains

At 5,800 feet between Wisdom and Dillon south of the Pioneer Mountains, Bannack is a ghost town on Grasshopper Creek—the site of Montana's first major gold discovery in 1862 and Montana's first territorial capital in 1864. Striking gold catapulted Bannack's population to 3,000 residents in one year, but other gold rushes lured residents away. Over 50 historic log and frame structures still stand in Bannock. You can look out the jail bars, sit in the schoolroom,

Bannack State Park is a preserved ghost town from Wild West mining days.

and even sidle up to the dusty bar. Short hiking trails lead to the gallows, cemetery, and mines. Grasshopper Creek also has fishing.

The state park has two campgrounds adjacent to each other on Grasshopper Creek 0.2 mile west of the ghost town. Road Agent camp sits across the creek to the left, and Vigilante camp sits to the right. Both have dirt roads that loop through the campgrounds, with unnumbered grassy sites tucked under cottonwoods. The open sunny sites are very close to each other, with no boundaries between many of them. Vigilante has several open walk-in sites on the grass along the creek and a tipi you can rent.

Campsites, facilities: The campgrounds have 15 RV or tent campsites plus three walk-in sites for tenters. RVs are limited to 35 feet. Facilities include picnic tables, fire rings with grills, vault toilets, drinking water, garbage service, horseshoe pits (horseshoes are available for rent), tipi rental, and firewood for sale. Pack out your trash if the garbage bins are not present. Leashed pets are permitted. A wheelchair-accessible toilet is available.

Reservations, fees: Reservations are not accepted. Camping costs $15 May–September

and $13 October–April. Tipi rental costs $25 per night. Entry fee for the ghost town is $5, but it's free for Montana residents. Cash or check. Open year-round.

Directions: From Dillon, drive south on I-15 to Exit 59 and drive west on Highway 278 for 17 miles. Turn south onto the paved Bannack Bench Road for three miles. Turn left onto the dirt Bannack Road and go 0.6 mile to the campgrounds, which are on the south side of the road. GPS Coordinates: N 45° 9.813' W 113° 0.144'

Contact: Montana Fish, Wildlife, and Parks, 4200 Bannack Rd., Dillon, MT 59725, 406/834-3413, http://fwp.mt.gov.

63 CLARK CANYON RESERVOIR

Scenic rating: 7

on Clark Canyon Reservoir south of Dillon

Located south of Dillon at 5,600 feet at the base of the Beaverhead Mountains, Clark

Canyon Reservoir is the site of Camp Fortunate, where the Lewis and Clark expedition met the Lemhi Shoshoni Tribe, Sacagawea reunited with her brother, and the expedition cached their supplies and boats for the return trip. The 4,935-acre reservoir surrounding an island is ringed with 17 miles of shoreline including four cement boat launch ramps. Its waters offer rainbow and brown trout fishing, plus ice fishing in winter. The Cattail Marsh Nature Trail, below Clark Canyon Dam, offers wildlife-watching opportunities for waterfowl, birds, pronghorn antelope, and yellow-bellied marmots.

Seven developed campgrounds and several dispersed primitive camping sites rim the reservoir. Six small campgrounds (the largest has 20 sites) offer free dry camping, and the largest campground offers pay RV hookups. Those campgrounds on the east and north shores are easiest to reach, including the RV park; the two south-side campgrounds require rough dirt road driving. Most of the campsites sit on broad, open sagebrush slopes, accompanied by expansive views of the reservoir and arid slopes. Be prepared for winds. Beaverhead Campground, on the east side squeezed between the interstate and the water, nestles under cottonwoods and willows for some shade, but the trade-off is road noise.

Campsites, facilities: The RV park has 55 sites with hookups for water, sewer, and electricity. Six campgrounds contain 41 campsites for RVs or tents without hookups. Many of the campsites can accommodate large RVs. Facilities include picnic tables with shelters, fire rings with grills, vault toilets, drinking water, garbage service, and campground hosts. Leashed pets are permitted. A wheelchair-accessible toilet is available.

Reservations, fees: Reservations are not accepted. Camping is free, except for the RV campsite with hookups that costs $20. Cash or check. Open year-round, although snow can close the roads and cover the campgrounds.

Directions: From I-15, take Exit 44 at Clark Canyon Reservoir. Drive east on Highway 324 across the dam to access the north shore campgrounds, or drive south before the dam to reach the east shore campgrounds. Access the two remote south shore campgrounds by taking exit 37 at Red Rocks Creek and driving west on Old Armstead Road.

GPS Coordinates: N 44° 59.566' W 112° 51.220' (Beaverhead Campground)

Contact: Bureau of Reclamation, 1200 Hwy. 41, Dillon, MT 59725, 406/683-6472.

NORTHERN YELLOWSTONE GATEWAYS

© BECKY LOMAX

BEST CAMPGROUNDS

Fishing
Palisades (Madison River), **page 249**.
Wade Lake, **page 253**.

Hiking
East Rosebud, **page 278**.
Island Lake, **page 286**.

Hot Springs
Bozeman KOA, **page 256**.

Lake Camping
Cliff Point, **page 254**.

Montana
Missouri Headwaters State Park, **page 241**.
Lewis and Clark Caverns State Park, **page 242**.
Red Mountain, **page 243**.
Beaver Creek, **page 251**.

Wildlife-Watching
Upper Red Rock Lake, **page 255**.

Wyoming
Beartooth Lake, **page 287**.

Yellowstone National Park feeds some of the

nation's most well-known blue-ribbon trout streams – waters that rush northward, forming its northern gateways. In Montana, these rivers wended their way into the history books, literature, and movies. From the Lewis and Clark expedition to the movie *A River Runs Through It*, the iconic image of wading thigh-deep in a river while casting a fly on its surface has sunk deep into the psyche of every angler.

For those who camp, the dream of lunker trout can become a reality in this region of rivers. Many of Yellowstone's northern gateway trout streams sit so far from towns brimming with hotels that tents and RVs become the way to travel if you want to savor days on the river. Campgrounds are much more frequent than lodges.

The northern Yellowstone gateway rivers flow mostly from south to north, lining up in a series of parallel valleys with roads running alongside. You'll be lucky to find yourself alone in midsummer on a stretch of the famous Madison, Gallatin, or Yellowstone Rivers – all three are feeders for the Mighty Mo, the Missouri River.

U.S. Forest Service and Bureau of Land Management campgrounds make up the largest camping options on the rivers. But in a testament to the popularity of fishing, rafting, floating, and kayaking, the state of Montana operates a horde of small, primitive campgrounds at fishing access sites. The rare RV park sidles up to the riverbank with hookups.

Of the larger river valleys, the Gallatin River draws the most crowds in campgrounds, due to its proximity to Bozeman, the largest town in the region, although it has only 4 percent of the population of Denver. The Gallatin campgrounds also lure campers for the outstanding hiking, climbing, rafting, and mountain biking in Gallatin National Forest. The 140 miles of the Madison River may be the most famous Montana blue-ribbon trout stream, hopping with rainbow and brown trout, but its canyon and sagebrush banks are largely public. Campgrounds are much more frequent on the Madison than on the Yellowstone River, which flows through more private land in Paradise Valley.

These three river valleys provide the main northern corridors to reach Yellowstone National Park. They are also the rivers where you'll see once-a-year vacationing anglers decked out in expensive Orvis garb and then a mile downstream find a local angler with a reel held on with duct tape. Most of the campgrounds along these three rivers are easily accessible via pavement with only a few dirt-road driving miles.

To escape the crowds of the three big-name rivers, head to the gaggle of smaller streams that plunge from the high peaks of the Absaroka-Beartooth Mountains. The Stillwater, Big Timber, Rosebud, and Rock Creek Rivers each offer something different for campers, hikers, mountain bikers, anglers, and rafters. However, routes into Montana's highest mountains along these rivers are mostly via long, dirt roads with wall-to-wall washboards and potholes sometimes large enough to swallow truck wheels. The smaller, more-primitive campgrounds along these rivers fill with tenters and only small to mid-size RVs due to the difficulty of the access.

These smaller rivers plummet from glaciers in the Absaroka-Beartooth Wilderness. As Rock Creek tumbles eastward, its valley also forms the eastern ascent from Red Lodge for the Beartooth Highway, which climbs over a two-mile-high pass en route to Yellowstone. Its paved route attracts scads of sightseers for the short three months it is snow-free, and six developed campgrounds are packed within a few miles of one another. You can, however, find solitude in the ream of primitive dispersed campsites along Rock Creek. The Beartooth Highway – touted by Charles Kuralt as "America's most beautiful highway" – lives up to its nickname and outclasses other Yellowstone gateways with its high alpine plateaus framed by snowcapped peaks.

Although Montana's gateways to Yellowstone are all rivers bouncing with trout, the state's highest mountains also provide unparalleled hiking and mountain biking. Camping is the way to see them best.

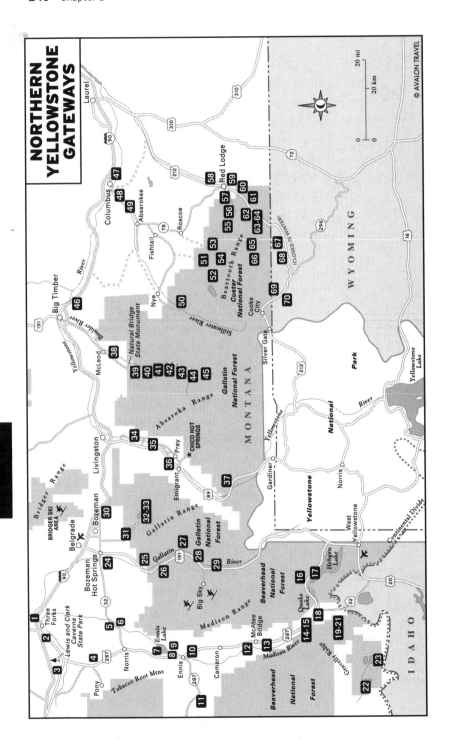

1 MISSOURI HEADWATERS STATE PARK

Scenic rating: 7

on the Madison River east of Three Forks

BEST (

Located at the confluence of the Gallatin, Madison, and Jefferson Rivers, Missouri Headwaters State Park marks the beginning of the Mighty Mo's 2,565-mile journey. The 506-acre state park at 4,045 feet in elevation devotes its interpretive endeavors to Native American use of the area, Lewis and Clark's time here, and the river ecosystems. Four miles of hiking trails tour the park. A concrete boat ramp allows boaters, rafters, kayakers, anglers, and floaters to launch to travel downstream eight miles to the next take-out. A paved six-mile bike trail connects with the town of Three Forks. The park provides superb habitat for wildlife-watching—moose, raptors, song-birds, and waterfowl.

The campground is crammed into one corner of the park adjacent to the Madison River. Due to the thick jungle of willows, cattails, and brush, you can't see the river from any of the sites. The grassy campground packs its sites close together; those at the front of the campground are wide open, but sites 17 and 18 at the back garner a little privacy. Faint freeway noise also floats into the campground. A few large cottonwoods lend a little shade, but on the whole, the campground is sunny and hot. But campers stay here for the history and park attributes rather than the campground itself.

Campsites, facilities: The campground has 18 RV or tent campsites that can accommodate RVs up to 35 feet long. Facilities include picnic tables, fire rings with grills, vault toilets, drinking water, campfire programs, and a campground host. Pack out your trash. Leashed pets are permitted. A wheelchair-accessible campsite (site 10) and toilet are available.

Reservations, fees: Reservations are not accepted. Campsites cost $15. Tipi rental costs $25. Day use is $5 per out-of-state vehicle but free for Montana residents. Cash or check. The park is open year-round, but camping is available only May–September.

Directions: From I-90 at Three Forks, take Exit 278 and head on Highway 205 toward Trident for 1.8 miles. Turn north onto Highway 286 and drive 1.6 miles to the park's information plaza on the right. Pay for campsites here; the campground entrance is on the opposite side of the road.

GPS Coordinates: N 45° 55.214' W 111° 29.927'

Contact: Montana Fish, Wildlife, and Parks, Missouri Headwaters State Park, 1400 S. 19th St., Bozeman, MT 59715, 406/994-4042, http://fwp.mt.gov.

2 CAMP THREE FORKS

Scenic rating: 6

west of Three Forks near the Jefferson River

Camp Three Forks is named for the nearby confluence of the Jefferson, Madison, and Gallatin Rivers, which together form the Missouri River. The Drouillard fishing access site is within a five-minute drive, providing access to the Jefferson River for fly-fishing, rafting, and floating. Within four miles, Three Forks has a golf course, groceries, gas, the paved six-mile Headwaters Trail system for hikers and bikers, and ponds for canoeing, kayaking, and children's fishing. The campground also sits less than seven miles from Missouri Headwaters State Park. The Wheat Montana store and deli is 1.3 miles to the north; this is the place to buy Montana flour. The campground conveniently lies at the junction of I-90 and the Madison and Jefferson River Valleys.

Flanked by flower beds, the mowed-lawn campground has loops of gravel roads with gravel parking pads. A variety of leafy trees lend partial shade. This ex-KOA campground has sites close together, and truck noise from the highway floats in at night. Some of the campsites have southeast-facing views of the Gallatin Mountains.

Campsites, facilities: The campground has 65 pull-through RV sites that can accommodate RVs up to 63 feet long, along with 21 tent campsites. Facilities include picnic tables, fire rings, vault toilets, drinking water, garbage service, a coin-operated launderette, a playground, wireless Internet, a swimming pool, and firewood for sale. Leashed pets are permitted.

Reservations, fees: Reservations are accepted. Hookups cost $22–36. Tent sites cost $20–24. Cash or check. Open May–September.

Directions: From I-90 west of Three Forks, take Exit 274 and drive south on Highway 287 for 1.1 miles. Turn right onto KOA Road for 0.1 mile and turn left into the campground. GPS Coordinates: N 45° 54.174' W111° 36.134'

Contact: Camp Three Forks, 15 KOA Rd., Three Forks, MT 59752, 406/285-3611 or 866/523-1773, campthreeforks.com.

© BECKY LOMAX

The Lewis and Clark Caverns hold otherworldly limestone formations.

☒ LEWIS AND CLARK CAVERNS STATE PARK

🚶 🚴 🎣 🏕 🛶 ♿ 🚐 ⛺

Scenic rating: 7

on the Jefferson River east of Three Forks

BEST (

On the Jefferson River, Lewis and Clark Caverns State Park offers a tour through the limestone caves with fantastical stalactites, columns, dripstones, ribbons, and cave popcorn. Guided two-hour tours of the caverns are available May–September only. You'll descend 600 steps and see utter darkness when the guide flips off the lights. The caverns are 1,400 vertical feet above the campground on a road not suitable for trailers. It's a 3.2-mile drive to get there from the campground. Across the highway, an access site allows for shore or wade fishing on the Jefferson River. Nine miles of hiking trails, including a 0.25-mile nature trail, tour the 2,920-acre park. Mountain bikes are allowed of some of these. The park also provides good wildlife-watching.

The campground, which sits at river level in the dramatic canyon, is good for tenters, with oodles of flat spaces. The grassy campground, which turns brown by the end of summer, offers no privacy, and only a couple of trees provide partial shade to a few sites. With the highway and the railroad tracks in the canyon, the campground is noisy at night. Watch for rattlesnakes.

Campsites, facilities: The campground has 40 RV or tent campsites that can accommodate RVs up to 60 feet long on back-in parking spurs. Facilities include picnic tables, fire rings with grills, flush toilets, showers, drinking water, garbage service, amphitheater programs, a disposal station, and a campground host. Leashed pets are permitted. A wheelchair-accessible toilet is available.

Reservations, fees: Reservations are not accepted. Campsites cost $15. Day-use fees are $5 per out-of-state vehicle; day use is free for Montana residents. Cash or check. Open year-round.

Directions: From I-90 east of Whitehall, take Exit 256. On the south side of the freeway, drive east on Highway 2 for 7.3 miles. From I-90 near Three Forks, take Exit 274 and go south on Highway 2/287 for 11.2 miles. Stay on Highway 2 as it splits off from 287 and head west for five miles. The signed park entrance is on the north side of the road. Drive 0.2 mile up and turn left to enter the campground.

GPS Coordinates: N 45° 49.422' W 111° 51.324'

Contact: Montana Fish, Wildlife, and Parks, Lewis and Clark Caverns, P.O. Box 489, Whitehall, MT 59759, 406/287-3541, http://fwp.mt.gov.

4 HARRISON LAKE

Scenic rating: 6

west of Harrison on Willow Creek Reservoir

Harrison Lake, elevation 4,741 feet, is a primitive fishing access site run by the state. Its real name is Willow Creek Reservoir, but it carries the Harrison name after the nearby town. The 713-acre lake contains brown and westslope cutthroat trout and is stocked regularly with rainbow trout. True to its name, the lake is surrounded by willow brush, making the best fishing via boat. The access road to get to the campground is rough, rutted, and bumpy. It turns to gumbo when wet and is dusty when dry. A concrete boat ramp and a primitive boat ramp aid launching onto the lake in two different locations of the campground. Near the community of Harrison, the lake is a locals' hangout for waterskiing, boating, and fishing.

The primitive campground spreads out in three different locations around a large peninsula with low mountain views in the distance. The weedy sites are rough, uneven, and dusty or muddy. Most of the sites are open, sunny, and visited by black flies. The campground sees more use on weekends and holidays, while weekdays have sparser visitation. When the campground is partly full, you can gain privacy by camping in sites across the peninsula from other campers. After boats pull off the lake in the evening, the area is exceptionally quiet, with only a songbird or two in the early morning.

Campsites, facilities: The campground has 12 RV or tent campsites that can accommodate midsized RVs. Facilities include picnic tables, fire rings with grills, and vault toilets. Leashed pets are permitted. A wheelchair-accessible toilet is available.

Reservations, fees: Reservations are not accepted. Campsites cost $7 with a Montana fishing license and $12 without a Montana fishing license. Cash or check. Open year-round.

Directions: From Highway 287 in Harrison, turn east onto Harrison Lake Road for four dirt-road miles.

GPS Coordinates: N 45° 41.982' W 111° 42.582'

Contact: Montana Fish, Wildlife, and Parks, Region 3, 1400 S. 19th Ave., Bozeman, MT 59718, 406/994-4042, http://fwp.mt.gov.

5 RED MOUNTAIN

Scenic rating: 8

east of Norris on the Madison River

BEST (

On the banks of the lower Madison River, Red Mountain Campground sits at the north end of Bear Trap Canyon, a narrow slice through 1,500-foot-tall red cliffs on the Madison River. The Madison River plummets through the canyon with the Class IV Kitchen Sink rapid in Lee Metcalf Wilderness. Paralleling the white water, the nine-mile Bear Trap Canyon

National Recreation Trail departs from Warm Springs Recreation Area (also the take-out for rafting the canyon) about two miles south on the highway. The river harbors 18-inch rainbow and brown trout, but the wade fishing is best before mid-July when the water warms up. The campground is convenient for cross-country bicyclists using Highway 287. It is also the closest campground to Norris Hot Springs, Montana's only wooden hot springs pool, eight miles to the west. Live bands often play there on weekends.

Sitting right on the Madison River and framed with juniper hillsides, the grassy campground's left loop has 10 sites lined up on the riverbank. A few small aspens and junipers dot the campground, but not enough for shade. Sun is pervasive, and the campground gets hot in August. The open vegetation allows you to see other campers, but the campsites are spaced out for privacy. Some of the campsites offer long, pull-over gravel parking pads off the gravel campground road; the remainder are back-ins. Watch for rattlesnakes in the area. Even though you'll hear some trucking noise from the adjacent highway at night, catbirds will wake you in the morning.

Campsites, facilities: The campground has 17 RV or tent campsites that can accommodate large RVs. Facilities include picnic tables, fire rings with grills, vault toilets, drinking water, firewood for sale, and a campground host. Pack out your trash. Leashed pets are permitted. A wheelchair-accessible toilet is available.

Reservations, fees: Reservations are not accepted. Campsites cost $8. An extra vehicle costs $5. Vehicles are limited to three per site. Cash or check. Open May–December.

Directions: From Highway 287 at Norris, drive 8.1 miles to the campground. The entrance is on the north side of the road as soon as it crosses the Madison River.

GPS Coordinates: N 45° 36.728' W 111° 34.214'

Contact: Bureau of Land Management, Dillon Field Office, 1005 Selway Dr., Dillon, MT 59725, 406/683-2337, www.blm.gov.

6 RED MOUNTAIN PRIMITIVE

Scenic rating: 8

east of Norris on the Madison River

On lower Madison River near Red Mountain Campground, several primitive campsites often fill up before the campground does due to their location right on the riverbank and their price—free. These primitive campsites are at the north end of Bear Trap Canyon. The nine-mile Bear Trap Canyon National Recreation Trail departs from Warm Springs Recreation Area (also the take-out when rafting the canyon) about two miles south on the highway. The river, good for wade fishing, harbors 18-inch rainbow and brown trout, but fishing is best before mid-July when the water warms up. These sites, convenient for cross-country bicyclists using Highway 287, are eight miles east of Norris Hot Springs. Access to these sites is via primitive dirt roads; scout them first to be sure you can get your rig in and turn around.

A few trees dot the riverbanks but provide minimal shade for the sunny, unmarked campsites. Some brush separates sites, but you can see across the river to the highway or to campers in the campground, depending on your choice of site. You'll hear highway noise at night, and in the sites across from the campground, you can hear people, too. Watch for rattlesnakes in the area.

Campsites, facilities: The area has eight primitive RV or tent campsites that can accommodate midsized RVs. Facilities include rock fire rings at some campsites. Use pre-existing rings rather than making new ones, and follow Leave No Trace ethics. Pack out your trash. Leashed pets are permitted.

Reservations, fees: Reservations are not accepted. Camping is free. Open May–December.

Directions: From Highway 287 at Norris, drive 8.1 miles to the bridge that crosses the Madison

River at Red Mountain Campground. Half of the primitive sites are located 0.8 mile south on the dirt road opposite the campground entrance. The remainder are spread out along 0.8 mile of the dirt road heading north along the river on the west side of the bridge.

GPS coordinates for south campsites: N 45° 35.906' W 111° 34.219'

GPS coordinates for north campsites: N 45° 36.813' W 111° 34.252'

Contact: Bureau of Land Management, Dillon Field Office, 1005 Selway Dr., Dillon, MT 59725, 406/683-2337, www.blm.gov.

◼ MEADOW LAKE

Scenic rating: 8

north of Ennis on the north shore of Ennis Lake

At 4,815 feet in elevation, Ennis Lake sits in the middle of the Madison River Valley surrounded by the Madison and Tobacco Root mountain ranges. The lake—a fishery known for its brown and rainbow trout—is also a haven for waterskiing, sailing, and boating. Kobayashi Bay, with its buoyed swimming area and boat ramp, is one mile east. From the campground, you can launch hand-carried boats, but no ramp is available. Due to the shallowness of the lake, it warms in summer but kicks up with whitecaps in afternoon winds. The outlet to the lake launches the Madison River through Bear Trap Canyon through a 1,500-foot-deep gorge and the Class IV Kitchen Sink rapid.

The sunny, treeless primitive campground—a fishing access run by the state—spreads out along the shore of the lake near the inlet for Meadow Creek, which is a mosquito-breeding haven. Five of the campsites back in on gravel parking pads to waterfront. Views look south to the Madison Range, which on a calm day reflects in the water. Some of the shoreline is brushy. Ennis Lake Road garners substantial

traffic during the summer from those heading to raft in the canyon or visit Kobayashi Bay, but the traffic dwindles at night.

Campsites, facilities: The campground has nine RV or tent campsites that can accommodate RVs up to 25 feet. Facilities include picnic tables, fire rings with grills, and vault toilets. Leashed pets are permitted. A wheelchair-accessible toilet is available.

Reservations, fees: Reservations are not accepted. Camping is free. Open year-round.

Directions: From Highway 287 six miles north of Ennis, turn east at milepost 55 onto North Ennis Lake Road and drive 1.4 miles to the fishing access sign. Turn right into the campground.

GPS Coordinates: N 45° 26.596' W 111° 42.414'

Contact: Montana Fish, Wildlife, and Parks, Region 3, 1400 S. 19th Ave., Bozeman, MT 59718, 406/994-4042, http://fwp.mt.gov.

◼ ENNIS RV VILLAGE

Scenic rating: 6

north of Ennis

One mile north of Ennis, this campground is convenient for shopping in the town's art galleries and western stores as well as for eating out in its restaurants. The town is best known for its Fourth of July parade and rodeo. Ennis Lake, good for swimming, fishing, boating, and waterskiing, sits five miles to the north, and the Kobayashi day-use area for swimming is less than seven miles north. Madison River fishing access sites are within two miles, and white-water rafting companies are available for guided trips through Bear Trap Canyon and its Class IV Kitchen Sink rapid. Madison Meadows Golf Course is also in Ennis, and the surrounding Gallatin and Beaverhead-Deerlodge National Forests offer hiking and mountain-biking trails.

The campground lines up its RV campsites

in parking-lot fashion along small patches of lawn on the sunny Madison River Valley floor. Views from the campground span the Madison Mountains to the east and the Tobacco Root Mountains to the northwest. In June, they are still snow-covered; in August, they are bare. You can hear some trucks along Highway 287 at night.

Campsites, facilities: The campground has 90 RV campsites that can accommodate RVs up to 80 feet long, plus 11 tent campsites. Facilities include picnic tables, flush toilets, showers, drinking water, garbage service, a disposal station, free wireless Internet, a convenience store, a coin-operated launderette, and hookups for sewer, water, and electricity up to 50 amps. Leashed pets are permitted. A wheelchair-accessible toilet is available.

Reservations, fees: Reservations are not accepted. Hookups cost $29–33. Tent sites and dry camping for small RVs costs $19–25. Rates are based on two people per site. Additional campers cost $2 each. Children under 12 years old camp for free. Use of the disposal station costs $6. Those staying a week can get the seventh night free. The 7 percent Montana bed tax will be added on. Cash, check, or credit card. Open mid-April–mid-November.

Directions: Drive 1.2 miles north of Ennis on Highway 287. Turn east and drive 300 feet to the campground entrance, which is straight ahead.

GPS Coordinates: N 45° 22.053' W 111° 43.700'

Contact: Ennis RV Village, 5034 Hwy. 287 N., Ennis, MT 59729, 406/682-5272 or 866/682-5272, www.ennisrv.com.

⑨ VALLEY GARDEN
🏊 🎣 🚤 ⛵ 🐕 ♿ 🚐 ⛺

Scenic rating: 7

northeast of Ennis on the Madison River

Valley Garden, elevation 4,885 feet, is a state-run fishing access site on the Madison River.

It is a popular location, as the town of Ennis, with its restaurants, shops, art galleries, and fishing outfitters, is less than a 10-minute drive away. The campground has a primitive gravel boat ramp where you can launch onto the river to float down to Ennis Lake (but fishing from boats is prohibited in this section of the river). The Madison River gains worldwide fame for its blue-ribbon trout fishing, which is catch-and-release only for rainbow trout.

A narrow, potholed dirt road accesses the campground, where an osprey nest sits on a platform above the pay station. Views from the campsites span the Tobacco Root Mountains to the northwest and the Madison Mountains to the east. Two sunny loops through the tall grass offer flat spaces mowed out for tents. Sites 5–8 overlook the river; other sites can access the river through the brushy willows. The sites are spaced out for privacy, but the openness means you can see other campers. The only noise is from the myriad songbirds and the river. The tall grass is green into July but fades to gold by the end of August.

Campsites, facilities: The campground has nine RV or tent campsites that can accommodate RVs up to 25 feet. Facilities include picnic tables, fire rings with grills, a boat ramp, and vault toilets. Leashed pets are permitted. A wheelchair-accessible toilet is available.

Reservations, fees: Reservations are not accepted. Camping costs $12 without a Montana fishing license or $7 with a fishing license. Open year-round.

Directions: From Ennis, drive south on Highway 287 about 1.5 miles to milepost 48. Turn north just after crossing Jeffers Creek and drive 1.9 miles. Turn left at the fishing access sign and drive over the cattle grate to reach the campground.

GPS Coordinates: N 45° 21.893' W 111° 42.313'

Contact: Montana Fish, Wildlife, and Parks, Region 3, 1400 S. 19th Ave., Bozeman, MT 59718, 406/994-4042, http://fwp.mt.gov.

10 ENNIS

Scenic rating: 4

in Ennis on the Madison River

At 4,938 feet in elevation, Ennis is a state-run fishing access site on the Madison River. It is a popular location, as you can walk five minutes into the town of Ennis, which offers restaurants, shops, art galleries, and fishing outfitters. The campground looks across the river at houses. A primitive gravel boat ramp allows a place to launch onto the river to float down to Valley Garden or Ennis Lake, but you can also go wade fishing here (it's catch-and-release only for trout above the bridge). The river harbors brown, rainbow, brook, and Yellowstone cutthroat trout along with mountain whitefish. Bicyclists also use this campground while cycling Highway 287.

A narrow, potholed dirt road accesses the campground's one big loop, which seems more like a maze due to the high brush. Campsites are tucked into the brush under several large willow trees that provide partial shade. Many of the campsites gain privacy from the 15-foot-high willow jungle in the campground, but a few are in sight of other campers. The three campsites on the river are not private, but open to other campsites and across the river to houses. The campsites, which are a mix of grass, dirt, and gravel, collect a combination of sounds, from the highway to songbirds. Be sure to locate the mowed path to the hand pump for drinking by site 13.

Campsites, facilities: The campground has 17 RV or tent campsites that can accommodate RVs up to 25 feet. Facilities include picnic tables, rock fire rings, a boat ramp, drinking water, and vault toilets. Leashed pets are permitted.

Reservations, fees: Reservations are not accepted. Camping costs $12 without a Montana fishing license or $7 with a fishing license. Open year-round.

Directions: From Ennis, drive south on Highway 287 about 0.1 mile. Turn right at the fishing access sign as soon as you cross the Madison River.

GPS Coordinates: N 45° 20.665' W 111° 43.449'

Contact: Montana Fish, Wildlife, and Parks, Region 3, 1400 S. 19th Ave., Bozeman, MT 59718, 406/994-4042, http://fwp.mt.gov.

11 VIRGINIA CITY RV PARK

Scenic rating: 4

southwest of Ennis

Surrounded by arid juniper and sagebrush hills, the campground is within a 10-minute walk to Virginia City's main street, where the town has preserved more than 100 historic buildings from its 1860s gold rush days, when it was the largest town in the inland Northwest. Shopping, restaurants, living history and frontier museums, galleries, and live theaters all operate out of the ghost town buildings, which are all connected by a boardwalk. You can also take rides in a 1910 refurbished steam locomotive, a stagecoach, or a 1941 fire engine. Kids can fish in the Virginia City ponds. Horseback riding and garnet or gold panning are also possibilities. Nevada City, a second ghost town, is 1.5 miles west of Virginia City.

The small, cramped campground is sunny and hot with only a few trees that shade a couple of sites. Most campers are here to see the ghost towns rather than spend time in their campsites, though, as this is the only campground within 13 miles of Virginia City. Some of the campsites overlook the graveyard, and full-time residents also live in the park. Even though sites can accommodate longer RVs on the paved parking pads, spaces between sites are dry and dusty.

Campsites, facilities: The campground has 50 RV campsites that can accommodate RVs up to 60 feet long, plus six tent campsites. Facilities include picnic tables, flush toilets, showers, drinking water, garbage service, a disposal station, free wireless Internet, and hookups for sewer, water, and electricity. Leashed pets are permitted.

Reservations, fees: Reservations are highly recommended. Hookups cost $26–30. Tent sites cost $22. Rates are based on four people per site. Additional campers cost $4 each. Children under four years old camp for free. The park offers a discount package for a three-night stay: pay for two nights at full price and get the third night half price. A 10 percent tax will be added. Cash, check, or credit card. Open mid-May–September.

Directions: On State Route 287 (not to be confused with Highway 287), from Ennis drive southwest for 13.1 miles, or from Virginia City drive 0.5 mile east. Turn south for 0.1 mile to enter the campground.

GPS Coordinates: N 45° 17.670' W 111° 55.660'

Contact: Virginia City RV Park, P.O. Box 235, Virginia City, MT 59755, 406/843-5493 or 888/833-5493, www.virginiacityrvpark. com.

12 RUBY CREEK

Scenic rating: 8

south of Ennis on the Madison River

Located on the west bank of the Madison River south of Ennis, Ruby Creek Campground attracts mostly anglers looking to hook trout. Sometimes, this upper Madison catch-and-release-only area fills with anglers at every river bend. The campground, however, also backs into the Wall Creek Wildlife Management Area, a wintering range for elk but also home to pronghorn antelope, moose, deer, black bears, and raptors. Designated roads, which are closed December–April, allow touring of the area

for wildlife-watching, hiking, or hunting. You can walk to the campground's boat launch south of the campground quicker than you can drive to it. By vehicle, you must drive out of the campground, turn left, and wrap 0.4 mile around to the boat launch, from which you can float the river north to McAtee Bridge.

Surrounded by sagebrush bench lands, the campground sits on an arid, bunchgrass prairie with large rocky outcroppings to the west and the Madison Mountains looming to the east. Unfortunately, you can also see a few houses up on the plateau, but the highway disappears—along with its noise—behind the plateau. Two gravel loops swing through the sunny campground, one on each side of Ruby Creek. The campground houses only a handful of 20-foot-high willows—not enough for shade or windbreaks. Sites 5–8 in the south loop sit closest to the river. Three sites have pull-over parking, which can accommodate those with trailers.

Campsites, facilities: The campground has 18 RV or tent campsites that can accommodate midsized RVs. Facilities include picnic tables, fire rings with grills, vault toilets, drinking water, and a campground host. Pack out your trash. Leashed pets are permitted. A wheelchair-accessible toilet is available.

Reservations, fees: Reservations are not accepted. Campsites cost $8. An extra vehicle costs $5. Only three vehicles are allowed per site. Cash or check. Open year-round; fees are collected May–December.

Directions: From Highway 287 south of Ennis, turn west at the campground sign at milepost 30.9 onto a wide gravel road and cross the Madison River. Turn left just past the McAtee Bridge fishing access site and drive 2.6 miles south to the campground entrance on the left.

GPS Coordinates: N 45° 3.619' W 111° 39.942'

Contact: Bureau of Land Management, Dillon Field Office, 1005 Selway Dr., Dillon, MT 59725, 406/683-2337, www.blm.gov.

13 PALISADES (MADISON RIVER)

Scenic rating: 7

south of Ennis on the Madison River

BEST (

On the east bank of the Madison River south of Ennis, Palisades Campground is named for the several-mile-long cliff band that runs along the hillside on the opposite side of the river. The cliffs light up in the morning sun. The boat ramp for launching rafts, drift boats, canoes, and kayaks onto the Madison River is in the Palisades picnic area, 0.9 mile south of the campground. You can float from here 8.5 miles to McAtee Bridge. Anglers can go wade fishing in the river here, which has a blue-ribbon reputation for its brown and rainbow trout. This area of the river can sometimes fill with anglers in every stretch, and the river here is catch-and-release only.

Surrounded by sagebrush bench lands, the tiny campground's sites are on a wide-open, arid, treeless bunchgrass prairie with views of the Madison Mountains. Unfortunately, those views also include a few homes up on the bluff, but the highway is hidden behind. Half of the sites sit on the river. You can see pronghorn antelope and deer from the campground as well as wake up to songbirds. All of the sites are sunny gravel back-ins with neighboring campers in sight.

Campsites, facilities: The campground has six RV or tent campsites that can accommodate midsized RVs. Facilities include picnic tables, fire rings with grills, vault toilets, and drinking water. Pack out your trash. Leashed pets are permitted. A wheelchair-accessible toilet is available.

Reservations, fees: Reservations are not accepted. Campsites cost $8. An extra vehicle costs $5. There's a three-vehicle limit per site. Cash or check. Open year-round; fees are collected May–December.

Directions: From Highway 287 south of Ennis, turn west at milepost 22.9 onto the gravel road. Drive a bumpy 0.4 mile to a junction and veer right for the campground, which you'll reach 0.6 mile later.

GPS Coordinates: N 44 ° 59.768' W 111° 39.533'

Contact: Bureau of Land Management, Dillon Field Office, 1005 Selway Dr., Dillon, MT 59725, 406/683-2337, www.blm.gov.

14 WEST FORK MADISON

Scenic rating: 5

on the West Fork of the Madison River in Beaverhead-Deerlodge National Forest

This tiny campground, elevation 6,000 feet, squeezes in between the West Fork of the Madison River in Beaverhead-Deerlodge National Forest and an RV park. It's an older national forest campground used mostly by anglers going after brown, rainbow, and cutthroat trout. A fishing access site with a boat ramp is located at Lyons Bridge 1.1 miles north. Anglers float the Madison River, where the trout fishing is catch-and-release only, with artificial lures.

Overhanging branches cramp the narrow campground loop, which can only handle truck-campers and other small RVs. Contrary to many of the river campsites on the Madison, sites 3–7 sit under the heavy shade of the forest with a floor covered with Douglas fir and spruce cones. Sites 3 and 4 claim waterfront along the river; they have flat tent spots and privacy from each other due to brush and willows, but the loop is so small that you can see other campers. Sites 1 and 2 sit north of the campground loop with two very small walk-in tent sites tucked into partly sunny willows. Wild roses bloom here in July. Despite the proximity of the burbling river, you can hear the highway. The campground also borders West Fork RV, where you can buy showers.

Campsites, facilities: The campground has five RV or tent campsites that can accommodate very small RVs. Trailers are not recommended. Two walk-in tent campsites are also available. Facilities include picnic tables, fire rings with grills, drinking water, bear boxes for food storage, and pit toilets. Pack out your trash. Leashed pets are permitted.

Reservations, fees: Reservations are not accepted. Campsites cost $10. Open year-round, but services are available only mid-May–early September.

Directions: At the rest area on Highway 287 at milepost 15.9, turn west and cross the Madison River, driving 1.1 miles south on Forest Road 209. Turn left onto a steep, single-lane road with turnouts for 0.3 mile and cross the West Fork of the Madison River. Turn right immediately to reach the campground loop, or go straight to find the walk-in tent sites on the left.

GPS Coordinates: N 44° 53.221' W 111° 34.929'

Contact: Beaverhead-Deerlodge National Forest, Madison Ranger District, 5 Forest Service Rd., Ennis, MT 59729, 406/682-4253, www.fs.fed.us/r1/b-d/.

15 WEST FORK CABINS AND RV

Scenic rating: 6

south of Ennis on the Madison River

Located at 6,000 feet in elevation along the Madison River, West Fork Cabins and RV offers fishing adjacent to the campground in the catch-and-release section of the river. This upper section of the Madison River often is packed in summer with wading anglers at every bend in the river due to its blue-ribbon reputation for catch-and-release wild trout. The company also offers guided fishing and float trips, plus rents rafts with trailers ($100/day) and personal kickboats ($30/day). The campground is surrounded by Beaverhead-Deerlodge National Forest and the Madison Mountains. Horses are also available for riding.

The campground has two loops surrounding a grassy lawn. While some trees surround the campground, they are not in locations to provide shade. But those looking for satellite reception will have a clear shot at the sky. The campsites are all visible from each other, but each has its own cement patio. You can hear the highway across the river in the campground.

Campsites, facilities: The campground has 24 RV campsites that can accommodate large RVs, and 20 tent sites. Facilities include picnic tables, fire pits, flush toilets, showers, drinking water, garbage service, a coin-operated launderette, tackle shop, satellite TV lounge, and hookups for sewer, water, and electricity. Leashed pets are permitted.

Reservations, fees: Reservations are accepted. Hookups cost $25. Tent spaces cost $12. A 7 percent Montana bed tax is added. Cash, check, or credit card. Open April–November.

Directions: From Ennis, drive 35 miles south on Highway 287. (From West Yellowstone, the drive is also 35 miles.) Exit Highway 287 to the west and cross the Madison River, veering left and driving 0.4 mile to the entrance.

GPS Coordinates: N 44° 52.921' W 111° 34.590'

Contact: West Fork Cabins and RV, 24 Sundance Bench Rd., Cameron, MT 59720, 406/682-4802 or 866/343-8267, www.wfork.com.

16 CABIN CREEK

Scenic rating: 6

northeast of Quake Lake in Gallatin National Forest

Cabin Creek Campground sits at 6,400 feet in elevation in the earthquake area of Gallatin National Forest. The Earthquake Scarp

Interpretive Area is adjacent to the campground. At the beginning of the Cabin Creek Scarp Trailhead, you'll pass a fault scarp, a 20-foot-high dirt bank where the ground dropped down and the earth rose up, trapping some campers during the 1959 earthquake. The trailhead for the Cabin Creek Scarp-Red Canyon complex of trails is across the creek from the campground. Many of the trails are open to hikers, mountain bikers, motorcycles, and ATVs. To the west, Quake Lake's boat launch is 2.3 miles away, followed by the Earthquake Center Visitor Area eight miles away. Fishing and boating are available on Quake Lake.

The campground rests alongside the busy highway. Sites are very close together, and many have views of the road. A canopy of Douglas firs shades the campground, but with only low ground cover and cow parsnips, you can see the entire campground from almost every site. Double-wide dirt parking pads allow for two vehicles or a trailer separated from its vehicle. Sites 10–13 line up along Cabin Creek.

Campsites, facilities: The campground has 15 RV or tent campsites that can accommodate RVs up to 30 feet long. Facilities include picnic tables, fire rings with grills, vault toilets, drinking water, bear boxes, garbage service, firewood for sale, and a campground host. Leashed pets are permitted. A wheelchair-accessible toilet is available.

Reservations, fees: Reservations are not accepted. Campsites cost $13. An extra vehicle costs $8. Cash or check. Open mid-May–mid-September.

Directions: On Highway 287 east of Quake Lake Visitor Center and west of Hebgen Lake, turn north off the highway at milepost 8.6 into the campground.

GPS Coordinates: N 44° 52.279' W 111° 20.680'

Contact: Gallatin National Forest, Hebgen Lake Ranger Station, 330 Gallatin Rd., West Yellowstone, MT 59758, www.fs.fed.us/r1/gallatin/.

17 BEAVER CREEK

Scenic rating: 9

overlooking Quake Lake in Gallatin National Forest

BEST (

Located in Gallatin National Forest's mountainous southwest corner at 6,500 feet, Beaver Creek is the closest campground to Quake Lake and the Earthquake Lake Visitor Center (open daily Memorial Day–mid-September) 4.6 miles to the west. The center marks the site of a 1959 earthquake landslide that killed 28 people and dammed up the Madison River, forming Quake Lake. You can hike five minutes to Memorial Rock and overlooks of the landslide path. Expert kayakers also run the 1.5 miles of Class IV–V river from Quake Lake's outlet. Two short hiking trails descend from the campground to the six-mile-long Quake Lake, and a boat launch 0.5 mile to the west allows access for boating and fishing for brown and rainbow trout. Mountain bikers, hikers, and ATVers can use many of the Cabin Creek trails 1.7 miles to the east.

Situated in three loops on meadow hilltops, the campground blooms prolifically in July with paintbrush, lupines, and harebells. Loose groves of aspens and thin lodgepoles provide partial shade; other sites draw full sun. Sites A7–9 flank the beaver ponds, where lily pads bloom with yellow flowers. The sites spread out for privacy, and thanks to the open forest, you get views of the surrounding peaks or Quake Lake but also can see other campers. The quiet campground rings with the sounds of songbirds or the light chatter of aspen leaves clacking in the breeze.

Campsites, facilities: The campground has 79 RV or tent campsites that can accommodate RVs up to 55 feet long. Facilities include picnic tables, fire rings with grills, vault toilets, drinking water, garbage service, firewood for sale, and a campground host. Leashed pets are permitted. A wheelchair-accessible toilet and campsite are available.

Reservations, fees: Reservations are accepted (877/444-6777, www.recreation.gov). Campsites cost $13. An extra vehicle costs $8. Cash or check. Open early June–mid-September.

Directions: On Highway 287, east of Quake Lake Visitor Center and west of Hebgen Lake, turn south off the highway at milepost 7 onto the paved narrow road. Climb 0.6 mile to the campground entrance junction, with loop A to the left and loops B and C to the right.

GPS Coordinates: N 44° 51.390' W 111° 22.384'

Contact: Gallatin National Forest, Hebgen Lake Ranger Station, 330 Gallatin Rd., West Yellowstone, MT 59758, www.fs.fed.us/r1/gallatin/.

18 RAYNOLD'S PASS

Scenic rating: 6

south of Ennis on the Madison River

The dead trees in Quake Lake are a reminder of the landslide that formed the lake.

At 6,178 feet in elevation, Raynold's Pass is a state-run fishing access site on the Madison River. The campground itself is just a dusty ring of campsites with picnic tables, but the river is the attraction. The Madison River is known for its wild trout fishery—particularly brown, rainbow, and Yellowstone cutthroat trout. This is a catch-and-release only section for trout; artificial lures must be used. You can go wade fishing in the river here or launch a drift boat, kayak, canoe, or raft from the primitive dirt boat ramp on the east side of the bridge. You can float from here three river miles west to Three Dollar Bridge or continue for a 10-mile float to Lyons Bridge. Earthquake Lake Visitor Center (open daily Memorial Day–mid-September), marking the site of the 1959 earthquake slide that killed 28 people and dammed up the Madison River, sits 3.2 miles to the east.

The arid, dusty campground loop sits in the open sagebrush and dry grass prairie with views of the Madison Mountains. No trees are available for shade or windbreaks, and the sites lack privacy because of the openness and the small loop. The proximity to the two highways adds noise from large trucks, even at night.

Campsites, facilities: The campground has six RV or tent campsites that can accommodate RVs up to 25 feet. Facilities include picnic tables, rock fire rings, a boat ramp, and vault toilets. Leashed pets are permitted.

Reservations, fees: Reservations are not accepted. Camping is free. Open year-round.

Directions: From Ennis, drive south on Highway 287 to the junction with Highway 87. Turn south onto Highway 87 and drive 0.4 mile. Turn right into the fishing access site.

GPS Coordinates: N 45° 49.649' W 111° 29.182'

Contact: Montana Fish, Wildlife, and Parks, Region 3, 1400 S. 19th Ave., Bozeman, MT 59718, 406/994-4042, http://fwp.mt.gov.

19 WADE LAKE

🚶 🏊 🛶 🚤 🎣 🐕 🚐 ⛺

Scenic rating: 7

on Wade Lake in Beaverhead-Deerlodge
National Forest

BEST (

At 6,200 feet in the Beaverhead-Deerlodge
National Forest, skinny Wade Lake, sunk
into a deep forest trough, is a popular lake,
especially with kids. Its sandy beach and turquoise water in the shallows lend conditions
for the lake water to warm a bit by August.
(Remember: In Montana, that means it's
above frigid, but nothing like the tropics.)
Anglers here have caught record-breaking
brown trout, and you can often see bald eagles
and ospreys fishing, plus river otters. Canoes
and kayaks are available to rent from the adjacent Wade Lake Resort. Only nonmotorized
watercraft are permitted. The surrounding
forested slopes contain hiking trails, one of
which is a nature trail that climbs one mile
to the Hilltop Campground.

The campground is stacked on a steep hillside above the boat ramp and swimming area.
The sites have steep trails between them. Sites
3–6 have outstanding water views but also
garner campground traffic on the way to the
boat launch. Several sites in the upper loop
have peek-a-boo views plummeting down to
the lake. The upper loop sites offer more privacy because people aren't tromping by all day.
Douglas firs shade most of the campground,
and hollyhocks, pink sticky geraniums, and
wild roses grow in sunny spots. Due to its
remote location, the campground is quiet.

Campsites, facilities: The campground has 25
RV or tent campsites that can accommodate
RVs up to 30 feet. Facilities include picnic
tables, fire rings with grills, vault toilets,
drinking water, and garbage service. Leashed
pets are permitted. A wheelchair-accessible
toilet is available.

Reservations, fees: Reservations are not
accepted. Campsites cost $12. Open mid-
May–September.

Directions: From Highway 287 south of
Ennis, turn off south at milepost 9.6 at the
Cliff and Wade Lake sign onto Wade Lake
Road (Forest Road 241). Drive over the
Madison River and pass the Three Dollar
Bridge fishing access site. Be prepared for
a long, bumpy drive with large rocks in the
road. At 3.4 miles, turn right at the fork and
climb steeply over the ridge down for 1.7
miles. Watch for cattle on the road. At the
signed fork in the road, turn right and drive
0.7 mile to the campground entrance.
GPS Coordinates: N 44° 48.376' W 111°
33.974'

Contact: Beaverhead-Deerlodge National Forest, Madison Ranger District, 5 Forest Service
Rd., Ennis, MT 59729, 406/682-4253, www.
fs.fed.us/r1/b-d/.

20 HILLTOP

🚶 🏊 🛶 🚤 🎣 🐕 🚐 ⛺

Scenic rating: 7

above Wade Lake in Beaverhead-Deerlodge
National Forest

At an elevation of 6,800 feet in the Beaverhead-Deerlodge National Forest, Hilltop
is aptly named, for it sits on the spine of a
ridge in between Wade and Cliff Lakes. A
one-mile trail drops from the campground
to Wade Lake, where you can swim, fish, and
rent canoes or kayaks from Wade Lake Resort.
The climb back up the hill requires more than
500 feet of ascent.

Hilltop is an older campground with
smaller, back-in dirt parking pads, overhanging branches on the campground road,
and trees that make for narrow turns. But it
also has sites with spacious flat tent spaces.
Douglas firs and lodgepole pines filter the
sunlight and lend partial shade. More open
campsites are rimmed with cow parsnip
and lupine. Sites 11–14 and 16–18 overlook
the canyon and opposite cliff wall, with a
rail fence marking the end lip of the cliff.

A few campsites offer peek-a-boo views of the Madison Mountains. Due to its remote location, the campground is quiet. Also, it is less crowded than Wade or Cliff Lake; you can often gain privacy just because of vacant neighboring campsites.

Campsites, facilities: The campground has 18 RV or tent campsites that can accommodate RVs up to 22 feet. Facilities include picnic tables, fire rings with grills, pit toilets, drinking water, and garbage service. Leashed pets are permitted.

Reservations, fees: Reservations are not accepted. Campsites cost $12. Open mid-May–September.

Directions: From Highway 287 south of Ennis, turn off south at milepost 9.6 at the Cliff and Wade Lake sign onto Wade Lake Road (Forest Road 241). Drive over the Madison River and pass the Three Dollar Bridge fishing access site. Be prepared for a long, bumpy drive with large rocks in the road. At 3.4 miles, turn right at the fork and climb steeply over the ridge down for 1.7 miles. Watch for cattle on the road. At the signed fork in the road, turn left for 0.1 mile and turn right to climb steeply for 0.8 mile to the campground.

GPS Coordinates: N 44° 47.775' W 111° 33.677'

Contact: Beaverhead-Deerlodge National Forest, Madison Ranger District, 5 Forest Service Rd., Ennis, MT 59729, 406/682-4253, www.fs.fed.us/r1/b-d/.

21 CLIFF POINT

Scenic rating: 8

on Cliff Lake in Beaverhead-Deerlodge National Forest

BEST (

At 6,350 feet in the Beaverhead-Deerlodge National Forest, the tiny Cliff Point Campground clusters around a small peninsula in Cliff Lake with popular campsites.

Surrounded by steep forested slopes, the narrow lake is actually twice as big as Wade Lake. The one-mile Fault Trail (#430) departs from the campground, touring through the canyon and connecting with the Wade Lake nature trail. As at Wade Lake, Cliff Lake's shallower bays shine turquoise because of the sandy bottom. Only nonmotorized boating is permitted, making it a quiet place for canoeing or kayaking. The lake's clear waters produce rainbow trout and cutthroat trout, and you can often watch bald eagles fish, plus see beaver.

These campsites are coveted for their locations on the point. Sites 3 and 4 claim the prime spots with big lake views and waterfront. Most of the sites have flat spaces for big tents. Due to the size of the campground, which is filled with pink sticky geraniums and has a few large Douglas fir trees for partial shade, you will see the neighbors, but you'll also get to wake up to the call of loons.

Campsites, facilities: The campground has 18 RV or tent campsites that can accommodate RVs up to 16 feet. Facilities include picnic tables, fire rings with grills, vault toilets, drinking water, bear boxes, and garbage service. Leashed pets are permitted. A wheelchair-accessible toilet is available.

Reservations, fees: Reservations are not accepted. Campsites cost $12. Open mid-May–September.

Directions: From Highway 287 south of Ennis, turn off south at milepost 9.6 at the Cliff and Wade Lake sign onto Wade Lake Road (Forest Road 241). Drive over the Madison River and pass the Three Dollar Bridge fishing access site. Be prepared for a long, bumpy drive with large rocks in the road. At 3.4 miles, turn right at the fork and climb steeply over the ridge down for 1.7 miles. Watch for cattle on the road. At the signed fork in the road, turn left for 0.4 mile to the boat ramp and continue another 0.6 mile to the campground. The road narrows to a single lane with curvy, blind corners.

GPS Coordinates: N 44° 47.600' W 111° 33.703'

Contact: Beaverhead-Deerlodge National Forest, Madison Ranger District, 5 Forest Service Rd., Ennis, MT 59729, 406/682-4253, www.fs.fed.us/r1/b-d/.

22 RIVER MARSH
🚶 🚴 🛶 🛥 ⛵ 🎣 🐕 🚐 ⛺

Scenic rating: 6

in Red Rock Lakes National Wildlife Refuge

At the outlet of Lower Red Rock Lake's west shore, this campground sits in the 45,000-acre Red Rock Lakes National Wildlife Refuge—an essential nesting area for trumpeter swans, with more than 2,000 of them using the lakes during the fall migration. The refuge is also an outstanding wildlife-watching area with 232 species of birds. The lakes are open for non-mechanized boats (except sailing) from mid-July to freeze out, and you can paddle between the two lakes. Fishing is permitted on Odell Creek east of the lower lake. Mountain bikers ride the refuge roads to Red Rock Pass, and around the lower lake the Idlewild and Odell trails lead to wildlife-watching areas from the refuge headquarters area about five miles from the campground. The refuge also permits antelope, elk, deer, and waterfowl hunting. Reaching the refuge requires miles of rough dirt road driving without any services; call the refuge to check road conditions, and gas up.

The primitive sunny campground sits in mixed prairie grass and sagebrush. With no trees, the campsites claim big views of the Centennial Mountains and the Continental Divide, but the marsh area produces voluminous summer mosquitoes, which, as long as the wind blows through, remain abated. When the wind blows, the campground is blustery. Very few people camp here, almost guaranteeing privacy, and you'll wake up to the sounds of birds.

Campsites, facilities: The campground has four RV or tent campsites that can accommodate small RVs. Facilities include fire pits and pit toilets. Water is available at refuge headquarters in Lakeview between the two lakes. Pack out your trash. Leashed pets are permitted.

Reservations, fees: Reservations are not accepted. Camping is free. Cash or check. Open year-round, although snow can close the roads and cover the campgrounds.

Directions: From Monida on I-15, take Exit 0 and drive north on Southside Centennial Road (#509) for 24.8 miles. Turn north and drive 2.6 miles, then turn right.

GPS Coordinates: N 44° 38.790' W 111° 52.806'

Contact: Red Rocks Lake National Wildlife Refuge, 27820 Southside Centennial Rd., Lima, MT 59739, 406/276-3536, www.fws.gov/redrocks/.

23 UPPER RED ROCK LAKE
🚶 🚴 🛶 🛥 ⛵ 🎣 🐕 ♿ 🚐 ⛺

Scenic rating: 8

in Red Rock Lakes National Wildlife Refuge

BEST (

On the south shore of Upper Red Rock Lake, the campground sits in the middle of the 45,000-acre Red Rock Lakes National Wildlife Refuge. The refuge is an essential nesting area for trumpeter swans, with more than 2,000 of them using the lakes during the fall migration. The lakes are open for nonmechanized boats (except sailing) from mid-July to freeze out, and you can paddle between the two lakes. Fishing is permitted in Red Rock and Elk Springs Creeks, plus three ponds east of the upper lake. Mountain bikers ride the refuge roads to Red Rock Pass, and two hiking trails connect to wildlife-watching areas around the lower lake. The refuge also permits antelope, elk, deer, and waterfowl hunting. Reaching the refuge requires miles of rough dirt-road driving without any services; call the refuge to check road conditions, and gas up.

Red Rock Lakes National Wildlife Refuge attracts hundreds of trumpeter swans during the fall migration.

Of the two campgrounds in the refuge, Upper Red Rock Lake is visited more, but more often than not, you'll have the place to yourself. It fills with summer mosquitoes but offers views of the upper lake and Centennial Mountains, and sits on a lush hillside with aspens, chokecherries, willows, nettles, and sticky pink geraniums. Most of the sites garner full sun; a few tuck under the aspens for partial shade. At night, you won't hear a sound until the sandhill crane calls wake you in the morning.

Campsites, facilities: The campground has seven RV or tent campsites that can accommodate small RVs. Facilities include picnic tables, fire pits, pit toilets, and drinking water from a spring. Pack out your trash. Leashed pets are permitted. A gravel-path wheelchair-accessible toilet and campsite are available.

Reservations, fees: Reservations are not accepted. Camping is free. Open year-round, although snow can close the roads and cover the campgrounds.

Directions: From Monida on I-15, take Exit 0 and drive north on Southside Centennial Road (#509) for 31.8 miles. The campground is on the north side of the road. From Highway 87/287 in Idaho at the north end of Henry's Lake, you can also drive over Red Rock Pass to reach the campground in 22 miles.

GPS Coordinates: N 44° 35.590' W 111° 43.736'

Contact: Red Rocks Lake National Wildlife Refuge, 27820 Southside Centennial Rd., Lima, MT 59739, 406/276-3536, www.fws.gov/redrocks/.

24 BOZEMAN KOA

Scenic rating: 6

south of Belgrade and west of Bozeman

BEST (

At 4,741 feet in elevation, about 10 minutes south of the freeway, the Bozeman KOA has two creek ditches running through the campground, which offer fishing. It also neighbors the Bozeman Hot Springs and Spa (open daily,

406/586-6492, www.bozemanhotsprings. com), which has nine pools between 59–106 degrees for dips ranging from icy to steaming. Two pools have cascading waterfalls, and the larger pool accommodates lap swimming. One pool is outdoors. Dry and wet saunas, a fitness facility, and spa services are available. The campground sits 0.5 mile from 27 holes of golf and 20 minutes from the Museum of the Rockies. Its location at the head of the Gallatin Valley makes it an easy 40-minute drive to Yellowstone National Park.

The campground sits on a busy highway— the main road heading down the Gallatin River Valley to Yellowstone National Park. Vehicle traffic is nonstop here in summer and during rush hours. The KOA has partially shaded campsites on mowed lawn, and in typical KOA fashion, the sites are very close together.

Campsites, facilities: The campground has 100 RV sites that can fit rigs up to 90 feet long, 50 tent sites, and one- and two-room cabins available. Hookups are available for water, sewer, and electricity up to 50 amps. Facilities include flush toilets, showers, picnic tables, fire rings with grills, garbage service, cable TV, modem dataport, free wireless Internet, a swimming pool, a hot tub, a sauna, a splash park, a playground, a disposal station, a pet walk, mini-golf, a camp store, firewood for sale, electrical hookups at tent sites, a kamping kitchen, and kamping kabins. Leashed pets are permitted.

Reservations, fees: Reservations are accepted (800/562-3036, www.koa.com). Hookups cost $30–51. Tent sites cost $27–33. Rates cover eight people. Children 14 and under stay free. A 7 percent Montana bed tax will be added on. Cash, check, or credit card. Open year-round.

Directions: On the west side of Bozeman at Belgrade on I-90, take Exit 298 and turn south on Jackrabbit Lane (Highway 85) for 7.7 miles. The campground entrance is on the west side of the road after the road becomes Highway 191.

GPS Coordinates: N 45° 39.583' W 111° 11.334'
Contact: Bozeman KOA, 81123 Gallatin Rd. (Hwy. 191), Bozeman, MT 59718, 406/587-3030, www.koa.com.

25 SPIRE ROCK

Scenic rating: 7

east of Gallatin Canyon in Gallatin National Forest

Spire Rock Campground nestles at 5,800 feet in a narrow canyon just south of Storm Castle Mountain in Gallatin National Forest. The canyon is home to several trailheads for hikers and mountain bikers. You can summit the 7,165-foot Storm Castle Mountain or 8,202-foot Garnet Mountain Lookout for views of the Spanish Peaks or head to Rat Lake. Just south of Storm Castle in the Gallatin Canyon, the Scorched Earth area offers sport climbing ranging in grade from 5.8 to 5.13. To the north in the canyon, rock climbers will find traditional routes on Gallatin Towers. The forested canyon yields a color drama in the evening with the limestone outcroppings lighting up.

Along a very skinny dirt road, the campground sprawls for one mile up the canyon with the campsites clumped together in twos and threes with 0.1 mile or so in between the clusters. That creates a feeling of camping in a tiny campground with only a couple campsites. Many of the campsites sit along the creek, with large, flat tent spaces. A lush undergrowth of thimbleberries, wild roses, and vine maples lends privacy between sites, many of which are partially shaded by Douglas firs. The first three sites are more open, with views of the mountain slope and meadow. The only sound you'll hear is the creek.

Campsites, facilities: The campground has 17 RV or tent campsites that can accommodate RVs up to 50 feet long. Facilities include picnic tables, fire rings with grills, pit toilets, bear boxes, garbage service, and firewood for sale. Leashed pets are permitted. A wheelchair-accessible toilet is available.

Reservations, fees: Reservations are accepted (877/444-6777, www.recreation.gov). Campsites cost $10. An extra vehicle costs $8. Cash or check. Open mid-May–late September.

Directions: West of Bozeman, travel south on Highway 191 to milepost 65.2. Turn east and cross the river. Turn immediately south onto the dirt road and drive past the helibase. The gravel road narrows along the river, with an abrupt drop-off and potholes for 1.6 miles, and then turns east for one mile, passing the trailhead for Storm Castle Mountain before reaching the campground. Turn right into the campground.

GPS Coordinates: N 45° 26.978' W 111° 11.731'

Contact: Gallatin National Forest, Bozeman Ranger District, 3710 Fallon St., Suite C, Bozeman, MT 59715, 406/522-2520, www.fs.fed.us/r1/gallatin/.

26 GREEK CREEK

Scenic rating: 7

in Gallatin Canyon in Gallatin National Forest

Located at 5,800 feet in elevation, Greek Creek Campground splits on both sides of the highway cutting through the Gallatin Canyon in Gallatin National Forest. The loops on the west side flank the river; those on the east side tuck into the forest up against a mountainside. For guided raft trips on the Class II-III river, Montana Whitewater Rafting Company is six miles north. Kayaker, rafters, and anglers going after brown and rainbow trout use the river here. The Lava Lake Trailhead is 3.2 miles north at Cascade Creek. The trail, for hikers only past the wilderness boundary, climbs into the Spanish Peaks of the Lee Metcalf Wilderness, reaching the lake in 3.5 miles after a 1,600-foot elevation gain. The trail is one of the most popular in the area, so you won't find solitude here—especially on weekends. Bicyclists riding to Yellowstone use this campground.

Due to the narrow canyon, the campground squeezes around the highway, making the sound of passing vehicles ubiquitous in the campground. Not even the river can drown out the larger trucks. Unfortunately, some campsites have views of the road, too. The Douglas fir forest admits filtered sunlight to the mountainside loops, which are more private, separated from each other by low brush, wild roses, and tall grass. The river loops, which are roomier with larger flat spaces for tents, are more open. On the left river loop, sites 14 and 15 overlook the river. The hot midsummer sun leaves the canyon early, cooling off the campground.

Campsites, facilities: The campground has 14 RV or tent campsites that can accommodate RVs up to 60 feet long. Facilities include picnic tables, fire rings with grills, vault toilets, drinking water, bear boxes, garbage service, and firewood for sale. Leashed pets are permitted. Wheelchair-accessible toilets and seven sites are available.

Reservations, fees: Reservations are accepted (877/444-6777, www.recreation.gov). Campsites cost $13. An extra vehicle costs $8. Cash or check. Open mid-May–late September.

Directions: West of Bozeman, travel south on Highway 191 to milepost 58.2. The campground splits on both sides of the highway, so turn right or left, depending on whether you want a site near the river or not.

GPS Coordinates: N 45° 22.818' W 111° 10.945'

Contact: Gallatin National Forest, Bozeman Ranger District, 3710 Fallon St., Suite C, Bozeman, MT 59715, 406/522-2520, www.fs.fed.us/r1/gallatin/.

27 SWAN CREEK

Scenic rating: 7

east of Gallatin Canyon in Gallatin National Forest

At 5,950 feet in elevation, Swan Creek Campground sits in a quiet side canyon east of Gallatin Canyon in Gallatin National Forest. The forested, steep-walled canyon pinches the narrow access road with overhanging branches, precluding many larger RVs from access. At the end of Swan Creek Canyon, a steep trail, #186, leads about 12 miles to Hyalite Peak. It is open to hikers, mountain bikers, and motorcycles. More hiking and mountain-biking trails are available from the Moose Creek area about 1.5 miles south on the highway. The nearby Gallatin River provides rafting, kayaking, and fishing.

Swan Creek Campground offers respite from the busy Gallatin Canyon campgrounds right on the highway. All of the campsites, which have back-in gravel parking spurs, line Swan Creek, where the burbling water is the sound you'll hear, rather than traffic. Douglas firs, spruces, and lodgepole pines lend partial to heavy shade to the campsites, and sunnier spots bloom with paintbrush, pink fireweed, and white yarrow. Several campsites have large, flat gravel spaces for tents. The two spread-out loops seem like two separate small campgrounds; the first loop has the pit toilets, and the second loop with more private sites has the wheelchair-accessible vault toilet.

Campsites, facilities: The campground has 13 RV or tent campsites that can accommodate RVs up to 45 feet long. Facilities include picnic tables, fire rings with grills, pit and vault toilets, hand pumps for drinking water, bear boxes, garbage service, and firewood for sale. Leashed pets are permitted. Wheelchair-accessible toilets and seven sites are available.

Reservations, fees: Reservations are accepted (877/444-6777, www.recreation.gov). Campsites cost $13. An extra vehicle costs $8. Cash or check. Open mid-May–late September.

Directions: West of Bozeman, travel south on Highway 191 to milepost 57.4. Turn east onto Swan Creek Road (Forest Road 481), a single-lane road with turnouts (trailers should be able to back up), and drive 0.5 mile. Use caution on turning off from the curvy highway here as locals drive fast on it. Both loops sit on the right side of the road about 0.6 mile apart. GPS Coordinates: N 45° 22.432' W 111° 9.117'

Contact: Gallatin National Forest, Bozeman Ranger District, 3710 Fallon St., Suite C, Bozeman, MT 59715, 406/522-2520, www.fs.fed.us/r1/gallatin/.

28 MOOSE CREEK FLATS

Scenic rating: 6

in Gallatin Canyon in Gallatin National Forest

At 5,800 feet in elevation in Gallatin Canyon in Gallatin National Forest, Moose Creek Flats Campground squeezes into an open meadow between the Gallatin River and the highway. The Class II–III river is popular here for whitewater rafting, kayaking, and wade-fishing. The campground works as both a take-out and put-in. For hikers and mountain bikers, the Moose Creek Trail (#187) departs on a spur road across the highway, leading eventually to the Gallatin Crest and Windy Pass Cabin. Other nearby trails for hikers access the Spanish Peaks of the Lee Metcalf Wilderness. Due to the campground's location right on the highway, bicyclists touring the Gallatin to Yellowstone stop here for camping.

A paved road with gravel back-in parking spurs and three pull-throughs weaves through the campground. Surrounded by a wide-open flat grassy meadow, all of the sunny campsites have views of the forested canyon walls as well as views of other campsites plus the highway, with its accompanying noise. A few Douglas firs are sprinkled along the river. Within the narrow Gallatin Canyon, the hot midsummer sun sinks out of sight earlier, which cools the campground. Sites 1–9 overlook the river.

Campsites, facilities: The campground has 13 RV or tent campsites that can accommodate RVs up to 60 feet long. One of the sites is for small groups. Facilities include picnic tables, fire rings with grills, vault toilets, drinking water, bear boxes, garbage service, and firewood for sale. Leashed pets are permitted. Toilets, four campsites, and a fishing access are wheelchair-accessible.

Reservations, fees: Reservations are accepted (877/444-6777, www.recreation.gov). Campsites cost $13. An extra vehicle costs $8. Cash or check. Open mid-May–mid-September.

Directions: West of Bozeman, travel south on Highway 191 to milepost 56.3. Be cautious about turning into the campground as locals drive fast in the canyon. The campground sits on the west side of the highway.

GPS Coordinates: N 45° 21.380' W 111° 10.291'

Contact: Gallatin National Forest, Bozeman Ranger District, 3710 Fallon St., Suite C, Bozeman, MT 59715, 406/522-2520, www.fs.fed.us/r1/gallatin/.

29 RED CLIFF

Scenic rating: 7

in Gallatin Canyon in Gallatin National Forest

At 6,250 feet in elevation in Gallatin National Forest, Red Cliff Campground is the only Forest Service campground in the upper Gallatin Canyon between Big Sky and Yellowstone National Park. The campground, which is named for the orange cliffs in the area, has places to carry rafts and kayaks to the Gallatin River for launching. The river houses rainbow, brown, brook, and Yellowstone cutthroat trout, plus mountain whitefish and arctic grayling. At the end of the south loop, the 4.8-mile Elkhorn Trail (#165) is open to hiking and horse-packing only, in a significant wildlife area. Bicyclists touring the Gallatin to Yellowstone National Park use this campground for its ease of access.

When you enter the campground on the gravel road, loops head off in both directions. The north loop contains the campsites without hookups; the south loop has those with electrical hookups. Although the campground is on the opposite side of the river from the highway, the water doesn't drown out the motor sounds. A young Douglas fir forest covers most of the campground, with both shady and partly sunny campsites available. In the south loop, which ends in a meadow blooming with pink sticky geraniums, the parking pads are gravel back-ins. In the north loop, sites 56–60 have views of the treed canyon, and several of the riverside sites have large flat spaces for tents where the door can sit right on the bank.

Campsites, facilities: The campground has 63 RV or tent campsites that can accommodate RVs up to 50 feet long. One of the sites is for small groups. Facilities include picnic tables, fire rings with grills, vault toilets, drinking water, bear boxes, garbage service, campground hosts, and firewood for sale. Leashed pets are permitted. Wheelchair-accessible toilets, tables, and water are available.

Reservations, fees: Reservations are accepted (877/444-6777, www.recreation.gov). No-hookup campsites cost $13; electrical hookup campsites cost $17. An extra vehicle costs $8. Cash or check. Open mid-May–late September.

Directions: West of Bozeman, travel south on Highway 191 to milepost 41.5. Be cautious about turning into the campground—locals drive fast in the canyon. Turn east off the highway and cross the Gallatin River.

GPS Coordinates: N 45° 10.604' W 111° 14.500'

Contact: Gallatin National Forest, Bozeman Ranger District, 3710 Fallon St., Suite C, Bozeman, MT 59715, 406/522-2520, www.fs.fed.us/r1/gallatin/.

30 BEAR CANYON

Scenic rating: 6

east of Bozeman on the Interstate

Located five minutes from downtown Bozeman, Bear Canyon Campground is convenient for shopping, nightlife, galleries, and restaurants along the main street as well as concerts in the Emerson Center. Bozeman is also home to golf courses, the Bozeman Hot Springs, and the Museum of the Rockies, with its celebrated dinosaur exhibits. A five-minute drive on the freeway also puts you at the entrance to Bridger Canyon, where the Bridger Bowl Ski Area hosts the annual Raptor Festival in early October. The free event takes place during the largest golden eagle migration in the United States, and you can hike to the ridge for a better view of the birds flying overhead. Hiking and mountain-biking trails are also in Bridger Canyon.

Bear Canyon Campground sits on a bluff above the freeway, but despite the proximity, some of the sites are surprisingly quiet. The campground commands views of the valley and surrounding mountains. Campsites are close together lined up in parking-lot fashion with some shorter trees providing partial shade. The campground has both pull-through and back-in gravel sites for RVs.

Campsites, facilities: The campground has 80 RV sites that can fit large RVs and 14 tent sites. Hookups are available for water, sewer, and electricity up to 50 amps. Facilities include flush toilets, showers, picnic tables, garbage service, free wireless Internet, an outdoor swimming pool, a playground, a launderette, a disposal station, and a camp store. Leashed pets are permitted.

Reservations, fees: Reservations are accepted. Hookups cost $28–33. Tent sites cost $20. Rates are for two people and one vehicle (includes trailer). Additional campers cost $5 per person. Children age three or younger stay free. An extra vehicle costs $2. Each pet costs $1. A 7 percent Montana bed tax will be added on. Cash or credit card. Open May–October.

Directions: From Bozeman, drive east on I-90 about 3.5 miles. Take Exit 313 and drive to the southwest side of the freeway, turning left into the campground in 400 feet.

GPS Coordinates: N 45° 39.080' W 110° 56.780'

Contact: Bear Canyon Campground, 5 Arnold St., Bozeman, MT 59715, 406/587-1575 or 800/438-1575, www.bearcanyoncampground. com.

31 LANGOHR

Scenic rating: 8

in Hyalite Canyon in Gallatin National Forest

At 6,250 feet in the Gallatin Range of Gallatin National Forest, Langohr Campground sits on the site of the first ranger station for the national forest. A short interpretive trail crosses the creek in the campground, and Hyalite Canyon is packed with hiking and mountain-biking trails, but the most popular trails depart from the Hyalite Reservoir area five miles farther up the road. The Blackmore picnic area and boat launch sits at the northwest corner of the reservoir. The lake is a no-wake zone. Hyalite Creek, which flows through the campground, harbors rainbow and Yellowstone cutthroat trout. Class IV–V stretches of white water in the canyon north of the campground draw expert kayakers.

The campground comprises two paved loops with paved campsite spurs lining up along Hyalite Creek with most of the campsites having creek frontage. The campground, which was reconstructed in 2005, sits in a wild garden of midsummer color with yarrow, sticky pink geraniums, cow parsnips, and bladder campions surrounded by a Douglas fir forest. The lush surroundings make up for the fact that you can see neighboring campers, despite the spread-out sites. After dark, a few late hikers still race back down the canyon to Bozeman on the adjacent road (which you can see above), but then only the sound of the stream remains. Most of the campsites have views of meadow hillsides and mixed forest slopes.

Campsites, facilities: The campground has 19 RV or tent campsites that can accommodate RVs up to 60 feet long. Facilities include picnic tables, fire rings with grills, vault toilets, drinking water, garbage service, bear boxes, firewood for sale, and a campground host. Leashed pets are permitted. A wheelchair-accessible toilet and two campsites are available.

Reservations, fees: Reservations are accepted (877/444-6777, www.recreation.gov). Campsites cost $13. An extra vehicle costs $8. Cash or check. Open mid-May–mid-September.

Directions: From downtown Bozeman, drive west on Highway 191 to Cottonwood Road. Turn south and drive 5.5 miles. Turn east onto South 19th Avenue and go one mile. Turn south onto Hyalite Canyon Road, which turns into Forest Road 62. Drive 5.9 miles to the campground entrance on the right.

GPS Coordinates: N 45° 31.827' W 111° 0.951'

Contact: Gallatin National Forest, Bozeman Ranger District, 3710 Fallon St., Suite C, Bozeman, MT 59715, 406/522-2520, www.fs.fed.us/r1/gallatin/.

Two campgrounds flank Hyalite Reservoir in Gallatin National Forest.

© BECKY LOMAX

32 HOOD CREEK

🚶 🚴 🏊 🛶 🚐 ⛵ 🏕 🎿 ♿ 🚙 ⛺

Scenic rating: 9

in Hyalite Canyon in Gallatin National Forest

At 6,730 feet in elevation, Hood Creek Campground sits on Hyalite Reservoir's northeast shore in Gallatin National Forest, with views up the canyon to Hyalite Peak. The lake is a no-wake zone, best for canoes, kayaks, and small sailboats, which can be launched from some campsites, but you can launch motorboats at the Blackmore picnic area less than a mile away. For anglers, the lake harbors Yellowstone cutthroat trout, brook trout, and arctic grayling. Across the road from the campground, Mystic Lake Trail (#436) leads 5.5 miles up to the lake. The trail is open to hikers, mountain bikers, and motorbikes.

The quiet campsites at Hood Creek are prized for their location right on the reservoir shore with big views of Hyalite Peak. The close proximity of the picnic tables and the tent sites is rare now because of concern for water quality. The sites vary from spread out with more privacy (sites 12–18) to closer together. Sites 8 and 9 sit on a bluff overlooking the lake. Large conifers lend partial shade to some of the sites; other sit in the open with junipers, lupines, and sage. The dirt campground road is potholed, rutted, and rough in places. This older campground is scheduled for reconstruction, which could alter the location of some of the campsites; call the ranger station to check on its status.

Campsites, facilities: The campground has 18 RV or tent campsites that can accommodate RVs up to 50 feet long. Facilities include picnic tables, fire rings with grills, pit toilets, drinking water, bear boxes, garbage service, firewood for sale, and a campground host. Leashed pets are permitted. A wheelchair-accessible toilet and two campsites are available.

Reservations, fees: Reservations are accepted (877/444-6777, www.recreation.gov). Campsites cost $13. An extra vehicle costs $8. Cash or check. Open mid-May–late September.

Directions: From downtown Bozeman, drive west on Highway 191 to Cottonwood Road. Turn south and drive 5.5 miles. Turn east onto South 19th Avenue and go one mile. Turn south onto Hyalite Canyon Road, which turns into Forest Road 62. Drive 10.5 miles to the campground entrance on the right. (You'll cross over Hyalite Dam.)

GPS Coordinates: N 45° 29.194' W 110° 58.272'

Contact: Gallatin National Forest, Bozeman Ranger District, 3710 Fallon St., Suite C, Bozeman, MT 59715, 406/522-2520, www.fs.fed.us/r1/gallatin/.

33 CHISHOLM

Scenic rating: 9

in Hyalite Canyon in Gallatin National Forest

Chisholm Campground, elevation 6,740 feet, sits on the west side of Hyalite Reservoir. But contrary to Hood Creek waterfront campsites, this campground offers only peek-a-boo water views through the trees and trails to the reservoir. However, its location lends easy access to several trails, including wheelchair-accessible trails. The paved 0.5-mile Palisades Falls trail, littered with 50-million-year-old basalt from volcanoes, departs one mile from the

campground and leads to the 80-foot waterfall. Trail #434 leads 5.5 miles to Emerald and Heather Lakes, and #427 saunters past 11 waterfalls en route to Hyalite Lake and the 10,299-foot summit of Hyalite Peak. You can launch boats at the Blackmore picnic area about 1.5 miles away. The lake, which harbors Yellowstone cutthroat trout and arctic grayling, is a no-wake zone. The East and West Forks of Hyalite Creek have fishing restrictions.

The campground has one loop with all back-in parking spurs. Sites are spread out for privacy; some have a thick forest of pines and firs between them, but others are more open, with neighboring campers in view. Most of the campsites sit under heavy shade or filtered sunlight. A creek runs along the northwest side of the campground, with three sites along it. Besides the creek, you'll hear only songbirds in the morning here.

Campsites, facilities: The campground has 10 RV or tent campsites that can accommodate RVs up to 60 feet long. Facilities include picnic tables, fire rings with grills, vault toilets, drinking water, bear boxes, garbage service, firewood for sale, and a campground host. Leashed pets are permitted. A wheelchair-accessible toilet is available.

Reservations, fees: Reservations are accepted (877/444-6777, www.recreation.gov). Campsites cost $13. An extra vehicle costs $8. Cash or check. Open mid-May–late September.

Directions: From downtown Bozeman, drive west on Highway 191 to Cottonwood Road. Turn south and drive 5.5 miles. Turn east onto South 19th Avenue and go one mile. Turn south onto Hyalite Canyon Road, which turns into Forest Road 62. Drive 11.7 miles to the campground entrance on the right. (You'll cross over Hyalite Dam.)

GPS Coordinates: N 45° 28.471' W 110° 57.236'

Contact: Gallatin National Forest, Bozeman Ranger District, 3710 Fallon St., Suite C, Bozeman, MT 59715, 406/522-2520, www.fs.fed.us/r1/gallatin/.

34 PARADISE VALLEY KOA

Scenic rating: 8

south of Livingston on the Yellowstone River

At 4,900 feet in elevation in the Paradise Valley, the KOA sits on the east bank of the Yellowstone River at the base of the Absaroka Mountains. The Yellowstone River, a blue-ribbon trout stream, is favored by anglers, who fish from drift boats and rafts in addition to wading. The river is also good for canoes here. A wheelchair-accessible 1.5-mile trail to Pine Creek Falls departs less than three miles from the campground, and the local roads off the highway work for bicycle touring. The campground is less than an hour's drive from Yellowstone National Park.

The campground is grassy, partly shaded by cottonwoods, and has 500 feet of river frontage. Those sites in the open sunny areas have views of the rugged Absaroka Mountains. Located on the opposite side of the river from the highway, the campground is quiet. As at most KOAs, the campsites are close together, with both back-in and pull-through parking pads.

Campsites, facilities: The campground has 52 RV campsites with a maximum length pull-through of 95 feet. Hookups include water, sewer, and electricity up to 50 amps. The campground also has 27 tent campsites, some with electricity. Facilities include picnic tables, fire rings, flush toilets, showers, an indoor swimming pool, a coin-operated launderette, drinking water, a playground, a swimming pool, a dog walk, wireless Internet, a modem dataport, a camp store, firewood and propane for sale, and bicycle rentals. Leashed pets are permitted.

Reservations, fees: Reservations are accepted (800/562-2805, www.koa.com). Hookups cost $35–40. Tent sites cost $25–30. Rates cover two adults. Extra campers cost $4 for adults and $3 for children 12–17 years old. Kids under 12 years old stay free. A 7 percent Montana bed tax will be added on. Open May–mid-October.

Directions: From Livingston, drive 10 miles south on Highway 89 toward Yellowstone Park

to around milepost 42.8. Turn east on Pine Creek Road and drive 1.25 miles across the river to the campground. Turn left at the entrance. GPS Coordinates: N 45° 30.718' W 110° 34.731'

Contact: Livingston/Paradise Valley KOA, 163 Pine Creek Rd., Livingston, MT 59047, 406/222-0992, www.koa.com.

35 MALLARD'S REST

Scenic rating: 6

south of Livingston on the Yellowstone River

At 4,701 feet in elevation south of Livingston, Mallard's Rest is a state-run fishing access on the Yellowstone River in Paradise Valley. A cement boat ramp with trailer parking is available for launching rafts, drift boats, canoes, and kayaks, and the river here is a blue-ribbon trout fishery. Located between Loch Leven and Pine Creek fishing access sites, Mallard's Rest is one of nine fishing access sites with boat ramps in the 56 river miles of the Yellowstone River between Livingston and Gardiner.

The dry, primitive campground sits on a tall grass and juniper bar on the river. Willow brush flanks some of the riverbanks, and a handful of big willow trees offer partial shade to only a couple of campsites. All of the campsites are open, with big views across the river of the Absaroka Mountains to the east. The sunny campground is green in early summer, but the grass turns gold by the end of July, and the dirt campground kicks up with dust. Although the highway sits on the bluff above the campground, you can still hear passing vehicles.

Campsites, facilities: The campground has 12 RV or tent campsites that can accommodate RVs up to 30 feet. Trailers are not recommended on the access road. Facilities include picnic tables, fire rings with grills, drinking water, and vault toilets. Leashed pets are permitted. A wheelchair-accessible toilet is available.

Reservations, fees: Reservations are not

accepted. Campsites cost $7 with a Montana fishing license and $12 without a Montana fishing license. Cash or check. Open year-round.

Directions: From Livingston, drive south on Highway 89 for approximately nine miles to milepost 41.5. Turn east onto the 0.2-mile steep dirt road, which drops through a sharp hairpin down to the river level and the campground. GPS Coordinates: N 45° 28.975' W 110° 37.235'

Contact: Montana Fish, Wildlife, and Parks, Region 3, 1400 S. 19th Ave., Bozeman, MT 59718, 406/994-4042, http://fwp.mt.gov.

36 YELLOWSTONE'S EDGE RV PARK

Scenic rating: 6

south of Livingston on the Yellowstone River

At 4,900 feet in elevation, the Yellowstone's Edge RV Park sits on the west bank of the Yellowstone River south of Livingston in the Paradise Valley. From the campground, you can launch hand-carried canoes, kayaks, or rafts and fish for brown and rainbow trout from the river's bank. A state-run fishing access site with a boat ramp and a fishing guide service is five miles south at Emigrant. Scenic floats are also available on the river. Chico Hot Springs is seven miles south. The campground is less than a 45-minute drive from Yellowstone National Park.

The campground sits on a sunny, flat bar with 3,000 feet of river frontage. More than one-third of the campsites line up along the river, but all sites have views of the surrounding Gallatin and Absaroka Mountains. Due to the proximity of the highway, vehicle noise is prevalent, but the highway is not a thoroughfare for trucking. The campground has evening campfires for socializing. Both back-in and pull-through sites—some with concrete patios—line up very close together with mowed lawn in between.

Campsites, facilities: The campground has 80 RV campsites that can accommodate RVs up to 90 feet long. Hookups are available for sewer, water, and electricity up to 50 amps. Facilities include picnic tables, flush toilets, showers, garbage service, a convenience store, wireless Internet, a coin-operated launderette,

© BECKY LOMAX

Chico Hot Springs in the Paradise Valley is open to the public for day visits.

a game room, horseshoe pits, and a dog walk. Leashed pets are permitted. A wheelchair-accessible toilet and shower are available.

Reservations, fees: Reservations are recommended. Campsites cost $42–47. Rates are based on two people. Additional adults cost $4.50; additional children ages 4–17 cost $2.50. A 7 percent Montana bed tax will be added on. Weekly and monthly rates are also available. Cash, check, or credit card. Open May–mid-October.

Directions: On Highway 89 between Livingston and Yellowstone National Park, find the campground on the east side of the road at milepost 35. It is 18 miles south of Livingston and 35 miles north of the park.

GPS Coordinates: N 45° 24.998' W 110° 41.077'

Contact: Yellowstone's Edge RV Park, 3502 Hwy. 89 S., Livingston, MT 59047, 406/333-4036 or 800/865-7322, www.mtrv.com.

37 CANYON

Scenic rating: 7

in Yankee Jim Canyon in Gallatin National Forest

At 5,350 feet in elevation in Gallatin National Forest, Canyon Campground nestles in Yankee Jim Canyon below Dome Mountain, about 20 minutes from the northwest entrance to Yellowstone National Park. The campground sits across the road from the Yellowstone River, which drops about 25 feet per mile in the five miles of Class III white water through the canyon. You can put in rafts and kayaks at Joe Brown Creek and take out at Carbella on either side of the campground. Due to the campground's ease of access adjacent to the highway, it works for those cycling the Paradise Valley to Yellowstone National Park. The canyon is also home to bighorn sheep.

Sitting at the base of a massive talus slope, the campground is a cluster of open junipers, Douglas firs, and giant granitic boulders, some bigger than vehicles. Between the trees and boulders, some of the arid campsites are partly shaded; others are sunny. With the highway running adjacent to the campground, you can hear passing vehicles, but the road is not a major trucking route. Sites 3, 4, and 6 tuck back in mini-canyons in the boulders and trees, with minimal views of the road. Of the campground's two loops, the right one features more open sites; the left one has more private sites that offer better protection when winds howl through the canyon. Watch for rattlesnakes.

Campsites, facilities: The campground has 18 RV or tent campsites that can accommodate RVs up to 50 feet, but the Forest Service discourages vehicles over 48 feet long due to the narrow road squeezing through large boulders. Facilities include picnic tables, fire rings with grills, vault toilets, and bear boxes. Pack out your trash. Leashed pets are permitted. Wheelchair-accessible toilets and tables are available.

Reservations, fees: Reservations are not accepted. Campsites cost $7. An extra vehicle costs $3. Cash or check. Open year-round.

Directions: From Livingston, travel south on Highway 89 to milepost 14.9. Turn north off the highway into the campground immediately after entering Gallatin National Forest. You can also locate the campground about 15 minutes northwest of Gardiner.

GPS Coordinates: N 45° 28.975' W 110° 37.235'

Contact: Gallatin National Forest, Gardiner Ranger District, P.O. Box 5, Hwy. 89 S., MT 59030, 406/848-7375, www.fs.fed.us/r1/gallatin/.

38 BOULDER FORKS

Scenic rating: 6

south of Big Timber on the Boulder River

At 4,780 feet in elevation south of Big Timber, Boulder Forks is a state-run fishing access on the Upper Boulder River at the confluence of the west, main, and east forks. The Boulder is a tributary of the Yellowstone River, drawing its water from the high reaches of the Absaroka-Beartooth Wilderness to the south—Montana's tallest peaks. You can launch rafts and kayaks (boats you can carry) from the primitive ramp to float 4.5 miles north to the highway bridge in Class III white water. The blue-ribbon trout stream houses brown trout and rainbow trout, plus mountain whitefish, and you can wade-fish here. Littered periodically with boulders, the river is aptly named.

On the perimeter of a sunny pasture with big views of the Absaroka Mountains, the campground spreads the campsites out along the river for privacy. Mature cottonwood trees line the river, but unfortunately, they produce little shade for the south-facing campground. The grass, weed, and rocky parking pads may pose a challenge to those trying to level an RV. Large spaces for tents are available, but they, too, are a little bumpy. Two sites are paired near each other on the loop, and two more are at the end of a spur jeep trail. Scout the space before you drive in with a large rig. The only sounds you'll hear are the river, the songbirds, and the wind. This is a popular fishing access; the sites frequently fill.

Campsites, facilities: The campground has four primitive RV or tent campsites that can accommodate midsized RVs. Facilities include rock fire rings and a vault toilet. Leashed pets are permitted. The toilet is wheelchair-accessible.

Reservations, fees: Reservations are not accepted. Camping is free. Open year-round.

Directions: From Big Timber, drive south on McLeod Street, which turns into Highway 298 for 16 miles to just past McLeod. At milepost 16.4, turn east onto the single-lane gravel road and drive over the cattle grate. Continue on the road for 0.3 mile.

GPS Coordinates: N 45° 39.445' W 110° 6.566'

Contact: Montana Fish, Wildlife, and Parks, Region 5, 2300 Lake Elmo Dr., Billings, MT 59105, 406/247-2940, http://fwp.mt.gov.

39 FALLS CREEK

Scenic rating: 7

on the Boulder River in Gallatin National Forest

At 5,350 feet in elevation in Gallatin National Forest, Falls Creek sits on the Boulder River's west bank, surrounded by 10,000-foot-high peaks of the Absaroka Mountains. It is 4.9 miles south of Natural Bridge Falls, an interpretive site with a wheelchair-accessible trail where the river flows over a 100-foot drop in high water—in low water, it disappears into an underground channel. The 5.5-mile Green Mountain Trail

© BECKY LOMAX

Natural Bridge Falls on the Boulder River

(#14), a route with less elevation gain than many of the other trails in the area, also departs from the falls. Summer homes and small ranches populate some of the private land around the campground. The fast plummet of the Boulder River slows here to riffles alternating with deep pools, coughing up 20-inch trout to expert fly-fishers. Kayakers and rafters tackle some of the river's Class II–III boulder-strewn white water above Natural Bridge through early summer.

Parking for the campground is in two common four-vehicle lots, with spur trails leading 20–50 feet to the campsites. Each campsite has a large, flat tent space along the creek with aspens, pines, and Douglas firs lending partial shade to some of the sites. The sites are spread out and some tuck under trees for privacy, but you can see the neighboring campsites. The sunnier campsites also have views of the canyon and forest. The nearby road is busy in midsummer but quiets at night, so you only hear the river.

Campsites, facilities: The campground has eight tent campsites and no turnaround for RVs. Facilities include picnic tables, fire rings with grills, pit toilets, drinking water, and bear boxes. Pack out your trash. Leashed pets are permitted. A wheelchair-accessible toilet is available.

Reservations, fees: Reservations are not accepted. Camping is free. Open year-round, but drinking water is available only Memorial Day–Labor Day.

Directions: From Big Timber, travel south on Highway 298 for 25.6 miles to the Gallatin National Forest boundary, where the road (Forest Road 6639) turns to bumpy dirt and gravel. (Locals call it the Boulder Road.) Drive to milepost 5.1 past the forest boundary and turn left onto the narrow campground road. GPS Coordinates: N 45° 29.424' W 110° 13.142'

Contact: Gallatin National Forest, Big Timber Ranger District, P.O. Box 1130, Hwy. 10 E., Big Timber, MT 59011, 406/932-5155, www.fs.fed.us/r1/gallatin/.

40 BIG BEAVER

Scenic rating: 7

on the Boulder River in Gallatin National Forest

At 5,500 feet in elevation in Gallatin National Forest, Big Beaver Campground sits on the east bank of the Boulder River surrounded by the 10,000-foot-high peaks of the West and East Boulder Plateaus in the Absaroka Mountains. The Absaroka-Beartooth Wilderness is across the river. One mile to the north, the Graham Creek Trail grinds up countless switchbacks to gain 4,500 feet in elevation and reach the flanks of Chrome Mountain in 11.8 miles. The Boulder River in this stretch services the expert trout angler who can wade-fish as well as Class II–III white-water rafters and kayakers through early summer. Those floating the rocky river put in at Chippy Park, about two miles upstream.

The campground squeezes between the road and the river, with flat tent spaces 10 feet from the water. The partly shaded sites, tucked under Douglas firs, are lined up both left and right of the entrance, with views of the canyon walls and talus slopes to the east, plus the road. This stretch of the river and road is quite populated, despite the road's deplorable condition, as a church camp borders the campground. The road kicks up dust all day long with traffic in midsummer, but quiets at night to where you'll just hear the sound of the river.

Campsites, facilities: The campground has five RV or tent campsites. The largest parking pad can accommodate an RV up to 42 feet, but the Forest Service warns the road is not suitable for vehicles longer than 32 feet. Facilities include picnic tables, fire rings with grills, and a pit toilet. Pack out your trash. Leashed pets are permitted. A wheelchair-accessible toilet is available.

Reservations, fees: Reservations are not accepted. Camping is free. Open year-round.

Directions: From Big Timber, travel south on Highway 298 for 25.6 miles to the Gallatin National Forest boundary, where the road (Forest Road 6639) turns to bumpy dirt and gravel that alternates between rocky washboards and large potholes. (Locals call it the Boulder Road.) Drive to milepost 7.3 past the forest boundary, crossing to the east side of the river, and turn right into the campground.
GPS Coordinates: N 45° 27.863' W 110° 11.896'

Contact: Gallatin National Forest, Big Timber Ranger District, P.O. Box 1130, Hwy. 10 E., Big Timber, MT 59011, 406/932-5155, www.fs.fed.us/r1/gallatin/.

41 BOULDER RIVER PRIMITIVE

Scenic rating: 8

on the Boulder River in Gallatin National Forest

Along the Boulder River in Gallatin National Forest, dispersed primitive campsites are sprinkled along the entire glaciated canyon length. These campsites, prized for their seclusion and privacy, sit between 5,350 and 6,700 feet in elevation on both the east and west banks of the river, flanked by the Absaroka Mountains and the Absaroka-Beartooth Wilderness. The river—a blue-ribbon trout stream—works best for wade fishing, but its boulders require care. From Fourmile to Boulder Falls, rafters and kayakers navigate the river's technical Class II–IV rapids. The floating season usually ends after early summer when water levels drop too low and expose too many boulders. Long hiking trails—requiring 3,000 feet or more of ascent—access the high summits in the wilderness. Mountain bikers and ATV riders tour the Boulder Road.

Most of the dispersed primitive campsites along the Boulder River sit right on the river. You'll find sites shaded under Douglas firs, in

filtered sunlight in aspens, and in full sun in grassy fields with big open views of the mountains. Find most of the sites by a small sign with a tent icon; a few are unmarked. Scout their dirt roads and turnaround space before you drive in blind. Etiquette dictates one site per party. Respect private property along the river.

Campsites, facilities: More than 30 dispersed, primitive RV or tent campsites sit along the Boulder River. The Forest Service recommends only RVs up to 32 feet in length on the Boulder Road. Facilities include rock fire rings. Use pre-existing fire rings rather than constructing new ones. Boil or purify river water before drinking. Follow Leave No Trace principles for human waste. Pack out your trash. Leashed pets are permitted.

Reservations, fees: Reservations are not accepted. Camping is free. Open year-round.

Directions: From Big Timber, travel south on Highway 298 for 25.6 miles to the Gallatin National Forest boundary, where the road (Forest Road 6639) turns to bumpy dirt and gravel that alternates between rocky washboards and large potholes. (Locals call it the Boulder Road.) After Falls Creek Campground at 5.1 miles past the forest boundary, it's 20 miles farther to the end of the road at Box Canyon.
GPS Coordinates: N 45° 28.691' W 110° 12.469' (first primitive site)

Contact: Gallatin National Forest, Big Timber Ranger District, P.O. Box 1130, Hwy. 10 E., Big Timber, MT 59011, 406/932-5155, www.fs.fed.us/r1/gallatin/.

42 ASPEN

Scenic rating: 7

on the Boulder River in Gallatin National Forest

At 5,500 feet in elevation in Gallatin National Forest, Aspen Campground sits on the Boulder River's east bank, tucked under the

10,000-foot-high summits of the Absaroka Mountains and the Absaroka-Beartooth Wilderness across the river. About 1.5 miles north, Graham Creek Trail grunts up 4,500 feet in elevation through innumerable switchbacks for 11.8 miles to Chrome Mountain. The boney Boulder River in this stretch services both the expert trout angler who can wade-fish as well as white-water rafters and kayakers with its Class II–III froth. Those floating the river (good only through early summer) put in at Chippy Park about 1.5 miles upstream. The campground is adjacent to an elk wintering range.

With its campsites divided into two loops, the campground sits in a thick grove of aspens and willows blooming with wild roses and bee balm. Unlike the other Boulder campgrounds, these campsites do not line up along the river. Site 7 is the only one adjacent to the river, and it has a view of the road. The partly sunny, private sites hear the sound of the river and some passing traffic, but the undergrowth blocks the view of the road for most. Short trails cut through the brush to the river. Several campsites grab views of the surrounding mountains.

Campsites, facilities: The campground has eight RV or tent campsites. The largest parking pad can accommodate RVs up to 42 feet. Facilities include picnic tables, fire rings with grills, drinking water, bear boxes, and both pit and vault toilets. Pack out your trash. Leashed pets are permitted. A wheelchair-accessible toilet is available.

Reservations, fees: Reservations are not accepted. Camping costs $5. Cash or check. Open year-round, although drinking water is available only Memorial Day–Labor Day.

Directions: From Big Timber, travel south on Highway 298 for 25.6 miles to the Gallatin National Forest boundary, where the road (Forest Road 6639) turns to bumpy dirt and gravel that alternates between rocky washboards and large potholes. (Locals call it the Boulder Road.) Drive to milepost 8 past the forest boundary, crossing to the east side of the river, and turn right down the skinny road into the campground.

GPS Coordinates: N 45° 27.389' W 110° 11.847'

Contact: Gallatin National Forest, Big Timber Ranger District, P.O. Box 1130, Hwy. 10 E., Big Timber, MT 59011, 406/932-5155, www.fs.fed.us/r1/gallatin/.

43 CHIPPY PARK

Scenic rating: 7

on the Boulder River in Gallatin National Forest

At 5,600 feet in elevation in Gallatin National Forest, Chippy Park Campground sits on the Boulder River's east bank, tucked under the 10,000-foot-high summits of the Absaroka Mountains. The Absaroka-Beartooth Wilderness flanks both sides of the river. About 2.5 miles south, Speculator Creek Trail climbs 4,500 feet in elevation for 7.3 miles to the West Boulder Plateau north of Boulder Mountain. Chippy Park serves as a starting point for rafters and kayakers to descend the river's Class II–III white water to Boulder Falls. The river from Speculator Creek to Chippy Park contains Class IV rapids. Both boulder-strewn sections are floatable only through early summer. The blue-ribbon trout stream is best fished by wading.

A forest of aspens and Douglas firs provides partial shade for the campground, which sits in tall grass. The campsites, which all (except site 5) line up along the riverbank, offer some sunny locations with views of the surrounding mountains. Back-in sites that can accommodate RVs sit to the left; two walk-in tent sites are to the right. Site 3 is very spacious, and site 4 garners more privacy at the end of the loop.

Campsites, facilities: The campground has seven RV or tent campsites. The largest parking pad can accommodate RVs up to 42 feet, but the Forest Service advises that only vehicles under 32 feet drive the access road. Facilities include picnic tables, fire rings with grills, drinking water, bear boxes, and both pit and vault toilets. Pack out your trash. Leashed pets are permitted. A wheelchair-accessible toilet and two campsites are available.

Reservations, fees: Reservations are not accepted. Camping costs $5. Cash or check. Open year-round, although drinking water is available only Memorial Day–Labor Day.

Directions: From Big Timber, travel south on Highway 298 for 25.6 miles to the Gallatin National Forest boundary, where the road (Forest Road 6639) turns to bumpy dirt and gravel that alternates between rocky washboards and large potholes. (Locals call it the Boulder Road.) Drive to milepost 9.5 past the forest boundary, crossing to the east side of the river, climbing a steep hill, and dropping to the campground road on the right. GPS Coordinates: N 45° 26.215' W 110° 11.332'

Contact: Gallatin National Forest, Big Timber Ranger District, P.O. Box 1130, Hwy. 10 E., Big Timber, MT 59011, 406/932-5155, www.fs.fed.us/r1/gallatin/.

44 HELLS CANYON

Scenic rating: 7

on the Boulder River in Gallatin National Forest

At 6,100 feet in elevation in Gallatin National Forest, Hells Canyon Campground sits on the Boulder River's west side, flanked by the Absaroka-Beartooth Wilderness and 10,000-foot-high pinnacles of The Needles to the west. Due to the constriction of the forested slopes, you won't see the summits of the Absaroka Mountains unless you slog up 4,500 feet in elevation. Trailheads are located about one mile to the north and south of the

campground. The Hawley Creek Trail climbs six miles to Breakneck Plateau, and the Fourmile Creek Trail ascends 7.8 miles to Silver Lake. The mountain slopes constrict here to form Hells Canyon, running with four miles of Class III–IV rapids between Fourmile to the south and Speculator Creek to the north, floatable only in early summer. The river, a blue-ribbon trout stream, is best fished by wading. Be prepared for tedious, slow-driving miles on the ragged Boulder Road.

The campground squeezes between the Boulder Road and the river. Most of the campground sits under the thick shade of conifers, with some campsites having snippets of views of the surrounding mountains. One large campsite to the left is sunny. Due to the rough road, traffic drops off considerably in this upper section of the river, filling the campground with the sound of the river instead. Several campsites overlook the river, with large flat tent spaces.

Campsites, facilities: The campground has 11 RV or tent campsites. The largest parking pad can accommodate vehicles up to 48 feet, but the Forest Service recommends that RVs on the campground road be no longer than 20 feet. Facilities include picnic tables, fire rings with grills, bear boxes, and pit toilets. Pack out your trash. Leashed pets are permitted.

Reservations, fees: Reservations are not accepted. Camping is free. Open year-round.

Directions: From Big Timber, travel south on Highway 298 for 25.6 miles to the Gallatin National Forest boundary, where the road (Forest Road 6639) turns to bumpy dirt and gravel that alternates between rocky washboards and large potholes. (Locals call it the Boulder Road.) Drive to milepost 15.5 past the forest boundary, crossing the river twice, and turn left into the campground. GPS Coordinates: N 45° 22.304' W 110° 12.595'

Contact: Gallatin National Forest, Big Timber Ranger District, P.O. Box 1130, Hwy. 10 E., Big Timber, MT 59011, 406/932-5155, www.fs.fed.us/r1/gallatin/.

45 HICKS PARK

🏃🚴🏊🛶♿🚙⛺

Scenic rating: 8

on the Boulder River in Gallatin National
Forest

At an elevation of 6,400 feet in Gallatin
National Forest, Hicks Park Campground
sits on the Boulder River's east side, flanked
by the Absaroka-Beartooth Wilderness and
10,000-foot-high pinnacles of Carbonate
Mountain and Hicks Peak. The blue-ribbon
trout stream is best when wade fishing. Requiring climbs of over 3,000 feet in elevation
in less than eight miles, Upsidedown Creek
Trail departs from the campground to switch-
back up to Horseshoe Lake, and Bridge Creek
Trail climbs to Bridge Lake. Be prepared for
long, slow-driving miles on the rough Boulder
Road. Hicks Park, the last designated campground, makes a base camp for exploring the
road's terminus at Box Canyon and continuing
farther on the boulder-filled, curvy trail via
mountain bike or ATV to the mining ghost
town of Independence. The road ends on Independence Peak, with a short trail to Blue
Lake set in an alpine cirque.

Grassy campsites line up along the river, with
a loose forest of conifers lending partial shade.
The open forest also permits views of the surrounding mountain slopes. The campsites are
spread out for privacy, but you can see one or
two neighboring campers through the trees.
With fewer people traveling the upper Boulder
Road, the river is the pervasive sound.

Campsites, facilities: The campground has
16 RV or tent campsites. The largest parking
pad can accommodate vehicles up to 51 feet,
but the Forest Service recommends that RVs
driving Boulder Road be no longer than 32
feet. Facilities include picnic tables, fire rings
with grills, bear boxes, drinking water, and pit
and vault toilets. Pack out your trash. Leashed
pets are permitted. A wheelchair-accessible
toilet is available.

Reservations, fees: Reservations are not
accepted. Campsites cost $5. Cash or check.
Open year-round, but drinking water is available only Memorial Day–Labor Day.

Directions: From Big Timber, travel south on
Highway 298 for 25.6 miles to the Gallatin
National Forest boundary, where the road
(Forest Road 6639) turns to bumpy dirt and
gravel that alternates between rocky washboards and large potholes. (Locals call it the
Boulder Road.) Drive to milepost 21 past the
forest boundary, crossing the river three times,
and turn right into the campground.
GPS Coordinates: N 45° 18.014' W 110°
14.431'

Contact: Gallatin National Forest, Big Timber
Ranger District, P.O. Box 1130, Hwy. 10 E.,
Big Timber, MT 59011, 406/932-5155, www.
fs.fed.us/r1/gallatin/.

46 BIG TIMBER KOA

🚴🏊🛶🚙🏕♿🚐⛺

Scenic rating: 4

east of Big Timber

Big Timber KOA is convenient for those road-
tripping along I-90. At 3,948 feet in elevation,
it's about a five-minute drive from Greycliff
Prairie Dog Town State Park (nonresidents
$5 per vehicle, Montana residents free), an in-
terpretive site where you can watch the black-
tailed prairie dogs skitter about their natural
habitat. The 9-hole Overland Golf Course also
is five minutes away. Adjacent to the campground, Big Timber Waterslide Park (KOA
campers can get a 20 percent discount) has an
outdoor pool and big slides for older kids and
adults as well as small slides for children. The
Yellowstone River parallels the freeway's north
side, offering fishing and floating.

The campground sits right next to the
freeway. You'll hear trucking noise at night.
The grassy campground offers partly shaded
campsites under large trees or sunny campsites tucked close to each other in parking-lot
fashion on gravel parking pads connected by a

gravel road. The campground swimming pool is open May 30–early September. The private hot tub and sauna are available for an extra fee. For kids, the campground has a 68-foot-long jumping pillow, one of only six in the United States, and also rents banana boat cycles.

Campsites, facilities: The campground has 17 RV campsites that can accommodate big rigs up to 100 feet in length. Hookups include water, sewer, and electricity up to 50 amps. The campground also includes eight tent sites. Facilities include picnic tables, pedestal grills, flush toilets, showers, a coin-operated launderette, drinking water, a playground, a swimming pool, a hot tub, a game room, horseshoe pits, mini-golf, free wireless Internet, cable TV, a café, a camp store, firewood for sale, and a disposal station. Leashed pets are permitted.

Reservations, fees: Reservations are accepted. Hookups cost $20–44. Tent campsites cost $20–29. Rates are based on two people. Extra adults cost $5 each; extra children cost $2.50 each. Cash, check, or credit card. Open mid-May–early September.

Directions: From I-90 nine miles east of Big Timber, take Exit 377. Drive to the south side of the freeway to Frontage Road (Highway 10) and turn west for 0.25 mile. Turn right into the campground entrance.

GPS Coordinates: N 45° 46.432' W 109° 47.990'

Contact: Big Timber KOA, 693 Hwy. 10 E., Big Timber, MT 59011, 406/932-6569 or 800/562-5869, www.bigtimberkoa.com.

47 ITCH-KEP-PE PARK

Scenic rating: 5

south of Columbus on the Yellowstone River

Located at 3,350 feet in elevation, Itch-Kep-Pe Park—a city park—sits between the railroad tracks, downtown Columbus, and the Yellowstone River. You can walk the half mile to town for restaurants, shops, and bars—including the first bar to be licensed in Montana. With a boat ramp at the east end of the park, the Yellowstone River offers fishing and floating in drift boats, rafts, kayaks, and canoes. Floaters and anglers also launch on the Stillwater River south of Columbus to float back to the park. The river diverts south of the campground around a few islands, making good places to swim before the water level drops too low. Children can bicycle the park roads, and free wood is sometimes delivered to the campground from a local timber company. The campground, which is popular because of its price, is maintained by the city and patrolled regularly by the city police.

The campground road makes several loops under huge cottonwood trees that provide shade to cool the grassy campground. Although no campsites command water frontage, many sit within sight of the river, and the long shoreline allows plenty of space for campers to spread out to enjoy the water. Campsites are a mix of shade, partial shade, and sunny, depending on location. Some tuck back in between trees for privacy, but most of the campsites are open, with views of other campsites. You'll hear the river, railroad, and trucks on the highway at night. Some sites are pull-throughs, but most are back-ins on gravel spurs.

Campsites, facilities: The campground has 30 RV or tent campsites that can accommodate RVs up to 55 feet long. Facilities include picnic tables, fire rings, flush and pit toilets, drinking water, and a concrete boat ramp. Leashed pets are permitted.

Reservations, fees: Reservations are not accepted. Camping is free, but donations are appreciated. Open April–October.

Directions: From Columbus, drive south on Highway 78 for 0.5 mile to just north of the bridge over the Yellowstone River. Turn left to enter the campground.

GPS Coordinates: N 45° 37.735' W 109° 15.187'

Contact: City of Columbus, P.O. Box 549, Columbus, MT 59019, 406/322-5313.

48 SWINGING BRIDGE

Scenic rating: 5

south of Columbus on the Stillwater River

At 3,730 feet in elevation, Swinging Bridge is a state-run fishing access site on the east bank of the Stillwater River. The river divides here around islands, making places to swim, but in high water the Swinging Bridge Rapid and the Beartooth Drop—both at the campground—require caution. The Stillwater runs past the campground with Class II–III rapids. Boaters usually put-in farther upstream at Whitebird and float past Swinging Bridge Campground to Fireman's Point, two miles south of Columbus, or Itch-Kep-Pe Park, after the Stillwater pours into the Yellowstone River. As the water level drops throughout the summer, large rocky bars extend as beaches along the shore. The Stillwater contains brook, rainbow, and Yellowstone cutthroat trout.

The campground shows wear from overuse at some sites, three of which sit right on the river. Junipers, large cottonwoods, and willows lend partial shade to the campground, and several sites have room for small tents. The gravel campground road kicks up dust when vehicles drive through, but the area is quiet at night.

Campsites, facilities: The campground has four primitive RV or tent campsites that can accommodate small RVs. Facilities include rock fire rings, a vault toilet, and a ramp for hand-carried watercrafts. Boil or purify river water before use. Leashed pets are permitted. The toilet is wheelchair-accessible.

Reservations, fees: Reservations are not accepted. Camping is free. Open year-round.

Directions: From Columbus, drive 5.3 miles south on Highway 78. Turn west at milepost 40.6 onto the one-lane gravel road. The 0.7-mile road jogs right, then left through private property before reaching the campground. Be ready to back up if you meet oncoming vehicles. The road has only a couple of narrow turnouts.

GPS Coordinates: N 45° 35.125' W 109° 19.869'

Contact: Montana Fish, Wildlife, and Parks, Region 5, 2300 Lake Elmo Dr., Billings, MT 59105, 406/247-2940, http://fwp.mt.gov.

49 WHITEBIRD

Scenic rating: 5

south of Columbus on the Stillwater River

At 3,747 feet in elevation, Whitebird is a state-run fishing access site on the east bank of the Stillwater River. It curves through arid juniper hillsides. The lower Stillwater, flanked with farms and small ranches, runs past the campground with Class II–III rapids. Rafters, kayakers, and white-water canoeists usually put-in here to float past Swinging Bridge Campground to Fireman's Point, two miles south of Columbus, or to Itch-Kep-Pe Park, after the Stillwater pours into the Yellowstone River. As the water level drops throughout the summer, large rocky bars extend as beaches along the shore. The Stillwater contains brook, rainbow, and Yellowstone cutthroat trout. The site offers archery and shotgun hunting in season.

None of the campsites have river frontage. The campground tucks its back-in campsites under tall cottonwoods, with a mix of willows providing partial shade. The location is still close enough to the highway to hear a little truck traffic at night. The grassy campground—being overgrown by brush, showing abuse, and missing a few picnic tables—is scheduled for improvements. Call to check on its status.

Campsites, facilities: The campground has seven primitive RV or tent campsites that can accommodate small RVs. Facilities include picnic tables, fire rings with grills, a vault toilet, and a ramp for hand-carried watercrafts. Boil or purify river water before use. Leashed pets are permitted. The toilet is wheelchair-accessible.

Reservations, fees: Reservations are not accepted. In summer 2009, camping was free, but with planned improvements, campsites will cost $7 with a Montana fishing license and $12 without a Montana fishing license. Cash or check. Open year-round.

Directions: From Columbus, drive about seven miles south on Highway 78. Turn west at milepost 39.8 onto the gravel Whitebird Creek Road, crossing the creek on a one-lane bridge. Drive 0.5 mile to the campground entrance. GPS Coordinates: N 45° 34.504' W 109° 20.192'

Contact: Montana Fish, Wildlife, and Parks, Region 5, 2300 Lake Elmo Dr., Billings, MT 59105, 406/247-2940, http://fwp.mt.gov.

50 WOODBINE

Scenic rating: 7

on the Stillwater River in Custer National Forest

At an elevation of 5,300 feet in Custer National Forest, Woodbine Campground is the only national forest campground on the Stillwater River. Sitting at the north edge of the Absaroka-Beartooth Wilderness in a primitive forest zone, the campground provides access to very remote country that few people visit. Cathedral Peak and the Granite Range make up the Absaroka and Beartooth peaks south of the campground. The 0.75-mile Woodbine Falls Trail (#93) departs from the campground for viewing the waterfall. While the 25-mile-long Stillwater Trail (#29) is mostly used by horses (hitching rails and loading ramps are at the trailhead) and some backpackers in its entirety, day hikers climb 3.1 miles to the marshy Sioux Charley Lake. Small Yellowstone cutthroat trout inhabit Woodbine Creek, and the Stillwater River harbors small rainbow and brook trout.

The two loops of the campground flank a meadow and forest hillside where you have a choice of sunny or partly shaded sites. The walk-in tent sites line up along Woodbine Creek, and many of the campsites command views of the Absaroka Mountains. Despite the miles of dirt road driving, the campground road and parking aprons are paved. The campground is also extremely quiet, with only the natural sounds of the wind or the creek.

Campsites, facilities: The campground has 34 RV or tent campsites that can accommodate trailers up to 32 feet. Another 10 walk-in tent campsites are also available. Facilities include picnic tables, fire rings with grills, vault toilets, drinking water, bear boxes, garbage service, and campground hosts. Leashed pets are permitted. A wheelchair-accessible toilet is available.

Reservations, fees: Reservations are not accepted. Campsites cost $20. An extra vehicle costs $10. Cash or check. Open late May–mid-September.

Directions: From Absarokee, drive west on County Road 420 (locals call it the Stillwater River Road) for 20.4 miles and left for one mile as the road swings south to Nye. The road is paved to Nye but potholed. Turn right onto County Road 419 and drive 7.8 miles southwest on the gravel road. The road becomes Forest Road 4200 at the boundary to the national forest. At the signed junction, turn east for 0.2 mile to reach the campground entrance. GPS Coordinates: N 45° 21.187' W 109° 53.858'

Contact: Custer National Forest, Beartooth Ranger District, 6811 Hwy. 212 S., Red Lodge, MT 406/446-2103, www.fs.fed.us/r1/custer/.

51 PINE GROVE

Scenic rating: 8

on the West Rosebud River in Custer National Forest

Located at 5,720 feet in elevation in Custer National Forest, Pine Grove is one of two Forest Service campgrounds in the West Rosebud

Creek valley on the northeast corner of the Absaroka-Beartooth Wilderness. The river attracts expert kayakers for its three miles of Class III–V white water from Emerald Lake to the campground. The river harbors brook, brown, rainbow, and Yellowstone cutthroat trout as well as mountain whitefish. Five miles south at the road's terminus at the power plant, trails depart for Mystic Lake (3.1 miles) and Island Lake (5 miles). For huge views, you can also climb scads of switchbacks up to the edge of Froze to Death Plateau (6.6 miles), on the flanks of the 11,765-foot Froze to Death Mountain. These three hikes are in the wilderness area.

Sitting at the base of a long, deep, glacier-carved valley, the quiet campground lies between West Rosebud Road and the river in a forested setting. Sites are partly shaded, but some garner outstanding views of the surrounding Beartooth Mountains. The campground was closed during 2009 due to storm damage. Call to check on its status.

Campsites, facilities: The campground has 27 RV or tent campsites that can accommodate RVs up to 28 feet. Another 19 campsites are for tents only. Facilities include picnic tables, fire rings with grills, vault toilets, drinking water, bear boxes, garbage service, and campground hosts. Leashed pets are permitted. A wheelchair-accessible toilet is available.

Reservations, fees: Reservations are not accepted. Campsites cost $9. Extra vehicles cost $5. Cash or check. Open late May–early September.

Directions: From Highway 78 south of Absarokee, take Highway 419 southwest to Fishtail. At a T intersection 0.5 mile south of Fishtail, turn left onto West Rosebud Road (Highway 425) for 6.5 miles to where the road turns to bumpy washboard and potholed gravel and continue 8.8 miles farther to the campground, which sits about 1.2 miles south of the Custer National Forest boundary. The campground has four entrances on the east side of the road, the first leading to the tent campsites and the last connecting with sites best for RVs.

GPS Coordinates: N 45° 16.718' W 109° 38.403'

Contact: Custer National Forest, Beartooth Ranger District, 6811 Hwy. 212 S., Red Lodge, MT 406/446-2103, www.fs.fed.us/r1/custer/.

52 EMERALD LAKE

Scenic rating: 9

on West Rosebud River in Custer National Forest

At 6,180 feet in elevation in Custer National Forest, Emerald Lake nestles in West Rosebud Creek valley below the immense Beartooth Mountains. Despite its name, the campground does not flank the lake's shore, but instead parallels the West Rosebud River. From Emerald Lake to Pine Grove Campground, the river attracts expert kayakers for its three miles of Class III–V white water. Flat-water paddlers and anglers also tour small Emerald Lake (no motors allowed), which you can also reach via a five-minute walk from the campground. The river harbors brook, brown, rainbow, and Yellowstone cutthroat trout as well as mountain whitefish. One mile south, the road terminates at the power plant, where trails depart into Absaroka-Beartooth Wilderness. Scenic hikes include Mystic Lake (3.1 miles), Island Lake (5 miles), and Froze to Death Plateau (6.6 miles), which are also accesses for rock climbing and mountaineering.

The quiet campground splits into two roads, both with gravel back-in parking. The left spur has no RV turnaround, but the right one does. Set on the edge of a heavily forested slope, the campsites vary between partly shaded to more open, garnering superb views of the snowy Beartooth Mountains in early summer.

Campsites, facilities: The campground has 19 RV or tent campsites that can accommodate RVs up to 40 feet, but the Forest Service recommends only trailers up to 30 feet. Another

12 campsites are for tents only. Facilities include picnic tables, fire rings with grills, vault toilets, drinking water, bear boxes, garbage service, and campground hosts. Leashed pets are permitted. A wheelchair-accessible toilet is available.

Reservations, fees: Reservations are not accepted. Campsites cost $9. Extra vehicles cost $5. Cash or check. Open late May–early September, but with good weather the Forest Service sometimes keeps the campground open later.

Directions: From Highway 78 south of Absarokee, take Highway 419 southwest to Fishtail. At a T intersection 0.5 mile south of Fishtail, turn left onto West Rosebud Road (Highway 425) for 6.5 miles to where the road turns to gravel and continue 13 miles farther, entering Custer National Forest about halfway, where the road turns to bumpy washboards and potholes. After passing Emerald Lake, turn east into the campground.

GPS Coordinates: N 45° 15.225' W 109° 41.936'

Contact: Custer National Forest, Beartooth Ranger District, 6811 Hwy. 212 S., Red Lodge, MT 406/446-2103, www.fs.fed.us/r1/custer/.

53 JIMMY JOE

Scenic rating: 9

on East Rosebud Creek in Custer National Forest

At 5,600 feet in elevation in Custer National Forest, Jimmy Joe Campground tucks into the northeast corner of the high Beartooth Mountains along East Rosebud Creek. Summer homes and small farms dot the prairie valley en route to the campground, which is flanked on both canyon walls by the Absaroka-Beartooth Wilderness. Anglers can wade-fish the stream for brown, rainbow, and Yellowstone cutthroat trout. Trailheads for hiking are located four miles farther south around East Rosebud Lake. Trail #17—the nearest one—ascends Phantom Creek up to Froze to Death Plateau, one of two access routes to climbing 12,799-foot Granite Peak, Montana's highest mountain, but you can day-hike 3.5 miles, gaining 3,900 feet to the saddle between Prairieview Mountain and Froze to Death Mountain.

Set at the bottom of the scooped-out glacier valley, the campground, which was renovated in 2008, commands big views of the surrounding Beartooth Mountains. A forest fire in 1995 swept through the area, which now blooms with cow parsnips, fireweed, and red paintbrush amid the new-growth lodgepole pines. A few surviving lodgepoles and cottonwoods partially shade a handful of the campsites, but full sun hits most of them. Eight of the campsites flank the river. Sites 8–11 cluster together, but others are more spread out. The wind and the river are the only sounds you'll hear at night. Hand pumps have been installed for drinking water, but were not functional yet in 2009.

Campsites, facilities: The campground has 12 RV or tent campsites that can accommodate trailers up to 32 feet. Facilities include picnic tables, fire rings with grills, and vault toilets. Pack out your trash. Leashed pets are permitted. A wheelchair-accessible toilet is available.

Reservations, fees: Reservations are not accepted. Camping is free. Open late May–early September.

Directions: From Highway 78 at Roscoe south of Absarokee, take East Rosebud Road south for 2.6 miles, where the rough pavement ends and the dusty, potholed, rutted dirt road begins. Go 1.2 miles farther and turn right, staying on East Rosebud Road for 6.5 miles to the campground entrance on the right. The campground is 10.3 miles south of Roscoe.

GPS Coordinates: N 45° 14.054' W 109° 36.149'

Contact: Custer National Forest, Beartooth Ranger District, 6811 Hwy. 212 S., Red Lodge, MT 406/446-2103, www.fs.fed.us/r1/custer/.

54 EAST ROSEBUD

🏕 🏊 🚐 ⚓ 🐕 ♿ 🚗 ⛰

Scenic rating: 10

south of East Rosebud Lake in Custer National
Forest

BEST (

At 6,400 feet in elevation in Custer National
Forest, East Rosebud Campground sits above
East Rosebud Lake in the Beartooth Mountains,
where rugged cliffs and scooped-out cirques dem-
onstrate the power of glaciers on the landscape.
Unfortunately, private property and summer
homes surround the lake, but the community
provides a primitive boat launch and parking
area (relock the gate after entering) for canoes,
kayaks, and rafts. The lake is stocked regularly
with rainbow trout. Two trails departing from
the campground enter the Absaroka-Beartooth
Wilderness. One climbs 5.9 steep miles to Sylvan
Lake at the timberline. The other tours the lake's
southeast rim on a more gentle 5.8-mile ascent to
Elk Lake, the first in a long string of backpacking
lakes along East Rosebud Creek.

The one campground loop—a narrow, steep,
rocky road—circles a hillside on the mixed fir
and pine forest fringe. Most of the back-in sites
tuck under trees for protection from the sun
and wind; the others sit in the sunny north-
facing meadows, with big views of the lake and
surrounding mountains. Buckwheat, bee balm,
and harebells bloom in the meadows. The quiet
campground packs its small sites close enough
that you'll see a neighboring campsite or two,
but those in the trees are more private.

Campsites, facilities: The campground has 14
RV or tent campsites that can accommodate
RVs up to 25 feet. Another 12 campsites are for
tents only. Facilities include picnic tables, fire
rings with grills, vault toilets, drinking water,
bear boxes, and garbage service. Leashed pets
are permitted. A wheelchair-accessible toilet
is available.

Reservations, fees: Reservations are not accepted. Campsites cost $9. A second vehicle
costs $5. Cash or check. Open late May–early
September.

Directions: From Highway 78 at Roscoe south
of Absarokee, take the East Rosebud Road
south for 2.6 miles, where the rough pavement
ends and the dusty, bumpy, potholed, dirt road
begins. Go 1.2 miles farther and turn right,
staying on East Rosebud Road for 9.9 miles
to a junction. Veer left for 0.6 mile over the
single-lane bridge and left at the next junction,
too. The campground entrance is on the left
just past the campground exit.
GPS Coordinates: N 45° 11.930' W 109°
38.061'

Contact: Custer National Forest, Beartooth
Ranger District, 6811 Hwy. 212 S., Red
Lodge, MT 406/446-2103, www.fs.fed.us/
r1/custer/.

55 CASCADE

🏕 🚲 🏊 🐕 ♿ 🚗 ⛰

Scenic rating: 8

on West Fork Rock Creek in Custer National
Forest

At 7,600 feet in elevation in Custer National Forest, Cascade Campground sits on
West Fork Rock Creek, known for its trout
fishing, surrounded by Montana's highest
mountains—the Beartooths. Within 1.5
miles west of the campground, trails depart
into the Absaroka-Beartooth Wilderness.
Climb 4.6 miles up to Timberline Lake, a
glacial cirque below the 12,500-foot Timberline Peak. A 4.3-mile trail grunts up to the
Red Lodge Creek Plateau, where the views
fly endlessly out onto the prairie. A shorter,
gentler trail of less than two miles leads to
Calamity Falls and Sentinel Falls. Backpackers continue farther to loop over the 11,037-
foot Sundance Pass, also a mountaineering
access for several peaks.

Although a 2008 fire burned the west tip
of the campground, the fast re-emerging vegetation will turn into a blooming meadow in
upcoming years as lodgepole pines regrow. The
campground comprises two loops, and most

sites still tuck under the partial shade of green lodgepole pines. On the smaller left loop, site 30 is a very private site at the end with a large, flat tent space. Twelve sites overlook the creek. Sites 11, 13, and 14 were burned by the fire, but the Forest Service has already cleared hazardous trees, which also opened up the views up-valley to the full scope of the fire and rocky peaks of the East Rosebud Plateau.

Campsites, facilities: The campground has 31 RV or tent campsites that can accommodate RVs up to 32 feet. Facilities include picnic tables, fire rings with grills, vault toilets, drinking water, garbage service, firewood for sale, bear boxes, and campground hosts. Leashed pets are permitted. A wheelchair-accessible toilet and two campsites are available.

Reservations, fees: Reservations are accepted (877/444-6777, www.recreation.gov). Campsites cost $14. An extra vehicle costs $8. Cash or check. Open late May–early September.

Directions: From Red Lodge on Highway 212 at the sign for the ski area, drive west on Ski Run Road for 2.8 miles and turn left onto West Fork Rock Creek Road (Forest Road 2071). Drive 7.7 miles to the campground entrance on the left. The last 3.3-mile stretch is on a single-lane road with turnouts rebuilt in 2009.

GPS Coordinates: N 45° 10.417' W 109° 27.049'

Contact: Custer National Forest, Beartooth Ranger District, 6811 Hwy. 212 S., Red Lodge, MT 406/446-2103, www.fs.fed.us/r1/custer/.

56 BASIN

Scenic rating: 7

on West Fork Rock Creek in Custer National Forest

At 6,800 feet in elevation in Custer National Forest, Basin Campground sits on West Fork Rock Creek, a brook trout fishery, in the eastern Beartooth Mountains. Three national recreation trails depart nearby. Across the road, the 3.8-mile Basin Lakes Trail climbs to a small glacial cirque. One mile east of the campground, the Silver Run Trail provides a 7.7-mile beginner mountain-bike loop, and a 15-minute nature trail loops around Wild Bill Lake. Wild Bill Lake also has wheelchair-accessible ramps and docks for fishing. Basin is the most popular campground in the West Fork drainage, not only because of the fire that swept through Cascade, but because the access and campground road are paved. Plan to arrive early in the day to claim a campsite.

The quiet campground sprinkles its spread-out, spacious campsites under the partial shade of a lodgepole forest. Unfortunately, because there's no undergrowth, you can see other campers, and at many of the sites you can see cars passing on the road. Pine needles and cones cover the forest floor of the campsites, which have plenty of big, level spaces for tents. Sites 3, 5, 7, 9, 11, and 12 overlook the creek. Sites 12, 14, 16, and 17 are more open, with views onto scorched hillsides from the 2008 fire. All of the gravel parking aprons are back-ins, but several are double-wide.

Campsites, facilities: The campground has 30 RV or tent campsites that can accommodate RVs up to 30 feet. Facilities include picnic tables, fire rings with grills, vault toilets, drinking water, garbage service, bear boxes, firewood for sale, and campground hosts. Leashed pets are permitted. A wheelchair-accessible toilet is available.

Reservations, fees: Reservations are accepted (877/444-6777, www.recreation.gov). Campsites cost $14. An extra vehicle costs $8. Cash or check. Open late May–early September.

Directions: From Red Lodge on Highway 212 at the sign for the ski area, drive west on Ski Run Road for 2.8 miles and turn left onto West Fork Rock Creek Road (Forest Road 2071). Drive 4.4 miles to the campground entrance on the right.

GPS Coordinates: N 45° 9.673' W 109° 23.498'

Contact: Custer National Forest, Beartooth Ranger District, 6811 Hwy. 212 S., Red Lodge, MT 406/446-2103, www.fs.fed.us/r1/custer/.

57 PALISADES (CUSTER NATIONAL FOREST)

🚶 🚲 ⛵ 🎣 ♿ 🚐 ⛺

Scenic rating: 6

west of Red Lodge in Custer National Forest

At 6,400 feet in elevation in Custer National Forest, Palisades Campground is named for the swath of limestone spires that poke up from a forested ridge on the eastern lip of the Beartooth Mountains. The campground tucks into the Willow Creek drainage tumbling from Red Lodge Ski Area. The Willow Creek Trail (#105) departs from the top of the campground to follow the creek upstream to the ski area. The trail is open to hikers and mountain bikers. Bikers can continue to loop back on the road from the ski area to reconnect with the campground.

Despite recent forest thinning around its entrance, the campground tucks into a draw along the creek that's forested with cottonwoods, aspens, and Douglas firs as well as lush meadows of sticky geraniums, fireweed, and tall grass. Half of the campsites sit along the creek, with the lowest one and the highest one having the most privacy and biggest tent spaces. Two sunny, open sites across the road from each other have views of the Palisades. The campground is also far enough from town to provide quiet, but close enough to run back in for supplies.

Campsites, facilities: The campground has six RV or tent campsites that can accommodate RVs up to 22 feet. Facilities include picnic tables, fire rings with grills, and a wheelchair-accessible vault toilet. Pack out your trash. Leashed pets are permitted.

Reservations, fees: Reservations are not accepted. Camping is free. Open late May–early September.

Directions: From Red Lodge on Highway 212, at the sign for the ski area, drive west on Ski Run Road for one mile and veer right onto the rough but paved Palisades Campground Road for 1.2 miles to the top of the hill. Turn right and then left on the road, which narrows and gets rougher with big potholes, reaching the campground in 0.6 mile.

GPS Coordinates: N 45° 10.294' W 109° 18.547'

Contact: Custer National Forest, Beartooth Ranger District, 6811 Hwy. 212 S., Red Lodge, MT 406/446-2103, www.fs.fed.us/r1/custer/.

58 RED LODGE KOA

🚲 🏊 ⛵ 🎣 🐕 🚻 🚐 ⛺

Scenic rating: 5

north of Red Lodge

At 5,148 feet in elevation, the Red Lodge KOA is a five-minute drive from downtown Red Lodge, with its restaurants, art galleries, shops, and funky western bars. The Red Lodge Mountain Golf Course sits about 10 minutes south of the campground, and the town is home to several fishing and rafting outfitters. Red Lodge is also the eastern portal to the Beartooth Highway. At the campground, the outdoor swimming pool is open late May–mid-September. A small children's fishing pond and banana bike rentals are also available.

The grassy campground, ringed by cottonwoods and aspens, offers a mix of shaded and sunny campsites. As at most KOAs, the campsites pack in tight to each other. Tent sites, which are a bit wider than the RV sites, ring the perimeter farthest from the highway. Due to the campground's location right on the highway, you'll hear trucks in the middle of the night, and vehicle traffic starts up in the early morning. The campground permits after-hours self-registration.

Campsites, facilities: The campground has

68 RV campsites that can fit vehicles up to 90 feet, along with 19 tent sites. Hookups include water, sewer, and electricity up to 50 amps. Facilities include picnic tables, rock fire rings, pedestal grills, flush toilets, showers, a coin-operated launderette, drinking water, a playground, a swimming pool, a dog walk, wireless Internet, modem dataports, a camp store, firewood for sale, and a disposal station. Leashed pets are permitted.

Reservations, fees: Reservations are accepted (800/562-7540, www.koa.com). Hookups cost $32–36. Tent sites cost $25–32. Rates cover two adults. Additional adults cost $4 each; kids ages 3–17 cost $3. Children under three years old stay free. Add on 7 percent Montana bed tax. Cash, check, or credit card. Open early May–September.

Directions: From Red Lodge, drive four miles north on Highway 212. Find the campground entrance on the east side of the road.

GPS Coordinates: N 45° 15.412' W 109° 13.706'

Contact: Red Lodge KOA, 7464 Hwy. 212, Red Lodge, MT 59068, 406/446-2364, www. koa.com.

59 PERRY'S RV PARK AND CAMPGROUND

Scenic rating: 6

south of Red Lodge

At 5,950 feet in elevation, Perry's RV Park and Campground is a three-minute drive or a 10-minute walk from downtown Red Lodge, with its restaurants, art galleries, shops, and funky western bars. The Red Lodge Mountain Golf Course sits about seven minutes north of the campground, and the town is home to several fishing and rafting outfitters. Red Lodge is also the eastern portal to the Beartooth Highway. Fishing is available for brook and brown trout on Rock Creek, which flanks the back of the campground.

The campground has two gravel road loops. A large, open, sunny parking-lot-type area houses bigger RVs and borders the highway. Other campsites, including the tent sites, tuck back under cottonwood trees, which offer partial shade. Several campsites line up on the bank of Rock Creek. Campsites are close together, and the highway noise is audible during the day but drops considerably at night. The campground does not permit after-hours self-registration.

Campsites, facilities: The campground has 30 RV campsites that can fit RVs up to 45 feet, as well as 13 tent sites. Hookups include water and electricity. Facilities include picnic tables, flush toilets, showers, drinking water, a camp store, and a disposal station. Leashed pets are permitted.

Reservations, fees: Reservations are accepted. Hookups cost $35. Tent sites cost $20. Rates cover two people. Additional campers cost $5 each. Add on 7 percent Montana bed tax. Cash or check only. Open late May–September.

Directions: From Red Lodge, drive two miles south on Highway 212. Find the campground entrance on the east side of the road.

GPS Coordinates: N 45° 9.082' W 109° 16.383'

Contact: Perry's RV Park and Campground, 6664 S. Hwy. 212, Red Lodge, MT 59068, 406/446-2722, www.perrysrv.us.

60 SHERIDAN

Scenic rating: 7

in the Beartooth Mountains in Custer National Forest

At 6,300 feet in elevation in Custer National Forest, Sheridan Campground is one of two Forest Service campgrounds at the eastern portal to the Beartooth Highway. Set in a narrow canyon on Rock Creek where you can fish for trout, the two campgrounds provide quick access to Red Lodge for supplies and a good jumping-off point for exploring the scenic highway. Departing 1.1 miles south of the campground, Corral Creek Trail (#9) climbs over 3,000 feet in 4.1 miles up to Line Creek Plateau, for views of the snowcapped Beartooth Mountains. You can also turn the route into a 12.7-mile loop with a waltz along the scenic plateau for views of Wyoming and the prairie before dropping down Maurice Creek. The loop ends about one mile north of the campground. Starting the loop at Maurice Creek lets you face the peaks as you hike. For experts kayakers and rafters, Rock Creek provides Class III–IV white water.

In a forest of cottonwoods, aspens, and Douglas fir, the campground offers a mix of partly shaded (sites 4–8) or sunny campsites with views of mountain slopes (sites 1–3) that are open to those driving in on the gravel campground road. Lyall's angelica, wild roses, and harebells bloom in the small meadows surrounding some of the sites. Light highway noise can be heard above the burbling creek, but it diminishes at night. Four campsites flank Rock Creek, with short paths through brush to the water.

Campsites, facilities: The campground has eight RV or tent campsites that can accommodate RVs up to 30 feet. Facilities include picnic tables, fire rings with grills, vault toilets, drinking water, garbage service, and firewood for sale. The campground hosts stay one mile west at Rattin. Leashed pets are permitted. A toilet and one campsite are wheelchair-accessible.

Reservations, fees: Reservations are accepted (877/444-6777, www.recreation.gov). Campsites cost $14. An extra vehicle costs $8. Cash or check. Open May–September.

Directions: From Red Lodge, drive 7.5 miles southwest on Highway 212 to milepost 61.8. Turn east onto the narrow, potholed, dirt East Side Road and cross the single-lane bridge. The campground entrance is on the left side of the road in 1.3 miles.

GPS Coordinates: N 45° 5.991' W 109° 18.534'

Contact: Custer National Forest, Beartooth Ranger District, 6811 Hwy. 212 S., Red Lodge, MT 406/446-2103, www.fs.fed.us/r1/custer/.

61 RATTIN

Scenic rating: 7

in the Beartooth Mountains in Custer National Forest

At 6,300 feet in elevation in Custer National Forest, Rattin Campground is one of two Forest Service campgrounds at the eastern portal to the Beartooth Highway. In a narrow canyon on Rock Creek where you can fish for trout, the campgrounds provide quick access to Red Lodge for supplies and a good jumping-off point for exploring the scenic highway. Departing 0.1 mile south of the campground, Corral Creek Trail (#9) climbs over 3,000 feet in 4.1 miles up to Line Creek Plateau for views of the snowcapped Beartooth Mountains. You can also turn the route into a 12.7-mile loop with an open walk along the crest of the scenic plateau for views of Wyoming and the prairie before dropping down Maurice Creek, which ends about two miles north of the campground. Starting the loop at Maurice Creek lets you face the peaks as you hike. For expert kayakers and rafters, Rock Creek provides Class III–IV white water.

In a forest of cottonwoods, aspens, pines, and Douglas fir, the campground is tucked along Rock Creek but doesn't have views of the water. You can hear it, though, along with vehicles on the highway, but the traffic dies down at night. Short paths cut through the brush to the creek. Some of the campsites have partial views of the mountains plus a bit of shade. Foliage limits visibility of other campsites to just a neighbor or two. The skinny, dusty campground road has no turnaround loop at the end.

Campsites, facilities: The campground has six RV or tent campsites that can accommodate RVs up to 25 feet. Facilities include picnic tables, fire rings with grills, vault toilets, drinking water, garbage service, firewood for sale, and campground hosts. Leashed pets are permitted. A wheelchair-accessible toilet is available.

Reservations, fees: Reservations are accepted (877/444-6777, www.recreation.gov). Campsites cost $14. An extra vehicle costs $8. Cash or check. Open May–September.

Directions: From Red Lodge, drive 7.5 miles southwest on Highway 212 to milepost 61.8. Turn east onto the narrow, potholed, dirt East Side Road and cross the single-lane bridge. The campground entrance is on the left side of the road in 0.3 mile.

GPS Coordinates: N 45° 5.276' W 109° 19.330'

Contact: Custer National Forest, Beartooth Ranger District, 6811 Hwy. 212 S., Red Lodge, MT 406/446-2103, www.fs.fed.us/r1/custer/.

62 PARKSIDE

Scenic rating: 8

in the Beartooth Mountains in Custer National Forest

At 7,200 feet in elevation in Custer National Forest, Parkside is one of three campgrounds clustered within 0.6 mile on Rock Creek Road at the eastern base of the Beartooth Highway, where the scenic highway begins its five-switchback climb to the Beartooth Plateau. From Vista Point at 9,100 feet, you can spot the campground on the valley floor. Cyclists on the Beartooth Highway opt to stay at Parkside to start the 4,000-foot climb up to Beartooth Pass first thing in the morning before the sun hits the switchbacks. The campground also sits adjacent to the Wyoming Creek Trailhead, a two-mile-long, hiking-only Parkside National Recreation Trail that links up four campgrounds along Rock Creek and tiny Greenough Lake. For anglers, Rock Creek harbors rainbow, brook, and Yellowstone cutthroat trout. Because of the campground's popularity in midsummer and on holidays, claim your site before noon.

Parkside Campground straddles Rock Creek on a paved road with a single-lane bridge. On the creek's west side, paved back-in parking pads line up sites closer together and visible from each other in the pine forest, which has an open understory with some peek-a-boo views of the peak. Sites 1, 2, 4, and 7–10 overlook Rock Creek. The loop on the creek's east side offers more private, shaded campsites under Douglas firs, aspens, and cottonwoods, with sites 17–19 overlooking the creek. Despite the proximity to the highway, the campground is quiet at night.

Campsites, facilities: The campground has 28 RV or tent campsites that can accommodate RVs up to 45 feet. Facilities include picnic tables, fire rings with grills, vault toilets, drinking water, garbage service, firewood for sale, bear boxes, and campground hosts. Leashed pets are permitted. A toilet and one campsite are wheelchair-accessible.

Reservations, fees: Reservations are accepted (877/444-6777, www.recreation.gov). Campsites cost $14. An extra vehicle costs $8. Cash or check. Open late May–early September.

Directions: From Red Lodge, drive 11.5 miles southwest on Highway 212 to milepost 57.2. Turn right onto the paved Rock Creek Road for 0.3 mile to the campground entrance on the right.

GPS Coordinates: N 45° 3.633' W 109° 24.285'

Contact: Custer National Forest, Beartooth Ranger District, 6811 Hwy. 212 S., Red Lodge, MT 406/446-2103, www.fs.fed.us/r1/custer/.

63 GREENOUGH LAKE

Scenic rating: 8

in the Beartooth Mountains in Custer National Forest

At 7,300 feet in elevation in Custer National Forest, Greenough Lake is one of three campgrounds clustered within 0.6 mile of each other on the Rock Creek Road at the eastern base of the Beartooth Highway. The campground, on Rock Creek's east bank, lies at the base of a glacier-carved valley flanked by the above-tree-line rocky plateaus of the Beartooth Mountains. At the north end of the campground, the two-mile hiking-only Parkside National Recreation Trail, which links up four campgrounds along Rock Creek, leads 0.25 mile to tiny Greenough Lake, a shallow mosquito pond that is stocked with rainbow trout. Campers often use mountain bikes and ATVs to tour two dirt roads—the continuation of Rock Creek Road and Forest Road 2004, which climbs to Hellroaring Plateau.

With paved internal roads, parking pads, and proximity to the Beartooth Highway, Greenough Lake is a popular campground that requires a before-noon arrival to get a site in midsummer and on holidays. Despite the nearness of the highway, the campground is quiet at night, with only the sound of the creek. Sites 1, 2, 3, 5, 7, 9, and 10 overlook Rock Creek and some of the Limber Pine campsites across the creek. A mixed forest of aspens, pines, and short willows lends partial shade and partial privacy to the campsites, some with views to mountain slopes. Site 13 houses a giant glacial erratic, a boulder dropped by receding ice.

Campsites, facilities: The campground has 18 RV or tent campsites that can accommodate RVs up to 50 feet. Facilities include picnic tables, fire rings with grills, vault toilets, drinking water, garbage service, firewood for sale, and bear boxes. The campground hosts stay at adjacent Parkside Campground. Leashed pets are permitted. A wheelchair-accessible toilet and two campsites (9 and 11) are available.

Reservations, fees: Reservations are accepted (877/444-6777, www.recreation.gov). Campsites cost $14. An extra vehicle costs $8. Cash or check. Open late May–early September.

Directions: From Red Lodge, drive 11.5 miles southwest on Highway 212 to milepost 57.2.

Turn right onto paved Rock Creek Road for 0.8 mile to the campground entrance on the left. GPS Coordinates: N 45° 3.375' W 109° 24.738'

Contact: Custer National Forest, Beartooth Ranger District, 6811 Hwy. 212 S., Red Lodge, MT 406/446-2103, www.fs.fed.us/r1/custer/.

64 LIMBER PINE

Scenic rating: 8

in the Beartooth Mountains in Custer National Forest

At 7,300 feet in elevation in Custer National Forest, Limber Pine is one of three campgrounds clustered within 0.6 mile on the Rock Creek Road at the eastern base of the Beartooth Highway. Flanked by the immense above-tree-line meadow plateaus of the snowcapped Beartooth Mountains, the campgrounds are dwarfed on the valley floor, where Limber Pine sits on the west bank of Rock Creek. The two-mile-long, hiking-only Parkside National Recreation Trail links up the four campgrounds along Rock Creek and leads 0.5 mile to Greenough Lake. Trout fishing is available at the lake and along Rock Creek. The dirt Forest Road 2004 (some use ATVs or mountain bikes on the road) departs Rock Creek Road near the campgrounds to climb onto the Hellroaring Plateau to the edge of the Absaroka-Beartooth Wilderness, where you can continue hiking on a trail for another 2.5 miles or farther cross-country with big views of alpine meadows and snowcapped peaks.

Limber Pine is a popular campground that requires a before-noon arrival to get a site in midsummer and on holidays. Its one paved loop connects campsites that vary from full shade to partial mountain views. Black-eyed susans, sagebrush, harebells, and yellow arrowleaf balsamroot bloom between stands of limber pine. Sites 1, 2, and 10 overlook the creek and campsites in Greenough Lake Campground across the creek. Despite sitting between the highway and Rock Creek Road, the campground quiets at night.

Campsites, facilities: The campground has 11 RV or tent campsites that can accommodate RVs up to 45 feet, plus two walk-in tent-only sites (7 and 11). Facilities include picnic tables, fire rings with grills, vault toilets, drinking water, garbage service, firewood for sale, and bear boxes. The campground hosts stay at adjacent Parkside Campground. Leashed pets are permitted. A wheelchair-accessible toilet and two campsites (sites 1 and 2) are available.

Reservations, fees: Reservations are accepted (877/444-6777, www.recreation.gov). Campsites cost $14. An extra vehicle costs $8. Cash or check. Open late May–early September.

Directions: From Red Lodge, drive 11.5 miles southwest on Highway 212 to milepost 57.2. Turn right onto paved Rock Creek Road for 0.9 mile to the campground entrance on the left. GPS Coordinates: N 45° 3.452' W 109° 24.742'

Contact: Custer National Forest, Beartooth Ranger District, 6811 Hwy. 212 S., Red Lodge, MT 406/446-2103, www.fs.fed.us/r1/custer/.

65 M-K

🚶 🚴 🛶 🐕 ♿ 🚐 ⛺

Scenic rating: 8

in the Beartooth Mountains in Custer National Forest

At 7,500 feet in elevation in Custer National Forest, M-K works as an overflow campground if Parkside, Greenough Lake, and Limber Pine are full. However, the two miles of dirt road between them is rough. Flanked by the immense above-tree-line meadow plateaus of the snowcapped Beartooth Mountains, the campground sits on the east bank of Rock Creek. At the end of Rock Creek Road (after five more miles of rough dirt road crossing into

Wyoming and back), a popular two-mile trail climbs into a scoured rocky cirque containing Glacier Lake. Anglers also go after rainbow, brook, and Yellowstone cutthroat trout in the lake as well as in Rock Creek. Rock Creek Road is a favorite of ATVers; mountain bikers also use it, but they must suck the dust of passing vehicles. M-K also sits at the south end of the two-mile, hiker-only Parkside National Recreation Trail, which leads to Greenough Lake.

M-K, a campground favored by tenters, is a quiet, partly shaded campground in a pine forest with an open understory and a pine needle and cone floor. Thanks to the lack of understory foliage, you can see neighboring campers; however, campsites are spread out for some privacy. The narrow, rough dirt road loops through the campground and connects the unnumbered sites. Those at the upper end overlook the creek, and most have huge flat spaces for multiple tents. A couple of unappealing sites flank Rock Creek Road. The sound of the creek filters through the whole campground.

Campsites, facilities: The campground has 10 RV or tent campsites that can accommodate RVs up to 22 feet. Facilities include picnic tables, fire rings with grills, and vault toilets. Pack out your trash. To use creek water, boil or purify it before drinking. Leashed pets are permitted. A wheelchair-accessible toilet is available.

Reservations, fees: Reservations are not accepted. Camping is free. Open May–September.

Directions: From Red Lodge, drive 11.5 miles southwest on Highway 212 to milepost 57.2. Turn right onto paved Rock Creek Road (Forest Road 2421) for 2.7 miles to the campground entrance on the right. The pavement disappears after one mile and the road disintegrates into potholes and washboards, which require slow driving. GPS Coordinates: N 45° 2.317' W 109° 25.715'

Contact: Custer National Forest, Beartooth

Ranger District, 6811 Hwy. 212 S., Red Lodge, MT 406/446-2103, www.fs.fed.us/r1/custer/.

66 ROCK CREEK PRIMITIVE

Scenic rating: 8

in the Beartooth Mountains in Custer National Forest

Located between 7,500 feet and 8,650 feet in elevation in Custer National Forest, Rock Creek tumbles along a forest road sprinkled on both sides with short spur roads and jeep trails. These offer campers privacy and solitude, accompanied by only the sound of the creek. The U-shaped, glacier-carved valley littered with large boulders left from receding ice sweeps up several thousand feet on both sides to the high alpine plateaus of the east Beartooth Mountains. Rock Creek Road crosses into Wyoming and back before terminating at a popular trailhead. A two-mile trail climbs into a scoured rocky cirque containing Glacier Lake. Anglers go after rainbow, brook, and Yellowstone cutthroat trout in the lake as well as in Rock Creek. Rock Creek Road is a favorite of highway-legal ATV riders.

Most of the dispersed primitive campsites along Rock Creek sit right on the river. You'll find sites shaded under cottonwoods and pines, in filtered sunlight in aspens, and in full sun in grassy fields with big open views of the mountains. Find most of the sites by a small sign with a tent icon; some are unmarked. Scout the dirt access roads and turnaround space before you drive in blind. Etiquette dictates one site per party.

Campsites, facilities: More than 25 primitive RV or tent campsites that can accommodate small RVs flank Rock Creek Road. Dispersed camping is permitted 300 feet on either side of the road from the centerline. The only facilities are rock fire rings. Use existing rings rather

than constructing new ones. Pack out your trash. To use creek water, boil or purify it before drinking. Follow Leave No Trace principles for human waste. Leashed pets are permitted.

Reservations, fees: Reservations are not accepted. Camping is free. Open May–September, or longer if there's no snow.

Directions: From Red Lodge, drive 11.5 miles southwest on Highway 212 to milepost 57.2. Turn right onto paved Rock Creek Road (Forest Road 2421). After passing Limber Pine Campground at 0.9 mile, the pavement disappears, and the road disintegrates into potholes and washboards, which require slow driving. Between Limber Pine and the road's terminus in 7.5 miles, look for spur roads and small posts with tent icons.

GPS Coordinates: N 45° 3.336' W 109° 25.018' (first primitive site)

Contact: Custer National Forest, Beartooth Ranger District, 6811 Hwy. 212 S., Red Lodge, MT 406/446-2103, www.fs.fed.us/r1/custer/.

67 ISLAND LAKE

Scenic rating: 10

on Beartooth Highway in Shoshone National Forest in Wyoming

BEST (

At 9,600 feet on top of the Beartooth Plateau in Wyoming's Shoshone National Forest, Island Lake is the highest campground along the Beartooth Highway as well as the highest drive-to campground in the entire Northern Rocky Mountains. In midsummer, huge alpine meadows overflowing with fuchsia paintbrush and bluebells sprawl between wind-blown pines and firs. The wildflower-rimmed lake containing a tiny island provides boating for small watercraft and fishing for small trout that can't grow big in the short ice-free season. (Fishing requires a Wyoming fishing license available one mile west at Top of the World store.) Canoeists and float tubers portage 100

© BECKY LOMAX

Hiking into the Absaroka-Beartooth Wilderness requires crossing streams without bridges.

functions; plan on bringing your own water or filling up at Beartooth Lake, two miles west.

Campsites, facilities: The campground has 20 RV or tent campsites that can accommodate RVs up to 32 feet. Facilities include picnic tables, fire rings with grills, pit toilets, garbage service, bear boxes, a boat ramp, and campground hosts. Leashed pets are permitted.

Reservations, fees: Reservations are not accepted. Campsites cost $10. Cash or check. Open July–mid-September, snow permitting.

Directions: On Highway 212, drive 29 miles southwest from Red Lodge, or from Yellowstone's northeast entrance drive 33 miles east. Turn north into the campground entrance. GPS Coordinates: N 44° 56.381' W 109° 32.492'

Contact: Shoshone National Forest, Clarks Fork Ranger District, 203A Yellowstone Ave., Cody, WY 82414, 307/527-6921, www.fs.fed.us/r2/shoshone/.

feet from Island Lake to Night Lake. A trail for hiking and horse-packing departs from the campground, touring the west shore and passing four more lakes within an hour of hiking. In 2.7 miles, it connects with the Beauty Lake Trail from Beartooth Lake. The trail also continues northeast into the Absaroka-Beartooth Wilderness, linking up lakes, backpacking and mountaineering routes, and rugged, remote granite summits, but mountain bikers may ride only six miles, to the wilderness boundary.

Bring DEET for the voracious mosquitoes bred in the boggy alpine meadows, prepare to be winded walking to the outhouse because of the altitude, and be ready for the regular afternoon thunderstorms that can pelt rain, hail, or snow—even in August. Set in loose-knit pine and fir clusters laced with large boulders, the campground has only a handful of campsites that can see the lake (on loop C), but trailers are not recommended on the narrow, steep loop. The campground's water system no longer

68 BEARTOOTH LAKE

Scenic rating: 10

on the Beartooth Highway in Shoshone National Forest in Wyoming

BEST (

At 9,000 feet on top of the Beartooth Plateau in Wyoming's Shoshone National Forest, Beartooth Lake sits below orange-streaked Beartooth Butte, a sedimentary anomaly amid the granite Beartooth Mountains. In midsummer, huge alpine bluebell meadows flank the butte's lower slopes across Beartooth Lake, a forest- and bog-rimmed lake with a boat ramp on its south end for launching small watercraft and fishing for small trout that can't grow big in the short ice-free season. A Wyoming fishing license is required, available at the Top of the World store one mile east. From the campground, two trails angle north; one waltzes past Beauty Lake, connecting with the

The Absaroka-Beartooth Mountains are the highest in Montana.

Island Lake trails in 2.4 miles and making a 7.9-mile loop. The loop also aims north into the Absaroka-Beartooth Wilderness, linking up lakes and backpacking and mountaineering routes, but mountain bikers may ride only five miles, to the wilderness boundary. One loop connects to Clay Butte Lookout (you can also drive to it), a 1942 fire lookout, elevation 9,811 feet, that commands a 360-degree panoramic view, open Wednesday–Sunday.

Mosquitoes breed armies here in the boggy alpine meadows: bring jumbo-sized bug juice. The air is thin; prepare to be winded walking from the lake up to your campsite. Afternoon thunderstorms roll in like clockwork; be ready for August rains, hail, or snow. The quiet-at-night campground packs its three forested, partly shaded loops tight with a few sites on the A loop having peek-a-boo lake views through the trees. Step outside at night to see brilliant stars light up the sky.

Campsites, facilities: The campground has 20 RV or tent campsites that can accommodate RVs up to 32 feet. Facilities include picnic tables, fire rings with grills, vault toilets, drinking water, garbage service, bear boxes, and campground hosts. Leashed pets are permitted. A wheelchair-accessible toilet is available.

Reservations, fees: Reservations are not accepted. Campsites cost $15. Cash or check. Open July–mid-September, snow permitting.

Directions: On Highway 212, drive 31 miles southwest from Red Lodge, or from Yellowstone's northeast entrance drive 31 miles east. Turn north into the campground entrance. GPS Coordinates: N 44° 56.673' W 109° 35.351'

Contact: Shoshone National Forest, Clarks Fork Ranger District, 203A Yellowstone Ave., Cody, WY 82414, 307/527-6921, www.fs.fed.us/r2/shoshone/.

69 FOX CREEK

Scenic rating: 8

on the Beartooth Highway in Shoshone National Forest in Wyoming

At 7,100 feet in elevation in Wyoming's Shoshone National Forest, Fox Creek

Campground sits on the western slopes of the Beartooth Highway. While you're driving down the west side of the highway, Index and Pilot Peaks, both over 11,000 feet in elevation, are the two prominent spires. At the base of these peaks, the campground's two loops sit between the Clarks Fork Yellowstone River and the highway. You can wade-fish for trout and mountain whitefish in the nationally designated Wild and Scenic River, but you need a Wyoming fishing license.

The loose mixed forest of spruce, lodgepole pine, grand fir, and Douglas fir lends a bit of shade to the sunny campsites surrounded by grassy wildflower meadows. The gravel and dirt campground road kicks up dust in late summer, and you'll hear some highway noise; however, the route into Yellowstone National Park does not permit commercial trucking, so the noise quiets at night. The forest provides a thick screen, so you don't see the highway, but the more open sites command views of Index and Pilot Peaks. Sites on the northeast ends of the loops sit nearest the river, but none have river views through the trees. A few campsites are double spaces that can accommodate two RVs. The Forest Service has plans for expansion of this campground, but it was closed in summer 2009 to house road crews working on the Beartooth Highway. Call for status.

Campsites, facilities: The campground has 27 RV or tent campsites that can accommodate RVs up to 50 feet. Facilities include picnic tables, fire rings with grills, hookups for water and electricity, vault toilets, garbage service, bear boxes, and campground hosts. Leashed pets are permitted.

Reservations, fees: Reservations are not accepted. Campsites cost $20. Cash or check. Open mid-June–mid-September.

Directions: On Highway 212, drive 51 miles southwest from Red Lodge, or from the northeast entrance to Yellowstone National Park drive 11 miles east. Turn north into the campground entrance.

GPS Coordinates: N 44° 58.469' W 109° 50.029'

Contact: Shoshone National Forest, Clarks Fork Ranger District, 203A Yellowstone Ave., Cody, WY 82414, 307/527-6921, www.fs.fed.us/r2/shoshone/.

70 CRAZY CREEK

Scenic rating: 7

on the Beartooth Highway in Shoshone National Forest in Wyoming

At 6,900 feet in elevation in Wyoming's Shoshone National Forest, Crazy Creek Campground tucks into the lower western slopes of the Beartooth Highway. The campground sits at the confluence of Crazy Creek with the Clarks Fork Yellowstone River, where anglers go after trout and mountain whitefish. Be sure to have a Wyoming license for fishing. Across the highway, the Crazy Lakes Trail (#612) climbs to a series of lakes on the southwestern flank of the Beartooth Plateau in the Absaroka-Beartooth Wilderness. Crossing back into Montana in 4.5 miles, the trail splits to various lakes—destinations for day hikers, backpackers, horse-packers, and anglers. (You'll need a Montana fishing license.) A five-minute walk on the trail leads to a waterfall. Cyclists going west to east on the Beartooth Highway stay here before the climb to Beartooth Pass.

Sitting in a spruce and lodgepole pine forest, Crazy Creek offers campsites that vary between sunny (sites 4–7) and shady (sites 1–3). Recent hazardous tree removal work thinned out some of the beetle-killed trees, opening up the forest more around the grassy sites and making it visually greener. The sunny open sites also have views of the cliffs on Jim Smith Peak. Unfortunately, the tree removal has also opened up the sites more, making them less private; however, sites 10 and 12, which work for smaller tents, have more privacy than the other campsites. You'll hear road noise in the campground, but the highway does not permit commercial hauling through Yellowstone National Park, so nighttime noise is minimal.

Campsites, facilities: The campground has 16 RV or tent campsites that can accommodate RVs up to 32 feet. Facilities include picnic tables, fire rings with grills, vault toilets, garbage service, bear boxes, and campground hosts. Bring your own drinking water, or if you use creek water, boil or purify it first. Leashed pets are permitted. A wheelchair-accessible toilet is available.

Reservations, fees: Reservations are not accepted. Campsites cost $10. Cash or check. Open May–September.

Directions: On Highway 212, drive 47 miles southwest from Red Lodge, or from the northeast entrance to Yellowstone National Park drive 15 miles east. Turn south into the campground entrance.

GPS Coordinates: N 44° 56.518' W 109° 46.429'

Contact: Shoshone National Forest, Clarks Fork Ranger District, 203A Yellowstone Ave., Cody, WY 82414, 307/527-6921, www.fs.fed. us/r2/shoshone/.

YELLOWSTONE AND TETONS

© BECKY LOMAX

BEST CAMPGROUNDS

Yellowstone Teton country wears the scars of a

volatile past. Mud bubbles, steam pours from clear blue cauldrons, vents hiss into roars, and boiling water spits several stories into the air. The fumings of a grumbling supervolcano rumble across Yellowstone National Park as molten rock swells a few miles below the feet of hikers. To the south, the fangs of Grand Teton National Park – one of the youngest ranges in the Rocky Mountains – gnaw on the sky, the result of equal violence. Upthrusting earth jutted Grand Teton up to 13,770 feet, where climbers scale cliffs scoured by ice.

Located a full day's drive south of Glacier National Park, Yellowstone and Teton Parks attract about three million visitors a year – most packed into a short summer season when sightseeing and hiking bring you face to face with bison, pronghorn antelope, and grizzly bears. While RV parks and national forest campgrounds ring the park's perimeters, camping inside the parks lets you smell the fuming caldera and hear the howl of wolves at night.

Yellowstone, the nation's first national park, spills from mountains to high plateaus, covering more land than Delaware and Rhode Island combined. Its forests and prairies hold 12 drive-up campgrounds. Small campgrounds cluster in the north, while large campgrounds verging on the size of small towns populate the Old Faithful, central canyon, and lake areas. For those looking to escape crowds, remote boat-in campsites rim the arms of Yellowstone and Shoshone Lakes. Surrounding Yellowstone, three small towns neighbor northern entrances: Gardiner, Cooke City, and West Yellowstone provide RV parks, nearby national forest campgrounds, and services for campers, plus outfitters for rafting, horseback riding, and fishing.

Inside Yellowstone National Park, the Grand Loop Road forms a figure-eight through the caldera, where shaggy brown bison graze next to steam billowing from hot pools. To camp closest to geysers, hot pools, and mud pots, head to Mammoth, Norris, Madison, or Canyon Campground. To camp near the famed wolf habitat of Lamar Valley, aim for Tower, Slough Creek, or Pebble Creek Campground in the northeast corner. To explore the park's lakes, go to Grant, Fishing Bridge, Bridge Bay, or Lewis Lake in the southeast corner. Better yet, hit the backcountry office in Bridge Bay for permits for remote, quiet boat-in campsites flanking Yellowstone Lake's 110 miles of shoreline, or kayak or canoe into Shoshone Lake. On both lakes, be ready for afternoon winds. Anglers looking to cast into blue-ribbon trout streams should camp at Madison Junction to fish the Madison River or at Fishing Bridge, Canyon, or Tower Fall to fish the Yellowstone River.

Grand Teton National Park, which connects to Yellowstone via the John D. Rockefeller, Jr. Memorial Parkway, strings its six large campgrounds along the east side of the mountain range and Jackson Lake, with only Flagg Ranch on the parkway between the two parks for camping. On the south end of the park, adjacent to the National Elk Refuge, Jackson Hole houses outfitters for rafting, fishing, hiking, horseback riding, mountaineering, and rock climbing. The surrounding Caribou-Targhee and Bridger-Teton National Forests also offer a few campgrounds within 15 minutes of the park.

Of Teton's campgrounds, Jenny Lake is by far the most popular, due to its access to hiking trails that climb up canyons toward the Teton Crest and the tour boat that runs across the lake. Signal Mountain, Colter Bay, and Lizard Creek Campgrounds rim the east shores of Jackson Lake, a large dammed reservoir on the Snake River. Gros Ventre Campground borders the National Elk Refuge, where 5,000 elk winter. Teton National Park also has boat-in campsites on Jackson Lake and the smaller, more wind-protected Leigh Lake.

Two of the national park campgrounds permit only certain camping units. Unlike other national parks, which have no campgrounds with hookups inside the park boundaries, Yellowstone offers Fishing Bridge, which has hookups for RVs and does not permit tents. In the Tetons, Jenny Lake is for tents only and does not permit RVs.

Yellowstone and Grand Teton National Parks are prime grizzly bear country. Practice safe food storage at all campgrounds.

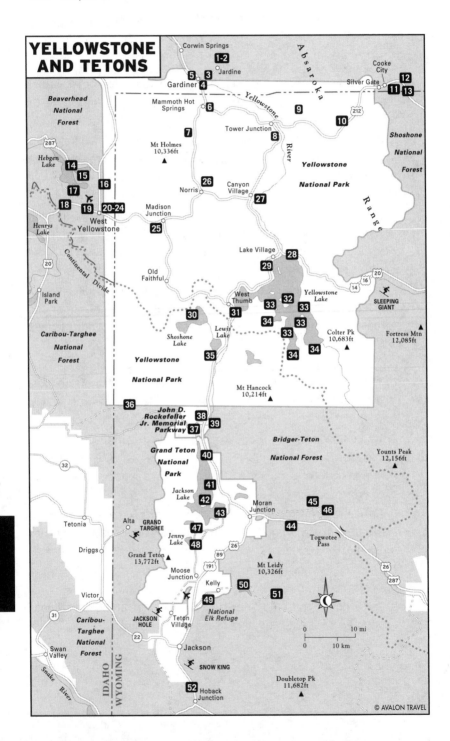

YELLOWSTONE AND TETONS

Corwin Springs
1-2
Jardine
5 3
Gardiner
4
Mammoth Hot Springs 6
7
Tower Junction 8
Mt Holmes 10,336ft
26
Norris
Canyon Village
27
Madison Junction
25
Lake Village
29 28
West Thumb
33 32
31
34 33
Old Faithful
30
Lewis Lake
33
Shoshone Lake
34 34
35
Mt Hancock 10,214ft
36
John D. Rockefeller Jr. Memorial Parkway
38
37 39
Grand Teton National Park
40
Jackson Lake
41
42
43
Moran Junction
45 46
Alta GRAND TARGHEE
47
44
Jenny Lake
48
Grand Teton 13,772ft
Moose Junction
Kelly
50
49
51
JACKSON HOLE
Teton Village
National Elk Refuge
Jackson
SNOW KING
52 Hoback Junction

Cooke City
Silver Gate
12
11 13
9
212
10

Yellowstone National Park

Shoshone National Forest

Absaroka Range

Yellowstone River

Colter Pk 10,683ft

SLEEPING GIANT

Fortress Mtn 12,085ft

Yellowstone Lake

16 20
14

Beaverhead National Forest

287
Hebgen Lake
14
15
16
17
18
19 20-24
West Yellowstone

Henrys Lake
20
Island Park

Continental Divide

Caribou-Targhee National Forest

32

Tetonia

Driggs

Victor
31

Caribou-Targhee National Forest

Swan Valley

Snake River

IDAHO
WYOMING

Bridger-Teton National Forest

Younts Peak 12,156ft

Mt Leidy 10,326ft

Togwotee Pass

26
287

89
191
26

22

Doubletop Pk 11,682ft

0   10 mi
0   10 km

© AVALON TRAVEL

1 BEAR CREEK

🚶 🚴 🐴 🚙 ⛺

Scenic rating: 5

in the west Absaroka Mountains northeast
of Gardiner in Gallatin National Forest in
Montana

In the west Absaroka Mountains in Gallatin
National Forest, Bear Creek Campground,
elevation 7,100 feet, sits on the edge of the
Absaroka-Beartooth Wilderness. The narrow,
forested Bear Creek Valley climbs up to peaks
topping out above 10,000 feet. Mountain bikes
and ATVs can tour the Forest Service roads
on the slopes of Ash Mountain east of the
campground, but not into the wilderness. Bear
Creek Trail, which departs from a trailhead
0.3 mile north of the campground, follows the
creek 2.4 miles to trail #620, which accesses
Knox and Fish Lake as well as the ridgeline
north of Ash Mountain.

The remote campground is for those seeking absolute privacy and quiet with only the
sounds of nature—jays squawking, squirrels
chattering, and a burbling creek. The campsites line up along the creek with flat spaces
for tents. The first two sites are well-used, but
the others show less wear as they are more difficult to reach. The shady campsites receive
filtered sun through the mixed fir and pine
forest. Small lupine and paintbrush meadows
weave through the campground.

Campsites, facilities: The campground has
four primitive RV or tent campsites. RVs are
limited to 21 feet. Trailers are not recommended due to lack of turnaround space. A
high-clearance vehicle is helpful to navigate
the campground's large potholes. Scout all
campground roads before driving them. Facilities include rock fire rings and a pit toilet. No
drinking water is available. Bring your own,
or boil or purify creek water. Pack out your
trash. Pets are permitted.

Reservations, fees: Reservations are not accepted. Camping is free. Open mid-June–
October, depending on snow.

Directions: From Gardiner, drive northeast
on Jardine Road for 5.4 miles. (The pavement ends quickly.) In Jardine, turn right
over the worn wooden bridge onto Bear
Creek Road (Forest Road 493) and climb on
the potholed, single-lane road with turnouts
for five miles to a Y. Take the left fork for
0.2 mile and turn left into the campground.
Warning: The campground road is extremely
narrow.
GPS Coordinates: N 45° 6.668' W 110°
36.024'
Contact: Gallatin National Forest, Gardiner
Ranger Station, P.O. Box 5, Hwy. 89 S., Gardiner, MT 59030, 406/848-7375, www.fs.fed.
us/r1/gallatin.

2 TIMBER CAMP

🚶 🚴 🐴 🚙 ⛺

Scenic rating: 7

in the west Absaroka Mountains northeast
of Gardiner in Gallatin National Forest in
Montana

At 7,100 feet in the west Absaroka Mountains,
Timber Camp enjoys a high alpine meadow
on the slopes of Ash Mountain, which tops
out over 10,000 feet. Due to the forest and
the steep terrain, the peak is not visible from
the campground. Across the road from the
campground, a Forest Service spur road climbs
up the west slope, a road explored by mountain
bikers and ATVers. Within three miles in both
directions on the road, hikers can access trails
into the Absaroka-Beartooth Wilderness. Bear
Creek Trailhead sits to the north, Pine Creek
Trailhead to the south.

The ultra-quiet campsites tuck under mature Douglas firs for protection from weather
and partial shade. The campsites surround
a large open meadow bursting with July
wildflowers—cow parsnips, lupines, sticky
geraniums. The unnumbered sites are spread
out for privacy, but they are in sight of each
other due to the open meadow. The forest

duff floors have spaces for tents. A creek runs along the camp's north side. Prepare for copious mosquitoes around the meadow.

Campsites, facilities: The primitive campground has five RV or tent campsites. RVs are limited to 21 feet. Facilities include picnic tables and fire rings with grills at three sites, rock fire rings at two sites, and a pit toilet. No drinking water is available. Bring your own, or if you use creek water, boil or purify it first. Pack out your trash. Pets are permitted.

Reservations, fees: Reservations are not accepted. Camping is free. Open mid-June–October, depending on snow.

Directions: From Gardiner, drive northeast on Jardine Road for 5.4 miles (the pavement ends quickly). In Jardine, turn right over the worn wooden bridge onto Bear Creek Road (Forest Road 493) and climb for 4.2 miles. The road narrows to a potholed single lane with turnouts. Turn left into the campground. Scout out the spur roads into the campsites—some have deep muddy potholes.

GPS Coordinates: N 45° 5.770' W 110° 36.301'

Contact: Gallatin National Forest, Gardiner Ranger Station, P.O. Box 5, Hwy. 89 S., Gardiner, MT 59030, 406/848-7375, www.fs.fed.us/r1/gallatin.

❸ EAGLE CREEK

Scenic rating: 8

in the west Absaroka Mountains northeast of Gardiner in Gallatin National Forest in Montana

Within three miles of Yellowstone National Park, Eagle Creek offers an inexpensive place to camp with expansive views of the park's north slopes. Eagle Creek is the closest Forest Service campground to the park's north entrance. While the campground is surrounded by an arid sagebrush slope, the terrain often is good for watching wildlife, such as elk. Bring binoculars! Hiking is available north of Jardine at Bear Creek, from Gardiner along the Yellowstone River, and in Yellowstone at Mammoth Hot Springs. Gardiner is also the local headquarters for rafting and fishing outfitters, and the Yellowstone River, which flows through town, provides white water for rafting and kayaking.

The campground sits on an open hillside, providing little shade and no privacy between most of the campsites. Site 7 at the top of the campground road has the most privacy and garners a little shade from aspens. Eagle Creek runs along the west side of the campground, surrounded by brush, aspens, and willows. The grassy campground—green in July, brown by August—is roomy enough for tents, but many of the sites are sloped. A stock corral sits adjacent to the main campground road; two campsites ring the dusty parking lot. Views from the campground extend across the valley to Mammoth Hot Springs and Yellowstone National Park's rugged northern peaks.

Campsites, facilities: The campground has 16 RV or tent campsites. RVs are limited to 48 feet. Facilities include picnic tables, fire rings with grills, bear boxes, stock facilities, and a vault toilet. No drinking water is available. Bring your own, or if you use creek water, boil or purify it first. Pack out your trash. Leashed pets are permitted. A wheelchair-accessible toilet is available.

Reservations, fees: Reservations are not accepted. Campsites cost $7. An extra vehicle costs $3. Cash or check. Open year-round.

Directions: From Gardiner, climb the hairpins northeast on Jardine Road for 2.1 miles. (The pavement ends in 0.3 mile.) Turn left into the campground.

GPS Coordinates: N 45° 2.581' W 110° 40.840'

Contact: Gallatin National Forest, Gardiner Ranger Station, P.O. Box 5, Hwy. 89 S., Gardiner, MT 59030, 406/848-7375, www.fs.fed.us/r1/gallatin.

4 ROCKY MOUNTAIN CAMPGROUND

Scenic rating: 8

in downtown Gardiner north of Yellowstone National Park's north entrance in Montana

Located at 5,357 feet in elevation, Rocky Mountain Campground sits in downtown Gardiner within walking distance to shopping, restaurants, the ranger station, visitors centers, art galleries, and groceries. The campground is four blocks from the Roosevelt Arch, the north entrance to Yellowstone National Park. Gardiner is a hub for fishing, rafting, and horseback-riding outfitters. Four raft companies guide trips on the Yellowstone River, which slices through town. Several fly shops can provide advice on the best places to fish the river and what flies to use when. From town, a trail traverses east along the Yellowstone River. Mountain bikers head to the five-mile abandoned railroad bed paralleling the Yellowstone River between Gardiner and the park boundary at Reese Creek.

On a bluff in Gardiner, the campground commands views of the town, Yellowstone River, and the north slopes of Yellowstone National Park. The park has three types of campsites: standard, deluxe, and premium. Many of the standard and deluxe sites rim the edge of the bluff, with the best views. Premium sites include all the amenities, with room for slide-outs. The campsites, which are stacked up in parking-lot fashion lacking in privacy, are grassy with gravel parking pads. Some sites are shaded by large trees. Traffic noise is audible.

Campsites, facilities: The campground has 87 RV campsites. Of those, 16 can accommodate tents. RVs are limited to 45 feet. The campground has 28 pull-through campsites, 50 sites that accommodate rigs with four slide-outs, and 60 with full hookups for water, sewer, and electricity up to 50 amps. Facilities include flush toilets, showers, a coin-op launderette, picnic tables, fire rings, drinking water, wireless Internet ($2.50 for standard sites), cable TV, propane, miniature golf, and a disposal station. Leashed pets are permitted, but only two per campsite. A wheelchair-accessible toilet is available.

Reservations, fees: Reservations are accepted. Campsites cost $38–51. Weekly rates are also available. Seniors can get a discount, and rates in April, May, late September, and October are cheaper. Cash, check, or credit card. Open mid-April–mid-October.

Directions: In Gardiner on Highway 89, turn northeast onto Jardine Road. Drive 0.1 mile up the hill and turn right.

GPS Coordinates: N 45° 1.988' W 110° 42.186'

Contact: Rocky Mountain Campground, 14 Jardine Rd., Gardiner, MT 59030, 406/848-7251 or 877/534-6931, www.rockymountain-campground.com.

5 YELLOWSTONE RV PARK

Scenic rating: 7

west of downtown Gardiner on the Yellowstone River north of Yellowstone National Park in Montana

At 5,200 feet in elevation, Yellowstone RV Park overlooks the Yellowstone River just outside downtown Gardiner. Views across the canyon sometimes lend sightings of wildlife—moose, antelope, bighorns, elk, deer, ospreys, and bald eagles. The campground is 1.3 miles from the Roosevelt Arch, the north entrance to Yellowstone National Park, and 0.3 mile from Gardiner. Gardiner is a hub for fishing, rafting, and horseback-riding outfitters. Four raft companies guide trips on the Yellowstone River. Several fly shops can provide advice on the best places to fish the river and what flies to use when. From town, a trail traverses east along the Yellowstone River. Mountain bikers head to the five-mile abandoned railroad bed paralleling the Yellowstone River between Gardiner and the park boundary at Reese Creek.

The campground has two rows of RV sites—one overlooks the river and the other lines up like a parking lot. The campsites are open, sunny, and speckled with a few low trees. A rail fence runs along the river canyon to mark where the slope drops to the water. A dirt road with gravel parking pads loops through the lawn sites but kicks up dust. Views span the brown, barren sagebrush canyon sweeping up from the river. With the campground squeezed between the river and the highway, the sounds of both permeate the campsites. Winds frequently blow through the canyon.

Campsites, facilities: This campground has 46 RV campsites and can accommodate tents in 10 of them. RV pull-throughs can accommodate rigs up to 70 feet. Facilities include picnic tables, flush toilets, showers, drinking water, hookups for water, sewer, and electricity up to 50 amps, cable TV, a coin-op launderette, a disposal station, a modem hookup, and wireless Internet. Leashed pets are permitted. A wheelchair-accessible toilet is available.

Reservations, fees: Reservations are accepted. Campsites cost $36–43. Rates are based on a maximum of six people per site. Cash, check, or credit card. Open May–October.

Directions: From downtown Gardiner where the bridge crosses the Yellowstone River, drive northwest on Highway 89 for 0.9 mile. Turn south at milepost 1.1 into the campground. GPS Coordinates: N 45° 2.324' W 110° 43.438'

Contact: Yellowstone RV Park and Campground, P.O. Box 634, 117 Hwy. 89 S., Gardiner, MT 59030, 406/848-7496.

⑥ MAMMOTH

🚶 🚲 🛶 🎣 🐎 ♿ 🚙 ⛺

Scenic rating: 8

at Mammoth Hot Springs on the northwest corner in Yellowstone National Park

BEST (

Located on an arid slope at 6,039 feet, Mammoth Campground at Mammoth Hot Springs

Mammoth Hot Springs form changing travertine terraces that boil and steam.

© BECKY LOMAX

offers a sweeping view of the dry, sagebrush canyon and Mount Everts. With elk hanging around the lawns, the town—historic Fort Yellowstone—contains restaurants, gift shops, Albright Visitor Center, and Yellowstone's park headquarters. Horseback rides are available. Boardwalks, stairs, and trails loop through steaming Mammoth Hot Springs. Upper Terrace Drive, which does not permit buses, RVs, or trailers on its narrow, curvy road, arcs through more mineral terraces. The six-mile Bunsen Peak Road is a mountain-bike trail looping around 8,564-foot Bunsen Peak. The Gardner River offers trout fishing in summer. Mammoth does not have a developed hot springs for soaking, but you can visit Boiling River. On the entrance road, locate parking lots 1.5 miles north of the campground and hike 0.5 mile to the volunteer-maintained natural hot pools on the Gardner River.

If Mammoth Campground were any other place, most people would bypass it.

The sagebrush and grass campsites have little privacy, little shade, and are exposed to winds and weather. Views include other campsites. Because the campground is tucked in a hairpin on the highway, you'll hear and see vehicles both above and below the campground. Nevertheless, it is a popular campground to access the Mammoth area; plan to arrive early in summer to claim a campsite. Evening ranger programs are offered in summer.

Campsites, facilities: Mammoth Campground has 85 RV or tent campsites. The gravel parking pads, which are all pull-throughs, can fit RVs up to 75 feet. Tent platforms are available in 51 campsites. Facilities include picnic tables, fire rings with grills, flush toilets, drinking water, and garbage service. Generators are permitted 8 A.M.–8 P.M. Leashed pets are permitted. A wheelchair-accessible toilet is available, and five campsites are wheelchair-accessible.

Reservations, fees: Reservations are not accepted. Campsites cost $14. Shared hiker and biker campsites cost $5 per person. Cash or check. Open year-round.

Directions: From the north entrance to Yellowstone National Park, drive south for five miles on the north entrance road. From park headquarters in Mammoth, drive 0.7 mile toward Gardiner. Turn west into the campground.

GPS Coordinates: N 44° 58.377' W 110° 41.600'

Contact: Yellowstone National Park, P.O. Box 168, Yellowstone, WY 82190-0168, 307/344-7381, www.nps.gov/yell.

⁊ INDIAN CREEK

🚶 🚴 ⛵ 🏕 ♿ 🚐 ⛺

Scenic rating: 8

between Mammoth and Norris in Yellowstone National Park

BEST (

Sitting at 7,298 feet in elevation, Indian Creek perches at the confluence of the Gardner River,

Obsidian Creek, and Indian Creek in Yellowstone National Park's northwest corner. In the four miles north of the campground, the Grand Loop Road passes the marshy meadows of Gardners Hole, which offers excellent wildlife-watching opportunities for moose, elk, and bears. Fishing is available for small brook trout in the Gardner River and the two creeks. The six-mile Bunsen Peak Road is a mountain-bike trail looping around 8,564-foot Bunsen Peak. Its Golden Gate Trailhead sits about four miles north of the campground. A separate hiking trail goes to its summit. The campground also sits at the junction of several older trails that go south along Obsidian Creek and west to Bighorn Pass.

Indian Creek sat in the midst of the 1988 wildfire that ripped through Yellowstone. While silvered trunks litter hillsides, fast-growing lodgepoles are converting the slopes to green again. The campground sits in a loose lodgepole forest with grassy meadows, offering a variety of campsites from shady to sunny. Views of the surrounding peaks include the 10,023-foot Antler Peak to the west. Due to its smaller size and location away from Yellowstone's big hubs, this campground is quieter and more relaxing than many of the park's larger ones. The campsites are also spaced out a little more for privacy, and those adjacent to larger meadows can offer evening and morning wildlife-watching.

Campsites, facilities: The campground has 71 RV or tent campsites. Ten campsites can accommodate RVs up to 40 feet; 35 campsites can fit RVs up to 30 feet. Generators are not permitted. Facilities include picnic tables, fire rings with grills, vault toilets, drinking water, firewood for sale, bear boxes, and garbage service. Leashed pets are permitted. A wheelchair-accessible toilet is available.

Reservations, fees: Reservations are not accepted. Campsites cost $12. Shared hiker and biker campsites cost $5 per person. Cash or check. Open mid-June–mid-September.

Directions: From Mammoth, drive 8.5 miles south on the Grand Loop Road. From Norris

Junction, drive 12.5 miles north. Turn west and drive 0.3 mile to the campground.

GPS Coordinates: N 44° 53.200' W 110° 44.093'

Contact: Yellowstone National Park, P.O. Box 168, Yellowstone, WY 82190-0168, 307/344-7381, www.nps.gov/yell.

8 TOWER FALL
🚶 🚵 ⛴ 🐕 ♿ 🚐 ⛺

Scenic rating: 7

between Tower-Roosevelt and Canyon Village in Yellowstone National Park

Located at 6,535 feet on the east side of the Grand Loop, Tower Fall Campground sits above the Tower Falls Complex in Yellowstone National Park. The area buzzes in summer with visitors stopping at the popular attraction, which includes a general store, picnic tables, and trail to view the 132-foot falls and the Yellowstone River. Fishing is available in the river. Roosevelt Lodge, 2.5 miles north, offers trail rides, stagecoach rides, and a nightly western cookout dinner. Mountain biking is permitted from the campground two miles on the Old Chittenden Service Road to Grand Loop Road. About six miles south of the campground, bikers can also ride three miles up Mount Washburn from the Chittenden Road parking area to the summit. You can also reach the Lamar Valley, famous for its wolves, in a 15-minute drive.

On a bluff above the Grand Loop Road, the campground sits on an arid north-facing hillside in a sparse, mixed forest of firs and pines that only shade some of the campsites. Dry grasses, dust, and forest duff make up the campsite floors, which are surrounded by green wild grasses in early July but brown in August. The open campground permits views of neighboring campers; sites around the outside of the loop have more privacy. Sites at the lower end of the campground overlook employee housing. Most of the campsites include views of forested and sagebrush slopes. Evening ranger programs may be offered in summer. Plan to arrive by 11 A.M. to claim a spot.

Campsites, facilities: The campground has 30 RV or tent campsites. RVs are limited to 30 feet, but the parking pads actually work better for smaller RVs, such as truck campers, minivans, and trailer popups. Facilities include picnic tables, fire rings with grills, vault toilets, drinking water, bear boxes, and garbage service. Generators are not allowed. Leashed pets are permitted. A wheelchair-accessible toilet is available.

Reservations, fees: Reservations are not accepted. Campsites cost $12. Shared hiker and biker campsites cost $5 per person. Cash or check. Open mid-May–late September.

Directions: From Tower-Roosevelt Junction, drive three miles south on the Grand Loop Road. From Canyon Village, drive 16 miles north. Turn west and drive 0.3 mile up the hill to the campground. The campground road has one hairpin turn.

GPS Coordinates: N 44° 53.376' W 110° 23.450'

Contact: Yellowstone National Park, P.O. Box 168, Yellowstone, WY 82190-0168, 307/344-7381, www.nps.gov/yell.

9 SLOUGH CREEK
🚶 ⛴ 🐕 ♿ 🚐 ⛺

Scenic rating: 7

on Slough Creek in the northeastern corner in Yellowstone National Park

BEST (

At an elevation of 6,249 feet, Slough Creek is one of Yellowstone National Park's smallest campgrounds—hence its popularity. The campground sits in the southwest corner of the Absaroka-Beartooth Mountains. Fly-fishing for Yellowstone cutthroat trout is available along Slough Creek and Buffalo Creek, the two creeks forming a confluence at the campground. The Slough Creek Trail—actually an old wagon road—departs south of the campground to meet the Buffalo Plateau Trail and then drops back down a trail that ends with fording the river at the campground, creating a 4.6-mile loop. For those looking to spot wolves, the famed Lamar Valley sits east of the campground. Go for a drive early or late in the day. Yellowstone Association Institute (406/848-2400, www.yellowstoneassociation. org), which is also located in the Lamar Valley, offers educational programs for all ages.

This campground is prized by those who enjoy quiet and solitude, so plan to arrive early to claim a site. Its remote location off the main park roads guarantees silence so that you can hear wolves howl and owls hoot at night. Various campsites are available, both sunny and shaded, many lining up along Slough Creek. Sites 16 and above are better suited for tents but not limited to them. The campground rims a huge sagebrush and wildflower meadow that can be good for spotting elk, bison, bighorn sheep, and foxes. Some sites are more private than others, tucked behind trees or brush, but from most, you'll see other campers.

Campsites, facilities: The campground has 14 RV or tent campsites and 15 campsites requiring a walk in that work better for tenting. Vehicle combinations are limited to 30 feet. Generators are not permitted. Facilities include picnic tables, fire rings with grills, vault toilets, bear boxes, drinking water, garbage service, and a campground host. Leashed pets are permitted. A wheelchair-accessible toilet is available.

Reservations, fees: Reservations are not accepted. Sites cost $12. Cash or check. Open late May–October.

Directions: From Tower-Roosevelt Junction, drive 5.8 miles east on the northeast entrance road. From the northeast entrance station, drive 23.2 miles west. Turn north onto the dirt road and drive 2.3 miles to the campground. GPS Coordinates: N 44° 56.938' W 110° 18.403'

Contact: Yellowstone National Park, P.O. Box 168, Yellowstone, WY 82190-0168, 307/344-7381, www.nps.gov/yell.

10 PEBBLE CREEK

Scenic rating: 7

on Pebble Creek in the northeast corner of Yellowstone National Park

BEST (

At 6,900 feet, Pebble Creek Campground sits in the mountains, in contrast to Yellowstone National Park's other campgrounds. High in the Soda Butte Valley at the south end of Icebox Canyon, the southeast Absaroka-Beartooth Mountains rise to 10,000 feet around it—snowcapped well into June. In summer, Soda Butte Creek is lined nearly wall-to-wall with anglers casting flies; it maintains a reputation for prime trout fishing. Pebble Creek offers fishing, too. The campground is also a superb wildlife habitat for grizzly bears, and the famed Lamar Valley about five miles south offers frequent bison- and moose-watching, plus the chance to see wolves. Yellowstone Association Institute (406/848-2400, www. yellowstoneassociation.org), which is also in the Lamar Valley, offers educational programs for all ages. The Pebble Creek Trail follows the creek 6.5 miles north to the Absaroka-Beartooth Wilderness. Mountain biking is available for one mile on the Rose Creek Service Road behind the Lamar Ranger Station.

Pebble Creek squeezes its campsites close together into two loops in a sparse aspen and lodgepole forest mixed with a wildflower meadow that blooms in July with cow parsnips, pink sticky geraniums, and yarrow. While views include neighboring campers, they also sweep up to the rugged, glacier-carved high peaks surrounding the campground. Even though the campground is removed from the more hectic areas of the park, vehicles stream by during the day. But at night, it quiets. Choices for campsites include partly shaded to sunny sites.

Campsites, facilities: The campground has 30 RV or tent campsites. RVs are limited to mid-sized rigs. Facilities include picnic tables, fire rings with grills, vault toilets, drinking water, garbage service, bear boxes, and campground hosts. Generators are not allowed. Leashed pets are permitted. A wheelchair-accessible toilet is available.

Reservations, fees: Reservations are not accepted. Sites cost $12. Shared hiker and biker campsites cost $5 per person. Cash or check. Open mid-June –September.

Directions: From Tower-Roosevelt Junction, drive 20 miles east on the northeast entrance road. From the northeast entrance station, drive nine miles west. Turn north onto the dirt road and drive 0.1 mile to the campground. GPS Coordinates: N 44° 55.018' W 114° 6.831'

Contact: Yellowstone National Park, P.O. Box 168, Yellowstone, WY 82190-0168, 307/344-7381, www.nps.gov/yell.

11 SODA BUTTE

Scenic rating: 7

on the Beartooth Scenic Byway east of Cooke City outside the northeast entrance to Yellowstone National Park in Montana

Sitting at 7,791 feet, Soda Butte Campground is the last Forest Service campground for those heading west into Yellowstone National Park. The campground sits 4.5 miles from the northeastern entrance. Located one mile east of Cooke City with 10,000-foot-high Sheep Mountain to the north, the campground is convenient for hooking up with local outfitters for fly-fishing or horse-packing trips into the Absaroka-Beartooth Wilderness about two miles north. Several nearby trails head into the wilderness, but mountain bikes are permitted only to the border. A 3.5-mile trail leads to Lady of the Lake. Another less-used trail climbs south up Republic Creek in the North Absaroka Wilderness to Republic Pass on the border of Yellowstone National Park.

Recent thinning of beetle-killed trees has opened up much of this campground. Cow parsnips, sticky pink geraniums, lupines, and grass meadows cover most of the campground, interspersed with a few lodgepole pines and spruces for shade (sites 11–12). Choose between open, sunny sites and those few with privacy from the trees. The road runs above the campground, so vehicle noise filters in, and you can also hear the stream burbling along the south end. Sites sit close together enough that you'll see what the neighbors are doing. Sites 11–21 offer better spaces for tents.

Campsites, facilities: This campground has 27 RV and tent campsites with the largest parking spur accommodating vehicle combinations up to 60 feet. Facilities include picnic tables, fire rings with grills, vault toilets, drinking water, bear boxes, garbage service, and a campground host. Bring your own firewood. Leashed pets are permitted. A wheelchair-accessible toilet is available.

Reservations, fees: Reservations are not accepted. Campsites cost $9. An extra vehicle costs $3. Cash or check. Open July–September., depending on snow.

Directions: From the Beartooth Scenic Byway (Highway 212) about one mile east of Cooke City or 14 miles west of the Chief Joseph Highway 296 junction, turn south at milepost 4.5 into the campground. GPS Coordinates: N 45° 1.388' W 109° 54.947'

Contact: Gallatin National Forest, Gardiner Ranger Station, P.O. Box 5, Hwy. 89 S., Gardiner, MT 59030, 406/848-7375, www.fs.fed.us/r1/gallatin.

12 COLTER

Scenic rating: 8

on the Beartooth Scenic Byway east of Cooke City outside the northeast entrance to Yellowstone National Park in Montana

At an elevation of 8,044 feet, Colter Campground sits two miles east of Cooke City,

Montana, and six miles from the northeast entrance to Yellowstone National Park. Surrounding peaks climb over 10,000 feet high, and the 900,000-acre Absaroka-Beartooth Wilderness is two miles to the north. Hiking and mountain-biking trails depart 0.2 mile west. The route heads 3.5 miles to Lady of the Lake, and farther to other lakes in the wilderness area. Mountain bikers can only travel as far as the wilderness boundary.

Campsites are packed in close together in this sunny campground. A loose forest of lodgepoles, spruces, and subalpine firs remains for specks of shade, with sites 5 and 7–11 garnering views of the mountains to the west. Noise from the road seeps into the campground, but the route is not a major trucking thoroughfare, so it quiets at night. The sites have small tent spaces.

Campsites, facilities: The campground has 23 RV or tent campsites. The largest gravel parking pad can accommodate vehicles up to 66 feet, but the Forest Service states that the gravel access road is not suitable for RV combinations longer than 48 feet. Facilities include picnic tables, fire rings with grills, bear boxes, vault toilets, drinking water, garbage service, and campground hosts. No firewood is available; bring your own. Leashed pets are permitted. A wheelchair-accessible toilet is available.

Reservations, fees: Reservations are not accepted. Campsites cost $9. An extra vehicle costs $3. Cash or check. Open mid-July–September.

Directions: From the Beartooth Scenic Byway (Highway 212), about two miles east of Cooke City or 13 miles west of the Chief Joseph Highway 296 junction, turn north at milepost 5.6 into the campground. (The sign is off the highway and difficult to see.)

GPS Coordinates: N 45° 1.685' W 109° 53.645'

Contact: Gallatin National Forest, Gardiner Ranger Station, P.O. Box 5, Hwy. 89 S., Gardiner, MT 59030, 406/848-7375, www.fs.fed.us/r1/gallatin.

13 CHIEF JOSEPH

Scenic rating: 7

on the Beartooth Scenic Byway east of Cooke City outside the northeast entrance to Yellowstone National Park in Montana

On the west end of the Beartooth Scenic Byway, Chief Joseph Campground, elevation 8,037 feet, sits four miles east of Cooke City, Montana, and seven miles from the northeast entrance to Yellowstone National Park. The campground is named after the Nez Perce chief who led his people across Idaho, Wyoming, and Montana while being chased by the U.S. Army. Across the road from the campground are interpretive sites for the Nez Perce National Historic Trail and Watchable Wildlife, along with the Clarks Fork Trailhead and Flume Interpretive Trail. Trails also access the 900,000 acre Absaroka-Beartooth Wilderness Area north of the campground. A two-mile trail leads to Curl Lake. Other short hikes lead to Rock Island Lake and Vernon Lake. Mountain bikers can access the local forest roads and trails only up to the wilderness boundary. Fishing is available in the Clarks Fork of the Yellowstone River, also across the highway from the campground.

Tucked into a mature lodgepole pine and spruce forest, Chief Joseph has partly shaded to filtered sunlight campsites. This campground has more large trees than neighboring Soda Butte or Colter Campground. The small campground sits close to the highway, so road noise is pervasive; however, it dwindles substantially at night. The campground was reconstructed in summer 2009.

Campsites, facilities: As of 2009, the campground had six RV or tent campsites, but the number of sites may change. The largest gravel parking pad can accommodate vehicles up to 60 feet, but the Forest Service advises that the access road is not suitable for vehicle combinations over 42 feet in length. Facilities include picnic tables, fire rings with grills, a vault toilet, drinking water, bear boxes, garbage service, and campground hosts. No firewood is available; bring your own. Leashed pets are permitted. A wheelchair-accessible toilet is available.

Reservations, fees: Reservations are not accepted. Campsites cost $9. An extra vehicle costs $3. Cash or check. Open mid-July–September.

Directions: From the Beartooth Scenic Byway (Highway 212), about four miles east of Cooke City or 11 miles west of the Chief Joseph Highway 296 junction, turn south at milepost 7 into the campground.
GPS Coordinates: N 45° 1.109' W 109° 52.347'

Contact: Gallatin National Forest, Gardiner Ranger Station, P.O. Box 5, Hwy. 89 S., Gardiner, MT 59030, 406/848-7375, www.fs.fed.us/r1/gallatin.

14 YELLOWSTONE HOLIDAY RV

Scenic rating: 8

on Hebgen Lake northwest of West Yellowstone in Montana

Located on the north shore of Hebgen Lake at 6,547 feet, Yellowstone Holiday RV Campground is flanked by the Madison Range. A 15-minute drive reaches West Yellowstone and the west entrance to Yellowstone National Park. Hebgen Lake is popular for boating, waterskiing, sailing, and fishing. The campground is part of a marina that includes a cement boat ramp, boat slips, fuel, rental boats, trailer parking, and a fish-cleaning station. The marina rents fishing boats, kayaks, canoes, and paddleboats and sells fishing licenses.

The campground sits on a low open plateau on the lake, within view of the highway, lake, and mountains, which are snowcapped in June. Mowed lawn surrounds the campsites, but very little shade is available. Because

of its openness, the afternoon winds cruise through and privacy is minimal, but the views encompass a broad panorama. Most of the sites, which are back-ins, are adjacent to the water. Sites 6–11 claim prime waterfront. The pull-through sites are behind a set of cabins nearer the highway.

Campsites, facilities: The campground has 36 RV campsites. Eight pull-through sites can accommodate big rigs. Hookups include water, sewer, and electricity up to 50 amps. Facilities include picnic tables, fire rings, flush toilets, showers, a coin-op launderette, a general store, propane, a marina, horseshoes, volleyball, tetherball, a camper kitchen, and a modem dataport desk. Leashed dogs are permitted.

Reservations, fees: Reservations are accepted. RV sites cost $39–49. Add on 7 percent Montana bed tax. Weekly, monthly, and seasonal rates are also available. Cash, check, or credit card. Open mid-May–early September.

Directions: From West Yellowstone drive north on Highway 191 for eight miles and then turn west onto Highway 287 for five miles. The entrance sits on the south side of the road.
GPS Coordinates: N 44° 48.202' W 111° 12.950'

Contact: Yellowstone Holiday, 16990 Hebgen Lake Rd., West Yellowstone, MT 59758, 406/646-4242 or 877/646-4242, www.yellowstoneholiday.com.

15 RAINBOW POINT

Scenic rating: 7

on Hebgen Lake north of West Yellowstone in Gallatin National Forest in Montana

Located at 6,541 feet, Rainbow Point Campground sits on Rainbow Bay, an east arm of Hebgen Lake, the site of Montana's largest earthquake in 1959. Views from the beach at the campground look northwest to the Madison Range. The campground, about 10 miles north of West Yellowstone and 11 miles from the west entrance to Yellowstone National Park, has a boat launch, which includes a cement ramp, docks, and trailer parking. The lake is popular for swimming, waterskiing, boating, and fishing—known for its dry fly trout fishing. Rainbow Bay is more sheltered from winds than the main lake, making it more appealing for canoeing and kayaking. The 16-mile-long lake is also surrounded by summer homes.

Four loops of campsites tuck into a thick shady forest of tall lodgepole pines that admit only filtered sunlight. Tree trunks act as privacy fences between the close campsites because little understory can grow beneath the trees. The loops are set back from the lake with only a few sites at the front of loops A and B catching glimpses of blue water across the road and between the trees. Paths lead from each loop to the beach. Big, flat spaces for tents are available. The campground is quiet at night.

Campsites, facilities: The campground has 86 RV and tent campsites. RV combinations are limited to 40 feet. Facilities include picnic tables, fire rings with grills, vault and pit toilets, drinking water, garbage service, electrical hookups at 15 campsites, bear boxes, a boat launch, firewood for sale, and campground hosts. Leashed pets are permitted. A wheelchair-accessible toilet is available, and site A1 is wheelchair-accessible.

Reservations, fees: Reservations are accepted (877/444-6777, www.recreation.gov). Campsites cost $14, plus $6 more for those with electrical hookups. An extra vehicle costs $6. Cash or check. Open mid-May–mid-September.

Directions: From West Yellowstone, drive north on Highway 191 for five miles and turn west onto the two-lane paved Rainbow Point Road (Forest Road 6954) for 3.2 miles. Then turn north onto the gravel Rainbow Point Road (Forest Road 6952) for 1.7 miles. The road veers right to the boat launch, but continue straight to reach the campground. GPS Coordinates: N 44° 46.726' W 111° 10.462'

Contact: Gallatin National Forest, Hebgen Lake District Office, P.O. Box 520, West Yellowstone, MT 59758, 406/823-6961.

16 BAKER'S HOLE

Scenic rating: 7

on the Madison River north of West Yellowstone in Gallatin National Forest in Montana

Baker's Hole Campground, which sits at 6,600 feet, is three miles north of West Yellowstone and four miles from the west entrance to Yellowstone National Park. The campground is strung along a narrow strip of forest in between the highway and the Madison River. In this stretch, the river slows to a crawl as it winds in convoluted oxbows through willow wetlands that provide habitat for moose and birds, plus churn out hordes of mosquitoes. The Madison River is famed for its trout fishing, and West Yellowstone is the headquarters for fishing outfitters. The 1.4-mile Riverside Trail for mountain bikers and hikers tours the river from West Yellowstone.

Due to its location adjacent to the highway, the campground picks up vehicle noise—especially from commercial trucks. Across the road is the Yellowstone Airport, which sees three commercial flights arrive and depart daily in the summer. A paved road loops through the campground, which is forested with short lodgepole pines and blooming with fireweed. Some campsites (42, 44, 46–48, 52, 55, and 57) have views of the mountains, and several campsites overlook the river. Sites, which vary from shady to sunny, are spread out for privacy, but the lack of undergrowth means you'll see a neighboring campsite or two.

Campsites, facilities: The campground has 73 RV and tent campsites. Large RVs can be accommodated in double-wide gravel parking pads up to 75 feet. Facilities include picnic tables, fire rings with grills, electrical hookups at 33 campsites, vault and pit toilets, drinking water, garbage service, bear boxes, firewood for sale, campground hosts, and a fishing platform. Leashed pets are permitted. A wheelchair-accessible toilet is available.

Reservations, fees: Reservations are not accepted. Campsites cost $14, plus $6 for those sites with electricity. An extra vehicle costs $6. Cash or check. Open mid-May–mid-September.

Directions: From West Yellowstone, drive north on Highway 191 for almost three miles. At milepost 2.9, turn east onto the paved road into the campground.

GPS Coordinates: N 44° 42.215' W 111° 6.023'

Contact: Gallatin National Forest, Hebgen Lake District Office, P.O. Box 520, West Yellowstone, MT 59758, 406/823-6961.

17 MADISON ARM RESORT

Scenic rating: 7

on Hebgen Lake north of West Yellowstone in Montana

Madison Arm Resort sits on the south shore of the Madison Arm of Hebgen Lake at 6,547 feet in elevation. Its sandy beach and marina tuck into a small bay protected by small islands of sand that grow larger as the water level in the lake drops throughout the summer. The lake is popular for boating, fishing, waterskiing, sailing, and swimming. Anglers go after rainbow and brown trout, and the resort rents out 14-foot aluminum boats with eight horsepower motors, canoes, paddleboats, kayaks, and water-bikes. A buoyed swimming area is available, along with a cement boat ramp and boat slips. The store sells fishing licenses. Bicyclists ride the dirt forest roads in the area. The resort sits 8.5 miles from West Yellowstone and 9.5 miles from the west entrance to Yellowstone National Park.

A forest of tall lodgepole pines surrounds the campground. Tent campsites are along the waterfront between trees, and RV campsites sit back in the trees and open areas. The quiet campground packs its campsites close together; privacy is available only inside the tent or RV. Also, back-in sites can pose difficulties for some RVs squeezing in. The resort tends to get families returning year after year.

Campsites, facilities: The resort has 52 RV campsites with hookups for water, sewer, and up to 30-amp electricity. Pull-through sites can accommodate large RVs. Twenty-two tent campsites are also available. Facilities include picnic tables, fire rings, flush toilets, hot showers, a coin-op launderette, a convenience store, propane, firewood, gifts, boat rentals, and wireless Internet. Leashed pets are permitted.

Reservations, fees: Reservations are accepted. RV hookups cost $34–36. Tent campsites cost $25. Rates are for two people. Each additional person costs $4. Add on the 7 percent Montana bed tax. Cash, check, or credit card. Open mid-May–September.

Directions: From West Yellowstone, drive north on Highway 191 for three miles. Turn west onto the dusty gravel Madison Arm Road (Forest Road 291) for 5.3 miles. The entrance to the resort is on the right side of the road.

GPS Coordinates: N 44° 44.142' W 111° 11.159'

Contact: Madison Arm Resort, P.O. Box 1410, 5475 Madison Arm Rd., West Yellowstone, MT 59758, 406/646-9328, www.madisonarmresort.com.

18 LIONSHEAD RV PARK

Scenic rating: 7

west of West Yellowstone in Montana

At 6,718 feet, Lionshead RV Park is seven miles west of West Yellowstone and eight miles from the west entrance to Yellowstone National Park. For those looking for the convenience of being near town with its activities, but who want a place less crowded and noisy, this campground provides an alternative to the West Yellowstone hubbub. The campground is behind a motel and Alice's Restaurant. Denny Creek flows past the back of the campground, with two bridges allowing access to a trail and constructed fishing ponds. Other fishing is available within 10 miles at Hebgen Lake or the Madison River.

Most of the RV area is open without trees, but the tent sites rim the perimeter in pines, which offer some shade. For RVers, 100 campsites are pull-throughs. A gravel road loops through the campground, which has mowed-lawn campsites set very close together with little privacy. The proximity to the highway means vehicle noise enters the campground.

Campsites, facilities: This campground has 109 RV campsites and 26 tent campsites. The campground can accommodate vehicle combinations up to 80 feet. Hookups are available for water, sewer, and electricity up to 50 amps. Facilities include picnic tables, fire rings, grills, flush toilets, showers, drinking water, a coin-op launderette, a convenience store, horseshoes, propane, a playground, a dog walk, a camping kitchen, and wireless Internet. Leashed pets are permitted. A wheelchair-accessible toilet is available.

Reservations, fees: Reservations are accepted. RV campsites cost $35–55. Tent campsites cost $22–31. Add on 7 percent Montana bed tax. Cash, check, or credit card. Open late May–mid-September.

Directions: From West Yellowstone, drive seven miles west on Highway 20 to the campground, on the north side of the road. GPS Coordinates: N 44° 41.242' W 111° 15.124'

Contact: Lionshead RV Resort, 1545 Targhee Pass Hwy., West Yellowstone, MT 59758, 406/646-7662 (summer), 406/646-9584 (winter), www.lionsheadrv.com.

19 YELLOWSTONE KOA

Scenic rating: 7

west of West Yellowstone in Montana

Sitting at 6,584 feet in elevation west of West Yellowstone, the Yellowstone KOA offers a place to camp away from the crowded West Yellowstone streets but convenient for exploring the town. The west entrance to Yellowstone National Park is seven miles east of the campground. Horseback rides and weekend rodeos are available nearby, along with fishing at Hebgen Lake or the Madison River. But not right at the campground.

In typical KOA fashion, the campground fills every niche of the property with close-set campsites. Due to its location outside of town and surrounded by open prairie, views encompass the mountains of the Madison Range. Pines near almost every campsite provide a bit of shade for the sunny, mowed-lawn campground, and tent sites are divided with split rail fences and pines. You can hear vehicles passing on the two-lane highway, but traffic dwindles at night. A paved road loops through the campground, but the parking pads are gravel.

Campsites, facilities: This KOA has 168 RV campsites and 84 tent campsites. Some of the campsites can accommodate big rigs, and hookups include sewer, water, and electricity up to 50 amps. Thirteen tent sites also have water and electricity. Facilities include picnic tables, fire rings, flush toilets, showers, drinking water, a coin-op launderette, a convenience store, an indoor pool, a hot tub, a camping kitchen, pancake breakfasts, nightly barbecue dinners, an ice cream and espresso kiosk, mini-golf, a playground, basketball, a dog walk, a game room, bike rentals, propane, and wireless Internet. Leashed pets are permitted. A wheelchair-accessible toilet is available.

Reservations, fees: Reservations are accepted. RV campsites cost $32–54. Tent campsites cost

$22–31. Rates cover two people. Each extra adult costs $6. Add on 7 percent Montana bed tax. Cash, check, or credit card. Open late May–September.

Directions: From West Yellowstone, drive west on Highway 20 for six miles. The campground is on the north side of the highway.

GPS Coordinates: N 44° 41.204' W 111° 13.008'

Contact: Yellowstone Park KOA, P.O. Box 348, 3305 Targhee Pass Hwy., West Yellowstone, MT 59758, 406/646-7606 or 800/562-7591, www.yellowstonekoa.com.

20 RUSTIC WAGON RV CAMPGROUND

Scenic rating: 4

in West Yellowstone in Montana

In West Yellowstone, the Rustic Wagon RV Campground sits on the opposite side of town from the busy shopping, restaurant, and tourist district. Yet, with town being only seven blocks wide, it still offers the convenience of walking to the visitors center, Yellowstone IMAX Theatre, Grizzly and Wolf Discovery Center, and Museum of the Yellowstone. The town is also headquarters for outfitters for horseback riding, white-water rafting, and fishing. The west entrance gate to Yellowstone National Park is one mile to the east. Hiking four miles or mountain biking 1.4 miles is available on the Riverside Trail, which tours along the Madison River about 1.5 miles east of the campground. Trout fishing is also available in the Madison River.

With its location on the west end of town, the campground is removed from the busy crowds downtown and quieter than the east side of town. The narrow campsites are close together. Spruce and pine trees help give it seclusion from the surrounding residential and commercial properties. Vehicle noise from the highway seeps in, but its side street is not busy. Tent campsites are in a grassy area.

Campsites, facilities: The campground has 45 RV campsites and 10 tent campsites. RV combinations are limited to 70 feet, and hookups have sewer, water, and electricity up to 50 amps. Facilities include picnic tables, flush toilets, showers, a coin-op launderette, cable TV, patios, horseshoes, a playground, and basketball. Leashed pets are allowed in RV sites, but not in tent sites.

Reservations, fees: Reservations are accepted. RV hookup sites cost $38–43. Tent sites cost $31. Rates cover two people. Each additional person older than three costs $3. Add on 10 percent tax. Cash, check, or credit card. Open year-round with 14 pull-through sites plowed in winter.

Directions: In West Yellowstone at the junction of Highways 20 and 191, drive west on Highway 20 (Firehole Avenue) and then angle north, staying on Highway 20 as it departs Firehole Avenue. Drive three blocks, turn north onto Iris Street, and immediately turn right onto Gibbon Street. The campground entrance is on the north side of the block.

GPS Coordinates: N 44° 40.006' W 111° 6.612'

Contact: Rustic Wagon RV Campground and Cabins, P.O. Box 608, 637 Hwy. 20, West Yellowstone, MT 59758, 406/646-7387 or 406/646-7872, www.rusticwagonrv.com.

21 WAGON WHEEL RV

Scenic rating: 4

in downtown West Yellowstone in Montana

At 6,663 feet in elevation, the Wagon Wheel RV Campground sits in downtown West Yellowstone surrounded by residential and commercial properties. The campground spans the length of one block. It is three blocks from the center of town and shopping, restaurants, groceries, and gas. The only reason for staying in town is for the convenience of walking to the visitors center, Yellowstone IMAX Theatre, Grizzly and Wolf Discovery Center, and Museum of the Yellowstone. The campground also sits eight blocks from the west entrance to Yellowstone National Park. Hiking four miles or mountain biking 1.4 miles is available on the Riverside Trail, which tours along the Madison River less than a mile east of the campground. Trout fishing is available in the Madison River. The town is headquarters for outfitters for horseback riding, white-water rafting, and fishing.

The location in downtown West Yellowstone means the campground comes with traffic noise and crowds—although its location off the main drags gives it some seclusion and quiet. The campsites are narrow and squeezed close together. Tall spruces and pines grant shade and a semblance of privacy to the RV sites, which have gravel pull-through or back-in parking pads and patios. Grassy tent sites are in a private area.

Campsites, facilities: The campground has 36 RV campsites and 15 tent campsites. RV combinations are limited to 60 feet. Hookups are available for water, sewer, and electricity up to 30 amps. Facilities include picnic tables, flush toilets, showers, drinking water, a coin-op launderette, a recreation room, cable TV, and wireless Internet. Leashed pets are allowed in the RV sites, but not in the tent sites.

Reservations, fees: Reservations are accepted. RV hookup sites cost $38–43. Tent sites cost $31. Rates cover two people. Each additional person older than three costs $3. Add on 10 percent tax. Cash, check, or credit card. Open mid-May–September.

Directions: In the center of West Yellowstone at the junction of Highway 20 and Highway 191, drive west on Highway 20 (Firehole Avenue) for three blocks. Turn right (north) onto Faithful Street and drive two blocks to Gibbon Avenue. Turn left and immediately left again into the campground.

GPS Coordinates: N 44° 39.829' W 111° 6.408'

Contact: Wagon Wheel RV Campground and Cabins, P.O. Box 608, 408 Gibbon Ave., West Yellowstone, MT 59758, 406/646-7872, www.wagonwheelrv.com.

22 HIDEAWAY RV PARK

Scenic rating: 7

in West Yellowstone outside the west entrance of Yellowstone National Park

Located 10 blocks from the west entrance to Yellowstone National Park, Hideaway RV Park, at 6,664 feet, allows convenient access to the park and the town of West Yellowstone. Shopping, restaurants, the visitors center, the Yellowstone IMAX Theatre, the Grizzly and Wolf Discovery Center, and the Museum of the Yellowstone are within three to seven blocks. The town is also headquarters for outfitters for horseback riding, white-water rafting, and fishing. The Riverside Trail along the Madison River offers hiking (four miles) and mountain biking (1.4 miles) about one mile east of the campground. Trout fishing is available in the Madison River. The campground is one block from a city park with a children's playground and a half block from a launderette.

Hideaway is West Yellowstone's smallest campground, and its location on the north edge of town in a residential area removes it from the busy tourist blocks. A gravel road loops through the campground, which has gravel pull-through or back-in parking pads. Tall conifers lend partial shade to many of the campsites, which are close together.

Campsites, facilities: This campground has 14 RV campsites and one tent campsite. RV combinations are limited to 45 feet, and hookups include water, sewer, and electricity up to 50 amps. Facilities include picnic tables, flush toilets, showers, patios, cable TV, and wireless Internet. Leashed pets are permitted.

Reservations, fees: Reservations are accepted.

RV sites cost $29–33. The tent site costs $18.50. Rates cover two people. Extra people over six years old cost $3 each. During May and September, the campground offers a "pay for six nights and stay for seven" deal. Add on 10 percent tax. Cash, check, or credit card. Open May–mid-October.

Directions: From downtown West Yellowstone at the intersection of Highways 20 and 191, drive west on Highway 20 (Firehole Avenue) for two blocks. Turn north onto Electric Street and drive 2.5 blocks. The entrance is on the left.

GPS Coordinates: N 44° 39.862' W 111° 6.263'

Contact: Hideaway RV Park, 320 Electric St., West Yellowstone, MT 59758, 406/646-9049, www.hideawayrv.com.

23 PONY EXPRESS RV PARK

Scenic rating: 4

in West Yellowstone in Montana

The Pony Express RV Park, at 6,668 feet, sits literally on the edge of West Yellowstone across the street from Yellowstone National Park. The west entrance gate to the park is five blocks away, along with the visitors center, Yellowstone IMAX Theatre, Grizzly and Wolf Discovery Center, and Museum of the Yellowstone. Shopping, restaurants, gas, and groceries are also within five blocks. The town is headquarters for outfitters for horseback riding, white-water rafting, and fishing. The Riverside Trail along the Madison River offers hiking (four miles) and mountain biking (1.4 miles) less than 0.5 mile east of the campground. Trout fishing is also available in the Madison River. The campground shares the block with the Pony Express Motel, part of the same business.

This small campground squeezes campsites close together in an open lot. Some of the campsites look across Boundary Street

into the park, but the view is of a forest—no geysers, mountains, or rivers. The territory comes with a certain amount of noise due to its location in downtown, but perched on the edge of town off the main drags, it is quieter than other locations. A handful of trees dot the campground with minimal shade. Those looking for clear satellite reception will find it here.

Campsites, facilities: The campground has 16 RV campsites. RVs are limited to 38 feet. Hookups include sewer, water, and electricity up to 50 amps. Facilities include picnic tables, flush toilets, showers, a coin-op launderette, wireless Internet, cable TV, and all pull-through sites. Leashed pets are permitted.

Reservations, fees: Reservations are accepted. Campsites cost $29–39. Add on 10 percent tax. Open April–November with full hookups and during winter for dry camping.

Directions: In downtown West Yellowstone, from the intersection of Highway 20 and Highway 191, turn east on Firehole Avenue and drive 1.5 blocks. The entrance is on the left.

GPS Coordinates: N 44° 39.742' W 111° 5.916'

Contact: Pony Express Motel and RV Park, P.O. Box 580, 4 Firehole Ave., West Yellowstone, MT 59758, 406/646-7644 or 800/217-4613, www.yellowstonevacations.com.

24 YELLOWSTONE GRIZZLY RV PARK

Scenic rating: 4

in West Yellowstone in Montana

Located on West Yellowstone's southern edge away from the crowded tourist streets, Yellowstone Grizzly RV—the area's newest campground—is bordered on two sides by the Gallatin National Forest. The west entrance to Yellowstone National Park, shopping, restaurants, visitors center, the Yellowstone

IMAX Theatre, the Grizzly and Wolf Discovery Center, Museum of the Yellowstone, and all outfitters for rafting, horseback riding, and fishing are within five blocks. The Riverside Trail along the Madison River offers hiking (four miles) and mountain biking (1.4 miles) about one mile east of the campground. Trout fishing is available in the Madison River.

The campground—West Yellowstone's largest—was expanded in 2006. Landscaped gardens, lawns, aspens, and lodgepole pines cover the campground, but the trees are still young and provide only partial shade. The RV sites, with paved back-in or pull-through parking pads, cement walkways, and patios, are positioned right next to each other, but they are roomy enough for slide-outs and awnings. The tent campsites ring a grassy area across from the playground and clubhouse, which has outdoor kitchen sinks.

Campsites, facilities: The campground has 261 RV campsites and 16 tent campsites. RV campsites can accommodate vehicle combinations up to 80 feet long, and hookups are available for water, sewer, and electricity up to 100 amps. Facilities include picnic tables, barbecue grills (bring your own charcoal), flush toilets, showers, drinking water, patios, cable TV, wireless Internet (free for premium sites; $4 per day for nonpremium sites), a dog walk, a game room, a playground, a convenience store, a coin-op launderette, and horseshoes. Leashed pets are permitted. A wheelchair-accessible toilet is available.

Reservations, fees: Reservations are accepted. RV campsites cost $47–57. Tent campsites cost $30, and bicycle campsites cost $10. Rates include six people. Each extra person costs $5. A 10 percent tax is added on. Cash, check, or credit card. Off-season rates are available in May and October. Open May–late October.

Directions: In downtown West Yellowstone from the junction of Highway 20 and Highway 191, drive west on Highway 20 for two blocks to Electric Street. Turn south and drive

0.5 mile. The campground entrance sits on the west side of the road opposite Gray Wolf Avenue.

GPS Coordinates: N 44° 39.330' W 111° 6.271'

Contact: Yellowstone Grizzly RV Park, 210 S. Electric St., West Yellowstone, MT 59758, 406/646-4466, www.grizzlyrv.com.

25 MADISON

Scenic rating: 8

on the western side of the Grand Loop in Yellowstone National Park

BEST (

Centrally located in Yellowstone National Park, Madison Campground is popular due to its quick access to the big geyser basins. Old Faithful erupts 16 miles south. Within five miles, Firehole Lake Drive offers short

© BECKY LOMAX

Bison in Yellowstone and the Tetons stand six feet tall and weigh over 2,000 pounds.

boardwalks to hot pools and the Great Fountain Geyser, which spurts 200 feet high, and a 0.5-mile trail winds through the Fountain Paint Pots, which feature multicolored mud pots, geysers, and fumaroles. The campground sits near the confluence of the Gibbon, Madison, and Firehole Rivers at 6,806 feet—all three are trout fisheries. Madison provides outstanding wildlife-watching as bison and elk usually hang out in the meadows along the river. In fall, you can hear the male elk bugling as they round up their harems. Hikers can climb three miles up Purple Mountain for a view of the Firehole and lower Gibbon Valleys. Mountain bikers can ride the 5.5-mile Fountain Flat Drive and the Daisy Geyser cut-off to Biscuit Basin.

Madison Campground comprises around a dozen loops, in a loose forest of tall pine trees for partial shade. With no understory—only tree trunks—campsites are visible to each other. Those at the west end of the campground are more open and sunny, but also garner peek-a-boo views onto the big meadows of the Madison. Paved roads with paved parking pads—both back-in and pull-through—weave through the campground. Although the campground is on the busy west entrance Road, it quiets after dark.

Campsites, facilities: Madison features 280 RV or tent campsites. RVs are limited to 40 feet. Facilities include picnic tables, fire rings with grills, flush toilets, drinking water, bear boxes, garbage services, a disposal station, and an amphitheater for evening interpretive programs. Generators are permitted 8 A.M.–8 P.M. Leashed pets are permitted. A wheelchair-accessible toilet is available.

Reservations, fees: Reservations are accepted (Xanterra Parks and Resorts, 307/344-7311 or 866/439-7375, www.travelyellowstone.com). Sites cost $18.50, plus sales tax and utility fee. Shared hiker and biker campsites cost $5 per person. Cash, check, or credit card. Open May–late October.

Directions: From the west entrance to Yellowstone National Park, drive 14 miles west on the west entrance road. The campground entrance is on the south side of the road. GPS Coordinates: N 44° 38.738' W 110° 51.672'

Contact: Yellowstone National Park, P.O. Box 168, Yellowstone, WY 82190-0168, 307/344-7381, www.nps.gov/yell.

26 NORRIS

Scenic rating: 8

at Norris Geyser Basin on the west side of the Grand Loop in Yellowstone National Park

Sitting at 7,555 feet on the Grand Loop Road's southwest corner, Norris Campground is less than one mile north of Norris Geyser Basin. A 10-minute walk connects the campground with the basin's boardwalks and trails. The geyser basin houses hot pools, steam vents, and Steamboat—the world's tallest geyser, which spouts to 380 feet. Porcelain Basin is a 1.6-mile loop through an austere landscape of colorful minerals, and Back Basin is a two-mile loop that houses the geysers, including the predictable Echinus, which begins eruptions with boiling water filling its basin. Fishing for small brook trout is possible at the campground, at the confluence of the Gibbon River and Solfatara Creek. Hiking trails depart from the campground east to Ice Lake (4.3 miles) and north along Solfatara Creek. Another Ice Lake trailhead sits 3.5 miles east of Norris Junction; it requires a 15-minute walk. But don't carry a fishing rod for the barren lake.

Plan on arriving around 11 A.M. in midsummer to claim a site at this popular campground. Set in a loose pine and fir forest and surrounded by the large Norris meadows, the campground provides an excellent location for spotting moose, elk, bears, and bison. Choose from among the roomy campsites for varying amounts of sun and shade. Neighboring campers are visible. Large, flat spaces are available for tents. Due to its location away from the more populated canyon and lake areas, the campground quiets at night.

Campsites, facilities: Norris has 100 RV or tent campsites. Two campsites are available for RVs up to 50 feet; five sites are available for RVs up to 30 feet. Generators are permitted 8 A.M.–8 P.M. Three campsites are walk-in tent sites. Facilities include picnic tables, fire rings with grills, flush toilets, drinking water, bear boxes, garbage service, and firewood for sale. Leashed pets are permitted. A wheelchair-accessible toilet is available.

Reservations, fees: Reservations are not accepted. Campsites cost $14. Shared hiker and biker campsites cost $5 per person. Cash or check. Open mid-May–September.

Directions: From Norris Junction, drive 0.8 mile north on the Grand Loop Road, or from Mammoth, drive 20.2 miles south. Turn east and drive 0.2 mile into the campground. GPS Coordinates: N 44° 44.269' W 110° 41.623'

Contact: Yellowstone National Park, P.O. Box 168, Yellowstone, WY 82190-0168, 307/344-7381, www.nps.gov/yell.

27 CANYON

🥾 🐕 ♿ 🚐 ⛺

Scenic rating: 9

at Canyon Village and the Grand Canyon of the Yellowstone in Yellowstone National Park

BEST (

Canyon Campground, elevation 7,944 feet, sits just off the busy junction of Grand Loop Road and Norris Canyon Road. The campground is within a five-minute walk of Canyon Village, which houses the Canyon Visitor Education Center. Displays feature live earthquake monitoring. The village also has a grocery, shopping, restaurants, gas, vehicle repairs, and a disposal station. Trail rides are also available. A two-mile road leads to Inspiration Point on the North Rim of the Grand Canyon of the Yellowstone, an

© BECKY LOMAX

The Yellowstone River flows through the Grand Canyon of the Yellowstone and tumbles with several falls.

immense 1,200-foot-deep chasm that plummets with a series of waterfalls. A two-mile trail connects with Grandview Point and Lookout Point, and a 0.5-mile trail switchbacks down to an overlook of the 308-foot Lower Falls. Driving north on the Grand Loop Road through Hayden Valley can yield views of hundreds of bison and sometimes wolves. While the campground does not sit on the Yellowstone River, a 10-minute drive south on the Grand Loop can yield several pullouts for accessing the river for fishing.

Canyon Campground is one of Yellowstone's more heavily forested campgrounds. Nine large loops pack the campsites close together. While the lodgepole pines offer shade, they have little understory, so other campsites are visible through the trunks. With all the traffic at Canyon Village and on the North Rim Road, vehicle noise trickles into the campground during the day, but not at night. The campground fills to capacity almost every day; plan to arrive by 11 A.M. to claim a campsite.

Campsites, facilities: The campground has 272 RV and tent campsites. The campground can accommodate RVs over 30 feet in a limited number of campsites; the campground operators recommend making reservations for rigs over 30 feet. Facilities include picnic tables, fire rings with grills, flush toilets, drinking water, bear boxes, coin-op showers, an amphitheater for interpretive programs, garbage service, and a coin-op launderette. Generators are permitted 8 A.M.–8 P.M. Leashed pets are permitted. A wheelchair-accessible toilet is available.

Reservations, fees: Reservations are accepted through Xanterra Parks and Resorts (307/344-7901 for same-day reservations, 307/344-7311 or 866/439-7375 for future reservations, www.travelyellowstone.com). Campsites cost $18.50, plus sales tax and utility fee. Shared hiker and biker campsites cost $5 per person. Cash, check, or credit card. Rates cover up to six people. Open early June–early September.

Directions: From Canyon Village Junction, drive 0.2 mile east on North Rim Drive. Turn left into the campground.

GPS Coordinates: N 44° 44.122' W 110° 29.253'

Contact: Yellowstone National Park, P.O. Box 168, Yellowstone, WY 82190-0168, 307/344-7381, www.nps.gov/yell.

28 FISHING BRIDGE RV

Scenic rating: 7

on the north shore of Yellowstone Lake in Yellowstone National Park

At 7,751 feet in thick forest, Fishing Bridge is 27 miles west Yellowstone National Park's east entrance and on the north side of Yellowstone Lake. Contrary to its name, fishing is not permitted from the famous Fishing Bridge on the Yellowstone River; however, it is allowed about one mile downstream and on Yellowstone Lake. All native species are catch-and-release only. The one-mile Pelican

The Yellowstone River, which starts at Yellowstone Lake, flows north to the Missouri River.

© BECKY LOMAX

Creek Nature Trail tours a marsh along Pelican Creek, where you can see American white pelicans and end at a black-sand beach on the lake. Fishing Bridge also has a grocery store, visitors center, restaurant, gas, and RV repair shop. A boat launch is available five miles southwest at Bridge Bay, although hand-carried watercraft can launch from picnic areas on the lake's north shore.

In a thick lodgepole forest, a paved road passes through the long campground loops, which all have paved, back-in campsites. Sites are close together, so privacy is minimal. Small patches of grass between the parking pads make up the campsites. Some campsites have one fir or lodgepole pine tree that offers a little shade; others are open and sunny. Little log tipis are available in a kids' play area. Located back in the woods, the campground is quiet once the generators turn off. The air at Fishing Bridge smells of sulfur.

Campsites, facilities: Fishing Bridge has 346 RV campsites for hard-sided vehicles only. No popup tent trailers or tent campers are allowed. RVs are limited to 40 feet. Hookups include water, sewer, and electricity up to 30 amps. Facilities include picnic tables, flush toilets, coin-op showers, a coin-op launderette, garbage service, and a disposal station. Generators are permitted 8 A.M.–8 P.M. Leashed pets are permitted. A wheelchair-accessible toilet is available.

Reservations, fees: Reservations are accepted and imperative for midsummer (Xanterra Parks and Resorts, 307/344-7311 or 866/439-7375, www.travelyellowstone.com). RV sites cost $35, plus sales tax and utility fee. Cash, check, or credit card. Open late May–late September.

Directions: From the east entrance from Cody, Wyoming, drive 27 miles west on the east entrance road. From Fishing Bridge Junction, drive one mile east. The entrance is on the north side.

GPS Coordinates: N 44° 33.820' W 110° 22.167'

Contact: Yellowstone National Park, P.O. Box 168, Yellowstone, WY 82190-0168, 307/344-7381, www.nps.gov/yell.

29 BRIDGE BAY

Scenic rating: 9

on Yellowstone Lake's west shore in Yellowstone National Park

Located at 7,784 feet on the west side of Yellowstone Lake, Bridge Bay Campground and Marina sits on a sheltered lagoon off Bridge Bay. Bridge Bay includes a ranger station, store, and boat launch with docks, boat slips, trailer parking, and cement ramp. One-hour tours of Yellowstone Lake are available several times daily; the *Lake Queen* loops around Stevenson Island for watching bald eagles and ospreys fish. Boat rentals (rowboats and motorboats), charter services, and a shuttle service to backcountry campsites are available. All boats—including canoes, kayaks, and float tubes—must have a permit, available at the marina or ranger station. Just south of the bridge over Bridge Bay, a 1.1-mile trail—open to hikers and mountain bikers—leads to Natural Bridge, a natural arch over a creek.

Bridge Bay is Yellowstone's largest campground; in high summer it can hold a population bigger than many small towns in the Northern Rockies. Its huge front loops circle on a gentle, grassy, sunny slope above the lake. Many campsites have views of the water and mountains in the distance as well as of other campers. Green June grasses are brown by August. Some of the back loops are more shaded, set in denser conifers. While Bridge Bay bustles during the day with marina traffic, it quiets at night.

Campsites, facilities: The campground has 432 RV or tent campsites. RV combinations are limited to 40 feet. Due to limited large RV parking pads, RVs over 30 feet should reserve sites. Facilities include picnic tables, fire rings with grills, flush toilets, drinking water, bear boxes, garbage service, a disposal station, and an amphitheater for evening ranger programs. Generators are permitted 8 A.M.–8 P.M. Leashed pets are permitted. A wheelchair-accessible toilet is available.

Reservations, fees: Reservations are accepted (Xanterra Parks and Resorts, 307/344/7901 for same day reservations and 307/344-7311 or 866/439-7375 for future reservations, www.travelyellowstone.com). Campsites cost $18.50, plus tax and utility fee. Shared hiker and biker campsites cost $5 per person. Cash, check, or credit card. Open late May–mid-September.

Directions: From the Fishing Bridge Junction on Grand Loop Road, drive 3.5 miles south. From the West Thumb Junction, drive 17.5 miles north. Turn west into Bridge Bay for 0.2 mile, and turn right into the campground entrance.

GPS Coordinates: N 44°32.065' W 110° 26.228'

Contact: Yellowstone National Park, P.O. Box 168, Yellowstone, WY 82190-0168, 307/344-7381, www.nps.gov/yell.

30 SHOSHONE LAKE

Scenic rating: 8

on Shoshone Lake in Yellowstone National Park

BEST (

Campers access the solitude of Shoshone Lake's primitive campgrounds by hiking, canoeing, or kayaking. Motorized boats are not permitted. The Howard Eaton Trail and the DeLacy Trail both connect to the Shoshone Lake Trail. Launch boats from the ramp at Lewis Lake Campground to paddle across the lake and up the Lewis River Channel between the two lakes. The last channel requires wading in frigid water while dragging boats. Because of the long

paddle, select a south shore site for the first night. Afternoon high winds on the lake are a daily occurrence.

The remote, quiet campsites are along the north, west, and south shores of the lake, tucked into the edge of the forest for protection from weather. Some campsites are for hikers only, some for boaters only, and some for both. These campsites fill consistently in summer; reservations are wise.

Campsites, facilities: The lake is rimmed with 21 tent campsites that each hold eight people maximum. Five campsites are accessed by trail only, 13 by boat only, and three via trail or water. These are primitive campsites, with no fires permitted. Facilities include pit or composting toilets and a bear pole or bar. Bring a 35-foot rope for hanging food, garbage, toiletries, and cooking gear. Pack out your trash. No pets are permitted.

Reservations, fees: Reservations are accepted ($20 cash, check, or money order). Applications (available online) may be submitted after January 1; reservation confirmations are issued starting April 1. Submit a reservation in March for a chance of getting coveted lake permits. Pick up the free permits in person at Bridge Bay, Grant Village, or the south entrance backcountry office no more than 48 hours before the trip. Boats also need permits ($10 for seven days, $20 annual for motorized; $5 for seven days for nonmotorized), obtained only in person at the south entrance, Lewis Lake Campground, Grant Village backcountry office, or Bridge Bay Ranger Station. Open June 15–October, depending on seasonal conditions and bear restrictions.

Directions: Drive 11 miles north of the south park entrance or 11 miles south of West Thumb Junction to reach Lewis Lake. Turn west into the Lewis Lake boat launch.

GPS Coordinates: N 44° 22.378' W 110° 42.250'

Contact: Yellowstone National Park, P.O. Box 168, Yellowstone, WY 82190-0168, 307/344-7381, www.nps.gov/yell.

31 GRANT

Scenic rating: 8

on West Thumb on Yellowstone Lake in
Yellowstone National Park

BEST (

Grant Campground sits at 7,733 feet on the
south shore of West Thumb—the large west-
side bay on Yellowstone Lake. South of the
campground, Grant Village has a visitors center, restaurant, interpretive sightseeing tours, a
lodge, a general store, gas, and a boat launch.
To the west, West Thumb Geyser Basin has a
0.6-mile loop trail through the basin, which
contains hot springs, the Abyss Pool, and the
Fishing Cone offshore, where anglers used to
cook their catch over the steam. Hikers can
grab a panoramic view of the park's largest
lake and Absaroka Mountains from the two-
mile Yellowstone Lake Overlook Trail.

A paved road with paved parking pads loops
through this giant campground. In summer
it houses a population larger than some Wyoming towns. In contrast to the other large
Yellowstone Lake campgrounds, this one sits
close to the beach. While none of the campsites overlook the water, trails lead to the large
pebble and sand beach. The campsites sit close
together under the partial shade of a loose
conifer forest. Loops near the back west side
of the main campground road are quite near
the parkway road.

Campsites, facilities: The campground has
425 RV or tent campsites. RV combinations
are limited to 40 feet. Due to limited large
RV parking pads, RVs over 30 feet should
reserve sites. Facilities include picnic tables,
fire rings with grills, flush toilets, drinking
water, bear boxes, firewood for sale, and
garbage service. Coin-op showers, a coin-op
launderette, and a disposal station are available 0.5 mile south in Grant Village. Generators are permitted 8 a.m.–8 p.m. Leashed
pets are permitted. A wheelchair-accessible
toilet is available.

Reservations, fees: Reservations are accepted

(Xanterra Parks and Resorts, 307/344/7901
for same day reservations, 307/344-7311 or
866/439-7375 for future reservations, www.
travelyellowstone.com). Campsites cost $18.50,
plus tax and utility fee. Shared hiker and biker
campsites cost $5 per person. Cash, check, or
credit card. Open late June–late September.

Directions: From West Thumb Junction, drive
south on Rockefeller Parkway for 1.8 miles.
From the park's south entrance, drive 22 miles
north. Turn east into Grant Village and drive
one mile. Turn left and drive 0.5 mile to the
campground.

GPS Coordinates: N 44° 12.666' W 110°
33.823'

Contact: Yellowstone National Park, P.O. Box
168, Yellowstone, WY 82190-0168, 307/344-
7381, www.nps.gov/yell.

32 FRANK ISLAND

Scenic rating: 8

on Yellowstone Lake in Yellowstone National
Park

At 136 square miles, Yellowstone Lake is the
second largest freshwater lake in the world that
is above 7,000 feet. That means cold water—
40 to 50 degrees in summer. Frank Island is
a unique place to camp in Yellowstone, but
camping here does require a self-contained
boat with a galley, berth, toilet, and anchor.
The island itself is for day visitation only, but
it's a good place to see bald eagles or ospreys.
Due to nesting, shore landings are not permitted prior to August 15, except at the dock
and picnic area, on the north side of the spit
in the south bay.

Boaters may camp at two anchorage locations within the eastern double cove of the
island: one in the north bay and one in the
south bay. Anchorage sites must be at least
100 feet from shore and 300 feet from the
dock. The coves, which face east, are open to
the lake's notorious afternoon winds, which

can whip up five-foot waves. Powerboats are limited to 45 mph. on the lake.

Campsites, facilities: Overnight camping is not permitted on the island, but two anchorage spots are available. No facilities are provided at the anchorage sites, and only one boat, with a maximum of eight people, is permitted per site.

Reservations, fees: Reservations are accepted ($20 cash, check, or money order). Applications (available online) may be submitted after January 1; reservation confirmations are issued starting April 1. Submit a reservation in March for a chance of getting a coveted lake permit. Pick up the free permits in person at Bridge Bay, Grant Village, or the south entrance backcountry office no more than 48 hours in advance of the trip. Boats also need permits ($10 for seven days, $20 annual for motorized; $5 for seven days for nonmotorized), obtained only in person at the south entrance, Lewis Lake Campground, Grant Village backcountry office, or Bridge Bay Ranger Station. Open June–October, depending on seasonal conditions.

Directions: To reach Frank Island, launch power boats from Bridge Bay for the 10-mile crossing.

GPS Coordinates: N 44° 24.001' W 110° 21.275'

Contact: Yellowstone National Park, P.O. Box 168, Yellowstone, WY 82190-0168, 307/344-7381, www.nps.gov/yell.

33 YELLOWSTONE LAKE

🏃 🏊 🛶 🚣 🎣 ⛺

Scenic rating: 9

on Yellowstone Lake's south arms in Yellowstone National Park

Yellowstone Lake—the second largest freshwater lake above 7,000 feet in the world—offers camping with boat access only on its east shore, three southern arms, and several bays east of West Thumb. Boats may be launched from Grant Village or Bridge Bay; hand-carried watercrafts can also launch from Sedge Bay picnic area. The 45-degree lake is notorious for daily afternoon winds with big whitecaps. Bridge Bay Marina (307/242-3893) provides a boat shuttle service for hikers and boaters mid-May–mid-September. Many campsites link to hiking trails, and the park service advocates fishing for lake trout to help restore the cutthroat trout fishery.

The popular campsites are prized for their quiet, solitude, scenery, and wildlife-watching. The campsites—some with sandy beaches—are set in the trees for protection. Most are within a few hundred feet of the shoreline. Three dock-accessed sites have three campsites each.

Campsites, facilities: Yellowstone Lake has 32 primitive tent campsites. Sites are limited to 8–12 people. Facilities include fire rings where campfires are permitted, bear boxes or poles, and pit toilets at some. Bring a 35-foot rope for hanging food, garbage, toiletries, and cooking gear. No drinking water is available; filter or boil lake water. Pack out your trash. Pets are not allowed.

Reservations, fees: Reservations are accepted ($20 cash, check, or money order). Submit applications (available online) after January 1; reservation confirmations are issued starting April 1. Pick up free required permits in person at Bridge Bay, Grant Village, or the south entrance backcountry office no more than 48 hours in advance of the trip. Permits are required for motorized ($10 for seven days, $20 annual) and nonmotorized ($5 for seven days, $10 annual) boats. Open June–October, depending on seasonal conditions; some campsites are closed because of bears until mid-July.

Directions: For launching from Grant Village, drive south on Rockefeller Parkway for 1.8 miles from West Thumb Junction, or from the park's south entrance drive 22 miles north. Turn east into Grant Village, drive 0.9 mile, and turn right, following the signs to the boat launch. To launch from Bridge Bay, drive south from Fishing Bridge Junction on

Grand Loop Road for 3.5 miles, or from the West Thumb Junction drive 17.5 miles north. Turn west into Bridge Bay for 0.2 mile.

GPS Coordinates for Bridge Bay: N 44° 32.020' W 110° 26.406'

GPS Coordinates for Grant Village: N 44° 23.520' 44° 23.520' W 110° 32.882'

Contact: Yellowstone National Park, P.O. Box 168, Yellowstone, WY 82190-0168, 307/344-7381, www.nps.gov/yell.

34 FLAT MOUNTAIN ARM, SOUTH ARM, AND SOUTHEAST ARM

🏃🛶🛶🚤🛶⛰️

Scenic rating: 9

on Yellowstone Lake's south arms in Yellowstone National Park

BEST (

Yellowstone Lake offers paddlers and hikers access to three remote south arms with views of the Absaroka Mountains. Only hand-propelled watercraft are permitted; a few campsites allow sailboats to anchor. Launch from Grant Village to paddle 19 miles to Flat Mountain Arm or 33–35 miles into South Arm; launch from Sedge Bay picnic area on the lake's northeast corner to paddle the east shore for 20 miles into Southeast Arm. Watch for daily afternoon winds that whip the 45-degree lake water into a chop of whitecaps. Hiking and fishing are available. Bridge Bay Marina (307/242-3893) provides a boat shuttle service for hikers and boaters mid-May–mid-September.

The popular campsites are prized for their quiet, solitude, scenery, wildlife-watching, and restrictions that preclude motorboats. The campsites are set in the trees for protection. Most are within a few hundred feet of the shoreline; one site requires a 0.25-mile walk.

Campsites, facilities: Yellowstone Lake has 10 primitive tent campsites spread between the nonmotorized bays. Sites are limited to 8–12 people. Facilities include fire rings where campfires are permitted, bear boxes or poles, and pit toilets at some. Bring a 35-foot rope for hanging food, garbage, toiletries, and cooking gear. No drinking water is available; filter or boil lake water. Pack out your trash. Pets are not allowed.

Reservations, fees: Reservations are accepted ($20 cash, check, or money order). Applications (available online) may be submitted after January 1; reservation confirmations are issued starting April 1. Pick up free required permits in person at Bridge Bay, Grant Village, or the south entrance backcountry office no more than 48 hours in advance of the trip. Boats also need permits ($5 for seven days). Open June–October, depending on seasonal conditions; seven campsites are closed because of bears until mid-July.

Directions: For launching from Grant Village, drive south on Rockefeller Parkway for 1.8 miles from West Thumb Junction, or from the park's south entrance drive 22 miles north. Turn east into Grant Village, drive 0.9 mile, and turn right, following the signs to the boat launch. To launch from Sedge Bay picnic area, drive the east entrance road 7.7 miles east of Fishing Bridge Junction.

GPS Coordinates for Grant Village: N 44° 23.520' 44° 23.520' W 110° 32.882'

GPS Coordinates for Sedge Bay Picnic Area: N 44° 31.177' W 110° 16.707'

Contact: Yellowstone National Park, P.O. Box 168, Yellowstone, WY 82190-0168, 307/344-7381, www.nps.gov/yell.

35 LEWIS LAKE

🏃🛶🛶🚤🛶🏕️♿🚐⛰️

Scenic rating: 8

on Lewis Lake on Rockefeller Parkway in Yellowstone National Park

BEST (

Coming north from the Tetons, Lewis Lake is the first Yellowstone National Park campground. The lake, which is the third largest in the park and sits at 7,830 feet, permits motorboats, which can be launched from the cement ramp down the hill from the campground. A boat dock and trailer parking are also available. The lake is a popular fishery for brown trout. Lewis Lake is also the gateway to Shoshone Lake via the Lewis Lake Channel. Only canoes and kayaks are permitted up the channel, though. The campground, which sits at the southeast corner of the lake, does not have trailheads that depart from it, but north of the lake, an 11-mile loop trail goes to Shoshone Lake.

By park standards, Lewis Lake is one of the smaller campgrounds, although it is still larger than most Forest Service campgrounds. Campsites are spaced out for privacy under the conifer canopy on a hillside, but the narrow parking pads may pose difficulties for those not used to backing in RVs. Campsites are partly shaded and partly sunny. Although the campground sits on Rockefeller Parkway, which connects Yellowstone with the Tetons, the area quiets at night. Most of the daytime activity is also concentrated around the boat launch. This campground is the one of the last to fill in the park, but in peak season, all the sites can fill by early afternoon.

Campsites, facilities: The campground has 85 RV or tent campsites. RVs are limited to 25 feet. Facilities include picnic tables, fire rings with grills, vault toilets, drinking water, garbage service, bear boxes, and a boat launch. Generators are not permitted. Leashed pets are permitted. A wheelchair-accessible toilet is available.

Reservations, fees: Reservations are not accepted. Sites cost $12. Shared hiker and biker campsites cost $5 per person. Cash or check. Open mid-June–October.

Directions: Drive 11 miles north of the south park entrance or 11 miles south of West Thumb Junction to reach Lewis Lake. Turn west into the Lewis Lake boat launch and campground entrance and immediately left again to the campground.
GPS Coordinates: N 44° 16.875' W 110° 37.644'

Contact: Yellowstone National Park, P.O. Box 168, Yellowstone, WY 82190-0168, 307/344-7381, www.nps.gov/yell.

36 CAVE FALLS

Scenic rating: 9

on the Falls River at the southwest corner of Yellowstone National Park in Caribou-Targhee National Forest

BEST (

At 6,200 feet in Caribou-Targhee National Forest, Cave Falls Campground requires a long drive through Idaho farmland and forest to reach this corner of Wyoming. The Bechler Ranger Station sits about two miles west, and the most remote entrance to Yellowstone National Park is one mile east on a very narrow road. The road ends at Cave Falls—a cascade only 20 feet high, but spanning 250 feet wide. A five-minute walk leads to the falls, and a path climbs above to look down on it. A 1.5-mile trail leads farther to Bechler Falls (1.5 miles). The Falls and Bechler Rivers are home to rainbow trout.

Set along the Falls River, the campground lines up most of its campsites overlooking the river. You can prop a chair on the edge of your campsite and listen to the roar of the river as you watch the sunset glow on the rocky outcroppings in the forest opposite. Paths drop down the steep bank to the water, too. A tall forest of aspens, subalpine firs, and lodgepoles alternates with meadows of arrowleaf balsamroot and huckleberries—offering a mix of part shade and sun. Flat tent spaces are available, and if the campground is full, you'll see a neighboring camper.

Campsites, facilities: The campground has 23 RV or tent campsites. RVs are limited to 24 feet. Facilities include picnic tables, fire rings with grills, pedestal grills, vault toilets, drinking water, bear boxes, and garbage service. Leashed pets are permitted. A wheelchair-accessible toilet is available.

Reservations, fees: Reservations are not accepted. Campsites cost $10. Extra vehicles cost $5. Cash or check. Open late May–September.

Directions: From five miles north of Ashton on Highway 47 in Idaho, drive east on Cave Falls

Cave Falls, a 250-foot-wide waterfall, tucks into the remote southwest corner of Yellowstone National Park.

Road (Greentimber Road or Forest Road 582) for 18 miles. At mile 5.5, the pavement ends and the bumpy ride begins. You'll hit pavement again at mile 16, where the road narrows and enters Wyoming. Turn right, drop 0.1 mile to the pay station, and swing right to the campsites. Note: From Flagg Ranch, the 52-mile rugged, narrow, dirt Grassy Lake Road takes 2.5 hours.

GPS Coordinates: N 44° 7.595' W 111° 0.777'

Contact: Caribou-Targhee National Forest, Island Park Ranger District, 3726 Hwy. 20, Island Park, ID 83429, 208/558-7301, www. fs.fed.us/r4/caribou-targhee.

37 GRASSY LAKE PRIMITIVE
🚲 🛶 ⛴ 🎣 🦌 🚐 ⛺

Scenic rating: 8

on Grassy Lake Road in Rockefeller Parkway and Caribou-Targhee National Forest

BEST (

An old Native American and wagon route, the 52-mile Grassy Lake Road through remote

wilderness connects Flagg Ranch with Ashton, Idaho, topping out at 7,306 feet. In winter, snowmobiles and dog-sleds travel the route. In summer, once the road dries (usually by August), those with tenacity and sturdy rigs drive it. (Trailers are not recommended.) The dirt road is rocky and narrow, has few turnouts, offers fewer views than one would expect, and will take 2.5 hours to drive. Mountain bikers can ride the road, too. Grassy Lake has a boat ramp and can be fished, paddled, or motored. On its east end, the Snake River is known for its trout fishery and can be floated.

The tiny camps—prized for their quiet and solitude—are about one mile apart with large tent spaces. Facing east within 10 minutes from Flagg Ranch, camps 1–4 command outstanding views of the Snake River and Teton Wilderness peaks. Camps 1 and 2 sit on the river in sage-brush, willow, and grass bottomlands. Camps 3 and 4 sit on partly shaded open-forest bluffs overlooking the river. With forest and meadow views, camps 5–8 line the road as it climbs toward Grassy Lake. Camp 5 sits the farthest back from the road in green lodgepoles. Camps

6–8 sit closer to the road in forested settings, broken by meadows of yarrow and asters.

Campsites, facilities: Eight tiny campgrounds with 14 RV or tent campsites between them line the first 10 miles from Flagg Ranch to Grassy Lake on Rockefeller Parkway. Camp 1 has four sites, camps 2–4 have two sites each, and camps 5–8 have one site each. Only small RVs are recommended. Facilities include picnic tables, fire rings with grills, vault toilets, bear boxes, and garbage service. Bring your own water. Seven additional primitive campsites sit in Caribou-Targhee National Forest at Grassy Lake and Lake of the Woods. The only facilities include rock fire rings. Leashed pets are permitted.

Reservations, fees: Reservations are not accepted. Camping is free. Open June–September.

Directions: From Flagg Ranch, Grassy Lake Road (Ashton-Flagg Ranch Road) heads west, crossing the Snake River. From Ashton, Idaho, the road begins two miles southeast of Ashton, heading east.

GPS Coordinates for the site nearest Flagg Ranch: N 44° 6.244' W 110° 41.233'

Contact: Grand Teton National Park, P.O. Drawer 170, Moose, WY 83102, 307/739-3300, www.nps.gov/grte/.

38 FLAGG RANCH

Scenic rating: 7

in Rockefeller Parkway between Yellowstone National Park and Grand Teton National Park

At 6,849 feet, Flagg Ranch is the only developed campground in Rockefeller Parkway between Yellowstone and the Tetons. On the Snake River, the large tourist center (lodge, restaurant, grocery, and gas station) offers guided fly-fishing, lake kayaking, horseback riding, and rafting trips. Skilled white-water rafters, kayakers, and canoeists can put in at Southgate Launch, 0.5 mile south of the south entrance of Yellowstone, for three miles

of Class III white water to the campground. The water mellows in the 10 miles from the ranch to Lizard Creek on Jackson Lake but requires route-finding through braided channels and paddling against strong lake winds. A nonmotorized boat park permit is required ($10 for seven days), available at Moose and Colter Bay Visitor Centers. From the campground, fishing is available on the river, mountain biking is possible on Grassy Lake Road heading west, and hiking to Huckleberry Lookout is an option from Sheffield Creek one mile south.

The forested campground sits near the Snake River with mountain views. Campsites vary from fully shaded under large conifers to partly sunny with views. RV campsites have gravel pull-throughs wide enough for slide-outs and awnings. Because of the lack of understory, views include neighboring campers. Paths lead from the campground to the Snake River. The eastern loops sit closest to the highway, but traffic dwindles at night, and commercial trucking isn't permitted.

Campsites, facilities: The campground has 100 RV campsites with hookups for sewer, water, and 20-amp electricity, plus 75 tent campsites. RV combinations are limited to 60 feet. Facilities include picnic tables, fire rings, flush toilets, showers, drinking water, garbage service, a coin-op launderette, and a convenience store. Leashed pets are permitted. A wheelchair-accessible toilet is available.

Reservations, fees: Reservations are recommended. RV campsites cost $50. Tent campsites cost $25. Rates are for two adults. Each additional adult costs $5. Cash, check, or credit card. Open late May–late September.

Directions: From Jackson Lake Junction in Grand Teton National Park, drive north on Highway 26/191/89 for 21 miles. From the south entrance to Yellowstone National Park, drive three miles south. Turn west into Flagg Ranch and drive 0.1 mile south to the campground entrance on the left.

GPS Coordinates: N 44° 6.305' W 110° 40.091'

Contact: Flagg Ranch Resort, P.O. Box 187, Moran, WY 83013, 800/443-2311, www.flaggranch.com.

39 SHEFFIELD CREEK

🚶 🚲 🛶 🎣 � 🛥 🏕 🐕 ♿ 🚐

Scenic rating: 7

south of Flagg Ranch in Bridger-Teton National Forest

The location of Sheffield Creek Campground makes it usable as overflow for Flagg Ranch or an option for a cheaper campsite in the area as it sits only five minutes from the ranch. At 7,000 feet, the campground cuddles next to a small tributary of the nearby Snake River below the 9,615-foot Huckleberry Mountain of the Teton Wilderness. Sheffield Creek Trail (#027) climbs five miles from the campground to the lookout, which is listed on the National Register of Historic Places. Views from the lookout include Jackson Lake, the Tetons, Yellowstone National Park, Absaroka Mountains, and Teton Wilderness. Mountain bikers can ride the Grassy Lake Road, departing from Flagg Ranch. Fishing, rafting, kayaking, and canoeing are available on the Snake River.

Sheffield Creek offers campsites in a loose conifer forest or sunny campsites with views of the surrounding mountains. A small stream runs west of the campground—one that the access road crosses. In June, scout the water depth before crossing. The campground is also located in a grizzly bear recovery area. It is a popular trailhead but quiets at night.

Campsites, facilities: The campground has five RV campsites for hard-sided vehicles only. No tent pop-ups or tent campers. Sites can fit midsized RVs only. Facilities include picnic tables, fire rings with grills, a vault toilet, horse facilities, and a bear box pole. No drinking water is available. Bring your own, or if you use creek water, boil or purify it first. Pack out your trash. Leashed pets are permitted. A wheelchair-accessible toilet is available.

Reservations, fees: Reservations are not accepted. Campsites cost $5. Cash or check. Open late May–September, weather permitting.

Directions: From Jackson Lake Junction in Grand Teton National Park, drive north on Highway 26/191/89 for 20 miles. From the south entrance to Yellowstone National Park, drive four miles south. Turn east onto the dirt road south of the bridge over the Snake River and drive 0.3 mile southeast into to the campground.

GPS Coordinates: N 44° 5.527' W 110° 39.813'

Contact: Bridger-Teton National Forest, Buffalo Ranger District, Hwy. 26/287, P.O. Box 278, Afton, WY 83110, 307/886-5300, www.fs.fed.us/r4/btnf/.

40 LIZARD CREEK

🛶 🎣 � 🏕 🐕 🚐 ⛺

Scenic rating: 9

at the north end of Jackson Lake in Grand Teton National Park

At the north end of Jackson Lake, Lizard Creek Campground, elevation 6,823 feet, stares across the lake at the jagged teeth of the northern Teton Mountains. While the campground offers enjoyment of the lakeshore (with several walk-in tent sites right on it), sometimes the lake level can drop so low that a huge mudflat surrounds the campground. The lake harbors cutthroat and lake trout, but fishing from the campground varies depending on water levels. The campground has no boat launch, but with high water levels, you can launch hand-carried rafts, kayaks, and canoes at a pullout about one mile south of the campground.

The partly sunny hillside campground is prized for its quiet location at the head of Jackson Lake, with outstanding views of the north end of the Teton Mountains. A thick spruce, fir, and lodgepole forest aids privacy, which is greater in the upper loop. Many of the lower loop prime campsites overlook the lake and the Tetons. Most of the walk-in tent sites, located in the lower loop, sit on the lake. Claim a campsite by early afternoon.

Campsites, facilities: The campground has 43 RV or tent campsites and 17 walk-in tent campsites. RV size is limited to 30 feet. Facilities include picnic tables, fire rings with grills, drinking water, flush toilets, garbage service, bear boxes, an amphitheater for interpretive programs, and campground hosts. Generators are permitted in the upper loop, but not the lower loop. Leashed pets are permitted.

Reservations, fees: Reservations are not accepted. Campsites cost $18. Shared hiker and biker campsites cost $5. Cash or check. Open early June–August.

Directions: From Jackson Lake Junction, drive 14 miles north on Highway 89/191/287, or from the south entrance to Yellowstone drive 10 miles south. Turn south onto the paved road for 0.1 mile into the campground.

GPS Coordinates: N 44° 0.350' W 110° 41.135'

Contact: Grand Teton National Park, P.O. Drawer 170, Moose, WY 83102, 307/739-3300, www.nps.gov/grte/.

41 COLTER BAY

Scenic rating: 10

on the east shore of Jackson Lake in Grand Teton National Park

Colter Bay, at 6,793 feet on Jackson Lake's east shore, sits north of islands and bays that provide canoeing, kayaking, and fishing sheltered from the big lake winds. The campground is part of the large Colter Bay Village, which contains a visitors center, restaurant, gas, grocery, and marina with a cement boat ramp, boat slips, trailer parking, docks, guided fishing, lake tours, and boat rentals (canoes, kayaks, and motorboats). The lake holds a variety of species for sport anglers. Hiking options are prolific. From the campground, trails loop the peninsula by the marina, and a multi-loop trail

The Teton Mountains rise higher than 12,000 feet.

system tours past Swan Lake and south around Hermitage Point. Trailheads to Two Ocean and Emma Matilda Lakes are also within five miles. Find three miles of scenic mountain biking on the Two Ocean Lake Road.

This giant campground sits on a forested bluff above Jackson Lake. The forest breaks with grassy meadows, allowing some of the spacious sites to garner views across to the Teton Mountains. Although it is a big, busy tourist center during the day, the campground quiets at night.

Campsites, facilities: The campground has 112 pull-throughs for large RVs with hookups for water, sewer, and electricity; 350 RV or tent campsites with no hookups; plus 11 group campsites. Facilities include picnic tables, fire pits with grills (except in RV hookup sites), flush toilets, drinking water, a disposal station, garbage service, and bear boxes. Coin-op showers and a coin-op launderette are available at Colter Bay Village. No tents, fires, or gas grills are permitted in the RV hookup campsites.

Generator use is restricted in the campsites without hookups. Leashed pets are permitted. Wheelchair-accessible toilets are available.

Reservations, fees: Reservations are accepted only for the RV hookup campsites and the group campsites (Grand Teton Lodge Company, 800/28-9988, 307/543-3100, www.gtlc. com). RV hookups cost $40–54. Campsites without hookups cost $19. Shared hiker and biker campsites cost $7. Cash, check, or credit card. Open late May–late September.

Directions: From Jackson Lake Junction, drive 5.5 miles north. From the south entrance to Yellowstone National Park, drive 18.5 miles south. Turn south into Colter Bay and drive 0.6 mile. Turn right into the campground. GPS Coordinates: N 43° 54.533' W 110° 38.493'

Contact: Grand Teton National Park, P.O. Drawer 170, Moose, WY 83102, 307/739-3300, www.nps.gov/grte/.

42 JACKSON LAKE

Scenic rating: 10

on Jackson Lake in Grand Teton National Park

One of the largest high-altitude lakes in the United States at 6,772 feet, Jackson Lake is 15 miles long, 7 miles wide, and 438 feet deep. The lake tucks into the base of the jagged Teton Mountain Range. The glacial lake trout waters are cold—below 60 degrees in August—and strong afternoon winds are common. Sailboats and motorboats are permitted with a 10-horsepower maximum. Four boat launches rim the lake's east shore: Leeks Marina, Colter Bay Marina, Signal Mountain, and Spalding Bay. Hiking is available only from the Hermitage Point group campsite. Motorboat, canoe, and kayak rentals are available at Leeks Marina, Signal Mountain, and Colter Bay.

Lake campsites are prized for their scenery, quiet, and solitude. Most campsites rim the lakeshore, set back into the trees for protection. Five campsites are on islands.

Campsites, facilities: Jackson Lake has 10 individual tent campsites and five group tent campsites. Six people are allowed per campsite, except for group campsites, which can hold 12. Facilities include fire rings, bear boxes, and pit toilets, and a few campsites have tent platforms. No drinking water is available; bring your own, or filter or boil lake water. Pets are not allowed in Jackson Lake campsites, except at Spalding Bay.

Reservations, fees: Reservations are available ($25, 307/739-3309 or 307/739-3397 for information, but all reservation requests must be via application). Applications are available online, and reservation requests are accepted January 1–May 15. Obtain the required free overnight camping permits at the Craig Thomas and Colter Bay Visitor Centers or Jenny Lake Ranger Station. Boats must also have permits. Motorboat permits cost $20 per week or $40 per season; nonmotorized boat permits cost $10 per week or $20 per season. Purchase boat permits at Moose and Colter Bay Visitor Centers. Open June–October.

Directions: From Jackson Lake Junction, drive Highway 89/191/287 north to reach Colter Bay Marina in 5.5 miles or Leeks Marina in 6.3 miles. From Jackson Lake Junction, drive Teton Park Road south to reach Signal Mountain Marina in three miles. To reach Spalding Bay (which only permits single-axle trailers and is a primitive launch), drive north on Teton Park Road for 1.3 miles from North Jenny Lake Junction and turn north for 2.1 miles on dirt Spalding Bay Road.

GPS Coordinates:

Leeks Marina: N 43° 55.797' W 110° 38.394'

Colter Bay Marina: N 43° 54.130' W 110° 38.611'

Signal Mountain Marina: N 43° 50.316' W 110° 36.976'

Spaulding Bay: N 43° 49.446' W 110° 40.532'

Contact: Grand Teton National Park, P.O. Drawer 170, Moose, WY 83102, 307/739-3300, www.nps.gov/grte/.

43 SIGNAL MOUNTAIN

Scenic rating: 10

on the west shore of Jackson Lake in Grand
Teton National Park

BEST (

Signal Mountain Campground, at 6,802 feet,
may command one of the best panoramic
views of the Teton Mountains from its perch
on the west shore of Jackson Lake. North of
the campground, Signal Mountain Lodge
houses a restaurant, a convenience store, and
gas station. South of the campground sits
the marina, with a cement boat ramp, dock,
trailer parking, sailboat tours, guided fishing, and boat rentals (canoes, kayaks, and
motorboats). The lake is popular for boating,
fishing, waterskiing, kayaking, and canoeing, although be prepared for cold water and
daily afternoon winds. Driving tours along
Teton Park Road often produce sightings
of bugling elk in fall. The campground is
named for the low mountain to the east.
You can drive, bike, or hike to its summit
for expansive views of the lake and peaks. A
15-mile gravel road also parallels the Snake
River eastward to Cottonwood—another
option for wildlife-watching expeditions or
mountain biking.

The campground loops around a hillside,
where some of the campsites have outstanding views of the lake and the jagged teeth
of the Teton Mountains. A mix of fir and
spruce provides some shade, but most of the
campsites are sunny in midday. The campsites are small, with low brush creating partial privacy along with the trees. The narrow
campground road and narrow parking pads
can pose challenges for RV drivers unskilled
in squeezing into tight spots. A steep walk
leads down to the waterfront. Because of its
location and scenery, plan on arriving before
noon to claim a campsite.

Campsites, facilities: The campground has 81
RV or tent campsites. Maximum length for
RVs is 30 feet. Facilities include picnic tables,
fire rings with grills, flush toilets, drinking
water, garbage service, and a disposal station.
Leashed pets are permitted.

Reservations, fees: Reservations are not accepted. Campsites cost $20. Shared hiker and
biker campsites cost $5. Cash or check. Open
early May–mid-October.

Directions: From Jackson Lake Junction, drive
south on Teton Park Road for three miles, or
from Jenny Lake Visitor Center drive nine
miles north. Turn west into Signal Mountain,
continuing straight past the road heading right
to the lodge to reach the campground.

GPS Coordinates: N 43° 50.524' W 110°
36.841'

Contact: Grand Teton National Park, P.O.
Drawer 170, Moose, WY 83102, 307/739-
3300, www.nps.gov/grte/.

44 HATCHET

Scenic rating: 7

west of Moran Junction in Bridger-Teton
National Forest

While Hatchet Campground isn't worth a
visit as a destination in itself, its location
provides a last-minute place to camp before
reaching Grand Teton National Park and access to scenic fly-fishing and floating. The
campground, elevation 6,800 feet, sits 0.2
mile west of the Buffalo Ranger Station and
at the base of the dirt Hatchet Road, which
climbs south along the foothills with dramatic
views across the valley to the toothy Teton
Mountains. The road, good for scenic drives,
ATVs, and mountain biking, also offers primitive campsites with big views overlooking
the valley and the Tetons. The Buffalo Fork
River parallels the highway heading west to
its confluence with the Snake River—both
trout fisheries. Paddling Jackson Dam to Pacific Creek on the Snake offers five miles of
scenic, calm water. Buffalo Fork is closed to
floating. Nonmotorized boats need a permit

($10 per week, $20 per season), available at the ranger station.

Rimmed with lodgepole pines and aspens, the sunny campground tucks its small campsites and small tent spaces around one loop. The best sites sit on the outside of the ring. Fireweed, wild roses, serviceberries, and sagebrush add to a short understory for some privacy. Sites 1 and 9 gaze north toward mountains, but unfortunately the highway is in sight, too. Due to the campground's proximity to the highway, road noise is inevitable.

Campsites, facilities: The campground has nine RV or tent campsites. Sites can fit midsized RVs only. Facilities include picnic tables, fire rings with grills, pit toilets, drinking water, garbage service, and bear boxes. Leashed pets are permitted. A wheelchair-accessible toilet is available.

Reservations, fees: Reservations are not accepted. Campsites cost $10. Cash or check. Open late May–September, weather permitting.

Directions: From Moran Junction, drive east on Highway 26/287 for 8.3 miles. Turn south onto Hatchet Road (Forest Road 30160) and immediately left into the campground.

GPS Coordinates: N 43° 49.463' W 110° 21.323'

Contact: Bridger-Teton National Forest, Buffalo Ranger District, Hwy. 26/287, P.O. Box 278, Afton, WY 83110, 307/886-5300, www.fs.fed.us/r4/btnf/.

45 BOX CREEK

Scenic rating: 6

west of Moran Junction in Bridger-Teton National Forest

Located in a valley of outfitters, Box Creek Campground at 7,300 feet is not a destination campground in itself, but one to use to access the Teton Wilderness Area. The trailhead campground is used mostly by horsepackers because corrals, hitch rails, and stock ramps are available. The Box Creek Trail climbs about five miles to 8,600 feet on Gravel Ridge. From the ridge, you can view the destruction from the 1987 Teton Tornado—the highest altitude recorded of a tornado touchdown. It cut a swath up to three miles wide across a 20-mile strip, snapping trees like toothpicks and uprooting others. Trout fishing is available in the Buffalo Fork River.

The campground—set in aspens and pines—circles on the end of a large, grassy meadow. Several of the campsites have views of the forest and mountains. Unfortunately, some of the forest includes beetle-killed trees, easily identified by their rust-colored needles. This sunny, little-used campground is ultra-quiet and secluded, but you'll see other campers, if any are there.

Campsites, facilities: The campground has six RV or tent campsites. Sites can fit midsized RVs. Facilities include picnic tables, fire grates, a vault toilet, bear boxes, garbage service, and stock facilities. Drinking water is not available. Bring your own, or fill up at Turpin Meadows 1.3 miles east. Leashed pets are permitted. A wheelchair-accessible toilet is available.

Reservations, fees: Reservations are not accepted. Campsites cost $10. Cash or check. Open late May–September, weather permitting.

Directions: From Moran Junction, drive east on Highway 26/287 for 3.4 miles and turn north onto Buffalo Valley Road for 8.7 miles. Turn north onto the narrow dirt road with no pullouts and climb 0.7 mile to the campground. Note: On Buffalo Valley Road, the only sign notes Box Creek Trailhead with no mention of the campground. An alternative route to the campground road departs Highway 26/287 at milepost 13, heading north on the gravel Forest Road 30050 for 4.2 miles to the bridge over the Buffalo Fork River and then one mile on pavement.

GPS Coordinates: N 43° 51.711' W 110° 17.697'

Contact: Bridger-Teton National Forest, Buffalo Ranger District, Hwy. 26/287, P.O. Box

278, Afton, WY 83110, 307/886-5300, www. fs.fed.us/r4/btnf/.

46 TURPIN MEADOW

Scenic rating: 8

west of Moran Junction in Bridger-Teton National Forest

Turpin Meadow Campground, at 7,300 feet, sits across the Buffalo Fork River from Turpin Meadow Guest Ranch in a high valley facing the Teton Mountains. From the river, the road, and the trailhead, you can see Mount Moran and the Teton Mountains in the distance, but not from the campground. The river is a popular trout fishery, but be aware of private property if you head downstream. Paths lead from the campground to the river, which can be wade-fished. A popular trailhead, often packed with horse trailers, sits northeast of the campground. The Clear Creek Trail makes an 18-mile loop with the Box Creek Trail, and the Buffalo Fork Trail follows the river west to the confluence of its north and south forks, where the trail divides to climb to the Continental Divide National Scenic Trail.

The gravel campground road weaves through a young lodgepole and fir forest surrounded by a lodgepole fence and huge sagebrush meadows. The first part of the loop features sunny campsites across from the outfitter camping area; the campsites at the end of the loop are more shaded—especially site 12. Big tent spaces are available. Mountain bluebirds frequent the campground.

Campsites, facilities: The campground has 18 RV or tent campsites. Sites can fit midsized RVs only. Facilities include picnic tables, fire rings with grills, a vault toilet, drinking water, garbage service, bear boxes, and stock facilities. Leashed pets are permitted. A wheelchair-accessible toilet is available.

Reservations, fees: Reservations are not accepted. Campsites cost $10. Cash or check. Open late May–September, weather permitting.

Directions: From Moran Junction, drive east on Highway 26/287 for 3.4 miles and turn north onto Buffalo Valley Road for 9.7 miles. Before the bridge over Buffalo Fork River, swing east onto the gravel road for 0.1 mile and veer right for 0.2 mile and turn right into the campground. An alternative route to the bridge departs Highway 26/287 at milepost 13, heading north on gravel Forest Road 30050 for 4.2 miles.
GPS Coordinates: N 43° 51.335' W 110° 15.834'

Contact: Bridger-Teton National Forest, Buffalo Ranger District, Hwy. 26/287, P.O. Box 278, Afton, WY 83110, 307/886-5300, www. fs.fed.us/r4/btnf/.

47 LEIGH LAKE

Scenic rating: 10

between Jenny Lake and Jackson Lake in Grand Teton National Park

Leigh Lake, a small 250-acre lake tucked at 6,877 feet below the giant toothy Teton Mountains, is a popular kayak and canoe destination for camping. Only human-powered boats are permitted on the lake, making it a quiet place to enjoy nature. Paddle trips to Leigh Lake start at String Lake, a three-mile-long small, shallow lake. A narrow, rocky, shallow stream requiring a 600-foot portage links the two lakes. Trails loop around String Lake and along Leigh Lake's east shore. Two islands—Mystic and Boulder—sit in Leigh Lake, good destinations for exploration. The Tetons are known for strong afternoon winds; plan paddling schedules accordingly.

These coveted campsites are set back into the forest on the east and west shores of Leigh Lake. They are prized for their quiet, solitude, wildlife-watching, and scenery. Those on the eastern shore can capture dramatic mountain reflections and sunsets on the water. Those on the western shore do not have trail access, thus guaranteeing more privacy.

Campsites, facilities: Leigh Lake has seven individual tent campsites, plus one group tent site. Six people maximum are allowed per permit, except at group sites, which can hold 12. Boaters may stay in a designated site for two consecutive nights. Facilities include fire pits, bear boxes, and pit toilets, and some sites have tent platforms. No drinking water is available; filter or boil lake water. Pack out your trash. Pets are not allowed.

Reservations, fees: Reservations are available ($25, 307/739-3309 or 307/739-3397 for information, but all reservation request must be via application). Applications are available online, and reservation requests are accepted January 1–May 15. Obtain the required free overnight camping permits at the Craig Thomas Visitor Center or Jenny Lake Ranger Station. Even kayaks and canoes must have permits ($10 per week, $20 per season). Open June–October.

Directions: From Teton Lake Road, turn west at North Jenny Lake Junction and drive 1.5 miles. Turn right at the sign for String Lake Trailhead. Drive 0.2 mile northwest, opting for the parking area on the left or the one where the road ends. Both require 170-foot portages to the shore. GPS Coordinates: N 43° 47.173' W 110° 43.817' (parking area)

Contact: Grand Teton National Park, P.O. Drawer 170, Moose, WY 83102, 307/739-3300, www.nps.gov/grte/.

48 JENNY LAKE

Scenic rating: 10

on Jenny Lake in Grand Teton National Park

BEST (

At 6,789 feet, Jenny Lake claims front-row seating below the immense Teton Mountains. A tourist complex—visitors center, ranger station, general store—sprawls along its southeast shore. A trail circles the lake, plus the 18-mile Paintbrush-Cascade Loop Trail draws those looking for dramatic backcountry and access

© BECKY LOMAX

From Jenny Lake, hikers loop through the Paintbrush-Cascade Canyons below the Grand Tetons.

to rock climbing. A shuttle boat speeds canyon hikers across the lake, and a tour boat circles the lake. While the lake offers fishing, you may line up along the shore with hordes of anglers. Motorboats are limited to 10 horsepower, a gravel boat launch is available, and permits are required for motorized ($20 weekly, $40 annual) and nonmotorized ($10 weekly, $20 annual) boats. The campground offers wildlife-watching, often with male elk rounding up harems in fall. A new bike trail running from Jenny Lake to Taggart Lake Trailhead opened in 2009.

Jenny Lake—the most popular campground in the park—fills by 10 A.M. each day. Its campsites, strung through the loose hilly forest and glacial boulders—are roomy. Some are partly shaded, but the best are open meadows claiming big views of the Tetons. Due to the campground's meadows, campsites are not private. But the trade-off in views is worth it. Trails run from the campground to the visitors center, lake, and boat dock. After day visitors retreat, the campground quiets at night. Listen in fall for elk bugling.

Campsites, facilities: The campground has 49 tent campsites and 10 sites designated for hikers and bicyclists. Trailers, truck campers, and generators are prohibited. Vehicles must be smaller than 8 feet wide and 14 feet long. Two tents, one vehicle or two motorcycles, and six people are the maximum allowed per site. Facilities include picnic tables, fire rings with grills, bear boxes, vault toilets, drinking water, and garbage service. Leashed pets are permitted. A wheelchair-accessible toilet is available.

Reservations, fees: Reservations are not accepted. Campsites cost $19. Shared hiker and biker campsites cost $7. Cash or check. Open mid-May–late September.

Directions: On Teton Park Road, drive toward Jenny Lake Visitor Center. Turn west, entering the visitors center complex, for 0.1 mile and turn right at the campground sign for 0.1 mile.

GPS Coordinates: N 43° 45.220' W 110° 43.261'

Contact: Grand Teton National Park, P.O. Drawer 170, Moose, WY 83102, 307/739-3300, www.nps.gov/grte/.

49 GROS VENTRE

Scenic rating: 8

on the Gros Ventre River in the south end of Grand Teton National Park

Gros Ventre Campground, at 6,568 feet, is not only the largest campground in Grand Teton National Park, but the closest national park campground to Jackson, about 12 miles south. The campground sits opposite the river from the National Elk Refuge, which attracts the largest collection of migrating elk each winter. Gros Ventre Road, a backroad cycling route, provides scenic opportunities for wildlife-watching for bison and elk. The campground's location is convenient for floating or fishing the lower stretches of the Snake River for 14 miles from Moose Landing to Wilson, which requires advanced boating skills. The Gros Ventre River, which flows past the campground, unfortunately often becomes a barren riverbed mid-July–September because of water diverted for irrigation.

The campground, which sits along the Gros Ventre River but with Black Butte blocking most of the Teton Mountains, sprawls its seven large loops on a flat sagebrush plateau beneath cottonwood trees for some shade. Paths lead to the river. Due to its road configurations and campsite parking pads, this campground is the best one in the national park for large trailers and RVs; it is also the last to fill up every day and often doesn't fill to capacity. Located several miles from the highway, the campground is quiet, secluded, and a respite from busy downtown Jackson or the more popular tourist areas of the park. With no understory, campsites lack privacy.

Campsites, facilities: The campground has 362 individual RV and tent campsites and five large group sites. Two tents, two vehicles, and six people are the maximum allowed per site.

The campsites can fit large RVs. Facilities include picnic tables, fire rings with grills, flush toilets, a disposal station, drinking water, an amphitheater for interpretive programs, and garbage service. Leashed pets are permitted. A wheelchair-accessible toilet is available.

Reservations, fees: Reservations are accepted only for group campsites (Grand Teton Lodge Company, 307/543-3100 or 800/628-9988). Campsites cost $19. Cash, check, or credit card. Open early May–mid-October.

Directions: From Gros Ventre Junction on Highway 89/191, turn northeast onto Gros Ventre Road for 4.6 miles. Turn south for 0.3 mile into the campground.

GPS Coordinates: N 43° 36.982' W 110° 40.001'

Contact: Grand Teton National Park, P.O. Drawer 170, Moose, WY 83102, 307/739-3300, www.nps.gov/grte/.

50 ATHERTON CREEK

Scenic rating: 8

on Lower Slide Lake in the Gros Ventre Mountains in Bridger-Teton National Forest

Atherton Creek Campground, elevation 7,250 feet, draws a varied boating crowd because of its location on the north shore of Lower Slide Lake in the colorful red- and orange-streaked Gros Ventre Mountains. Canoeists explore the shoreline, which has silvered trunks buried by water when the lake was formed by a 1925 landslide. Anglers fish for brook, lake, and cutthroat trout. Water-skiers weave a white trail across calm, blue water. When daily winds crop up, windsurfers hit the waves. The Gros Ventre Slide Geological Area still shows the track of the landslide, and an interpretive trail tells the story of the lake's creation. Mountain biking is an option on Gros Ventre Road, with bucolic views west of the Teton Mountains. A boat dock and ramp are available. May–July the Lower Gros Ventre River offers kayakers Class III–IV white water.

The sunny quiet hillside campground gleans a little shade from aspens, spruces, firs, and small willow bushes strung around its interconnected loops, which have back-in gravel parking pads. Sagebrush and wild roses complete the understory for campsites that range from shady and private to sunny and open. Sites 16 and 17 sit on the water, while sites 18 and 20 overlook the water; many of the other campsites have no view of the lake, but some have views of surrounding forest slopes. In the breeze, the aspen leaves clatter with a soothing background sound, but prepare for strong afternoon winds.

Campsites, facilities: The campground has 23 RV or tent campsites. Sites can fit midsized RVs only. Facilities include picnic tables, fire rings with grills, a vault toilet, drinking water, garbage service, bear boxes, tent platforms, and campground hosts. Leashed pets are permitted. A wheelchair-accessible toilet is available.

Reservations, fees: Reservations are not accepted. Campsites cost $12. Cash or check. Open late May–September.

Directions: From Moose Junction, drive north 1.2 miles and turn east onto Antelope Flats Road for 3.2 miles. Turn south onto Lower Gros Ventre Road for 2.5 miles. Turn east onto Gros Ventre Road for 5.5 miles of bumpy paved road to the campground entrance on the right.

GPS Coordinates: N 43° 38.270' W 110° 31.341'

Contact: Bridger-Teton National Forest, Jackson Ranger District, 25 Rosencrans Ln., Jackson, WY 83001, 307/739-5400, www.fs.fed.us/r4/btnf/.

51 RED HILLS AND CRYSTAL CREEK

Scenic rating: 8

on the Gros Ventre River in Bridger-Teton National Forest

Sitting at 7,300 feet in the Gros Ventre Mountains of Bridger-Teton National Forest,

Red Hill and Crystal Creek are a pair of small, older, adjacent campgrounds that allow exploration of the range facing the Teton Mountains. Red Hills is named for the red-orange sagebrush hills that create such a dramatic contrast in color. Crystal Creek Campground sits at the confluence of Crystal Creek with the Gros Ventre River. Both offer native cutthroat trout fishing, mountain biking on forest roads and nearby trails, and hiking. Trails run south along Crystal Creek into the Gros Ventre Wilderness, but only hikers may travel into the wilderness for climbing its 10,000-foot peaks, an important wildlife enclave for bighorn sheep, elk, and bears. Raft, kayaks, and canoes put in at the Warden Bridge to float eight miles of Class II–III rapids to Lower Slide Lake.

Both campgrounds squeeze in between the road and the river in a forest of spruces and firs. Willows line the riverbank. In Red Hills, sites 1, 2, 4, and 5 claim river frontage, with views of the red-orange hills surrounded by sagebrush. In Crystal Creek, sites 3 and 4 overlook the river, with big views of the richly colored countryside. The quiet, older campgrounds are popular with locals but rarely crowded.

Campsites, facilities: The campgrounds have 11 RV or tent campsites—five at Red Hills and six at Crystal Creek. Sites and the narrow campground roads can fit midsized RVs only. Red Hills has no turnaround. Facilities include picnic tables, fire rings with grills or rock fire rings, pit toilets, drinking water, and bear boxes. Leashed pets are permitted.

Reservations, fees: Reservations are not accepted. Campsites cost $10. Cash or check. Open late May–September.

Directions: From Moose Junction, drive north 1.2 miles and turn east onto Antelope Flats Road for 3.2 miles. Turn south onto Lower Gros Ventre Road for 2.5 miles. Turn east onto Gros Ventre Road for 10 miles of bumpy paved and dirt road. The campground entrances are on the left 0.4 mile apart.

GPS Coordinates for Red Hills: N 43° 36.691' W 110° 26.266'
GPS Coordinates for Crystal Creek: N 43° 36.643' W 110° 25.865'
Contact: Bridger-Teton National Forest, Jackson Ranger District, 25 Rosencrans Ln., Jackson, WY 83001, 307/739-5400, www.fs.fed.us/r4/btnf/.

52 SNAKE RIVER PARK KOA

Scenic rating: 7

on the Snake River between Hoback Junction and Jackson

The Snake River Park KOA, elevation 5,090 feet, is a combination campground and white-water rafting business on the Snake River north of Hoback Junction. Those camping at the park can get 10 percent off white-water rafting trips or saddle and paddle trips. The corral is across the street from the campground. The campground is 20 minutes from the entrance to Grand Teton National Park and 15 minutes from Jackson. Fishing is available on the Snake River from the campground.

Tucked into a deep narrow canyon, the campground squeezes between the busy two-lane highway rumbling with commercial haul trucks and the Snake River. Tent campsites sit along Horse Creek and the river with partial shade and views. The sunny RV campsites are lined up in parking-lot fashion with mowed lawns between sites. Stairs lead from the campground to the sandy riverbank.

Campsites, facilities: This campground has 47 RV back-in campsites and 10 tent campsites. RVs are limited to 36 feet. Hookups are available for water, sewer, and electricity up to 50 amps. Facilities include picnic tables, fire rings with grills, flush toilets, showers, drinking water, a coin-op launderette, a game room, firewood for sale, a playground, a pet walk, a convenience store, and wireless Internet. Leashed pets are permitted.

Reservations, fees: Reservations are accepted (800/562-1878, www.koa.com). RV hookups sites range $59–62, plus $5 extra for 50-amp hookups. Tent sites range $39–43. Rates cover two people; each extra person costs $8; kids under six camp for free. A 6 percent sales tax is added on. Cash, check, or credit card. Open mid-April–early October.

Directions: On Highway 26/89/197/191, drive 12 miles south of Jackson or 1.5 miles north of Hoback Junction. Turn west into the campground.

GPS Coordinates: N 43° 20.450' W 110° 43.400'

Contact: Jackson South/Snake River KOA, 9705 S. Hwy. 89, Jackson, WY 83001, 307/733-7078, www.srpkoa.com.

SOUTHERN YELLOWSTONE GATEWAYS

© BECKY LOMAX

BEST CAMPGROUNDS

《 Fishing
Riverside, **page 346.**
Green River Warren Bridge Access Area, **page 374.**

《 Hiking
Big Sandy, **page 376.**

《 Idaho
Big Springs, **page 341.**
Grandview, **page 347.**

《 Hot Springs
Granite Creek, **page 372.**

《 River Camping
Warm River, **page 348.**

《 Wyoming
Clearwater, **page 354.**
Brooks Lake, **page 360.**
Pinnacles, **page 361.**

Surrounding Yellowstone and Grand Teton National

Parks, mountain ranges spring up from high desert plateaus in Wyoming and Idaho. The Continental Divide skips across the top of glacier-rimmed peaks stretching over 12,000 feet tall and dips through grassy sagebrush saddles. Prime camping spots in Yellowstone's southern gateways hold a collision of habitats that support abundant wildlife, from waterfowl to grizzly bears.

The southern perimeter of the national parks is ringed with three national forests, giving campers the opportunity to explore what appeals most to them – thick pine forests, blue-green lakes, trout-filled rivers, rugged mountains, or arid sage grasslands. The Caribou-Targhee National Forest in Idaho and Wyoming flanks the western boundaries. The Bridger-Teton National Forests surrounds the south and east. Shoshone National Forest flanks the eastern boundary.

To the west of Yellowstone and Grand Teton National Parks, the Caribou-Targhee National Forest holds three large reservoirs fed by waters streaming west from the two national parks. The area appeals to many for its spectacular "back-side" views of the Teton Mountains. Its campgrounds are smaller than the gigantic national park campgrounds, plus they feel more remote and less crowded.

The northern portion of the forest holds Island Park, two calderas formed 2.1 million years ago. The high, forested Idaho plateau playground cradles lakes and rivers with more than 15 campgrounds. Campgrounds on Henrys Lake or Island Park Reservoir appeal to boaters, water-skiers, and anglers. Campers head to the Henrys Fork of the Snake River for canoeing, kayaking, and rafting. Anglers camp along Henrys Fork or the Buffalo River for blue-ribbon trout fishing.

East of Driggs, Idaho, national forest roads shimmy into the west flank of the Teton Mountains to reach Wyoming campgrounds, where trails lead into wilderness areas and Grand Teton National Park. At the south end of the national forest, a dam on the Snake River forms the popular Palisades Reservoir north of Alpine, which attracts boaters and anglers to its several campgrounds.

Wyoming's Bridger-Teton National Forest, which arcs around Grand Teton National Park's southern and eastern boundaries, is characterized by high mountain ranges broken by deep river gorges. Flowing south from Jackson Hole, a mecca of outdoor recreation, the Snake River tumbles through a rugged canyon, while to the east the Green River spills from the Wind River Mountains – both blue-ribbon trout fisheries with riverside campgrounds. River rafters and kayakers splash through their canyons while canoeists paddle calmer stretches.

Two high mountain ranges dominate the Bridger-Teton National Forest – both crisscrossed with hiking and horseback-riding trails through remote wilderness. The Gros Ventre Range sits to the east of the Teton Mountain Range. Its campgrounds line up along river canyons such as Granite Creek and Hoback Canyon. By far, the Wind River Range attracts the most campers to the national forest, with Wyoming's second largest natural lake and trails leading into the alpine glaciated peaks of three wilderness areas. The mountain range – with the Continental Divide tripping across its peak tops – attracts campers for hiking, rock climbing, mountaineering, backpacking, horse-packing, boating, fishing, mountain biking, and hunting.

To the east of Yellowstone National Park, Shoshone National Forest runs from its north boundary on the Montana-Wyoming border to the Continental Divide in the Wind River Range. Campgrounds line up along river valleys and scenic byways, which lead to the popular eastern entrances for both Yellowstone and Grand Teton National Parks. From Cody, the Chief Joseph Scenic Byway, following the route of the Nez Perce through Wyoming, parallels much of the Clarks Fork of the Yellowstone River, a reputable trout fishery. The route connects with the Beartooth Highway and the northeast entrance to Yellowstone National Park.

Also from Cody, the Buffalo Bill Scenic Byway follows the North Fork of the Shoshone to Yellowstone's most popular eastern entrance. Campgrounds litter the river corridor, providing opportunities for fishing, floating, hiking, and mountain biking.

The Wind River Valley provides a third access to Grand Teton National Park via Togwotee Pass. Long dirt roads lead into the Wind River Range for quiet, remote camping. Northwest of Togwotee Pass, the Pinnacles provide some of Wyoming's most photographed natural art.

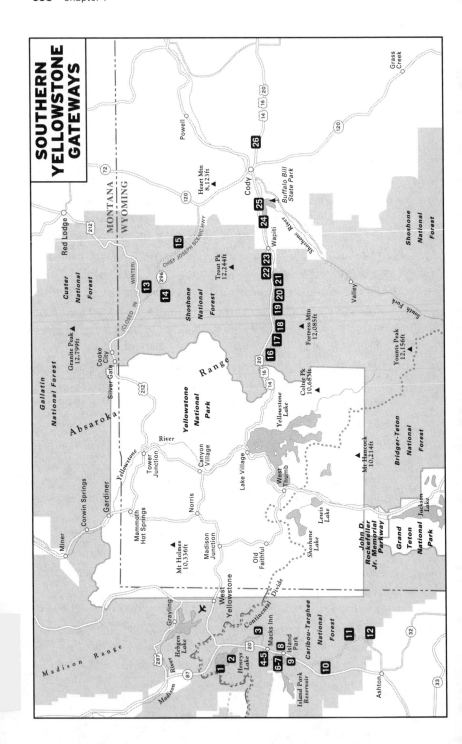

SOUTHERN YELLOWSTONE GATEWAYS

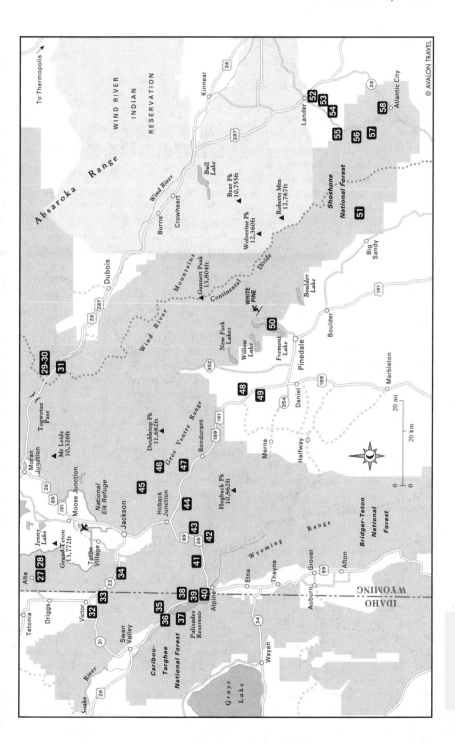

© AVALON TRAVEL

◼ BILL FROME COUNTY PARK

🚶 🛶 🚤 🎣 🐕 ♿ 🚐 ⛺

Scenic rating: 7

on Henrys Lake north of Island Park and west of Yellowstone National Park in Idaho

At 6,450 feet in elevation, Henrys Lake State Park sits on the west side of the 6,000-acre Henrys Lake about 15 miles from the west entrance to Yellowstone National Park. A boat launch includes a cement ramp, dock, and trailer parking. Henrys Lake is popular for boating, waterskiing, and fishing for Yellowstone cutthroat, brook, and rainbow trout. You can take a scenic 25-mile dirt road drive west to Red Rocks Pass and Red Rocks National Wildlife Refuge. Within a 10-minute drive east, the Targhee Creek Trailhead launches a 14-mile loop past five alpine lakes at the base of Targhee Peak.

Surrounded by sagebrush prairie, the quiet campground is on the west shore of the lake. A few small perimeter aspens help shade some of the sunny campsites and act as windbreaks for the common strong afternoon gusts. The open area, however, provides big views of the lake and the surrounding mountains, including Sawtell Peak to the south and Black Mountain to the north. A single gravel road drops through the campground to the boat launch; all campsites line up on the grass and gravel back-in parking pads in close proximity.

Campsites, facilities: The campground has 30 RV or tent campsites that can accommodate large RVs. Facilities include some rock fire rings, vault toilets, a boat launch, pet area, and campground hosts. Pack out your trash. Leashed pets are permitted. A wheelchair-accessible toilet is available.

Reservations, fees: Reservations are not accepted. Camping is free. Open May–October.

Directions: From the junction of Highway 87 and Highway 20, drive south toward Island Park for 1.2 miles and turn right at the state park sign for 1.7 miles to the park entrance station.

GPS Coordinates: N 44° 38.997' W 111° 26.275'

Contact: Fremont County, 151 West 1st North, St. Anthony, ID 83445, 208/624-7332.

◼ HENRYS LAKE STATE PARK

🚶 🚴 🛶 🎣 🚤 🐕 ♿ 🚐 ⛺

Scenic rating: 7

on Henrys Lake north of Island Park and west of Yellowstone National Park in Idaho

Henrys Lake State Park, elevation 6,470 feet, sits on the southeast corner of the 6,000-acre Henrys Lake north of Island Park and 15 miles from the west entrance to Yellowstone National Park. Within a 10-minute drive, the Targhee Creek Trailhead launches a 14-mile loop past five alpine lakes at the base of Targhee Peak. A paved bicycle and walking trail loops through the park, including a wheelchair-accessible Aspen Loop Nature Trail. Guided nature walks are available. A boat ramp allows for launching onto the lake for boating, waterskiing, and fishing. The lake harbors Yellowstone cutthroat, brook, and rainbow trout. The park also has good wildlife-watching: birds, pronghorn antelope, and moose. For kids, the park has a Junior Ranger Program.

Surrounded by wetlands and sagebrush prairie, the campground's two large paved loops are on the southeast shore of Henrys Lake, where few trees provide shade or act as windbreaks for the common strong afternoon gusts. The open area, however, provides big views of the lake and the surrounding mountains, including Sawtell Peak to the south and Black Mountain to the north. Paved back-in parking pads are surrounded by mowed lawn, with campsites spread out for privacy, although you will see everyone around your site. When the winds die down, you can hear a faint truck or two on the highway.

Campsites, facilities: The campground has 45 RV or tent campsites. RVs are limited to

40 feet. Hookups are available for electricity and water. Facilities include picnic tables, fire rings with grills, flush toilets, showers, drinking water, garbage service, a disposal station, firewood for sale, horseshoe pits, interpretive programs, a boat launch, a fish-cleaning station, and campground hosts. Leashed pets are permitted. A wheelchair-accessible toilet is available.

Reservations, fees: Reservations are accepted (888/922-6743, www.parksandrecreation. idaho.gov). Campsites cost $16–20, plus 6 percent Idaho sales tax. Cash, check, or credit card. Open late May–October.

Directions: From the junction of Highway 87 and Highway 20, drive south toward Island Park for 1.2 miles and turn right at the state park sign for 1.7 miles to the park entrance station.

GPS Coordinates: N 44° 37.095' W 111° 22.130'

Contact: Henrys Lake State Park, 3917 East 5100 North, Island Park, ID 83429, 208/558-7532, www.parksandrecreation.idaho.gov.

3 BIG SPRINGS

Scenic rating: 8

in Island Park in Caribou-Targhee National Forest in Idaho

BEST (

At an elevation of 6,400 feet in Caribou-Targhee National Forest, Big Springs Campground sits adjacent to Big Springs, an idyllic natural pool fed by snowmelt and rain that seeps through the Yellowstone plateau. The exceptionally clear water of the National Natural Landmark stays at 52 degrees year-round, providing habitat for trout, moose, bald eagles, and herons. Wheelchair-accessible trails connect the campground with the pond. A one-mile hiking-only trail (paved halfway) traverses downstream along the Henrys Fork of the Snake River. Big Springs does not permit wading, swimming, fishing, or boating along this route to protect the underwater gardens for spawning. One mile west of the campground, a river put-in allows paddlers to tour the four-mile National Recreation Water Trail, which is closed to fishing to its outlet. Mountain bikers access the 42-mile dirt Union Pacific Railroad Right of Way Trail.

Set in a young lodgepole forest, the campground loops one paved road around its campsites, many of which have rough-paved pull-through parking. The campsites are spread out for privacy, and the lodgepoles are thick enough to shield sites from one another. The nighttime quiet is broken only by the yipping of coyotes or the call of the herons. The spacious campsites vary between sunny (site 11) and partly shaded. Sites 1–3 view Big Springs Road.

Campsites, facilities: The campground has 16 RV or tent campsites. RVs are limited to 32 feet. Facilities include picnic tables, fire rings with grills, cookstove pedestals, vault toilets, drinking water, garbage service, and campground hosts. Leashed pets are permitted. A wheelchair-accessible toilet is available.

Reservations, fees: Reservations are accepted (877/444-6777, www.recreation.gov). Campsites cost $12. Extra vehicles cost $6. Cash or check. Open late May–mid-September.

Directions: From Highway 20, two entrances onto Big Springs Loop Road swing east to the campground. Coming from Henrys Lake, turn east at Island Park Village onto N. Big Springs Loop Road (Forest Road 059) for 4.3 miles mostly on dirt. Coming from Ashton, turn east at Mack's Inn onto S. Big Springs Loop Road for 4.7 paved miles. Locate the campground entrance south of the Big Springs Bridge.

GPS Coordinates: N 44° 29.800' W 111° 15.329'

Contact: Caribou-Targhee National Forest, Island Park Ranger District, 3726 Hwy. 20, Island Park, ID 83429, 208/558-7301, www. fs.fed.us/r4/caribou-targhee.

4 FLAT ROCK

🚴 🎣 🚌 ⚓ 🐴 ♿ 🚐 ⛺

Scenic rating: 6

in Island Park in Caribou-Targhee National Forest in Idaho

At 6,400 feet in Island Park caldera in Caribou-Targhee National Forest, Flat Rock sits on the banks of the Henrys Fork of the Snake River, a blue-ribbon trout fishery. A five-minute walk leads to Mack's Inn, where you can rent canoes, kayaks, and rafts. Outfitters for fishing and horseback riding are available, as well as groceries, restaurants, and gas. The campground also sits at the lower end of the Henrys Fork of the Snake River National Recreation Water Trail—a four-mile paddle. Fishing is not permitted on the trail until Henrys Fork Outlet Creek; however, fishing is permitted along the riverbank at the campground, and you can launch hand-carried watercrafts from the campground. The river harbors native Yellowstone cutthroat, plus rainbow and brook trout. For bicyclists on Highway 20, the campground is one of the most convenient due to its location on the highway.

The campground is divided into an upper and lower loop. The upper loop has electrical hookups in sites 2–9; the lower includes sites along the river (18–23). You can pick from sunny or shady campsites under lodgepole pines, and the grassy meadows between campsites bloom with asters in August. You'll see several other campsites from your picnic table, and both loops pick up substantial highway noise.

Campsites, facilities: The campground has seven RV campsites with electrical hookups and 34 tent or RV campsites. RVs are limited to 32 feet. Hookups include electricity. Facilities include picnic tables, fire rings with grills, cookstove pedestals, vault and flush toilets, drinking water, garbage service, and campground hosts. Leashed pets are permitted. A wheelchair-accessible toilet is available.

Reservations, fees: Reservations are accepted (877/444-6777, www.recreation.gov).

Many campgrounds in Island Park have been upgraded with cookstove and cooler platforms, in addition to picnic tables and fire rings with grills.

Hookups cost $17. Nonhookup campsites cost $12. Extra vehicles cost $6. Cash or check. Open late May–mid-September.

Directions: From Highway 20 south of Mack's Inn at milepost 393, turn west into the campground.

GPS Coordinates: N 44° 29.965' W 111° 20.328'

Contact: Caribou-Targhee National Forest, Island Park Ranger District, 3726 Hwy. 20, Island Park, ID 83429, 208/558-7301, www.fs.fed.us/r4/caribou-targhee.

5 UPPER COFFEE POT

Scenic rating: 7

in Island Park in Caribou-Targhee National Forest in Idaho

Located at 6,300 feet in elevation in the Island Park caldera of Caribou-Targhee National Forest, Upper Coffee Pot sits on the Henrys Fork of the Snake River, a blue-ribbon trout stream. Kayakers, rafters, and canoeists can float the river one mile from Mack's Inn to the campground or five miles to the campground, starting at the upper end of the Henrys Fork of the Snake River National Recreation Water Trail. However, boaters must take out at the campground due to the dangerous rapids downstream. Fishing is not permitted on the water trail until the confluence with the Henrys Fork Outlet Creek, but fishing is permitted at the campground. A 2.5-mile hiking trail tours the shoreline from the campground southeast to Coffee Pot Rapids. Mountain bikers and ATV riders tour the network of old Forest Service roads around the campground.

The campground lines up in two sections along the river. The right loop contains electrical sites (8–15). Campsites 1, 3, 6, 7, 9, 11, 13, 14, and 15 overlook the river. Campsites 1 and 15 at each loop turnaround have the most privacy. The loose lodgepole forest and grassy meadow campground has sites that are close enough that you'll see neighboring campers. Sites vary between sunny and partly shaded. Due to its location away from the highway, the only sound in the campground is the river.

Campsites, facilities: The campground has eight RV campsites with electrical hookups plus seven RV or tent campsites. RVs are limited to 32 feet. Facilities include picnic tables, fire rings with grills, vault toilets, drinking water, garbage service, and campground hosts. Leashed pets are permitted. A wheelchair-accessible toilet is available.

Reservations, fees: Reservations are accepted (877/444-6777, www.recreation.gov). Hookups cost $17. Nonhookup campsites cost $12. Extra vehicles cost $6. Cash or check. Open late May–mid-September.

Directions: From 0.5 mile south of Mack's Inn on Highway 20, turn west onto Forest Road 130 at milepost 392.5. Drive one mile and turn right onto Forest Road 311. Drive 0.4 mile. Turn right, and drive 0.2 mile to the campground.

GPS Coordinates: N 44° 29.442' W 111° 21.974'

Contact: Caribou-Targhee National Forest, Island Park Ranger District, 3726 Hwy. 20, Island Park, ID 83429, 208/558-7301, www.fs.fed.us/r4/caribou-targhee.

6 MCCREA BRIDGE

Scenic rating: 6

in Island Park in Caribou-Targhee National Forest in Idaho

At 6,200 feet in elevation in the Island Park caldera in Caribou-Targhee National Forest, McCrea Bridge Campground sits where the Henrys Fork of the Snake River flows into the northeast arm of Island Park Reservoir. The campground has a boat launch with four docks and a cement ramp, which allows access to the reservoir for boating, waterskiing, and fishing for kokanee salmon, rainbow trout, and Yellowstone cutthroat trout. Water levels drop in late season; call the Forest Service to check on levels. Mountain bikers can tour the maze of forest roads in the area.

Sitting on the narrow arm of the reservoir, the campground flanks a western-facing hillside of lodgepole and sagebrush and looks across at summer homes. The campground comprises two interconnected loops, with the A loop closest to the water. Three sites (3, 4, and 6) overlook the water. Several sites (2, 3, 4, 10, and 12) are wide open and sunny; the others have partial shade and some privacy created from the forest. Although the campground is removed from the trucking noise on Highway 20, the Yale-Kilgore Road is a main thoroughfare for accessing private homes on the reservoir. Most of the campsites are gravel back-ins; the campground road is also gravel.

Campsites, facilities: The campground has 24 RV or tent campsites. RVs are limited to 32 feet. Facilities include picnic tables, fire rings with grills, vault toilets, drinking water, garbage service, a boat launch, and campground hosts. Leashed pets are permitted. A wheelchair-accessible toilet is available.

Reservations, fees: Reservations are accepted (877/444-6777, www.recreation.gov). Campsites cost $12. Extra vehicles cost $6. Cash or check. Open late May–mid-September.

Directions: From Highway 20 two miles north of the Island Park Ranger Station, turn west onto Yale-Kilgore Road at milepost 389.2. Drive 2.1 miles and turn south before the bridge into the campground.

GPS Coordinates: N 44° 27.774' W 111° 23.880'

Contact: Caribou-Targhee National Forest, Island Park Ranger District, 3726 Hwy. 20, Island Park, ID 83429, 208/558-7301, www.fs.fed.us/r4/caribou-targhee.

⑦ BUTTERMILK

Scenic rating: 6

in Island Park in Caribou-Targhee National Forest in Idaho

In the Island Park caldera in Caribou-Targhee National Forest, Buttermilk Campground, elevation 6,200 feet, sits on the tip of a peninsula on Island Park Reservoir's east end. The campground is the biggest on the reservoir—empty on weekdays in early and late season, but hopping busy in peak summer. The campground's boat launch, with five docks, a double-side concrete ramp, and trailer parking, accommodates those getting onto the reservoir for boating, waterskiing, and fishing. Anglers go after kokanee salmon, rainbow trout, and Yellowstone cutthroat trout. Mountain bikers and ATVers ride the local network of forest roads.

Buttermilk Campground's two loops spread the campsites out, but you can see through the trees to other campsites. Some campsites are doubles—with double-wide parking pads and two picnic tables—that allow for two RVs to camp together for double the price. Although the access to the campground is via paved road, the campground loops and parking pads, most of which are pull-throughs, are gravel. The campsites are partly shaded, with some in B loop receiving more sun. Only three sites in loop A and five sites in loop B have peek-a-boo views of the water through the trees. After the boating stops, the campground is quiet at night. Paths cut from the campground loops to the water.

Campsites, facilities: The campground has 53 RV or tent campsites. One additional RV campsite (site 38) has a hookup for electricity. RVs are limited to 32 feet. Facilities include picnic tables, fire rings with grills, vault toilets, drinking water, tent platforms, garbage service, a boat launch, and campground hosts. Leashed pets are permitted. A wheelchair-accessible toilet is available.

Reservations, fees: Reservations are accepted (877/444-6777, www.recreation.gov). Campsites cost $12, except for site 38 with an electrical hookup, which costs $17. Extra vehicles cost $6. Cash or check. Open late May–mid-September.

Directions: From Highway 20 two miles north of the Island Park Ranger Station, turn west onto Yale-Kilgore Road at milepost 389.2. Drive 1.9 miles and turn south onto Buttermilk Road for 2.5 miles. Turn right into the campground.

GPS Coordinates: N 44° 25.934' W 111° 25.568'

Contact: Caribou-Targhee National Forest, Island Park Ranger District, 3726 Hwy. 20, Island Park, ID 83429, 208/558-7301, www.fs.fed.us/r4/caribou-targhee.

8 BUFFALO

Scenic rating: 7

in Island Park in Caribou-Targhee National Forest in Idaho

At 6,200 feet in elevation in the Island Park caldera of Caribou-Targhee National Forest, Buffalo is the largest national forest campground in the Island Park area. The campground sits right on the Buffalo River, where anglers go after a variety of trout. A wheelchair-accessible boardwalk and fishing platforms sit adjacent to the G loop. Kayakers, canoeists, tubers, and rafts also float the river. Boaters, water-skiers, and anglers can access Island Park Reservoir via the Island Park boat ramp, two miles from the campground. Cyclists on Highway 20 use this campground for its convenience to the highway. Evening interpretive programs include appearances by Smokey Bear.

A paved road winds through the seven loops of Buffalo Campground with paved pull-through or back-in parking pads. Surrounded by grass, fireweed, and purple asters, the campsites are partly shaded by doghair lodgepole and aspens, which also make the sites semiprivate. A and B loops sit closest to the highway, which rumbles with commercial trucking. Loops A, D, F, and G each have a handful of campsites that border the river, although trees, serviceberries, and willows block some views. G5 has the best river view. Double sites at double the price are available to accommodate two RVs.

Campsites, facilities: The campground has 105 RV or tent campsites. RVs are limited to 34 feet. Hookups in C loop include electricity. Facilities include picnic tables, fire rings with grills, flush and vault toilets, drinking water, tent platforms, garbage service, an amphitheater for interpretive programs, and campground manager and hosts. Leashed pets are permitted. A wheelchair-accessible toilet is available.

Reservations, fees: Reservations are accepted (877/444-6777, www.recreation.gov). Campsites cost $12, except for electrical hookups in C loop, which cost $17. Extra vehicles cost $6. Cash or check. Open late May–mid-September.

Directions: On Highway 20, drive 0.25 mile north of the Island Park Ranger Station to milepost 387.5. Turn east off the highway into the campground.

GPS Coordinates: N 44° 25.457' W 111° 22.075'

Contact: Caribou-Targhee National Forest, Island Park Ranger District, 3726 Hwy. 20, Island Park, ID 83429, 208/558-7301, www.fs.fed.us/r4/caribou-targhee.

9 BOX CANYON

Scenic rating: 7

in Island Park in Caribou-Targhee National Forest in Idaho

Located at 6,320 feet in elevation in the Island Park caldera of Caribou-Targhee

National Forest, Box Canyon sits on the Henrys Fork of the Snake River. The blue-ribbon fishery is favored by trout anglers for its wild Yellowstone cutthroat and rainbow trout. In this section, the river is catch-and-release only with barbless hooks. Box Canyon is also a favorite section of the river for rafts, kayaks, and experienced canoeists with its Class II rapids. The two-hour float goes from the Island Park Dam Road launch to Last Chance. Mountain bikers tour the maze of dirt Forest Service roads in the area, and hikers can walk Box Canyon via a three-mile trail along its rim. Gas, groceries, and outfitters for fishing and floating are within five miles.

Box Canyon is one of the best campgrounds in Island Park for those who like privacy and seclusion. One gravel loop accesses all the campsites with gravel back-in parking pads. Set back from the highway, the quiet campground has spacious campsites tucked into shade of lodgepoles and Douglas firs. The large, grassy sites, which are spread out for privacy, are surrounded by purple asters, huckleberries, and serviceberries. Several campsites sit near the river, without views of the water, but with paths cutting through the trees to the riverbank. Site 16 is a double site, which allows two camping units for double the price.

Campsites, facilities: The campground has 19 RV or tent campsites. RVs are limited to 32 feet. Facilities include picnic tables, fire rings with grills, vault toilets, drinking water, garbage service, tent platforms, and campground hosts. Leashed pets are permitted. A wheelchair-accessible toilet is available.

Reservations, fees: Reservations are not accepted. Campsites cost $12. Extra vehicles cost $6. Cash or check. Open late May–mid-September.

Directions: From Highway 20 one mile south of the Island Park Ranger Station, turn west at milepost 386 onto the gravel Forest Road 134 for 0.4 mile. Turn right onto Forest Road

284 for one mile to reach the campground entrance.

GPS Coordinates: N 44° 24.584' W 111° 23.799'

Contact: Caribou-Targhee National Forest, Island Park Ranger District, 3726 Hwy. 20, Island Park, ID 83429, 208/558-7301, www.fs.fed.us/r4/caribou-targhee.

10 RIVERSIDE

Scenic rating: 8

on Henrys Fork of the Snake River in Caribou-Targhee National Forest in Idaho

BEST

At an elevation of 6,200 feet in the Caribou-Targhee National Forest, Riverside is Island Park's southernmost campground. It sits five miles south of Harriman State Park ($4 for entrance), a wildlife refuge where you can see elk, moose, sandhill cranes, and trumpeter swans. The park is also renowned for its blue-ribbon fishery, and it holds 20 miles of trails for hikers and mountain bikers. Guided horseback trail rides and tours of historic ranch buildings are also available. From the campground, you can fish the Henrys Fork of the Snake River. Upstream of the campground is catch-and-release only with barbless hooks. Downstream of the campground there's a two-fish limit. Expert boaters can launch from the campground to float Cardiac Canyon to Hatchery Ford; less-skilled boaters should float the upstream section seven miles from Last Chance to take out at the campground.

The campground has two loops with an additional row of campsites along the road connecting the two loops. The A sites line up along with river, with many of them overlooking the water and the volcanic rock falls flanking the opposite shore. While many of these grab the views, they do so at a cost to privacy as they are more sunny and open amid small stands of aspens and lodgepoles. Those seeking privacy and shade will find both in the hillside camps of loops B and C under tall lodgepoles. The river froths here, filling the campground with its sound.

Campsites, facilities: The campground has 16 RV or tent campsites. RVs are limited to 34 feet. Facilities include picnic tables, fire rings with grills, cookstove pedestals, vault toilets, drinking water, garbage service, and campground hosts. Leashed pets are permitted. Wheelchair-accessible toilets and 15 sites with paved parking pads and cement patios are available.

Reservations, fees: Reservations are accepted (877/444-6777, www.recreation. gov). Campsites cost $12. Extra vehicles cost $6. Cash or check. Open late May–mid-September.

Directions: From Highway 20 about 16 miles north of Ashton, turn east off the highway at milepost 375.6. Head southeast on the narrow, rough-paved Forest Road 304 for 0.8 mile to the campground entrance.

GPS Coordinates: N 44° 15.830' W 111° 27.382'

Contact: Caribou-Targhee National Forest, Island Park Ranger District, 3726 Hwy. 20, Island Park, ID 83429, 208/558-7301, www. fs.fed.us/r4/caribou-targhee.

11 GRANDVIEW

Scenic rating: 9

on Mesa Falls Scenic Byway in Caribou-Targhee National Forest in Idaho

BEST (

Located on the Mesa Falls Scenic Byway at 5,800 feet in elevation in Caribou-Targhee National Forest, Grandview perches on the lip of a deep canyon that houses the Henrys Fork of the Snake River where it roars through Mesa Falls. A four-wheel-drive road drops from the back of the campground 0.5 mile to the river for fishing, rafting, or kayaking. The route also makes a good hike, since the climb back up gains 500 feet in elevation. From the campground, a two-minute walk leads to the overlook

© BECKY LOMAX

The Henrys Fork of the Snake River's Mesa Falls plummets 114 feet in Caribou-Targhee National Forest.

for the 65-foot-high Lower Mesa Falls, but the larger 114-foot-high and 300-foot-wide Upper Mesa Falls thunders about a mile upstream, looking like a smaller clone of Niagara Falls. At the site ($5 or America the Beautiful Interagency Pass), paths lead to decks overlooking various points of the falls, including the lip.

The campground sits in a loose forest of fir, aspen, and lodgepole trees with brushy mountain ash and willows lending a thick understory. The short gravel road puts the partly shaded campsites close to each other, but the underbrush lends privacy. Once the day traffic on the scenic byway disappears, the campground is so quiet that you can hear the faint roar of Lower Mesa Falls below in the canyon.

Campsites, facilities: The campground has eight RV or tent campsites. RVs are limited to 28 feet. Facilities include picnic tables, fire rings with grills, cookstove pedestals, vault toilets, drinking water, garbage service, and campground hosts. Leashed pets are permitted. A wheelchair-accessible toilet is available.

Reservations, fees: Reservations are not accepted. Campsites cost $12. Extra vehicles cost $6. Cash or check. Open from late May until snow closes the byway. The water is shut off in mid-September.

Directions: From Highway 20 at Ashton or one mile north of Harriman State Park, turn east onto the Mesa Falls Scenic Byway (also Route 47 and Forest Road 294). From Ashton, drive 16 miles northeast. From the north entrance to the byway, drive 14 miles. The campground entrance is on the southwest side of the byway adjacent to Lower Mesa Falls Overlook and 0.5 mile southeast from the entrance to Upper Mesa Falls.
GPS Coordinates: N 44° 10.470' W 111° 18.860'

Contact: Caribou-Targhee National Forest, Island Park Ranger District, 3726 Hwy. 20, Island Park, ID 83429, 208/558-7301, www.fs.fed.us/r4/caribou-targhee.

12 WARM RIVER

Scenic rating: 6

on Mesa Falls Scenic Byway in
Caribou-Targhee National Forest in Idaho

BEST (

At 5,200 feet in elevation along the Mesa Falls Scenic Byway in Caribou-Targhee National Forest, Warm River Campground sits adjacent to a tiny burg of three houses. The river's slow-moving water is popular for floating with tubes. Fed by water from the Yellowstone plateau via underground springs, the clear water maintains a year-round temperature of 50 degrees. Wading anglers go after native trout, and a wheelchair-accessible fishing platform is available. The campground is also the south entrance to the 42-mile Railroad Right of Way Trail, which includes one tunnel, with its first two miles open only to hikers and mountain bikers. ATV and motorcycle riders must start at the Bear Gulch Trailhead to the north.

Surrounded by sagebrush and aspen slopes, the popular campground tucks into a lush river corridor. Many of the grassy campsites sit right on the Warm River. Mature willows provide shade for some of the sites, but the lack of understory allows you to see other campers. The campground is in several sections: a collection of shady RV sites, walk-in tent sites, a large group pavilion, and a sunny loop of campsites accessed via a narrow bridge across the river. Once the byway traffic dies at night, the campground quiets to the sound of the river and birds.

Campsites, facilities: The campground has 13 RV campsites and 12 tent campsites. RVs are limited to 24 feet. Facilities include picnic tables, fire rings with grills, pedestal grills, cookstove pedestals, vault toilets, drinking water, garbage service, horseshoe pits, tent pads, and campground hosts. Leashed pets are permitted. A wheelchair-accessible toilet and one accessible campsite (site 13) are available.

Reservations, fees: Reservations are accepted (877/444-6777, www.recreation.gov). Campsites cost $12. Extra vehicles cost $6. Site 12, which has an electrical hookup, costs $18. Cash or check. Open late May–mid-September.

Directions: From Highway 20 at Ashton or one mile north of Harriman State Park, turn east onto the Mesa Falls Scenic Byway (also Route 47 and Forest Road 294). From Ashton, drive nine miles northeast, or from the north entrance to the byway drive 20 miles. At milepost 8.9, turn east along the river and drive 0.5 mile into the campground.

GPS Coordinates: N 44° 7.208' W 111° 18.814'

Contact: Caribou-Targhee National Forest, Island Park Ranger District, 3726 Hwy. 20, Island Park, ID 83429, 208/558-7301, www.fs.fed.us/r4/caribou-targhee.

13 LAKE CREEK

Scenic rating: 6

on Chief Joseph Highway in Shoshone National Forest

About 65 miles northwest of Cody and 20 miles east of Yellowstone National Park, Lake Creek, elevation 7,000 feet, sits at the base of the Beartooth Mountains just south of the Beartooth Highway on Chief Joseph Highway—both outstanding drives for the distinctly different scenery. The campground isn't a destination, but a place to camp for convenience. For those who love scenic drives, the campground provides a good launch point for exploring two of Wyoming's most scenic roads—the rugged lake-strewn west flank of the Beartooth Highway and arid canyons of the Chief Joseph Highway up to Dead Indian Pass. Cross-country cyclists use this campground before beginning the steep climb 3,000 feet in elevation over Beartooth Pass. Anglers can fish for brook, rainbow, and Yellowstone cutthroat trout in the Wild and Scenic–designated Clarks Fork of the Yellowstone River, which parallels Chief Joseph Highway. The Clarks Fork upstream of the campground offers experts-only Class IV–V+ white water.

Some campers prefer staying at this lower elevation campground than high on the Beartooth Plateau, as it stays warmer and drier, plus some people sleep better at lower elevations. Lake Creek fills the campground with its burbling, but not enough to drown out passing cars on the close highway. Commercial trucking noise, however, is sparse, as trucks do not climb over the Beartooth Highway or travel through Yellowstone National Park. In midsummer, the campground meadows bloom with sticky pink geraniums, wild roses, and grasses. Lodgepole pines provide partial shade. Sites 4 and 5 tuck in more private locations under the trees, but more open sites garner mountain views.

Campsites, facilities: The campground has six RV or tent campsites. RVs are limited to 22 feet. Facilities include picnic tables, fire rings with grills, pit toilets, bear boxes, garbage service, and campground hosts. No drinking water is available. If you opt to use creek water, boil or purify it first. Leashed pets are permitted.

Reservations, fees: Reservations are not accepted. Campsites cost $10. Cash or check. Open late June–early September.

Directions: From the junction of the Beartooth Highway (Highway 212) and Chief Joseph Highway (Highway 296), drive south on Highway 296 for 1.5 miles. Turn left into the campground.

GPS Coordinates: N 44° 55.277' W 109° 42.419'

Contact: Shoshone National Forest, Clarks Fork Ranger District, 203A Yellowstone Ave., Cody, WY 82414-9313, 307/527-6921, www.fs.fed.us/r2/shoshone/.

14 HUNTER PEAK

Scenic rating: 7

on the Clarks Fork of the Yellowstone in Shoshone National Forest

At 6,680 feet in elevation about 60 miles northwest of Cody and 25 miles east of Yellowstone

National Park, Hunter Peak Campground squeezes in between the scenic Chief Joseph Highway and the Wild and Scenic–designated Clarks Fork of the Yellowstone River. It sits at the base of the 9,034-foot Hunter Peak, where it attracts elk hunters in the fall. Anglers can fish the river for trout (artificial flies and lures only) from several campsites. Across the highway from the campground, the Clark's Fork Trailhead departs for a 17-mile trek along the rugged canyons of the river as it heads downstream. A 300-foot waterfall awaits about 90 minutes down the trail. The trail, a popular horse-packing route, is also open to mountain bikes and ATVs. North Crandell Trail, which departs three miles south of the campground, climbs 16 miles up North Crandell Creek into Yellowstone National Park.

Most of the campsites ring a loop on the left; the campground hosts usually camp on the spur to the right. The campground tucks under tall lodgepole pines and spruces on a flat grassy plateau on the river. Views from several campsites include large boulders across the river. Meadows bloom throughout the campground with penstemon, buckwheat, and pink sticky geranium. Sites 2, 4, 5, and 6 claim river frontage, but all remaining campsites have access via trails. The sound of the river helps you forget the road passes right above the campground, and sites vary between partly shaded and sunny.

Campsites, facilities: The campground has nine RV or tent campsites. RVs are limited to 28 feet. Facilities include picnic tables, fire rings with grills, vault toilets, drinking water, bear boxes, garbage service, and campground hosts. Leashed pets are permitted. A wheelchair-accessible toilet is available.

Reservations, fees: Reservations are accepted (977/444-6777, www.recreation.gov). Campsites cost $15. Cash or check. Open late May–mid-October.

Directions: From the junction of Highway 212 (Beartooth Highway) and Highway 296 (Chief Joseph Highway) drive southeast for 4.7 miles. Turn right, descending into the campground.

GPS Coordinates: N 44° 53.095' W 109° 39.327'

Contact: Shoshone National Forest, Clarks Fork Ranger District, 203A Yellowstone Ave., Cody, WY 82414-9313, 307/527-6921, www. fs/fed/us/r2/shoshone/.

15 DEAD INDIAN CREEK
🥾 🚴 🏊 🎣 🚙 ⛰️

Scenic rating: 7

on Chief Joseph Highway in Shoshone National Forest

At an elevation of 6,100 feet in Shoshone National Forest, surrounded by sagebrush hills broken by orange and white sandstones, Dead Indian Creek Campground, named for the creek and the 8,000-foot-high pass above the campground, sits on the scenic Chief Joseph Highway in between Dead Indian Pass and Sunlight Bridge. The Dead Indian Pass Overlook includes interpretive stories about the escape of Chief Joseph from the army and the trek of the Nez Perce across Wyoming. The panoramic view spans the rugged country of the Beartooth Mountains to the Absaroka Range. West of the campground, the Sunlight Bridge, the highest bridge in Wyoming, spans a deep gorge. Road cyclists pedal the switchbacking grade of the highway up to the pass. The Dead Indian Creek Trail walks a portion of the Nez Perce National Historic Trail, reaching the Clarks Fork of the Yellowstone River in less than five miles.

The arid campground is divided in two parts by the creek, with five campsites on each side. Most of the campsites sit very near the creek but out of its view due to the thick brush. Short paths cut through the brush to the creek. Bits of shade come from cottonwoods, alder, and junipers, but most of the campsites are sunny and hot in midsummer. The highway completely

West of Dead Indian Creek Campground, the Sunlight Bridge, the highest bridge in Wyoming, spans the deep gorge of Sunlight Creek.

GPS Coordinates: N 44° 45.194' W 109° 25.132'

Contact: Shoshone National Forest, Clarks Fork Ranger District, 203A Yellowstone Ave., Cody, WY 82414-9313, 307/527-6921, www. fs.fed.us/r2/shoshone/.

16 THREE MILE

Scenic rating: 8

on the North Fork of the Shoshone River in Shoshone National Forest

On the North Fork of the Shoshone River in Shoshone National Forest, Eagle Creek Campground, elevation 6,700 feet, allows the quickest access into Yellowstone National Park from the Buffalo Bill Scenic Byway. Debating whether to camp here or push on into the park? Consider that the drive to Fishing Bridge Campground requires more than an hour. Three Mile snuggles into the narrow canyon between the Absaroka Mountains and Washakie Wilderness. From the campground, anglers wade-fish the river for rainbow, brown, and Yellowstone cutthroat trout. Rafters and kayakers put in here to float the Class I–III white water. As the river level drops throughout the summer in front of the campground, sand and rock bars form beaches. Sitting one mile west, Pahaska Tepee Resort features a lodge built by Buffalo Bill Cody in 1904. The resort offers trail rides and has a convenience store, gas, restaurant, bar, and gift shop. The 22-mile Pahaska Trail (#751) allows hikers and horse-packers a route into the Absaroka Mountains.

The campground, which used to have plenty of shade with trees, was thinned in 2009 to remove beetle-killed trees. Now much of it is wide open and sunny. Views from many of the campsites span the forested hills and the river; however, they also now include the highway and other campsites. Road noise is pervasive in the campground, but it does quiet down a

circles the campground; every campsite hears vehicles, but the road is not a heavy trucking route, and traffic dwindles at night. The campsites are spread out for privacy.

Campsites, facilities: The campground has 12 RV or tent campsites. RVs are limited to 32 feet. Facilities include picnic tables, fire rings with grills, pit toilets, garbage service, and campground hosts. Drinking water is not available; if you use creek water, filter or boil it first. Leashed pets are permitted.

Reservations, fees: Reservations are not accepted. Campsites cost $10. Cash or check. Open early May–October.

Directions: From the junction of Highway 212 and Highway 296, drive southeast for 25 miles, or from Highway 120 north of Cody, drive 21 miles west on Highway 296. The campground has two entrances, both on the north side of the road and set on each side of the creek.

bit at night. With fewer trees, the cow parsnip meadows around the campground should grow thicker.

Campsites, facilities: The campground has 21 RV campsites. RVs are limited to 32 feet. Due to the prevalence of bears, only hard-sided camping units are permitted (no tents, tent pop-ups, or tent trailers). Facilities include picnic tables, fire rings with grills, vault toilets, drinking water, lantern poles, bear boxes, garbage service, and campground hosts. Leashed pets are permitted. A wheelchair-accessible toilet is available.

Reservations, fees: Reservations are not accepted. Campsites cost $15. Cash or check. Open late May–early September.

Directions: On the Buffalo Bill Scenic Byway (Highway 14/16/20), drive three miles east of Yellowstone National Park or 47.5 miles west of Cody. Turn south off the highway into the campground.

GPS Coordinates: N 44° 29.783' W 109° 56.854'

Contact: Shoshone National Forest, Wapiti Ranger District, 203A Yellowstone Ave., Cody, WY 82414-9313, 307/527-6921, www.fs.fed.us/r2/shoshone/.

17 EAGLE CREEK

Scenic rating: 6

on the North Fork of the Shoshone River in Shoshone National Forest

At 6,500 feet in elevation on the North Fork of the Shoshone River in Shoshone National Forest, Eagle Creek Campground allows quick access into Yellowstone National Park, about six miles west. The 10-mile Eagle Creek Trail (#755) departs from the campground, crossing the North Fork on a hiker and horse bridge, heading into the Washakie Wilderness. From the campground, anglers wade-fish both the river and Eagle Creek for rainbow, brown, and Yellowstone cutthroat trout. Rafters and kayakers drive 10 minutes west to put in at Pahaska Tepee to float the Class I–III North Fork of the Shoshone. As the river level drops in front of the campground, sand and rock bars form beaches.

Eagle Creek sits in a loose lodgepole forest with meadows of hollyhock, cow parsnips, fireweed, harebells, and black-eyed susans. Wild roses are thick enough to scent the air. The two loops are crammed in between the river and the highway, which, unfortunately, adds vehicle noise that you can hear above the sound of the river. You can also see the highway from a few campsites in the left loop. All of the campsites in the left loop have river frontage, although some of the views include cabins across the river. About half of the right loop's campsites overlook the river. You'll have your choice of sunny or partly shaded campsites. Recent thinning projects have removed many of the beetle-killed trees, giving the campground a fresher, more open appearance than some of the surrounding canyon slopes.

Campsites, facilities: The campground has 20 RV campsites. RVs are limited to 22 feet. Due to the prevalence of bears, only hard-sided camping units are permitted (no tents, tent pop-ups, or tent trailers). Facilities include picnic tables, fire rings with grills, vault toilets, drinking water, bear boxes, lantern hangers, garbage service, and campground hosts. Leashed pets are permitted. A wheelchair-accessible toilet is available.

Reservations, fees: Reservations are not accepted. Campsites cost $15. Cash or check. Open late May–early September.

Directions: On the Buffalo Bill Scenic Byway (Highway 14/16/20), drive seven miles east of Yellowstone National Park or 43.8 miles west of Cody. Turn south off the highway into the campground.

GPS Coordinates: N 44° 23.310' W 109° 53.323'

Contact: Shoshone National Forest, Wapiti Ranger District, 203A Yellowstone Ave., Cody, WY 82414-9313, 307/527-6921, www.fs.fed.us/r2/shoshone/.

18 NEWTON CREEK

Scenic rating: 8

on the North Fork of the Shoshone River in Shoshone National Forest

Located at 6,300 feet in elevation along the North Fork of the Shoshone River in Shoshone National Forest, Newton Creek is the last campground en route toward Yellowstone National Park that allows tents, tent trailers, and bicycle-touring campers. All campgrounds upriver require hard-sided camping units. Newton Creek also defines the abrupt shift from the arid sagebrush and juniper forest to the thicker fir and pine forests of the Absaroka Mountains. The campground is popular for fishing, rafting, and kayaking on the Class I–III North Fork of the Shoshone River; however, fishing is closed below Newton Creek April–June due to spawning trout. (Upriver, there's no closure.) The surrounding canyon walls often have bighorn sheep grazing in early summer. The trailhead for the Blackwater National Recreation Trail is on a spur road one mile east; the trail climbs four miles to a memorial for 15 firefighters who died fighting a blaze in 1937. Hunters use this campground in fall.

The two gravel campground loops tuck under a forest of Douglas firs and tall junipers with a sagebrush, wild rose, grass, and pine needle duff floor. The spacious campsites include large flat spaces for tents, and those in the left loop, which is bisected by a small creek, are spread farther apart from each other. Over half of the campsites have river frontage, either sitting adjacent to it or overlooking it from a small bluff. Views include the dramatic pinnacles across the river. Unfortunately, while this campground is popular for its ambiance, it comes with highway noise, which dwindles after dark.

Campsites, facilities: The campground has 31 RV and tent campsites. RVs are limited to 22 feet. Facilities include picnic tables, fire rings with grills, vault toilets, drinking water, bear boxes, garbage service, and campground hosts.

Leashed pets are permitted. A wheelchair-accessible toilet is available.

Reservations, fees: Reservations are not accepted. Campsites cost $15. Cash or check. Open May–November.

Directions: On the Buffalo Bill Scenic Byway (Highway 14/16/20), drive 14.5 miles east of Yellowstone National Park or 36 miles west of Cody. Turn south off the highway into the campground.

GPS Coordinates: N 44° 22.152' W 109° 45.477'

Contact: Shoshone National Forest, Wapiti Ranger District, 203A Yellowstone Ave., Cody, WY 82414-9313, 307/527-6921, www.fs.fed.us/r2/shoshone/.

19 REX HALE

Scenic rating: 7

on the North Fork of the Shoshone River in Shoshone National Forest

At an elevation of 6,100 feet, along the North Fork of the Shoshone River in Shoshone National Forest, Rex Hale is one of the last two campgrounds en route toward Yellowstone National Park that allows tents, tent trailers, and bicycle touring campers. The campground is popular for fishing, rafting, and kayaking on the Class I–III North Fork of the Shoshone River; however, fishing is closed along the campground section April–June due to spawning trout. The surrounding canyon walls often have bighorn sheep grazing in early summer. The trailhead for the Blackwater National Recreation Trail is on a spur road 1.5 miles west; the trail climbs four miles to a memorial for 15 firefighters who died fighting a blaze in 1937. Hunters use this campground in fall.

The campground was renovated in 2006, with the gravel parking pads leveled, new picnic tables, bear boxes, and the addition of lantern hangers and electrical hookups. The wide, open sagebrush plateau blooming with yellow clover in July offers neither privacy nor shade, but it is popular due to the electrical hookups that are available. Only a few fir, pines, and junipers dot the campground, allowing every campsite to have big canyon views, which unfortunately includes the highway. Highway noise dies down somewhat at night as the route is not a major trucking thoroughfare. Campsites are spread out, rather than squashed together, and sites 16, 17, 18, 20, 22, 24, 26, 28, and 30 overlook the river. The flat sites offer big tent spaces.

Campsites, facilities: The campground has 30 RV and tent campsites. RVs are limited to 40 feet. Facilities include picnic tables, lantern hangers, fire rings with grills, vault toilets, drinking water, hookups for electricity, bear boxes, garbage service, a group campfire area for interpretive programs, and campground hosts. Leashed pets are permitted. A wheelchair-accessible toilet is available.

Reservations, fees: Reservations are accepted (877/444-6777, www.recreation.gov). Campsites cost $20 for electrical hookups and $15 without hookups. Cash or check. Open mid-June–mid-September.

Directions: On the Buffalo Bill Scenic Byway (Highway 14/16/20), drive 16 miles east of Yellowstone National Park or 34 miles west of Cody. Turn south off the highway into the campground.

GPS Coordinates: N 44° 27.241' W 109° 43.745'

Contact: Shoshone National Forest, Wapiti Ranger District, 203A Yellowstone Ave., Cody, WY 82414-9313, 307/527-6921, www.fs.fed. us/r2/shoshone/.

20 CLEARWATER

Scenic rating: 8

on the North Fork of the Shoshone River in Shoshone National Forest

BEST (

Along the North Fork of the Shoshone River in Shoshone National Forest, Clearwater

Campground, elevation 6,000 feet, is aptly named, for after spring runoff, the river runs with very clear water. The river, which wraps under a rusty-orange cliff wall opposite the campground, attracts anglers wade-fishing for rainbow, brown, and Yellowstone cutthroat trout, but due to the spawning trout, fishing here is closed April–June. As the river level drops during the summer, large sandy and pebble beaches form along the campground. From Pahaska Tepee to Buffalo Bill Reservoir, the North Fork of the Shoshone River runs with Class I–III white water. The river works for floating in a raft or kayak usually through July. The campground is popular with tenters; only one other campground between here and the east entrance to Yellowstone National Park permit tents. Cyclists touring the Buffalo Bill Scenic Byway will want to stay here.

The campground tucks next to the river on an open sagebrush plateau under a mix of limber pine, junipers, and cottonwoods. The sparse trees allow for big views of the dramatic canyon walls from many of the grassy campsites. Sites 1–8 overlook the river. The open campsites do not afford much privacy. The sound of the river is not enough to block out vehicle traffic on the highway.

Campsites, facilities: The campground has 18 RV or tent campsites. RVs are limited to 40 feet. Two additional campsites (sites 1 and 2) are walk-ins for tenters. Facilities include picnic tables, fire rings with grills, vault toilets, bear boxes, garbage service, and campground hosts. Drinking water is not available; boil or purify river water if you use it. Leashed pets are permitted. A wheelchair-accessible toilet is available.

Reservations, fees: Reservations are not accepted. Campsites cost $10. Cash or check. Open mid-June–early September.

Directions: On the Buffalo Bill Scenic Byway (Highway 14/16/20), drive 20 miles east of Yellowstone National Park or 31 miles west of Cody. Turn south off the highway into the campground.

GPS Coordinates: N 44° 27.690' W 109° 40.103'

Contact: Shoshone National Forest, Wapiti Ranger District, 203A Yellowstone Ave., Cody, WY 82414-9313, 307/527-6921, www.fs.fed.us/r2/shoshone/.

21 ELK FORK

Scenic rating: 6

on Elk Fork Creek in Shoshone National Forest

Located at 6,000 feet in elevation along Elk Fork Creek in Shoshone National Forest, Elk Fork Campground is popular with horse-packers and hunters. Across the Buffalo Bill Scenic Byway from Wapiti Campground, it also offers an alternative for tenters who may not want to be around so many RVs, plus it is one of the last few campgrounds that permit tents heading toward Yellowstone National Park. At the back of the campground, a popular horse-packing trail follows Elk Fork Creek upstream into the Washakie Wilderness of the Absaroka Range. Horse facilities at the trailhead include trailer parking, corrals, and a stock ramp. Elk Fork Creek is closed to fishing, but across the highway, anglers can wade-fish the North Fork of the Shoshone River for trout after July 1 (it is closed April–June for spawning trout). Rafters, kayakers, and skillful canoeists can float the river, which runs with Class I–III white water. Cyclists touring the Buffalo Bill Scenic Byway stay here.

Surrounded by an arid sagebrush canyon, the campground contrasts with a lush cottonwood bottomland on the east side of Elk Fork Creek. The partly shaded or sunny campsites are spread out for privacy; however, many are open enough to see the neighboring campsite. The brush that surrounds the grassy campsites comprises junipers, willows, and fireweed. The paved campground road connects with paved parking pads, most of which are back-ins. Due to the campground's proximity to the highway, you'll hear traffic, but it does die down somewhat at night.

Campsites, facilities: The campground has 13 RV or tent campsites. RVs are limited to 22 feet. Facilities include picnic tables, fire rings with grills, vault toilets, drinking water, bear boxes, garbage service, and campground hosts. Leashed pets are permitted. A wheelchair-accessible toilet is available.

Reservations, fees: Reservations are not accepted. Campsites cost $10. Cash or check. Open year-round.

Directions: On the Buffalo Bill Scenic Byway (Highway 14/16/20), drive 22 miles east of Yellowstone National Park or 29 miles west of Cody. At milepost 22.4 just east of the bridge over Elk Fork, turn south off the highway into the campground.

GPS Coordinates: N 44° 27.816' W 109° 37.722'

Contact: Shoshone National Forest, Wapiti Ranger District, 203A Yellowstone Ave., Cody, WY 82414-9313, 307/527-6921, www.fs.fed.us/r2/shoshone/.

22 WAPITI

Scenic rating: 8

on the North Fork of the Shoshone River in Shoshone National Forest

At an elevation of 6,000 feet along the North Fork of the Shoshone River in Shoshone National Forest, Wapiti Campground is named for the elk herds that inhabit the valley. Across the highway at Elk Fork Campground, a popular horse-packing trail follows Elk Fork Creek upstream into the Washakie Wilderness of the Absaroka Range. The river attracts anglers wade-fishing for its wild trout (rainbow and Yellowstone cutthroat), but due to the spawning trout, fishing here is closed

April–June. From Pahaska Tepee to Buffalo Bill Reservoir, the North Fork of the Shoshone River runs with Class I–III white water, navigated usually through July in a raft or kayak. Cyclists touring the Buffalo Bill Scenic Byway stay here.

Surrounded by red canyon walls with dramatic eroded spires, the popular, well-maintained, partly shaded campground's two loops sit under tall cottonwoods and junipers on each side of the forest road crossing the river. Campsites are spread out for privacy, plus tall brush makes some ultra-private. Ten sites (8, 10, 12, 14, 15, 17, 27, 28, 31, and 33) overlook the river; for the remainder of the campsites, paths access the river. As the river level drops throughout the summer, sandy beaches grow larger. Passing vehicles on the highway can be heard, but traffic dwindles at night as the route is not a major trucking thoroughfare.

Campsites, facilities: The campground has 42 RV or tent campsites. RVs are limited to 50 feet. Facilities include picnic tables, fire rings with grills, vault toilets, drinking water, hookups for electricity, bear boxes, garbage service, and campground hosts. Leashed pets are permitted. A wheelchair-accessible toilet is available.

Reservations, fees: Reservations are accepted (877/444-6777, www.recreation.gov). Campsites cost $20 with electrical hookups and $15 without hookups. Cash or check. Open late May–late September.

Directions: On the Buffalo Bill Scenic Byway (Highway 14/16/20), drive 22.5 miles east of Yellowstone National Park or 28.5 miles west of Cody. At milepost 22.5, turn north off the highway onto Sweetwater Creek Road (Forest Road 423) for 0.1 mile. Campground loops sit on both sides of the road.
GPS Coordinates: N 44° 27.925' W 109° 37.462'

Contact: Shoshone National Forest, Wapiti Ranger District, 203A Yellowstone Ave., Cody, WY 82414-9313, 307/527-6921, www.fs.fed.us/r2/shoshone/.

23 BIG GAME

🚵 🛶 🎣 ⛵ 🥾 🚐 ⛺

Scenic rating: 7

on the North Fork of the Shoshone River in Shoshone National Forest

At 5,900 feet in elevation along the North Fork of the Shoshone River in Shoshone National Forest, Big Game Campground is surrounded by sagebrush hills broken by eroded orange pinnacles. The Wapiti Wayside, 0.5 mile west of the campground, offers interpretive information on grizzly bears. The river attracts fly-fishers for its wild trout, but due to the spawning trout, fishing here is closed April–June. From Pahaska Tepee to Buffalo Bill Reservoir, the river runs with Class I–III white water, runnable usually through July in a raft or kayak. Canoeists can run part of the river. As river levels drop during the summer, a large pebble and sand bar forms between the campground and the water. Cyclists touring the Buffalo Bill Scenic Byway stay here.

Compared to the arid surrounding hillsides, the campground is lush—partly shaded by giant willow trees, junipers, and lodgepoles with privacy created by short brushy willows. Due to the vegetation, none of the sites overlook the river, but paths weave through the brush to the bank. Some open, grassy sites have views of the pinnacles. A few pull-through gravel parking pads are available for RVs, and flat spaces are available for tents. Because the sites are squeezed between the highway and the river, the sound of passing vehicles enters the campground, but it dwindles at night as the route is not a major trucking thoroughfare.

Campsites, facilities: The campground has 17 RV or tent campsites. RVs are limited to 32 feet. Facilities include picnic tables, fire rings with grills, pit toilets, bear boxes, garbage service, and campground hosts. Drinking water is not available; purify or boil water taken from the river. (You can also get potable water 0.5 mile west at Wapiti Campground.) Leashed pets are permitted.

Reservations, fees: Reservations are accepted (877/444-6777, www.recreation.gov). Campsites cost $10. Cash or check. Open mid-June–mid-September.

Directions: On the Buffalo Bill Scenic Byway (Highway 14/16/20), drive 23 miles east of Yellowstone National Park or 28 miles west of Cody. At milepost 23.1, turn north off the highway into the campground.

GPS Coordinates: N 44° 27.717' W 109° 36.443'

Contact: Shoshone National Forest, Wapiti Ranger District, 203A Yellowstone Ave., Cody, WY 82414-9313, 307/527-6921, www.fs.fed.us/r2/shoshone/.

24 NORTH FORK

Scenic rating: 7

on the North Fork of the Shoshone River in Buffalo Bill State Park

At 5,500 feet in elevation, North Fork Campground sits at the confluence of Trout Creek with the North Fork of the Shoshone River in Buffalo Bill State Park about 36 miles from Yellowstone National Park's east entrance station. Buffalo Bill Reservoir sits less than one mile to the east. An east-end boat launch nearby allows for fishing, boating, and waterskiing, plus the reservoir's consistent winds make it popular for windsurfing. The campground's Trout Creek Nature Trail, a 0.25-mile walk, tours riparian habitat on Trout Creek. About four miles west, the Four Bears Trail tours the eroded badlands country for 4.5 miles to a ridgeline viewpoint below Four Bears Mountain. The North Fork of the Shoshone River from Pahaska Tepee to the reservoir contains Class I–III water for rafting, canoeing, and kayaking, floated best in June. The river is closed to fishing April–June for spawning trout.

The North Fork campground with lush, mowed, green lawns is strikingly opposite from the arid North Shore Bay Campground, but as at its sister campground, every campsite has views of the surrounded eroded hills. A few short cottonwood trees sprinkle throughout the three interconnected paved loops with paved pull-through parking pads, but the trees aren't tall enough yet to yield shade. While the campground sits on the Shoshone River, none of the campsites overlook the water. You can hear the highway, but often the wind replaces the traffic noise.

Campsites, facilities: The campground has 56 RV or tent campsites that can accommodate large RVs. Six other tent-only campsites are also available. Facilities include picnic tables, fire rings with grills, vault toilets, drinking water, garbage service, a playground, a disposal station, and a campground host. Leashed pets are permitted. A wheelchair-accessible toilet and three accessible campsites (32, 41, and 42) are available.

Reservations, fees: Reservations are accepted (877/996-7275, www.usedirect.com/cdweb). Campsites cost $10 for Wyoming residents and $17 for nonresidents. Cash, check, or credit card. Open May–September.

Directions: From Cody, drive west for 13 miles on the Buffalo Bill Scenic Byway (Highway 14/16/20) towards Yellowstone National Park. At milepost 36.7, turn south off the highway and drive 0.1 mile. Turn right into the campground entrance.

GPS Coordinates: N 44° 29.174' W 109° 19.935'

Contact: Buffalo Bill State Park, 47 Lakeside Rd., Cody, WY 82414, 307/587-9227, http://wyoparks.state.wy.us/.

25 NORTH SHORE BAY

Scenic rating: 8

on Buffalo Bill Reservoir in Buffalo Bill State Park

North Shore Bay Campground, elevation 5,500 feet, sits on the north shore of Buffalo

Bill Reservoir in Buffalo Bill State Park about 42 miles from Yellowstone National Park's east entrance station. Surrounded by eroded sandstone formations, the reservoir draw locals for its fishing, boating, windsurfing, swimming, and waterskiing. The campground's boat launch includes a cement ramp, dock, and fish-cleaning station. Fish species in the reservoir include rainbow, brown, lake, and Yellowstone cutthroat trout. The wheelchair-accessible Eagle Point Trail, which will eventually traverse the north shore, is in the Eagle Point Day Use Area four miles east. Buffalo Bill Dam maintains a museum open to the public, and the walk across the dam lets you view the Shoshone Canyon gorge from above.

The campground, with a paved road and paved parking pads at most of its campsites, squeezes its three loops in between the reservoir and the highway. Even though the highway is a major traffic route into Yellowstone, it does not serve as a major trucking highway; much of the noise diminishes after dark. The arid campground sits on a natural sparse grass and sagebrush plateau exposed to the wind and sun with only a handful of small cottonwoods. Half of the campsites overlook the lake, which makes it popular, and all of the campsites have views encompassing the rock spires to the north. The tent-only sites sit on a terraced hillside with windscreens.

Campsites, facilities: The campground has 32 RV or tent campsites that can accommodate large RVs. Five additional walk-in sites are for tents only. Facilities include picnic tables, fire rings with grills, vault toilets, drinking water, garbage service, a boat launch, a disposal station, and park personnel on-site in the entrance station. Leashed pets are permitted. A wheelchair-accessible toilet and campsite (site 31) are available.

Reservations, fees: Reservations are accepted (877/996-7275, www.usedirect.com/cdweb). Campsites cost $10 for Wyoming residents and

$17 for nonresidents. Cash, check, or credit card. Open May–September.

Directions: From Cody, drive west for nine miles on the Buffalo Bill Scenic Byway (Highway 14/16/20) towards Yellowstone National Park. Locate the entrance to the campground at milepost 42 on the south side of the highway. GPS Coordinates: N 44° 30.092' W 109° 14.100'

Contact: Buffalo Bill State Park, 47 Lakeside Rd., Cody, WY 82414, 307/587-9227, http://wyoparks.state.wy.us/.

26 CODY KOA

Scenic rating: 5

east of Cody

At an elevation of 5,097 feet just east of Cody, the KOA is convenient for visiting sights in town. Buffalo Bill Historical Center wraps five museums about the West (including the life of Buffalo Bill Cody) under one roof. The Cody Rodeo, the longest-running rodeo in the United States, runs every night June–August with bull riding, calf roping, and barrel racing. (The KOA provides a shuttle to the rodeo.) Cody also is home to local outfitters for white-water river rafting, fishing, and horseback riding. The Shoshone River, west of Cody, froths with Class II–III white water through Red Rock Canyon for rafters and kayakers, with water runnable through September. The KOA's three outdoor pools include a swimming pool, a kiddie play pool, and a hot tub. Nearby Beck Lake offers fishing for kids.

The open, sunny campground affords an easy place for satellite reception. Only a few small cottonwood trees cluster in the mowed lawn campground for a bit of shade. Located outside of town, the campground is removed from the hubbub of town but has highway noise, which does include some commercial trucking. The KOA offers social events: an all-you-can-eat pancake breakfast for $2, ice cream socials, kids crafts, bingo, and s'mores.

Campsites, facilities: The campground has 161 RV campsites. The maximum length for RV pull-through is 80 feet. Twelve tent campsites are also available. Hookups include water, sewer, and electricity up to 50. Facilities include picnic tables, fire rings with grills, flush toilets, showers, coin-operated launderette, drinking water, a playground and jumping pillow, horseshoe pits, a swimming pool, a hot tub, a game room, a dog walk, wireless Internet, modem dataports, cable TV, a camp store, firewood for sale, propane for sale, and a dump station. Leashed pets are permitted.

Reservations, fees: Reservations are accepted (800/562-8507, www.koa.com). Hookups cost $40–54. Tent sites cost $29. Rates cover two people. Extra campers cost $7 for adults and $5 for kids 6–17 years old. Kids under six stay free. Taxes and a $3 resort fee will be added on. Open May–September.

Directions: From Cody, drive three miles east on Highway 14/16/20, passing the airport. Turn left into the campground.

GPS Coordinates: N 44° 30.775' W 109° 0.487'

Contact: Cody KOA, 5561 Greybull Hwy., Cody, WY 82414, 307/587-2369, www.codykoa.com.

27 REUNION FLATS

Scenic rating: 9

on the west flank of the Teton Mountains in Caribou-Targhee National Forest

Located at 6,900 feet in Caribou-Targhee National Forest, Reunion Flats Group Camping area sits on the west flank of the Teton Mountains. It is the closest campground to Grand Targhee Resort, which offers summer scenic lift rides, horseback riding, and lift-accessed mountain biking and hiking.

You'll stare at Grand Teton from Targhee's slopes. The resort's annual bluegrass festival takes place in late August. Trailheads into the Jedediah Smith Wilderness and Grand Teton National Park depart 1.8 miles to the east near Teton Canyon Campground. Due to spawning of Yellowstone cutthroat trout, fishing is not permitted in Teton Creek until July 1.

After reconstruction of this group campground in 2000, five individual camping sites were added to the three group sites. Unfortunately, the individual sites sit in between the group camping sites. While a pine, fir, and aspen forest surrounds the campground, many of the grassy sites are open, allowing big views of Teton Canyon and the tips of the Teton Range in the distance. Paths connect to Teton Creek, which runs past the campground. The spacious sites have flat, roomy spots for tents. If large groups are not present, the campground is very quiet.

Campsites, facilities: The campground has nine RV or tent campsites. RVs are limited to 60 feet. Facilities include picnic tables, fire rings with grills, pedestal grills, vault toilets, drinking water, garbage service, and a campground host. Leashed pets are permitted. A wheelchair-accessible toilet is available.

Reservations, fees: Reservations are accepted (877/444-6777, www.recreation.gov). Campsites cost $10. Extra vehicles cost $5. Cash or check. Open early June–September.

Directions: From Highway 33 in Driggs, Idaho, turn east at Little Street/Ski Hill Road for one mile to a Y intersection. Bear left onto Ski Hill Road and go 5.6 miles, passing Alta and the state line into Wyoming, to the campground sign. Turn right onto the gravel Forest Road 009 and drive 2.7 miles, turning right into the campground.

GPS Coordinates: N 43° 45.449' W 110° 57.032'

Contact: Caribou-Targhee National Forest, Teton Basin Ranger District, 515 S. Main, P.O. Box 777, Driggs, ID 83422, 208/354-2312, www.fs.fed.us/r4/caribou-targhee.

28 TETON CANYON

Scenic rating: 9

on the Teton Mountain's west slope in
Caribou-Targhee National Forest

At an elevation of 7,200 feet in Caribou-Targhee
National Forest, Teton Canyon Campground
sits on the edge of the Jedediah Smith Wilderness
on the west flank of the Teton Mountains.
En route to the campground, the scenic drive,
which enters Wyoming, lends views of Grand
Teton National Park's rugged panorama of
peaks. From the campground, a popular trailhead
departs into the wilderness via the South
and North Forks of Teton Creek. Reach Alaska
Basin Lakes in seven miles, Grand Teton National
Park in nine miles, or 11,106-foot Table
Mountain in six miles for views of the Grand
Teton. Stock facilities sit 0.1 mile west of the
campground. Surrounding granitic rock outcroppings
and cliffs have rock-climbing routes.
Teton Creek is closed to fishing until July 1.

The campground's two interconnected
loops provide different environments. The
southern loop weaves through a thick conifer
forest that shades the campsites dark, keeping
them cool and protected from the elements.
Teton Creek flows nearest sites 6–8,
and most of the sites are gravel back-ins. The
open understory permits some views of nearby
campers. Campsites in the north loop ring
an open wildflower field dotted with only a
handful of aspens. While the open sites, most
of which are pull-throughs, do not afford
privacy, they command views of the canyon's
cliffs and sweeping mountain slopes. The
trailhead draws in day hikers, but at night,
the campground is ultra quiet.

Campsites, facilities: The campground has 20
RV or tent campsites. RVs are limited to 24 feet.
Facilities include picnic tables, fire rings with
grills, vault toilets, drinking water, garbage service,
and a campground host. Bring your own
firewood. Leashed pets are permitted.

Reservations, fees: Reservations are accepted
(877/444-6777, www.recreation.gov). Campsites
cost $10. Extra vehicles cost $5. Cash or
check. Open early June–September.

Directions: From Highway 33 in Driggs,
Idaho, turn east at Little Street/Ski Hill Road
for one mile to a Y intersection. Bear left onto
Ski Hill Road and go 5.6 miles, passing Alta
and the state line into Wyoming, to the campground
sign. Turn right onto the gravel Forest
Road 009 and drive 4.3 miles, turning right
into the campground.
GPS Coordinates: N 43° 45.411' W 110°
55.258'

Contact: Caribou-Targhee National Forest,
Teton Basin Ranger District, 515 S. Main,
P.O. Box 777, Driggs, ID 83422, 208/354-2312,
www.fs.fed.us/r4/caribou-targhee.

29 BROOKS LAKE

Scenic rating: 10

on Brooks Lake and the Continental Divide in
Shoshone National Forest

BEST (

Located at 9,185 feet in elevation in Shoshone
National Forest, Brooks Lake sits on the
Continental Divide, squeezed between large
orange buttresses of rock. The campground
looks across the lake to the Pinnacles, spires
that capture the alpenglow of the setting
sun. The Continental Divide Trail departs
from the lake, and trails loop around the Pinnacles.
Trails also lead to Upper Jade Lake,
Upper Brooks Lake, and Rainbow Lake. At
the campground, a primitive boat ramp aids
those launching small boats (motors are okay)
for paddling the shoreline of the 234-acre
lake or fishing for rainbow and brook trout.
The lake has exceptionally clear water in early
summer, but as it overturns at the end of
August, it takes on a green cast from algae.
Historic Brooks Lake Lodge sits behind the
campground, with its horses grazing near
the lake.

Recent thinning due to fungus in the pine

© BECKY LOMAX

Brooks Lake, known for its trout fishing, sits on the Continental Divide, northeast of Togwotee Pass.

trees at the ultra-quiet campground changed some of the campsites from deep shade to partial shade. Two short gravel spurs and one gravel loop make up the campground, with the loop offering sites 10–13 overlooking the lake and pinnacles. Most of the loop sites are open, close together, and substitute privacy for stunning location; the spur campsites are more private.

Campsites, facilities: The campground has 13 RV or tent campsites. RVs are limited to 32 feet. Facilities include picnic tables, fire rings with grills, vault toilets, bear boxes, garbage service, and campground hosts. Drinking water is not available; purify or boil water taken from the lake. (You can also get potable water one mile east at Pinnacles Campground.) Leashed pets are permitted. A wheelchair-accessible toilet is available.

Reservations, fees: Reservations are not accepted. Campsites cost $10. Cash or check. Open July–early September.

Directions: On Highway 26/287, drive 22 miles west from Dubois or 33 miles east from Moran Junction. At milepost 33, turn north

onto Brooks Lake Road (Forest Road 515). Drive four miles and veer left at the fork. At the signed junction, turn left for 0.6 mile, and turn sharp right at Brooks Lake Lodge, dropping 0.2 mile to the lake.

GPS Coordinates: N 43° 44.980' W 110° 0.307'

Contact: Shoshone National Forest, Wind River Ranger District, 1403 W. Ramshorn, Dubois, WY 82513, 307/455-2466, www. fs.fed.us/r2/shoshone/.

30 PINNACLES

Scenic rating: 10

on Brooks Lake and the Continental Divide in Shoshone National Forest

BEST (

Located at 9,142 feet in elevation in Shoshone National Forest, this campground nestles below an orange butte of fantastical pinnacles—hence its name. The Pinnacles are a photographer's delight, best shot in

Wyoming's red Pinnacles rise above Brooks Lake to catch the setting sun.

late afternoon and evening light. The campground also sits on Brooks Lake and borders its outlet creek. The Continental Divide Trail departs from the lake, and trails loop around the Pinnacles. Trailheads within two miles also lead to Bonneville Pass and the Pinnacles. You can launch boats, canoes, and kayaks from Brooks Lake Campground one mile to the west. Both the lake and the creek harbor rainbow and brook trout along with splake, a cross between the two. The lake has exceptionally clear water in early summer, but as it overturns at the end of August, it takes on a green cast from algae. Be ready at this high elevation for afternoon thunderstorms.

In contrast to nearby Brooks Lake Campground, Pinnacles offers more private, shadier campsites spread out across a bigger area. The hilly campground has one loop with some campsites tucked directly under the Pinnacles (site 10 grabs a good view of them) and six campsites overlooking Brooks Lake (but these can be windy). The ultra-quiet campground in the mixed subalpine fir and pine forest has both gravel pull-through and back-in parking

pads. Sites 1 and 2, unfortunately, are positioned for snippets of Pinnacle views, but with traffic at the entrance.

Campsites, facilities: The campground has 21 RV or tent campsites. RVs are limited to 32 feet. Facilities include picnic tables, fire rings with grills, vault toilets, bear boxes, drinking water, garbage service, and campground hosts. Leashed pets are permitted. A wheelchair-accessible toilet is available.

Reservations, fees: Reservations are not accepted. Campsites cost $15. Cash or check. Open July–early September.

Directions: On Highway 26/287, drive 22 miles west from Dubois or 33 miles east from Moran Junction. At milepost 33, turn north onto Brooks Lake Road (Forest Road 515). Drive four miles and veer left at the fork. At the signed junction, turn left for 0.6 mile, crossing the bridge into the campground. GPS Coordinates: N 43° 45.065' W 109° 59.447'

Contact: Shoshone National Forest, Wind River Ranger District, 1403 W. Ramshorn, Dubois, WY 82513, 307/455-2466, www. fs.fed.us/r2/shoshone/.

31 FALLS

Scenic rating: 8

east of Togwotee Pass on Wyoming's Centennial Scenic Byway in Shoshone National Forest

In Shoshone National Forest, Falls Campground, elevation 8,000 feet, sits just east of Togwotee Pass on Wyoming's Centennial Scenic Byway. The campground is one convenient for cyclists touring the highway and those needing a campground before hitting Grand Teton National Park, 40 minutes west. An interpretive wheelchair-accessible trail leads to an overlook of the falls that gives the campground its name. Hiking trails, boating, canoeing, and fishing are available five miles to the north at Brooks Lake.

Due to the campground's location on the busy highway, the area hums with vehicle noise. However, the road is not a major trucking thoroughfare, so traffic does quiet somewhat after dark. The partly shaded campsites tuck under a loose mixed forest of pines and subalpine firs in two loops. Neighboring campsites are visible, but not stacked close like a parking lot. Gravel back-in and pull-through parking spurs access the campsites, some of which grab snippets of views of the Pinnacles to the north. Double sites are also available for double the price. The campground was renovated in 2009, to enlarge parking spurs, add more electrical hookups, and replace toilets.

Campsites, facilities: The campground has 54 campsites. Loop A is geared toward RVs with 20 campsites with electrical hookups, and loop B is geared more toward tent campers with 34 sites, including five walk-ins. RVs are limited to 32 feet. Facilities include picnic tables, fire rings with grills, vault toilets, bear boxes, drinking water, garbage service, and campground hosts. Leashed pets are permitted. Wheelchair-accessible toilets and campsites are available.

Reservations, fees: Reservations are not accepted. Campsites cost $15, or $20 with electricity. Cash or check. Open mid-June–September.

Directions: On Highway 26/287, drive 22.5 miles west from Dubois or 32.5 miles east from Moran Junction. At milepost 32.5, turn southeast off the highway onto the campground road.

GPS Coordinates: N 43° 45.065' W 109° 59.447'

Contact: Shoshone National Forest, Wind River Ranger District, 1403 W. Ramshorn, Dubois, WY 82513, 307/455-2466, www.fs.fed.us/r2/shoshone/.

32 PINE CREEK

Scenic rating: 8

in the Big Hole Mountains west of Victor in Caribou-Targhee National Forest in Idaho

At 6,600 feet in Caribou-Targhee National Forest, Pine Creek sits nearly at the summit of Pine Creek Pass over the Big Hole Mountains. A trail along the crest of the Big Hole Mountains departs northward just west of the pass. Hikers use the trail for its expansive views across the Teton Valley to the Grand Teton and Teton Mountains. Mountain bikers ride the 17 miles across the crest trail to the Horseshoe Canyon Trailhead west of Driggs.

The curvy gravel campground road and back-in gravel parking pads may pose difficulties for those with large trailers, but spacious, spread out campsites make it appealing. A mixed forest of firs, lodgepoles, and aspens provides a thick overhead canopy for shade. Pink wild roses and a brushy understory shield the campground from the highway, but Pine Creek Summit is not a major thoroughfare for trucking, so night traffic is minimal. Sites 1 and 2 sit closest to the road. Two of the campsites have small bridges crossing the creek to their tables and tent spaces.

Campsites, facilities: The campground has

10 RV or tent campsites. RVs are limited to 30 feet. Facilities include picnic tables, fire rings, and vault toilets. No water is available; bring your own. When the creek through the campground is running, you can use its water, but purify or boil it first. Pack out your trash. Leashed pets are permitted.

Reservations, fees: Reservations are not accepted. Campsites cost $8. Extra vehicles cost $4. Cash or check. Open mid-June–mid-September.

Directions: From Victor, drive Highway 31 southwest for six miles. Turn left into the campground. Coming from Swan Valley, locate the campground entrance about 0.7 mile on the east side of Pine Creek Pass.

GPS Coordinates: N 43° 34.387' W 111° 12.320'

Contact: Caribou-Targhee National Forest, Teton Basin Ranger District, 515 S. Main, P.O. Box 777, Driggs, ID 83422, 208/354-2312, www.fs.fed.us/r4/caribou-targhee.

33 MIKE HARRIS

Scenic rating: 8

in the Snake River Range in Caribou-Targhee National Forest in Idaho

In Caribou-Targhee National Forest at 6,200 feet, Mike Harris Campground sits in the Snake River Range south of Victor. At the bottom of the long, 10 percent grade climb over Teton Pass, the campground is popular with hikers and mountain bikers. With the trailhead departing from the 90-degree bend in the campground entrance road, the Mikesell Canyon Trail (#049) climbs four miles to the top of 8,987-foot Oliver Peak for views of the southern Teton Mountains and Snake River Range. Another four-mile stretch crosses the state line into Wyoming to connect with Mosquito Pass on the Teton Crest. Stream fishing is available in Trail Creek adjacent to the highway.

The one gravel campground loop tucks

under a green canopy of firs, lodgepole pines, and aspens, with two gravel pull-throughs and the remainder back-in parking pads. Meadows of grass, paintbrush, and fireweed weave through the trees, which partly shade the campsites. The roomy campsites are spread out for privacy, but spaces for tents are small. With its proximity to the highway, morning and evening noise is abundant with the commuter traffic from the Teton Valley to Jackson Hole.

Campsites, facilities: The campground has 12 RV or tent campsites. RVs are limited to 30 feet. Facilities include picnic tables, fire rings with grills, pedestal grills, vault toilets, drinking water, bear boxes, garbage service, and a campground host. Leashed pets are permitted. A wheelchair-accessible toilet is available.

Reservations, fees: Reservations are accepted (877/444-6777, www.recreation.gov). Campsites cost $10. Extra vehicles cost $5. Cash or check. Open mid-May–mid-September.

Directions: From Victor, drive southeast on Highway 33 for 3.8 miles. At milepost 153.5, turn west for 300 feet, and turn south for 0.3 mile, arcing right into the campground. Coming from Teton Pass, locate the turnoff 1.5 miles northwest of the Idaho-Wyoming state line.

GPS Coordinates: N 43° 33.363' W 111° 4.144'

Contact: Caribou-Targhee National Forest, Teton Basin Ranger District, 515 S. Main, P.O. Box 777, Driggs, ID 83422, 208/354-2312, www.fs.fed.us/r4/caribou-targhee.

34 TRAIL CREEK

Scenic rating: 8

in the Snake River Range in Caribou-Targhee National Forest

Located at 6,600 feet in Caribou-Targhee National Forest, Trail Creek Campground sits in the Snake River Range on the highway over Teton Pass. It is convenient for those traveling over the pass to reach Grand Teton and Yellowstone National Parks, but those who drive the steep road with trailers will feel its 10 percent grade. The campground is less than 0.2 mile east of the Idaho-Wyoming state line. The trailhead at Coal Creek Meadows leads through the Jedediah Smith Wilderness to the Teton Crest Trail, with views north to the Grand Teton. A three-mile steady climb reaches the meadows. Cyclists traveling over Teton Pass use this campground for its convenience to the highway, and mountain bikers use the national forest trails in the Snake River Range.

The campground road parallels the highway, squeezed by traffic on the north and Trail Creek on the south. Most of the campsites are open to the highway, which buzzes with commuters traveling between Teton Valley and Jackson Hole in the morning and evening. At night, after the traffic dies down, you can hear the creek. The sunny campsites have little privacy; however, a few snuggled against the aspen and fir forest carve out little nooks for a semblance of privacy. Surrounded by pink fireweed in midsummer, the grassy campsites are spread out, with big, flat tent spaces available. Six of the campsites have gravel pull-through parking pads.

Campsites, facilities: The campground has 11 RV or tent campsites. RVs are limited to 20 feet. Facilities include picnic tables, fire rings with grills, vault toilets, drinking water, bear boxes, garbage service, and campground hosts. Leashed pets are permitted. A wheelchair-accessible toilet is available.

Reservations, fees: Reservations are accepted (877/444-6777, www.recreation.gov). Campsites cost $10. Extra vehicles cost $5. Cash or check. Open mid-May–mid-September.

Directions: From Victor, drive southeast on Highway 33 for 5.6 miles. At milepost 155, turn south into the campground. Coming from Teton Pass, locate the turnoff 3.5 miles past the Coal Creek Meadows pullout. GPS Coordinates: N 43° 32.322' W 111° 2.185'

Contact: Caribou-Targhee National Forest, Teton Basin Ranger District, 515 S. Main, P.O. Box 777, Driggs, ID 83422, 208/354-2312, www.fs.fed.us/r4/caribou-targhee.

35 PALISADES CREEK
🥾 🏊 🛶 🦌 🚐 ⛺

Scenic rating: 7

on Palisades Creek in the Snake River Range in Caribou-Targhee National Forest in Idaho

At an elevation of 5,700 feet in Caribou-Targhee National Forest, Palisades Creek Campground snuggles into the Palisades Creek Canyon at the base of 10,000-foot-high peaks of the Snake River Range. It houses the most popular trail in the range, busy on hot summer days when hikers head to the cool subalpine lakes for fishing and swimming. A gentle trail leads four miles to Lower Palisades Lake, surrounded by willow brush, and continues through Waterfall Canyon to the larger Upper Palisades Lake with its scenic shoreline (7.5 miles total). The trailhead departs from the east side of the campground. A stock ramp is available at the separate trailhead for horses. You can often see mountain goats on the canyon cliffs high above the trail and moose at the lakes. Anglers enjoy the lakes and Palisades Creek for its native cutthroat trout.

The tiny campground tucks its loop into a shady forest of mixed conifers at the bottom of the Palisades Creek Canyon. The creek runs adjacent to the campground. Underbrush and small trees contribute to the privacy of the campsites. Once day hikers depart, the campground is very quiet, prized by those who seek solitude.

Campsites, facilities: The campground has eight RV or tent campsites. RVs are limited to 22 feet. Facilities include picnic tables, fire rings with grills, vault toilets, drinking water, and garbage service. Leashed pets are permitted.

Reservations, fees: Reservations are not accepted. Campsites cost $10. Extra vehicles cost $5. Double campsites are available for $20. Cash or check. Open from late May until closed by snow. Fees are reduced after late October when water is turned off.

Directions: On Highway 26, drive 7.1 miles south of Swan Valley. Turn north onto Palisades Creek Road (Forest Road 255) for two dirt miles to the campground entrance, passing the hiker parking for the trailhead just before the entrance. Coming from the south on the highway, locate the turnoff 3.7 miles north of Palisades Dam.

GPS Coordinates: N 43° 23.803' W 111° 12.892'

Contact: Caribou-Targhee National Forest, Palisades Ranger District, 3659 E. Ririe Hwy., Idaho Falls, ID 83401, 208/523-1412, www.fs.fed.us/r4/caribou-targhee.

36 RIVERSIDE PARK

Scenic rating: 7

on the Snake River north of Palisades Dam in Caribou-Targhee National Forest in Idaho

In Caribou-Targhee National Forest, Riverside Park, elevation 5,300 feet, sits on the Snake River below Palisades Dam. Fishing is available right from the campground. The river in this stretch, referred to as the South Fork, is renowned for its fly-fishing, which runs from early July in to autumn. Drift boats full of anglers fishing for brown trout float from the dam downstream to Swan Valley. The Class II river also works for scenic float trips for rafts, kayaks, and canoes. American pelicans often nest in the area, and wildlife-watching includes sandhill cranes, golden eagles, and moose. The river corridor is home to the largest riparian cottonwood forest in the West, which provides habitat for 126 bird species, including 21 raptors. The area is designated as a National Important Bird Area.

The campground squeezes in between the river and the highway, with noise being pervasive in the campground. Built on a flat river bar, the location offers roomy campsites with big, flat, raised gravel tent platforms. The electrical hookup sites are very open, sunny, back from the river, and lined up in parking-lot fashion. The other campsites sit on a loop in the cottonwoods down by the river. Sites 5–9, 17, and 18 overlook the river. Most of these campsites are partly shaded.

Campsites, facilities: The campground has 23 RV or tent campsites that can accommodate large RVs. Nine additional RV campsites have electrical hookups. Some double campsites are available for $20. Facilities include picnic tables, fire rings with grills, vault toilets, drinking water, garbage service, firewood for sale, tent platforms, and a campground host. Leashed pets are permitted. A wheelchair-accessible toilet is available.

Reservations, fees: Reservations are not accepted. Campsites cost $10; electrical hookup sites cost $13. Extra vehicles cost $5. Cash or check. Open from late May until closed by snow.

Directions: On Highway 26, drive eight miles south of Swan Valley. At milepost 387, turn west into the campground. Coming from the south on the highway, locate the turnoff one mile north of Palisades Dam.

GPS Coordinates: N 43° 20.413' W 111° 12.343'

Contact: Caribou-Targhee National Forest, Palisades Ranger District, 3659 E. Ririe Hwy., Idaho Falls, ID 83401, 208/523-1412, www.fs.fed.us/r4/caribou-targhee.

37 CALAMITY

Scenic rating: 7

on Palisades Reservoir in Caribou-Targhee National Forest in Idaho

Located at 5,800 feet in Caribou-Targhee National Forest, Calamity Campground is the largest of the campgrounds on Palisades

Reservoir. It sits on the northwest corner south of Palisades Dam. A landslide in spring 2009 temporarily closed access to the campground; the active landslide area, which covers 13 acres, is being monitored, and warnings on the dam will note concerns for motorists and campers. The reservoir is popular for fishing, swimming, boating, waterskiing, and sailing. The boat launch includes concrete ramps, a dock, and trailer parking. Due to the campground's location across the reservoir from the highway, it is quieter than other Palisades campgrounds. Bear Creek Trailhead, about six miles south of the campground on a rough road, leads into the Caribou Range.

Built on a steep hillside with constructed steps and gravel terraces for campsites, the campground comprises three loops with spacious campsites that have big, flat spaces for tents. A loose forest of aspen, fir, and lodgepole adds partial shade to some sites; others are sunny with big views of the reservoir. Most lack privacy. You can hear faint trucking noise from the highway across the reservoir. For tents only, loop C, on a steeper hillside with more privacy, has the best views. Look for huckleberries in season.

Campsites, facilities: The campground has 30 RV or tent campsites. RVs are limited to 32 feet. Eleven additional campsites for tents only are available. Facilities include picnic tables, fire rings with grills, vault toilets, drinking water, garbage service, firewood for sale, a boat launch, and a campground host. Leashed pets are permitted. A wheelchair-accessible toilet is available.

Reservations, fees: Reservations are not accepted. Campsites cost $12. Extra vehicles cost $6. Cash or check. Open from late May until closed by snow. Fees are reduced after late September when water is turned off.

Directions: From Alpine Junction, where Highway 26 and Highway 89 join on the Snake River, drive 18.5 miles northwest on Highway 26. At milepost 388, turn west over the dam on Bear Creek Road (Forest Road 058) and drive one mile of rough dirt road, veering left into the campground. Coming from the north on the highway, locate the turnoff at Palisades Dam.

GPS Coordinates: N 43° 19.621' W 111° 12.915'

Contact: Caribou-Targhee National Forest, Palisades Ranger District, 3659 E. Ririe Hwy., Idaho Falls, ID 83401, 208/523-1412, www.fs.fed.us/r4/caribou-targhee.

38 BIG ELK CREEK

Scenic rating: 7

north of Palisades Reservoir in Caribou-Targhee National Forest in Idaho

At 5,800 feet in Caribou-Targhee National Forest, Big Elk Creek Campground sits northeast of Palisades Reservoir in a forested side canyon below the 10,000-foot-high peaks of the Snake River Range. While it is not on the reservoir, it is close enough to launch boats from two nearby primitive ramps or the concrete ramps at Blowout or Calamity Campground. The reservoir is popular for fishing, swimming, boating, waterskiing, and sailing. Due to the campground's location in a side canyon, it is quieter than the Palisades campgrounds right on the highway. Big Elk Creek Road terminates 0.4 mile farther, where a gentle trail heads up the open Big Elk Creek canyon with views of the drainage and the Snake River Range. A stock ramp is available. The trail reaches Dry Canyon in 2.5 miles, Hells Hole Canyon in 3.4 miles, and Idaho-Wyoming border in 4.5 miles.

The grassy campground loops on an open, sunny, south-facing gentle slope. A few conifers sprinkle through the campground but provide minimal shade. Surrounded by a large sagebrush field, the wide-open sites garner big views of the Big Elk Creek drainage, but at the cost of privacy, and some sites are quite close together. A gravel road loops through the campground to access gravel and grass parking pads. Overflow primitive camping is available at Little Elk Creek boat ramp.

Campsites, facilities: The campground has

18 RV or tent campsites. RVs are limited to 22 feet. Facilities include picnic tables, fire rings with grills, vault toilets, drinking water, and garbage service. Leashed pets are permitted. A wheelchair-accessible toilet is available.

Reservations, fees: Reservations are not accepted. Campsites cost $10. Extra vehicles cost $5. Cash or check. Open from late May until closed by snow. Fees are reduced after late September when water is turned off.

Directions: From Alpine Junction, where Highway 26 and Highway 89 join on the Snake River, drive 15.1 miles northwest on Highway 26. At milepost 390.8, turn north onto Big Elk Creek Road (Forest Road 262) and drive 1.6 miles. The campground entrance is on the left. Coming from the north on the highway, locate the turnoff about 3.4 miles southeast of Palisades Dam.

GPS Coordinates: N 43° 19.331' W 111° 7.051'

Contact: Caribou-Targhee National Forest, Palisades Ranger District, 3659 E. Ririe Hwy., Idaho Falls, ID 83401, 208/523-1412, www.fs.fed.us/r4/caribou-targhee.

39 BLOWOUT

Scenic rating: 7

on Palisades Reservoir in Caribou-Targhee National Forest in Idaho

At an elevation of 5,800 feet in Caribou-Targhee National Forest, Blowout Campground is situated on the northeast side of the 16,000-acre Palisades Reservoir, surrounded by steep forested mountains. Due to its location, it is one of the most popular campgrounds on the lake. Anglers will need to ensure they have an Idaho license for fishing. Fed by the Snake River, the reservoir, which is known for wind and summer thunderstorms, is popular for fishing, swimming, boating, waterskiing, and sailing. The campground's large boat launch includes a double-wide concrete ramp, dock, and trailer parking. The reservoir harbors cutthroat, brown, and lake trout, along with kokanee salmon. Thanks to its location on the highway, cross-country cyclists find this campground convenient. In fall, the hillsides around the lake light up with color—especially when the aspens turn gold.

The aspen and lodgepole forest provides partial shade for the tight campsites with gravel back-in parking pads; you'll have your pick between varying amounts of privacy and sites overlooking the reservoir. Only small spaces for tents are available. Unfortunately, sites 2 and 15 plop next to the highway and chain-link fence. Due to commercial trucking on the highway, this campground picks up road noise during the night. Overflow parking for large RVs is available at the boat launch.

Campsites, facilities: The campground has 16 RV or tent campsites. RVs are limited to 32 feet. A few are double campsites at double the price. The gravel back-in parking pads can accommodate large RVs. Facilities include picnic tables, fire rings with grills, vault toilets, drinking water, garbage service, a boat launch, and campground hosts. Leashed pets are permitted. A wheelchair-accessible toilet is available.

Reservations, fees: Reservations are not accepted. Campsites cost $10. Extra vehicles cost $5. Cash or check. Open from late May until closed by snow. Fees are reduced after late September when water is turned off.

Directions: From Alpine Junction, where Highway 26 and Highway 89 join on the Snake River, drive 12 miles northwest on Highway 26. At milepost 394, turn south into the campground. Coming from the north on the highway, locate the campground entrance about 6.5 miles southeast of Palisades Dam.

GPS Coordinates: N 43° 17.130' W 111° 7.351'

Contact: Caribou-Targhee National Forest, Palisades Ranger District, 3659 E. Ririe Hwy., Idaho Falls, ID 83401, 208/523-1412, www.fs.fed.us/r4/caribou-targhee.

40 ALPINE

🚴 🏊 🛶 🛥️ ⚓ 🐎 ♿ 🚐 ⛺

Scenic rating: 6

on Palisades Reservoir in Caribou-Targhee
National Forest

Located at 5,800 feet in elevation in Caribou-Targhee National Forest, Alpine Campground is near the east end of the 16,000-acre Palisades Reservoir, surrounded by steep forested mountains. While it actually sits in Wyoming, it is adjacent to the Idaho border. Anglers will need to ensure they have the appropriate state licenses depending on where they drop in lines. The reservoir, fed by the Snake River, is shallow along the shoreline near the campground. When the lake water level drops low in late August, the area in front of the campground can become a muddy maze of braided streams. The reservoir, which is known for wind and summer thunderstorms, is popular for fishing, swimming, and boating. The closest boat ramp is in Alpine. Another is located mid-lake on the east side at Indian Creek. The reservoir harbors cutthroat, brown, and lake trout along with kokanee salmon. Due to its location on the highway, cross-country cyclists find this campground convenient.

The campground tucks into a loose lodgepole pine, aspen, and spruce forest, which admits partial and full sun to campsites. Contrary to the surrounding steep hillsides, the campground is in flatter terrain. High undergrowth blooming with pink fireweed under the forest canopy gives the roomy, grassy campsites privacy. With the highway so close—a commercial trucking route—road noise enters the campground.

Campsites, facilities: The campground has 16 RV or tent campsites. Three are double campsites at double the price. Three additional group camping areas are available. RVs are limited to 45 feet. Facilities include picnic tables, fire rings with grills, vault toilets, drinking water, firewood for sale, garbage service, and campground hosts. Leashed pets are permitted. A wheelchair-accessible toilet is available.

Reservations, fees: Reservations are accepted (877/444-6777, www.recreation.gov). Campsites cost $10. Extra vehicles cost $5. Cash or check. Open late May–mid-September.

Directions: From Alpine Junction, where Highway 26 and Highway 89 join on the Snake River, drive two miles northwest on Highway 26. At milepost 402, turn south into the campground. Coming from the north on the highway, look for the campground entrance 0.5 mile southeast of Forest Road 402.
GPS Coordinates: N 43° 11.992' W 111° 2.375'

Contact: Caribou-Targhee National Forest, Palisades Ranger District, 3659 E. Ririe Hwy., Idaho Falls, ID 83401, 208/523-1412, www.fs.fed.us/r4/caribou-targhee.

41 WOLF CREEK

🚶 🚴 🛶 🛥️ ⚓ 🐎 ♿ 🚐 ⛺

Scenic rating: 8

in Snake River Canyon in the Wyoming Range
in Bridger-Teton National Forest

In the Wyoming Range of Bridger-Teton National Forest, Wolf Creek Campground, elevation 5,800 feet, sits in the southwest end of the Snake River Canyon. The canyon walls narrow, forcing the campground to climb a hillside, but this Class III stretch of river through the canyon, designated in March 2009 as Wild and Scenic, is favored by kayakers and rafters for eight miles of white water. Taco Hole kayak playboat area is 3.5 miles northwest of the campground. Anglers on the shore or in drift boats go after brown and Yellowstone cutthroat trout. Outfitters for fishing and rafting are available in Hoback Junction. The Wolf Creek Trailhead, 1.5 miles east of the campground, leads eight miles to Red Pass on the west flank of 9,483-foot Wolf Mountain. Due to the campsite's location on the highway, it is convenient for cross-country cyclists.

Despite sitting in the Snake River Canyon, the campground does not afford enjoyment of the river from campsites, but a few paths across the highway lead to the shore. On a hillside on the opposite side of the road from the river, the campsites have views of the highway, with its accompanying noise and power lines crossing above the campground. Of the three loops, C loop climbs the farthest from the highway, with its upper campsites (16–20) having views of the cliffs across the canyon. The open sagebrush hillside—blooming with fireweed and mountain hollyhock—sprinkles in a few fir trees that lend a little shade to some campsites. A gravel road loops through the campground with gravel parking pads.

Campsites, facilities: The campground has 20 RV or tent campsites. Some parking pads can fit midsized RVs. Facilities include picnic tables, fire rings with grills, vault toilets, drinking water, bear boxes, garbage service, tent platforms, and campground hosts. Leashed pets are permitted. A wheelchair-accessible toilet is available.

Reservations, fees: Reservations are not accepted. Campsites cost $15. Cash or check. Open late May–September.

Directions: On Highway 26/89/6, from Hoback Junction drive southwest for 16 miles, or from Alpine drive seven miles northeast. At milepost 124.9, turn north into the campground.

GPS Coordinates: N 43° 11.932' W 110° 54.197'

Contact: Bridger-Teton National Forest, Jackson Ranger District, 25 Rosencrans Ln., P.O. Box 1689, Jackson, WY 83001, 307/739-5400, www.fs.fed.us/r4/btnf/.

42 STATION CREEK

Scenic rating: 8

in Snake River Canyon in the Wyoming Range in Bridger-Teton National Forest

Located at 5,800 feet in the Wyoming Range of Bridger-Teton National Forest, Station Creek Campground sits midway through the Snake River Canyon. The canyon walls narrow, forcing the campground onto a bluff above the river without access to the shore from the campground. This Class III stretch of river through the canyon, designated in March 2009 as Wild and Scenic, is favored by kayakers and rafters for its eight miles of white water, which peaks in early June and rips through Big Kahuna, Lunch Counter, and Ropes wave train rapids at the end. The campground is convenient for floaters as it sits midway between the put-in at West Table launch site and take-out at Sheep Gulch. Taco Hole, a kayak playboat area with a 30-foot-wide wave hole and the accompanying Burrito Hole, sits 0.5 mile west. Anglers, floating the upper section of the river in drift boats, go after brown and Yellowstone cutthroat trout. Outfitters for fishing and rafting are available in Hoback Junction. Due to the campsite's location on the highway, it is convenient for cross-country cyclists.

Station Creek Campground sits high above the Snake River on a bluff, with half of its campsites (3–10) overlooking the river. Due to the steep drop to the river, fences rim the ledges. Lodgepole pines and firs shade the campsites, which are ringed with meadows of fireweed. The sites sit within view of neighboring campers, and road noise is pervasive, even above the roar of the river below.

Campsites, facilities: The campground has 16 RV or tent campsites. Some parking pads can fit midsized RVs. Facilities include picnic tables, fire rings with grills, pedestal grills, vault toilets, drinking water, bear boxes, garbage service, tent platforms, and campground hosts. Leashed pets are permitted. A wheelchair-accessible toilet is available.

Reservations, fees: Reservations are not accepted. Campsites cost $15. Cash or check. Open late May–September.

Directions: On Highway 26/89/6, from Hoback Junction drive southwest for 12 miles, or from Alpine drive 11 miles northeast. At milepost 128.7, turn south into the campground.

GPS Coordinates: N 43° 12.296' W 110° 50.074'

Contact: Bridger-Teton National Forest, Jackson Ranger District, 25 Rosencrans Ln., P.O. Box 1689, Jackson, WY 83001, 307/739-5400, www.fs.fed.us/r4/btnf/.

43 EAST TABLE CREEK

Scenic rating: 8

in Snake River Canyon in the Wyoming Range in Bridger-Teton National Forest

At an elevation of 5,800 feet in the Wyoming Range of Bridger-Teton National Forest, East Table Campground sits toward the upper end of the Snake River Canyon. The slopes on the opposite canyon wall burned recently, but vegetation is regrowing fast. Even though this is the only Snake River Canyon campground that accesses the water, boat launching is not permitted from the campground. Instead, launch from the huge West Table boat ramp west of the campground. The river, designated in March 2009 as Wild and Scenic, is calmer above the campground, where anglers float drift boats from Hoback Junction to fish for brown and Yellowstone cutthroat trout. You can also fish from the shore along the campground and wade-fish in late summer. Below the campground, an eight-mile stretch of Class III white water amuses kayakers and rafters. Outfitters for fishing and rafting are available in Hoback Junction. Due to the campsite's location on the highway, it is convenient for cross-country cyclists.

The campground sits on a large, aspen- and lodgepole-covered river bar crisscrossed with paths leading to the water. Campsites 4–9, 11, and 13 overlook the river and have views of the burn area. Tall, mature pines shade many of the campsites, but with little understory, the campsites are not private. The sites are within view of neighboring campers, and road noise is pervasive, even above the sound of the river. If

the campground is full, you can use the overflow sites and walk-in tent campsites across the highway, but no services are available.

Campsites, facilities: The campground has 18 RV or tent campsites. Some parking pads can fit midsized RVs. Facilities include picnic tables, fire rings with grills, pedestal grills, vault toilets, drinking water, bear boxes, garbage service, tent platforms, and campground hosts. Leashed pets are permitted. A wheelchair-accessible toilet is available.

Reservations, fees: Reservations are not accepted. Campsites cost $15. Cash or check. Open late May–September.

Directions: On Highway 26/89/6, from Hoback Junction drive southwest for 11 miles, or from Alpine drive 12 miles northeast. At milepost 130, turn south into the campground. GPS Coordinates: N 43° 12.762' W 110° 48.459'

Contact: Bridger-Teton National Forest, Jackson Ranger District, 25 Rosencrans Ln., P.O. Box 1689, Jackson, WY 83001, 307/739-5400, www.fs.fed.us/r4/btnf/.

44 HOBACK

Scenic rating: 8

in Hoback Canyon in the Gros Ventre Range in Bridger-Teton National Forest

In the Gros Ventre Range in Bridger-Teton National Forest, Hoback Campground, elevation 6,250 feet, tucks into deep gray- and red-cliffed Hoback Canyon, where ospreys fish the Hoback River. Trout fishing runs sluggish during June runoff, but during the salmon fly hatch in early July, fishing picks up. The Hoback froths with Class I–III white water through the canyon. You can put in at the campground and take out at Hoback Junction, or put in at Granite Creek and take out at the campground. Due to its white-water sections, this river requires some skill to navigate by kayak or raft. The river was designated Wild and Scenic in March 2009. Because of its proximity to the highway, the campground attracts cross-country cyclists, too.

Tucked under big spruce, firs, and aspens, the campground squeezes in between the highway and the river; a couple campsites, such as site 7, suffer right near the highway noise. Open, sunny campsites are interspersed with partly shaded campsites, offering campers a choice. Those in the open garner views of the canyon walls. Sites 2, 4, 5, 11, and 12 sit on the river. A paved road loops through the campground with paved back-in parking pads.

Campsites, facilities: The campground has 13 RV or tent campsites. Some parking pads can fit midsized RVs. Facilities include picnic tables, fire rings with grills, pedestal grills, vault toilets, drinking water, bear boxes, garbage service, and campground hosts. Leashed pets are permitted. A wheelchair-accessible toilet is available.

Reservations, fees: Reservations are not accepted. Campsites cost $15. Cash or check. Open late May–September.

Directions: From Hoback Junction, drive eight miles southeast on Highway 189/191. At milepost 155.5, turn south into the campground. GPS Coordinates: N 43° 16.876' W 110° 35.628'

Contact: Bridger-Teton National Forest, Jackson Ranger District, 25 Rosencrans Ln., P.O. Box 1689, Jackson, WY 83001, 307/739-5400, www.fs.fed.us/r4/btnf/.

45 GRANITE CREEK

Scenic rating: 9

south of Granite Hot Springs in the Gros Ventre Range in Bridger-Teton National Forest

BEST (

Located at 6,850 feet in the Gros Ventre Range in Bridger-Teton National Forest, Granite Creek Campground lies below the massive Open Door rock slab, a slice of orange rock with a horizontal hole like a doorway. Granite Hot Springs

($6, open daily 10 A.M.–8 P.M. year-round) and Granite Falls sit within one mile. The hot springs (with a changing room, restrooms, and outdoor cement pool built by the CCC in 1933) heat to 93 degrees in the summer, when rains and snowmelt dilute the hot water, and to 112 degrees in the winter. Primitive hot pools also sit below Granite Falls. Granite Creek flows past the campground, although its thick willows make wade-fishing for Yellowstone cutthroat trout and mountain whitefish more difficult. Granite Creek Trail runs along the opposite side of the river from the bridge south of the campground two miles to the falls and hot springs before continuing farther north into the Gros Ventre Wilderness. Rafting and kayaking—best late May–mid-June—start at the wooden bridge seven miles up the road from the highway.

Several campsites on the campground's three loops have views of the Open Door. Large lodgepoles and subalpine firs shade most of the campsites, except for a handful of sunny, open sites in loop A. The sites are spaced out for privacy—many with spacious tent areas—but with forest pine needle and duff floors, the minimal vegetation between sites lets you see neighboring campers. Despite the narrow high elevation canyon, sandhill cranes fly in over the willows around the creek, squawking as they land.

Campsites, facilities: The campground has 53 RV or tent campsites. Some parking pads can fit midsized RVs. Facilities include picnic tables, fire rings with grills, pedestal grills, vault toilets, drinking water, bear boxes, garbage service, tent platforms, and campground hosts. Leashed pets are permitted. A wheelchair-accessible toilet is available.

Reservations, fees: Reservations are not accepted. Campsites cost $15. Cash or check. Open late May–September.

Directions: From Hoback Junction, drive 11 miles southeast on Highway 189/191. Turn north onto dirt Granite Creek Road (Forest Road 30500) for 8.6 miles. The campground entrance is on the right.

Granite Hot Springs is a pool constructed in 1933 by the Civilian Conservation Corps in Bridger-Teton National Forest.

GPS Coordinates: N 43° 21.567' W 110° 26.802'

Contact: Bridger-Teton National Forest, Jackson Ranger District, 25 Rosencrans Ln., P.O. Box 1689, Jackson, WY 83001, 307/739-5400, www.fs.fed.us/r4/btnf/.

46 GRANITE CREEK PRIMITIVE

Scenic rating: 9

south of Granite Hot Springs in the Gros Ventre Range in Bridger-Teton National Forest

Located 6,400 to 6,850 feet in the Gros Ventre Range in Bridger-Teton National Forest, Granite Creek primitive campsites are popular for their beauty, solitude, and quiet as well as options for camping in shoulder seasons when Granite Creek Campground is closed. Granite Hot Springs ($6, open daily 10 A.M.–8 P.M. year-round) and Granite Falls (with primitive hot pools at the base) sit at the end of the 10-mile dirt road. The hot springs' outdoor cement pool, built by the CCC in 1933, heats to 93 degrees in the summer when rains and snowmelt dilute the hot water and to 112 degrees in the winter. From the hot springs, Granite Creek Trail runs two miles along the river south past the falls and also north into the Gros Ventre Wilderness. Anglers wade-fish for Yellowstone cutthroat trout and mountain whitefish in Granite Creek at primitive campsites. Rafters and kayakers float the river's bottom seven miles, best from late May to mid-June.

All campsites command river frontage along Granite Creek. The first few sit within sight of the road, but the upper ones tuck into private locations behind aspens, firs, and pines. Some have sweeping views of the Gros Ventre Mountains at the end of the drainage. Many of the spur accesses are narrow and rough; scout them first.

Campsites, facilities: The area has 12 RV or tent campsites; some can accommodate mid-sized RVs. Facilities include rock fire rings. Bring your own drinking water, or boil or purify creek water. Pack out your trash. Use Leave No Trace principles for managing human waste. Store all food, meat, pet food, beverages, toiletries, and garbage inside hard-sided vehicles or bear-resistant containers. Pets are permitted.

Reservations, fees: Reservations are not accepted. Camping is free. Open May–early November.

Directions: From Hoback Junction, drive 11 miles southeast on Highway 189/191. Turn north onto Granite Creek Road (Forest Road 30500). Locate the entrances to the primitive campsites on the right side of the road along the seven miles after milepost 1.3 and 1.3 miles before the end of the road, where a sign denotes the end of primitive camping.

GPS Coordinates: N 43° 17.833' W 110° 30.115' (first primitive site)

Contact: Bridger-Teton National Forest, Jackson Ranger District, 25 Rosencrans Ln., P.O. Box 1689, Jackson, WY 83001, 307/739-5400, www.fs.fed.us/r4/btnf/.

47 KOZY

Scenic rating: 8

in Hoback Canyon in the Gros Ventre Range in Bridger-Teton National Forest

At an elevation of 6,500 feet in the Gros Ventre Range in Bridger-Teton National Forest, tiny Kozy Campground tucks into deep gray- and red-cliffed Hoback Canyon, where ospreys fish the Hoback River. Trout fishing runs sluggish during June runoff, but during the salmon fly hatch in early July, fishing picks up. The Hoback froths with Class I–III white water through the canyon. You can put in at the campground and take out at Hoback Junction, or put in at Bondurant and take out at the campground. Due to its white-water sections, this river requires some skill to navigate by kayak or raft. The river was designated Wild and Scenic in March 2009. Because of its proximity to the highway, the campground attracts cross-country cyclists.

The tiny campground nestles in Hoback Canyon, squeezed between the highway and the river. It's close to the highway, and even the river can't drown out the trucking noise at night. Surrounded by sagebrush and pine hills, the campground tucks several of the campsites into the loose forest, but you can still see the highway as well as other campers. Sites 3, 4, 5, 7, and 8 claim river frontage. Site 3, at the end of the turnaround loop, offers the most privacy. A paved road loops through the campground, and each campsite has a paved parking pad.

Campsites, facilities: The campground has eight RV or tent campsites. Some parking pads can fit midsized RVs. Facilities include picnic tables, fire rings with grills, pedestal grills, vault toilets, drinking water, bear boxes, and garbage service. Leashed pets are permitted. A wheelchair-accessible toilet is available.

Reservations, fees: Reservations are not accepted. Campsites cost $12. Cash or check. Open late May–mid-September.

Directions: From Hoback Junction, drive 13 miles southeast on Highway 189/191. At milepost 151.9, turn north into the campground.

GPS Coordinates: N 43° 16.204' W 110° 30.911'

Contact: Bridger-Teton National Forest, Jackson Ranger District, 25 Rosencrans Ln., P.O. Box 1689, Jackson, WY 83001, 307/739-5400, www.fs.fed.us/r4/btnf/.

48 GREEN RIVER WARREN BRIDGE ACCESS AREA

Scenic rating: 8

north of Pinedale on the Green River

BEST (

Located between 7,600 and 8,000 feet, the Green River floats through a series of convoluted oxbows in its gentle descent through the valley from the Wind River Range. Nine miles of mini-campgrounds line the river's western shore at 12 developed river access points. During early-summer high water, the river runs at Class I–II, good for canoes, rafts, drift boats, and kayaks. Late-summer low water may require negotiating gravel bars. Anglers go after rainbow, brown, and Yellowstone cutthroat trout via wade-fishing or by boat in Green River. Boat ramps—which work for standard trucks and cars with trailers—are provided at four of the river access sites. Most vehicles can reach the river access sites, but wet, muddy conditions may require four-wheel drive, and many require steep descents.

The sunny campgrounds offer quiet places away from hordes of people. In the height of the boating season, you will, however, see plenty of river traffic and day use visitors. At night, the campgrounds are very quiet. Sagebrush prairies cover the slopes around the campgrounds, with brushy willows along the riverbanks. Be ready to cope with biting blackflies.

Campsites, facilities: The river access area has 12 locations on the west side of the Green River with 23 RV or tent campsites. Five of the river accesses (3, 4, 7, 10, and 12) can accommodate large RVs; the others can only fit RVs less than 31 feet. Vehicles must be parked at least 50 feet from the water. Facilities include picnic tables, fire rings with grills, vault toilets, and boat ramps at sites 1, 2, 4, and 12. Drinking water is not available. Bring your own, or boil or purify river water. Pack out your trash. Leashed pets are permitted.

Reservations, fees: Reservations are not accepted. Camping is free. Open mid-May–September.

Directions: From Highway 191 about 20 miles north of Pinedale, turn east onto the gravel road 200 yards north of Warren Bridge over the Green River. Road conditions vary, depending on the season. The 12 river access locations are on the right side of the road in the nine miles upstream from Warren Bridge. GPS Coordinates for first site: N 43° 1.713' W 110° 6.365'

Contact: Bureau of Land Management, Pinedale Field Office, 1625 W. Pine St., P.O.

Box 768, Pinedale, WY 82941, 307/367-5300, www.blm.gov/wy/st/en/field_offices/Pinedale/recreation/developed_sites.html.

49 WARREN BRIDGE

Scenic rating: 8

north of Pinedale on the Green River

At 7,600 feet facing the Wind River Range, Warren Bridge Campground flanks the Green River in its upper miles en route to its confluence several states away with the Colorado River. Across Warren Bridge, a gravel road parallels the Class I and II river upstream with 12 different places to launch drift boats, kayaks, rafts, or canoes. High water runs in early summer, but even as the water level drops, the river remains floatable through August. September flows may require pulling boats over shallow gravel bars. Wildlife—particularly sage grouse and pronghorn antelope—use the prairies around the river. Anglers go after rainbow, Yellowstone cutthroat, and brown trout in the Green. Cross-country cyclists use this campground for its ease of access adjacent to the highway.

Warren Bridge Campground is adjacent to the highway, where commercial trucking delivers noise to the campground at night. Only the howling wind can drown out the highway. The sagebrush and purple lupine plateau can be hot or windy, but the treeless campground offers big views of the Wyoming Range to the west and the Wind River Range to the east. Sites 1, 3, and 5 sit closest to the river. The wide-open prairie offers no natural fences between sites, but they are spaced out for privacy.

Campsites, facilities: The campground has 16 RV or tent campsites. Some parking pull-throughs can fit large RVs. Facilities include picnic tables, fire rings with grills, pedestal grills, vault toilets, drinking water, a disposal station, and campground hosts. Leashed pets are permitted. A wheelchair-accessible toilet is available.

Reservations, fees: Reservations are not accepted. Campsites cost $10. Use of the waste disposal costs $5. Cash or check. Open mid-May–September.

Directions: From Highway 191 north of Pinedale, turn west at milepost 120 just south of the bridge over the Green River.

GPS Coordinates: N 43° 0.995' W 110° 7.261'

Contact: Bureau of Land Management, Pinedale Field Office, 1625 W. Pine St., P.O. Box 768, Pinedale, WY 82941, 307/367-5300, www.blm.gov/wy/st/en/field_offices/Pinedale/recreation/developed_sites.html.

50 FREMONT LAKE

Scenic rating: 8

in the southern Wind River Range in
Bridger-Teton National Forest

In the Wind River Range in Bridger-Teton National Forest, Fremont Lake Campground, elevation 7,400 feet, sits on the east shore of Fremont Lake, where the landscape changes from sagebrush prairie to forest. The nine-mile-long and 600-foot-deep glacier-carved lake, which supplies Pinedale's water, is the second-largest natural lake in Wyoming. The lake is popular for boating, sailing, waterskiing, personal watercraft riding, swimming, kayaking, canoeing, and fishing for lake, rainbow, and brown trout. The campground's boat launch has a ramp, dock, and trailer parking. Sandy swimming beaches rim part of the campground shore. Mornings bring calm water; winds usually pick up in the afternoon, bringing whitecaps, and late afternoon thunderstorms are common. Accessible by boat, short hiking trails into the Bridger Wilderness depart from the head of the lake. The location of the campground near the lake's upper canyon blocks views of the snow-covered peaks of the Wind River Range; drive or boat to the lake's south end for the views.

The campground—the largest in the Pinedale area—offers a mix of shaded, partly shaded, and sunny campsites sprawled in several loops along the lakeshore hillside. A mixed forest of Douglas fir, junipers, spruce, and aspens provides the shade for some sites; others are surrounded by brushy growth of wild roses, sagebrush, balsamroot, and willows. Privacy varies between sites: From some, you can see several other campsites. In brushier parts of the campground, the sites are more private. Once the Jet Skis clear the lake, the campground is quiet.

Campsites, facilities: The campground has 54 RV or tent campsites. Some parking pads can fit RVs up to 45 feet. Facilities include picnic tables, fire rings with grills, vault and pit toilets, drinking water, a boat launch, and campground hosts. Leashed pets are permitted. Two wheelchair-accessible toilets are available, as well as six barrier-free campsites.

Reservations, fees: Reservations are accepted (977/444-6777, www.recreation.gov). Campsites cost $12. Cash or check. Open late May–early September.

Directions: From Highway 191 in Pinedale, turn northeast onto Fremont Lake Road for four miles. At the T junction, turn left for 0.2 mile. At the Y junction, turn right for 3.1 miles to the campground.

GPS Coordinates: N 42° 56.742' W 109° 47.497'

Contact: Bridger-Teton National Forest, Pinedale Ranger District, 29 E. Fremont Lake Rd., P.O. Box 220, Pinedale, WY 82941, 307/367-4326, www.fs.fed.us/r4/btnf/.

51 BIG SANDY

Scenic rating: 7

in the southern Wind River Range in
Bridger-Teton National Forest

BEST (

At an elevation of 9,100 feet in the southern Wind River Range in Bridger-Teton National Forest, remote Big Sandy Campground requires hours of laborious, bumpy dirt-road driving to reach it. Despite the rough roads, you'll arrive to parking areas brimming with 50–60 cars due to the popular trailhead, which accesses both the Bridger and Popo Agie Wildernesses, lakes for fishing, and the Cirque of the Towers rock-climbing area. Day hikes lead to three small lakes within 3.5 miles, Big Sandy Lake (5.3 miles), and Jackass Pass (7.7 miles), the latter with stunning views into the Cirque of the Towers. Horse facilities (corrals, ramps, and hitch rails) are available. Big Sandy River flows past the campground, offering wade-fishing for brook and Yellowstone cutthroat trout.

Despite the number of cars, the campground is quiet. Grassy campsites vary between sunny and open with views of vehicles to shaded under mature lodgepoles within sound of the river. All have large flat spaces for tents. The three spacious campsites at the end of the turnaround may see each other, but not the hordes of vehicles, plus they are shaded from the late afternoon heat.

Campsites, facilities: The campground has 12 RV or tent campsites. Some grassy parking pads can accommodate midsized RVs, but leveling is difficult and the access road brutal. Facilities include picnic tables, fire rings with grills or fire pits, pit toilets, and bear boxes. Drinking water is not available. Bring your own, or if using river water, boil or purify it first. Leashed pets are permitted.

Reservations, fees: Reservations are not accepted. Campsites cost $9. Cash or check. Open late June–early September.

Directions: From Highway 191 south of Pinedale, drive 19 miles east on Highway 353 to where pavement ends. Turn east onto Big Sandy Elkhorn Road for 8.6 miles. Turn east onto the Lander Cutoff Road for seven miles. Turn north onto Big Sandy Road for 10 miles. Plan on one hour to drive the rugged, narrow Big Sandy Road. From Highway 28 at South Pass, you can also drive the dirt Lander Cutoff Road for 25 miles to reach Big Sandy Road.

GPS Coordinates: N 42° 41.304' W 109° 16.183'

Contact: Bridger-Teton National Forest, Pinedale Ranger District, 29 E. Fremont Lake Rd., P.O. Box 220, Pinedale, WY 82941, 307/367-4326, www.fs.fed.us/r4/btnf/.

52 SAWMILL
🚶 🏊 🏕 🚴 ♿ 🚐 ⛰

Scenic rating: 8

south of Lander in Sinks Canyon State Park

At an elevation of 6,200 feet in Sinks Canyon State Park, Sawmill is one of two state park campgrounds in the narrow, arid sagebrush canyon. Sinks Canyon, an ice age feature, acquired its name due to the disappearance of the Middle Fork of the Popo Agie River (pronounced po-PO-zha). The river enters a limestone cave and sinks underground only to emerge 0.25 mile lower in a pool called The Rise. The park's visitors center (open Labor Day–Memorial Day) sits 0.5 mile up the highway, where hikers can access the one-mile Popo Agie Nature Trail and the four-mile Canyon Loop Trail. The Sinks area is near the visitors center; a 0.25-mile trail leads to The Rise. Fishing is available in portions of the Popo Agie River but not permitted in The Rise pond.

Tucked along the roaring, boulder-strewn river in the bottom of the canyon, Sawmill is a small, sunny campground right on the highway. However, traffic dwindles after dark, as the road is a forest access rather than a trucking route. A few cottonwoods lend partial shade, and several campsites are open to the road. Tent space is limited as the sites are very small and cramped. The campground is best suited as an overflow site for Popo Agie Campground one mile southwest. A wildlife-watching area—visible from several campsites—sits on the opposite side of the highway. Look for bighorn sheep and golden eagles.

Campsites, facilities: The campground has four RV or tent campsites that can fit only small RVs. Facilities include picnic tables, fire rings with grills, vault toilets, drinking water, a playground, and garbage service. Leashed pets are permitted. A wheelchair-accessible toilet is available.

Reservations, fees: Reservations are not accepted. Campsites cost $6 for Wyoming residents, $11 for nonresidents. Day use costs $4 for Wyoming residents, $6 for nonresidents. Cash or check. Open May–September.

Directions: From Lander, drive south on Highway 131 for six miles. At milepost 7, turn left into the campground.

GPS Coordinates: N 42° 45.423' W 108° 47.982'

Contact: Sinks Canyon State Park, 3079 Sinks Canyon Rd., Lander, WY 82520, 307/332-6333 or 307/332-3077, http://wyoparks.state.wy.us.

53 POPO AGIE

Scenic rating: 8

south of Lander in Sinks Canyon State Park bordering Shoshone National Forest

In Sinks Canyon State Park, Popo Agie Campground (pronounced po-PO-zha), elevation 6,750 feet, is the largest of the two state park campgrounds in the narrow, arid sagebrush canyon housing the Middle Fork of the Popo Agie River. Sinks Canyon, an ice age feature, acquired its name due to the disappearance of the river, which enters a limestone cave and sinks underground only to emerge 0.25 mile lower in a pool called The Rise. The park's visitors center (open Labor Day–Memorial Day) sits 0.5 mile down the highway. The Sinks cavern is near the visitors center; a 0.25-mile trail leads to The Rise. From the campground, a bridge crosses the river to access the one-mile Popo Agie Nature Trail and the four-mile Canyon Loop Trail. Fishing for rainbow trout is available in portions of the Popo Agie River but not permitted in The Rise pond.

Set in junipers, cottonwoods, and sagebrush, the sunny campground squeezes in between the highway and the river. The roar of the river with early summer high runoff drowns out vehicle noise from the highway. The route, a forest access, is also not used for commercial trucking, so traffic dwindles after dark. A paved road winds through the campground, connecting paved parking pads, but most sites can only accommodate small tents. The campground offers a mix of privacy, with some sites very open and others more sheltered from other campsites. Sites 13, 15, 16, 19, and 20–23 overlook the river.

Campsites, facilities: The campground has 21 RV or tent campsites plus three walk-in tent sites. RVs are limited to 35 feet, although one site can fit a 45-footer. Facilities include picnic tables, fire rings with grills, vault toilets, drinking water, and garbage service. Leashed pets are permitted. A wheelchair-accessible toilet is available.

Reservations, fees: Reservations are not accepted. Campsites cost $6 for Wyoming residents, $11 for nonresidents. Day use costs $4 for Wyoming residents, $6 for nonresidents. Cash or check. Open May–September.

Directions: From Lander, drive south on Highway 131 for seven miles. At milepost 8.2, turn left into the campground.

GPS Coordinates: N 42° 44.560' W 108° 49.206'

Contact: Sinks Canyon State Park, 3079 Sinks Canyon Rd., Lander, WY 82520, 307/332-6333 or 307/332-3077, http://wyoparks.state.wy.us.

54 SINKS CANYON

Scenic rating: 8

south of Lander in Sinks Canyon in Shoshone National Forest

At an elevation of 6,850 feet in Sinks Canyon in Shoshone National Forest, Sinks Canyon

Campground squeezes between the Middle Fork of the Popo Agie River and the canyon highway. Sinks Canyon, an ice age feature, acquired its name from the disappearing river, which enters a limestone cave and sinks underground only to emerge 0.25 mile lower in a pool called The Rise. The state park visitors center (open Labor Day–Memorial Day), The Sinks, and The Rise sit one mile down the highway. Fishing for rainbow trout is available along the river. From the campground, a bridge crosses the river to access the four-mile Canyon Loop Trail. From Bruces picnic area 1.5 miles southeast, a trail leads 1.6 miles to Popo Agie Falls, a series of roaring cascades. Bicyclists and scenic drivers also tour the Loop Road, which climbs above the campground in a series of switchbacks and continues 33 miles to Highway 28. The pavement ends after eight miles.

In a forest of aspens, lodgepoles, and junipers, the sunny campground tucks between the highway and the river. Most of the campsites are open to the highway, but the views also yield sights of the streaked canyon walls and the split habitat of the canyon's sagebrush north slopes and forested south slopes. The highway—a forest access road—sees traffic in midsummer but quiets after dark, as the route is not used for commercial trucking. The river, which is strewn with large boulders, roars in early summer. Tenters find more space here than at the two state park campgrounds; sites 1–3 offer shaded walk-in sites for tents.

Campsites, facilities: The campground has 11 RV or tent campsites. RVs are limited to 20 feet. Three walk-in tent campsites are also available. Facilities include picnic tables, fire rings with grills, vault toilets, drinking water, bear boxes, garbage service, firewood for sale, tent platforms, and campground hosts. Leashed pets are permitted. A wheelchair-accessible toilet is available.

Reservations, fees: Reservations are not accepted. Campsites cost $15. Cash or check. Open May–October.

Directions: From Lander, drive Highway 131 eight miles southeast. Turn right into the campground at milepost 9.

GPS Coordinates: N 42° 44.193' W 108° 50.163'

Contact: Shoshone National Forest, Washakie Ranger District, 333 E. Main St., Lander, WY 82520, 307/332-5460, www.fs.fed.us/r2/shoshone/.

55 WORTHEN MEADOWS

Scenic rating: 8

south of Lander in the Wind River Range in Shoshone National Forest

At 8,800 feet in the Wind River Range in Shoshone National Forest, Worthen Meadows Campground sits on the south shores of cold Worthen Meadows Reservoir, which provides water for the city of Lander. Surrounded by large granite boulders and lodgepoles, the reservoir is named for the high elevation sagebrush and lupine meadows in the area. A trailhead accesses Roaring Fork, Stough Creek Lakes, and the Sheep Bridge Trail in Popo Agie Wilderness. Anglers go after brook and rainbow trout in the reservoir, best fished from a boat, and the small lake offers canoeists and kayakers a place to paddle. Water levels can drop in the reservoir by late summer; call the Forest Service for status. Mountain bikers tour the dirt Loop Road (Highway 131) to Louis Lake.

The campground is divided into two sections—one sitting on each side of the boat ramp. Eight sites sprawl around the Hilltop loop on a peninsula, with sites 4 and 5 overlooking the water on the end. The Lakeside loop comprises 20 campsites, with sites 9, 10, and 12–15 overlooking the reservoir. The partly shaded campsites tuck under aspens and lodgepoles with whortleberry and pine needle duff forest floors. Sites are spread out for privacy, but the lack of understory allows visibility of neighboring campers from some campsites. Both gravel pull-through and back-in sites are available. The campground is extremely quiet, except for the loud squawking of Clark's nutcrackers.

Campsites, facilities: The campground has 28 RV or tent campsites. RVs are limited to 24 feet. Facilities include picnic tables, fire rings with grills, vault toilets, drinking water, bear boxes, garbage service, tent platforms, and campground hosts. Leashed pets are permitted. A wheelchair-accessible toilet is available.

Reservations, fees: Reservations are not accepted. Campsites cost $15. Cash or check. Open July–September.

Directions: From Lander, drive Highway 131 (also known as The Loop or Louis Lake Road) for 16 miles south, climbing up the series of Loop switchbacks. Turn right at the signed junction and the end of the pavement onto Forest Road 302. Drive 2.4 miles, veering left at the youth camp and the unmarked entrance to the reservoir. Turn right into the campground.

GPS Coordinates: N 42° 41.908' W 108° 55.610'

Contact: Shoshone National Forest, Washakie Ranger District, 333 E. Main St., Lander, WY 82520, 307/332-5460, www.fs.fed.us/r2/shoshone/.

56 FIDDLERS LAKE

Scenic rating: 8

south of Lander in the Wind River Range in Shoshone National Forest

At 9,400 feet in elevation in the Wind River Range in Shoshone National Forest, the remote 57-acre Fiddlers Lake houses a beaver lodge, yellow water lilies, brook trout, a boat ramp, boat dock, and campground. The lake, which is also stocked annually with rainbow trout, is cold, retaining ice often through May. The trailhead to Christina Lake (#721)—a scenic popular fishing lake—is 0.5 mile south on The Loop. Stock facilities are available at the trailhead. The 4.3-mile trail climbs to the lake. The same trailhead also leads four miles into the Popo Agie Wilderness to Upper Silas Lake. A 0.7-mile trail, one mile north of Fiddlers Lake, also leads to Blue Ridge Lookout, an abandoned fire lookout at 9,998 feet with views of the Wind River Range. Mountain bikers also ride The Loop road.

If you're looking for solitude and quiet, Fiddlers Lake offers both in abundance. The campground sprawls along the north and west sides of the idyllic lake, with sunny or shaded campsites spread out for privacy; however, some sites are open to the campground road. Sites 5, 7, 8–10, and 18–20 overlook the lake. Many of the lake sites have pull-over gravel parking pads; the other campsites have back-ins. The surrounding lodgepole forest is broken by grassy meadows of purple lupine and white yarrow.

Campsites, facilities: The campground has 16 RV or tent campsites. RVs are limited to 40 feet. Four walk-in tent campsites are also available. Facilities include picnic tables, fire rings with grills, benches, pedestal grills, vault toilets, drinking water, bear boxes, garbage service, tent platforms, and campground hosts. Leashed pets are permitted. A wheelchair-accessible toilet is available.

Reservations, fees: Reservations are not accepted. Campsites cost $15. Cash or check. Open July–September.

Directions: From Lander, drive Highway 131 (also known as The Loop or Louis Lake Road) for 21 miles southeast. The last five miles are on a narrow dirt road. Turn right and drive 0.3 mile into the campground.

GPS Coordinates: N 42° 38.025' W 108° 52.877'

Contact: Shoshone National Forest, Washakie Ranger District, 333 E. Main St., Lander, WY 82520, 307/332-5460, www.fs.fed.us/r2/shoshone/.

57 LITTLE POPO AGIE

Scenic rating: 7

south of Lander in the Wind River Range in Shoshone National Forest

At 8,800 feet in elevation, Little Popo Agie (pronounced po-PO-zha) sits on the east side of the Wind River Range in Shoshone National Forest. A long, rough dirt road drive is required to reach it. Compared to the other three developed lake campgrounds on The Loop, this one sits near the Little Popo Agie River, which spills from Christina Lake. Trout fishing is available a three-minute walk from the campground near the single-lane bridge crossing the river. Watch for black bears and moose along the river. Hiking trails are available within 2–3 miles at Fiddlers and Louis Lakes. One mile south of the campground, the adjacent Maxon Basin loops with mountain-bike and ATV trails, which become snowmobile trails in winter.

The four sites are located around the circumference of a gravel parking lot of this older, little-used campground surrounded by lodgepole and aspen trees. Whortleberries and lupines cover the ground, and some willow brush grows nearby, but the partly shaded campsites are open to each other. Ponds in the area can produce prodigious mosquitoes in July, but they abate by the end of August. The campground is, however, very quiet.

Campsites, facilities: The campground has four RV or tent campsites. RVs are limited to 16 feet. Facilities include picnic tables, fire grates, vault toilets, and garbage service. Drinking water is not available. Bring your own, or if you choose to use the stream water, boil or purify it first. (You can also get water at Fiddlers Lake Campground two miles northwest.) Leashed pets are permitted. A wheelchair-accessible toilet is available.

Reservations, fees: Reservations are not accepted. Camping is free. Open July–September.

Directions: From Lander, drive Highway 131 (also known as The Loop or Louis Lake Road) for 23.5 miles. The last 7.5 miles are on a narrow, rough dirt road. Turn right into the campground.

GPS Coordinates: N 42° 36.503' W 108° 51.298'

Contact: Shoshone National Forest, Washakie Ranger District, 333 E. Main St., Lander, WY 82520, 307/332-5460, www.fs.fed.us/r2/shoshone/.

58 LOUIS LAKE

Scenic rating: 8

south of Lander in the Wind River Range in Shoshone National Forest

In the Wind River Range in Shoshone National Forest, remote small Louis Lake, elevation 8,600 feet, offers boating, fishing, and swimming, but be prepared for cold water. The high elevation lake retains ice until late May. A boat launch with a ramp, dock, and trailer parking is available on the campground entrance road, and picnic areas with sandy swimming beaches sit on the opposite side of the lake. The Louis Lake Lodge runs a tiny camp store on the lake's west shore, plus rents canoes, kayaks, and fishing boats and guides horseback tours. A Forest Service guard station also sits on the lake. A trail leads 4.5 miles to Christina Lake and 1.7 miles farther to Atlantic Lake in the Popo Agie Wilderness. Two miles north, mountain-bike and ATV trails also loop with Maxon Basin.

The campground tucks at the bottom of a tall talus slope in a loose forest of aspens and lodgepoles. The small sunny sites are clustered close together with sites 6 and 7 overlooking the lake. A trickling stream, which flows only in early summer, runs through the campground loop. Louis Lake is very quiet at night.

Campsites, facilities: The campground has

nine RV or tent campsites. RVs are limited to 24 feet. Facilities include picnic tables, fire rings with grills, vault toilets, bear boxes, and garbage service. Drinking water is not available. Bring your own, or if you choose to use lake water, boil or purify it first. Leashed pets are permitted. A wheelchair-accessible toilet is available.

Reservations, fees: Reservations are not accepted. Campsites cost $10. Cash or check. Open July–September.

Directions: From Lander, drive Highway 131 (also known as The Loop or Louis Lake Road) 26.5 miles (the final 10.5 are dirt). Watch for ATVs on the road, which narrows to one lane frequently. Turn left and drive 0.8 mile through giant potholes into the campground. Trailers may have trouble with some of the deeper potholes. Louis Lake can also be reach via an eight-mile drive on Forest Road 300 from Highway 28.

GPS Coordinates: N 42° 35.561' W 108° 50.595'

Contact: Shoshone National Forest, Washakie Ranger District, 333 E. Main St., Lander, WY 82520, 307/332-5460, www.fs.fed.us/r2/shoshone/.

IDAHO PANHANDLE

© BECKY LOMAX

BEST CAMPGROUNDS

Like no other place in Idaho, the landscape of the

Panhandle is littered with lakes. Some swell to the size of small seas, while others dot rural farmlands with just enough room to set down a flock of migrating geese. Their waters all shimmer with a blue that mirrors the sky, while forests of conifers lend a lush green to the backdrop of rugged mountains.

The slender strip of Idaho's Panhandle houses four large lakes that could swamp one-fifth of Rhode Island and two national forests that could smother Connecticut. At the narrowest section, the Panhandle is a 75-mile-wide slice that squeezes between Montana and Washington. On the interstate, you can drive across it in a little over an hour, but crossing on any two-lane highway takes two to three hours. Most of the Panhandle's developed campgrounds cluster around the four large lakes and the lifeline rivers that feed the lakes.

In the north, the Selkirk Mountains cradle Priest Lake, whose 72-mile shoreline still retains some of the feel of the 1950s, with small cabins rather than monstrous mansions and resorts that only the wealthy can afford to visit. State and national forests encompass the lake, which is rimmed with campgrounds – far more campgrounds than the Panhandle's other three huge lakes. Islands, plus a sister lake to the north connected via a slow-moving slough called the Thorofare, offer boat-in havens for tent campers, while Priest Lake State Park and Idaho Panhandle National Forest campgrounds line the main lake's shore for boating, waterskiing, fishing, paddling, and swimming.

At Sandpoint, Lake Pend Oreille – which is pronounced "POND-o-RAY" – sits at the junction between the Selkirk and Cabinet Mountains. The Clark Fork River feeds Idaho's biggest lake with prodigious volumes of water captured near the Continental Divide in Montana, and the Pend Oreille River drains it toward Washington. The shorelines sprout with homes, cabins, and farms, with public access sprinkled in between. Where the national forest borders the waterway, you'll find waterfront campgrounds for boating and fishing for kamloops rainbow trout, where you can work at breaking the lake's 37-pound world record.

In the center of the Panhandle, Lake Coeur d'Alene is the easiest lake to reach, adjacent to the interstate. Gathering water from the Bitterroot Mountains on the Idaho-Montana border, the St. Joe and Coeur d'Alene Rivers – both rife with wildlife – spill into the 25-mile-long lake. Lake Coeur d'Alene – which contains the world's only floating golf green – is flanked by the Trail of the Coeur d'Alenes, a 72-mile paved bicycle trail. Within a day trip, campers can ride the 15-mile Hiawatha Trail, which leads mountain bikers over seven trestles and through nine tunnels, the longest of which spans 1.7 miles under the Idaho-Montana border. The lake also harbors one of the largest populations of nesting osprey in the West. Unfortunately, due to the bulk of the shoreline being built up with private homes, public access is limited to only a handful of national forest and state park campgrounds.

In the southern Panhandle, the remote North Fork of the Clearwater River also springs from the Bitterroot Mountains on the Idaho-Montana border to fill Dworshak Reservoir, a lake with narrow arms like Norwegian fjords. Camping on the reservoir's shores demands battling skinny paved roads and hilly scenic byways. Until July 4, while the lake fills to full pool, the 54 miles of waterway offer campgrounds for boating, fishing, and swimming. But as the reservoir water drains throughout July, campground boat ramps are stranded above the water, rendering them unusable.

Across the Panhandle, two national forests – the Idaho Panhandle and the Clearwater – dominate the mountainous landscape. Half of their campgrounds cluster in pockets of wet, damp rain forests under a canopy of western red cedars and hemlocks; the others garner sunshine in swaths of drier, loosely spaced, rusty-barked ponderosa pines. In the higher elevations, larch trees turn gold in autumn and drop their needles to carpet the campground forest floors in October.

Lakes define camping in the Idaho Panhandle. Bring the kayak, canoe, mountain bike, fishing rod, and hiking boots to savor all the lakes offer.

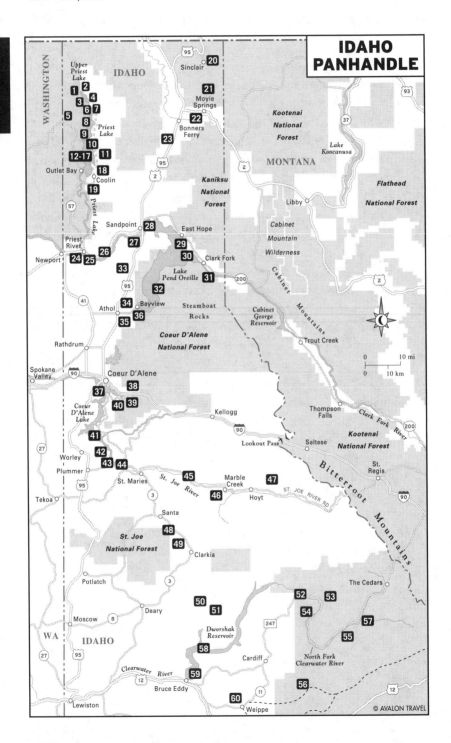

IDAHO PANHANDLE

1 NAVIGATION

🧍‍♂️🚴‍♂️🏊‍♂️🛶🚤⛵🐎⛺

Scenic rating: 9

on Upper Priest Lake in Idaho Panhandle National Forest

BEST (

Located on the west shore of 3.5-mile-long Upper Priest Lake in the Selkirk Mountains of Idaho Panhandle National Forest, Navigation is the most remote lakeshore campground in the Priest Lake area. Hikers, mountain bikers, and horseback riders access it via the 8.1-mile Navigation Trail (#291). Boaters and paddlers reach it via the 2.5-mile Thorofare, a slow-moving slough rife with wildlife between Priest Lake and Upper Priest Lake. Power-boats are restricted to no-wake speed. From Priest Lake, paddlers portage 50 feet across the sand to avoid the jetty. Boaters, including paddlers, launch from the free boat ramp south of Beaver Creek Campground. A longer drive up Priest Lake's east side leads to Lionhead Campground's boat ramp, which charges a fee. Paddlers have two other launches: One is a short canoe portage from Beaver Creek Campground (fee), but to avoid Priest Lake winds, park at the Navigation Trailhead (free) to portage 1,000 feet directly onto the Thorofare. To reach Navigation requires six miles of paddling. Upper Priest Lake is catch-and-release fishing only.

The quiet campground sits on the north-west end of Upper Priest Lake among firs and pines, where it has views from the beach of the Selkirk Mountains. The campground does not have a dock, but the sandy beach provides a good place to beach boats overnight. Of the four upper lake campgrounds, this one is prized for the most wilderness feel.

Campsites, facilities: The campground has four tent campsites. Facilities include picnic tables, fire rings with grills, vault toilets, and bear boxes, but no drinking water. You can haul water from nearby Deadman Creek or the lake, but boil or purify it before use. Pack out all trash. Leashed pets are permitted.

Reservations, fees: Reservations are not accepted. Camping is free, but two launch sites charge fees. The Forest Service charges $6 to use the short canoe portage and park at Beaver Creek Campground. Lionhead Campground charges an entrance fee of $4. Cash or check. Open May–October.

Directions: From Priest River, drive 39 miles north on Highway 57 to Nordman. Turn right onto Reeder Bay Road (Forest Road 2512) for 12 miles to Beaver Creek Campground.
GPS Coordinates: N 48° 47.653' W 116° 54.472

Contact: Priest Lake Ranger District, Idaho Panhandle National Forest, 32203 Hwy. 57, Priest River, ID 83856, 208/443-2512, www.fs.fed.us/ipnf/priestlake.

2 TRAPPER CREEK

🧍‍♂️🏊‍♂️🛶🚤⛵🐎⛺

Scenic rating: 8

on Upper Priest Lake in Idaho Panhandle National Forest

Located on Upper Priest Lake's east shore, Trapper Creek is one of the more remote lakeshore campgrounds in the Selkirk Mountains of Idaho Panhandle National Forest. Hikers, mountain bikers, and horseback riders access it via the 4.3-mile Upper Priest Lake Trail (#302). Boaters, canoeists, and kayakers enter Upper Priest Lake via the 2.5-mile Thorofare, convoluted oxbows filled with bald eagles and birds, to reach the smaller 3.5-mile-long lake north of Priest Lake. Powerboats are restricted to no-wake speed. From Priest Lake, paddlers portage 50 feet across the sand to avoid the jetty. Boaters, including paddlers, launch from the free boat ramp south of Beaver Creek Campground. (A longer drive up Priest Lake's east side leads to Lionhead Campground's boat ramp, where a fee is charged.) Paddlers have two other launches: One is a short canoe portage from Beaver Creek Campground (fee), but to avoid Priest Lake winds, park at the

Navigation Trailhead (free) to portage 1,000 feet directly onto the Thorofare. To reach Trapper Creek requires about 5.5 miles of paddling. Upper Priest Lake and the upper Priest River are catch-and-release fishing only.

The quiet campground with spread-out campsites for privacy sits on the northeast side of Upper Priest Lake facing Plowboy Mountain. The campsites are tucked into the forest edge of the lake, which offers protection from winds. The sandy beach makes it easier to pull canoes and kayaks from the lake.

Campsites, facilities: The campground has five tent campsites. Facilities include picnic tables, fire rings with grills, vault toilets, and bear boxes, but no drinking water. Haul water from nearby Trapper Creek or the lake, but boil or purify it before use. Pack out all trash. Leashed pets are permitted.

Reservations, fees: Reservations are not accepted. Camping is free, but two sites charge launch fees. The Forest Service charges $6 to use the short canoe portage and park at Beaver Creek Campground. Lionhead Campground charges an $4 entrance fee. Cash or check. Open May–October.

Directions: From Priest River, drive 39 miles north on Highway 57 to Nordman and turn right onto Reeder Bay Road (Forest Road 2512) for 12 miles to Beaver Creek Campground. GPS Coordinates: N 48° 47.858' W 116° 53.957'

Contact: Priest Lake Ranger District, Idaho Panhandle National Forest, 32203 Hwy. 57, Priest River, ID 83856, 208/443-2512, www.fs.fed.us/ipnf/priestlake.

3 PLOWBOY

Scenic rating: 9

on Upper Priest Lake in Idaho Panhandle National Forest

Located on the west shore of Upper Priest Lake, which is devoid of the summer homes and resorts of the big lake, Plowboy Campground faces the Selkirk Mountains of the Idaho Panhandle National Forest. Hikers, mountain bikers, and horseback riders access it via the three-mile rolling Navigation Trail (#291). Boaters, canoeists, and kayakers enter Upper Priest Lake via the 2.5-mile Thorofare, the slough connecting the upper lake to the lower lake. Powerboats are restricted to no-wake speed. From Priest Lake, paddlers portage 50 feet across the sand to avoid the jetty. Boaters, including paddlers, launch from the free boat ramp south of Beaver Creek Campground. (A longer drive up Priest Lake's east side leads to Lionhead Campground's boat ramp, which charges a fee.) Paddlers have two other launches: One is a short canoe portage from Beaver Creek Campground (fee), but to avoid Priest Lake winds, park at the Navigation Trailhead (free) to portage 1,000 feet directly onto the Thorofare. To reach Plowboy requires 3.5 miles of paddling. Upper Priest Lake is catch-and-release fishing only.

The campground sits on the southeast side of Upper Priest Lake, a half-mile from Geisingers Campground on the opposite side of the Thorofare. Plowboy gets more traffic than the campgrounds on the upper end of the lake due to hikers using it as a destination to see the upper lake, but at night it quiets. The shaded campsites tuck into the mixed forest for privacy and protection from winds.

Campsites, facilities: The campground has four tent sites. Facilities include picnic tables, fire rings with grills, vault toilets, and bear boxes, but no drinking water. You can haul water from the lake, but boil or purify it before use. Pack out all trash.

Reservations, fees: Reservations are not accepted. Camping is free, but two launch sites charge fees. The Forest Service charges $6 to use the short canoe portage and park at Beaver Creek Campground. Lionhead Campground entrance costs $4. Cash or check. Open May–June.

Directions: From Priest River, drive 39 miles

north on Highway 57 to Nordman and turn right onto Reeder Bay Road (Forest Road 2512) for 12 miles to Beaver Creek Campground. GPS Coordinates: N 48° 46.196' W 116° 52.832'

Contact: Priest Lake Ranger District, Idaho Panhandle National Forest, 32203 Hwy. 57, Priest River, ID 83856, 208/443-2512, www. fs.fed.us/ipnf/priestlake.

4 GEISINGERS

Scenic rating: 8

on Upper Priest Lake in Idaho Panhandle National Forest

Located on Upper Priest Lake's south end, Geisingers Campground—which is accessed only by trail or by water—sits in the Selkirk Mountains of the Idaho Panhandle National Forest. Hikers, mountain bikers, and horseback riders access it on Upper Priest Lake Trail (#302) via Trapper Creek Campground. Boaters, canoeists, and kayakers enter Upper Priest Lake via the 2.5-mile Thorofare, a slow-moving river that links with Priest Lake. From Priest Lake, paddlers portage 50 feet across the sand to avoid the jetty. Boaters, including paddlers, launch from the free boat ramp south of Beaver Creek Campground. (A longer drive up Priest Lake's east side leads to Lionhead Campground's boat ramp, where there's a fee.) Paddlers have two other launches: One is a short canoe portage from Beaver Creek Campground (fee), but to avoid Priest Lake winds, park at the Navigation Trailhead (free) to portage 1,000 feet directly onto the Thorofare. To reach Geisingers requires 3.25 miles of paddling. Upper Priest Lake is catch-and-release fishing only.

The campground sits under hemlocks and pines on the south side of Upper Priest Lake at the outlet. Due to its location at the end of the Thorofare, it sees lots of day traffic,

good for people-watching, but it quiets at night. The view from the beach spans the entire 3.5-mile length of the lake with a backdrop of mountains. Ancient rusted relics from early logging days can be found around the camp.

Campsites, facilities: The campground has two tent sites. Facilities include one picnic table, fire rings with grills, vault toilets, and bear boxes, but no drinking water. You can haul water from the lake, but boil or purify it before use. Pack out all trash. Leashed pets are permitted.

Reservations, fees: Reservations are not accepted. Camping is free, but two launch sites charge fees. The Forest Service charges $6 to use the short canoe portage and park at Beaver Creek Campground. Lionhead Campground charges an entrance fee of $4. Cash or check. Open May–October.

Directions: From Priest River, drive 39 miles north on Highway 57 to Nordman and turn right onto Reeder Bay Road (Forest Road 2512) for 12 miles to Beaver Creek Campground (where you can launch your boat). Access via the Upper Priest Lake Trail #302 (through Trapper Creek Campground) on a mountain bike, horseback, or on foot. GPS Coordinates: N 48° 45.948' W 116° 51.844'

Contact: Priest Lake Ranger District, Idaho Panhandle National Forest, 32203 Hwy. 57, Priest River, ID 83856, 208/443-2512, www. fs.fed.us/ipnf/priestlake.

5 STAGGER INN

Scenic rating: 7

northwest of Priest Lake in Idaho Panhandle National Forest

Up a long stretch of washboard gravel road in the Idaho Panhandle National Forest, Stagger Inn Campground garnered its name from the manner in which the 1926 firefighters

© BECKY LOMAX

Granite Falls is one of the attractions on Priest Lake's west side, at Stagger Inn Campground.

stumbled into fire camp after trekking from Nordman on Priest Lake's west side without a road. Today, the campground, elevation 3,200 feet, is adjacent to Granite Falls and Roosevelt Grove of the Ancient Cedars Scenic Area. Granite Falls tumbles with crashing and frothing white water through its carved canyon. A two-minute walk leads to the base of the falls, but a one-mile loop trail (#301) tours higher for a dramatic look at the lower falls and then a peek at the upper falls. The cedar grove, named after Teddy Roosevelt, was nearly destroyed in a 1926 fire, but two small segments remain that house giants, some up to 12 feet in diameter and averaging 800 years old. Explore the upper grove off the trail, reached via one mile of walking from the top of the loop trail.

Tucked under lush cedars with a forest floor of ferns, the campground sits in the other surviving grove. The area has one small loop that doubles as the parking lot and picnic area for grove visitors during the day and acts as a primitive quiet campground at night. Due to the heavy cedar canopy, the campground is very shady and almost dark.

Campsites, facilities: The campground has four RV or tent campsites that can accommodate small RVs. Facilities include picnic tables, fire ring, and a vault toilet. Bring your own water, or if you plan on using water from Granite Creek, boil or purify it first. Haul the water from lower downstream where access is safer. Leashed pets are permitted. A wheelchair-accessible toilet is available.

Reservations, fees: Reservations are not accepted. Camping is free. Open late May–September.

Directions: From Priest River, drive 37 miles north on Highway 57 to Nordman. Continue north for 1.6 miles until the pavement ends and the road turns into Forest Road 302. Drive another 10.7 miles on the rough dirt road to reach the campground, which is on the left.

GPS Coordinates: N 48° 46.006' W 117° 3.671'

Contact: Priest Lake Ranger District, Idaho Panhandle National Forest, 32203 Hwy. 57, Priest River, ID 83856, 208/443-2512, www.fs.fed.us/ipnf/priestlake.

6 BEAVER CREEK

Scenic rating: 9

on Priest Lake's west shore in Idaho
Panhandle National Forest

BEST (

Located the farthest north of the Idaho Panhandle National Forest campgrounds on the west side of Priest Lake, Beaver Creek is in the best vicinity to boat the Thorofare to Upper Priest Lake. The narrow, flat-water river provides wildlife-watching for moose, ospreys, bald eagles, and bears. To avoid running aground, be sure to follow the channel markers when entering and exiting the Thorofare. Powerboats take the Thorofare at no-wake speeds, while kayakers paddle its 2.5 miles. Several hiking trails depart from the campground. Navigation Trail (#291) heads for three miles to Upper Priest Lake and then continues on for another five miles up-lake. Lakeshore Trail (#294) begins near the swimming area and travels south along the shoreline to dispersed campsites.

Tucked under lush cedars and hemlocks, the popular campground has two paved loops with paved parking aprons, some of which are double-wide. Campsites 13, 15, 33, and 34 sit closest to the lake, but views of the water are blocked. While the campsites are large and spaced out, you can still see the neighbors through the trees. From the sandy swimming beach, the views span the Selkirk Mountains, including Lookout Mountain. The boat launch sits on a gravel spur road south of the campground.

Campsites, facilities: The campground has 41 RV or tent campsites that can fit RVs 50–60 feet in length and up to 22 feet wide. Facilities include picnic tables, fire rings with grills, drinking water, vault toilets, a campground host, firewood for sale, a swimming area, a canoe portage, and a boat launch. Leashed pets are permitted. A wheelchair-accessible toilet is available.

Reservations, fees: Reservations are accepted (877/444-6777, www.recreation.gov). Campsites cost $16. An extra vehicle costs $7. Cash or check. Open late May–September.

Directions: From Priest River, drive 39 miles north on Highway 57 to Nordman and turn right onto Reeder Bay Road (Forest Road 2512) for 12 miles to Beaver Creek Campground. GPS Coordinates: N 48° 44.160' W 116° 51.702'

Contact: Priest Lake Ranger District, Idaho Panhandle National Forest, 32203 Hwy. 57, Priest River, ID 83856, 208/443-2512, www. fs.fed.us/ipnf/priestlake.

7 LIONHEAD

Scenic rating: 8

on Priest Lake's east shore in Priest Lake State Park

Located on Squaw Bay on the east side of Priest Lake, Lionhead Campground is named for large, rocky Lions Head Peak in the Selkirk Mountains to the east. The campground is the one farthest north on the state park side of the lake, but the location is convenient for paddling up the Thorofare or hiking to Upper Priest Lake. The campground itself has an intricate web of trails, and the three-hour hike up to Lookout Lake and Mountain puts you above both lakes with views of the Selkirk Mountains. The campground's boat dock aids those launching for sightseeing, boating, waterskiing, and fishing.

The East Lakeshore access road turns to gravel several miles before Lionhead, and the parking aprons for the campsites are gravel. The south-facing swimming beach is a favorite of many because of its 0.25-mile-long sandy shore with oodles of room for sunbathing. Eleven campsites sit in the trees in a prime waterfront location overlooking the beach. The bay is also very sheltered and gets less wind than the central corridor of the lake. The campsites have ample room for tents, but the parking aprons can only accommodate small RVs less than 25 feet, and only six campsites have pull-through parking.

Campsites, facilities: The campground has 47 RV or tent campsites. Facilities include picnic tables, fire rings with grills, drinking water, vault toilets, a boat launch with a dock, a swimming beach, campground rangers, firewood for sale, and an amphitheater for naturalist presentations. The Lionhead Group Campsite has a cabin with a kitchen and nine RV hookup sites. Leashed pets are permitted. A wheelchair-accessible toilet is available.

Reservations, fees: Reservations are accepted (888/922-6743, http://parksandrecreation. idaho.gov). Campsites cost $12 per night, plus Idaho tax. Cash, check, or credit card. The day-use fee is $4. Open early May–late October.

Directions: From Priest River, drive 22 miles north on Highway 57 and turn right at the Dickensheet Road. Stay on that to Coolin and turn right onto East Lakeshore Road. The drive from Highway 57 to Lionhead is 26 miles. Find the campground entrance on the left.

GPS Coordinates: N 48° 43.918' W 116° 49.371'

Contact: Priest Lake State Park, 314 Indian Creek Park Rd., Coolin, ID 83821, 208/443-2200, http://parksandrecreation.idaho.gov/parks/priestlake.aspx.

8 NORTH SHORE PRIEST LAKE

Scenic rating: 9

on Priest Lake's west shore in Idaho Panhandle National Forest

Priest Lake has several non-drive-in campgrounds on its west shore—all on the north end of the lake in the bottleneck and most where the lake narrows to one mile across. They are best accessed by boat, kayak, or canoe from the water, or by foot, horse, or mountain bike on the Lakeshore Trail. For water access, launch from the Reeder Bay public boat launch on the west side or Indian Creek Campground on the east side. You can also launch from farther north at Beaver Creek on the west side or Lionhead Campground on the east side. For trail access, the heavily used Lakeshore Trail (#294) route runs seven miles along the lakeshore, paralleling Forest Road 2512. Its southern trailhead sits on the Copper Bay Cutoff Road (milepost 4.7), and the north end is at the Beaver Creek Campground (milepost 12). Two other trailheads are spaced out on side roads at mileposts 4.9 and 7.8. Spur paths cut off the Lakeshore Trail to reach the campground beaches. Trail entrances for Bottle Bay and Teacher Bay are signed with small pullouts for parking.

This string of developed lakefront campgrounds runs from Distillery Bay to Tule Bay. Primitive campsites are also sprinkled in between the developed campgrounds. Most campsites overlook the lake, with flat spaces for tents under the partial shade of firs and cedars. Some of the primitive campsites are very private. Those at Teacher and Bottle Bays have less privacy and attract more campers.

Campsites, facilities: Tule Bay has seven tent campsites; Bottle Bay has 10 tent sites. Tripod, Distillery, and Teacher Bay have two or three tent sites each. Facilities at the five developed campgrounds include vault toilets, picnic tables, and fire rings with grills. Primitive campsites have only rock fire rings. None of the campsites have water; bring your own or, if you plan on using lake water, boil or purify it. Pack out your garbage. Leashed pets are permitted.

Reservations, fees: Reservations are not accepted. Campsites are free. Open May–October.

Directions: From Priest River, drive 37 miles north on Highway 57 to Nordman and turn right onto Reeder Bay Road (Forest Road

2512). In the next 12 miles heading north toward Beaver Creek Campground, this road accesses boat launches and trailheads for reaching the north shore campgrounds.

GPS Coordinates for Bottle Bay: N 48° 42.154' W 116° 51.934'

Contact: Priest Lake Ranger District, Idaho Panhandle National Forest, 32203 Hwy. 57, Priest River, ID 83856, 208/443-2512, www.fs.fed.us/ipnf/priestlake.

9 REEDER BAY

Scenic rating: 9

on Priest Lake's west shore in Idaho Panhandle National Forest

Halfway up Priest Lake's west side, Reeder Bay Campground squeezes in between a few small resorts on Reeder Bay east of Nordman, where you can buy propane and minor camping supplies. The bay sits south of the Priest Lake bottleneck, where the span narrows to one mile across. The Lakeview Mountain Trail (#269)—a 5.3-mile trek up and over the mountain to Highway 57 for hikers, mountain bikers, horses, and trail motorcycles—begins on the Reeder Bay side of the mountain. The summit requires a 1,500-foot climb but does not afford views until you drop 0.25 mile down the west side to a marked junction to a rocky viewpoint. The 4.2-mile Kalispell-Reeder Bay Trail (#365) is a multi-use trail for mountain bikers, hikers, horses, and trail motorcycles that runs south to Kalispell Bay.

The campground sits under a heavy canopy of huge cedar trees—indicative of the moisture this area receives. The paved campground road loops beneath the cedars, with large sites spread out for privacy. Reeder also has the most waterfront campsites of any of the west-side campgrounds: Sites 14–24 all have views and lake frontage. You can see Chimney Rock poking up in the Selkirks across the

lake. The campground does not have a boat launch, but you can carry kayaks or canoes to the shore. Launch other boats just north of the campground.

Campsites, facilities: The campground has 24 RV or tent campsites. Most of the campsites can fit RVs and trailer combinations 30–45 feet. Site 16 can fit a 50-foot RV, and site 14 can fit a 60-foot RV. Facilities include picnic tables, fire rings with grills, pedestal grills, vault toilets, drinking water, and a campground host. Leashed pets are permitted. A wheelchair-accessible toilet is available.

Reservations, fees: Reservations are accepted for 14 of the campsites (www.recreation.gov, 877/444-6777). The waterfront sites cost $18. Sites 1–13 cost $16. An extra vehicle costs $7. Cash or check. Open mid-May–September.

Directions: From Priest River on Highway 57, go 37 miles north to Nordman. Turn right onto Reeder Road and drive 2.6 miles to the campground entrance on the right.

GPS Coordinates: N 48° 37.850' W 116° 52.979'

Contact: Priest Lake Ranger District, Idaho Panhandle National Forest, 32203 Hwy. 57, Priest River, ID 83856, 208/443-2512, www.fs.fed.us/ipnf/priestlake.

10 INDIAN CREEK

Scenic rating: 8

on Priest Lake's east shore in Priest Lake State Park

BEST (

On the east side of Priest Lake about halfway up, Indian Creek sits on the protected south bay of Cape Horn at the base of the Selkirk Mountains. Both beaches on either side of the park are lined with summer homes. The campground offers forest hiking to places like the Old Flume, a three-mile-long path for loggers in the 1940s and 1950s to shoot logs down to the bay. The campground is also the closest for hiking to Hunt Lakes, Mount Roothaan, and the dramatic Chimney Rock. Anglers go after trophy-sized lake trout. In winter, the park becomes a base for snowmobilers.

The beach area has a huge, long sandy swimming beach with a buoyed-off area for safety as well as a boat launch area, which has a dock, cement ramp, and large paved parking lot for boat trailers. The campsites tuck into a mixed cedar forest with the burbling Indian Creek running by some. A paved road loops through the Indian Creek campsites, which are nearer the beach, and the White Pine campsites, which sit on two loops farther back in the woods. Reservations are imperative in July and August.

Campsites, facilities: The campground has 73 RV campsites. Some can accommodate vehicles up to 40 feet. Hookups include water, sewer, and electricity. The campground also has 20 tent campsites. Facilities include picnic tables, fire rings with grills, drinking water, flush toilets, showers, a disposal station, an amphitheater for interpretive programs, horseshoes, basketball, a camp store, a swimming beach, and a boat launch. Pack out your trash. Leashed pets are permitted. A wheelchair-accessible toilet is available.

Reservations, fees: Reservations are recommended (888/922-6743, http://parksandrecreation.idaho.gov). Hookup campsites cost $20–23. Tent campsites cost $12. Extra vehicles cost $6. Add on the 6 percent Idaho sales tax. Day use entry costs $4. Cash, check, or credit card. Open all year.

Directions: From Priest River, drive 22 miles north on Highway 57 and turn right at the Dickensheet Road. Stay on that to Coolin and turn right onto East Lakeshore Road. From Highway 57 to Indian Creek is 17 miles. The campground entrance sits on the left.
GPS Coordinates: N 48° 36.686' W 116° 49.816'
Contact: Priest Lake State Park, 314 Indian Creek Park Rd., Coolin, ID 83821, 208/443-2200, http://parksandrecreation.idaho.gov.

11 HUNT CREEK PRIMITIVE

Scenic rating: 6

in the Selkirk Mountains east of Priest Lake in Priest Lake State Forest

On the east side of Priest Lake, Hunt Creek primitive campground sits on a large, previously logged plateau in the Selkirk Mountains. While the campground has no services, it attracts a few campers—especially hunters—for its price. It's free. The dirt access road continues farther to the trailhead to Hunt Lakes, requiring a one-hour drive and a 90-minute hike. The route passes through a boulder field where you must follow orange dots on the rocks. The campground is also adjacent to Hunt Creek Falls, in a gorgeous mossy gorge. In spring the falls roar with water roiling through the multiple cascades. Rough log benches allow you to sit and listen. While you can drive to the falls,

© BECKY LOMAX

Hunt Creek Falls roars on the east side of Priest Lake.

the last half mile is a very rough road with no turnaround. You're better off parking in the campground and walking to the falls.

A rough, rocky dirt road loops around the plateau holding the campsites. Most of the large campsites sit on sunny, grassy areas surrounded by brush and shaded by only a few pines. The first campsite, however, is easier to access and set under the trees with more shade and a forest duff floor.

Campsites, facilities: The campground has four primitive RV or tent campsites that can fit small RVs. Facilities include only rock fire rings. Use Leave No Trace practices here for human waste, and pack out your trash. Bring your own water. The gorge is slippery at the falls; do not attempt to get water here. Pets are permitted.

Reservations, fees: Reservations are not accepted. Camping is free. Open April–November.

Directions: From Priest River, drive 22 miles to the Dickensheet Road, turning right and heading toward Coolin. At Coolin, turn right to follow the East Lakeshore Road four miles to Forest Road 23. Turn right, heading up the steep hill on the dirt road. At the top of the hill, turn left at the state lands sign. You'll find the first campsite on the right and the others sprawled around the loop.

GPS Coordinates: N 48° 33.799' W 116° 49.481'

Contact: Priest Lake State Park, 314 Indian Creek Park Rd., Coolin, ID 83821, 208/443-2200, http://parksandrecreation.idaho.gov.

12 KALISPELL ISLAND

🧍🌊🛶🚤⚓🐎🛶

Scenic rating: 9

on Priest Lake in Idaho Panhandle National Forest

BEST (

Kalispell Island, the largest, most popular of the Priest Lake islands, is completely public property, best accessed from the west side. The island also sits opposite the Indian Rock pictographs, which are best seen from the water. A 2.5-mile trail circles the island between all of the campgrounds, with views of the Selkirk Mountains to the east.

The island has two day-use sites and 13 campgrounds, three of which are group sites. The smallest campgrounds—Shady and Peninsula—have two campsites each. An island host cabin at West Shores is flagged for visibility from the water. Kalispell boat launch has a free SCAT machine boaters may use to clean and sanitize portable toilets, including five-gallon buckets and ammo boxes. Most of the campsites are tucked into the forest for wind protection, but they overlook the lake.

Campsites, facilities: Kalispell Island campgrounds have 42 tent campsites. Facilities include picnic tables, fire rings with grills, and vault toilets at Schneider, North Cove, Silver Cove, Silver, Three Pines, and Rocky Point. Portable toilets, including self-contained boat toilets, are required for camping at West Shores, Selkirk, Shady, Peninsula, and Cottonwood, which have privacy screens for setting up privies. Island rangers will check for these. None of the campsites have water: bring your own, or if you plan on using lake water, boil or purify it. Pack out your garbage to the Kalispell boat launch dumpster. Leashed pets are permitted.

Reservations, fees: Reservations are accepted only for the group campsites for 10 people or more. Call the ranger station for reservations. Campsites cost $10 per night. You can pay for campground fees at the boat launch or in the fee collection tubes located on the island at the Kalispell host site, Schneider, Silver Cove, Three Pines, Rocky Point, and North Cove. Parking for island campers at Kalispell boat launch is free for one car and one launch. Additional vehicles cost $5 for the first day and $3 per day thereafter. Cash or check. Open May–October.

Directions: From Priest River, drive 31 miles north on Highway 57 to Kalispell Bay Road. Turn right and drive 1.7 miles to the Kalispell boat launch on the right.

GPS Coordinates: N 48° 34.191' W 116° 54.445'

Contact: Priest Lake Ranger District, Idaho Panhandle National Forest, 32203 Hwy. 57, Priest River, ID 83856, 208/443-2512, www.fs.fed.us/ipnf/priestlake.

13 BARTOO ISLAND

Scenic rating: 9

on Priest Lake in Idaho Panhandle National Forest

Bartoo Island, an oblong island southeast of Kalispell Island on Priest Lake's west side, includes a strip of private property on the north side. Those paddling to the island will cross an expanse of open water between Kalispell and Bartoo, broken only by the miniature Papoose Island.

The island has two day-use sites, six campgrounds, and the Sunrise group site. For ultra privacy, head to Solo Two, Bartoo Solo, or Cedars—all with single campsites. When launching from the Kalispell boat launch, you can check what sites are available. An island host cabin near Cedars is flagged for visibility from the water. The Kalispell boat launch has a free SCAT machine boaters may use to clean and sanitize portable toilets, including five-gallon buckets and ammo boxes.

Campsites, facilities: Bartoo campgrounds have 21 tent campsites. Facilities include picnic tables and fire rings with grills (except for the solo sites). Sunshine campground has the only vault toilet. Those staying at other sites (North Bartoo, Solo Two, South Bartoo, Bartoo Solo, Sunrise group site, and Cedars) are required to have self-contained toilets in boats or portable toilets—labeled with the owner's name, address, phone number, and driver's license number. Privacy screens for setting up privies are available at the campsites. None of the campsites have water: bring your own, or if you plan on using lake water, boil or purify it. Pack out your garbage. Leashed pets are permitted.

Reservations, fees: Reservations are accepted only for the group campsites for 10 people or more. Call the ranger station for reservations. Campsites cost $10 per night. Pay for your campsite at the boat launch or in the fee tubes at North Bartoo, South Bartoo, and Sunshine. Parking for island campers at Kalispell boat launch is free for one car and one launch. Additional vehicles cost $5 for the first day and $3 per day thereafter. Cash or check. Open May–October.

Directions: From Priest River, drive 31 miles north on Highway 57 to Kalispell Bay Road. Turn right and drive 1.7 miles to the Kalispell boat launch on the right.

GPS Coordinates: N 48° 32.652' W 116° 53.050'

Contact: Priest Lake Ranger District, Idaho Panhandle National Forest, 32203 Hwy. 57, Priest River, ID 83856, 208/443-2512, www.fs.fed.us/ipnf/priestlake.

14 PRIEST LAKE RV RESORT AND MARINA

Scenic rating: 8

on Priest Lake's west shore

Located on Kalispell Bay on the west side of Priest Lake, Priest Lake Marina attracts RVers who want to spend more of their time on the lake. For boaters, the 26,000-acre lake has 70 miles of shoreline to explore—plus the 2.5-mile no-wake Thorofare connects to Upper Priest Lake. Priest Lake is also renowned for its trophy-sized mackinaws or lake trout. The cold, clear lake is a perfect breeding ground for the voracious predator to reach 40 inches long and weigh up to 25 pounds. The lake also harbors some kokanee, cutthroat, and bull trout. The marina is within a 10-minute drive of the Priest Lake Museum and Visitor Center and Priest Lake Golf Course. The six-mile hiker-only Beach Trail (#48) departs just south of the marina, touring the shoreline to Outlet Campground. About a five-minute drive north, find the trailhead for the 4.2-mile Kalispell-Reeder Bay Trail (#365), which allows hikers, horseback riders, mountain bikes, and trail motorcycles.

The campground portion of the resort forms a grassy semicircle banked against the trees on the south side of the property. Due to the tight quarters, privacy is nonexistent. The marina, which provides boat moorage for guests, has several large docks with covered slips. The marina often attracts RVers and boaters who come in for the season, so call for reservations for both campsites and boat moorage.

Campsites, facilities: The marina maintains 11 campsites with a maximum trailer length of 30 feet. Hookups include water, sewer, and electricity. Other amenities include flush toilets, showers, a launderette, a convenience store, a restaurant, a lounge, and the marina.

Reservations, fees: Reservations are highly recommended. Campsites cost $25. Boat moorage costs $15 per night. Cash, check, or credit card. Open May–October.

Directions: From Priest River, take Highway 57 north for 28.6 miles. Turn right onto Luby Bay Road (also Forest Road 1337), driving north for 1.4 mile. Turn right onto West Lakeshore Road and follow it north for 1.5 miles to the marina.

GPS Coordinates: N 48° 33.722' W 116° 55.725'

Contact: Priest Lake RV Resort & Marina, 6515 W. Lakeshore Rd., Priest Lake, ID 83856, 208/443-2405.

15 LUBY BAY

Scenic rating: 9

on Priest Lake's west shore in Idaho Panhandle National Forest

On Priest Lake's west side, Luby Bay links onto the six-mile Beach Trail (#48) along the shoreline, which is for hikers only. The 5.3-mile Woodrat Trail (#235) for hikers and mountain bikers cruises through the forest, paralleling Forest Road 237. The campground is 0.5 mile north of the Priest Lake Museum and Visitor Center. A public boat launch is 0.8 mile north.

Luby Bay Campground has two looping sections with a paved road. Due to the hillside on lower Luby, some of the campsites are crammed together and have less privacy than those at upper Luby. Sites 1–11 sit near the waterfront, with sites 7, 9, 10, and 11 boasting lake frontage, which makes them in high demand. Upper Luby has lusher campsites tucked into the hemlock-cedar forest, is more level, and is not as cramped. Sites 27–40 are large and private with room for tents. Sites 47–54 can accommodate those with bigger rigs. Trails, including one paved, lead to the long sandy beach.

Campsites, facilities: Luby Bay has 85 RV or tent sites. Several campsites can accommodate a maximum RV length of 55 feet. Facilities include picnic tables, fire rings with grills, pedestal grills, flush and vault toilets, some double-wide parking pads, garbage service, drinking water, an amphitheater for interpretive programs, campground hosts, and a disposal station. Leashed pets are permitted. A wheelchair-accessible toilet is available.

Reservations, fees: Reservations are accepted (877/444-6777, www.recreation.gov). Sites near the waterfront cost $18. All other sites cost $16. An extra vehicle costs $7. The day-use fee is $6. The disposal station costs $6 (but you can drive about 10 minutes south to the Priest River Information Center to use free disposal stations). Cash or check. Open mid-May–early October.

Directions: From Priest River, drive 28.6 miles north on Highway 57 to Luby Bay Road, otherwise known as Forest Road 1337. Turn right and drive 1.3 miles to West Lakeshore Road (Forest Road 237). Turn left and drive 0.6 mile to the campground. Lower Luby Bay campground is to the right, and Upper Luby Bay campground is to the left.

GPS Coordinates: N 48° 32.925' W 116° 55.532'

Contact: Priest Lake Ranger District, Idaho Panhandle National Forest, 32203 Hwy. 57, Priest River, ID 83856, 208/443-2512, www.fs.fed.us/ipnf/priestlake.

16 OSPREY

Scenic rating: 9

on Priest Lake's west side in Idaho Panhandle National Forest

On the southwest side of Priest Lake, Osprey Campground sits right on the six-mile Beach Trail (#48) about 0.5 mile north of Outlet Campground and 5.5 miles south of Luby Bay. You can launch hand-carried watercraft from the campground, but the nearest boat launch is about five miles north. Within a 10-minute drive, you'll find the Priest Lake Golf Course, Priest Lake Museum and Visitor Center, and Priest Lake Marina. RVers looking for a disposal station can find a free one at the Priest Lake Information Center five miles to the south.

Even though the access is via one mile of dirt road, the campground road is paved, with gravel parking aprons. Compared to Outlet and Lower Luby campgrounds, Osprey has very spacious sites with lots of privacy because of their distance from each other. The campground's one loop sits under a mixed canopy with a heavy dose of cedars. Sites 8–15 claim a premium price with waterfront, although sites 14 and 15 have peek-a-boo views through the trees rather than beach frontage, which is across the campground loop road. Trails from the campground access the shoreline.

Campsites, facilities: Osprey has 16 RV or tent campsites that can accommodate a maximum RV length of 20 feet. Facilities include picnic tables, raised tripod fire pans on cement pads, flush toilets, drinking water, garbage collection, and a campground host. Leashed pets are permitted. A wheelchair-accessible toilet is available.

Reservations, fees: Reservations are accepted (877/444-6777, www.recreation.gov). Waterfront sites cost $16. Other sites cost $14. Extra vehicles cost $7. Cash or check. Open June–early September.

Directions: From Priest River, go 26 miles north on Highway 57. At milepost 26, turn right onto Outlet Bay Road. Drive 0.5 mile and turn left at the sign onto the dirt West Lakeshore Drive (Forest Road 237). Drive one mile and turn right into the campground.

GPS Coordinates: N 48° 30.455' W 116° 53.340'

Contact: Priest Lake Ranger District, Idaho Panhandle National Forest, 32203 Hwy. 57, Priest River, ID 83856, 208/443-2512, www.fs.fed.us/ipnf/priestlake.

17 OUTLET BAY

Scenic rating: 9

on Priest Lake in Idaho Panhandle National Forest

As you drive north on the west side of Priest Lake, Outlet Bay is the first campground on the lake with views across to the Selkirk Mountains. The location is convenient for those who want to explore both sides of the lake; the road to the east side sits less than four miles south on Highway 57. The Beach Trail—a hiker-only trail—runs six miles from the campground to Luby Bay along the shoreline. The popular 5.3-mile Woodrat Trail (#235)—for mountain bikers and hikers—also departs across the road from the campground entrance. Paddlers in rafts or kayaks aiming for the Class II–III white water of Priest River can start paddling from Outlet Campground. The one mile of flat water leads to a dam requiring a portage before hitting the Binarch Rapids section.

Tucked under tall cedars, the shady campground has large sites but only small paved parking pads. The narrow, curvy campground road loops through tight trees. Prime waterfront campsites (3–5, 24–27) have peek-a-boo views of the lake. Trailers are not permitted in sites 24–27, and those sites, which are best for tents, are paired to work for two parties camping together in two sites. Check on the status for this campground, as a windstorm blew down trees in sites 6–12. A portion or the complete campground may be closed in 2010 for reconstruction.

Campsites, facilities: Outlet Bay has 27 RV or tent campsites. The maximum RV length is 35 feet, but most of the sites can only fit those 25 feet or less. Facilities include picnic tables, fire rings with grills, flush toilets, drinking water, campground hosts, and garbage service. Leashed pets are permitted. A wheelchair-accessible toilet is available.

Reservations, fees: No reservations are accepted. Waterfront campsites cost $16. Other campsites cost $14. Extra vehicles cost $7. Cash or check. Open late May–early September.

Directions: From Priest River, go 26 miles north on Highway 57. At milepost 26, turn right onto Outlet Bay Road. Drive 0.5 mile and turn left onto the dirt West Lakeshore Drive—also known as the Forest Road 237—at the sign. Drive 0.5 mile and turn right into the campground.

GPS Coordinates: N 48° 29.958' W 116° 53.616'

Contact: Priest Lake Ranger District, Idaho Panhandle National Forest, 32203 Hwy. 57, Priest River, ID 83856, 208/443-2512, www.fs.fed.us/ipnf/priestlake.

18 INN AT PRIEST LAKE

🏃 🚴 🏊 🛶 🎣 ❄️ 🦌 ♿ 🚐 ⛺

Scenic rating: 6

in Coolin near Priest Lake

Located in Coolin, a small town on Priest Lake's south end, the Inn at Priest Lake is

Sundance Lookout towers above Priest Lake, with huckleberry picking and views of the Idaho Panhandle National Forest.

© BECKY LOMAX

a hub for both summer lake recreation and winter snowmobiling. In Coolin, you can rent boats and personal watercraft. To get a scenic panoramic view of the entire Priest Lake area or pick huckleberries, take a drive up to Sundance Lookout. To reach the lookout, the 90-minute drive on a maze of narrow, bumpy rough dirt roads requires a four-wheel rig to ascend about 3,700 feet up from the lake. Get directions from the state park office in Coolin before departing. Due to Coolin's location at the south end of the lake, the town makes a good base for exploring both the east, state park side and the west, national forest side of Priest Lake. The Chipmunk Rapids National Recreation Trail is within a 10-minute drive.

A paved road loops through the campground, which has paved parking pads and small concrete aprons for tables and chairs. Small trees lend partial shade to some of the sites. The wide-open area lends itself to RVers who need to get a clear shot of the sky for satellite reception. This is the only private campground in the Priest Lake area that can handle big rigs.

Campsites, facilities: The inn's 12 RV spaces are all 75-foot-long pull-throughs surrounded by mowed lawn. Hookups include water, sewer, and electricity up to 50 amps. Undesignated space for five tents is available on the grass, too. Facilities include flush toilets, showers, and the use of the inn's swimming pool. Small leashed pets are permitted. A wheelchair-accessible toilet is available.

Reservations, fees: Reservations are accepted, and highly recommended for July and August. Hookup campsites cost $25. Tent sites cost $15. Add on the 6 percent Idaho sales tax. During holidays, a two-night minimum stay is required. Cash, check, or credit card. Open year-round.

Directions: From Priest River, drive north on Highway 57 for 22 miles, turning right at Dickensheet Road. Follow the road to Coolin for five miles, turning right onto East Lakeshore Road. The inn sits on the right side of the road with the RV park behind it.

GPS Coordinates: N 48° 28.480' W 116° 50.710'

Contact: The Inn at Priest Lake, 5310 Dickensheet Rd., Coolin, ID 83821, 208/443-2447, www.innatpriestlake.com.

19 DICKENSHEET

Scenic rating: 7

on Priest River in Priest Lake State Park

Located on Priest River between Binarch and Chipmunk Rapids, Dickensheet is the southernmost campground in the Priest Lake Area. The river, which you can float in a day, starts at the lake and ends at the town of Priest River at the Mudhole Campground and the confluence with the Pend Oreille

River. Sections of Class II and III rapids litter the river; Binarch and Eight Mile Rapids are the most hazardous in high water. The river has seven accesses: Outlet Campground, the put-in below the dam, Dickensheet, Saddlers Creek, and the take-out at Mudhole are just off Highway 57; White Tail Butte Landing and Big Creek are reached via the East Side and West Side Roads. A connector trail departs from camp, crossing the river on the old bridge, to link up with the West Priest Lake Trails. You can scout the rapids just below the camp on the Chipmunk Rapids National Recreation Trail at the Priest Lake Information Center, a five-minute drive away.

Tucked under cedar trees right next to the road and river, Dickensheet is a cramped, small campground, but perfect for those who float the river as you can launch right from the campground. The sites have little privacy. D2, D4, and D5 sit right on the river. Campsite 10 can handle larger tents. Only two pull-through sites are available.

Campsites, facilities: Dickensheet has 11 RV or tent campsites, suitable only for small RVs. Facilities include picnic tables, fire pits with grills, and a wheelchair-accessible vault toilet, but no drinking water. Boil or purify water taken from the river. Pack out your trash. At the south end of the campground, a small area for parking for floating or boat trailers is available. Leashed pets are permitted.

Reservations, fees: Reservations are accepted (888/922-6743, http://parksandrecreation. idaho.gov). Campsites cost $12, plus 6 percent Idaho tax. Cash or check. Extra vehicles cost $6. Open May–September.

Directions: From Priest River, drive 22 miles north on Highway 57. Turn right onto Dickensheet Road and drive one mile, crossing Priest River. The campground sits immediately on the right.

GPS Coordinates: N 48° 27.115' W 116° 53.989'

Contact: Priest Lake State Park, 314 Indian Creek Park Rd., Coolin, ID 83821, 208/443-2200, http://parksandrecreation.idaho.gov.

20 COPPER CREEK

Scenic rating: 7

on Moyie River in Idaho Panhandle National Forest

Sitting at 2,800 feet on the east bank of the Moyie River in the Purcell Mountains, Cooper Creek is a favorite for river rafters and kayakers. From the put-in at Copper Creek in the Idaho Panhandle National Forest to the take-out upstream of the Moyie Falls Dam is 18 miles. You can also float the three miles from the border to Copper Creek. From Copper Creek to Meadow Creek, the Class II rapids work for canoes, with shallow, rocky riffles. Below Meadow Creek, the river enters a canyon containing two Class III rapids at old Eileen Dam and Hole-in-the-Wall. These require technical finesse from river rafters and kayakers. About two miles from the campground, a 0.5-mile trail leads to Copper Falls, where water plunges 225 feet in two pitches over a rocky lip. In winter, the waterfall freezes to become a lure for ice climbers. The river also harbors rainbow, brook, and westslope cutthroat trout.

The campsites sit around one loop on a forested hillside above the Moyie River, but none with river frontage. The mixed forest offers partial shade and some privacy between sites. The sound of passing trains filters into the camp from across the river.

Campsites, facilities: The campground has 15 RV or tent campsites. Some of the campsites can handle RVs and trailer combinations up to 45 feet. Facilities include picnic tables, fire rings with grills, vault toilets, and drinking water. Pack out your trash. Leashed pets are permitted. A wheelchair-accessible toilet is available.

Reservations, fees: No reservations are accepted. Campsites cost $6 per night. Cash or check. Open mid-May–September.

Directions: From the Canadian border at Eastport, drive 0.8 mile south on Highway 95 to the campground sign and turn onto Copper Creek Road (Forest Road 2517). From Bonners Ferry, drive Highway 95 north for 29.8 miles to Forest Road 2517. Turn east onto the dirt, single-lane road and drive 0.6 mile to the campground entrance. The road has pullouts in case you meet an oncoming vehicle, and the signed campground entrance is on the right. GPS Coordinates: N 48° 59.123' W 116° 10.074'

Contact: Idaho Panhandle National Forest, Bonners Ferry Ranger District, 6286 Main St., Bonners Ferry, ID 83805, 208/267-5561, www.fs.fed.us/ipnf.

21 MEADOW CREEK

Scenic rating: 8

on Moyie River in Idaho Panhandle National Forest

Sitting at 2,350 feet in the Purcell Mountains on the west side of the Moyie River where it oxbows around the campground, Meadow Creek is favored by river rafters and kayakers in May and June. From the put-in at Copper Creek to the take-out upstream of the Moyie Falls Dam is 18 miles. The section from Copper Creek Campground to Meadow Creek is filled with Class II rapids, but skilled canoeists can navigate its smaller, rocky rapids. Below Meadow Creek, the river dives into a canyon with two Class III rapids—old Eileen Dam and Hole-in-the-Wall. These should be left to skilled whitewater river rafters and kayakers. For anglers, the river also harbors rainbow, brook, and westslope cutthroat trout, along with mountain whitefish. The 1.3-mile Queen Lake Trail (#152) leads to huckleberry-picking opportunities. Locate Forest Road 2542 to the trailhead about four miles south of the campground.

The campsites have gravel parking aprons and sit in a thick pine and birch forest around two loops surrounded by the river. Some of the campsites right on the river are walk-in sites best for tents. As water levels drop during the summer, sandbars open up the shoreline.

Campsites, facilities: The campground has 22 RV or tent campsites. Some of the campsites can handle RVs and trailer combinations up to 60 feet. Facilities include picnic tables, fire rings with grills, vault toilets, and drinking water. Pack out your trash. Leashed pets are permitted.

Reservations, fees: No reservations are accepted. Campsites cost $6. Cash or check. Open mid-May–September.

Directions: From Bonners Ferry, drive north three miles on Highway 95 to the junction with Highway 2. Turn right and drive 2.5 miles to Meadow Creek Road. Turn north and drive 10 miles. The signed campground entrance is on the right.

GPS Coordinates: N 48° 49.193' W 116° 8.889'

Contact: Idaho Panhandle National Forest, Bonners Ferry Ranger District, 6286 Main St., Bonners Ferry, ID 83805, 208/267-5561, www.fs.fed.us/ipnf.

22 TWIN RIVERS CANYON RESORT

Scenic rating: 8

on Highway 2 east of Bonners Ferry

At the confluence of the Kootenai and Moyie Rivers in the Purcell Mountains, Twin Rivers Canyon Resort has the advantages of two rivers on its borders. The Moyie River Overlook and bridge—one of the highest in the state—sits a half mile to the west. This bridge offers terrific views of the river and dam. River rafters and kayakers tackle the Moyie's rapids, and those looking to float the bigger, slower waters of the Kootenai can rent a raft for the day for self-guided floating. The resort offers a shuttle service to an upriver launching area where you can float back down to the park. Anglers go after 20-pound trout in the Kootenai, and you can fish along the banks of the Moyie.

Located across the Moyie River from a lumber yard, the resort has its own lake with a dock for swimming and fishing. Other activities include mini-golf, picnicking, a playground for small children, basketball/pickleball court, softball diamond, volleyball courts, and horseshoe pits. The shaded campsites are available in pull-through and back-in sites, but the tenting campsites line up nearest the Moyie River. Some trees offer partial shade to some sites, but many are open and sunny.

Campsites, facilities: The campground has 50 RV campsites that can fit large rigs, plus 16 tent campsites. Hookups include 30-amp electricity, water, and sewer. Facilities include picnic tables, fire rings, flush toilets, showers, a convenience store, a launderette, modem hookups, covered pavilion with gas barbecue, and boat ramp. Leashed pets are permitted.

Reservations, fees: Reservations are accepted. Hookups cost $28–30. Tent campsites cost $20. Cash or credit card. Open April–October.

Directions: From Moyie Springs, drive one mile east on Highway 2 and turn right onto Twin Rivers Road. From the border with Montana, drive nine miles west on Highway 2 and turn left. Follow the road as it switchbacks down to the river.

GPS Coordinates: N 48° 43.175' W 116° 11.069'

Contact: Twin Rivers Canyon Resort, 1823 Twin Rivers Rd., Moyie Springs, ID 83845, 208/267-5932 or 888/258-5952, www.twin-riversresort.com.

23 BLUE LAKE RV RESORT

Scenic rating: 6

on Highway 2/95 between Sandpoint and Bonners Ferry

Located in the Purcell Trench—the lowlands between the Purcell and Selkirk Mountains—Blue Lake is a tiny, spring-fed lake in a private resort. New owners took over the 20-acre Blue

Lake RV Resort and renovated the campground in 2009. They have upgraded the resort to include 11 big-rig sites, seven supersites with 50 and 100 amps, plus concrete patios, boutique camping in canvas pole tents, a lakeside deck and tiered amphitheater, wood-fired sauna, and a new sport dock on the lake.

The small lake has a dock for swimming and fishing for rainbow trout, catfish, and brown bluegill, and the resort permits nonmotorized boats on the lake. A gravel road loops through the grassy, treed campground; parking pads are gravel. Some sites garner partial shade from tall conifers, but they are close together; others sit in full sun. Many of the big-rig sites have views of the lake. Tent campsites tuck into the trees right on the lake.

Campsites, facilities: The campground has 36 RV campsites. Big-rig sites can accommodate a maximum RV length of 60 feet. Hookups are available for water, sewer, and electricity up to 200 amps at extended stay sites. The campground also has six tent campsites. Facilities include picnic table, fire rings, flush toilets, showers, wireless Internet, a launderette, kayak and canoe rentals, propane and firewood for sale, an off-leash pet run, and a disposal station. The resort also rents boutique pole tents and cabins. Two leashed pets are permitted; inquire about breeds not allowed. A wheelchair-accessible toilet is available.

Reservations, fees: Reservations are accepted. Hookups cost $27–45. Tent campsites cost $16–20. Rates are for two adults and two children. Extra people cost $3–5. Extra vehicles and boats cost $5. Open April–October.

Directions: From Sandpoint, drive north on Highway 95 for 22 miles to milepost 498. Turn left onto Blue Lake Road across the railroad. From Bonners Ferry, drive 5.5 south on Highway 95 to reach Blue Lake Road. Drive 0.25 mile to the south end of the lake. GPS Coordinates: N 48° 34.877' W 116° 23.290'

Contact: Blue Lake Resort RV Park, 242 Blue Lake Rd., Naples, ID 83847, 208/946-3361, www.bluelakervresort.com.

24 ALBENI COVE RECREATION AREA

Scenic rating: 7

on Pend Oreille River west of Sandpoint

BEST (

At the Idaho-Washington border, the Pend Oreille River is dammed into a slow-moving lake by Albeni Falls Dam. Upstream from the dam, Albeni Cove Recreation Area sits where high water can close the boat ramp and swim beach during May and June. The Albeni Falls Dam Visitor Center has exhibits on history and natural history, plus offers tours of the dam daily Memorial Day to Labor Day from the visitors center located on Highway 2 two miles east of Newport, Washington, and 3.7 miles west of Priest River. On opposite sides of the river, the visitor centers sits on the north and Albeni Cove on the south. To get between the two, you must drive around through Newport, Washington. The cove is home to bald eagles, ospreys, bears, deer, skunks, and porcupines.

Albeni Cove is the smallest of the Pend Oreille River campgrounds. It tucks its small campsites on a shady, east-facing hillside with built-up platforms among firs, cedars, and pines overlooking the cove. Two large sandy spits create the cove and are great places to explore.

Campsites, facilities: Albeni Cove has 14 RV or tent campsites. RVs must be 30 feet or shorter. Facilities include picnic tables, fire rings with grills, flush toilets, showers, a boat ramp, a swimming beach, drinking water, and interpretive programs. Leashed pets are permitted. A wheelchair-accessible toilet is available.

Reservations, fees: Reservations are accepted (877/444-6777, www.recreation.gov). Campsites cost $16 per night. The fee covers one vehicle plus a trailer or up to two tents. Each site can hold a maximum of eight people. An extra vehicle costs $10. Open mid-May–early September.

Directions: From Priest River, drive six miles

west, crossing into Washington and continuing two miles across the Pend Oreille River to Newport, Washington. Turn south onto State Avenue, crossing on an overpass over the railroad tracks, and then left onto 4th Street. Follow it as it turns into Albeni Cove Road. The pavement becomes a rough dirt road as it crosses back into Idaho. Stay on it, veering left at the fork in the road. At the power lines the road becomes paved again. Follow it into the campground.

GPS Coordinates: N 48° 10.562' W 116° 59.933'

Contact: Army Corps of Engineers, 2376 E. Hwy. 2, Oldtown, ID 83882, 208/437-3133.

25 PRIEST RIVER RECREATION AREA (MUDHOLE)

Scenic rating: 6

on Pend Oreille River west of Sandpoint

BEST (

Located on the east edge of the town of Priest River, the Priest River Recreation Area earned a nickname—the Mudhole—for its large beach in a protected bay where Priest River meets the Pend Oreille River. However, the water isn't muddy. The water runs clear most of the year, and the fine sand beach enlarges as water levels drop in August. Hot summer days see scads of day-use visitors for swimming, boating, and fishing. The adjacent Priest River Wildlife Area adds bird-watching—especially for ospreys, songbirds, and waterfowl. The nine-hole Ranch Club Golf Course sits two miles west, as do grocery stores and gas. Anglers and boaters head out on both rivers; kayakers and canoeists enjoy the slough along the Pend Oreille River southeast of the campground. The campground is also the last take-out for those rafting or kayaking the white water on Priest River.

Tucked under shady pines and hemlocks,

the campground squeezes in between the highway and the railroad, so be ready for some noise rather than hoping for the quiet of wilderness. The campground has a large, grassy baseball/soccer field. Sites 10–13 sit closest to the river. Campsites 12 and 13 also are on a side spur from the one main campground loop. The entrance gate is locked 10 P.M.–7 A.M. On weekends and holidays, plan on a noon arrival for this popular campground.

Campsites, facilities: The campground has 20 RV or tent campsites. RVs are limited to 35 feet. Facilities include picnic tables, fire rings with grills, flush toilets, showers, drinking water, garbage service, a disposal station, camp hosts, a boat ramp, and a swimming beach. Leashed pets are permitted. A wheelchair-accessible toilet is available.

Reservations, fees: Reservations are available for all of the sites (877/444-6777, www.recreation.gov). Campsites cost $16. The fee covers one vehicle plus a trailer or two tents. Up to eight people are permitted per site. An extra vehicle costs $10. Open mid-May–late September.

Directions: From the town of Priest River, drive one mile east on Highway 2, crossing Priest River. The campground is on the right. From Sandpoint, you'll reach the campground entrance in 21 miles on Highway 2.

GPS Coordinates: N 48° 10.722' W 116° 53.408'

Contact: Army Corps of Engineers, 2376 E. Hwy. 2, Oldtown, ID 83822, 208/437-3133.

26 RILEY CREEK RECREATION AREA

Scenic rating: 7

on Pend Oreille River west of Sandpoint

Of the campgrounds located on the Pend Oreille River, Riley Creek is the largest, tucked at the base of the Selkirk Mountain foothills along Highway 2. With water on three sides, Riley Creek sits at the end of a peninsula in the Pend Oreille River, facing west, making it a prime location for boating, personal watercraft riding, fishing, hiking, bicycling, and swimming. However, it is also adjacent to waterfront homes. A multi-lane cement boat ramp, dock, boat basin for mooring, and parking for boat trailers aid those heading out on the water. A bicycling and hiking trail also loops through the recreation area, and a large grassy field is available for Frisbee, football, and soccer games.

Campsites cluster around two loops under a thick evergreen canopy for shade. Sites 12, 13, 15, 17, 19, 20, 21, 43, 47, 48, and 50 sit closest to the water. Campsites are close enough together that you can see neighboring campers, but tree trunks help to act as privacy shields. The campground locks the park gates 10 P.M.– 7 A.M. for security. Railroad and highway noise creeps into the campground after it quiets at night. Riley Creek is popular, requiring a noon arrival on weekends and holidays.

Campsites, facilities: The campground has 67 RV or tent campsites; some can fit vehicles up to 40 feet. Hookups include water and electricity up to 50 amps. Facilities include picnic tables, fire rings with grills, flush toilets, showers, a disposal station, a boat launch, garbage service, horseshoe pits, firewood for sale, amphitheater programs, camp hosts, and a swimming beach. Leashed pets are permitted. A wheelchair-accessible toilet is available.

Reservations, fees: Reservations are accepted (877/444-6777, www.recreation.gov). Campsites cost $16 per night. The fee covers one vehicle plus a trailer or up to two tents and eight people. An extra vehicle costs $10. Cash or check. Open mid-May–early September.

Directions: From Priest River, go eight miles east on Highway 2. From Sandpoint, drive 14 miles west on Highway 2. In Laclede, turn south onto Laclede Ferry Road for 0.4 mile. Then turn right onto Riley Creek Park Road for 0.9 mile. The entrance is on the right.

GPS Coordinates: N 48° 9.584' W 116° 46.343'
Contact: Army Corps of Engineers, 2376 E. Hwy. 2, Oldtown, ID 83822, 208/437-3133.

27 SPRINGY POINT RECREATION AREA

🚴 ⛴ 🏊 🚤 🎣 🐕 ♿ 🚐 ⛺

Scenic rating: 6

west of Sandpoint on Lake Pend Oreille

On Lake Pend Oreille's west arm, which becomes the Pend Oreille River, Springy Point is the only public campground on the south side of the river. Its north-facing beach and small bay are protected by Springy Point. With its location off the main lake, the bay is also more protected than the open, windy expanses on the main part of Lake Pend Oreille. The paved access road passes large waterfront homes and summer cabins en route to the campground—indicative of the number of boaters you'll encounter in the area. A 10-minute drive puts you right in downtown Sandpoint for restaurants, gas, groceries, and shopping.

The campground itself squeezes onto a heavily treed slope. Two paved campground loops curve through narrow openings between the trees. Only smaller RVs and trailers can fit through these, and most of the parking pads are fairly small. Even though underbrush provides fences between some of the campsites, most are crammed in close together with little privacy from each other. In the Birch loop, campsites 23 and 24 sit right above the boat ramp area, with log rails keeping campers from falling down the steep hill. In Cedar loop, campsites 30, 33, and 35 are closest to the swimming beach. These campsites also have snippets of lake views through the trees. The sandy beach is divided into two sections—the buoyed swimming beach reached by a trail and the boat launch area with a small cement ramp and dock.

Campsites, facilities: The campground has 40 RV or tent campsites that can fit RVs up to 35 feet. Facilities includes picnic tables, fire rings with grills, flush toilets, showers, drinking water, a disposal station, garbage service, a campground host, a boat ramp, boat trailer parking, and a swimming beach. Leashed pets are permitted. A wheelchair-accessible toilet is available.

Reservations, fees: No reservations are accepted. A campsite costs $16 for one vehicle plus a trailer or up to two tents and eight people. An extra vehicle costs $10. Cash or check. Open mid-May–early October.

Directions: From Sandpoint, go 1.5 miles south on Highway 95 and turn right onto Lakeshore Drive for three miles. The entrance sits on the right.

GPS Coordinates: N 48° 14.164' W 116° 35.207'

Contact: Army Corps of Engineers, 2376 E. Hwy. 2, Oldtown, ID 83882, 208/437-3133.

28 EDGEWATER RESORT

Scenic rating: 6

in Sandpoint

The Edgewater Resort is actually a Best Western hotel with a parking lot that has RV hookups. While it doesn't have the feel of a campground, those looking to be right in the heart of downtown Sandpoint will find it convenient. The resort is a five-minute walk from downtown Sandpoint restaurants, shopping, and art galleries. (Sandpoint has an art walk with 20 shops featuring regional artists.) A pedestrian walking bridge crosses Sand Creek into town. City Beach sits adjacent to the resort and has two boat launch ramps, sand volleyball courts, horseshoe pits, swimming areas with lifeguards, picnic tables, pedestal barbecues, a basketball court, two tennis courts, restrooms, a playground, and food concessions. A bicycling

and walking path circles the perimeter of the beach and links up with a path running across the bridge over Lake Pend Oreille's west arm. A marina sits on the east side of the resort, and businesses in town offer boat and Jet Ski rentals, parasailing, scuba diving, and scenic cruises. The nine-hole Elks Golf Club sits on Highway 200 on the east side of town.

The campground is a parking lot for RVs, rather than a traditional campground. It sits below the train tracks. Bring earplugs, for nearly 40 trains a day rumble through here. Those staying in the RV parking lot have access to amenities in the hotel—indoor swimming pool, hot tub, and fitness center. The hotel also has a restaurant.

Campsites, facilities: The resort has 20 RV parking stalls for large RVs. Hookups include sewer, water, and electricity. Facilities include cable TV hookup, a disposal station, and wireless Internet. Flush toilets and showers are in the hotel.

Reservations, fees: Reservations are accepted. Campsites cost $15–50. Open year-round.

Directions: In downtown Sandpoint, turn south at Bridge Street. After crossing through the railroad underpass, turn left into the hotel parking lot.

GPS Coordinates: N 48° 16.484' W 116° 32.661'

Contact: Edgewater Resort, 56 Bridge St., Sandpoint, ID 83809, 208/263-3194 or 800/635-2534, www.bestwestern.com.

29 SAM OWEN RECREATION AREA

Scenic rating: 8

on Lake Pend Oreille's north shore on the David Thompson Game Preserve

BEST (

Sitting on the north shore of Lake Pend Oreille two miles east of Hope, Sam Owen Recreation Area is on the David Thompson Game Preserve in Idaho Panhandle National Forest.

Drive slowly to avoid deer. From the campground, interpretive trails lead to the day-use area and boat-launch area. The boat ramp allows launching onto the lake for boating, waterskiing, and fishing for monster kamloops rainbow trout. Hiking and mountain biking are available on trails outside of Hope; those looking for a big view of the lake should climb the 7,009-foot Scotchman Peak. A three-mile steep ascent leads to its summit—the tallest in the area—where mountain goats live. It's the site of an old lookout.

In 2009, the campground renovated its water system. The campsites are tucked back under a thick canopy of pines, cedars, and firs back from the water. A paved road winds through the campground, but the parking aprons are gravel. Very little underbrush separates the campsites; however, they are set apart from each other, and some of the large old-growth trunks form barriers between the sites. The campsites surround four loops, with Skipping Stone loop (sites 29–43) the closest to the beach. Red Sun loop sits behind the day-use area and boat ramp. Dancing Shadow and Scented Leaf loop are farther back uphill in the woods.

Campsites, facilities: The campground has 81 RV or tent campsites. The maximum RV length is 36 feet. Facilities include picnic tables, fire rings with grills, drinking water, flush toilets, a disposal station, camp hosts, firewood for sale, an amphitheater for naturalist programs, a swimming beach, and a boat launch. Leashed pets are permitted. A wheelchair-accessible toilet is available.

Reservations, fees: Reservations are accepted (877/444-6777, www.recreation.gov). Premium sites closer to the lake cost $18. All others cost $16. An extra vehicle costs $7. Day use or boat launching costs $7. Cash or check. Open May–September.

Directions: From Hope, drive two miles east on Highway 200 and turn right onto Peninsula Road. Drive 0.8 mile, swinging left at the fork, and turn right onto Sam Owen Road. GPS Coordinates: N 48° 13.125' W 116° 17.113'

Contact: Idaho Panhandle National Forest, Sandpoint Ranger District, 1500 Hwy. 2, Sandpoint, ID 83864, 208/263-5111, www.fs.fed.us/ipnf.

30 ISLAND VIEW RESORT

Scenic rating: 8

on Lake Pend Oreille's north shore on the David Thompson Game Preserve

East of both Sandpoint and Hope on the north shore of Lake Pend Oreille, Island View Resort is aptly named, for it looks out on a few of the northern islands, the nearest of which is Memaloose Island. The campground sits on the David Thompson Game Preserve: deer, ospreys, and sometimes bald eagles are common sights. Because of the game preserve, drive slowly on the paved access road.

The office sits right on the waterfront, with a handful of pull-in campsites for RVs on both sides. These spots have prime lake views; however, they are virtually parking stalls perpendicular to the shore and just inches from each other. All of the other sites are across the street in a grassy setting under firs and pines with more room. The open sites afford little privacy and offer a bucolic setting among the nearby small farms. The resort has a small marina formed by a narrow, rocky, treed reef just offshore. A small, primitive boat launch sits just east of the resort. Instead of individual campsite fire rings, a community fire pit with benches is available in the grass near the beach. Some long-term residents also stay here.

Campsites, facilities: The campground has 61 RV campsites that can fit trailer combinations up to 60 feet. Hookups include water, sewer, and electricity. Facilities include picnic tables, flush toilets, showers, a community fire pit, a launderette, a store, cable TV hookups, and propane gas. Leashed pets are permitted.

Reservations, fees: Reservations are accepted. Hookups cost $30. Open year-round.

Directions: From Hope, drive two miles east on Highway 200 and turn right onto Peninsula Road. Drive 1.7 miles, swinging left at the fork. Locate the campground just east of Sunray Drive.

GPS Coordinates: N 48° 12.555' W 116° 17.284'

Contact: Island View Resort, 1767 Peninsula Rd., Hope, ID 83836, 208/264-5509.

31 RIVER LAKE RV PARK

Scenic rating: 6

on the Clark Fork River east of Sandpoint

Drive slowly on the access road that leads to this RV campground tucked on the south shore of the Clark Fork River. The bucolic farm area lends itself to horseback riding and pleasant bike tours. The campground appeals to anglers because it sits right on the Clark Fork River, where you can fish for brown, bull, cutthroat, and rainbow trout. The river slows to a crawl here. You can get updates on fishing from the owners.

The small, cramped campground offers views of the low, forested mountains to the north. Due to its proximity to the railroad tracks, the highway across the river, and a private airstrip, be prepared for noise. While the road to the campground is paved, the campground road is gravel. All the sites are grassy and open with no privacy, but perimeter shade trees cool the area. Some campers are seasonal residents, taking the few prime spots on the river, but the riverfront has room to pull up a chair to sit in the evening. The campground has a fenced area for dogs.

Campsites, facilities: There are 31 RV campsites with full hookups that can fit RVs up to 40 feet. Facilities include flush toilets, showers, a launderette, a disposal station, and dock. Pets are permitted.

Reservations, fees: Reservations are accepted. Campsites cost $18–20. Open May–September.

Directions: From Sandpoint, go 27 miles east on Highway 200 to Clark Fork. From Clark Fork, go south for two miles on Stephen Road and across the railroad tracks and the Clark Fork River. The road becomes River Road. Turn left at River Lake Drive. A steep climb and drop crosses the railroad tracks again. Take another left at the T intersection. The campground is 0.1 mile ahead on the right.

GPS Coordinates: N 48° 7.536' W 116° 9.732'

Contact: River Lake RV Park, 145 N. River Lake Rd., Clark Fork, ID 83811, 208/266-1115.

32 WHISKEY ROCK

Scenic rating: 7

on Lake Pend Oreille's east shore

In a remote location on Lake Pend Oreille's east side, Whiskey Rock Campground demands a tough drive to get there. Pack supplies and gas up; you won't find convenience stores in the neighborhood. Even though you'll only be driving 30 miles from Clark Fork, the dirt road, which is littered with potholes, steep drops, curves, and switchbacks, requires over an hour to drive. Smaller RVs can handle the rugged road after it dries out in late spring. Some campers boat across the lake to reach the campground, launching from Garfield Bay on the west side about 13 miles to the north. While the legends about Whiskey Rock are many—a transfer point for rum runners, a maroon site for three days for a pair of pioneers with only a jug of whiskey—the area today holds a few lodges and summer homes. Hiking and mountain-biking are available on Packsaddle Mountain.

Located at the base of Packsaddle, the largest mountain surrounding Lake Pend Oreille, the partially forested campground has three campsites right on the lake. The others sit back in the woods. From the campground, trails lead to the water, the day-use picnic area with a sandy beach for swimming, viewpoints of the lake, and a cove. A boat ramp and large dock are also available for boaters and anglers. Because of the area's location on the lake, Whiskey Rock can get hammered by winds. Secure all boats overnight.

Campsites, facilities: The campground has nine RV or tent campsites that can fit RVs only up to 16 feet. Facilities include picnic tables, fire rings with grills, vault toilets, and drinking water. Pack out your trash. Leashed pets are permitted.

Reservations, fees: No reservations are accepted, and camping is free. Open mid-May–September.

Directions: From Sandpoint, drive 27 miles east on Highway 200 to Clark Fork. Turn right onto Stephen Road and drive across the Clark Fork River. Take the first right at the Sportsman Access sign and follow Forest Road 278 (also called Johnson Creek Road) for 2.5 miles. Turn right onto the dirt road to reach the dock and fishing access. Boaters should head to Garfield Bay. Drive south out of Sandpoint on Highway 95 for 5.3 miles. Turn left at Sagle Road and drive 7.1 miles. At the fork, veer right onto Garfield Bay Road and drive 1.2 miles to the road's end.

GPS Coordinates: N 48° 3.049' W 116° 27.345'

Contact: Idaho Panhandle National Forest, Sandpoint Ranger District, 1500 Hwy. 2, Sandpoint, ID 83864, 208/263-5111, www.fs.fed.us/ipnf.

33 ROUND LAKE STATE PARK

Scenic rating: 6

south of Sandpoint

South of Sandpoint at the 142-acre Round Lake State Park, a small 58-acre lake is the remnant of a depression made by ice age glaciers chewing on the landscape. Fed by Cocolalla Creek, the lake is named appropriately, for it is round. The shallow lake—37 feet at its deepest point—warms up much more than its larger neighbor, Lake Pend Oreille, making it a favorite for swimming. A two-mile nature trail tours the lake. Ringed with grasses and water lilies, the lake chimes with bullfrog choruses in the evening, and it attracts songbirds, herons, deer, raccoons, and porcupines. For anglers, it is also home to brook trout, largemouth bass, pumpkinseed sunfish, yellow perch, and black crappie. Only electric boats and hand-powered watercraft are permitted. In winter, the lake offers ice fishing, ice skating, and cross-country skiing. The ski and snowshoe trail converts to a hiking and mountain-biking trail in summer.

The campground, with its narrow, looping road, sits on the north side of the lake. Campsites cluster under the shade of huge cedars, hemlocks, and Douglas firs. Filtered sunlight reaches the campsite floors, which are covered with forest duff and cones. The dirt back-in campsites are very close together with little underbrush; you can see several other campsites.

Campsites, facilities: The campground has 51 RV or tent campsites. RVs are limited to 24 feet in length. Facilities includes picnic tables, fire rings, flush toilets, showers, drinking water, a disposal station, a boat ramp and dock, canoe rentals, guided walks, educational campfire programs, horseshoes, firewood for sale, and a swimming beach. Leashed pets are permitted. A wheelchair-accessible toilet is available.

Reservations, fees: Reservations are available for mid-May–early September (888/922-6743, http://parksandrecreation.idaho.gov). Campsites cost $12 per night, plus 6 percent Idaho sales tax. Cash or check. Open year-round.

Directions: From Sandpoint drive 10 miles south on Highway 95, or from Coeur d'Alene go north on Highway 95 approximately 34 miles. Turn west onto Dufort Road, driving two miles to the campground, on the south side of the road.

GPS Coordinates: N 48° 9.913' W 116° 38.246'

Contact: Round Lake State Park, 1880 W. Dufort Rd., Sagle, ID 83860, 208/263-3489, http://parksandrecreation.idaho.gov.

34 SILVERWOOD THEME PARK

Scenic rating: 5

on Highway 95 north of Coeur d'Alene

The largest theme park in the Northern Rockies, Silverwood Theme Park and Boulder Beach sits 15 minutes north of Coeur d'Alene. Campers who stay at the RV park can purchase discounted tickets for the theme park and beach. The theme park has 65 rides, including monster roller coasters and whitewater river splash rides. Its other attractions include a 1915 steam engine train, a Victorian village of restaurants and souvenir shops, magic and ice shows, and climbing trees. Boulder Beach features water slides, wave pools, springs, creeks, and a cabana island.

The paved highway accesses the gravel roads through the campground. With gravel parking pads, campsites sprawl throughout the park-like grassy grounds under a thick, shady canopy of pines and firs. The open area beneath the canopy affords little privacy from neighbors. Loops A, B, C, and D sit farthest away from the highway, while loops E, F, and sites 55–70 on the main loop are adjacent to the highway. The campground connects to the theme park via a pedestrian tunnel and also has an overflow camping area minus hookups. You can hear the highway, railroad, and theme park in the campground.

Campsites, facilities: The campground has 126 RV or tent campsites that can fit large RVs. Hookups are available for water, sewer, and electricity. Facilities include picnic tables, flush toilets, showers, drinking water, a launderette, propane, volleyball courts, horseshoes, and a camp store. Fires are not permitted. Each campsite is allowed one RV or one to two tents. Leashed pets are permitted in the campground, but not in the theme park.

Reservations, fees: Reservations are accepted. Campsites cost $34, plus 6 percent Idaho tax. Open daily June–early September. Open weekends and holidays in May and early September–October. Note: Boulder Beach is only open June–early September.

Directions: From I-90 in Coeur d'Alene, take exit 12. Drive north on Highway 95 for 15 miles. The entrance to the campground is on the east side of the highway opposite the theme park to the west.

GPS Coordinates: N 47° 54.465' W 116° 42.048'

Contact: Silverwood Theme Park and Boulder Beach, 27843 N. Hwy. 95, Athol, ID 93801, 208/683-3400, www.silverwoodthemepark.com.

35 ALPINE COUNTRY RV PARK

Scenic rating: 4

on Highway 95 north of Coeur d'Alene

Located 10 miles north of Coeur d'Alene, this campground works for Highway 95 travelers looking to be out of the I-90 corridor bustle between Post Falls and Coeur d'Alene. The campground is seven miles south of Silverwood Theme Park. It is not a destination in itself, but it can provide overflow camping for Silverwood or even Farragut State Park. Recent highway reconstruction added a newly paved bike trail adjacent to the road.

The campground sits off the four-lane highway behind a gas station and minimart. Although the store blocks the campground from the highway, some traffic noise creeps in, especially from the trains, which toot their horns as they pass the road crossing. Bring earplugs if you're a light sleeper. The campground's gravel road loops through a parked-out, grassy, no privacy setting with firs and willows for shade. The tent-only sites (1–6) sit in their own loop adjacent to a large pet area—both separated from the RV sites.

Campsites, facilities: The campground has 19 RV campsites with pull-through sites that can accommodate slide-out big rigs up to 70 feet long. Hookups for water, sewer, and electricity are available. One loop has six tent campsites. Facilities include picnic tables, pedestal grills, flush toilets, showers, drinking water, modem hookups, and a minimart. Leashed pets are permitted. A wheelchair-accessible toilet is available.

Reservations, fees: Reservations are accepted. Campsites cost $24–28. Open early spring–late fall.

Directions: From I-90 in Coeur d'Alene, take exit 12 and head north on Highway 95 for 10 miles. The store and campground sit on the east side of the highway.

GPS Coordinates: N 47° 49.785' W 116° 46.740'

Contact: Alpine Country Store and RV Park, 17568 N. Hwy. 95, Hayden Lake, ID 83835, 208/772-4305.

36 FARRAGUT STATE PARK

Scenic rating: 7

north of Coeur d'Alene on Lake Pend Oreille's south end

Farragut State Park, which used to be the world's second largest naval training station, is now a 4,000-acre park covering a huge knoll between two bays at the southwest end of Lake Pend Oreille. It features several campgrounds, swimming, a boat launch, fishing, disc golf courses, an orienteering course, a model airplane field, sand volleyball courts, horseshoes, and 40 miles of trails for hiking, mountain biking, and horseback riding.

Campsites sit on slopes well above the shore. Some sites are open and sunny; others tuck under partial mixed conifer shade. All are close together. Gilmore, Snowberry, Redtail, and Nighthawk areas contain serviced RV sites. Whitetail has only tent sites. The Ward Primitive area (no services, tables, or fires) permits self-contained RVs to park for the night; tents are not permitted. Snowberry and Whitetail sit nearest the boat launch, disc golf courses, and a disposal station. Gilmore is closer to the visitors center and Beaver Bay Beach. The park also has a Corral campsite section, for those traveling with stock, and three additional large, group camping areas.

Campsites, facilities: The park has 88 RV campsites, some that can hold a maximum vehicle length of 60 feet. Hookups are available for water and electricity. The park also has 60 tent campsites with tent pads. Facilities include picnic tables, fire rings, flush toilets, drinking water, showers, campground hosts, a boat ramp, and a disposal station. Companion sites that permit more than eight people and double the equipment are also available. Leashed pets are permitted. A wheelchair-accessible toilet is available.

Reservations, fees: Reservations are accepted (888/922-6743, http://parksandrecreation. idaho.gov). RV hookup sites cost $20–33. Tent campsites cost $12–22. RV camping in the Ward Primitive area costs $9. Cash, check, or credit card. The park is open all year with camping available late March–early November, but water is available only mid-April–mid-October.

Directions: Drive Highway 95 to Athol, about 15 minutes north of Coeur d'Alene. From Athol, turn east onto Highway 54 and drive four miles to the park entrance sign. Drive 0.2 mile farther to reach the visitors center for camper registration. The visitors center is on the south side of the road.

GPS Coordinates for Camper Registration: N 47° 57.097' W 116° 36.122'
Contact: Farragut State Park, 13550 E. Hwy. 54, Athol, ID 83801, 208/683-2425, http://parksandrecreation.idaho.gov.

37 BLACKWELL ISLAND RV RESORT

Scenic rating: 4

in Coeur d'Alene on the Spokane River

Located in Coeur d'Alene on the Spokane River, this RV-only campground is convenient for those traveling I-90 and needing to pop off the freeway for the night. Its location on the Spokane River gives boating access to Lake Coeur d'Alene, but the area is more protected than the open water of the lake. The campground has 500 feet of sand and pebble beach for swimming. A boat launch accesses the river or lake for fishing, waterskiing, and sightseeing. Across the river, the paved 24-mile North Idaho Centennial Trail for walkers and bicyclists parallels the river to the Washington border and also connects in 1.5 miles with downtown Coeur d'Alene. Downtown has golfing (including a floating green), dining, shopping, art walks, boat cruises, parasailing, and live theater concerts. Cedars Floating Restaurant sits across the river from the campground.

A paved road weaves through the sunny, open campground, which is landscaped with tiny grassy islands, young trees, and gravel parking pads. The open sites yield no privacy, and while the campground overlooks the Spokane River, it also views industrial and residential areas. For large RVs, 140 sites are pull-throughs—some up to 40 feet wide to accommodate slide-outs. You'll hear noise from the adjacent highway and the railroad tracks across the river. Bring earplugs if you are a light sleeper. Sites 113–122 overlook the beach and river.

Campsites, facilities: The campground has 182 RV campsites, some that can fit RVs up to 60 feet. Hookups are available for water, sewer, electricity up to 50 amps, and cable TV. Facilities include flush toilets, showers, wireless Internet, modem dataports, a launderette, propane, a minimart, a game room, a boat launch and moorage, 18-foot and 24-foot pontoon rental, canoes, water bike rentals, a playground, dog walk and swim areas, and a swimming beach. Leashed pets are permitted. A wheelchair-accessible toilet is available.

Reservations, fees: Reservations are accepted. Campsites cost $35–48, plus 6 percent Idaho tax. Cash or credit card. Open April–mid-October.

Directions: From I-90 in Coeur d'Alene, take exit 12. Drive south on Highway 95 for 1.5 miles, driving over the Spokane River. Turn east onto Marina Drive and take the first left to reach the park entrance on the left.

GPS Coordinates: N 47° 40.844' W 116° 48.160'

Contact: Blackwell Island RV Park, 800 S. Marina Dr., Coeur d'Alene, ID 83814, 208/665-1300 or 888/571-2900, www.idahorvpark.com.

38 WOLF LODGE

Scenic rating: 6

adjacent to I-90 east of Lake Coeur d'Alene

Eight miles east of Coeur d'Alene in the Coeur d'Alene Mountains on the edge of Idaho Panhandle National Forest, Wolf Lodge Campground sits adjacent to I-90. A public boat launch is about two miles west. The paved, 24-mile North Idaho Centennial Trail for walking and bicycling along the lake starts at Higgens Point, about four miles to the west. You can swim in the campground creek or rent canoes ($5/hour) to paddle it, but fishing is not permitted since it is a spawning creek.

The campground also sponsors a nightly group campfire and outdoor movie.

The campground sits in a grassy meadow on a creek with trees for shade, but without underbrush, the sites have little privacy from each other. By midsummer, the creek shrinks down considerably. Some of the campsites are open with clear shots of the sky for satellite reception, and the proximity to the freeway adds traffic noise. For RV sites, one RV and one towed vehicle are permitted; all other vehicles (boats, trailers, extra cars) must be parked for a fee in the overflow parking area. Tent sites 1–16 and 31–33 border the creek.

Campsites, facilities: The campground has 57 RV campsites, some that can fit large RVs. Hookups include water, sewer, and electricity up to 50 amps. The campground also has 34 tent campsites. Facilities include picnic tables, fire rings, flush toilets, showers, volleyball, badminton, horseshoes, shuffleboard, a launderette, a camp store, three-wheeled bike and canoe rentals, wireless Internet, a large group tenting site, and several cabins. Six people are permitted per site. Leashed pets are permitted. A wheelchair-accessible toilet is available.

Reservations, fees: Reservations are accepted. Sites with hookups cost $28–35. Tent sites cost $22. Rates are based on two people; each additional person costs $3. Extra vehicles, boats, and trailers cost $10. Cabins run $50–115. Cash or credit card. Open mid-May–September.

Directions: From I-90 at the east end of Lake Coeur d'Alene, take Exit 22. Drive to the freeway's north side and turn east onto Frontage Road for 1.75 miles, passing the Wolf Lodge Inn and Steakhouse. The campground entrance is on the left and crosses over the creek.

GPS Coordinates: N 47° 37.829' W 116° 36.982'

Contact: Wolf Lodge Campground, 12329 E. Frontage Rd., Coeur d'Alene, ID 83814, 866/664-2812 or 208/664-2812, www.wolflodgervcampground.com.

39 LAKE COEUR D'ALENE CAMPING RESORT

Scenic rating: 6

on Lake Coeur d'Alene east of downtown Coeur d'Alene

Lake Coeur d'Alene Camping Resort sits on the east end of Lake Coeur d'Alene's Wolf Lodge Bay at 2,650 feet in the Coeur d'Alene Mountains. Adjoining Lake Coeur d'Alene via no-wake zone wetland ponds and a river, this camping resort can be a destination by itself. Launch small, hand-carried watercraft, canoes, and kayaks from the campground's ramp, but for larger boats, a public boat ramp sits 0.5 mile west. The campground also rents paddleboats, canoes, and powerboats.

The campground has two parts, split by the access road—a primitive tent section that sprawls adjacent to the water, and an RV section that climbs up the terraced slope that houses the swimming pool, adults-only hot tubs, and showers. The grassy, open tent sites are partly shaded by willows and divided by thigh-high rail fences. A few walk-in tent sites sit on peninsulas right on the water. The RV terraces are both back-in and pull-through; some are quite narrow, cramming in two RVs. The campground is close enough to the freeway to hear truck noise.

Campsites, facilities: The campground has 70 RV campsites, some fitting vehicles up to 45 feet. Hookups include water, sewer, and electricity up to 50 amps. The tenting area has 25 tent campsites. Facilities include picnic tables, fire barrels, flush toilets, showers, wireless Internet, cable TV hookups, camping cabins, drinking water, a disposal station, a launderette, propane, a camp store, a playground, a swimming pool, and hot tubs. Leashed pets are permitted in the RV campsites, but not tent campsites.

Reservations, fees: Reservations are accepted. Hookups run $32–43. Tent sites cost $27–30. Six people are permitted in each site. Rates are based on two people; each additional person costs $3. Boat mooring and extra vehicles cost $10 per night. Cash or credit card. Open April–September.

Directions: From I-90 east of Coeur d'Alene, take Exit 22. Turn south for 0.5 mile, passing over the wetlands and the lake. Take the first left onto E. Wolf Lodge Bay Road. Drive 0.2 mile to the campground, which spans both sides of the road. Find the office on the uphill side of road.

GPS Coordinates: N 47° 37.163' W 116° 38.629'

Contact: Lake Coeur d'Alene Camping Resort, 10588 E. Wolf Lodge Bay Rd., Coeur d'Alene, ID 83814, 208/664-4771 or 888/664-4471, www.campcda.com.

40 BEAUTY CREEK

Scenic rating: 7

on Coeur d'Alene Lake's east side in Idaho Panhandle National Forest

Located on Coeur d'Alene Lake's east side on Beauty Creek rather than on the lake, the campground squeezes in between the tall, forested ridges of the Coeur d'Alene Mountains flanking Beauty Bay. The Mineral Ridge public boat launch is less than two miles east. This campground sits along the Lake Coeur d'Alene Scenic Byway, a slow, curvy paved road touring the lake's east side. Bicyclists on the byway need to watch for narrow-to-nonexistent shoulders. From the campground, a trail climbs the ridge above, but trees block much of the views. To hike an interpretive trail with 22 educational stations, take the 3.3-mile-long trail that climbs through the Mineral Ridge Scenic Area; the national recreation trailhead is 0.1 mile north of the campground turnoff. Another trail, about 2.5 miles south on the scenic byway after a steep, twisting ascent uphill, loops 0.5 mile through the Beauty Bay Recreation Area for a soaring lake view.

Snuggled into the mixed forest along Beauty Creek, the quiet campground has two types of campsites. Those at the front sit in open grassy sites that have little privacy from each other. Due to more trees and thick underbrush, the sites at the back half are more secluded—particularly sites 14, 16, 17, 18, and 19. Sites 3–8 are designated for tents only, with walk-in sites off a joint parking area. A few sites have cabanas over their picnic tables. The access road, campground road, and parking pads are paved.

Campsites, facilities: The campground has 20 RV or tent campsites that can fit RVs up to 32 feet. Facilities include picnic tables, fire rings with grills, vault toilets, garbage service, campground host, and drinking water. Leashed pets are permitted. A wheelchair-accessible toilet is available.

Reservations, fees: No reservations are accepted. Campsites cost $16. An extra vehicle costs $7. Cash or check. Open late May–early September.

Directions: From I-90 east of Coeur d'Alene, Idaho, take Exit 22 and drive 2.3 miles southeast on Lake Coeur d'Alene Scenic Byway (Route 97). Turn left onto Forest Road 438. Drive 0.6 mile to the campground entrance on the right.

GPS Coordinates: N 47° 36.451' W 116° 40.151'

Contact: Idaho Panhandle National Forest, Coeur d'Alene River Ranger District, 2502 E. Sherman Ave., Coeur d'Alene, ID 83814-5899, 208/664-2318, www.fs.fed.us/ipnf.

41 BELL BAY

Scenic rating: 9

on Lake Coeur d'Alene's east shore in Idaho Panhandle National Forest

On the east side of Lake Coeur d'Alene, Bell Bay Campground sits right on the lake. A trail leads from the campsites down to two boat docks for mooring, but the closest public boat

© BECKY LOMAX

The Chacolet Bridge is part of the 72-mile paved Trail of the Coeur D'Alenes, which runs from Plummer to Mullan, Idaho.

launch is at Harrison, a 12-minute drive south. For bicyclists, runners, and walkers, Harrison also has trailheads for the paved 72-mile Trail of the Coeur d'Alenes, which meanders through pastoral farmland, wetlands housing abundant nesting birds, and Lake Coeur d'Alene's shoreline to the Chacolet Bridge. Harrison also includes a bike shop, several restaurants, and an ice cream shop.

The campground is divided into upper and lower sections, one mile apart and connected via the Bell Bay Trail. The upper section is for group reservations only. The lower section sits on the lake in a mixed forest. While the access road requires washboard gravel driving, the campground road and parking pads are paved. The campsites sit above the lake in mixed forest with several sites (5, 6, 7, 10, 11, and 15) overlooking the water. Sites 6, 7, 10, and 11 are walk-in sites for tents. Campsite 15 commands seclusion and a primo lake view.

Campsites, facilities: The campground has 12 RV and tent campsites that can accommodate vehicles up to 22 feet and four walk-in tent campsites. The upper, group loop contains 10 RV and tent spaces. Facilities include picnic tables, fire rings with grills, vault toilets, drinking water, a campground host, and garbage service. Leashed pets are permitted. A wheelchair-accessible toilet is available.

Reservations, fees: Reservations are accepted only for the group loop (877/444-6777, www.recreation.gov). Campsites in the lower loop cost $14. Extra vehicles cost $7. Cash or check. Open late May–early September.

Directions: From I-90 east of Coeur d'Alene, take Exit 22. Drive south on the Lake Coeur d'Alene Scenic Byway (Route 97) for 25 slow, curvy miles. At milepost 71.4, turn west at the campground sign for three miles. After 0.7 mile of pavement, you'll hit two miles of gravel before reaching pavement again. At the entrance, follow the left fork for 0.9 mile down steep switchbacks to the lower loop. GPS Coordinates: N 47° 28.353' W 116° 50.483'

Contact: Idaho Panhandle National Forest, Coeur d'Alene River Ranger District, 2502 E. Sherman Ave., Coeur d'Alene, ID 83814-5899, 208/664-2318, www.fs.fed.us/ipnf.

42 CHACOLET

Scenic rating: 8

in Heyburn State Park south of Lake Coeur
d'Alene

Heyburn State Park flanks a series of small
lakes that connect to the south end of Lake
Coeur d'Alene, surrounded by the Coeur
d'Alene Indian Reservation. In Heyburn
State Park, Chacolet Campground—which
sits on Chacolet Lake, although most campers
think they are on the larger lake—is popular
for boating, hiking, and biking. For boaters,
water-skiers, and anglers, the campground
has a marina with a boat ramp, dock, and
moorage. The cruise boat *Idaho* also departs
from the marina. The Plummer Point swimming area is 0.9 mile from the campground
and easily reached via the Trail of the Coeur
d'Alenes, a paved 72-mile trail for bicyclists,
runners, and walkers. Most cyclists departing
from the campground opt for a ride across
the Chacolet Bridge and touring Lake Coeur
d'Alene's east shoreline. Bird-watchers will
enjoy nesting ospreys from the Chacolet
Bridge. Within two miles, trailheads depart
for the Plummer Creek Marsh interpretive
boardwalk for wildlife-watching opportunities, the three-mile Indian Cliffs Trail, and
the one-mile, hiking-only CCC Nature Trail.
Over 12 miles of mountain-biking trails also
loop through the park.

Chacolet, the least developed of the park's
three campgrounds, has small, cramped together, and sloped partially shaded campsites.
A dusty dirt road loops through the quiet
campground, and most of the small, narrow
parking pads are back-ins that can accommodate only smaller RVs. Some of the sites
have peek-a-boo lake views.

Campsites, facilities: The campground has 38
RV or tent campsites that can fit vehicles up
to 18 feet. Facilities include picnic tables, fire
pits with grills, flush toilets, drinking water,
a campground host, and garbage service.

Leashed pets are permitted. A wheelchair-
accessible toilet is available.

Reservations, fees: Reservations are accepted
(888/922-6743, http//:parksandrecreation.
idaho.gov/). Campsites cost $12, plus 6 per-
cent Idaho sales tax. Cash or check. The park
is open year-round, but Chacolet is only open
mid-May–mid-September.

Directions: From Coeur d'Alene, drive south
on Highway 95 for 34 miles to Plummer. Turn
east onto Highway 5 for 6.4 miles to Hawley's
Landing. Turn north and drive west through
the parking lot onto the Chacolet Road for
1.9 miles. Veer left at the fork for 0.2 mile and
again left at the junction at the cabins for 0.2
mile, staying on Upper Chacolet Road.
GPS Coordinates: N 47° 22.557' W 116°
45.825'

Contact: Heyburn State Park, 1291 Chatcolet Rd., Plummer, ID 83851, 208/686-1308,
http//:parksandrecreation.idaho.gov/.

43 HAWLEY'S LANDING

Scenic rating: 8

in Heyburn State Park near the south end of
Lake Coeur d'Alene

BEST (

The 5,500-acre Heyburn State Park, created
in 1908, is the oldest park in the Northwest.
Surrounded by Coeur d'Alene Indian Reservation, it houses small lakes connected to
Lake Coeur d'Alene. Hawley's Landing sits
on Chatcolet Lake in a western red cedar and
hemlock forest mixed with drier tall ponderosa pines, some 400 years old. One mile east,
boaters, water-skiers, and anglers can launch
at the Rocky Point Marina or rent rowboats,
kayaks, canoes, and paddleboats. A one-mile
bicycle ride on a paved road connects to the
72-mile Trail of the Coeur d'Alenes. A 0.6-mile
hiking trail tours the lakeshore and meets with
the Plummer Creek Marsh interpretive trail,
where you can see muskrats, great blue herons, and loons. Other mountain-biking and

hiking trailheads are one mile away, as is the Plummer Point swimming beach. In winter, cross-country skiers and snowshoers tour the park's trails.

The shady campsites are cramped; neighbors are squeezed close together, and some sites are on slopes where a picnic table cannot sit flat. Most of the small, narrow gravel parking pads are back-ins, but a few are pull-throughs. With a common parking lot, four of the sites are walk-ins for tents, with the best views overlooking the lake. You'll hear nearby trains.

Campsites, facilities: The campground has 36 RV or tent campsites that can fit vehicles up to 40 feet. Hookups are available for water, sewer, and electricity. An additional 16 tent campsites with tent pads are available. Facilities include picnic tables, fire pits with grills, flush toilets, showers, a disposal station, firewood, drinking water, interpretive programs, a campground host, and garbage service. Leashed pets are permitted. A wheelchair-accessible toilet is available.

Reservations, fees: Reservations are accepted (888/922-6743, http//:parksandrecreation. idaho.gov/). Hookups cost $16–22. Tent campsites cost $12. Idaho sales tax (6 percent) is added on. Cash or check. The park is open year-round, but Hawley's Landing is only open April–October.

Directions: From Coeur d'Alene, drive south on Highway 95 for 34 miles to Plummer. Turn east onto Highway 5 and turn left into Hawley's Landing at milepost 6.4. The campground is on the right.

GPS Coordinates: N 47° 21.303' W 116° 46.229'

Contact: Heyburn State Park, 1291 Chatcolet Rd., Plummer, ID 83851, 208/686-1308, http//:parksandrecreation.idaho.gov/.

44 BENEWAH LAKE

Scenic rating: 7

in Heyburn State Park on Benewah Lake west of St. Maries

Heyburn State Park includes Benewah Lake, which connects to Chacolet Lake via the St.

© BECKY LOMAX

Benewah Lake, a wildlife-rich waterway, connects to Chacolet and Coeur D'Alene Lakes, plus the St. Joe River.

Joe River. Chacolet Lake in turn connects with Lake Coeur d'Alene. Due to the connected waterways, many campers mistakenly think they are still on Lake Coeur d'Alene. Boaters will find a boat ramp, dock, and trailer parking. Benewah Lake harbors islands, a railroad trestle, and wetlands, which offer protection and good destinations for canoeists, kayakers, and bird-watchers. A 0.4-mile walking or mountain-biking trail departs from the campground for touring the shoreline or fishing. Due to its location on the east end of Heyburn, most of the park's hiking, mountain-biking, and horse trails—along with the 72-mile paved Trail of the Coeur d'Alenes—sit about 10 minutes to the west.

As at all three of Heyburn's campgrounds, camping at Benewah provides an excellent location for enjoying the lake, but there's no privacy in its three loops. The forested campsites scrunch so close to each other that you can hear the snores in the neighbors' tent. The first loop on the left can only accommodate RVs up to 20 feet because it dead-ends with skimpy turnaround space. Nine sites have lake views—all located on the unserviced loops. Passing train sounds carry into the campground.

Campsites, facilities: The campground has 26 RV campsites, most of which fit vehicles up to 35 feet. Hookups are available for water and electricity. Another 19 RV or tent sites ring two other loops, with an additional four walk-in tent sites. Facilities include picnic tables, fire rings with grills, flush toilets, showers, a disposal station, drinking water, campground host, firewood for sale, and garbage service. Leashed pets are permitted. A wheelchair-accessible toilet is available.

Reservations, fees: Reservations not accepted. Campsites with hookups cost $16–22. Unserviced campsites cost $12. Idaho sales tax (6 percent) is added on. Cash or check. The park is open year-round, but Benewah is only open mid-May–mid-September.

Directions: From Coeur d'Alene, drive south on Highway 95 for 34 miles to Plummer to reach Highway 5. From St. Maries, turn west on Highway 5. At milepost 11.8, turn north onto Benewah Lake Road and drive 1.3 miles, veering left at the trailer park.
GPS Coordinates: N 47° 20.976' W 116° 41.222'

Contact: Heyburn State Park, 1291 Chatcolet Rd., Plummer, ID 83851, 208/686-1308, http//:parksandrecreation.idaho.gov/.

45 SHADOWY ST. JOE

Scenic rating: 7

on the St. Joe River in Idaho Panhandle National Forest

BEST (

East of St. Maries at 2,100 feet in elevation in the Idaho Panhandle National Forest, the St. Joe River—nicknamed the Shadowy St. Joe—gathers its headwaters from the Bitterroot Mountains along the Idaho-Montana border. The blue-ribbon trout fishery holds cutthroat, rainbow, brook, and bull trout. In its lower stretches, the water calms into deep slow-moving flats traveling about 0.5 mile per hour, where the river is popular for motorboats and floating. From St. Joe City (don't let the name fool you; it's just a blip), the river runs for 31 miles to reach Chacolet and Coeur d'Alene Lakes. The river here has the reputation of being the world's highest navigable river; tugs haul logs to Coeur d'Alene mills.

Shadowy St. Joe Campground tucks between the road and the river. With only a few trees—cottonwoods and birch—the open, grassy, sunny campground offers minimal shade. Hit it around July 4 and the surrounding green grass will be as tall as a human. The campsites, however, are mowed. The campground—with a paved road and paved parking pads—also has a boat ramp, dock, and trailer parking. Sites 10–12 border the river, but with the tall grass and brush, they don't offer views of it.

Campsites, facilities: The campground has

14 RV or tent campsites. The parking pads can fit RVs up to 45 feet. Facilities include picnic tables, fire rings with grills, a vault toilet, drinking water, garbage service, campground host, and a boat launch. Leashed pets are permitted. A wheelchair-accessible toilet is available.

Reservations, fees: No reservations are accepted, and camping costs $6. Cash or check. Open late May–early September.

Directions: From St. Maries, drive north on State Route 3 to the outskirts of town to find the paved St. Joe River Road (Forest Road 50). Drive 10 miles east. The campground entrance sits on the right.

GPS Coordinates: N 47° 19.490' W 116° 23.622'

Contact: Idaho Panhandle National Forest, St. Joe Ranger District, P.O. Box 407, St. Maries, ID 83861, 208/245-2531, www.fs.fed.us/ipnf.

46 HUCKLEBERRY

Scenic rating: 7

on the St. Joe River in Idaho Panhandle National Forest

On the St. Joe River surrounded by the Idaho Panhandle National Forest, Huckleberry Campground sits about midway in between the tiny burgs of Calder and Avery. The section of river here is mixed with Class I and II water—gentle for canoeing, rafting, and float tubing. The St. Joe maintains a reputation as a prime trout fishery. It harbors endangered bull trout and cutthroat trout whose numbers are declining due to hybridization with other trout. Both trout are catch-and-release only, using barbless, unbaited hooks. The surrounding national forest is also popular with elk hunters.

Squeezed in between the road and the river, the long, narrow, sunny campground packs almost half of its sites along the river. The

campground, having a paved road and parking pads, sits in two sections, with one-third of the sites along the east road and the remainder along the west. The mowed-lawn sites with few trees have little to block the view of the road or other campers. Some pull-through sites are available. With the proximity to the St. Joe River Road, busy traffic passes most of the day but quiets somewhat at night.

Campsites, facilities: The campground has 33 RV or tent campsites, some which can fit large RVs. Hookups are available for electricity and water. Facilities include picnic tables, fire rings with grills, vault toilets, garbage service, horseshoe pits, a disposal station, gravel tent pads, a campground host, and drinking water. Three sites are for groups. Leashed pets are permitted. A wheelchair-accessible toilet is available.

Reservations, fees: No reservations are accepted. Campsites cost $12 for tents and $15 for hookups. A second vehicle costs $4. Cash or check. Open year-round.

Directions: From the north side of St. Maries on Highway 3, drive east on the St. Joe River Road (Forest Road 50). At milepost 29.5, turn north at the sign into the campground entrance.

GPS Coordinates: N 47° 16.122' W 116° 5.185'

Contact: Bureau of Land Management, Coeur d'Alene Field Office, 3815 Schreiber Way, Coeur d'Alene, ID 83815, 208/769-5000, www.blm.gov.

47 NORTH FORK ST. JOE

Scenic rating: 7

in Idaho Panhandle National Forest on the North Fork of the St. Joe River

On the remote North Fork of the St. Joe River surrounded by the Idaho Panhandle National Forest, the renamed North Fork St. Joe Campground may be identified

The 15-mile Route of the Hiawatha bike trail passes through a 1.7-mile tunnel beneath the Idaho-Montana border.

© BECKY LOMAX

on some older maps as Squaw Creek. The campground requires dusty dirt road driving from Avery. The area trails attract ATVers, hikers, and mountain bikers. Anglers go after 18-inch cutthroat trout in the river, and May–June, rafters and kayakers tackle the river's Class III rapids. The campground is the closest to Pearson (a 20-minute drive), the lower trailhead of the Route of the Hiawatha trail, a 15-mile railroad grade with 10 tunnels and seven trestles that has been converted to a mountain-bike trail ($9 for adults and $6 for kids). En route to Pearson, you'll drive through seven tunnels—all single-lane and a scenic drive in itself. Honk to alert oncoming traffic, and turn on lights for safety.

This quiet campground, renovated in 2007, sits on a hillside in an open pine forest that permits some views of the surrounding North Fork of the St. Joe River canyon. Filtered sunlight reaches the campsite floor made of forest duff and cones. There's very little underbrush, so you'll see your neighboring campers through the trees. Trailers are not recommended on Old Moon Pass Road.

Campsites, facilities: The campground has five RV or tent campsites that can fit only small RVs. Facilities include picnic tables, fire rings with grills and benches, and vault toilets, but no drinking water is available. If using river or stream water, boil or purify it first. Pack out your trash. Leashed pets are permitted. A wheelchair-accessible toilet is available.

Reservations, fees: No reservations are accepted. Camping is free. Open late May–September.

Directions: From Avery on the St. Joe River Road (Forest Road 50), drive north on dusty, washboarded Moon Pass Road (Forest Road 456) for six miles to the high bridge over the North Fork of the St. Joe River. At the northwest corner of the bridge, drop onto Old Moon Pass Road for one mile. It plummets to the river, where you'll turn right and cross the river to the campground entrance. GPS Coordinates: N 47° 17.825' W 115° 46.504'

Contact: Idaho Panhandle National Forest, St. Joe Ranger District, P.O. Box 407, St. Maries, ID 83861, 208/245-2531, www.fs.fed.us/ipnf.

48 EMERALD CREEK

Scenic rating: 7

west of the St. Maries River in Idaho Panhandle National Forest

Emerald Creek, a tributary of the St. Maries River in the Idaho Panhandle National Forest between St. Maries and Clarkia, is known for its gemstones. Located four miles southwest of the campground, the Emerald Creek Garnet Area (open 9 A.M.–5 P.M. Friday–Tuesday,

Memorial Day–Labor Day) is best known for star garnets, the 12-sided crystals that are found only in Idaho and India. A 0.5-mile hike reaches the site, and permits for collecting are available on site: $10 for adults, $5 for children ages 6–12. Buckets, shovels, and two sluices are available for screening and washing. You can keep up to five pounds of garnets daily, but bring a bag or container for your gems.

The campground is a welcome reprieve from crowded, cramped campgrounds because the thick Douglas fir and pine forest yields privacy. Spread out campsites are surrounded by a lush thimbleberry undergrowth. Some of the sites are fully shaded; others see filtered sunlight during the day. Despite its gravel road access, the campground loop is paved, with gravel back-in parking pads. (Campsite 16, however, is a pull-through.) Due to its distance from the highway, this is a very quiet campground.

Campsites, facilities: The campground has 18 RV or tent campsites that can fit vehicles up to 45 feet. Facilities include picnic tables, fire rings with grills, vault toilets, drinking water, garbage service, and a campground host. Leashed pets are permitted. A wheelchair-accessible toilet is available.

Reservations, fees: Reservations are not accepted. Camping costs $6. Cash or check. Open late May–early September.

Directions: From St. Maries, drive south on Highway 3 for 25 miles. Turn west at the signed turnoff onto Forest Road 447 to drive the five miles to the campground entrance. After 0.3 mile, the pavement ends. Continue on the washboard gravel road, veering left at 3.3 miles. From here, the road narrows, with pullouts for passing. Find the campground entrance on the left.

GPS Coordinates: N 47° 0.463' W 116° 19.560'

Contact: Idaho Panhandle National Forest, St. Joe Ranger District, St. Maries Office, 222 S. 7th St., Ste. 1, St. Maries, ID 83861-0407, 208/245-2531, www.fs.fed.us/ipnf/.

49 CEDAR CREEK

Scenic rating: 5

on the St. Maries River in Idaho Panhandle National Forest

The area along Highway 3 is timber country, dotted by small towns, like Clarkia, that depend on the forest for their economic base. Huge bare swaths flank mountaintops where logging operations have clear-cut portions of the Idaho Panhandle National Forest. The tiny campground is more a convenient place to stay while driving or bicycling Highway 3 than a destination. Cedar Creek Campground sits at 2,800 feet in elevation, with access to the St. Maries River for fishing. Clarkia, three miles south, has groceries and gas.

The campground has a small day-use area, plus small campsites. Sunny site 1 sits within sight of the highway with no room for a tent. Site 2 and 3 are tucked back in the woods with more privacy. Cottonwoods, firs, pines, and hawthorns partially shade them. Sites 1 and 2 have short gravel parking pads that are wide enough for two cars. Site 3 has a longer parking pad. Site 2 has the most flat space for a tent.

Campsites, facilities: The campground has three RV or tent campsites that can accommodate small RVs. Facilities include picnic tables, fire rings with grills, and a vault toilet, but no drinking water. Bring your own water, or if you use river water, boil or purify it first. Pack out your trash. Leashed pets are permitted. A wheelchair-accessible toilet is available.

Reservations, fees: Reservations are not accepted. Camping costs $6. Cash or check. Open late May–early September.

Directions: Find the campground at milepost 57.2 on Highway 3, three miles north of Clarkia. The signed entrance to the campground is on the west side of the road.

GPS Coordinates: N 47° 3.043' W 116° 17.298'

Contact: Idaho Panhandle National Forest, St. Joe Ranger District, St. Maries Office, 222 S. 7th St., Ste. 1, St. Maries, ID 83861-0407, 208/245-2531, www.fs.fed.us/ipnf/.

50 ELK CREEK

Scenic rating: 6

on Elk Creek in Clearwater National Forest

Elk Creek Campground sits one mile north of the town of Elk River—a funky backwoods village with cafés, groceries, lodging, bars, and gas in the Clearwater National Forest north of Dworshak Reservoir. The area is a favorite haunt for ATV riders, offering dusty rides on a web of dirt national forest roads. Forest Road 382 north from Elk River houses short 0.5- to 1-mile scenic hikes. Three waterfalls at Elk Creek Falls plummet through a deep basalt gorge. Morris Creek Cedar Grove protects 90 acres of old growth trees up to 500 years old. The 18-foot-diameter giant red cedar is 3,000 years old. Elk Creek harbors brook trout. Elk Creek Reservoir, a five-minute drive from the campground, also has a primitive ramp for launching boats and canoes. The campground sits at the north end of the Elk River Backcountry Byway, a curvy half-gravel/half-paved, steep graded road along Dworshak Reservoir's east side.

A mixed pine and fir forest lends filtered shade to this campground, which was built in 2006. While the gravel road and several double-wide parking pads accommodate RVs, the campsites themselves are small—most with very little room for tents. The sites are open to the campground road but spaced out from each other to afford some privacy.

Campsites, facilities: The campground has 14 RV or tent campsites with 40-foot-long parking pads. Hookups are available for electricity. Facilities include picnic tables, fire rings with grills, drinking water, vault toilets, and a campground host. Pack out your trash. In addition, an overflow parking lot area can fit 10 additional camping vehicles. Leashed pets are permitted. A wheelchair-accessible toilet and campsite are available.

Reservations, fees: Reservations are accepted for six of the sites (877/444-6777, www.recreation.gov). Campsites cost $15. Extra vehicles cost $2. Cash or check. Open late May–early September.

Directions: From Elk River, follow the signs from town north one mile. Turn left, climbing over a small hill where the pavement changes to gravel. Veer right at the second sign and left after crossing the bridge. The campground entrance sits on the left. You can also reach the campground entrance by heading toward Elk Creek Reservoir and turning left.

GPS Coordinates: N 46° 47.581' W 116° 10.337'

Contact: Clearwater National Forest, Palouse Ranger District, Potlatch Ranger Station, 1700 Hwy. 6, Potlatch, ID 83855, 208/875-1131, www.fs.fed.us/r1/clearwater/.

51 ELK CREEK RESERVOIR

Scenic rating: 8

on Elk Creek Reservoir in Clearwater National Forest

Sprawled along Elk Creek Reservoir, this camping area combines a selection of different campsites—lakeshore, forest, grassy, and parking lot. The reservoir has a dock for swimming and a primitive boat launch (electric motors only permitted), and the water harbors largemouth and smallmouth bass, bluegill, and stocked rainbow trout. The town of Elk River, with cafés, groceries, and gas, is a mecca for summer ATV riders and winter snowmobilers exploring the miles of trails and roads in the Clearwater National Forest. Forest Road 382 north from Elk River houses natural sightseeing: short 0.5- to 1-mile hikes to three waterfalls in a basalt gorge at Elk Creek Falls Recreation Area, 500-year-old trees in the Morris Creek Cedar Grove, and a 3,000-year-old giant red cedar. This reservoir sits as the northern gateway to the curvy Elk River Backcountry Byway, which links by steep gravel grades with Dent Acres, Dworshak Reservoir, and Orofino. Between here and Dent Acres, the washboarded gravel road throws steep, nearly 10 percent grade climbs and descents at drivers. Don't be fooled by the map; the road is not straight, but snakes the entire way.

The campground comprises several units sprawled along one mile of the reservoir's western shore. You'll find open gravel parking lots suited for the largest RVs overlooking the reservoir, shaded campsites tucked under trees on the shoreline, grassy and treed tent sites across the road, and a series of more private campsites across the road in the forest.

Campsites, facilities: The campground has 64 RV and tent campsites. Some can fit the largest RVs. Facilities include picnic tables, fire rings (rock or metal rings with grills), and vault or pit toilets. Bring your own drinking water. If you choose to use reservoir water, filter or boil it first. Leashed pets are permitted. A wheelchair-accessible toilet is available.

Reservations, fees: Reservations are not accepted. Campsites cost $6. A park host comes around to collect the fees. Cash or check. Open mid-April–October.

Directions: Find the various units between mileposts 36 and 37 on the Elk River Backcountry Byway.
GPS Coordinates: N 46° 46.518' W 116° 10.309'

Contact: Idaho State Fish and Game, Clearwater Division, 3316 16th St., Lewiston, ID 83501, 208/799-5010, http://fishandgame.idaho.gov.

52 AQUARIUS CREEK

Scenic rating: 8

on the North Fork of the Clearwater River in Clearwater National Forest

BEST (

In the Bitterroot Mountains along the North Fork of the Clearwater River, the remote Aquarius Creek Campground sits south of the 30,000-acre Mallard-Larkins Pioneer Area, a proposed wilderness area. The area skyrockets 5,000 feet off the valley floor into high alpine cliffs, glacial cirques, and 21 lakes. The six-mile Smith Ridge Trail (#240), which climbs Larkin Peak, departs about 14 miles from the campground. From the campground, a multi-use trail runs downriver. Aquarius Creek is the only North Fork campground accessed via pavement, and the pavement ends right after the campground. Several good swimming holes sit just east of the campground. The river is a popular trout fishery. Anglers are limited to two fish of 14 inches or longer. Float the river above Aquarius to take out here, as the road goes no farther downstream.

Aquarius sits on the north side of the river adjacent to the bridge. All of the campsites line up along the river; those at the back of the campground have more shade, from the thicker cedars and alders. Sites 1–5 garner more sunshine. Due to their location at the end, surrounded by patches of thimbleberry, elderberry, and ferns, sites 7–9 feature more privacy. Sites 2 and 3 include large flat areas for tents. The campground's narrow gravel road and short, dirt parking pads are only suitable for shorter RVs.

Campsites, facilities: The campground has nine RV or tent campsites that can fit RVs up to 21 feet. Facilities include picnic tables, fire rings with grills, drinking water, and vault toilets. Pack out your trash. Leashed pets are permitted. A wheelchair-accessible toilet is available.

Reservations, fees: Reservations are not

accepted. Campsites cost $7. Cash or check. Open late May–September.

Directions: From Headquarters, drive north on Forest Road 247 for 25 miles to reach the North Fork of the Clearwater River. Cross the river on the bridge and turn into the campground entrance on the right. You can also reach the campground from Pierce by driving 29 miles on Forest Road 250 to Bungalow junction and then turning west onto Forest Road 247 for 27 miles.

GPS Coordinates: N 46° 50.463' W 115° 37.128'

Contact: Clearwater National Forest, North Fork Ranger District, 12730 Hwy. 12, Orofino, ID 83544, 208/476-4541, www.fs.fed.us/r1/clearwater/.

53 NORTH FORK OF THE CLEARWATER RIVER PRIMITIVE

Scenic rating: 8

on the North Fork of the Clearwater River in Clearwater National Forest

BEST (

In Idaho's Bitterroot Mountains, the North Fork of the Clearwater River runs for 45 miles, paralleled by narrow dirt forest roads. Primitive dispersed camps line the entire river corridor, popular for fishing, mountain biking, hiking, rafting, kayaking, canoeing, and float tubing. These afford free places to camp in the utmost solitude. Three primitive campgrounds—Riviara, Bungalow, and Death Creek—also offer multiple sites and toilets.

Look for the undeveloped sites where you see unmarked spur roads turn right or left off the road. Some sit on shaded bluffs overlooking the river; others access sunny, rocky, river bar campsites. Do not drive blindly on the spurs; walk them first to be sure you can turn around or back out. Locate Riviara (it's signed) under alders and cedars along a sunny rocky river bar between Aquarius Creek and Washington Creek.

Find the unsigned grassy and partially shaded Bungalow campsites on both sides of Orogrande Creek on the south side of the bridge over the North Fork at the junction of Forest Roads 247 and 250. Locate the unsigned, heavily shaded Death Creek camp north of the road and river between Weitas Creek and Noe Creek.

Campsites, facilities: The corridor contains around 30 primitive dispersed campsites, plus three primitive campgrounds with flat spaces for tents: Riviara (three sites), Bungalow (four sites), and Death Creek (six sites). Some of the campsites can fit RVs up to 25 feet. All of the campsites have rock fire rings; use them rather than making new ones. The three primitive campgrounds also have vault or pit toilets. No drinking water is available. Bring your own, or if you use river water, boil or purify it. Pack out your trash. Leashed pets are permitted.

Reservations, fees: Reservations are not accepted. Camping is free. Open May–November.

Directions: From Headquarters, drive north on Forest Road 247 for 25 miles to reach the North Fork of the Clearwater River. Cross the river on the bridge and turn right. You can also reach the river from Pierce, by driving 29 miles on Forest Road 250 to Bungalow junction and then turning west onto Forest Road 247 or east onto Forest Road 250.

GPS Coordinates: N 46° 37.854' W 115° 30.486' (Bungalow)

Contact: Clearwater National Forest, North Fork Ranger District, 12730 Hwy. 12, Orofino, ID 83544, 208/476-4541, www.fs.fed.us/r1/clearwater/.

54 WASHINGTON CREEK

Scenic rating: 9

on the North Fork of the Clearwater River in Clearwater National Forest

BEST (

In the Bitterroot Mountains along the North Fork of the Clearwater River, Washington

Creek sits on the opposite side of the river from the dusty road. The Wild and Scenic River runs into a deep pool above the bridge and shallower past the campground, with big rocky bars. The river provides top-notch trout fishing and is gentle enough for float tubes, canoes, and beginning rafters. The Washington Ridge Trail (#600) departing from the campground reaches Hornby Creek Road in three miles and farther to Elk Mountain.

Washington Creek, the largest of the North Fork's campgrounds, tucks its shaded campsites under tall cedars and alders. In early summer, wild roses and syringa—Idaho's state flower—bloom along the river here. Sites 2–8 overlook the river across the campground road. Sites 9, 11, and 13 have their own waterfront. The group campsite sits on an open grassy area with plenty of flat space for tents. The campsites at the back of the campground tuck under heavier shade.

Campsites, facilities: The campground has 23 RV or tent campsites. Some of the larger campsites can fit RVs up to 32 feet. Each has a picnic table and fire ring with grill. Amenities include drinking water, vault toilets, a campground host (sometimes), and a horseshoe pit. Pack out your trash. Leashed pets are permitted. A wheelchair-accessible toilet is available.

Reservations, fees: Reservations are not accepted. Campsites cost $7. A $15 small group site is available, too, for two to four vehicles. Cash or check. Open late May–early September.

Directions: From Pierce, drive 29 miles up the half-paved, half-gravel, narrow, curvy French Mountain Road, also known as Forest Road 250, to Bungalow junction. Cross the North Fork of the Clearwater River on the bridge and turn left. Drive seven miles west on the narrow, single-lane washboard and potholed gravel road. Be prepared to back up into turnouts for passing vehicles. At the campground sign, cross the North Fork on the single-lane bridge to enter the campground. You can also arrive via headquarters by driving 25 miles

northeast on Forest Road 247, crossing the bridge at Aquarius, and then continuing east and south for 20 miles.

GPS Coordinates: N 46° 42.116' W 115° 33.382'

Contact: Clearwater National Forest, North Fork Ranger District, 12730 Hwy. 12, Orofino, ID 83544, 208/476-4541, www.fs.fed.us/r1/clearwater/.

55 WEITAS CREEK

Scenic rating: 7

on the North Fork of the Clearwater River in Clearwater National Forest

In the Bitterroot Mountains, Weitas Creek Campground sits at the confluence of the North Fork of the Clearwater River and Weitas Creek. The North Fork runs with shallow riffles here around small grassy islands. The campground requires a long, bumpy, dusty drive, which guarantees quiet and solitude. You can fish both rivers, plus float the North Fork of the Clearwater River on rafts, kayaks, canoes, or float tubes. A multi-use trailhead departs from the back of the campground for Hemlock Butte. It's a popular ATV destination, connecting to the Lolo Motorway, the historic trail of the Nez Perce and the Lewis and Clark expedition.

The quiet campground sits in tall grass and lady ferns under large cedar trees that admit filtered sunlight. Ox-eye daisies and self-heal flowers bloom in early July. Three of the sites sit on Weitas Creek, but those along the North Fork of the Clearwater River have larger flat spaces for tents. After driving across the bridge, you'll find one private campsite to the left and five of the sites to the right.

Campsites, facilities: The campground has six RV or tent campsites. RVs are limited to 18 feet. Facilities include picnic tables, fire rings with grills, and a pit toilet, but no drinking water. Bring your own water or you can use water from Weitas Creek or the river, but you should boil or purify it first. Pack out your trash. Leashed pets are permitted.

Reservations, fees: Reservations are not accepted. Camping is free. Open late May–September.

Directions: From Pierce, drive 29 miles up the half-paved, half-gravel, narrow, curvy French Mountain Road, also known as Forest Road 250, to Bungalow junction. Cross the North Fork of the Clearwater River on the bridge and turn right. Drive five miles east on the narrow, single-lane washboard and potholed gravel road. Be prepared to back up into turnouts for passing vehicles. At the campground sign, cross the North Fork on the single-lane, rusty bridge to enter the campground.

GPS Coordinates: N 46° 38.161' W 115° 25.918'

Contact: Clearwater National Forest, North Fork Ranger District, 12730 Hwy. 12, Orofino, ID 83544, 208/476-4541, www.fs.fed.us/r1/clearwater/.

56 NOE CREEK

Scenic rating: 7

on the North Fork of the Clearwater River in Clearwater National Forest

Located in the Bitterroot Mountains along the North Fork of the Clearwater River, Noe Creek is a campground that grants solitude and quiet, guaranteed by its long, bumpy, dusty access. The North Fork of the Clearwater River contains westslope cutthroat, bull, brook, and rainbow trout, along with kokanee salmon. The river is also gentle enough for beginner floaters—rafts, kayaks or canoes, or float tubes. Departing up Mush Creek five miles from the campground, the trail to Pot Mountain Ridge (#144) climbs 1,000 feet for views of the drainage.

A gravel road drops through the campground, with a small turnaround loop at the end. With the sound of the river, all of the campsites line up along the riverbank. Site 6 has the best views, overlooking the water. Those tucked deep under the shade-giving firs and pines have short trails through the lady ferns and thimbleberry to reach the beach. The road is visible from most of the sites, but the sites are spaced out for privacy.

Campsites, facilities: The campground has six RV or tent campsites. RVs are limited to 22 feet. Facilities include picnic tables, fire rings with grills, a hand pump for drinking water, and vault toilets. Pack out your trash. Leashed pets are permitted. A wheelchair-accessible toilet is available.

Reservations, fees: Reservations are not accepted. Campsites cost $7. One group campsite (two vehicle minimum, four vehicle maximum) costs $15. Cash or check. Open late May–September.

Directions: From Pierce, drive 29 miles up the half-paved, half-gravel, narrow, curvy French Mountain Road, also known as Forest Road 250, to Bungalow junction. Cross the North Fork of the Clearwater River on the bridge and turn right. Drive 10.3 miles east on the narrow, single-lane washboard and potholed gravel road. Be prepared to back up into turnouts for passing vehicles. The campground sits on the south side of the road on the river.

GPS Coordinates: N 46° 41.087' W 115° 21.402'

Contact: Clearwater National Forest, North Fork Ranger District, 12730 Hwy. 12, Orofino, ID 83544, 208/476-4541, www.fs.fed.us/r1/clearwater/.

57 KELLY FORKS

Scenic rating: 8

on the North Fork of the Clearwater River in Clearwater National Forest

In the Bitterroot Mountains, Kelly Forks sits at the confluence of Kelly Creek with the North Fork of the Clearwater River and adjacent to Kelly Forks Ranger Station. Only those who really want to see the area suffer the miles of bumpy dirt road to reach Kelly Forks, but they are rewarded with beauty, solitude, and quiet. Despite its name, Kelly Creek is really a blue-ribbon trout river, loaded with 12- to 15-inch westslope cutthroat trout, plus a few mountain whitefish and rainbow trout. Fishing is equally good on the North Fork of the Clearwater River, which also attracts rafters, canoeists, and float tubers for its gentle waters. Hiking and mountain-biking trails are available up the Kelly Creek and North Fork drainages.

The Kelly Forks Campground sits on Kelly Creek rather than on the North Fork of the Clearwater River. Sites 6, 7, 8, 10, 14, and 15 sit adjacent to the creek, with trails to the shore. A mixed forest of firs and alders (alive with the sounds of songbirds into July) provides shade for most of the campsites, while a healthy dose of thick brush adds privacy. You'll hear only the creek and river here.

Campsites, facilities: The campground has 14 RV or tent campsites. RVs are limited to 40 feet. Facilities include picnic tables, fire rings with grills, drinking water, vault toilets, a campground host, and interpretive programs. Pack out your trash. Leashed pets are permitted. A wheelchair-accessible toilet is available.

Reservations, fees: Reservations are not accepted. Campsites cost $7. One group campsite (two-vehicle minimum, four-vehicle maximum) costs $15. Cash or check. Open late May–early September.

Directions: From Pierce, drive 29 miles up the half-paved, half-gravel, narrow, curvy French Mountain Road, also known as Forest Road 250, to Bungalow junction. Cross the North Fork of the Clearwater River on the bridge and turn right. Drive 18 miles east on the narrow, single-lane washboard and potholed gravel road. Be prepared to back up into turnouts for passing vehicles. The campground sits on the right-hand side

of the road 0.25 mile past the Kelly Forks Ranger Station.

GPS Coordinates: N 46° 43.022' W 115° 15.308'

Contact: Clearwater National Forest, North Fork Ranger District, 12730 Hwy. 12, Orofino, ID 83544, 208/476-4541, www.fs.fed.us/r1/clearwater/.

58 DENT ACRES

Scenic rating: 9

on Dworshak Reservoir in Clearwater National Forest

BEST (

When you drive into Dent Acres, the campground host can tell whether you came on the Elk River Backcountry Byway via the gravel road from Elk River or on the paved road from Orofino. The dust on the vehicle is testament to the route. Regardless of the access, you will travel miles of steep curvy grades—despite the appearance on some maps of the road being a straight line. Located on the north shore of Dworshak Reservoir's eastern arm and surrounded by the Clearwater National Forest, the campground sits about 10 minutes from Dent Bridge, which crosses the reservoir. The reservoir is popular in early summer for bass and kokanee salmon fishing, boating, and waterskiing before water levels drop low. The campground accommodates boaters with a large paved trailer parking area, cement boat ramp, dock, and fish-cleaning station. Unfortunately, you can't swim at the boat launch area, and much of the remaining shoreline is steep and rocky. Most people swim from their boats. The reservoir is usually at full pool through July 4.

The quiet campground sits on a sunny, grassy south-facing hillside with three paved loops and a few token trees between the open sites. All campsites except site 43 are paved pull-throughs. This popular campground books out months in advance for holiday weekends and is a hunter's favorite in fall. Most of the picnic tables are covered with small shade canopies.

Campsites, facilities: The campground has 50 RV or tent campsites. Some of the campsites can fit RVs up to 50 feet. Hookups include electricity up to 50 amps. Facilities include picnic tables, fire rings with grills, flush toilets, showers, summer campground hosts, a disposal station, a playground, summer garbage service, a marine pump-out station, and a weather station. Pack out your trash in the off-season. Leashed pets are permitted. A wheelchair-accessible toilet is available.

Reservations, fees: Reservations are accepted (877/444-6777, www.recreation.gov). Campsites cost $10–18. Cash or check. Open early April–November.

Directions: From Dent Acres Bridge on the Elk River Backcountry Byway, climb one mile north up the curvy road and turn south at the recreation area sign. Descend 1.9 miles on the steep, curvy, gravel road.

GPS Coordinates: N 46° 37.635' W 116° 13.152'

Contact: U.S. Army Corps of Engineers, P.O. Box 48, Ahsahka, ID 83520, 208/476-1261 or 800/321-3198, www.nww.usace.army.mil.

59 CANYON CREEK

Scenic rating: 8

on Dworshak Reservoir in Clearwater National Forest

Dworshak Reservoir is popular in spring and summer for boating. With the lake at full pool around July 4, most of the campgrounds fill up, including this remote one on the east side of the reservoir about halfway between Orofino and Dent Bridge. Once you depart the paved Elk River Backcountry Byway, a long gravel drive leads to the 96-acre campground, dropping from the ranchland to the reservoir on a narrow, curvy road in its last miles. Use second or first gear for the final very steep descent to avoid the burning brake smell. Via water, the campground sits about seven miles from Big Eddy marina. The primitive campground has a single-lane boat ramp with a dock in a sheltered bay. The launch ramp is usable in the spring and summer months when the lake level sits at elevations of 1,560 to 1600 feet. Call 800/321-3198 for a 24-hour recorded message on the current reservoir information to check for pool levels.

The quiet campground tucks under a shady canopy of trees and the steep wall of the reservoir's gorge. Sunlight finds the area late in the day. Most of the sites are close together in the open loop under the trees for protection from lake winds, but three campsites above the shoreline have great sunset views. Some of the campsites in the middle of the loop have large, flat tent spaces.

Campsites, facilities: The campground has 17 RV or tent campsites. RVs are limited to 22 feet in length. Facilities include picnic tables, fire pits with grills, and vault toilets. Pack out your garbage. Take drinking water, or if you plan on consuming lake water, boil or purify it first. Leashed pets are permitted. A wheelchair-accessible toilet is available.

Reservations, fees: Reservations are not accepted. Camping is free. Open May–November.

Directions: From Orofino, 11 miles north on Elk River Road via Wells Bench and Eureka Ridge Road, follow the signs to Canyon Creek Campground. From the turnoff at Elk River Backcountry Byway, drive west through scenic Palouse ranchland for eight miles on a gravel road. At 3.9 miles, turn right and continue as the road plummets to the campground.

GPS Coordinates: N 46° 33.364' W 116° 14.005'

Contact: U.S. Army Corps of Engineers, P.O. Box 48, Ahsahka, ID 83520, 208/476-1255, www.nww.usace.army.mil.

60 FRASER PARK

Scenic rating: 6

between Orofino and Weippe

Located on the high plateau above the Clearwater River Canyon, 10-acre Fraser Park sits south of Weippe on the Gold Rush Historic Byway, which runs between Orofino and Pierce. The county campground offers a place to stay en route to the North Fork of the Clearwater River and the Clearwater National Forest. Interpretive signs at the campground relate the Lewis and Clark Corps of Discovery expedition, which passed through here, as well as the 1860 gold rush at Pierce. Several plants Lewis and Clark identified in their journals are found in the park. The town of Weippe is also on the Lewis and Clark Trail; historic sites around town and murals on the public library chronicle the activities of the explorers in the area.

Contrary to the surrounding sprawling wheat fields, the campground sits in a tall stand of pine trees. The park houses a baseball field, covered picnic areas, a playground, horseshoe pits, and the campground. Several of the sites have large, flat, grassy areas good for tents, and some can fit larger trailers. Six of the campsites tuck against the back of the forest farthest from the road traffic, but they are visible to each other.

Campsites, facilities: The campground has 10 RV or tent campsites that can fit midsized RVs. Facilities include picnic tables, fire rings with grills, drinking water, vault toilets, and garbage service. Water use per camp unit is limited to 50 gallons per day. Campers are limited to a three-night stay. Leashed pets are permitted. A wheelchair-accessible toilet is available.

Reservations, fees: Reservations are not accepted. Camping is free. Open year-round.

Directions: Locate Fraser Park at milepost 12.7 on Highway 11 about 11 miles south of Weippe and 14 miles north of Orofino. The campground sits on the north side of the road.

GPS Coordinates: N 46° 23.285' W 116° 2.814'

Contact: Clearwater County Parks, P.O. Box 586, Orofino, ID 83544.

EASTERN CENTRAL IDAHO

© BECKY LOMAX

BEST CAMPGROUNDS

❰ **Boat-in Camping**
Redfish Inlet, page 470.

❰ **Fishing**
Johnson Bar, page 442.
Salmon River, page 461.

❰ **Hiking**
Iron Creek, page 463.
Pettit Lake, page 470.

❰ **Hot Springs**
Jerry Johnson, page 436.
Easley, page 473.

❰ **Idaho**
Wilderness Gateway, page 435.
Stanley Lake, page 461.
Sockeye, page 469.

❰ **Lake Camping**
Outlet, page 467.

❰ **River Camping**
Wild Goose, page 441.
O'Hara Bar, page 443.
Upper and Lower O'Brien, page 458.
Mormon Bend, page 459.

Marked by a gigantic swath of roadless remote

wilderness, eastern-central Idaho attracts campers for its rugged scenery and wild big rivers. The mountainous terrain skyrockets to steep, toothy peaks and plummets into deep canyons. National Wild and Scenic Rivers bounce between raging white water and streams running clear enough to see trout swim.

Because of the region's wilderness, which is accessible only by hiking, horseback riding, rafting, and kayaking, vehicle-accessible campgrounds line rivers to the north and south of the roadless regions. The Lochsa and Selway Rivers border the north, while the Salmon River rims the south. All three provide corridors loaded with national forest campgrounds that offer hiking, mountain biking, fishing, rafting, kayaking, canoeing, and floating.

Two wilderness areas make up the vast mountainous expanse between the Lochsa and Salmon Rivers: the 1.3-million-acre Selway-Bitterroot Wilderness and the 2.3-million-acre Frank Church–River of No Return Wilderness, the largest wilderness in the Lower 48. Both contain rivers designated as Wild and Scenic, but the latter houses the Salmon River, the longest free-flowing river in the lower 48.

Forming the northern boundary of the wilderness, the 70-mile-long Lochsa River churns in its upper stretches from the Bitterroot Mountains with huge sustained rapids that have the reputation of flipping boats. In addition to its Class IV white water, the river also runs with riffles that give it its blue-ribbon trout stream status. Highway 12 offers easy access to most of the river, with campgrounds every few miles along its length. The corridor also resounds with history, as it served as the route of Lewis and Clark heading west and the Nez Perce traveling to and from buffalo lands. Their routes followed the ridges above the Lochsa, now known as the Lolo Motorway – a 73-mile single-lane dirt road with primitive camping.

Converging with the Lochsa River, the Selway River rips through the heart of the Selway-Bitterroot Wilderness, flowing 60 miles. The river's blue-ribbon trout fishing comes from its crystalline waters filled with westslope cutthroat trout. While the upper river requires a flight or horse-packing trip into the wilderness for rafting the Class IV white-water rapids, the more sedate lower Selway parallels a rough dirt road, giving campers easy access for floating or fishing. Vehicle-accessible campgrounds line the route up to the wilderness boundary east of Selway Falls.

To the south, the 425-mile Main Salmon River curves northward from the Sawtooth Mountains and turns west, cutting through the Frank Church–River of No Return Wilderness en route to the Snake River. Portions are calm enough for canoes; other stretches cut through steep-walled, narrow canyons with white-water drops. The Salmon River attracts anglers for its trout, steelhead, and chinook salmon. Many federal campgrounds line the river for fishing and floating access, and campgrounds increase in number in the canyon northeast of Stanley – a summer hub for rafting, fishing, horseback riding, and mountain biking.

The Salmon River, which originates in the 217,088-acre Sawtooth Wilderness, flows through a valley of ranches at the base of the ragged Sawtooth Mountains, which top 10,000 feet. Small streams tumble from the glacier-carved peaks, forming lakes that attract campers for stunning scenery, boating, and swimming on sandy beaches. Kayakers and canoeists ply the waters, along with water-skiers and anglers. The Sawtooth National Recreation Area includes trails for hikers and horseback riders that head to wilderness destinations of alpine lakes. Mountain climbers head for the jagged summits, while rock climbers aim for the Sawtooths' granite faces. Mountain bikers tour reams of national forest trails surrounding the Sawtooth Mountains. The Sawtooth National Recreation Area extends camping south over Galena Pass to Sun Valley, where you can mountain bike or walk portions of the gravel 18-mile Harriman Trail from campgrounds flanking the Big Wood River.

When camping in eastern-central Idaho, pack along your favorite toys, including the hiking boots and mountain bikes. For river camping, pack the fishing tackle, rafts, canoes, and kayaks. For camping at the Sawtooth National Recreation Area lakes, bring the boats. You can easily spend days camping in this region.

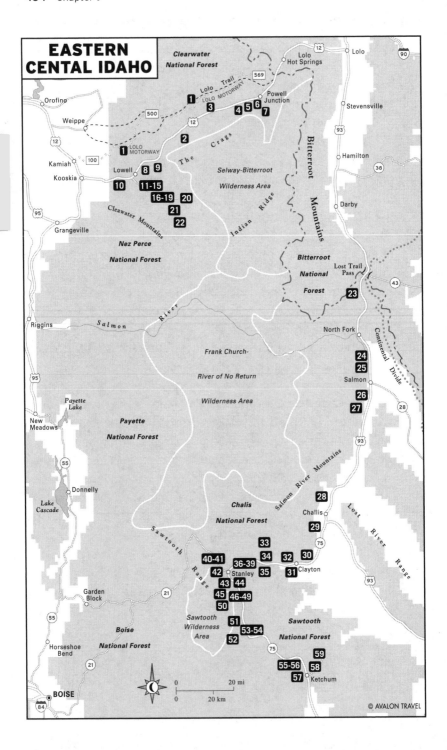

1 LOLO MOTORWAY AND TRAIL

🚶 🚴 🛶 🏕 🚐 ⛺

Scenic rating: 9

north of the Lochsa River in Clearwater National Forest

The 73-mile Lolo Motorway, which follows the Lolo Trail National Historic Landmark, is a primitive ridgetop road that parallels Highway 12 and the Lochsa River. Western tribes used the trail, which tops out at 6,800 feet, to reach buffalo hunting grounds; eastern tribes used it to reach salmon-fishing streams. Lewis and Clark used the trail, and in 1877, the Nez Perce followed it to flee General Howard's army. After the Civilian Conservation Corps built the road in the 1930s, the Lolo Motorway (Forest Road 500) became a winding dirt roadbed through lodgepole and ponderosa forests alternating with green meadows and interpretive sites. Most of the road is single-lane, rocky, steep, good for mountain bikes, and only has a few pullover spots. You'll need a sturdy high-clearance vehicle, good tires, a full-sized spare, and the wits to back up a long distance when you meet an oncoming car. Trailers are not recommended. Protruding rocks, trees, and branches can scrape large vehicles. Watch for large potholes, downed trees, rocks, and early snowstorms. Check current road conditions before you depart, and gas up the car. You'll find no services!

Plan for 2–5 days to drive the motorway. No developed campgrounds exist, but you'll find plenty of primitive campsites. Use previous fire rings to avoid additional scars on the landscape.

Campsites, facilities: None of the primitive campsites have any facilities besides a rock fire ring. RVs are limited to 23 feet. Pack out your trash, and take drinking water along. Should you choose to drink lake or creek water, boil or purify it first. A scant handful of toilets can be found, but most campers will need to follow Leave No Trace ethics for human waste. Leashed pets are permitted.

Reservations, fees: No reservations are accepted. Camping is free. The motorway generally is snow-free by July 4 and open until the snows bury it.

Directions: From the Powell area, access the Lolo Motorway via Parachute Hill Road (Forest Road 569). From the Wilderness Gateway area, connect via Saddle Camp Road (Forest Road 107). From the Kamiah area, locate the access to Forest Road 100 at the junction of Highway 12 and the Kamiah bridge over the Clearwater River. GPS Coordinates at Powell Junction: N 46° 34.746' W 114° 43.121'

Contact: Clearwater National Forest, Powell Ranger District, 192 Powell Rd., Lolo, MT 59847, 208/942-3113, www.fs.fed.us/r1/clearwater/.

2 WILDERNESS GATEWAY

🚶 🚴 🏊 🛶 🎣 🚴 🐕 ♿ 🚐 ⛺

Scenic rating: 9

on the Lochsa River in Clearwater National Forest

BEST (

Located at 2,100 feet, Wilderness Gateway is so named for its access to the Selway-Bitterroot Wilderness to the south. As the largest Forest Service campground in the Lochsa-Selway drainage, it sits away from the highway on the south side of the Lochsa River as it churns white through a boulder garden. At the campground's far end, a trail outfitter offers horseback rides. Across the highway about one mile from the campground is the Lochsa Historical Ranger Station, and the Sherman Creek Trailhead (#211) launches the eastern end of the 16-mile "downriver" trail—the Lochsa Historical Trail. Fishing for trout upstream of the bridge over the Lochsa is catch-and-release only, using barbless hooks, but below the bridge and in Boulder Creek, you can keep trout. Rafting or kayaking this section of the Lochsa requires technical expertise.

The campground is divided into two parts, with two paved loops on each side of Boulder Creek. Loop C has campsites right on the Lochsa River, with the remaining partly shaded campsites under a mixed forest of firs and pines flanked by thimbleberry bushes. Loop D, equipped with hitching rails, feeders, and a stock ramp, is only for campers with horses. A birding trail runs behind loops A and B. Loop C also has a short trail that overlooks the Lochsa and dead-ends in 0.5 mile.

Campsites, facilities: The campground has 91 RV or tent campsites. Some of the paved parking pads can fit RV combinations up to 60 feet long. Facilities include picnic tables, fire rings with grills, vault toilets, drinking water, an amphitheater with interpretive programs, a campground host, a disposal station, and garbage service. Leashed pets are permitted. A wheelchair-accessible toilet is available.

Reservations, fees: Reservations for 25 of the campsites are accepted for Memorial Day weekend–Labor Day weekend (877/444-6777, www.recreation.gov). Campsites cost $8. An extra vehicle costs $2. Cash or check. Open mid-May–late October.

Directions: From Kooskia, drive 48 miles east on Highway 12. Locate the bridge crossing the Lochsa at milepost 122.2 on the south side of the road. (The bridge is about 52 miles west of Lolo Pass.) After crossing the wide two-lane bridge, drive less than 0.1 mile to the campground. GPS Coordinates: N 46° 20.531' W 11115° 18.531'

Contact: Clearwater National Forest, Lochsa Ranger District, Kooskia Ranger Station, 502 Lowry, Kooskia, ID 83539, 208/926-4274, www.fs.fed.us/r1/clearwater/.

3 JERRY JOHNSON

Scenic rating: 8

on the Lochsa River in Clearwater National Forest

BEST (

At 3,100 feet, Jerry Johnson is popular for its hot springs. Three natural soaking pools

A bridge leads across the Lochsa River to reach Jerry Johnson Hot Springs by trail.

© BECKY LOMAX

sit across the Lochsa River from the campground along Warm Springs Creek. Two of the pools can be used year-round, but the waterfall pools are submerged under spring's high runoff until late summer. The rock-ringed pools are open 6 A.M.–8 P.M. From the campground, a trail connects with the Warm Springs Trail, which crosses the Lochsa on a bridge to reach the hot pools in one mile. Although the campground does not have a put-in, it is popular in spring for rafting and kayaking on the Lochsa; this stretch of river has Class II and III rapids. The river here is catch-and-release only for trout. Barbless hooks must be used, and no bait is permitted. Two miles west, the 1.2-mile Colgate Licks National Recreation Trail tours a fire zone and natural wildlife mineral lick.

The campground sits on an open, sunny hillside covered with bear grass and huckleberry bushes surrounded by a thick forest of evergreens. Due to disease, the Forest Service removed the campground's trees, so you can see neighboring campers, but a new fast-growing crop of conifers sprouting may alter that in the future. A paved road loops through the campground, with back-in paved parking pads. You can see the highway from several campsites.

Campsites, facilities: The campground has 19 RV or tent campsites. Large RVs are okay. Facilities include picnic tables, fire rings with grills, vault toilets, and drinking water. Pack out your trash. Leashed pets are permitted. A wheelchair-accessible toilet is available.

Reservations, fees: No reservations are accepted. Campsites cost $8. An extra vehicle costs $2. Cash or check. Open mid-April–late May and early September–early November. In summer, when Jerry Johnson Campground is closed, the closest campgrounds to the hot springs are Wendover and Whitehouse, both six miles east.

Directions: From Kooskia, drive 76 miles east on Highway 12. Locate the turnoff into the campground at milepost 150.5 on the north side of the road. The campground sits about 24 miles west of Lolo Pass.

GPS Coordinates: N 46° 28.548' W 114° 54.319'

Contact: Clearwater National Forest, Powell Ranger District, 192 Powell Rd., Lolo, MT 59847, 208/942-3113, www.fs.fed.us/r1/clearwater/.

⁴ WENDOVER

Scenic rating: 8

on the Lochsa River in Clearwater National Forest

Located at an elevation of 3,300 feet in the Clearwater National Forest, Wendover Campground sits on the Lochsa River on the site where Lewis and Clark passed on September 15, 1805. The campground is popular in spring for rafting and kayaking on the Lochsa; this stretch of river has Class II and III rapids, but the campground has no river put-in. The river here is catch-and-release only for trout. Barbless hooks must be used, and no bait is permitted. For those looking to hike to Jerry Johnson Hot Springs on the Warm Springs Trail, the campground sits six miles east and is the closest campground to the hot pools in summer when the Jerry Johnson Campground is closed. The campground is three miles west of Lochsa Lodge, where gas, minimal groceries, and a restaurant are available. About 12 miles west, the 1.2-mile Colgate Licks National Recreation Trail tours a fire zone and natural wildlife mineral lick.

Wendover's campsites spread out for privacy under a thick canopy of cedars, pines, and firs, with an undergrowth of wild roses and tall, white bear grass that blooms in July. Sites 9, 10, 11, 13, and 15 have river frontage. Between loops A and B, the paved campground road dips through a water crossing;

the sharp drop and climb may cause long trailers to drag. During high water, loop B is closed.

Campsites, facilities: The campground has 26 RV or tent campsites. Some of the paved parking pads, which are all back-ins, can fit RV combinations up to 50 feet. Facilities include picnic tables, fire rings with grills, vault toilets, hand pumps for drinking water, garbage service, and a campground host. Leashed pets are permitted. A wheelchair-accessible toilet is available.

Reservations, fees: No reservations are accepted. Campsites cost $8. An extra vehicle costs $2. Cash or check. Open late May–September.

Directions: From Kooskia, drive 84 miles east on Highway 12. Locate the turnoff into the campground at milepost 158.1 on the south side of the road. The campground sits about 16 miles west of Lolo Pass.

GPS Coordinates: N 46° 30.624' W 114° 47.001'

Contact: Clearwater National Forest, Powell Ranger District, 192 Powell Rd., Lolo, MT 59847, 208/942-3113, www.fs.fed.us/r1/clearwater/.

5 WHITEHOUSE

Scenic rating: 8

on the Lochsa River in Clearwater National Forest

The Lochsa River riffles with froth here past Whitehouse and neighboring Wendover Campgrounds. At an elevation of 3,300 feet in the Clearwater National Forest, Whitehouse is popular in spring for rafting and kayaking on the Lochsa; this stretch of river has Class II and III rapids, but the campground has no river put-in. The river here is catch-and-release only for trout. Barbless hooks must be used, and no bait is permitted. For those looking to hike to Jerry Johnson

Hot Springs on the Warm Springs Trail, the campground sits six miles east and is one of the closest campgrounds to the hot pools in summer when the Jerry Johnson Campground is closed. Three miles east is Lochsa Lodge, where gas, minimal groceries, and a restaurant are available. About 12 miles to the west, the 1.2-mile Colgate Licks National Recreation Trail tours a fire zone and natural wildlife mineral lick.

The campground sits right on the Lochsa River and has more sites right on the river than neighboring Wendover. Sites 1, 2, 4, 5, and 7–11 have river frontage and their own slice of private beach. The first few sit higher above the river, while the others drop to river level. For the other campsites, trails lead to the beach for fishing or enjoying the water. The campsites are shaded by firs, cedars, and alders, and a thick undergrowth of willows and corn lilies adds privacy. Both the campground road and back-in parking pads are paved.

Campsites, facilities: The campground has 13 RV or tent campsites. A loop turnaround at the end of the line of campsites aids trailers, and the campground can accommodate RVs up to 45 feet. Facilities include picnic tables, fire rings with grills, vault toilets, garbage service, and hand pumps for drinking water. Leashed pets are permitted. A wheelchair-accessible toilet is available.

Reservations, fees: No reservations are accepted. Campsites cost $8. An extra vehicle costs $2. Cash or check. Open late May–September.

Directions: From Kooskia, drive 84 miles east on Highway 12. Locate the turnoff into the campground at milepost 158.3 on the south side of the road. The campground sits about 16 miles west of Lolo Pass.

GPS Coordinates: N 46° 30.488' W 114° 46.714'

Contact: Clearwater National Forest, Powell Ranger District, 192 Powell Rd., Lolo, MT 59847, 208/942-3113, www.fs.fed.us/r1/clearwater/.

⑥ POWELL

🚶 🚵 🏊 🎣 🚤 ⛵ 🐕 ♿ 🚐 ⛺

Scenic rating: 8

on the Lochsa River in Clearwater National
Forest

In Clearwater National Forest, Powell
Campground, at 3,400 feet, sits on a side
spur in between Lochsa Lodge and the Powell
Ranger Station. You can get gas, fishing gear,
and minimal groceries at Lochsa Lodge, and
the ranger station has maps and handouts
on hiking trails. Powell is popular in spring
for rafting and kayaking on the Wild and
Scenic Lochsa; this stretch of river has Class
II and III rapids, but the campground has
no river put-in. The river here is catch-and-
release only for trout. Barbless hooks must be
used, and no bait is permitted. Powell is also
a jump-off point for those aiming to drive
the primitive Lolo Motorway, the historic
Nez Perce and Lewis and Clark Trail, via the
Parachute Hill Road.

The campground tucks under firs and
pines in two loops. Loop A houses the sites
with electrical hookups and has campsites
crammed in close to each other. Some of the
sites are more open, and a few have river frontage. Loop B campsites have more privacy and
two campsites have river frontage. The campground road is paved, as are the parking pads,
most of which are back-ins. Five campsites
have pull-through parking.

Campsites, facilities: The campground has
39 RV or tent campsites, 22 of which have
electrical hookups. (No water or sewer hookups.) Some sites can accommodate RVs up
to 50 feet. Facilities include picnic tables,
fire rings with grills, flush and vault toilets,
drinking water, a campground host, garbage
service, and an amphitheater with interpretive programs. Leashed pets are permitted. A
wheelchair-accessible toilet is available.

Reservations, fees: Reservations are accepted
for late May–early September (877/444-6777,
www.recreation.gov). Campsites cost $8

without hookups, $15 for hookups. An extra
vehicle costs $2. Cash or check. Open late
May–mid-October.

Directions: From Kooskia drive 88 miles east
on Highway 12, or from Lolo Pass drive 12
miles west. Locate the road to Powell at milepost 161.8 on the south side of the highway.
Drive 0.2 mile past the entrance to Lochsa
Lodge and continue toward the ranger station, turning right at the campground sign.
GPS Coordinates: N 46° 30.701' W 114°
43.247'

Contact: Clearwater National Forest, Powell
Ranger District, 192 Powell Rd., Lolo, MT
59847, 208/942-3113, www.fs.fed.us/r1/
clearwater/.

⑦ WHITE SANDS

🚶 🏊 🎣 🚤 ⛵ 🐕 ♿ 🚐 ⛺

Scenic rating: 7

at the confluence of the Crooked Fork and
Lochsa Rivers in Clearwater National Forest

At 3,500 feet at the beginning of the road to
Elk Summit, White Sands sits in the Clear-
water National Forest on a forested sandy bar
adjacent to the confluence of the Crooked
Fork with the Wild and Scenic Lochsa River.
The Lochsa is popular in spring for rafting
and kayaking; this stretch of river has Class
II and III rapids, and you can put in to the
river on the bridge over the Lochsa. Crooked
Fork also has a short, highly technical Class
III–V two-mile section for rafting and kayaking from Hopeful Creek to Brushy Creek.
The Lochsa here is catch-and-release only for
trout. Barbless hooks must be used, and no
bait is permitted. On Crooked Fork, you can
keep two trout over 14 inches per day. Fishing
is also permitted in the small pond between
the campground and the bridges. From the
campground, you can continue a bumpy,
dusty scenic drive 20 miles to Elk Summit to
see moose and views of the Selway-Bitterroot
Wilderness. The 1.5-mile Walton Lakes Trail

(#79) departs from Forest Road 362 to drop into a glacier-carved cirque.

A dusty gravel road accesses the campground, which has one potholed dirt loop with short dirt parking pads that can accommodate smaller RVs. All of the sites line up adjacent to the Lochsa River, with short trails to the shore. Sites 1 and 2 have prime river views. Most of the sites—except for 6 and 7—are spread out for privacy under a mixed forest canopy that admits filtered sunlight.

Campsites, facilities: The campground has seven RV or tent campsites. The campsites are best for small RVs only. Facilities include picnic tables, fire rings with grills, vault toilets, a hand pump for drinking water, and garbage service. Leashed pets are permitted. A wheelchair-accessible toilet is available.

Reservations, fees: Reservations are not accepted. Campsites cost $8. An extra vehicle costs $2. Cash or check. Open late May–mid-October.

Directions: From Kooskia, drive 89 miles east on Highway 12, or from Lolo Pass, drive 11 miles west. Locate the road heading to Elk Summit at milepost 163.2 on the south side of the highway. Drive one mile downhill on the washboarded, gravel Forest Road 111. The entrance to the campground sits on the right just before bridge.

GPS Coordinates: N 46° 30.470' W 114° 41.198'

Contact: Clearwater National Forest, Powell Ranger District, 192 Powell Rd., Lolo, MT 59847, 208/942-3113, www.fs.fed.us/r1/clearwater/.

8 APGAR CREEK
[icons]

Scenic rating: 8

on the Lochsa River in Clearwater National Forest

At 1,600 feet in Clearwater National Forest on the curvy paved two-lane Northwest Passage Scenic Byway, Apgar Creek sits on a rock and sand bar on the Lochsa River. The campground is across the road from a trailhead; Apgar Creek Trail (#111) grunts up 2,800 feet in 4.3 miles for views of the Coolwater Ridge area. This section of the Lochsa River flattens out compared to its upper reaches, but Class II–IV rapids still require experience to navigate. The fishing season runs May 23–November 30, with a daily bag limit of two trout over 14 inches long. Using bait is prohibited.

Pinched in between the river and the highway, the campground loops under western red cedars with minimal sword fern undergrowth, allowing you to see your neighbors. Sites 5–7 are more shaded than sites 1–4, which have river frontage with peek-a-boo views. Site 1 is a walk-in tent site with a private area along the river. A group fire pit surrounded by benches is available on an open patch of grass with views of the forested mountains and river. A trail accesses the river between campsites 4 and 5. Due to its proximity to the highway, noise seeps in at night from long-haul trucks.

Campsites, facilities: The campground has seven RV or tent campsites. The narrow dirt road and dirt back-in parking pads are suitable only for smaller RVs. Facilities include picnic tables, fire rings with grills, vault toilets, drinking water, and garbage service. Leashed pets are permitted. A wheelchair-accessible toilet is available.

Reservations, fees: No reservations are accepted. Campsites cost $8. An extra vehicle costs $2. Cash or check. Open Memorial Day weekend–early September.

Directions: From Kooskia, drive 30 miles east on Highway 12. Turn into the campground on the south side of the highway at milepost 104.3. The campground sits about 70 miles west of Lolo Pass.

GPS Coordinates: N 46° 12.847' W 115° 32.200'

Contact: Clearwater National Forest, Lochsa Ranger District, Kooskia Ranger Station, 502 Lowry, Kooskia, ID 83539, 208/926-4274, www.fs.fed.us/r1/clearwater/.

9 KNIFE EDGE

🏃 🚴 🛶 🛷 🚐 ⛴ 🐕 ♿ 🚙 ⛺

Scenic rating: 8

on the Lochsa River in Clearwater National
Forest

In Clearwater National Forest on the curvy,
paved, two-lane Northwest Passage Scenic
Byway, Knife Edge, elevation 1,700 feet, is a
river access site for those putting in or taking
out from the Lochsa River. The rapids in this
stretch of the river run Class III and IV, requiring technical skills to avoid rocks even at lower
water levels. Right in front of the campground,
the river flows deeper where the canyon narrows. The fishing season is May 23–November
30, with a daily bag limit of two trout over 14
inches long. Using bait is prohibited. Built in
the 1920s, the Lochsa River Historical Trail
has its Split Creek Trailhead 2.5 miles east
on the highway. It runs 16 miles east to the
Sherman Creek Trailhead near the Lochsa
Historical Ranger Station and offers views of
the Lochsa Canyon. The path is also part of
the Idaho Centennial Trail.

Squeezed in between the river and the highway, the campground has shaded sites under a
canopy of cedars and firs. Two parking pads
are small pull-throughs. Sites 3 and 5 have
river frontage. As a river access site, the campground includes a place to launch rafts and
kayaks, plus a trailer turnaround and parking
space. Due to its proximity to the highway,
noise from long-haul trucks competes with
that of the river at night.

Campsites, facilities: The campground has
five RV or tent campsites. The gravel campground road and dirt parking pads are suitable
for smaller RVs and trailers. Facilities include
picnic tables, fire rings with grills, vault toilets, and garbage service. No drinking water
is available. Bring your own, or if you plan
on using river water, boil or purify it first.
Leashed pets are permitted. A wheelchair-
accessible toilet is available.

Reservations, fees: No reservations are

accepted. Camping is free. Open May–early
September.

Directions: From Kooskia, drive 34 miles
east on Highway 12. Locate the campground
on the south side of the highway at milepost
108.7. The campground sits about 66 miles
west of Lolo Pass.

GPS Coordinates: N 46° 13.631' W 115°
28.471'

Contact: Clearwater National Forest, Lochsa
Ranger District, Kooskia Ranger Station, 502
Lowry, Kooskia, ID 83539, 208/926-4274,
www.fs.fed.us/r1/clearwater/.

10 WILD GOOSE

🚴 🛶 🛷 🚐 ⛴ 🐕 ♿ 🚙 ⛺

Scenic rating: 8

on the Middle Fork of the Clearwater River in
Clearwater National Forest

BEST (

Located at 1,500 feet on the banks of the Middle Fork of the Clearwater River, Wild Goose
Campground is popular for its sandy beaches
and its ease of access en route to Lolo Pass.
The campground sits within a few miles either
direction of two companies that guide rafting
trips on both the Selway and the Lochsa. The
tamer Middle Fork of the Clearwater, also a
designated national Wild and Scenic River,
runs 22 miles with Class I and II water—gentle enough for canoes and float tubes. Thanks
to the campground's close proximity to the
confluence of the Selway and the Middle Fork,
you can launch rafts, float tubes, and canoes
from the Selway's lower stretches and float
back to camp. A float downriver to Kooskia
(pronounced "KOOS-kee" by the locals) is a
21-mile, all-day adventure. The river is also
known for its 15-pound steelhead.

Squeezed between the highway and the
river, the coveted campground lines up all
but one of its campsites along the riverfront
under large cedar trees. Two stairways lead
to the sandy beaches along the swift-moving
river. The proximity of the highway adds

noise from long-haul trucks during the night. Site 6, on the turnaround loop, is geared for groups, with two double-long picnic tables and a huge fire ring with three benches. Most of the sites—accessed by the narrow campground road with short parking pads—have flat spots for tents.

Campsites, facilities: The campground has six RV or tent campsites. Most are only suitable for RVs under 30 feet, but leveling may be difficult in some sites. Facilities include picnic tables, fire rings with grills, vault toilets, drinking water, and garbage service. Leashed pets are permitted. A wheelchair-accessible toilet is available.

Reservations, fees: Reservations are not accepted. Campsites cost $8. An extra vehicle costs $2. Cash or check. Open Memorial Day weekend–early September.

Directions: From Kooskia, drive 21 miles east on Highway 12. Locate the campground on the south side of the highway at milepost 95.4. The campground sits about 79 miles west of Lolo Pass.

GPS Coordinates: N 46° 8.147' W 115° 37.525'

Contact: Clearwater National Forest, Lochsa Ranger District, Kooskia Ranger Station, 502 Lowry, Kooskia, ID 83539, 208/926-4274, www.fs.fed.us/r1/clearwater/.

11 JOHNSON BAR

🚴 🏊 🛶 🚣 ⛵ 🎣 ♿ 🚐 ⛺

Scenic rating: 8

on the Selway River in Nez Perce National Forest

BEST (

Johnson Bar, at 1,600 feet, is the first in a long string of campgrounds running up the Selway River. Its sandbar is popular for swimming, and the river is tamer here than at its upper end. May and June runoff makes for good kayaking. After water levels drop in July, the lower river works for canoeing, rafting, and float tubing. Anglers go after trout,

chinook salmon, and steelhead. The daily bag limit is two trout (no limits on salmon or steelhead); none can be under 14 inches. Only artificial flies and lures are permitted. The historic Fenn Ranger Station—open weekdays for visitor information—is 0.6 mile southwest of the campground. Across from the ranger station, Fenn Pond, with its boardwalk and wheelchair-accessible trail, is stocked annually with rainbow trout. The pond (limit of six fish) is great for teaching kids to fish.

The Selway Road is paved to the campground entrance, but the campground roads and parking pads are gravel. The campground is a combination of large, open, grassy fields and partially shaded sites flanked with mixed deciduous trees and cedars. Sites 3, 4, 6, 7, and 8 have riverfront locations. The group campsite sits in a large grassy field. Sites 7 and 8 are more private in their own loop. Even without a boat ramp, you can launch rafts, kayaks, and canoes easily from several locations in the campground. Extra parking areas for trailers are available. Be cautious about rattlesnakes.

Campsites, facilities: The campground has eight RV or tent campsites. RVs are limited to 20 feet. Facilities include picnic tables, fire rings and grills, vault and portable toilets, drinking water, and garbage service. Leashed pets are permitted. A wheelchair-accessible toilet is available.

Reservations, fees: Reservations are not accepted, except for the group site (877/444-6777, www.recreation.gov). If the group site is not reserved, it is available for anyone to use. Camping costs $6. An extra vehicle costs $2. Cash or check. Open mid-May–mid-September.

Directions: From Lowell on Highway 12, turn southeast onto the Selway Road, also called Forest Road 223. Drive to milepost 4. The campground entrance is on the right.

GPS Coordinates: N 46° 6.123' W 115° 33.430'

Contact: Nez Perce National Forest, Moose

Creek Ranger District, Fenn Ranger Station, 831 Selway Rd., Kooskia, ID 83539, 208/926-8925, www.fs.fed.us/r1/nezperce.

12 CCC CAMP

Scenic rating: 7

on the Selway River in Nez Perce National Forest

Located at 1,600 feet in elevation on the Selway River in Nez Perce National Forest, the CCC Camp on the Selway Road works as a spillover campground for crowded holiday weekends. The easily accessed riverbank across the road from the campground has a large sandbar that increases in size as the river level drops during the summer. The bar is popular for day use for swimming, fishing, and floating. Adjacent to the campground, the six-mile-long CCC Trail (#734), which is restricted to hiking and horses only, ascends 4,000 feet in elevation to the Coolwater Ridge Road 317 on an open bear grass ridge with views of the Selway. The trailhead includes a stock ramp and hitching post.

The campground, shaded by tall cedars, has large flat spaces for tents. Two sites sit between the campground loop road and the Selway Road in full view of all passing vehicles, but with great views of the river. A third walk-in campsite is more secluded under larger cedars on a raised bench above the campground loop with peek-a-boo views of the river.

Campsites, facilities: The campground has three primitive RV or tent campsites. Midsized RVs can fit in this campground. Two campsites have fire rings with grills, but a third only has a rock fire ring. Facilities include a vault toilet. You can get water for drinking from the river across the road, but boil or purify it first. You can also get potable water at nearby O'Hara or Johnson Bar Campground. Pack out your trash. Leashed pets are permitted. A wheelchair-accessible toilet is available.

Reservations, fees: No reservations are not accepted. Camping is free. Open late April–October.

Directions: From Lowell on Highway 12, turn southeast onto the Selway Road, also called Forest Road 223. Drive to milepost 6. The campground is on the left and is unsigned. GPS Coordinates: N 46° 5.447' W 115° 31.217'

Contact: Nez Perce National Forest, Moose Creek Ranger District, Fenn Ranger Station, 831 Selway Rd., Kooskia, ID 83539, 208/926-8925, www.fs.fed.us/r1/nezperce.

13 O'HARA BAR

Scenic rating: 8

on the Selway River in Nez Perce National Forest

BEST (

O'Hara Bar sits at 1,600 feet at the confluence of O'Hara Creek with the Selway River. Its location on the river is convenient for fishing, rafting, or floating right from camp, and the bar has a mix of sand, river rocks, and grass. O'Hara, the largest of the Selway campgrounds, is also the last campground upriver accessed via pavement. A one-mile interpretive trail tours up O'Hara Creek, home to beavers, belted kingfishers, and ospreys. Stream improvement efforts restored chinook salmon, trout, and steelhead spawning to the once fishless creek, which was damaged from timber harvesting and road building sediments. You can also drive or mountain bike the dirt Hamby Road 3.5 miles to hike the 2.1-mile O'Hara Creek trail. A steep, six-mile trail (#335) climbs from the campground to Stillman Point, an old fire lookout.

The paved campground loop road has paved, back-in parking pads. Over half of the campsites have Selway River frontage; river views through the lush thimbleberries, yews, and sword ferns vary. Cedars and alders shade most of the sites, too. Sites 26–32 are grassy, more open, and sunnier. Despite the campground's rainforest appearance, be cautious of rattlesnakes. Many of the sites include large, flat spaces for tents. Because of its location across the river from the Selway Road, the campground is quiet. A RV disposal station is adjacent to the Fenn Ranger Station, 2.5 miles to the northwest.

Campsites, facilities: The campground has 32 RV or tent campsites. The largest parking pads can accommodate RV combinations up to 45 feet. Facilities include picnic tables, fire rings with grills, vault toilets, drinking water, garbage service, and a campground host. Leashed pets are permitted. A wheelchair-accessible toilet is available.

Reservations, fees: Reservations are accepted for 60 percent of the campsites (877/444-6777, www.recreation.gov). Campsites cost $10. An extra vehicle costs $3. Cash or check. Open mid-May–late September.

Directions: From Lowell on Highway 12, turn southeast onto the Selway Road, also called Forest Road 223. Drive to milepost 7 and turn right onto the bridge. After crossing over the Selway River, take an immediate left for 0.1 mile to the campground.

GPS Coordinates: N 46° 5.138' W 115° 30.773'

Contact: Nez Perce National Forest, Moose Creek Ranger District, Fenn Ranger Station, 831 Selway Rd., Kooskia, ID 83539, 208/926-8925, www.fs.fed.us/r1/nezperce.

14 RACKLIFF

Scenic rating: 7

on the Selway River in Nez Perce National Forest

In Nez Perce National Forest, Rackliff, elevation 1,600 feet, is the first campground

up the Selway River Road after leaving the pavement. The road narrows at milepost 7, offering a rough, curvy, jouncing ride for its remaining 12 miles upriver. Many aiming for the upper campgrounds give up after one mile of washboards and potholes to camp here instead. Large sandbars both up- and down-river from the campground work for fishing, swimming, rafting, canoeing, and floating. The Rackliff Ridge Trail (#702) climbs a steep six miles to Coolwater Lookout.

This shaded campground tucked under thick firs and cedars is best for tents only. The tight, dirt-road access, narrow parking areas, and cramped turnaround space don't lend themselves to RV maneuvering. Most of the sites have flat spaces to accommodate large tents. Some of the sites have room for more than one tent. The campground—in two parts on both sides of Rackliff Creek—sits on a bench above the road and has peek-a-boo views of the river. Access to the river for fishing, swimming, or floating is easy; drop across the road and climb down the short bank.

Campsites, facilities: The campground has six tent campsites. Facilities include picnic tables, fire rings with grills, and vault toilets, but no drinking water. You can get water from Rackliff Creek, but boil or purify it before use. Pack out your trash. Leashed pets are permitted.

Reservations, fees: No reservations are accepted. Camping is free. Open mid-May–mid-September.

Directions: From Lowell on Highway 12, turn southeast onto the Selway Road, also called Forest Road 223. After milepost 7, the road turns to gravel and narrows to one lane with turnouts. Drive to milepost 7.9. The first part of Rackliff sits on the left before Rackliff Creek, and the second half is on the left after the creek. The campground sign is difficult to see tucked in the brush.

GPS Coordinates: N 46° 5.146' W 115° 29.897'

Contact: Nez Perce National Forest, Moose Creek Ranger District, Fenn Ranger Station, 831 Selway Rd., Kooskia, ID 83539, 208/926-8925, www.fs.fed.us/r1/nezperce.

15 TWENTYMILE BAR
🏊 ⛵ 🚤 🎣 🏇 ⛰️

Scenic rating: 7

on the Selway River in Nez Perce National Forest

At 1,600 feet in Nez Perce National Forest along the Selway River, Twentymile Bar is a small, primitive campground for those looking for privacy. The campground sits along the Selway where the river widens into shallow riffles alternating with slower deeper pools. A large rock and sandy bar good for fishing, swimming, and floating flanks the river below the road.

A dirt-road spur cuts off the rugged Selway Road into the campground parking lot above both the road and river. One site with room for small tents sits on the left, virtually in the parking lot; a more spacious walk-in site sits just uphill on the right. It has room for a large tent. Both sites are heavily shaded under a mixed forest with peek-a-boo views of the water.

Campsites, facilities: The campground has two tent campsites. Facilities include picnic tables, fire rings with grills, and a vault toilet, but no drinking water. Bring water with you, or get it from O'Hara or Johnson Bar. You can also get water from the river here, but boil or purify it before use. Pack out your trash. Leashed pets are permitted.

Reservations, fees: No reservations are accepted. Camping is free. Open May–September.

Directions: From Lowell on Highway 12, turn southeast onto the Selway Road, also called Forest Road 223. After milepost 7, the road turns to gravel and narrows to one lane with turnouts. Drive to milepost 9.5. The campground is not signed in advance on the road.

Look for the sign at the entrance of the road spur on the left.

GPS Coordinates: N 46° 5.222' W 115° 27.909'

Contact: Nez Perce National Forest, Moose Creek Ranger District, Fenn Ranger Station, 831 Selway Rd., Kooskia, ID 83539, 208/926-8925, www.fs.fed.us/r1/nezperce.

16 SLIDE CREEK
🏊 ⛵ 🚤 🎣 🏇 ⛰️

Scenic rating: 7

on the Selway River in Nez Perce National Forest

In Nez Perce National Forest along the Selway River, Slide Creek, elevation 1,600 feet, works for tent campers driving the Selway Road as well as those floating the river. This section of the river works for float tubing, rafting, and canoeing in summer, but rafting and kayaking are best in the early summer high runoff. The fishing season on the Selway runs May 23–November 30. On this section of the river, the daily bag limit is two trout over 14 inches long.

Slide Creek is a walk-in campground with both sites on a rocky, sandy bar right on the river. It is one place you can camp with your tent door just a few feet from the water. From the parking pullouts on the Selway Road, drop 30 feet down the steep embankment trails to the bar. One site (with the picnic table and fire ring) is protected a bit more under cedars and firs; the other is grassy, more open, and sunny. The first pullout can only accommodate a small vehicle; the second, larger, grassy parking pullout can fit trucks and bigger cars. An alternative primitive site is available above the road on the creek should these two be claimed.

Campsites, facilities: The primitive campground has two tent campsites. One has a picnic table and fire ring with grill; the other has only a rock fire ring. A pit toilet is available, but there's no drinking water. Bring water with you, or get it from O'Hara or Johnson Bar on your way upriver. You can also get water from the river or creek here, but boil or purify it before use. Pack out your trash. Leashed pets are permitted.

Reservations, fees: No reservations are accepted. Camping is free. Open May–September.

Directions: From Lowell on Highway 12, turn southeast onto the Selway Road, also called Forest Road 223. After milepost 7, the road turns to gravel and narrows to one lane with turnouts. Drive to milepost 10.5. The campground is not signed in advance on the road. Look for the Slide Creek sign on the right-hand side near a small pullout. The larger parking pullout is a few seconds farther down the road, also on the right.

GPS Coordinates: N 46° 5.037' W 115° 27.062'

Contact: Nez Perce National Forest, Moose Creek Ranger District, Fenn Ranger Station, 831 Selway Rd., Kooskia, ID 83539, 208/926-8925, www.fs.fed.us/r1/nezperce.

17 BOYD CREEK

Scenic rating: 8

on the Selway River in Nez Perce National Forest

Boyd Creek, at 1,600 feet in the Nez Perce National Forest, is a tributary of the Selway River. The western trailhead to the 23-mile-loop East Boyd–Glover–Roundtop National Recreation Trail (#703 and #704) departs across the Selway Road from the campground. A stock ramp and hitching post are also available. The trail is open to motorbikes, too. Access to the shoreline for fishing, swimming, or floating is via the lower campsites.

The campground has two parts. Two sites (1 and 2) are on a cedar and hemlock bluff

overlooking the river and adjacent to the Selway Road. One is on an open grassy knoll, while the other is tucked under the trees with a large cement pad. Access the remaining sites (3–6) by dropping down a steep, narrow gravel road to the river level. Sites 3, 4, and 6 have river frontage. Site 3 is the most secluded as a walk-in tent site. Sites 5 and 6 sit very close together on an open, sunny bench—a good option for two parties traveling together.

Campsites, facilities: The campground has six RV or tent campsites. The campground can accommodate smaller RVs up to 20 feet. Facilities include picnic tables, fire rings with grills, and a vault toilet, but no drinking water. Bring your own, or pick it up at O'Hara or Johnson Bar. Pack out your trash. Leashed pets are permitted.

Reservations, fees: No reservations are accepted. Campsites cost $5. Cash or check. Open May–September.

Directions: From Lowell on Highway 12, turn southeast onto the Selway Road, also called Forest Road 223. After milepost 7, the road turns to gravel and narrows to one lane with turnouts. Drive to milepost 10.8. The campground is on the right in two parts—the upper sites off Selway Road and the lower sites on the river.

GPS Coordinates: N 46° 4.866' W 115° 26.565'

Contact: Nez Perce National Forest, Moose Creek Ranger District, Fenn Ranger Station, 831 Selway Rd., Kooskia, ID 83539, 208/926-8925, www.fs.fed.us/r1/nezperce.

18 TWENTYFIVE MILE BAR

Scenic rating: 8

on the Selway River in Nez Perce National Forest

Located in Nez Perce National Forest at 1,700 feet along the Wild and Scenic Selway River,

Twentyfive Mile Bar sits far up the jarring washboard and potholed Selway Road, but those going here will be rewarded with privacy and the perfect beach for a sunny day. Here, the river moves slowly, and the larger sandbar swells even bigger throughout the summer as the water level drops. The river in this section is good for canoeing and floating, although you'll need to watch out for the sporadic rocks just upstream from the campground. Anglers may only keep two trout over 14 inches long in this section of the river, and the use of bait is prohibited.

Access to the campground requires a steep descent down a narrow road to reach the large sandy bar on the river. The access is suitable for trucks with campers, but not trailers or larger RVs. Both campsites are tucked under large cedars and hemlocks with several flat spaces that can fit large tents. Lady fern and thimbleberry bushes mound high in the campground, separating the two campsites.

Campsites, facilities: The campground has two RV or tent campsites. The parking pads can accommodate only small RVs. Facilities include picnic tables, fire rings with grills, and a vault toilet, but no drinking water. Bring water with you, or get it from O'Hara or Johnson Bar when you drive upriver. You can also get water from the Glover Creek here, but boil or purify it before use. Pack out your trash. Leashed pets are permitted.

Reservations, fees: No reservations are accepted. Camping is free. Open May–September.

Directions: From Lowell on Highway 12, turn southeast onto Selway Road, also called Forest Road 223. After milepost 7, the road turns to gravel and narrows to one lane with turnouts. Drive to milepost 15.1. Look for a steep road climbing up to the left.

GPS Coordinates: N 46° 4.379' W 115° 22.589'

Contact: Nez Perce National Forest, Moose Creek Ranger District, Fenn Ranger Station, 831 Selway Rd., Kooskia, ID 83539, 208/926-8925, www.fs.fed.us/r1/nezperce.

19 GLOVER

Scenic rating: 7

on the Selway River in Nez Perce National Forest

At 1,700 feet in Nez Perce National Forest along the Wild and Scenic Selway River, Glover Campground sits far up the jarring washboarded and potholed single-lane Selway Road. (Watch for ATVers on the road.) While the lesser-used campground sits on a sloped plateau above the road, trails cut below the road to a large rocky bar along the river for fishing, swimming, and floating. The eastern trailhead to the 23-mile-loop East Boyd–Glover–Roundtop National Recreation Trail (#703 and #704) departs across the Selway Road from the campground. A stock ramp and hitching post are also available. The trail is open to mountain bikes and motorbikes, too.

Access to the campground requires a steep climb up a narrow road with a sharp hairpin. The hairpin turn is not suitable for trailers or large RVs, but smaller rigs such as trucks with campers can negotiate the sharp corner. One campsite sits on Glover Creek at the end of the hairpin. The others are sprinkled around an open grassy hillside with a few cedars for partial shade. One campsite at the upper end tucks along Glover Creek. Two along the edge of the plateau have views of the river.

Campsites, facilities: The campground has seven campsites. Only small RVs are suitable. Facilities include picnic tables, fire rings with grills, and a vault toilet, but no drinking water. Bring water with you, or get it from O'Hara or Johnson Bar when you drive upriver. You can also get water from the Glover Creek here, but boil or purify it before use. Pack out your trash. Leashed pets are permitted.

Reservations, fees: No reservations are accepted. Camping is free. Open May–September.

Directions: From Lowell on Highway 12, turn southeast onto Selway Road, also called Forest Road 223. After milepost 7, the road turns to gravel and narrows to one lane with turnouts. Drive to milepost 15.1. Look for a steep road climbing up to the left.

GPS Coordinates: N 46° 4.147' W 115° 21.795'

Contact: Nez Perce National Forest, Moose Creek Ranger District, Fenn Ranger Station, 831 Selway Rd., Kooskia, ID 83539, 208/926-8925, www.fs.fed.us/r1/nezperce.

20 RACE CREEK

Scenic rating: 7

on the Selway River in Nez Perce National Forest

Over 12 miles of narrow, bumpy dirt-road driving is required to reach Race Creek. At an elevation of 1,750 feet in the Nez Perce National Forest only a few miles from the Selway-Bitterroot Wilderness boundary, Race Creek is a springboard for those accessing the wilderness on either foot or horseback on the Selway-Bitterroot Trail (#4). Moose Creek Ranger Station, which is not staffed full-time, sits one mile back on the road. Only catch-and-release fishing is permitted above the Selway Falls Bridge.

Race Creek is not a campground one enjoys as a destination (go for Slims Camp or Selway Falls instead), but rather for utilitarian reasons. The campground is made up of parking-lot terraces crammed with cars and Forest Service trucks due to the popular wilderness entry point here. Most campers here are preparing to follow the trail as it continues up the river 25 miles into the Selway-Bitterroot Wilderness. One campsite sits under cedars across from the toilet, and another tucks into an alcove of firs and thimbleberries. Located right on the river under a few trees for protection,

the best site is a walk-in tent site below the parking area.

Campsites, facilities: The campground has three RV or tent campsites. Only small RVs are suitable. Facilities include picnic tables, fire rings with grills, and a vault toilet, but no drinking water. Bring water with you, or get it from O'Hara or Johnson Bar when you drive upriver. You can also get water from the river here, but boil or purify it before use. Pack out your trash. As a wilderness entrance, it also has a stock ramp, hitch rail, and feeding trough. Leashed pets are permitted. A wheelchair-accessible toilet is available.

Reservations, fees: No reservations are accepted. Camping is free. Open May–September.

Directions: From Lowell on Highway 12, turn southeast onto the Selway Road, also called Forest Road 223. After milepost 7, the road turns to gravel and narrows to one lane with turnouts. Drive to milepost 19.5, where the road ends.

GPS Coordinates: N 46° 2.653' W 115° 17.032'

Contact: Nez Perce National Forest, Moose Creek Ranger District, Fenn Ranger Station, 831 Selway Rd., Kooskia, ID 83539, 208/926-8925, www.fs.fed.us/r1/nezperce.

21 SELWAY FALLS

Scenic rating: 7

south of the Selway River in Nez Perce National Forest

One reason to drive the 12 miles of bumpy gravel road to Selway Falls Campground is to see Selway Falls. The falls—broken by titanic boulders—roar at a deafening volume in early summer high water. Even after the river level drops in summer, the white water still churns through here. Fishing above the Selway Falls Bridge is catch-and-release only, and no fishing is permitted between the cable car below the falls and the bridge. At 1,800 feet, the campground, however, is about a mile to the southwest on the Meadow Creek tributary of the Selway. The Meadow Creek drainage is lush with sword ferns and vine maples. The campground is also popular with ATV riders and mountain bikers, who continue on to Falls Point (7 miles) and Elk City (30 miles). A large swimming sandbar sits between the campground and the bridge above the falls.

The campground sprawls its campsites along the Meadow Creek Road. The first four sites are near one toilet, and the last three are near another. All of the sites are open to the road, but most are quite shaded under western red cedar trees with large flat spaces for tents. Campsite 4's hillside has scarring from ATVs and motorcycles.

Campsites, facilities: The campground has seven RV or tent campsites. The dirt parking pads can accommodate small RVs, but trailers will have trouble turning around. Facilities include picnic tables, fire rings with grills, and vault toilets, but no drinking water. Bring water with you, or get it from O'Hara or Johnson Bar when you drive upriver. You can also get water from Meadow Creek here, but boil or purify it before use. Pack out your trash. Leashed pets are permitted. A wheelchair-accessible toilet is available.

Reservations, fees: No reservations are accepted. Campsites cost $5. Cash or check. Open late May–early September.

Directions: From Lowell on Highway 12, turn southeast onto Selway Road, also called Forest Road 223. After milepost 7, the road turns to gravel and narrows to one lane with turnouts. Drive to milepost 18.5 and turn right onto the one-lane bridge. After crossing the Selway, continue 0.7 mile on narrow, potholed dirt Meadow Creek Road to the campground.
GPS Coordinates: N 48° 2.685' W 116° 17.838'

Contact: Nez Perce National Forest, Moose Creek Ranger District, Fenn Ranger Station, 831 Selway Rd., Kooskia, ID 83539, 208/926-8925, www.fs.fed.us/r1/nezperce.

22 SLIMS CAMP

Scenic rating: 9

south of the Selway River in Nez Perce National Forest

Located at 1,875 feet in the Nez Perce National Forest, Slims Camp sits far up the Selway drainage on Meadow Creek. Departing from the campground loop, the Meadow Creek Trail (#726) climbs 15 miles up the drainage and fords the creek to reach Meadow Creek Cabin, which you can rent. The first three miles are open to motorcycles and mountain bikes, but the trail permits only hikers and horses after that. From the campground, Forest Road 290 continues on for 12 more miles from Slims Camp to Indian Hill Lookout, perched on the boundary of the Selway-Bitterroot Wilderness. Fishing is permitted in Meadow Creek, with two trout for a daily bag limit.

The campground tucks into a lush forest of thimbleberries, elderberries, and ferns. The two cedar-shaded campsites on the river have large, flat grassy areas for tents. Despite the rough road to get here and small dirt parking pads, the campsites can accommodate small RVs, and the loop at the end of the campground makes it easier to turn around. The campground is also more private than Selway Falls.

Campsites, facilities: The campground has two RV or tent campsites. Only small RVs are suitable. Facilities include picnic tables, fire rings with grills, and a vault toilet, but no drinking water. Bring water with you, or get it from O'Hara or Johnson Bar when you drive upriver. You can also get water from Meadow Creek here, but boil or purify it before use. Pack out your trash. Leashed pets are permitted. A wheelchair-accessible toilet is available.

Reservations, fees: No reservations are not accepted. Camping is free. Open late May–early September.

Directions: From Lowell on Highway 12, turn southeast onto the Selway Road, also called

Forest Road 223. After milepost 7, the road turns to gravel and narrows to one lane with turnouts. Drive to milepost 18.5 and turn right onto the one-lane bridge. After crossing the Selway, continue 1.6 miles on narrow, pot-holed dirt Meadow Creek Road, past the Sel-way Falls campsites and crossing the creek on a single-lane bridge to reach Slims Camp.
GPS Coordinates: N 48° 47.653' W 116° 54.472

Contact: Nez Perce National Forest, Moose Creek Ranger District, Fenn Ranger Station, 831 Selway Rd., Kooskia, ID 83539, 208/926-8925, www.fs.fed.us/r1/nezperce.

23 TWIN CREEK

Scenic rating: 6

west of the North Fork of the Salmon River in Salmon-Challis National Forest

At 5,100 feet in elevation south of Lost Trail Pass in Salmon-Challis National Forest, Twin Creek Campground sits five minutes off the Salmon River Scenic Byway in a forested side canyon. The campground is on the Lewis and Clark National Historical Trail. Fishing is available on the North Fork of the Salmon along the highway. Find easy access to the river via the paved loop of old highway across from Forest Road 449. Paths through the woods access Twin Creek.

Set in a diverse forest of firs and ponderosas, the partly shaded campground sprouts with a lush ground cover of snowberry, Oregon grape, and bear grass. The spacious campsites—including one large, double campsite—feature huge flat spaces for tents. Since the forest lacks a midstory, one or two other campsites are visible even though they are spread out for privacy around the two loops. The location in a side canyon off the highway contributes to nighttime quiet. A small creek runs through the woods south of the campground.

Campsites, facilities: The campground has 46 RV or tent campsites. RVs are limited to 32

feet. Facilities include picnic tables, fire rings with grills, pedestal grills, vault toilets, drinking water, garbage service, stock ramps, and campground hosts. Leashed pets are permitted. Horses are also permitted in the campground. A wheelchair-accessible toilet is available.

Reservations, fees: Reservations are not accepted. Campsites cost $5. Cash or check. Open June–October.

Directions: From Highway 93 between Gibbonsville and Lost Trail Pass (Idaho-Montana border), turn west at milepost 342.4 onto Forest Road 449. Drive for 0.5 mile, passing the picnic area, and turn left at the camping sign into the campground.
GPS Coordinates: N 45° 36.621' W 113° 58.563'

Contact: Salmon-Challis National Forest, Challis-Yankee Fork Ranger District, HC 63 Box 1669 Hwy. 93, Challis, ID 83226, 208/879-4100, www.fs.fed.us/r4/sc/.

24 TOWER ROCK

Scenic rating: 7

on the Salmon River between North Fork and Salmon

The Salmon River flows north past Tower Rock, a site where Lewis and Clark camped on their journey through the area in 1805. Surrounded by arid, orange-colored sagebrush hills, the rock outcropping towers above the campground, which sits at 3,850 feet. The sandstone feature eroded 57 million years ago. Boating facilities at the campground include two cement ramps and trailer parking to aid those floating the Salmon River with rafts, kayaks, canoes, and drift boats. Fishing for steelhead and trout is available in the campground from two wheelchair-accessible fishing platforms. Due to the campground's convenient location on the highway, it attracts cross-country cyclists riding the Salmon River Scenic Byway. A large osprey nest is on site,

© BECKY LOMAX

Lewis and Clark camped at Tower Rock on their journey along the Salmon River.

as well as historical and geological interpretive displays.

Sitting on a wide-open flat river bar below Tower Rock, the sunny campground borders a trailer park; however, it is fenced off to minimize views into neighboring yards. With no trees, the mowed-lawn campground with its newly paved loop road and paved parking pads affords no privacy, but it does provide views of the river from some of the campsites. Tucked between the river and the highway, the campground picks up the sound of the river and the two-lane highway. Site 5 includes a tent platform.

Campsites, facilities: The campground has six RV or tent campsites. RVs are limited to 28 feet. Facilities include picnic tables, fire rings with grills, pedestal grills, vault toilets, drinking water, garbage service, one tent platform, and a boat ramp. Leashed pets are permitted. A wheelchair-accessible toilet is available.

Reservations, fees: Reservations are not accepted. Campsites cost $5. An extra

vehicle costs $2. Cash or check. Open May–October.

Directions: From Highway 93 about 11 miles north of Salmon, turn west into the campground at milepost 315.

GPS Coordinates: N 45° 18.716' W 113° 54.391'

Contact: Bureau of Land Management, Salmon Field Office, 1207 S. Challis St., Salmon, ID 83467, 208/756-5400, www.blm.gov/id/.

25 MORGAN BAR

Scenic rating: 7

on the Salmon River between North Fork and Salmon

Backed up against sagebrush hills of the Salmon River Mountains to the west at 3,850 feet, Morgan Bar sits on a former homestead and still has a remnant orchard. The Salmon River flows north past the campground, with the 10,000-foot-high Beaverhead Mountains to the east. In early summer, they are still snow-covered. The campground also sits on the Lewis and Clark National Historic Trail. A trail tours around a wetland pond and along a mile of the Salmon River's west bank. A cement boat ramp aids launching canoes, kayaks, rafts, and drift boats onto the river for floating and fishing.

The sunny campground has the advantage of sitting across the river and fields away from the highway, so river sounds provide the backdrop for its campsites. The mowed-grass campground's one gravel loop circles through thickets of willows and a few cottonwoods for a bit of shade. Most of the campsites have views of the Beaverhead Mountains. Sites 1–3 line up in a field without views of the river. Site 4 claims privacy at the east end of the loop, with both views and partial shade. Sites 7–9 overlook the river.

Campsites, facilities: The campground has eight RV or tent campsites. RVs are limited to

28 feet. Facilities include covered picnic tables, fire rings with grills, vault toilets, drinking water, garbage service, horseshoes, volleyball, firewood for sale, and a campground host. Leashed pets are permitted. A wheelchair-accessible toilet is available.

Reservations, fees: Reservations are not accepted. Campsites cost $5. An extra vehicle costs $2. Cash or check. Open May–September.

Directions: From Highway 93 about seven miles north of Salmon, turn west at milepost 309 onto Diamond Creek Road. Drive 0.5 mile on pavement and veer left where the road turns to gravel. Drive 0.3 mile to a Y, taking the right fork. Drive 1.3 miles and turn right into the campground.

GPS Coordinates: N 45° 15.135' W 113° 54.471'

Contact: Bureau of Land Management, Salmon Field Office, 1207 S. Challis St., Salmon, ID 83467, 208/756-5400, www.blm.gov/id/.

26 SHOUP BRIDGE

🚴 🎣 🛶 ⛵ 💫 🐕 ♿ 🚙 ⛺

Scenic rating: 6

on the Salmon River between Salmon and Challis

Located at 4,150 feet on the south side of the Shoup Bridge over the Salmon River, the campground is one of the popular launch points for floating the river that borders the east edge of the Salmon River Mountains. The surrounding arid slopes, covered with sagebrush, flank the bucolic river corridor, which is rimmed with small ranches and farms. A cement boat ramp helps those launching kayaks, canoes, rafts, and drift boats. Fishing for steelhead requires barbless hooks. Only hatchery steelhead—identified by a clipped adipose fin—may be kept. Cyclists on the Salmon River Scenic Byway use the campground for its ease of access. The campground is also convenient to Salmon (five

miles north) for gas, groceries, ice, and fishing supplies. Fishing and floating outfitters are also based in Salmon, as are outfitters for horseback riding and hunting. The town is the birthplace of Sacajawea and on the Lewis and Clark National Historic Trail. It also houses the developed Salmon Hot Springs (open year-round, 248 Hot Springs Rd., Salmon, ID 83467, 208/756-4449, fee charged).

Tucked under big shady cottonwood trees, the tiny mowed-lawn campground sits between the highway, the river, and the bridge. Noise from passing vehicles comes with the territory; however, the highway is only a two-laner. A paved road loops through the campground, which squeezes its paved parking pads for campsites very close together. Site 3 claims waterfront.

Campsites, facilities: The campground has six RV or tent campsites. RVs are limited to 28 feet. Facilities include picnic tables, fire rings with grills, pedestal grills, vault toilets, drinking water, and garbage service. Leashed pets are permitted. A wheelchair-accessible toilet is available.

Reservations, fees: Reservations are not accepted. Campsites cost $5. An extra vehicle costs $2. Cash or check. Open April–October.

Directions: From Highway 93 about five miles south of Salmon, turn west at milepost 299.4 into the campground.

GPS Coordinates: N 45° 5.877' W 113° 53.601'

Contact: Bureau of Land Management, Salmon Field Office, 1207 S. Challis St., Salmon, ID 83467, 208/756-5400, www.blm.gov/id/.

27 WILLIAMS LAKE

🥾 🏊 🎣 🛶 ⛵ 🐕 ♿ 🚙 ⛺

Scenic rating: 7

northeast of Williams Lake in the Salmon River Mountains

On the arid sagebrush-covered eastern edge of the Salmon River Mountains, Williams

Lake, elevation 5,400 feet, sits in a pocket formed about 6,000 years ago. A landslide—most likely triggered by an earthquake—blocked Lake Creek, damming up the flow to create the lake. Today, homes surround the southeast and east sides of the lake. A boat launch is 1.5 miles west of the campground, which sits on a small, loose-forested parcel northeast of the lake, but without lake views or frontage. Boat launch facilities include a steep cement ramp and trailer parking. Boaters, water-skiers, canoeists, and kayakers all use the lake, as well as anglers going after rainbow trout. The fish are reputedly large—up to two pounds. The trailhead for Thunder Mountain National Historic Trail sits two miles west of Williams Lake.

The single-lane dirt road through the campground gets more eroded at its far end, but the larger sites at the upper ends see more use anyway. Mature firs lend partial shade to many of the sites, which have forest duff floors surrounded by burnt-red boulders or grass. Large, flat tent spaces are available, as well as peek-a-boo views of cliffs above the campground on sagebrush hills. Due to its distance from the highway, the campground is quiet. With grass and three kinds of sagebrush, the campground's open midstory admits views of neighboring campsites.

Campsites, facilities: The campground has 11 RV or tent campsites. RVs are limited to 28 feet. Facilities include picnic tables, fire rings with grills, vault toilets, drinking water, and garbage service. Leashed pets are permitted. A wheelchair-accessible toilet is available.

Reservations, fees: Reservations are not accepted. Campsites cost $5. An extra vehicle costs $2. Cash or check. Open late May–October.

Directions: From Highway 93 about four miles south of Salmon, turn west at milepost 299.4 across the one-lane Shoup Bridge over the Salmon River. At 0.7 mile, turn left onto Williams Lake Road. Drive 3.6 miles to where the road turns to gravel and climbs another 2.7

miles to a junction. Turn right and drive 0.4 mile uphill. Turn left into the campground. GPS Coordinates: N 45° 1.472' W 113° 57.914'

Contact: Bureau of Land Management, Salmon Field Office, 1207 S. Challis St., Salmon, ID 83467, 208/756-5400, www. blm.gov/id/.

28 COTTONWOOD

Scenic rating: 7

north of Challis on the Salmon River

Sitting at 4,800 feet along the north-flowing Salmon River along the east edge of the Salmon River Mountains, Cottonwood Campground provides river access for floaters and anglers in a section of canyon surrounded by arid, sagebrush slopes. A large sandbar south of the boat launch provides access to a swimming hole. The boat launch area—a cement ramp with trailer parking—aids those launching drift boats, rafts, kayaks, and canoes for the Class I–II water. You can put in at the campground to float 17 miles to Kilpatrick takeout, or put in upriver at Spring Gulch to float six miles back to the campground. Anglers go after trout and steelhead in the river. Cyclists on the Salmon River Scenic Byway use this campground for its convenience. Cronks Canyon Hot Springs, an undeveloped rock pool on the Salmon River, sits five miles north of the campground.

As the name implies, the campground sits under mature cottonwood trees, which provide shade for some of the campsites; however, sunny, open campsites are also available. Brushy willows separate some of the sites—particularly those that back up to the highway—into private niches. Mowed lawn surrounds the paved pull-through and back-in parking pads. Sites 1–4, 6, and 7–9 overlook the river. Sites 1–3 line up very close together. Sites 5, 8, 9, and 11 have tent platforms; sites 8

© BECKY LOMAX

The Salmon River provides sandy swimming holes as well as fishing and floating.

and 9 are walk-in tent sites. With the highway above the campground, the road noise is less obnoxious, but still audible.

Campsites, facilities: The campground has 11 RV or tent campsites. RVs are limited to 65 feet. Two additional walk-in tent campsites are available. Facilities include picnic tables, fire rings with grills, pedestal grills, vault toilets, drinking water, a disposal station, garbage service, horseshoe pits, a boat ramp, two tent platforms, and campground hosts. Leashed pets are permitted. A wheelchair-accessible toilet is available.

Reservations, fees: Reservations are not accepted. Campsites cost $10. Use of the disposal station costs $3. Cash or check. Open mid-May–October.

Directions: From Highway 93 about 14 miles north of Challis, turn west at milepost 261.3 into the campground.

GPS Coordinates: N 44° 40.103' W 114° 4.752'

Contact: Bureau of Land Management, Challis Field Office, 1151 Blue Mountain Rd., Challis, ID 83226, 208/879-6200, www.blm.gov/id/.

29 BAYHORSE

Scenic rating: 7

southwest of Challis on the Salmon River

Named for an old mining community in the area, Bayhorse Campground sits at 5,200 feet on the upper Salmon River, tucked into a narrow, arid, sagebrush-walled canyon on the southeast edge of the Salmon River Mountains. The campground provides boating, kayaking, canoeing, and fishing access to Class I–II portions of the Upper Salmon River between Stanley and Challis. A cement boat ramp and trailer parking are available. Two miles southwest of the campground and accessed via rough dirt roads, Deadman Hole Recreation Site contains a deep swimming pool below a rocky cliff. Put in at East Fork to float nine miles back to Bayhorse, or float downstream from the campground for two miles to Dugway or eight miles to the Challis Bridge to take out. Cyclists on the Salmon River Scenic Byway use the campground for its ease of access. Outfitters for rafting, fishing, and horseback riding are in Challis, 10 miles north. ATVers ride the Bayhorse Trails, a series of old mining roads.

The wide-open, sunny campground loops with three interconnected gravel roads through the river bar. Mowed lawns surround the level, gravel parking pads, and grass has started to invade the gravel tent platforms—both provide large flat spaces for tents. Brushy willows and sage line the riverbank, with a few aspens and cottonwoods along the perimeter. Due to the proximity to the two-lane highway, the campground garners noise from passing vehicles—even above the sound of the river. Sites 5 and 7–11 overlook the river. Power lines cross the upper end of the campground.

Campsites, facilities: The campground has 11 RV or tent campsites. RVs are limited to 45 feet. Facilities include picnic tables, fire rings with grills, pedestal grills, vault toilets, drinking water, garbage service, a boat ramp, and campground hosts. Leashed pets are permitted. A wheelchair-accessible toilet is available.

Reservations, fees: Reservations are not accepted. Campsites cost $10. Cash or check. Open mid-May–October.

Directions: From Highway 75 about 10 miles southwest of Challis, turn west at milepost 237 into the campground.

GPS Coordinates: N 44° 23.130' W 114° 15.634'

Contact: Bureau of Land Management, Challis Field Office, 1151 Blue Mountain Rd., Challis, ID 83226, 208/879-6200, www.blm.gov/id/.

30 EAST FORK

Scenic rating: 6

at the confluence of the East Fork of the Salmon River with the Upper Salmon River

At 5,600 feet on the confluence of the East Fork of the Salmon River with the Upper Salmon River, the campground provides access to both rivers. A primitive boat ramp sits on the highway's south side on the East Fork for launching rafts, kayaks, and canoes. On the Upper Salmon, you can paddle from East Fork seven miles to Deadman Hole, or from Torrey's Bar 16 miles to the campground. You can also float 22 miles of the East Fork, which has been nominated for designation as a national Wild and Scenic River. Put in at Little Boulder Creek and take out at the campground. Within three miles up the East Fork canyon, a trail departs for Jimmy Smith Lake, a 1.2-mile hike. The Snake Ridge ATV trail, also a route for mountain bikers, connects with the national forest. The East Fork also accesses hot springs and is the eastern portal for hiking and mountain biking in the White Cloud Mountains.

Sitting on a willow and cottonwood bluff above both rivers, the campground offers sunny or partly shaded campsites surrounded by mowed lawn. Sites offer views of the dry, sagebrush canyon hills. Several sites overlook the East Fork, while others overlook the Salmon. Site 4 overlooks both. Three tent camping sites line up along the East Fork. Sites 8 and 9 have big views of the highway bridge, too. Despite the sound of the rivers, the noise of passing vehicles invades the campground, but the number of vehicles lessens substantially at night. Watch for rattlesnakes in the campground.

Campsites, facilities: The campground has seven RV or tent campsites. RVs are limited to 45 feet. Three additional tent camping sites are available. Facilities include covered picnic tables, fire rings with grills, vault toilets, drinking water, garbage service, a boat ramp, and campground hosts. Leashed pets are permitted. A wheelchair-accessible toilet is available.

Reservations, fees: Reservations are not accepted. Campsites cost $10. Cash or check. Open mid-May–October.

Directions: From Highway 75 about four miles north of Clayton and 19 miles southwest of Challis, turn north at milepost 227 into the campground.

GPS Coordinates: N 44° 16.042' W 114° 19.582'

Contact: Bureau of Land Management, Challis Field Office, 1151 Blue Mountain Rd., Challis, ID 83226, 208/879-6200, www.blm.gov/id/.

31 HOLMAN CREEK

Scenic rating: 6

on the Upper Salmon River east of Sunbeam in Sawtooth National Recreation Area

Sitting at 5,625 feet on Holman Creek between Challis and Stanley on the north edge of the White Cloud Mountains, the campground is the first Forest Service campground lining the Upper Stanley River when you drive west. Tucked into a sagebrush canyon with a Douglas fir forest on its north-facing slopes, the campground is convenient for travelers but doesn't provide the river access that many of the other Upper Salmon River campgrounds do. Anglers can reach the river by walking across the highway to the south bank, but no developed river access exists. A primitive boat launch is 0.25 mile west. A few expert rafters and kayakers float the Class IV river from Sunbeam to Holman Creek. Cyclists use the campground for its convenience to the highway.

At the entrance, the campground seems to have little appeal thanks to power lines overhead and the highway between the campsites and the river. But drive the gravel road past the first six sunny, open sagebrush campsites, and the campground runs a spur of four campsites south into a narrow, forested side canyon along Holman Creek. Sites 8–10 have short bridges that cross the creek to reach their tables, fire pits, and tent spaces. Site 8 is also a double campsite at double the price. The spur campsites are shadier, cooler, and quieter than those in front, but the front sites claim the views of the canyon. Large tent spaces are available at many of the sites.

Campsites, facilities: The campground has 10 RV or tent campsites. RVs are limited to 22 feet. Facilities include picnic tables, fire rings with grills, vault toilets, drinking water, and garbage service. Leashed pets are permitted. A wheelchair-accessible toilet is available.

Reservations, fees: Reservations are not accepted. Campsites cost $8. An extra vehicle costs $2. Cash or check. Open late May–mid-October.

Directions: From Highway 75 between Stanley and Challis and seven miles west of Clayton, turn south into the campground at milepost 214.7.

GPS Coordinates: N 44° 14.967' W 114° 31.940'

Contact: Sawtooth National Forest, Stanley Ranger Station, HC 64 Box 9900, Stanley, ID 83278, 208/774-3000, www.fs.fed.us/r4/sawtooth/.

32 WHISKEY FLATS

Scenic rating: 5

on the Upper Salmon River east of Sunbeam in Sawtooth National Recreation Area

Sitting at 5,700 feet, Whiskey Flats is one of the more primitive river bar campgrounds along the Upper Salmon River. Expert boaters can raft or kayak this Class IV section of river from below Sunbeam to Holman Creek, and fishing is available from the riverbanks. Cross-country cyclists can easily access this campground along the Salmon River Scenic Byway. On the east side of the bridge, Slate Creek Road (Forest Road 666) terminates in eight miles at a trailhead. A 0.25-mile walk leads to rustic Slate Creek hot springs. The road and springs both have problems with spring flooding; call the Forest Service for conditions before driving. From the road's terminus, mountain-biking and hiking trails access the White Cloud Mountains.

The tiny, wide-open campground sits on a

tall grass and sagebrush bench with a couple cottonwoods, junipers, and firs. Be prepared for a rough, eroded dirt loop through the sunny campground. From any site, you can see campers at all the others and will hear the highway. Site 1 sits on the river, the farthest from the highway, but it still has views of the highway bridge. Sites 2 and 4 can see the river across the campground road. Site 3, which overlooks the river, is the closest to the highway bridge. Large tent spaces are available.

Campsites, facilities: The campground has four RV or tent campsites. RVs are limited to midsized rigs. Facilities include picnic tables, fire rings with grills, and pit toilets. No drinking water is available. If you use river water, boil or purify it first. Pack out your trash. Leashed pets are permitted. A wheelchair-accessible toilet is available.

Reservations, fees: Reservations are not accepted. Campsites cost $5. An extra vehicle costs $2. A double campsite costs $10. Cash or check. Open May–October.

Directions: From Highway 75 east of Sunbeam, turn north at milepost 213.3 on the west side of the Whiskey Flats Bridge onto a dirt road. Swing immediately right into the campground loop.

GPS Coordinates: N 44° 15.297' W 114° 33.118'

Contact: Sawtooth National Forest, Stanley Ranger Station, HC 64 Box 9900, Stanley, ID 83278, 208/774-3000, www.fs.fed.us/r4/sawtooth/.

33 FLAT ROCK AND POLE FLAT

Scenic rating: 7

on the Yankee Fork River in the Salmon River Mountains in Salmon-Challis National Forest

At 6,200 feet, Flat Rock and Pole Flat are a pair of campgrounds along the Yankee Fork River and the rugged 46-mile gravel Custer Motorway. The campgrounds sit on the opposite side of the road from the river with paths accessing the bank. Only members of the Shoshone-Bannock Tribe can fish for salmon in the Yankee Fork, but non-tribal members can go after rainbow trout and mountain whitefish. The campgrounds sit seven miles south of two ghost mining towns—Custer and Bonanza City. Since a portion of the road is paved from Sunbeam, these campgrounds are popular for their convenience for exploring the ghost towns and the surrounding mining relics.

Located along one mile of the river, the two quiet campgrounds plus an extension loop function as one campground. Set close to the road, Flat Rock has a six-campsite loop and the Flat Rock extension has three campsites. Both have an open understory that admits views of neighboring campers as well as passing vehicles. Site 5 garners the most privacy. Pole Flat loops up a hillside with sites 4, 6, 7, and 8 away from the road. Pole Flat also has two double campsites for the double the price. Shaded and sunny campsites, with large tent spaces, tuck into a mixed loose forest of firs, lodgepoles, spruce, and aspens with peek-a-boo views of gray talus slopes and spires. Unfortunately, power lines also pass overhead.

Campsites, facilities: The campgrounds have 19 RV or tent campsites. RVs are limited to 32 feet. Facilities include picnic tables, fire rings with grills, vault toilets, and drinking water. Pack out your trash. Leashed pets are permitted. A wheelchair-accessible toilet is available.

Reservations, fees: Reservations are not accepted. Campsites cost $5. Cash or check. Open June–September.

Directions: From Sunbeam on Highway 75 between Challis and Stanley, turn north at milepost 202.5 onto Yankee Fork Road (Forest Road 013). Drive north for two miles to Flat Rock Campground. Flat Rock extension and Pole Flat sit within 0.7 mile to the north.

GPS Coordinates for Flat Rock: N 44° 17.411' W 114° 43.106'

GPS Coordinates for Pole Flat: N 44° 18.197' W 114° 43.188'

Contact: Salmon-Challis National Forest, Challis-Yankee Fork Ranger District, HC 63 Box 1669 Hwy. 93, Challis, ID 83226, 208/879-4100, www.fs.fed.us/r4/sc/.

34 BLIND CREEK

Scenic rating: 7

on the Yankee Fork River in the Salmon River Mountains in Salmon-Challis National Forest

At 6,100 feet in the Salmon River Mountains of Salmon-Challis National Forest, Blind Creek Campground is the only campground sitting on the Yankee Fork River between Sunbeam and the ghost towns nine miles north. Its location one mile from Sunbeam makes it popular for touring the Sunbeam Dam Interpretive Site to see the remnants of the dam installed in 1910. It provided power for mining up the Yankee Fork, and the subsequent breaching of the dam in 1934 permitted the return of salmon and steelhead to spawning grounds. Sunbeam also offers Gold Dredge Tours and Upper Salmon River rafting trips. The Sunbeam hot springs—natural undeveloped springs—are one mile west on the highway. Only members of the Shoshone-Bannock tribe can fish for salmon in the Yankee Fork, but non-tribal members can go after rainbow trout and mountain whitefish.

The tiny campground tucks its five campsites on a forested plateau 15 feet above the river, where the sound of rushing water pervades the campsites. Unfortunately, you'll also hear cars driving up the Yankee Fork to its ghost towns. Rimmed with gray boulders and a lush understory of thimbleberry, fireweed, and wild roses, the campsites overlooking the river (2–4) have some privacy. Aspens, firs, and spruce partly shade the sites. Sites 1 and 5 border the road. Site 2 is a double site. At night, the campground quiets to the sound of the river.

Campsites, facilities: The campground has five RV or tent campsites. RVs are limited to 32 feet. Facilities include picnic tables, fire

rings with grills, and vault toilets. No drinking water is available; if you use river water, boil or purify it first. Pack out your trash. Leashed pets are permitted. A wheelchair-accessible toilet is available.

Reservations, fees: Reservations are not accepted. Camping is free. Open June–September.

Directions: From Sunbeam on Highway 75 between Challis and Stanley, turn north at milepost 202.5 onto Yankee Fork Road (Forest Road 013). Drive north for 1.1 mile, turning east into the campground. No sign marks the campground. GPS Coordinates: N 44° 16.856' W 114° 43.952'

Contact: Salmon-Challis National Forest, Challis-Yankee Fork Ranger District, HC 63 Box 1669 Hwy. 93, Challis, ID 83226, 208/879-4100, www.fs.fed.us/r4/sc/.

35 UPPER AND LOWER O'BRIEN

Scenic rating: 7

on the Upper Salmon River east of Sunbeam in Sawtooth National Recreation Area

BEST (

Located at 6,000 feet on the Upper Salmon River, the O'Brien campgrounds are popular because of their location across the river from the highway. Expert boaters can raft or kayak this Class IV section of river to Holman Creek, and fishing is available from the riverbanks. Mountain bikers can tour the forest road that parallels the river and the highway for seven miles east. Sunbeam, with guided white-water rafting and gold dredge tours, sits two miles west, and the Sunbeam hot springs on the Upper Salmon River are one mile farther west. Sunbeam is also the access for the Yankee Fork and the historical Custer Motorway, a 46-mile gravel mining road with two ghost towns.

Both the upper and lower campgrounds sit on flat river bar benches; however, the upper sits above the river along rapids and the lower sits at river level with a rocky beach and only small riffles. Douglas firs lend shade to both campgrounds; however, a couple of sunny sites are available, too. With the highway high above the campgrounds, the sound of the river is more pervasive than the sound of vehicles. Big, flat spaces for tents are available. At least half of the campsites in both campgrounds overlook the river, and sites are spaced out for privacy, although you'll see neighboring campers.

Campsites, facilities: The campgrounds have 19 RV or tent campsites. RVs are limited to small rigs. Facilities include picnic tables, fire rings with grills, pit toilets, and drinking water. Pack out your trash. Leashed pets are permitted.

Reservations, fees: Reservations are not accepted. Campsites cost $13. Cash or check. Open May–November. Fees are reduced around mid-September when services are limited.

Directions: From Highway 75 between Stanley and Challis, turn south into the campground at milepost 204.3 to drop on a steep, narrow dirt road (Forest Road 454) to cross the Upper Salmon River on a one-lane bridge. Find the upper campground entrance on the left 0.3 mile from the highway and the lower campground entrance on the left 0.2 mile farther. GPS Coordinates for Upper O'Brien: N 44° 15.552' W 114° 41.931' GPS Coordinates for Lower O'Brien: N 44° 15.445' W 114° 41.731'

Contact: Sawtooth National Forest, Stanley Ranger Station, HC 64 Box 9900, Stanley, ID 83278, 208/774-3000, www.fs.fed.us/r4/sawtooth/.

36 MORMON BEND

🚲 ⛵ 🛶 🏕️ 🎣 〰️ 🐾 ♿ 🚐 🏕️

Scenic rating: 7

on the Upper Salmon River east of Stanley in Sawtooth National Recreation Area

BEST (

Sitting at 6,100 feet on the Upper Stanley River, Mormon Bend is a popular site for rafting and kayaking the Class III–IV white-water section

of the river from the campground to Sunbeam Dam. The campground has a cement boat ramp and trailer parking available. You can float from Stanley to the campground, or from the campground to Torrey's Hole before Sunbeam. (Total distance from Stanley is about 13 miles.) From the campground to Yankee Fork, the river is closed to floating mid-August–late September. Across the river from the campground there are natural undeveloped hot springs, which are best in fall and reached by wading the river. The Basin Creek hot springs (also called Kem or Cove hot springs) are 1.5 miles east on the highway. Cyclists on the Salmon River Scenic Byway use the campground for its ease of access.

Recent logging in the campground due to beetle kill opened up the sagebrush and small pine campsites to more sun and, unfortunately, to the highway, too. Views now include the surrounding arid slopes of the canyon. Although several campsites line up along the river, only sites 6 and 7 actually have views of the water due to heavy willows and brush. Most of the sites off the paved campground loops are paved back ins, and sites 1 and 2 on a side spur offer no trailer turnaround. In spring, the campground packs out with kayakers and rafters, and in fall, with hunters. Arrive early to claim a campsite. Expect to hear road noise above the river.

Campsites, facilities: The campground has 16 RV or tent campsites. RVs are limited to mid-sized rigs. Facilities include picnic tables, fire rings with grills, vault toilets, drinking water, garbage service, tent platforms, and campground hosts. Leashed pets are permitted. A wheelchair-accessible toilet is available.

Reservations, fees: Reservations are not accepted. Campsites cost $13. Cash or check. Open May–October, but fees are reduced starting mid-September, when services are limited.

Directions: From Highway 75 about seven miles east of Stanley, turn south at milepost 196.1 into the campground. GPS Coordinates: N 44° 15.721' W 114° 50.535'

Contact: Sawtooth National Forest, Stanley

Ranger Station, HC 64 Box 9900, Stanley, ID 83278, 208/774-3000, www.fs.fed.us/r4/sawtooth/.

37 RIVERSIDE

Scenic rating: 7

on the Upper Salmon River east of Stanley in Sawtooth National Recreation Area

At 6,100 feet in elevation, Riverside is one of three campgrounds sitting close together on the Salmon River Scenic Byway on the Upper Salmon River. Part of the campground squeezes between the highway and the river; the other portion sits north of the highway. Rafters and kayakers float the Class III–IV river from Stanley to Mormon Bend or farther to Torrey's Hole west of Sunbeam. Anglers fish for trout, chinook salmon, and steelhead; check fishing regulations for catch-and-release regulations and seasonal closures for spawning. Cyclists use this campground for its ease of access on the Salmon River Scenic Byway.

Sprawled around paved loops set on either side of the highway, this campground has views not only of the surrounding sagebrush and forest canyon, but of the two-lane highway with its accompanying noise. Those areas with views of the river also look across to private homes and cabins along the river. The grass and sagebrush sites sit under a thinned-out lodgepole forest; both sunny and partly shaded sites are available. Because there's no midstory, you'll see neighboring campers. Riverside is more shaded than Salmon River and Mormon Bend.

Campsites, facilities: The campground has 17 RV or tent campsites. RVs are limited to midsized rigs. Facilities include picnic tables, fire rings with grills, vault toilets, drinking water, garbage service, and campground hosts. Leashed pets are permitted. A wheelchair-accessible toilet is available.

Reservations, fees: Reservations are not accepted. Campsites cost $13. Cash or check.

Open June–September, but sometimes closes in mid-August during salmon spawning.

Directions: From Highway 75 about six miles east of Stanley, turn south or north at milepost 195.2 into the campground, which has loops on both sides of the highway.

GPS Coordinates: N 44° 15.923' W 114° 51.088'

Contact: Sawtooth National Forest, Stanley Ranger Station, HC 64 Box 9900, Stanley, ID 83278, 208/774-3000, www.fs.fed.us/r4/sawtooth/.

38 CASINO CREEK

Scenic rating: 7

on the Upper Salmon River east of Stanley in Sawtooth National Recreation Area

At 6,100 feet in elevation, Casino Creek has the advantage of being on the south side of the Upper Salmon River, in contrast to most of the other campgrounds in the vicinity. Due to its location on the river, it provides the same fishing, rafting, and kayaking opportunities as the three campgrounds that sit on the highway side of the river between Stanley and Sunbeam. The Big Casino Creek (#646) trailhead for hikers, mountain bikers, and horse-packers sits at the end of the campground. It is equipped with a stock ramp and hitch rail. The trail provides a strenuous 19-mile mountain-bike loop with Little Casino Creek.

A lodgepole fence with gates for access lines the willow-covered riverbank. The sagebrush-and lupine-filled campground sits on a dry river bar in a loose lodgepole forest with gravel back-in parking pads. Most of the sites are sunny and open. Sites 1–8, 10 and 11 overlook the river. Site 8 is a double site, and sites 18 and 19 are walk-in tent sites, with the campsites set uphill on a bench. Site 17 has the most privacy. Even though the campground sits across the river from the highway, the sound of passing vehicles still comes into the campground.

Campsites, facilities: The campground has 17 RV or tent campsites. RVs are limited to midsized rigs. Two additional walk-in tent campsites are available. Facilities include picnic tables, fire rings with grills, vault toilets. No drinking water is available. If you use river or creek water, boil or purify it first. Pack out your trash. Leashed pets are permitted. A wheelchair-accessible toilet is available.

Reservations, fees: Reservations are not accepted. Campsites cost $5. An extra vehicle costs $2.50, except in a double site, where the campsite costs $10. Cash or check. Open May–October.

Directions: From Highway 75 about 5.5 miles east of Stanley, turn south onto Forest Road 651, crossing the Upper Salmon River. Drive 0.2 mile on a potholed dirt road to the campground pay station.

GPS Coordinates: N 44° 15.338' W 114° 51.327'

Contact: Sawtooth National Forest, Stanley Ranger Station, HC 64 Box 9900, Stanley, ID 83278, 208/774-3000, www.fs.fed.us/r4/sawtooth/.

39 SALMON RIVER

Scenic rating: 7

on the Upper Salmon River east of Stanley in Sawtooth National Recreation Area

BEST (

Located at 6,100 feet in elevation, Salmon River is the first of three campgrounds in a row heading east on the Salmon River Scenic Byway along the Upper Salmon River. Part of the campground squeezes between the highway and the river; the other portion sits north of the highway. Rafters and kayakers float the 13-mile, Class III–IV river from Stanley to Mormon Bend or farther to Torrey's Hole west of Sunbeam. Anglers fish for trout, chinook salmon, and steelhead; check fishing regulations for catch-and-release regulations and seasonal closures for spawning. Cyclists use this campground for its ease of access on the Salmon River Scenic Byway. Elkhorn hot springs (also called Boat Box), offering a wooden tub and rock-rimmed, user-built pools, are 1.5 miles to the west on the river.

Sprawled around paved loops set on both sides of the highway, this campground has views of forested slopes to the south across the river and arid sagebrush slopes to the north. The campground used to be shaded with mature lodgepoles, but thinning to remove beetle-killed trees has opened up the campground to make it sunny. Only a handful of trees remain for a sprinkle of shade. You'll see neighboring campers, hear the highway, and see the road.

Campsites, facilities: The campground has 30 RV or tent campsites. RVs are limited to 32 feet. Facilities include picnic tables, fire rings with grills, vault toilets, drinking water, garbage service, and campground hosts. Leashed pets are permitted. A wheelchair-accessible toilet is available.

Reservations, fees: Reservations are not accepted. Campsites cost $13. Cash or check. Open May–September, but sometimes closed in mid-August during salmon spawning.

Directions: From Highway 75 about four miles east of Stanley, turn south or north at milepost 193.8 into the campground, which has loops on both sides of the highway.

GPS Coordinates: N 44° 14.964' W 114° 52.210'

Contact: Sawtooth National Forest, Stanley Ranger Station, HC 64 Box 9900, Stanley, ID 83278, 208/774-3000, www.fs.fed.us/r4/sawtooth/.

40 STANLEY LAKE

Scenic rating: 10

on Stanley Lake northwest of Stanley in Sawtooth National Recreation Area

BEST (

Stanley lake, which sits at 6,500 feet at the north end of the jagged Sawtooth Mountains, offers fishing and boating. Large boats can launch at the lake's primitive west end ramp, but canoes, kayaks, and rafts can launch from the day-use area between Lakeview and Stanley Lake Campgrounds. From the west end of the lake, trails depart into the Sawtooth Wilderness with Bridal Veil Falls (3.5 miles) as the closest destination. Stock facilities are available at the trailhead, plus one mile of trail is gravel for wheelchair-accessibility. Mountain bikers head to the 11.5-mile Elk Mountain Loop. In 2009, the lake had three developed campgrounds, plus a huge area of dispersed primitive free camping. The Forest Service plans to close the dispersed area, reconstruct Stanley Lake Campground, and convert the Inlet Campground at the lake's west end to day-use only with a developed boat launch, larger parking, and paved trail along the north shore.

The quiet campground sits at the west end of Stanley Lake, with views of McGown and Mystery Mountains. Spindly lodgepoles lend partial shade to the campsites, but the forest has no midstory to add privacy beyond the tree trunks. Look for mountain bluebirds around the campsites. In 2009, the campground looped on a potholed dirt road with several sites right on the lakeshore and the outlet riverbank. The Forest Service is planning to rebuild this campground east of its current location, but farther from the beach to protect water quality. The new campground with 25–30 campsites should be completed in 2011 or 2012.

Campsites, facilities: The campground has 19 RV or tent campsites. RVs are limited to midsized rigs. Facilities include picnic tables, fire rings with grills, vault toilets, drinking water, garbage service, and campground hosts. Leashed pets are permitted. A wheelchair-accessible toilet is available.

Reservations, fees: Reservations are accepted (877/444-6777, www.recreation.gov). Campsites cost $15. Cash or check. Open May–October.

Directions: From 4.6 miles north of Stanley on Highway 21, turn west at milepost 125.9 onto the paved Stanley Lake Road (Forest Road 455). Drive 1.1 miles and turn left. Turn left again into Stanley Lake Campground.

GPS Coordinates: N 44° 14.971' W 115° 3.295'

Off-trail routes in the Sawtooth Wilderness lead to hidden lakes and jagged summits.

Contact: Sawtooth National Forest, Stanley Ranger Station, HC 64 Box 9900, Stanley, ID 83278, 208/774-3000, www.fs.fed.us/r4/sawtooth/.

41 LAKE VIEW

🏃 🚴 🏊 🎣 ⛵ 🚣 🐕 ♿ 🚐 ⛺

Scenic rating: 10

on Stanley Lake northwest of Stanley in Sawtooth National Recreation Area

Stanley Lake, which sits at 6,500 feet at the north end of the jagged Sawtooth Mountains, offers fishing for rainbow, lake, and brook trout as well as kokanee salmon. Large boats can launch at the lake's primitive west end ramp, but canoes, kayaks, and rafts can launch from the day-use area between Lakeview and Stanley Lake Campgrounds. From the west end of the lake, trails depart into the Sawtooth Wilderness; Bridal Veil Falls (1.5 miles) is the closest destination. Stock facilities are available at the trailhead, plus one mile of trail is gravel for wheelchair-accessibility. Mountain bikers head to the 11.5-mile Elk Mountain Loop. In 2009, the lake had three developed campgrounds, plus a huge area of dispersed primitive free camping. The Forest Service plans to close the dispersed area, reconstruct Stanley Lake Campground, and convert the Inlet Campground at the lake's west end to day-use only with a developed boat launch, larger parking, and a paved trail along the north shore connecting with Lake View Campground.

Lake View Campground is popular for its views of McGown and Mystery Mountains, rising up over 9,000 feet to reflect in the lake on calm days. The campground's one potholed loop circles a small bluff overlooking the lake, which is surrounded by aspens and lodgepoles. The sunny, quiet campsites give up privacy in favor of the views. However, site 4 at the end of the loop commands both lake views and privacy. Site 5 is a huge, double campsite with a long pull-through overlooking the lake.

Campsites, facilities: The campground has six RV or tent campsites. RVs are limited to midsized rigs. Facilities include picnic tables, fire rings with grills, vault toilets, drinking water, and garbage service. Leashed pets are permitted. A wheelchair-accessible toilet is available.

Reservations, fees: Reservations are not accepted. Campsites cost $15. Cash or check. Open May–October.

Directions: From 4.6 miles north of Stanley on Highway 21, turn west at milepost 125.9 onto the paved Stanley Lake Road (Forest Road 455). Drive 1.1 miles and turn left. Veer right for 0.1 mile, passing the day use area, into the campground.

GPS Coordinates: N 44° 14.907' W 115° 3.441'

Contact: Sawtooth National Forest, Stanley Ranger Station, HC 64 Box 9900, Stanley, ID 83278, 208/774-3000, www.fs.fed.us/r4/sawtooth/.

42 IRON CREEK

🏃 🎣 🐕 ♿ 🚐 ⛺

Scenic rating: 7

on Iron Creek west of Stanley in Sawtooth National Recreation Area

BEST (

In the Sawtooth National Recreation Area at 6,700 feet, Iron Creek is one of the few Sawtooth Mountain campgrounds that does not sit on a lake. Campers use this campground to access the Sawtooth Wilderness Area. The trailhead, which is equipped with a stock ramp and hitch rail, leads 5.5 miles and 1,700 feet in elevation to Sawtooth Lake. Steep switchbacks finish the trail into the scenic lake, flanked by the 10,190-foot Mount Regan. The lake harbors rainbow trout. You can also access Alpine Lake from this trailhead.

The campground tucks one loop into a spindly lodgepole forest, the remaining healthy pines left after removal of the larger beetle-killed trees. The pines do contribute partial shade to the campsites. After the loop passes the trailhead, the campsites line up along the creek. Most of the campsites are open to the road, and neighboring campers are visible. On weekends there's a stream of vehicles to the popular trailhead, which can see 40 people a day in summer, but at night, the campground quiets.

Campsites, facilities: The campground has nine RV or tent campsites. RVs are limited to midsized rigs. Facilities include picnic tables, fire rings with grills, vault toilets, drinking water, and garbage service. Leashed pets are permitted. A wheelchair-accessible toilet is available.

Reservations, fees: Reservations are not accepted. Campsites cost $12. Cash or check. Open May–October.

Directions: From 2.1 miles north of Stanley on Highway 21, turn south onto Iron Creek Road (Forest Road 619) and drive 2.7 miles of dirt to the campground loop.

GPS Coordinates: N 44° 11.990' W 115° 0.378'

Contact: Sawtooth National Forest, Stanley Ranger Station, HC 64 Box 9900, Stanley, ID 83278, 208/774-3000, www.fs.fed.us/r4/sawtooth/.

43 CHINOOK BAY AND MOUNTAIN VIEW

🚶 🚴 🏊 🛶 🚤 🎣 🐴 ♿ 🚐 ⛺

Scenic rating: 9

on Little Redfish Lake south of Stanley in Sawtooth National Recreation Area

Located at 6,500 feet in elevation on the northeast end of tiny Little Redfish Lake, these adjacent campgrounds sit at the base of the rugged Sawtooth Mountains. The lake, which does not permit motorboats, is small enough to avoid the big whitecaps of the larger lake. Hand-carried watercraft can be launched from both campgrounds. Since the lake is so shallow, it does not offer the same quality of fishing as Redfish Lake, but fish pass through its waters.

Mountain bikers tour the 12-mile Decker Flat Loop, which parallels Highway 75. The Redfish complex, 1.5 miles south, includes hiking trailheads, boat launches, horseback rides, bicycle and boat rentals, a convenience store, showers, a disposal station, and a lodge with a restaurant.

Lodgepole pines dominate the two adjacent grass and sagebrush campgrounds, but they are sparse enough for sun. Because there's little midstory, neighboring campers are visible. Of all the Redfish complex campgrounds, these two are the noisiest—vehicles can be heard on the highway and the Redfish entrance road. Some sites even have views of the road. Both campgrounds, however, garner views of Heyburn Mountain. In Mountain View, sites 2, 3, and 4 grab prime views of the jagged Sawtooths. In Chinook Bay, sites 9 and 11 pick up lake views with sites 4, 5, 7, and 8 lining up along the riverbank. Power lines pass over a few sites in Chinook Bay.

Campsites, facilities: The campgrounds have 20 RV or tent campsites. RVs are limited to midsized rigs. Facilities include picnic tables, fire rings with grills, flush toilets, drinking water, garbage service, and campground hosts. Leashed pets are permitted. A wheelchair-accessible toilet is available.

Reservations, fees: Reservations are not accepted. Campsites cost $16. Cash or check. Open May–October.

Directions: From 4.3 miles south of Stanley on Highway 75, turn southwest at milepost 185 onto Redfish Lake Road (Forest Road 214). Drive 0.4 mile to Chinook Bay Campground entrance and 0.1 mile farther to Mountain View Campground. Both entrances are on the right.

Chinook Bay GPS Coordinates: N 44° 9.847' W 114° 54.215'

Mountain View GPS Coordinates: N 44° 9.715' W 114° 54.263'

Contact: Sawtooth National Forest, Stanley Ranger Station, HC 64 Box 9900, Stanley, ID 83278, 208/774-3000, www.fs.fed.us/r4/sawtooth/.

44 SUNNY GULCH
![icons]

Scenic rating: 9

on the Upper Salmon River south of Stanley in Sawtooth National Recreation Area

At 6,400 feet in elevation along the Upper Salmon River, Sunny Gulch is a convenient campground for visiting the town of Stanley. Fishing and rafting outfitters are headquartered in town, plus groceries, ice, and gas are available. A seasonal bakery is worth a stop in summer. For cyclists traveling through the Sawtooth National Recreation Area, this campground is the only one located on the highway between Stanley and Galena Pass to the south. The Upper Salmon River harbors rainbow trout, steelhead (mid-March–April), and chinook salmon (until late July). Trails within a 10-minute drive depart into the White Clouds or Sawtooth Mountains. Mountain-biking trails are also available near Redfish Lake. If Sunny Gulch and the Redfish Lake campgrounds fill up, a primitive overflow camping area sits south of Sunny Gulch Campground. A disposal station is available at the ranger station 1.1 miles north of the campground.

The sunny campground sits surrounded by sagebrush, grass, and a loose lodgepole forest with peek-a-boo views of the Sawtooth Mountains and White Cloud foothills. Through the open forest, much of the campground is visible, but so are the dramatic peaks. A paved road makes two loops around the campground with paved parking pads that are mostly back ins. While the campground does hear highway noise, sites at the back overlooking the river canyon also hear the river. Sites 35, 37–39, 42, 44, and 45 not only sit farthest from the highway, but also overlook the river. A lodgepole fence divides the campsites from the abrupt canyon edge. The loop with campsites 27–45 sits on a higher plateau with bigger views.

Campsites, facilities: The campground has 45 RV or tent campsites. RVs are limited to 35 feet. Facilities include picnic tables on cement pads, fire rings with grills, cookstove pedestals, vault toilets, drinking water, garbage service, tent platforms, and campground hosts. Leashed pets are permitted. A wheelchair-accessible toilet is available.

Reservations, fees: Reservations are accepted (877/444-6777, www.recreation.gov). Campsites cost $16. Cash or check. Open May–October.

Directions: From 3.6 miles south of Stanley on Highway 75, turn northeast into the campground at milepost 185.8.

GPS Coordinates: N 44° 10.431' W 114° 54.624'

Contact: Sawtooth National Forest, Stanley Ranger Station, HC 64 Box 9900, Stanley, ID 83278, 208/774-3000, www.fs.fed.us/r4/sawtooth/.

45 POINT

Scenic rating: 10

on Redfish Lake south of Stanley in Sawtooth National Recreation Area

Tucked below the jagged Sawtooth Mountains on Redfish Lake's northwest side, Point Campground is popular for its location, views, sandy swimming beach, and kokanee salmon fishing. It is also the closest Redfish complex campground to the lodge, bicycle and boat rentals, and boat tours. Horseback rides, showers, and a disposal station are also available within one mile. Bench Lakes trail (3.4 miles) departs near the campground entrance, climbing 1,200 feet to lakes filled with yellow-blooming lily pads. Hand-carried watercraft can launch from the campground or picnic area, but larger boats must launch from the lake's opposite side.

The campground splits on both sides of the day-use picnic area. Skinny lodgepoles provide partial shade for the grassy campsites but are also open enough for views of the lake and Sawtooth Mountains as well as neighboring campers. Sites 1–8 are walk-in sites for tents only. Hand carts

Redfish Lake in the Sawtooth National Recreation Area is surrounded by six campgrounds, one of which is accessed only by boat.

are available to transfer camping gear to the campsites from a parking area 15 minutes away. Overnight parking is available near the day-use area. Sites 11, 12, 14, 16, and 17 overlook the water in the eastern loop. While Redfish Lake hums with the noise of motorboats during the day, at night the campground is quiet.

Campsites, facilities: The campground has nine RV or tent campsites plus eight tent-only sites. RVs are limited to camper vans and trucks with campers only. No motorhomes, trailers, or pop-up tent trailers are permitted. Facilities include picnic tables, fire rings with grills, cookstove pedestals, vault toilets, drinking water, bear boxes, tent platforms, garbage service, firewood for sale, and campground hosts. Leashed pets are permitted. A wheelchair-accessible toilet is available.

Reservations, fees: Reservations are not accepted. Campsites cost $8. An extra vehicle costs $2. Cash or check. Open late May–mid-September. During summer, the campground is periodically closed for 24 hours for irrigation to mitigate fire conditions.

Directions: From 4.3 miles south of Stanley

on Highway 75, turn southwest at milepost 185 onto Redfish Lake Road (Forest Road 214). Drive 1.7 miles and turn right for 0.7 mile, passing the lodge. The road terminates at the campground.

GPS Coordinates: N 44° 8.399' W 114° 55.535'

Contact: Sawtooth National Forest, Stanley Ranger Station, HC 64 Box 9900, Stanley, ID 83278, 208/774-3000, www.fs.fed.us/r4/sawtooth/.

46 GLACIER VIEW

Scenic rating: 9

at Redfish Lake south of Stanley in Sawtooth National Recreation Area

North of Redfish Lake at 6,600 feet, Glacier View is somewhat a misnomer. While a monstrous glacier carved the lake basin, the Sawtooth Mountains have no active glaciers remaining today. The campground has access to the lake at the North Shore picnic area, which sits across the road. It offers stunning views of the Sawtooths and a sandy swimming beach. Canoes and kayaks can launch from the picnic area, but larger boats must drive 0.9 mile south to the boat launch. The lake, which is best fished from boats, harbors several species of trout plus kokanee salmon. The 12-mile Decker Mountain Bike Loop is nearby, and trailheads depart from various locations around the lake—some for destinations in the Sawtooth Wilderness Area. Bicycle and boat rentals, horseback rides, boat tours, a disposal station, a convenience store, and showers all sit within two miles.

Set on a knoll above the lake, Glacier View campsites rim three loops in a loose lodgepole forest that is open enough for views of the Sawtooth or White Cloud Mountains. With only short vegetation between the trees—sagebrush, lupines, and grass—views of neighboring campers are also available. The A loop overlooks the outlet stream drainage, and paths connect to the banks. Since the campground is set back from the lakeshore, it is quieter than the Redfish campgrounds with lake frontage.

Campsites, facilities: The campground has 65 RV or tent campsites. RVs are limited to midsized rigs. Facilities include picnic tables on paved pads, fire rings with grills, pedestal grills, flush toilets, drinking water, tent platforms, garbage service, firewood for sale, double campsites, and campground hosts. Leashed pets are permitted. A wheelchair-accessible toilet is available.

Reservations, fees: Reservations are accepted (877/444-6777, www.recreation.gov). Campsites cost $16. Cash or check. Open late May–October. During summer, the campground is closed periodically for 24 hours for irrigation to mitigate fire conditions.

Directions: From 4.3 miles south of Stanley on Highway 75, turn southwest at milepost 185 onto Redfish Lake Road (Forest Road 214). Drive 2.2 miles, swinging east at the lake. Turn left into the campground and drive 0.1 mile uphill to the pay station.

GPS Coordinates: N 44° 8.746' W 114° 54.906'

Contact: Sawtooth National Forest, Stanley Ranger Station, HC 64 Box 9900, Stanley, ID 83278, 208/774-3000, www.fs.fed.us/r4/sawtooth/.

47 OUTLET

Scenic rating: 10

on Redfish Lake south of Stanley in Sawtooth National Recreation Area

BEST (

Located at 6,500 feet on Redfish Lake's northeast shore, Outlet Campground sits on a sandy bay with views of Mount Heyburn and the Grand Mogul—two of the Sawtooth Mountains' more dramatic peaks. The campground also has a day-use picnic area, with a buoyed swimming beach. Canoes and kayaks can launch from the picnic area, but larger boats must drive 0.6 mile south to the boat launch. The lake, which is best fished from boats, harbors several species of trout plus kokanee salmon. It is also stocked with sockeye salmon. The 12-mile Decker Mountain Bike Loop and the trail to the end of the lake depart 0.7 mile south. Bicycle and boat rentals, horseback rides, boat tours, a disposal station, a convenience store, and showers all sit within two miles.

The long, narrow campground squeezes between the lake and the busy road, which accesses two more campgrounds plus the boat launch for Redfish Lake. Young lodgepole pines partly shade the spacious campsites, many of which have peek-a-boo views of the lake and Mount Heyburn. Sagebrush and grasses cover the ground surrounding the campsites. At the campground's north end, sites are more open, and views include neighboring campers. At the southern end, the trees are thicker, allowing more privacy. Sites 8, 11, 13, and 15 sit nearest the water. The campground also has six double campsites.

Outlet Campground offers a sandy beach on Redfish Lake.

Campsites, facilities: The campground has 19 RV or tent campsites. RVs are limited to midsized rigs. Facilities include picnic tables on cement pads, fire rings with grills and pot hangers, cookstove pedestals, vault toilets, drinking water, garbage service, and campground hosts. Leashed pets are permitted. A wheelchair-accessible toilet is available.

Reservations, fees: Reservations are accepted (877/444-6777, www.recreation.gov). Campsites cost $16. Cash or check. Open late May–October. During summer, the campground is closed periodically for 24 hours for irrigation to mitigate fire conditions.

Directions: From 4.3 miles south of Stanley on Highway 75, turn southwest at milepost 185 onto Redfish Lake Road (Forest Road 214). Drive 2.5 miles, swinging east at the lake. Turn right and immediately left into the campground.

GPS Coordinates: N 44° 8.602' W 114° 54.682'

Contact: Sawtooth National Forest, Stanley Ranger Station, HC 64 Box 9900, Stanley, ID 83278, 208/774-3000, www.fs.fed.us/r4/sawtooth/.

48 MOUNT HEYBURN

Scenic rating: 9

at Redfish Lake south of Stanley in Sawtooth National Recreation Area

Mount Heyburn, which sits at 6,600 feet on the east side of Redfish Lake, is popular with boaters. The campground, which sits on the south side of the road, is a five-minute walk from the beach at the Mount Heyburn day-use picnic area. The day-use area houses the lake's boat launch, with docks, a cement ramp, trailer parking, and a buoyed swimming area with a sandy beach. The lake, which is best fished from boats, harbors kokanee salmon, sockeye salmon, and several species of trout. The 12-mile Decker Mountain Bike Loop and the trail to the end of the lake depart 0.3 mile south. Bicycle and boat rentals, horseback rides, boat tours, a disposal station, a convenience store, and showers all sit within 2.5 miles.

Mount Heyburn Campground tucks into a lodgepole forest. Its one large, paved loop is treed with a thin forest of spindly lodgepole pines—all that remain after logging the campground clean of beetle-killed trees. Sagebrush and wild grass surround the campsites, which are now sunny and open. Some have views to the road. Due to the campground's location off the lake, it is quieter than some of the other Redfish campgrounds and tends to fill up later than the others.

Campsites, facilities: The campground has 20 RV or tent campsites. RVs are limited to midsized rigs. Facilities include picnic tables, fire rings with grills, vault toilets, drinking water, garbage service, and campground hosts. Leashed pets are permitted. A wheelchair-accessible toilet is available.

Reservations, fees: Reservations are not accepted. Campsites cost $16. Cash or check. Open late May–early September. During summer, the campground is closed periodically for 24 hours for irrigation to mitigate fire conditions.

Directions: From 4.3 miles south of Stanley on Highway 75, turn southwest at milepost 185 onto Redfish Lake Road (Forest Road 214). Drive 3.1 miles, swinging east around the lake. Turn left into the campground.

GPS Coordinates: N 44° 8.155' W 114° 54.934'

Contact: Sawtooth National Forest, Stanley Ranger Station, HC 64 Box 9900, Stanley, ID 83278, 208/774-3000, www.fs.fed.us/r4/sawtooth/.

49 SOCKEYE

Scenic rating: 10

on Redfish Lake south of Stanley in Sawtooth National Recreation Area

BEST (

Sockeye Campground, named for the salmon stocked in Redfish Lake, sits at 6,500 feet on the east shore of the Sawtooth Mountains' largest lake. The campground entrance is 0.1 mile from Mount Heyburn day-use picnic area, which houses the docks, a cement boat ramp,

trailer parking, and a buoyed swimming area with a sandy beach. Adjacent to campsite 20, a trailhead departs for Redfish Ridge, Decker Flat, and Redfish Lake inlet at the head of the lake. The 12-mile Decker Mountain Bike Loop permits mountain bikes. Bicycle and boat rentals, horseback rides, boat tours, a disposal station, a convenience store, and showers sit at the lodge and Redfish corral complex less than three miles north of the campground.

Sockeye Campground gains appeal because it sits at the road's terminus. While noise from motorboats on the lake enters the campground during the day, it quiets at night. The newly remodeled campground looks across the lake to Mount Heyburn, and a lodgepole fence borders the water, permitting access to the rocky shoreline only at certain places to prevent habitat damage. Sites 1–5 have views of the water from across the campground road, but sites 6, 7, 9, 12, 14, and 15 overlook the lake through lodgepoles. The campground includes six double campsites. The thinned doghair lodgepole forest permits views of neighboring campers, but the campsites are spread out. Most of the campsites are sunny with only a little shade.

Campsites, facilities: The campground has 23 RV or tent campsites. RVs are limited to midsized rigs. Facilities include picnic tables on cement pads, fire rings with grills, campstove pedestals, vault toilets, drinking water, garbage service, tent platforms, firewood for sale, and campground hosts. Leashed pets are permitted. A wheelchair-accessible toilet is available.

Reservations, fees: Reservations are not accepted. Campsites cost $8. An extra vehicle costs $2. Cash or check. Open May–November.

Directions: From 4.3 miles south of Stanley on Highway 75, turn southwest at milepost 185 onto Redfish Lake Road (Forest Road 214). Drive 3.2 miles, swinging east around the lake until the road ends at the campground.

GPS Coordinates: N 44° 8.106' W 114° 55.041'

Contact: Sawtooth National Forest, Stanley Ranger Station, HC 64 Box 9900, Stanley,

ID 83278, 208/774-3000, www.fs.fed.us/r4/ sawtooth/.

50 REDFISH INLET

Scenic rating: 10

on Redfish Lake south of Stanley in Sawtooth National Recreation Area

BEST (

Tucked below the jagged Mount Heyburn on Redfish Lake's southwest side, Redfish Inlet Campground requires a boat or five-mile hike to reach. From the Mount Heyburn boat launch on the lake's opposite side, the crossing is three miles. From the lodge at the north end of the lake, the crossing is five miles. Motorboats, canoes, and kayaks are available to rent at the lodge, and a boat shuttle service runs about five times per day to the transfer camp. When crossing the lake, look for the Guardians of the Lake, the large rocks flanking both sides. Beach canoes, kayaks, and boats overnight for safety from winds. From the camp, a 0.5-mile walk leads to Lily Lake. Trails circle Redfish Lake and head up Redfish Lake Creek into the Sawtooth Wilderness Area. The south slopes of Mount Heyburn contain the Redfish Slab rock-climbing routes. For anglers, the lake harbors kokanee salmon and rainbow trout.

The campground sits back in the forest on the north side of Redfish Lake Creek. The sites sprinkle across an open forest flat bench with peek-a-boo views of the lake and Grand Mogul. Sites are partly shaded by lodgepole pines, many of which have been damaged by pine bark beetles. The campsites are within sight of each other and trails. During the day, the area hums with activity as the tour boat disgorges visitors on its dock, but nighttime is exceptionally quiet.

Campsites, facilities: The campground has six tent campsites. Facilities include picnic tables, fire rings with grills, bear boxes, and a vault toilet. Drinking water is not available. Bring your own, or if you use water from the lake

or Inlet Creek, boil or purify it first. Pack out your trash. Leashed pets are permitted.

Reservations, fees: Reservations are not accepted. Camping is free. Open mid-June–mid-September.

Directions: From 4.3 miles south of Stanley on Highway 75, turn southwest at milepost 185 onto Redfish Lake Road (Forest Road 214). Drive 3.1 miles, swinging east around the lake to Mount Heyburn boat launch. The entrance is on the right.

GPS Coordinates: N 44° 8.399' W 114° 55.535'

Contact: Sawtooth National Forest, Stanley Ranger Station, HC 64 Box 9900, Stanley, ID 83278, 208/774-3000, www.fs.fed.us/r4/ sawtooth/.

51 PETTIT LAKE

Scenic rating: 9

on Pettit Lake south of Stanley in Sawtooth National Recreation Area

BEST (

On other Sawtooth Mountain lakes, no summer homes line the shores. On Pettit Lake, elevation 7,000 feet, homes string along the south lakeshore and the point that houses the campground, which is on the northeastern end. A boat launch is available 0.5 mile southeast, but canoes and kayaks can launch from the campground to tour the shallow east bays. The lake harbors rainbow, brook, and westslope cutthroat trout. At the back of the campground, the trail departs for Yellow Belly Lake (2.7 miles) or Alice Lake (6.3 miles). The 18-mile Toxaway-Pettit Loop strings together a series of lakes through 10,000-foot peaks of the Sawtooth Wilderness Area. Listen for loons on the lake.

The campground sits on two loops on a shallow east-side bay with summer homes surrounding a portion of the lake. Circling under skinny lodgepoles, the campground's two loops weave campsites through shade and sun, now open due to logging of beetle-killed trees.

The open understory with only low sagebrush, grass, and lupine permits visibility of other campsites. Sites 1–3 unfortunately sit under power lines and along the campground road that leads to the busy trailhead. Sites 4–6 sit adjacent to trailhead parking, but sites 7–13, located on the left loop, sit nearer the lake. A lodgepole fence surrounds the campground, with gates to access the water. The campsites have large, flat tent spaces. Three double sites are available.

Campsites, facilities: The campground has 13 RV or tent campsites. RVs are limited to midsized rigs. Facilities include picnic tables, fire rings with grills, vault toilets, drinking water, garbage service, and campground hosts. Leashed pets are permitted. A wheelchair-accessible toilet is available.

Reservations, fees: Reservations are not accepted. Campsites cost $12. Cash or check. Open May–October. Fees are reduced in mid-September when services are limited.

Directions: From Highway 75 about 17 miles south of Stanley, turn west at milepost 171.3 onto the gravel Pettit Lake Road (Forest Road 208). Expect some small potholes and washboards. Drive 1.6 miles to a junction with the picnic area and boat launch. Turn right and drive 0.5 mile to the campground pay station.

GPS Coordinates: N 43° 59.098' W 114° 52.178'

Contact: Sawtooth National Forest, Stanley Ranger Station, HC 64 Box 9900, Stanley, ID 83278, 208/774-3000, www.fs.fed.us/r4/sawtooth/.

52 ALTURAS LAKE INLET

Scenic rating: 9

on Alturas Lake south of Stanley in Sawtooth National Recreation Area

At 7,050 feet at the west end of Alturas Lake, the Alturas Lake Inlet Campground marks one of the southernmost campgrounds in the Sawtooth Mountains and the best one for swimming on the lake. Visitors opt for camping here as a quieter alternative to the Redfish complex crowds. Canoes and kayaks can launch from the day-use beach, which has a sandy buoyed swimming area. The developed boat launch for boaters and anglers is 2.3 miles east at Smokey Bear. Mountain bikers can ride up-valley along Alturas Lake Creek—partway on road, part on trail. With a trailhead one mile north of the lake, the Cabin Creek Lakes Trail climbs a steep 1,998 feet in 4.5 miles. Watch for loons, ospreys, and tundra swans on the lake.

The quiet campground tucks into the forest between the forest road heading up-valley to trailheads, the day-use picnic area at the lake's head, and Alturas Lake Creek. Sitting in a loose, open forest of firs and lodgepoles, the sunny campground's one large loop contains eight double campsites that can fit two parties camping together. A few trails whack through the willow brush to the creek, and a trail leads to the beach at the picnic area. Flat spaces for tents are available. Sites at the west end have views up-valley across the meadows.

Campsites, facilities: The campground has 28 RV or tent campsites. RVs are limited to 40 feet. Facilities include picnic tables, fire rings with grills, vault toilets, drinking water, garbage service, firewood for sale, and campground hosts. Leashed pets are permitted. A wheelchair-accessible toilet is available.

Reservations, fees: Reservations are accepted (877/444-6777, www.recreation.gov). Campsites cost $15. Cash or check. Open May–October.

Directions: From Highway 75 about 21 miles south of Stanley, turn east onto Alturas Lake Road (Forest Road 205) at milepost 167.5. Drive 4.8 miles and turn left and then immediately right into the campground.

GPS Coordinates: N 43° 54.396' W 114° 52.813'

Contact: Sawtooth National Forest, Stanley Ranger Station, HC 64 Box 9900, Stanley,

ID 83278, 208/774-3000, www.fs.fed.us/r4/sawtooth/.

53 NORTH SHORE

Scenic rating: 9

on Alturas Lake south of Stanley in Sawtooth National Recreation Area

Located on Alturas Lake at the south end of the Sawtooth Mountains, North Shore Campground sits at 7,050 feet on the north shore of the lake. It sits west of Smokey Bear Campground, which has the lake's one developed boat launch, equipped with a dock, cement ramp, and boat trailer parking. Motorboats are permitted on the lake, but not personal watercraft. The lake, which frequently sees afternoon winds, supports a fish population of rainbow and westslope cutthroat trout as well as kokanee salmon. Mountain biking is permitted on the forest roads in the area that connect to Pettit Lake, and hiking trails tour the lakeshore. Sandy beaches are available for swimming near the boat launch. Visitors opt for camping at Alturas as a quieter alternative to the busy Redfish complex. Watch for bald eagles, ospreys, and grebes on the lake.

North Shore is a sprawling, quiet campground situated on a hillside rimmed with tall firs and lodgepole pines. Grass and sagebrush meadows make up most of the sunny campground. Campsites in meadow areas glean big views up-valley to the southern Sawtooth Mountains. Those near the trees are partly shaded, but that may change as beetle-killed trees are removed. Flat tent spaces are available. Some of the campsites overlook the lake. Trails connect with the shore.

Campsites, facilities: The campground has 15 RV or tent campsites. RVs are limited to 32 feet. Facilities include picnic tables, fire rings with grills, vault toilets, drinking water, garbage service, firewood for sale, and campground hosts. Leashed pets are permitted. A wheelchair-accessible toilet is available.

Reservations, fees: Reservations are not accepted. Campsites cost $15. Cash or check. Open May–early September.

Directions: From Highway 75 about 21 miles south of Stanley, turn east onto paved Alturas Lake Road (Forest Road 205) at milepost 167.5. Drive 3.7 miles and turn left into the campground.

GPS Coordinates: N 43° 55.195' W 114° 51.969'

Contact: Sawtooth National Forest, Stanley Ranger Station, HC 64 Box 9900, Stanley, ID 83278, 208/774-3000, www.fs.fed.us/r4/sawtooth/.

54 SMOKEY BEAR

Scenic rating: 9

on Alturas Lake south of Stanley in Sawtooth National Recreation Area

Located on Alturas Lake at the south end of the Sawtooth Mountains, Smokey Bear Campground sits at 7,050 feet on the north shore of the lake. The campground has the lake's one developed boat launch, equipped with a dock, cement ramp, and boat trailer parking. Motorboats are permitted on the lake, but not personal watercraft. The lake supports a fish population of rainbow and westslope cutthroat trout as well as kokanee salmon. The lake frequently sees afternoon winds. Mountain biking is permitted on the forest roads in the area that connect to Pettit Lake, and hiking trails tour the lakeshore. Sandy beaches are available for swimming. Visitors opt for camping at Alturas as a quieter alternative to the busy Redfish complex. Watch for loons and tundra swans on the lake in spring and fall.

The quiet Smokey Bear campground used to be thick forest, but pine beetles killed many of the trees, which have been subsequently logged out. Much of the campground receives more sun now than it did in the past. With dirt pull-through or back-in parking pads, campsites with forest duff floors are surrounded by doghair lodgepoles that only lend a bit of shade. Several of the sites are spacious with flat sites for tents, but neighbors are still visible. Sites 4–7 and 10 overlook the lake. Three campsites accommodate two parties camping together.

Campsites, facilities: The campground has 11 RV or tent campsites. RVs are limited to 16 feet. Facilities include picnic tables, fire rings with grills, vault toilets, drinking water, and garbage service. Leashed pets are permitted. A wheelchair-accessible toilet is available.

Reservations, fees: Reservations are not accepted. Campsites cost $15. Cash or check. Open May–October.

Directions: From Highway 75 about 21 miles south of Stanley, turn east onto paved Alturas Lake Road (Forest Road 205) at milepost 167.5. Drive 3.5 miles, and turn left into the campground. Campsites sit to the right of the pay station and the boat launch to the left. GPS Coordinates: N 43° 55.263' W 114° 51.757'

Contact: Sawtooth National Forest, Stanley Ranger Station, HC 64 Box 9900, Stanley, ID 83278, 208/774-3000, www.fs.fed.us/r4/sawtooth/.

55 EASLEY

🚶 🚴 🛶 🎣 ♨️ 🐕 ♿ 🚐 ⛺

Scenic rating: 8

on the Big Wood River north of Ketchum in Sawtooth National Recreation Area

BEST (

At 6,600 feet along the Big Wood River and the Sawtooth Scenic Byway, Easley Campground is popular for the developed hot springs 0.3 mile across the river from the campground. Run by the Idaho Baptist Convention, the swimming complex (open Memorial Day–Labor Day, 208/726-7522, www.cathedralpines.org) has a full-size chlorine-free swimming pool, two

98-degree hot tubs, and changing rooms with showers. Views from the pools include the Boulder Mountains. The campground also sits on the 18.8-mile Harriman Trail, a double-track hiking, mountain biking, and horseback riding trail that connects SNRA Headquarters with Galena, where more mountain-biking and hiking trails are available. The Big Wood River is known for its rainbow and brook trout fishery. Across the river, the 10-site Boulder View Campground, which provided additional campsites near Easley and the hot springs, has been closed following flooding. Contact the Forest Service about its status.

Spread out for privacy, the campsites line up along one dirt road with a small turnaround loop at the end in an open aspen forest. A few Douglas firs and pines also contribute partial shade to some of the campsites. With the Big Wood River flowing along the south side of the campground through willow bogs, the area can buzz with mosquitoes. Highway sounds are audible.

Campsites, facilities: The campground has 10 RV or tent campsites. RVs are limited to 40 feet. Facilities include picnic tables, fire rings with grills, vault toilets, garbage service, firewood for sale, and campground hosts. No drinking water is available. Bring your own or fill up at Wood River Campground four miles east. Leashed pets are permitted. A wheelchair-accessible toilet is available.

Reservations, fees: Reservations are accepted (877/444-6777, www.recreation.gov). Campsites cost $10. An extra vehicle costs $5. Cash or check. Open June–mid-September.

Directions: From Highway 75 about 12 miles north of downtown Ketchum, turn south at milepost 142.4 onto Forest Road 160. Drive 0.2 mile and turn right for 0.1 mile to reach the campground. GPS Coordinates: N 43° 46.798' W 114° 32.199'

Contact: Sawtooth National Forest, Sawtooth National Recreation Area Headquarters, HC 64 Box 8291, Ketchum, ID 83340, 208/727-5000, www.fs.fed.us/r4/sawtooth/.

56 WOOD RIVER

Scenic rating: 7

on the Big Wood River north of Ketchum in Sawtooth National Recreation Area

On the Sawtooth Scenic Byway, Wood River Campground, elevation 6,400 feet, sits on the Big Wood River, a rainbow trout fishery tumbling from Galena Pass and surrounded by steep-sloped peaks climbing above 9,000 feet. The campground also sits on the 18.8-mile Harriman Trail, a double-track trail for hiking, mountain biking, and horseback riding. The trail passes through the campground, linking 2.5 miles south to SNRA Headquarters and 16.3 miles north to Galena, where another network of mountain-bike and hiking trails is available. A nature trail also tours the forest from the back of the campground.

This campground, set in a deeper forest than the North Fork Campground, fills up faster due to its location and ambiance. A thicker forest of aspens, lodgepoles, and Douglas firs shades many of the campsites, although some of the dying pines may need to be removed in the future. The campground also sits on the opposite side of the river from the highway. Unfortunately, those sites along the river (1–3, 8, 26, 28, and 29) also hear the highway and view it, too. Sites 9–19 at the back of the campground garner more shade and a bit more privacy for those that back up to the forest slope. The campground also has a paved road and paved parking pads—only two of which are pull-throughs. Sites 19 and 20 garner views up valley.

Campsites, facilities: The campground has 30 RV or tent campsites. RVs are limited to mid-sized rigs. Facilities include picnic tables, fire rings with grills, vault toilets, drinking water, garbage service, firewood for sale, an amphitheater for interpretive programs, and campground hosts. Leashed pets are permitted. A wheelchair-accessible toilet is available.

Reservations, fees: Reservations are not accepted. Campsites cost $12. An extra vehicle costs $5. Cash or check. Open May–October.

© BECKY LOMAX

Campgrounds along the Wood River in the Sawtooth National Recreation Area also parallel the Harriman Trail.

Directions: About 10 miles north of downtown Ketchum, turn south off Highway 75 at milepost 138.4 and drive 0.1 mile across the single-lane bridge over the Big Wood River into the campground.

GPS Coordinates: N 43° 47.614' W 114° 27.459'

Contact: Sawtooth National Forest, Sawtooth National Recreation Area Headquarters, HC 64 Box 8291, Ketchum, ID 83340, 208/727-5000, www.fs.fed.us/r4/sawtooth/.

57 NORTH FORK

Scenic rating: 6

on the Big Wood River north of Ketchum in Sawtooth National Recreation Area

At 6,300 feet in the Big Wood Valley north of Ketchum on the Sawtooth Scenic Byway, the North Fork is named for the river flowing into the Big Wood River just downstream of the campground; however, the campground does not sit up the North Fork Canyon but rather on the main river surrounded by sagebrush. It is the nearest campground to Ketchum, where rafting, fishing, and horseback riding outfitters are headquartered. The Big Wood River harbors rainbow trout for fishing. The campground's popularity is due to its placement on the south end of the Harriman Trail, an 18.8-mile double-track trail for hiking, mountain biking, and horseback riding. The trail parallels the river and highway running from SNRA Headquarters to Galena. The nearest destination is Baker Creek at seven miles.

Located in between the highway and the river, the campground's two loops circle through an aspen forest dotted with a few dying pines. Sites are partly shaded by the trees; brushy willows add privacy to some campsites, while others are more open with wildflower meadows. The sounds of both the river and the highway pervade the campground, along with winds that cause the aspen leaves to clack together in song.

Sites 11–14, 16–18, 21, and 22 sit adjacent to the river. Two sites are doubles, allowing for two parties to camp together. The small campsites with small tent spaces are spread out for privacy, some with views of low sagebrush slopes.

Campsites, facilities: The campground has 28 RV or tent campsites. RVs are limited to 40 feet. Facilities include picnic tables, fire rings with grills, vault toilets, drinking water, garbage service, and campground hosts. Leashed pets are permitted. A wheelchair-accessible toilet is available.

Reservations, fees: Reservations are accepted (877/444-6777, www.recreation.gov). Campsites cost $12. An extra vehicle costs $5. Cash or check. Open May–October.

Directions: About eight miles north of downtown Ketchum, turn south off Highway 75 at milepost 136.6 into the campground.

GPS Coordinates: N 43° 47.261' W 114° 25.517'

Contact: Sawtooth National Forest, Sawtooth National Recreation Area Headquarters, HC 64 Box 8291, Ketchum, ID 83340, 208/727-5000, www.fs.fed.us/r4/sawtooth/.

58 MURDOCK

Scenic rating: 7

in the North Fork Canyon north of Ketchum in Sawtooth National Recreation Area

At an elevation of 6,500 feet, Murdock Campground sits in the North Fork Canyon along the North Fork of the Big Wood River. The river, which flows past the campground on the opposite side of the road, provides rainbow and brook trout habitat. Mountain bikers ride the North Fork Canyon Road to access single-track trails. The Murdock Trailhead, adjacent to the campground's south side, is equipped with a stock ramp and hitch rails. The trail follows Murdock Creek for 3.5 miles. A disposal station is on North Fork Canyon Road, 0.7 mile from the entrance.

One dirt road loops through the sunny campground, which tucks under a few aspens and large lodgepoles for shade in a sage and grass meadow. South of the campground, a large open meadow allows views down-valley for sites 1–4, which border it. On the north end of the campground, sites 9 and 10 grab views up-valley. In addition to the views, the open forest permits seeing neighboring campers. Even though the campground is adjacent to North Fork Canyon Road and Murdock Trailhead, the campground quiets at night.

Campsites, facilities: The campground has 11 RV or tent campsites. RVs are limited to mid-sized rigs. Facilities include picnic tables, fire rings with grills, vault toilets, drinking water, garbage service, firewood for sale, and a campground host. Leashed pets are permitted.

Reservations, fees: Reservations are not accepted. Campsites cost $12. Cash or check. Open May–October.

Directions: From Highway 75 about eight miles north of downtown Ketchum, turn north at milepost 136.4 onto North Fork Canyon Road (Forest Road 146). Drive north past the Sawtooth National Recreation Area Headquarters for 1.4 miles to the campground entrance on the right. (Pavement turns to dirt at 0.4 mile. Be ready for potholes and a single-lane bridge.) GPS Coordinates: N 43° 48.289' W 114° 25.244'

Contact: Sawtooth National Forest, Sawtooth National Recreation Area Headquarters, HC 64 Box 8291, Ketchum, ID 83340, 208/727-5000, www.fs.fed.us/r4/sawtooth/.

59 CARIBOU

Scenic rating: 6

in the North Fork Canyon north of Ketchum in Sawtooth National Recreation Area

At 6,600 feet in the North Fork Canyon, Caribou Campground sits between North Fork Canyon Road and the North Fork of the Big Wood River. The river supports a rainbow and brook trout fishery. Trails for hiking, mountain biking, and horseback riding tour up all three forks of the river drainage: the East Fork, the North Fork, and the West Fork. Access these trails within four miles of the campground at the end of North Fork Canyon Road. A disposal station is on North Fork Canyon Road, 0.7 mile from the entrance.

Caribou is a quiet campground where you can listen to the sound of the river, which flows along its west side. Set in a loose forest of Douglas firs and lodgepole pines (some dying from beetle infestations), the campground offers partial shade with views of forested slopes. Site 6, however, is very shady. Large, flat spaces are available for tents. Sites 1, 3, 5, and 7 sit on the river side of the campground, which has a dirt-road loop with back-in parking pads. With only low grass and brush between the trees, neighboring campers are visible. Paths lead to the river.

Campsites, facilities: The campground has seven RV or tent campsites. RVs are limited to 22 feet. Facilities include picnic tables, fire rings with grills, vault toilets, campground host, firewood for sale, and garbage service. Drinking water is not available at Caribou but is available at Murdock Campground 0.6 mile south. Leashed pets are permitted. A wheelchair-accessible toilet is available.

Reservations, fees: Reservations are not accepted. Campsites cost $10. Cash or check. Open May–October. Fees drop in mid-September when services are limited.

Directions: From Highway 75 about eight miles north of downtown Ketchum, turn north at milepost 136.4 onto North Fork Canyon Road (Forest Road 146). Drive north for two miles. (Pavement turns to dirt at 0.4 mile. Be ready for potholes and a single-lane bridge.) Turn left onto the single-lane campground road for 0.1 mile. GPS Coordinates: N 43° 48.812' W 114° 25.453'

Contact: Sawtooth National Forest, Sawtooth National Recreation Area Headquarters, HC 64 Box 8291, Ketchum, ID 83340, 208/727-5000, www.fs.fed.us/r4/sawtooth/.

RESOURCES

RESERVATIONS

National Recreation Reservation Service

The National Recreation Reservation Service (NRRS) books reservations for federal campgrounds in Montana, Wyoming, and Idaho. While not all campgrounds offer reservations, the Forest Service, Bureau of Land Management, and National Park Service each offer some campgrounds on the NRRS reservation system.

877/444-6777 or 518/885-3639, TDD 877/833-6777

www.recreation.gov

State Parks

Montana does not offer reservations for state park campgrounds, but Idaho and Wyoming do.

Idaho State Parks

888/922-6743

http://idahostateparks.reserveamerica.com

Wyoming State Parks

877/996-7275

www.usedirect.com/cdweb

NATIONAL RESOURCES

Passes

The annual interagency pass—America the Beautiful—grants access to federal recreation lands that charge entrance fees. The $80 pass ($10 for seniors and free to disabled U.S. citizens) provides free entrance to national parks, Bureau of Land Management areas, U.S. Wildlife Refuges, and U.S. Forest Service lands. For seniors and disabled citizens, the passes also grant half-price camping fees. Passes may be purchased at entrance stations or online.

America the Beautiful National Pass

888/275-8747

http://store.usgs.gov/pass/index.html

National Park Service Sites

Big Hole National Battlefield

16425 Highway 43 W.
Wisdom, MT 59761
406/689-3155
www.nps.fov/biho

Glacier National Park

P.O. Box 128
West Glacier, MT 59936
406/888-7800
www.nps.gov/glac

Grand Teton National Park

P.O. Drawer 170
Moose, WY 83012
307/739-3300
www.nps.gov/grte

Grant-Kohrs Ranch National Historic Site

266 Warren Lane
Deer Lodge, MT 59722
406/846-2070
www.nps.gov/grko

Ice Age Floods National Geologic Trail

Since Congress just established the trail, federal contact information is not set up yet. In the meantime, you can get travel information from the Ice Age Floods Institute.

Ice Age Floods Institute
c/o Columbia River Exhibition of History,
    Science, and Technology
95 Lee Boulevard
Richland, WA 99352
509/943-9000 or 877/789-9935
www.iafi.org/trail.html

Lewis and Clark National Historic Trail

601 Riverfront Drive
Omaha, NE 68102
402/661-1804
www.nps.gov/lecl

Nez Perce National Historic Trail

12730 Highway 12

Orofino, ID 83544
208/476-8334
www.fs.fed.us/npnht

Yellowstone National Park
P.O. Box 168
Yellowstone National Park, WY 82190
307/344-7381
www.nps.gov/yell

National Recreation Areas
Sawtooth National Recreation Area
HC 64, Box 8291
5 North Fork Canyon Road
Ketchum, ID 83340
208/727-5000 or 800/260-5970
www.fs.fed.us/r4/sawtooth/

National Forests
Many national forests keep current campground information on their websites. On the road, contact the district ranger stations for updated information. You can also get maps and camping, hiking, boating, fishing, and hunting information at the district offices.

BEAVERHEAD-DEERLODGE NATIONAL FOREST
Supervisor's Office
420 Barrett Street
Dillon, MT 59725
406/683-3900
www.fs.fed.us/rl/b-d

Butte Ranger District
1820 Meadowlark
Butte, MT 59701
406/494-2147

Jefferson Ranger District
3 Whitetail Road
Whitehall, MT 59759
406/287-3223

Madison Ranger Station
5 Forest Service Road
Ennis, MT 59729
406/682-4253

Pintler Ranger District
88 Business Loop
Philipsburg, MT 59858
406/859-3211

Wisdom Ranger District
P.O. Box 238
Wisdom, MT 59761
406/689-3243

Wise River Ranger District
P.O. Box 100
Wise River, MT 59762
406/832-3178

BITTERROOT NATIONAL FOREST
Supervisor's Office
1801 N. 1st Street
Hamilton, MT 59840
406/363-7100
www.fs.fed.us/r1/bitterroot

Darby Ranger District
712 N. Main
Darby, MT 59829
406/821-3913

Stevensville Ranger District
88 Main Street
Stevensville, MT 59870
406/777-5461

Sula Ranger District
7338 Highway 93 S.
Sula, MT 59871
406/821-3201

West Fork Ranger District
6735 West Fork Road
Darby, MT 59829
406/821-3269

BRIDGER-TETON NATIONAL FOREST
P.O. Box 1888
Jackson, WY 83001
307/739-5500
www.fs.fed.us/r4/btnf

Buffalo Ranger District
Highway 26/287
P.O. Box 278
Moran, WY 83013
307/543-2386

Jackson Ranger District
25 Rosencrans Lane
P.O. Box 1689
Jackson, WY 83001
307/739-5400

Pinedale Ranger District
29 E. Fremont Lake Road
P.O. Box 220
Pinedale, WY 82941
307/367-4326

CARIBOU-TARGHEE NATIONAL FOREST
Supervisor's Office
1405 Hollipark Drive
Idaho Falls, ID 83401
208/524-7500
www.fs.fed.us/r4/caribou-targhee

Ashton Ranger District
P.O. Box 858
Ashton, ID 83420
208/652-7442

Dubois Ranger District
127 W. Main
P.O. Box 46
Dubois, ID 83423
208/374-5422

Island Park Ranger District
3726 Highway 20
Island Park, ID 83429
208/558-7301

Palisades Ranger District
3659 E. Ririe Highway
Idaho Falls, ID 83401
208/523-1412

Teton Basin Ranger District
515 S. Main
P.O. Box 777
Driggs, ID 83422
208/354-2312

CLEARWATER NATIONAL FOREST
Supervisor's Office
12730 Highway 12
Orofino, ID 83544
208/476-4541
www.fs.fed.us/r1/clearwater

Lochsa Ranger District
Kamiah Ranger Station
903 3rd Street
Kamiah, ID 83536
208/935-2513

Kooskia Ranger Station
502 Lowry
Kooskia, ID 83539

North Fork Ranger District
12730 Highway 12
Orofino, ID 83544
208/476-4541

Powell Ranger District
192 Powell Road
Lolo, MT 59847
208/942-3113

CUSTER NATIONAL FOREST
Supervisor's Office
1310 Main Street
Billings, MT 59105
406/657-6200
www.fs.fed.us/r1/custer

Beartooth Ranger District
HC 49, Box 3420
Red Lodge, MT 59068
406/446-2103

FLATHEAD NATIONAL FOREST
Supervisor's Office
650 Wolfpack Way
Kalispell, MT 59901
406/758-5200
www.fs.fed.us/r1/flathead

Hungry Horse and Glacier View Ranger Districts
10 Hungry Horse Drive
Hungry Horse, MT 59919
406/387-3800

Spotted Bear Ranger District
P.O. Box 190310
Hungry Horse, MT 59919
406/758-5376

Swan Lake Ranger District
200 Ranger Station Road
Bigfork, MT 59911
406/837-7500

Tally Lake Ranger District
650 Wolfpack Way
Kalispell, MT 59901
406/758-5200

GALLATIN NATIONAL FOREST
Supervisor's Office
P.O. Box 130
Bozeman, MT 59771
406/587-6701
www.fs.fed.us/r1/gallatin

Big Timber Ranger District
P.O. Box 1130
225 Big Timber Loop Road
Big Timber, MT 59011-1130
406/932-5155

Bozeman Ranger District
3710 Fallon Street, Suite C
Bozeman, MT 59718
406/522-2520

Gardiner Ranger District
P.O. Box 5
Highway 89 S.
Gardiner, MT 59030
406/848-7375

Hebgen Lake Ranger District
P.O. Box 520
West Yellowstone, MT 59758
406/823-6961

Livingston Ranger District
5242 Highway 89 S.
Livingston, MT 59047
406/222-1892

HELENA NATIONAL FOREST
Supervisor's Office
2880 Skyway Drive
Helena, MT 59602
406/449-5201
www.fs.fed.us/r1/helena

Helena Ranger District
2001 Poplar
Helena, MT 59601
406/449-5490

Lincoln Ranger District
1569 Highway 200
Lincoln, MT 59639
406/362-4265

Townsend Ranger District
415 S. Front
Townsend, MT 59644
406/266-3425

KOOTENAI NATIONAL FOREST
Supervisor's Office
1101 Highway 2 W.
Libby, MT 59923
406/293-6211
www.fs.fed.us/r1/kootenai

Cabinet Ranger District
2693 Highway 200

Trout Creek, MT 59874-9503
406/827-3533

Fortine Ranger District
12797 Highway 93 S.
P.O. Box 116
Fortine, MT 59918-0116
406/882-4451

Libby Ranger District
12557 Highway 37
Libby, MT 59923-8212
406/293-7773

Rexford Ranger District
949 Highway 93 N.
Eureka, MT 59917-9550
406/296-2536

Three Rivers Ranger District
12858 Highway 2
Troy, MT 59935-8750
406/295-4693

IDAHO PANHANDLE NATIONAL FOREST
Supervisor's Office
3815 Schreiber Way
Coeur d'Alene, ID 83815
208/765-7223
www.fs.fed.us/ipnf

Bonners Ferry Ranger District
6286 Main Street
Bonners Ferry, ID 83805-9764
208/267-5561

Coeur d'Alene Ranger District
Silver Valley Office
173 Commerce Drive
Smelterville, ID 83868
208/783-2100

Coeur d'Alene River Ranger District
Fernan Office
2502 E. Sherman Avenue
Coeur d'Alene, ID 83814-5899
208/664-2318

Priest Lake Ranger District
32203 Highway 57
Priest River, ID 83856-9612
208/443-2512

Sandpoint Ranger District
1500 Highway 2, Suite 110
Sandpoint, ID 83864-9509
208/263-5111

St. Joe Ranger District
Avery Office
HC Box 1
Avery, ID 83802-9702
208/245-4517

Clarkia Office
54495 Highway 3
Clarkia, ID 83812
208/245-1134

St. Maries Office
222 S. 7th Street, Suite 1
St. Maries, ID 83861-0407
208/245-2531

LEWIS AND CLARK NATIONAL FOREST
Supervisor's Office
1101 15th Street N.
Great Falls, MT 59401
406/791-7700
www.fs.fed.us/r1/lewisclark

Augusta Information Station
405 Manix Street
P.O. Box 365
Augusta, MT 59410
406/562-3247

Lewis and Clark Interpretive Center
4201 Giant Spring Road
P.O. Box 1806
Great Falls, MT 59403-1806
406/453-6157

Rocky Mountain Ranger District
1102 Main Avenue NW

P.O. Box 340
Choteau, MT 59422
406/466-5341

LOLO NATIONAL FOREST
Fort Missoula, Building 24
Missoula, MT 59804
406/329-3750
www.fs.fed.us/r1/lolo

Missoula Ranger District
Fort Missoula, Building 24
Missoula MT 59804
406/329-3814

Ninemile Ranger District
20325 Remount Road
Huson, MT 59846
406/626-5201

Plains-Thompson Falls Ranger District
P.O. Box 429
408 Clayton
Plains, MT 59859
406/826-3821

Seeley Lake Ranger District
3583 Highway 83
Seeley Lake, MT 59868
406/677-2233

Superior Ranger District
P.O. Box 460
209 W. Riverside
Superior, MT 59872
406/822-4233

NEZ PERCE NATIONAL FOREST
Supervisor's Office
104 Airport Road
Grangeville, ID 83530
208/983-1950
www.fs.fed.us/r1/nezperce

Moose Creek Ranger District
831 Selway Road

Kooskia, ID 83539
208/926-4258

Red River Ranger District
300 American River Road
Elk City, ID 83525
208/842-2245

Salmon River Ranger District
304 Slate Creek Road
White Bird, ID 83554
208/839-2211

SALMON-CHALLIS NATIONAL FOREST
Supervisor's Office
1206 S. Challis Street
Salmon, ID 83467
208/756-5100
www.fs.fed.us/r4/sc

Challis-Yankee Fork Ranger District
HC 63, Box 1669, Highway 93
Challis, ID 83226
208/879-4100

Leadore Ranger District
176 N. Railroad Street
P.O. Box 180, Highway 28
Leadore, ID 83464
208/768-2500

Lost River Ranger District
716 W. Custer
P.O. Box 507
Mackay, ID 83251
208/588-3400

Middle Fork Ranger District
P.O. Box 750, Highway 93
Challis, ID 83226
208/879-4101

North Fork Ranger District
11 Casey Road
P.O. Box 180, Highway 93 N.
North Fork, ID 83466
208/865-2700

Salmon/Cobalt Ranger District
311 McPherson Street
Salmon, ID 83467
208/756-5200

SAWTOOTH NATIONAL FOREST
Supervisor's Office
2647 Kimberly Road E.
Twin Falls, ID 83301
208/737-3200
www.fs.fed.us/r4/sawtooth

Ketchum Ranger District
P.O. Box 2356
206 Sun Valley Road
Ketchum, ID 83340
208/622-5371

Stanley Ranger Station
HC 64, Box 9900
Stanley, ID 83278
208/774-3000

SHOSHONE NATIONAL FOREST
Supervisor's Office
808 Meadowlane Avenue
Cody, WY 82414
307/527-6241
www.fs.fed.us/r2/shoshone

Clarks Fork Canyon, Wapiti, and Greybull Ranger Districts
203A Yellowstone Avenue
Cody, WY 82414-9313
307/527-6921

Washakie Ranger District
333 E. Main Street
Lander, WY 82520-3499
307/332-5460

Wind River Ranger District
1403 W. Ramshorn
Dubois, WY 82513-0186
307/455-2466

National Wildlife Refuges
Lee Metcalf National Wildlife Refuge
4567 Wildfowl Lane
Stevensville, MT 59870
406/777-5552
www.fws.gov/refuges

Lost Trail National Wildlife Refuge
6295 Pleasant Valley Road
Marion, MT 59925
406/858-2216
www.fws.gov/refuges

Red Rocks National Wildlife Refuge
27820 Southside Centennial Road
Lima, MT 59739
406/276-3536
www.fws.gov/redrocks

Swan River, Pablo, and Ninepipe National Wildlife Refuges and National Bison Range
58355 Bison Range Road
Moiese, MT 59824
406/644-2211
www.fws.gov/refuges

Bureau of Land Management
Idaho Bureau of Land Management
1387 S. Vinnell Way
Boise, ID 83709
208/373-4000
www.blm.gov/id

Montana Bureau of Land Management
5001 Southgate Drive
Billings, MT 59101
406/896-5000
www.blm.gov/mt

Wyoming Bureau of Land Management
5353 Yellowstone Road
Cheyenne, WY 82009
307/775-6256
www.blm.gov/wy

STATE RESOURCES

Montana
Montana Department of Transportation
2701 Prospect Avenue
P.O. Box 201001
Helena, MT 59620
406/444-6201
www.mdt.mt.gov/mdt

Montana Fish, Wildlife, and Parks
1420 E. 6th Avenue
P.O. Box 200701
Helena, MT 59620
406/444-2535
www.fwp.mt.gov

Montana Office of Tourism
301 S. Park Avenue
P.O. Box 200533
Helena, MT 59620
800/847-4868
www.visitmt.com

Idaho
Idaho Division of Tourism Development
700 W. State Street
Boise, ID 83720
208/334-2470
www.visitidaho.org

Idaho Fish and Wildlife
600 S. Walnut
Boise, ID 83712
208/334-3700
www.fishandgame.idaho.gov

Idaho Transportation Department
3311 W. State Street
P.O. Box 7129
Boise, ID 83707
208/334-8000
www.itd.idaho.gov/

State of Idaho Parks and Recreation
P.O. Box 83720
Boise, ID 83720
208/334-4199
www.parksandrecreation.idaho.gov/

Wyoming
Wyoming Department of Transportation
5300 Bishop Blvd.
Cheyenne, WY 82009
307/777-4375
www.dot.state.wy.us/wydot

Wyoming Game and Fish
5400 Bishop Boulevard
Cheyenne, WY 82006
307/777-4600
www.gf.state.wy.us/

Wyoming State Parks
2301 Central Avenue
Cheyenne, WY 82002
307/777-6323
www.wyoparks.state.wy.us/

Wyoming Travel and Tourism
1520 Etchepare Circle
Cheyenne, WY 82007
307/777-7777 or 800/225-5996
www.wyomingtourism.org

NATIVE AMERICAN RESERVATIONS
Blackfeet Nation
1 Agency Square
Browning, MT 59417
406/338-7521
www.blackfeetnation.com

Coeur d'Alene Indian Reservation
401 Anne Antelope Road
Plummer, ID 83851
208/686-5302
www.cdatribe-nsn.gov

Confederated Salish and Kootenai Tribes
51383 Highway 93 N.
Pablo, MT 59855

406/675-2700
www.cskt.org

Wind River Indian Reservation
P.O. Box 538
Fort Washakie, WY 82514
307/332-3532
www.easternshoshone.net

RECREATION

Maps
Beartooth Publishing
406/585-7205 or 800/838-1058
www.beartoothpublishing.com
Regional recreation maps for southern Montana, northwestern Wyoming, and eastern Idaho; maps include latitude and longitude grids, trail mileages, and campgrounds.

National Geographic Trails Illustrated
800/962-1643
www.natgeomaps.com
Maps can be acquired for Glacier, Grand Teton, and Yellowstone National Parks.

Cycling

Missoula's Adventure Cycling Association
800/721-8719
www.adventurecycling.org
Provides route descriptions and maps.

Route of the Hiawatha
208/744-1301
www.ridethehiawatha.com
Info for Idaho's 15-mile mountain bike trail.

Fishing

Idaho fishing licenses
http://fishandgame.idaho.gov/fish/

Montana fishing licenses
http://fwp.mt.gov/fishing/license/default.html

Wyoming fishing licenses
http://gf.state.wy.us/fish/fishing/index.asp

Index

Acknowledgments

I would like to thank the innumerable rangers, biologists, and campground hosts that I spoke with on my camping trips. As I plied them with odd questions about birds, plants, geology, wildlife, and camping spots, they employed patience in their answers. I applaud their dedication to their work and extend a giant thank you to those maintenance personnel and volunteers who keep the campgrounds clean and safe for visitors.

In writing this book, I needed assistance from family and friends. My husband, Michael, helped on the home front, while friends signed on for traveling adventures with me. Little did they know I would shove a GPS or notebook in front of them, putting them to work on their vacations. My niece, Erin, invented codes (PTFRG meant picnic tables, fire rings with grills) to speed up the note-taking process. Those accompanying me after her week in the Bitterroot and Pioneer Mountains fell in to using her codes, too. We even spoke in code. "The campground has DR and GS (drinking water and garbage service)."

As I collated my trip notes into text for the book, I stumbled across tidbits left by my assistants. Kjell noted that one campground was nicely appointed (what the heck does that mean?). Babs drew pictures and added words that shouldn't be in print to describe long, washboard, and pothole dirt roads. Weezie didn't even want to take notes, but instead did all the driving so I could be the scribe—but I had the worst handwriting of all of us.

A huge thank you goes to all my assistants—Michael, Syd, Chris, Sarah, Erin, Gail, Kjell, Barb, Steve, Lou, Mary, Kellie, and Bill. Your encouragement, companionship, and laughter made this book happen.

Last, I must thank my editors at Avalon. They pulled together my rambling convolutions of thought to make a book.

www.moon.com

DESTINATIONS | ACTIVITIES | BLOGS | MAPS | BOOKS

MOON.COM is ready to help plan your next trip! Filled with fresh trip ideas and strategies, author interviews, informative travel blogs, a detailed map library, and descriptions of all the Moon guidebooks, Moon.com is all you need to get out and explore the world—or even places in your own backyard. While at Moon.com, sign up for our monthly e-newsletter for updates on new releases, travel tips, and expert advice from our on-the-go Moon authors. As always, when you travel with Moon, expect an experience that is uncommon and truly unique.

MOON IS ON FACEBOOK—BECOME A FAN!
JOIN THE MOON PHOTO GROUP ON FLICKR